APPLIED PSYCHOLOGY FOR TEACHERS

A BEHAVIORAL COGNITIVE APPROACH

DEDICATION

To my children:

Jill
Jeff
Linda
Jim
Karen
David
Brandin

Whose love and caring have constantly kept my adult life attuned to the importance of good teachers.

Applied Psychology For Teachers

A Behavioral Cognitive Approach

WESLEY C. BECKER

SRA®

SCIENCE RESEARCH ASSOCIATES, INC.
Chicago, Henley-on-Thames, Sydney, Toronto

An IBM Company

Acquisitions Editor.......Phil Gerould
Development Editor.... Byron Riggan
Text and Cover
Designer...............William Marvin
Typographer .... Compositors, Inc.

Library of Congress Cataloging-in-Publication Data
Becker, Wesley C., 1928-
Applied psychology for teachers.
Bibliography: p.
Includes index.
1. Behavior modification. 2. Classroom management.
3. Lesson Planning. 4. Cognition in Children.
I. Title.
LB1060.2.B43 1986 371.1'024 85-24982
ISBN 0-574-23125-0

Printed in the United States of America.
10-9-8-7-6-5-4-3-2
This is a revised edition of *Teaching: A Course in Applied Psychology,* © 1971.

CONTENTS

PREFACE

This book is designed primarily for teachers in training at the undergraduate level, although it could easily be used for inservice and some graduate courses. It attempts to systematically cover areas of Educational Psychology important to teachers. It is designed to be a two-term course of three hours each term or a one-semester course of four or five hours. Of course other arrangements are possible through being selective in assigning chapters.

A number of areas of psychology (the study of individuals and groups) have generated empirical principles useful to the teacher in decision making. These areas include developmental psychology, individual differences, personality theory, cognitive psychology, social psychology, measurement theory, learning theory, instructional psychology, and behavior theory.

The implications of empirical behavior theory cut across many different aspects of teacher decision making and provide a set of *core concepts* that one can build from to understand more complex events. In understanding how students in different social environments develop differently, behavior principles apply. In understanding good classroom management practices, behavior principles are a factor. In understanding effective teaching practices, behavior principles enter consideration. In understanding effective ways of monitoring student progress, behavior principles are pertinent. Because the basic principles of behavior underly much of what this text is about, I cover them in early chapters.

In addition to having an understanding of the *empirical* principles underlying learning processes, teachers need to have a *logical* understanding of the structure of knowledge systems and how such knowledge is important to teaching strategies. For example, in teaching basic concepts, there are logically derivable principles for sequencing examples that will facilitate student learning. In teaching more complex problem-solving routines, it is important to be able to analyze subskills assumed by the routine and teach them first. Knowledge of how to analyze and carry out general-case instruction is very important to the breadth of applications the student can make for any given instruction. It adds *power* to teaching. In the past two decades, considerable progress has been made in analyzing the nature of concepts, principles, problem-solving routines, problem-solving strategies, and some of the metacognitive processes related to managing one's thinking processes. In approaching these areas, our attempt is to present a systematic viewpoint, showing where possible how more complex forms of behavior and thinking grow out of simpler forms. In the process, it is our hope that our students will develop a systematic, empirically based frame of reference for approaching the professional problems faced by teachers.

Teachers also need a background for understanding students' individual differences and developmental changes. Learning processes are continually interacting with our biological bases and maturation processes. Unlike most texts in this area, I did not begin with developmental processes because it is my belief that a background in behavior theory and the analysis of cognitive knowledge would provide a stronger foundation for approaching the psychological implications of developmental processes for teachers.

My goal was to collect and synthesize what psychology has to offer teachers in a cohesive, practically oriented fashion. Alternative viewpoints are examined, but within the framework of a systematic *empirical* orientation.

ORGANIZATION OF THE TEXT

After an introductory chapter that discusses some of the issues involved in taking an empirical, scientific approach to human behavior, the text has four major parts, plus a concluding chapter that discusses some of the technological changes likely to affect teachers before too long.

Part I examines how teachers can use the basic principles of behavior to strengthen, weaken, and maintain behavior. The chapters explore systematic application of such principles for instruction at the elementary level, the secondary level, in physical education, in coaching, and in music education. Part I concludes by examining cognitive-motivational processes and group processes for their implications for teachers.

Part II explores the design of quality instruction through the use of mastery learning strategies and the careful, *logical* analysis of what is to be taught. The goal is to learn how teaching sequences can be designed that will lead to efficient learning and generalizable learning.

Part III examines developmental issues and individual differences. Chapters analyze the nature of intelligence, cognitive development, personal and social development, sex-related issues, how to deal with problems in student social behavior, and the special needs of special children.

Finally, Part IV describes issues involved in monitoring and evaluating instruction in more detail. Chapters cover criterion-referenced tests, norm-referenced tests, and an introduction to norm-referenced test theory.

SPECIAL FEATURES OF THIS TEXT

1. While building from the practical (readily usable) principles of behavior, there is up-to-date coverage of higher-cognitive processes.

2. It provides a systematic frame of reference for viewing classroom activities, and yet it provides a broad coverage of such topics as developmental processes, group process, cognitive-motivational processes, sex differences and equity issues, intelligence, behavior problems, and special education.

3. It is the only book of its type to systematically examine the design of quality instruction covering such areas as the basic structure of effective teaching (mastery learning models), the structure of cognitive knowledge, strategies for teaching different kinds of knowledge including concepts, facts, rules, principles, transformations, fact systems, problem-solving routines, and problem-solving strategies.

4. It illustrates program-design principles with an analysis of teaching reading and mathematics.

5. It teaches the basic principles for strengthening, weakening, and maintaining

behavior and shows how to apply them to design effective teaching-management systems for both elementary and secondary education. Use of special reinforcement systems for hard-to-teach students is discussed. Applications of principles to improving physical education, music education, and coaching are detailed.

6. It is the only text of its kind to outline a system-wide plan for systematically teaching responsibility to students, both in social areas and academic areas.

7. The text examines system designs for monitoring student learning using criterion-referenced tests.

8. Norm-referenced tests and their interpretation are examined.

9. Finally, some promising technologies of the near future—microcomputers, classroom network systems, and videodisc systems are illustrated with programs now in the developmental stage.

SUPPLEMENTS

A *Student Workbook* and an *Instructor's Manual* have been designed to accompany this text. The *Workbook* contains "Study Questions" which should be read before starting a chapter to help focus your study. After reading a chapter (or occasionally at various points in a chapter) go to the *Concept Practice* programmed instruction in the *Workbook* and (when included) the "Essential Definitions". Finally, return to the "Study Questions" and attempt to answer the questions in your own words. Answers are provided in the *Workbook* so you can check your answers. The *Workbook* also contains some projects to be carried out to apply what you are learning.

The *Instructor's Manual* contains test items, supplemental reading lists, suggestions for classroom presentations, and a guide for evaluating projects.

ACKNOWLEDGEMENTS

I am indebted to the following people for their assistance in preparation of this text by reviewing parts of the text: Douglas Carnine, Randy Sprick, Hill Walker, Lloyd Lovell, Richard Schmuck, and James Enochs. Richard Rankin, Dan Hursh, and Galen Alessi made major contributions by reviewing the full manuscript. A number of others, including Siegfried Engelmann, made strong substantive contributions to this work. They are specifically acknowledged at the appropriate points in the text.

Wesley C. Becker
Eugene, Oregon
September, 1985

CHAPTER

1

SCIENCE, HUMAN VALUES, AND TEACHING-INTEGRATING POLARITIES

When first faced with a scientific approach to the understanding of human behavior, as taken by psychologists, students often have many questions. This opening chapter examines some of those questions with the goal of helping you to understand the potential value of such an approach.

SOME QUESTIONS

- Does taking an objective view of human behavior detract from a personal view of humans as feeling-thinking persons?
- Are humanist values incompatible with a scientific approach to the study of people?
- Is freedom of choice incompatible with scientific determinism?
- How does scientific control differ from social control?

These and related questions are examined in this first chapter to clarify for you the assumptions about values and the philosophy of science that underpin our views.

A PERSONAL PERSPECTIVE

A year ago I had a student named Carl in my undergraduate educational psychology class—a class many students perceived as behaviorally oriented. I was presenting an objective view of human behavior that had grown out of the experimental study of behavior change processes (learning). Carl was also taking a course from another professor. His other professor, who had recommended my class, was focusing on a phenomenological perspective that emphasized the role of our personal learning history (especially the language we use) in structuring what we see; his goal was to make students aware of their own biases. What was noteworthy about Carl was his orientation to the world. Carl's personal orientation was Zen Buddhist. He dressed differently and approached the class differently than any student I have known. He was constantly trying to integrate the views of two professors and was also trying to translate back and forth between his Zen philosophy and behavioral principles. In his view, a person is a *unity* that can be looked at from the inside or the outside. I admired the wisdom of his position. I was pleased when he later told me that he had learned much from me that would be useful in his teaching career. In discussions with this student, I recalled what I had learned from Robert Pirsig's *Zen and the Art of Motorcycle Maintenance* (1974).

Pirsig's thesis was that we need a way of looking at the world that unites the polarities that have dominated philosophic history—logical-emotional, technology-art, objective-subjective, deductive-intuitive, physical-spiritual, classical-romantic, "square" and "hip"—*without doing violence to either.* In today's psychology a major polarity is the cognitive approach versus the behavioral approach; another is the humanistic orientation versus the behavioral. Within the behavioral approach is yet another expression of Pirsig's classical-romantic polarity, namely, respondent behavior (emotional, reflexive) versus operant behavior (which has the potential to be logical and intelligent).

Pirsig's pursuit of an integration of these polarities led to the study of values (qualities). For him values lie not in the object or the subject, but in *the reactions of the subject to the environment* (objects). *The most important aspect of our existence is neither objective or subjective, but an event relating both.* To illustrate his point, Pirsig uses the example of the amoeba placed in a plate of water with a drop of sulfuric acid in it. If the amoeba could think and talk, it would quickly say "This environment has poor quality." And it would likely (if it could) behave in a way that would change that environment.

Pirsig goes on to show that both classical (logical) and romantic (emotional) views of the world deal with values. The romantic (or artistic or existential) view treasures the values in immediate perceptions, while the classical (or logical or technological) view looks for value in events that relate the present to the past and the future. While it happens that "squares" in their analytic habits may fail to see the beauty before them, this is not a necessary outcome of intellectually oriented learning. Just as you might enjoy the beauty of the countryside and the wind in your face on a BMW bike, you can also learn to attend to what has happened in the past and might happen in the future if the oil, tires, and engine timing are not attended to (the art of motorcycle maintenance). Taking a romantic view of students (young and old) for all the ways they can please us, does not exclude the possibility that with a little teaching technology, we might come to better meet our goals for them. We are all both emotional-feeling beings with an internal view of ourselves, and rational-intelligent beings capable of taking an objective view of our world and how it works (including ourselves).

Because we see value in the scientific study of behavior does not mean that we have become (or will become) inhuman. If you love someone, you can still decide rationally to disagree with him or her on some choice. It is important to keep an open mind and heart in looking for value. Those taking a more scientific approach to the "art of teaching" (empirical behaviorists) have often been criticized by humanists as being simplistic, rigid, and impersonal. They have also been criticized by cognitive psychologists as being wrong. As far as I can see, we are all "blindmen" describing the same "elephant" from different perspectives, and there is likely to be truth in each of the so-called opposing positions.

My personal point of view grows out of empirical behavior theory, but it doesn't stop there. I see value in studying how logical analysis can help us develop a theory of instruction about cognitive learning, and how emotions and feelings can be developed and changed through learning processes. Finally, I believe that a continuous sequence of value judgments underlies all that we do as scientists, as teachers, as parents, and as friends.

A SCIENTIFIC PERSPECTIVE

One goal of science is to study orderliness in nature—to find out what leads to what. Most of us are convinced that there is lawfulness in the physical world. The sun rises predictably; A-bombs explode on signal; and ice melts at 32°F. That *behavior* is lawful is sometimes quite obvious. After a day on a hot desert with no water, people will drink. In different learning environments around the world, we see remarkable consistencies in language, dress, gesture, and patterns of relating. For example, Russians speak Russian, not Italian. The more we as scientists investigate the environmental conditions that control learning (behavior change), the more convinced we are that *all learning follows lawful processes,* which can be known. This is equivalent to saying that behavior is determined by causes. It does not mean that we know enough about the variables affecting a given individual at a given point in time to precisely predict his or her every behavior. It simply means that they are potentially knowable.

After millions of corroborating observations, the initial assumption that behavior is determined has assumed the status of an empirical law: All behavioral events have causes. This same lawfulness is also found in the rest of the physical world.

HUMANISTIC VALUES AND BEHAVIOR SCIENCE

Historically, humanists have been concerned with the problems of people, here and now, rather than in some afterlife that might be. It was the early humanist movement that helped to create the Renaissance and foster the development of modern science. Humanists are still concerned for the individual. They value such qualities as self-determination, self-knowledge, personal responsibility, individuality, diversity, and openness. But some humanists today oppose making human behavior the object of scientific study because they feel that such study of man as seen from the outside will somehow destroy what they value in man as seen from the inside. This argument seems to contradict their concern with self-knowledge. To become mature involves developing a more objective frame of reference about oneself.

When we examine the values held by most behaviorally oriented professionals, we find that they also must be called humanists. They are concerned with helping others as individuals find solutions to their here-and-now problems. The major difference seems to be not in the *values* held, but in the *methods of knowing* considered acceptable. The behavioral scientist insists on dealing with observations that can be verified by others. While thoughts and feelings are observable to the person experiencing them, they are not subject to verification by others.[1] Also many value-related terms like *concern, self-knowledge,* and *openness* are not sufficiently specific for the behavioral scientist. The behavioral scientist would have to ask, "What do you mean by openness; that is, how does this value affect your behavior?" In the process, the value terms are given some observable action equivalents. For example:

Concern	"I will volunteer as a classroom aide working with disadvantaged children."
Self-knowledge	"When I do a job for others, like giving a lecture, I ask for feedback on my performance. I try to know how I affect others."

[1] B.F. Skinner (1953) has proposed that we use what we know from studying observable behavior and indirect methods of assessment to study the unobservables.

Individuality	"I support the right to be different."
Openness	"I let others know what I am thinking and feeling. I encourage others to talk to me."

People may have the same actions in mind when they use a particular value term, or they may not. One person's concern may not be another's. The behaviorist would seek to clarify such terms before studying their role in human behavior. But it does not mean that his or her values are different. It only means that the terms are not acceptable in a science of behavior until they have been defined in terms of observables. The issue is one of methods, not value differences.

The Problem of Control

If we agree that behavior is lawful, we have accepted the assumption that behavior is *determined* (controlled) by causes. These causes are environmental events, called *stimuli.* Thus, to the behavioral scientist, it is correct to say that behavior is controlled by stimulus events. But this is not the kind of control that we personally find upsetting. We are content when we can do what we have found is rewarding for us. The fact that we have learned to do things in a determined world poses no problem; it is when someone tries to *prevent us* from doing what we have learned to do that we get upset. We object to controls by others that are coercive.

But control by others need not be coercive. In fact we are all social controllers to the extent that we teach each other. Much of what each of us does determines how others behave. Parents teach children, children teach parents, husbands teach wives, wives teach husbands, caring people teach each other. In a very real sense we are each reponsible for what others learn—how they learn to behave with us. We have the power to make others better people. With a knowledge of behavior principles we can facilitate what we value in people and their social systems.

THE PROBLEMS OF FREE WILL AND RESPONSIBILITY

In the history of philosophy, the concept of free will has had two features: (1) it refers to the behavior of making choices without being hampered, and (2) it involves an assumption that choices are not caused by physical or divine events. The problem that arises is this: If all behavior is determined, then human beings cannot have a free will. If humans do not have free will, how can they be held responsible for their actions?

As we know them today, the facts are: (1) people do make choices at times without being coerced by others, but (2) this choice behavior is determined by physical events or causes. Where, then, does that leave responsibility? To see the issue more clearly, we need to discriminate between *physical principles* that influence our behavior and *rules established by a society that humans created.* The former are the laws of science, and they *describe* what leads to what. The latter are "laws of society," and they *prescribe* what one should do. It is within the context of human social-rule systems that questions of freedom, coercion, and responsibility arise. Some societies are structured to provide more freedom (individual choice); others have more restrictive rules. Social-rule systems are subsystems within nature. People within society still behave according to their "nature," but society has now specified some consequences that can influence the choices that we make. Figure 1.1 illustrates the relation, showing social systems as subsystems within nature.

Responsibility can be personal or legal. Legal responsibility is *assumed* (for example, by entering into a marriage contract) or *assigned* by social rules.

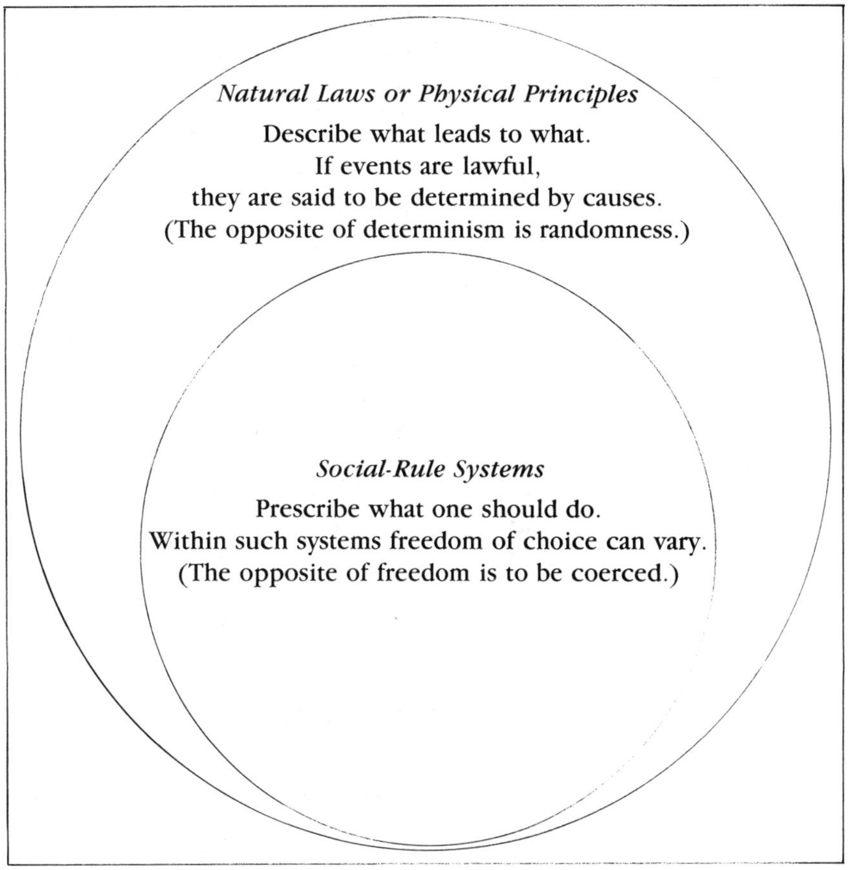

Figure 1-1 *The relation of natural law and social-rules system*

For example, the law states that parents are responsible for the care of their children. Parents can be punished for a failure to meet this responsibility. But the laws do not make a person responsible. We need to be taught to be law-abiding. Behavior principles can help us do this teaching.

What about personal, rather than legal, responsibility? This is an *assumed* responsibility based on an *implicit* contract with others to take care of each other. It is assumed because of an understanding of our mutual dependence on each other for important human satisfactions—such as love, affection, sharing, giving, safety, and nourishment.

THE PROBLEM OF SIMPLICITY AND MISREPRESENTATION

Nancy Cooke (1984) recently analyzed some of the ways in which behavioral viewpoints are presented in texts for teachers. Besides the fact that the technical terms of behavior theory are often misused and misdefined, many texts for teachers go out of their way to present a view of behavior theory that focuses on the work of Ivan Pavlov (1927) and John B. Watson (1919). They focus on the mechanisms for classical conditioning (what this text calls respondent or reflexive behavior) and largely ignore the far reaching contributions of B. F. Skinner in the study of operant (intelligent) behavior (1938, 1948, 1953, 1954, 1957, 1958, 1968, 1969). Behaviorists are often characterized as stimulus-response psychologists, operating within a rigid, simplistic view of human learning. Modern behavior theory is characterized as too simplistic to deal with the complexities of human cognitive process. Some assert that concept formation, problem solving, and operational thought are not covered by behavior theory, and that behavior theory explains only habits and reflexes. Such a characterization presents a false view of behavior theory.

Through the study of *individual organisms,* Skinner developed the basic principles for teaching organisms and showed us how to apply them to teaching humans. A large percentage of the principles presented in the early part of this text come directly from the work of B. F. Skinner and his students or are extensions of that work by others. From the beginning, Skinner dealt with concepts and operations, rather than fixed stimuli and responses. He described how *intelligent* organisms learn, not just how reflexes are conditioned. As you will see as you progress through this text, basic behavioral principles provide a solid foundation for understanding how more complex intellectual skills are learned. With a simple extension, "thinking" becomes the problem-solving behavior that we humans do in our heads through the manipulation of words and symbols, rather than through operating physically on the environment.

Operant behavior classes (physical operations) are closely related to Piaget's mental operations, except that one is overt while the other covert. For example, when the operation of addition is first learned, it usually involves adding members to a physical group (an overt operation). When such operations are carried out symbolically through a chain of words and mental pictures, addition becomes a mental operation. Mental operations are *concepts* about physical operations. Modern behavior theory is not restricted to the simple or trivial aspects of human behavior.

FALSE EXPLANATIONS FOR BEHAVIOR

History is full of false explanations for behavior. As recently as 1692 people were executed as witches in this country, as late as 1782 in Switzerland. Devil, gods, and ghosts have carried a big load in the accounting for behavior in the past. Unfortunately, there are continuing misconceptions cloaked in the guise of scientific explanations to bedevil the teacher.

Circular Explanations

In *a circular explanation,* a hypothetical cause is inferred from behavior and then said to cause the behavior, but all the human observer can know about is the behavior itself. A hyperactive student is referred to a psychologist who infers that the child has "minimal brain damage." But there is no evidence for brain damage and all the psychologist knows is that the student moves around in the class a lot and does not get her work done. Later in the text you will see illustrations of several classrooms where such behavior was radically changed simply by changing when and how the teachers showed attention to such students. (This does not imply that there may not be some physical factors operating with some hyperactive children. The point is simply that it may be dangerous to make assumptions about causes without first exploring the possible causes.)

Early psychologists often used terms like *needs, instincts,* and *ego forces* to explain behavior. Their accounts of the reasons for behavior became circular. In our personal attempts to account for the behavior of others, humans often make this same error in logic. Here are some examples:

"Why is he so suspicious and jealous?" (Behavioral effect)
"He's paranoid." (Pseudo cause)
"How do you know that?" (Investigation)
"See how suspicious and jealous he is." (Circular reason)

"Why can't he learn to read?" (Behavioral effect)
"He has a learning disability." (Pseudo cause)

"How do you know that?" (Investigation)
"See, he can't read." (Circular reason)

The logical structure of a circular explanation is *A* is *A:* he does it because he does it. However, this structure is hidden by a label for the behavior to be explained. He does not read because he has a *learning disability.* But investigation shows that the only information available is that he does not read because he does not read. No independent variable or cause is specified.

In the following examples, a cause is specified.

Cause	*Effect*
Rivers that hinder food-gathering	Builds bridges
Poor reading instruction	Can not read
No reinforcement for sitting and working	Stays out of seat (called hyperactive)
Reinforcement for schoolwork	Does well in school

Purposeful Explanations

Another common error in explaining behavior is to assert that a person is going to do something in order to acquire or achieve something—for a purpose. "I am going to go to the store to get milk." While statements like this are easily understood and aid communication, they must be false *as explanations* because *causes have to come before their effects.* Causes, which are events in time, can only move forward. An event that has not yet occurred cannot be the cause of an event that has occurred. In his debates with Carl Rogers, B. F. Skinner gave the example of a spider to make his point (because spiders obviously do not have purposes). "Why do spiders spin webs?" "In order to catch flies" is a common answer. But this cannot possibly be true because the cause comes after the behavior to be explained. More likely, the answer lies in a long evolutionary history where spiders who developed web-spinning capabilities were able to get food and were more likely to reproduce. Later in this book you will explore the assertion that consequences control what is learned. You will find that this actually means that consequences affect the *future probability* of behavior; they do not cause the response in the first instance. As you shall see, other events that are a part of a technology of teaching can be used to get responses to occur so that they can be reinforced. When you come across a purposeful explanation, look to the genetic and learning history of the organism for the real causes. Humans do plan and set goals, but these plans are made because of what we have learned to do in the past.

SOME VALUES OF A SCIENTIFIC APPROACH

If in fact there are tested principles and procedures that can be applied as a technology of teaching, it is possible that knowing about them will make you a better teacher. Teacher decision making can be guided by this technology, rather than by trial and error, or by what other teachers did to you. Knowing how the motorcycle goes together, how it operates, and its periodic maintenance needs is valuable information in keeping it running. Knowing how students learn, how to motivate them, and how to build on what they know to teach what they need to know can be valuable information. When we first went to Tupelo, Mississippi, in the summer of 1968 with a project called Follow Through, a program for disadvantaged students in kindergarten through third grade, one teacher had completely failed the year before to teach reading to five of her first grade black children. After four weeks of training that summer in cognitive-behavioral procedures underlying the Direct Instruction Model, she was able to go back to her classroom that fall and teach these same students to read quite well by Christmas. Even though she had been teaching for over 30 years, she quickly become a devotee to a new technology because she saw that *it worked.*

A scientific understanding of behavior cannot only help you to be a better teacher, but perhaps even a better person. Much of the thoughtlessness in our own behavior goes on because we do not understand what we are doing. A number of teachers' primary mode of interaction with their students (and spouses) is to criticize behavior they do not like and ignore appropriate behavior. This text discusses this problem later, calling it the *criticism trap.* In the criticism trap, behavior that you are trying to weaken by criticism is found to actually *increase.* Experimental studies in the classroom have revealed ways to make a positive approach to reducing classroom problems very effective.

Finally, with an appropriate knowledge of teaching technology, the teacher can discard the misconception that teaching failures should be blamed on the students: "He failed because of his home background, his IQ," "She had a learning disability," or "His motivation was poor." You should no longer accept the conclusion: "I can't teach students if they do not want to learn." With effective teaching technology, the teacher is able to accept responsibility for students' progress in learning, as the physician does when children are ill.

SUMMARY

Many college students preparing for the teaching profession have been taught to distrust objective, experimental-based approaches to classroom practice as dehumanizing, unfeeling, and so on. This chapter examined this problem in the context of the classical romantic polarity in the history of Western thought. It is important to keep an open mind, to decide for yourself whether or not there is *value* or potential value in taking a scientific approach to the technology of teaching. As Pirsig might say, while the beauty of the moment may be very important to people, there may also be value in a technology for creating beauty (relating the past to the present) and preserving it for the future.

Probably one of the most important lessons any of us can learn is how to integrate apparently opposite views. Pirsig found a way to integrate the subjective and the objective in the definition of value. For him value lies neither in the object nor the subject, but in the reactions of subject to object. As you begin your study of the analysis of behavior in the next chapter, you should see that what Pirsig calls values is very closely related to what behavioral scientists call reinforcing and punishing stimuli. In addition, these consequent events are not defined as *objects* in the environment, but as *events* relating the person (subject) to objects in the environment. The major tenets of modern behavior theory are expressed in functional definitions that relate stimulus events to behavior.

The study of behavior has shown that behavior is related in systematic ways to stimulus events. Behavior has *causes* that you can come to know and use in a technology of teaching. These procedures are codified as scientific principles. They are statements of what leads to what. If behavior has causes that can be known, it can be controlled. However, be careful to distinguish *scientific control* from the common meaning of *control,* which is more appropriately called *social control.* Scientific control is just another way of saying that you know the cause of something, and how to make it happen or not happen. Having scientific control of a process can be used to produce good (positive value) or evil (negative value) for people. The control that humans typically dislike is aversive social control—when other people make them do things (under threat of punishment) that they would not otherwise choose to do. With an adequate knowledge of behavior, it is potentially possible to design social systems that are less coercive and more reinforcing. It is a question of seeking what has long-term value for the most people. The course of history can be viewed as an expression of this perspective (with a few dramatic setbacks now and then).

The historic-philosophic-religious necessity to deny scientific determinism in order to save "free will" and responsibility can be resolved by recognizing that the problem of freedom of choice arises within social-rule systems. We all make choices, and we like to do so without being coerced by others. But even when we make choices, the choices are determined by our personal genetic and learning histories. Some societies permit more freedom than others. But all societies operate within the framework of deterministic natural law.

Issues of responsibility also arise within social-rule systems and are based on contracts between people and laws made by people. Personal responsibility is *assumed* through an implicit contract people make with other people to be mutually supporting.

Accusations that behavior theory is too simplistic to handle the complexities of human cognition are usually based on a confusion of early behavior theories with modern behavior theories.

Several false explanations for behavior were discussed. Although sounding like causal statements, circular explanations contain no cause and, in reality, say nothing. That people do things for a purpose has to be logically incorrect, since causality runs only forward in time. Of course people make plans and follow them, but they do so because of behaviors and outcomes learned in the past.

Explanations of student behavior that place the blame (cause) for teaching failures on the students are no longer acceptable. The teacher is *responsible.* Present knowledge of behavior can be used to help you learn to become an effective teacher. It can also be used to help you better manage your own life and to contribute to a better world.

PART I

CLASSROOM MANAGEMENT

To build an understanding of classroom management strategies, Chapter 2 begins with an overview of the key principles underlying behavior theory. Because this overview comes thick and fast and there are many new concepts to learn, instructions to go to *Concept Practice* exercises in your *Workbook* appear at four places in this chapter. A careful study of definitions and examples of concepts is needed.

Chapters 3 to 6 develop the basic principles from Chapter 2 into generalizable procedures useful in the classroom for both instruction and behavior management. First, five procedures are discussed for strengthening behavior, then three procedures for weakening behavior, and finally, five procedures for maintaining behavior. These provide a powerful set of tools for good classroom management. Chapters 7 to 9 develop more specialized applications of the basic principles. First, you will learn about token systems and point-contract systems that might be useful in a resource room, a special education classroom, or with the more difficult student in the regular classroom. Next, you will look at the necessary planning to set up both elementary and secondary classrooms for the start of a new year. Then, applications to physical education, coaching, and music education are considered. The final two chapters in Part I look at issues involving cognitive-motivational processes and group processes and are designed to broaden your view of interaction processes.

CHAPTER

2

BASIC PRINCIPLES OF BEHAVIOR

In this chapter you will consider a few basic principles which control the learning that leads to the complexities of the adult human. Two classes of behavior are identified which are differentially related to four different kinds of stimuli that have effects on behavior (called functional stimuli). Beyond these basic classes of responses and functional stimuli, there are simple processes for converting neutral stimuli (stimuli that do not at first have an effect on behavior) into functional stimuli and procedures for undoing such learning. But first, consider these dramatic changes that took place in a first grade classroom through the application of some of the principles you will be learning.

USING BEHAVIOR PRINCIPLES TO RAPIDLY CHANGE AN OUT OF CONTROL CLASS

Observations on February 1: "Six children were in a reading group and fifteen were working on individual projects. The noise level for the entire classroom was extremely high and went higher just before recess. Some behavior noted included whistling, running around the room (five occasions), yelling at another child (many times), loud incessant talk, and hitting each other in recess line. Mrs. E. would reestablish quiet by counting to ten after giving a threat."

Mrs. E. was a young teacher who had not been taught how to manage children. She attempted to control the children by shouting and scolding, but it would only slow down the unwanted behavior for a short time, and she would have to "get on them" again. Two boys in Mrs. E.'s class were studied closely.

Edward was six years nine-months old and of average ability. His teacher described him as distractable, with poor attention and poor work habits. He did not comprehend what he read. He never finished assignments. He was often seen wandering about the room or turning in his seat. He made odd noises with his mouth. He was in speech therapy and was being seen by the social worker.

Elmer was two months older than Edward and was also of average intelligence. He apparently started out the school year working well, but got worse. He was described as nervous and very active. He would not work. He cried or threw a tantrum if his work was criticized. Observers thought Elmer might have brain damage, since he was so very active. He did not stay in one place or on any task very long.

Figure 2.1 tells the story of the change in these two boys. You first need to understand that observers in the classroom were recording a variety of deviant behaviors shown by these boys using a twenty-second observation interval. Before attempting to change the situation, the boys were observed for five weeks

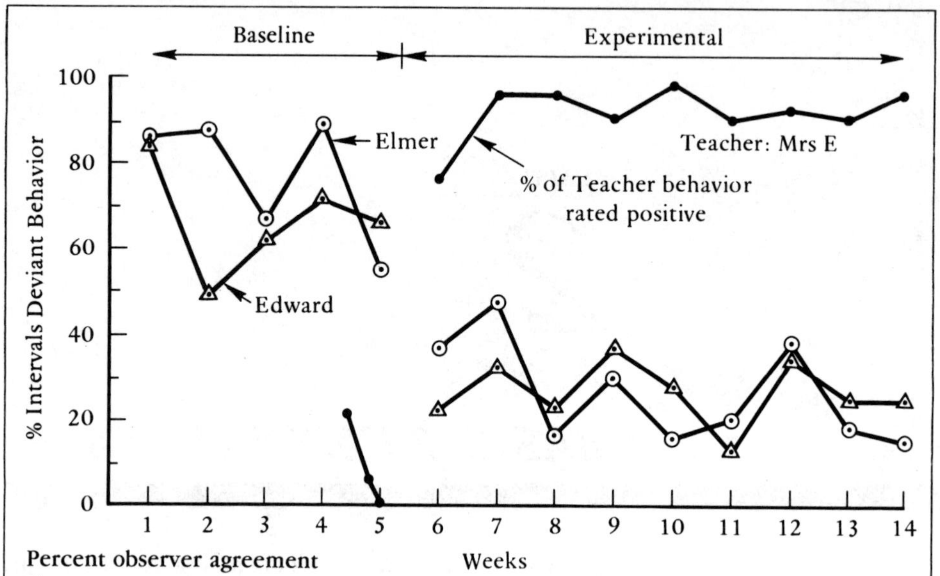

Percent observer agreement	1	2	3	4	5	6	7	8	9	10	11	12	13	14
Elmer	98	95	92	89	90	–	–	–	–	91	96	–	98	97
Edward	87	94	91	92	90	–	–	95	–	–	–	100	91	90

Figure 2.1 *Changes in behavior for two children and their teacher*

(the baseline condition). Elmer was showing deviant behavior in nearly 80 percent of the observation intervals, and Edward was showing deviant behavior in over 60 percent of them. In Figure 2.1, the vertical axis represents the percent of deviant behavior for the two boys. It also represents the percent of positive behavior shown by Mrs. E. If you look carefully at the solid circles between week four and week five, you will see that Mrs. E. rarely used praise in the classroom.

Beginning in week six (the experimental condition), Mrs. E. was asked to follow these procedures:

1. *Give clear signals.* Specify the desired behavior. Make your rules clear, so that the children will know what is expected to them. Repeat the rules as necessary.

2. *Ignore disruptive behavior.* Do not attend to the behavior you wish to weaken. Get involved with other children showing behavior you wish to strengthen. Praise a child showing behavior incompatible with the disruptive behavior. Play deaf and dumb.

3. *Praise the children for improvement in behavior.* Catch the children being good, rather than bad. Tell them what it is you like that they're doing. Award privileges to those showing good behavior. For example, say "You can lead the salute because you are paying attention so well."

Prior to week six, this teacher used very little praise. After week six, over 90 percent of her comments to children were positive rather than negative. Elmer and Edward changed greatly, as did the teacher and other members of the class. It took some time for the teacher to become comfortable in her new role of being a reinforcer for children, but the children responded to her new behavior whether she felt comfortable about it or not. The classroom became quieter; many members learned to work on-task for long periods of time. There was order and cooperation. The teacher found she had more time to teach now that she spent less time trying to control the children (Becker, Madsen, Arnold & Thomas, 1967).

The study of Mrs. E. shows how knowledge of behavior change principles can be very valuable to teachers. To become skillful in this area, one first needs to acquire a technical understanding of behavior principles and then to study and practice their applications in the classroom. This chapter requires you to learn the technical language so that you later can correctly apply the principles. The more effort you apply in this basic learning, the easier it will be later to master applications.

STIMULUS FUNCTIONS

In unraveling the genetic code, James Watson and Francis Crick (*The Double Helix*) were able to demonstrate that the development of the most complex organisms on this earth is controlled by a genetic code built out of five simple elements: hydrogen, carbon, oxygen, nitrogen, and phosphorus. With this understanding, biological scientists are making great strides in what has come to be called genetic engineering, and in showing the high similarities in gene structures across species. This knowledge is also of great importance for research on the causes and cures of cancer.

For years, arguments have been made that the human being is much too complex a creature to ever be fully understood. Our complex genetic structures and the learning events of a lifetime make each of us truly unique. But now we are beginning to see some simplicities in principles underlying this complex uniqueness. Just as five basic elements underlie genetic variability, it appears that only four major stimulus functions can help us to understand behavioral uniqueness (and one of these functions is derived from two of the others).

A *stimulus* is an aspect of the environment that can be specified in a way that two or more observers can agree on when it is present and when it is not.

Table 2-1 Two responses classes and four stimulus functions

<table>
<tr><th colspan="2">Two Response Classes</th></tr>
<tr><td>Respondent Behavior
(reflexive)</td><td>Operant Behavior
(voluntary)</td></tr>
<tr><td colspan="2">Four Stimulus Functions</td></tr>
<tr><td>1. Eliciting function.
Unconditioned stimulus (US) makes an unconditioned response (UR) happen.
$US \rightarrow UR$</td><td>2. Reinforcing function.
A reinforcing stimulus (S^R) strengthens the operant behavior it follows.
$R \rightarrow S^R$

3. Punishing function.
A punishing stimulus (S^P) weakens the operant behavior it follows.
$R \rightarrow S^P$

4. Discriminative function.
A preceding stimulus (S^d) "tells" us when to do (or not to do) what.
$S^d \rightarrow R \rightarrow S^R$
or$\rightarrow S^P$</td></tr>
</table>

Any stimulus has the potential to exert some control over behavior. Stimuli include visual properties of objects, objects, sounds, movements, smells, etc.

Some stimuli can be shown to control behavior. They are functional stimuli because they *do* influence behavior. The concept of ***stimulus functions*** is very important. There are millions of stimulus events going on around us all the time. The concept of stimulus functions focuses our attention on those events that are ***systematically related to behavioral outcomes.*** Some stimuli elicit reflexive or respondent behavior, some stimuli strengthen or weaken "voluntary" or operant behavior, and some become discriminative stimuli for operant behavior. By noting the common strengthening function of such stimuli as a smile, a pat on the back, a good grade, a hug, or a piece of gum, we are able to greatly simplify our understanding of the causes of behavior. In Chapter 1, value was defined as an event relating subject and object; so too it is with stimulus functions. The functions of environmental stimuli are defined by how they affect behavior. By using *functional definitions* (rather than arbitrarily just assuming something is a reinforcer or punisher), the psychologist or teacher is required to respect the unique genetic and learning history of each student. What is reinforcing for one child may not be for another. We have to check carefully to see if our assumptions are true by seeing if what we call reinforcers actually function to strengthen behavior for particular persons. The four stimulus functions are previewed in Table 2.1.

RESPONDENTS AND OPERANTS

Modern behavior theory distinguishes between two classes of behavior: respondent and operant. *Respondent behavior* involves reactions of the smooth muscles and glands; it includes such reflexive reactions as sweating, salivating, secreting digestive juices, shivering, and the activation syndrome (secretion of adrenalin, increased blood sugar, increased heart rate, increased respiration rate). *Operant behavior* involves the striated muscular system (or the muscles that we normally talk about as under voluntary control). Behaviors such as talking, walking, eating, and problem solving are examples of operant behavior. Although currently there are controversies about the distinction between operants and respondents, this distinction has proved to be useful in applied work.

Repondent behavior is controlled by preceding stimuli. For example:

US	→	UR
Unconditioned Stimulus *(Preceding Stimulus)*	→	Unconditioned Response *(Respondent Behavior)*
Lemon juice in mouth	→	Salivation
Sudden loud noise	→	Startle reaction
Bright light in eye	→	Pupil contraction
Tap to knee	→	Knee jerk
Crushing of finger	→	Activation syndrome

In the case of respondent behavior, preceding stimuli are said to *elicit* (or cause) the response. Present the stimulus and you get the response. Certain stimuli (called *unconditioned stimuli or US,*) function to elicit respondents. They have an eliciting function.

In contrast, operant behavior is controlled by stimulus events that immediately follow the operant. As noted in Chapter 1, a following stimulus cannot cause the operant response (because causes must come before their effects), but once an operant behavior occurs, *its future rate of occurrence* depends upon its consequences. Consequent stimuli can have either a reinforcing or a punishing function. *Reinforcers* are stimuli that strengthen operant behavior, and *punishers* are stimuli which weaken operant behavior.

A specific preceding stimulus (or class of stimuli) can become the signal for an operant response (that is, it can acquire a *discriminative* function). To make this happen, it is necessary to reinforce an appropriate response only in the presence of that stimulus. For example, to teach the discrimination of the color *red* and to respond with its name "red," you would demonstrate through modeled examples what is *red* and *not-red.* Then you would test the student with additional examples and reinforce right responses and correct wrong responses. The result is that the child now knows *when* to say "red" and "not-red."

In a similar way, discriminative stimuli followed by punishing consequences can become signals not to do something (this is known as *avoidance behavior*). Green lights are discriminative stimuli or S^ds indicating that going through an intersection is likely (not guaranteed) to be safe. Red lights are S^ds indicating that going through an intersection could be punishing.

Thus, both respondents and operants can be controlled by *preceding* stimuli, but there is a difference in the nature of the control. The respondent reflex is caused by an appropriate preceding stimulus that has an *eliciting function.* In the case of an operant, we would be hard put to say that the redness in the red ball caused the response "red." In fact looking at the learning history reveals that initially the red ball brought out no response. Only after many teaching examples in which positive and negative consequences were applied did saying "red" to red stimuli occur. The *consequences* of the child's answers caused the child to learn to name red-colored objects correctly. The red objects themselves only *set the occasion* when saying "red" would be reinforced. In sum, preceding stimuli can have an eliciting function for respondent behavior and a discriminative function for operant behavior.

Thus far we have distinguished between two types of behavior and discussed the way antecedent and consequent stimuli relate to each. These distinctions may be diagramed as follows:

Model 1

US ——————→ UR

Eliciting stimulus   Respondent Behavior

Model 2

S^d ————→ R ————→ S

Discriminative Stimulus   Operant Response   Consequent Stimulus

Operant behavior usually involves a three-part contingency (discrimnative stimulus, response, consequent stimulus). It is this behavioral model that is most important to the teacher. In fact, you will see the respondent model at only two other places in this text—in the analysis of conditioned reinforcers and conditioned emotional reactions. The operant model provides the basis for a model of teaching. Teaching is changing what children do or say (responses) under particular stimulus conditions. We make learning happen by systematically controlling stimuli that precede a child's response and those that follow it.

The teacher basically uses discriminative stimuli and consequent stimuli to change behavior.

Go to *Concept Practice 2A and 2B* in your *Workbook*, complete the programed exercises, and then return to text.

A Technical Note

As mentioned earlier, there is much controversy over the operant-respondent distinction even though it has proved very useful in applied work. Teitelbaum (1977) probably comes closest to expressing the "truth" in the matter. Teitelbaum sees a continuum of gradations between respondent and operant behavior. He sees the respondent as the *idealized* pure reflex, "prewired," and the operant at the *idealized* purely adaptable behavior (any stimulus can be conditioned to any response). These are models that help us to understand what is going on. But like Newton's laws, which only operate in a vacuum, they are only part of the truth. In every operant, there is likely some built-in selectivity in what we respond to and how we respond that is not changeable. And, in every respondent there is likely some adaptability.

CONDITIONING AND EXTINCTION OF STIMULUS FUNCTIONS

Extinction of Discriminative Functions

In the presence of an S^d, operant approach responses can be strengthened by reinforcers and avoidance responses can be strengthened by preventing punishment. As noted earlier, discriminative stimuli are learned cues for behavior. A reversal of this learning can occur, however, if an operant is no longer followed by reinforcers at least some of the time. *Extinction* of responding to the S^d is said to occur. Extinction of avoidance responses is also likely to occur if the situation makes clear that punishment is not likely to happen. However, in many cases the avoidance behavior prevents one from learning about a threat that may no longer be there. Many neurotic behaviors such as phobias and compulsive behaviors are thought to be of this nature. As long as you perform the avoidance behavior, you do not get punished. But it may be unrealistic behavior and costly in terms of time and effort.

There are also complications in the extinction of approach behaviors. One reinforcer may be removed, but others may still operate. How long it takes for extinction to occur is complicated by the effects of schedules of reinforcement. The more important practical issues concerning extinction and resistance to extinction will be discussed later.

Conditioning and Extinction of Other Stimulus Functions

Eliciting (US), reinforcing (S^R), and punishing stimuli (S^P) can also have conditioned (learned) forms. If a neutral stimulus (one that does not have that function) is *repeatedly* followed immediately by a US, S^R, or S^P), it can acquire the same function.

- A neutral stimulus (say a tone) that is quickly followed by an eliciting stimulus (shock) will come to elicit some of the fearful reactions caused by the shock.

- A neutral stimulus (money to the young child) that is soon exchanged for a reinforcer (say candy) will become a conditioned reinforcer (if the candy was reinforcing for that child). The child will then come to do things to get money.

- A neutral stimulus ("No") that is followed by a punishing stimulus (say a spanking for running into the street) will come to be a conditioned punisher.

The conditioned property of a stimulus can be ***extinguished*** (weakened) if the conditioned stimulus is repeatedly presented without pairing it with the unconditioned stimulus. In the three examples, repeated use of the tone without the shock would come to weaken its eliciting properties. If money could no longer be exchanged for "goodies," it would lose its conditioned reinforcing properties. If "No" was never backed up with an effective punisher, it would lose its punishing properties. Table 2.2 summarizes these new conditioning and extinction procedures. (Note that we use *capital* R and P for unconditioned reinforcers and punishers, and *lower case* r and p for conditioned forms.)

Table 2-2 Summary of conditioned stimulus functions and extinction of such functions (does not include S^d)

<table>
<tr><td colspan="2">Conditioning
General Procedure: Pair a neutral stimulus with an effective stimulus, repeatedly.</td></tr>
<tr><td>Respondent Behavior</td><td>Operant Behavior</td></tr>
<tr><td>1. A neutral stimulus repeatedly followed by an eliciting stimulus (US) becomes a conditioned stimulus (CS) capable of eliciting some part of the unconditioned response (UR). The response to a conditioned eliciting stimulus is called a conditioned response (CR).</td><td>2. A neutral stimulus repeatedly followed by an effective reinforcing stimulus becomes a conditioned reinforcer (S^r).

3. A neutral stimulus repeatedly followed by a punishing stimulus becomes a conditioned punisher (S^p).</td></tr>
<tr><td colspan="2">Extinction
General Procedure: Present conditioned form without the unconditioned form, repeatedly.</td></tr>
<tr><td>Respondent Behavior</td><td>Operant Behavior</td></tr>
<tr><td>1. Results in a weakening or loss of a conditioned eliciting function (CS).</td><td>2. Results in a weakening or loss of the conditioned reinforcing function (S^r).

3. Results in a weakening or loss of the conditioned punishing function (S^p).</td></tr>
</table>

Go to *Concept Practice 2C* in your *Workbook*, complete the programed exercises, and then return to text.

TYPES OF REINFORCERS AND PUNISHERS

There are two types of reinforcers and two types of punishers. Generally, those consequences we could call "rewards" tend to function as reinforcers (but we have to check, because this may not be true), but in addition, *the stopping of "painful" or "unpleasant" events* will also usually function as reinforcers of behaviors. Getting in out of the hot sun can be reinforcing, as is taking your hand off the hot stove. Those consequences we would label as punishing or "painful" tend to function as punishers and weaken the future occurrence of the behavior they follow. But *the stopping or taking away of rewarding events* can also weaken the behavior they follow.

Table 2.3 illustrates the relations between the two types of punishment and two types of reinforcement.

Table 2-3 Two types of reinforcing and punishing stimulus events

Effect on Behavior	*Procedure*	
	Present a stimulus following behavior	*Withdraw a stimulus following behavior*
Strengthens	Reinforcement by presenting a stimulus (Positive reinforcement)	Reinforcement by withdrawing a stimulus (Negative reinforcement) (Reinforces avoidance and escape behavior)
Weakens	Punishment by presenting a stimulus (Punishment)	Punishment by withdrawing a stimulus (Time out and response cost)

NOTE: Some textbooks use negative reinforcement as another word for punishment. When you see this word used, look carefully for the meaning intended.

This text will use the terms *reinforcement* and *positive reinforcement* interchangeably. When you see the term *negative reinforcement* used here, the text will try to make clear what it is that is escaped from or avoided. The term *escape* is used to refer to turning off an unconditioned aversive stimulus (such as a shock) and the term *avoidance* to refer to the turning off of a conditioned aversive stimulus (such as nagging).

There are two major varieties of punishment by withdrawing or turning off a positive stimulus. One is *time out* from positive reinforcement and the other *response cost.* In *time out,* the punishment might consist of placing a tantruming child in a nonreinforcing environment until the tantrum is over. In *response cost,* a valued reinforcer is lost. For example, we might lose $30 to the judge for speeding. A reinforcing stimulus, money, is taken away as a punishment. Other response-cost procedures might involve loss of privileges or free time as a consequence for misbehavior.

EXTINCTION VERSUS TIME OUT

Since extinction of behavior controlled by reinforcers and time out both involve withholding reinforcers, the procedures are sometimes confused. The difference is this: in time out, no reinforcers are given for any response; in extinction, responses other than those being extinguished may be reinforced. If a child is placed in his or her room until tantruming stops (time out), the parent has to be careful to see that other reinforcers (besides being with the parent) are not present. When Mrs. E. ignored disruptive behavior (extinction), she was withholding a social reinforcer (attention) from that behavior. At the same time, she was using reinforcement to strengthen on-task behavior.

Go to *Concept Practice 2D* in your *Workbook*, complete the programed exercises, and then return to summary.

SUMMARY

There are two main classes of behavior. *Respondent* behavior consists of reflexes, the actions of the smooth muscles and glands. Much emotional behavior can be understood as respondent conditioning. Loves, fears, and hates have much of their bases in conditioned emotional reactions. *Operant* behavior is intelligent or "voluntary" behavior.

Three of the four basic stimulus functions relate to operant behavior. The fourth relates to respondent behavior. These functions are:

- *Eliciting function.* We are "prewired" to respond to certain stimuli in automatic ways. These stimuli elicit respondent behavior. They make it happen. Think of how you jump if someone makes a loud noise right behind you. Your heart beats faster, and maybe you perspire.

- Stimuli that function as *reinforcers, punishers,* and *discriminative* stimuli affect operant behavior. Reinforcers are stimuli that will increase the future occurrence of the behavior they follow. Punishers are stimuli that decrease the future occurrence of the behavior they follow. Discriminative stimuli are signals or *cues* that tell us "when to do (or not to do) what." These cues that precede operant behavior are important because they have been associated with responses that have led to reinforcement or the avoidance of punishment in the past. As you will see later, much of what is called intelligent behavior can be understood as operant behavior under the control of discriminative stimuli. Concept learning will be shown to be multiple-discrimination learning, and problem-solving behavior can be viewed as chains of operants under discriminative control.

Extinction of the discriminative control of approach behavior can occur when appropriate reinforcers are no longer presented following a response. S^d control of avoidance behavior can also be extinguished, but it is sometimes more difficult to accomplish because the avoidance behavior prevents learning that the punisher is no longer there.

Eliciting, reinforcing, and punishing stimuli can have conditioned (learned) forms and like learned discriminative stimuli (S^d's) are subject to extinction. If a neutral stimulus is repeatedly followed closely by one of these three stimuli, it can acquire its function. We can come to "hate the sight of" those that hurt us (a negative conditioned stimulus or CS) and love be near those who have been associated with good events (a positive CS). Conditioned reinforcers (such as praise) are very important to the teacher. If parents have effective conditioned punishers ("stop that"), they will have less need to use stronger punishment in keeping children safe and out of trouble.

What can be learned, can be "unlearned." The technical process of "unlearning" is called *extinction* of a stimulus function. If a conditioned eliciting, reinforcing, or punishing stimulus is repeatedly presented without occasionally being paired with its unconditioned form, extinction will occur. That means the conditioned form will lose its stimulus function. If money could no longer be used to buy reinforcing goods, we would no longer work for money.

Two classes of reinforcers can function to strengthen behavior—one involves presenting a stimulus (positive reinforcement) and one involves terminating a stimulus (negative reinforcement). Similarly, there are two classes punishing stimuli. You can use traditional punishment and present an aversive stimulus (such as a spanking, assuming it was legal to do so), or you can punish by taking away reinforcers, as in time out and response cost.

CHAPTER

3

APPLICATIONS OF PRINCIPLES: STRENGTHENING BEHAVIOR, PART 1

In viewing classroom behavior it is a relatively easy decision to determine whether your goal is to strengthen some behavior, weaken some behavior, or just keep a good thing going (maintain behavior). By keeping this basic question in mind: "What do I want to do, strengthen, weaken, or maintain?", your decision-making process is greatly simplified. We will now look in detail at procedures for strengthening behavior.

PROCEDURE 1. REINFORCE THE DESIRED BEHAVIOR

When we follow behavior with reinforcing consequences, that behavior is more likely to occur in the future in similar situations. This principle is probably the most important principle for teachers to keep in mind. It has the virtue of keeping your decision-making processes *positively* focused on where you are trying to take your students in terms of social and academic learning goals, rather than simply trying to control misbehavior. The practical questions in applying this principle are:

- What are the potential reinforcers available to me?
- How can I be fairly sure they will be effective for particular students?
- How do I use reinforcers most effectively?

Unconditioned and Conditioned Reinforcers

Some reinforcers "come with the baby," so to speak. These are called *unconditioned reinforcers* or unlearned reinforcers. Stimulus events such as food, water, warmth, activity, and probably novelty will usually strengthen the behavior they follow without having to be first paired with some other reinforcer. Some of these, however, are more effective as reinforcers if the individual is not *satiated* with (already had too much of) that kind of reinforcer at the time.

Other reinforcers can be learned or *conditioned* (as noted in the last chapter) if they are repeatedly followed by effective reinforcers. For example, to teach Jimmy to respond to teacher praise, the teacher might tell Jimmy, who just completed his seatwork, "Jimmy, you did such a good job completing your work that you can choose a puzzle from the shelf to play with for the next ten minutes." Similar statements would be repeated as other occasions arise to pair praise with a reinforcing consequence.

Here are two more examples of the same idea: Susie's teacher decided to use stars on a card at Susie's desk to help motivate her to work more. Susie was told that she would get one star for each worksheet she completed. Each star earned could be traded for playtime in the activity corner where there was a doll house she liked. The first day, Susie needed only two stars to earn five minutes of play; after that each star could be exchanged for one minute of play. The stars were closely followed by a reward. Susie learned to like to earn stars.

To the turned-off adolescent who has repeatedly failed in school because he or she was never taught to read well, a stronger reinforcer than stars may be needed. The answer may be: a program that will effectively teach him or her to read or a home-school contract that provides stronger reinforcers for progress, such as earning an allowance or getting driving lessons.

Types of Conditioned Reinforcers

Social Reinforcers. Social reinforcers involve the teacher's behavior—tone of voice, words of praise, giving attention, smiling, touching, and being near. Most teaching is based on the use of social reinforcers as the immediate consequence for good behavior. For example, the teacher says, "That's right," when Billy answers correctly. He may *pat Aaron on the back* for working well or tell Tony to *bring his work to be checked* when he is finished. In each of these examples, the italicized words are aspects of teacher behavior that can function as social reinforcers.

For most children, social reinforcers are established as important early in life because parents repeatedly give attention and physical contact along with reinforcers such as food, warmth, and relief from painful events.

The following are examples of social reinforcers:

Praising Words and Phrases

Good.
That's right.
Excellent.
That's clever.
Exactly.
Fine answer.
Good job.
Good thinking.
Thank you.
I'm pleased with that.
Great.

That shows a great deal of work.
You really pay attention.
You should show this to your parents.
I like that.
Show the class your picture.
That's interesting.
See how well Joan is working.
Jimmy got right down to work after recess; he's going to finish on time.
Let's all give John a round of applause.
That was very kind of you.

Facial Expressions

Smiling
Winking
Nodding

Looking interested
Laughing

Nearness

Walking among students
Sitting in their group

Joining the class at recess
Eating with the children

Physical Contact

Touching	Stroking arm
Patting head, shoulder, or back	Shaking hand
Hugging	Holding hand
Holding on lap	

Token Reinforcers. Token reinforcers are another important kind of learned reinforcer. They consist of such things as points, gold stars, or poker chips that have been made reinforcing by being paired with other reinforcers. Money is a very important token reinforcer in our society. But money by itself is useless. It has value to us because it is a basis for obtaining other reinforcers.

We can make a variety of objects token reinforcers and use them to motivate students to do things. Tickets, bottle caps, and bubble gum cards have been used at various times. It is very useful for teachers to know how to use token and social reinforcers in teaching.

Activity Reinforcers–The Premack Principle. David Premack is a psychologist whose basic studies demonstrated that more-preferred activities can be used to reinforce less-preferred activities (Premack, 1965). The Premack principle states that any higher-frequency behavior that is *contingent* on a lower-frequency behavior is likely to increase the rate of the lower-frequency behavior. Here, contingent means that if the less-preferred behavior occurs, the student is then permitted to perform some more-preferred behavior. The preferred activity is used to reinforce behavior the teacher wants to strengthen.

The following examples use the Premack principle:

- "You may go home when you finish your assignment."
- "When the whole class is quiet and seated, we can go out to recess, a row at a time."

IT'S THE FIRST STEP IN A SURVEY OF HIGH-FREQUENCY BEHAVIOR.

- "Jimmy, you raised your hand, so I'm going to call on you to answer."
- "Alice is all finished. She can help me hand out these corrected papers."
- "Those who score 100 percent on this spelling test may go out to recess five minutes early today."
- "Jeff has been working hard. He can clean the erasers for me today."

The next two examples are *not* examples of the Premack principle:

- "You can go play if you will do your homework later."
- "We'll have an extra five minutes of recess if you will work harder when we get back to class."

In the last two examples, the order of behavior is backwards. The more-preferred activity comes before rather than after the less-preferred activity.

A Teacher Learns to Use the Premack Principle

Mrs. Stone had been battling with Justin. She had deprived him of recess because he had not completed his exercises, and Justin just pouted for the rest of the day. He could see no point to finishing his exercises, since he could not go to recess anyway. Mrs. Stone happened to mention this difficulty to the school social worker in the lounge. The social worker recognized the problem as an ineffective use of punishment and suggested a slight modification of procedure. "Tomorrow you tell Justin at the beginning of the work period that when he finishes his assignment he can go to recess. If he finishes before recess, he can go out early. If he finishes after recess starts, he can go out for as much recess as there is left." The early recess possibility was cleared with the principal and Mrs. Stone tried it. Justin was finished seven minutes before recess and extremely pleased with himself. Mrs. Stone was amazed at the difference made by using recess to reward working rather than using loss of recess to punish not working.

Student teachers often ask what this does to the other class members. If the teacher simply explains: "Justin needs some special help in learning to get his work done. You are fortunate that you don't need that kind of help." This will usually take care of the possible problem.

Choosing Reinforcers

Even though one can never be sure a suspected reinforcer will work without trying it, the task of finding reinforcers is not all that difficult. Most students respond positively to such things and events as food, candy, toys, games, praise, attention, hugs, smiles, warmth, money, and free time. We have some common genetic and learning histories that make us more alike than different when it comes to "what turns us on." In addition, knowledge of the Premack principle can be a great asset.

If preferred activities can function as reinforcers, then by observing what children do frequently, the teacher can determine when might be used as a reinforcer for a particular child. This is an extremely valuable idea for teachers learning how to motivate children in positive ways. Lloyd Homme once observed that four preschool children he wanted to teach to read spent most of their classroom time "running and screaming." So he made a rule. "Sit and listen for two minutes, and I'll let you run and scream." Gradually, he required more sitting, listening, and working for less running and screaming. In a short time, the children were hardworking and well-behaved.

With careful observation the teacher can find a host of activities readily available to be used as reinforcers.

Finally, students often can tell you what they would like to work for when you need a special reinforcer. Ask them.

How to Use Reinforcers

The focus here is on social reinforcers and activity reinforcers. The first general rule is: *Never use a stronger reinforcer than you need to get the job done.* Most of the time, this means you are simply using your verbal behavior (praise), perhaps grades, and definitely activity reinforcers. There are several important points to be made about how to use these effectively.

If Praise Does Not Come "Naturally," Practice. In Chapter 2 the study of Mrs. E. and her classroom revealed some interesting changes. Initially, Mrs. E. did not know how to say nice things to children. She primarily criticized them. Just telling her to praise more was not enough. She had to practice a lot of different ways before she could do it in class. Even then, for three weeks the classroom observers reported that she gave phony praise. However, her students showed great improvement; the praise was not phony to them, but very important. New behavior is often stilted and somewhat disorganized. Well-practiced behavior becomes natural. It took a while for Mrs. E. to be comfortable with her new behavior.

We learned two things from this experience. First, some people have to be *taught how to praise.* We cannot assume that everybody knows how. Second, initial efforts at praising might seen quite uncomfortable or unnatural for the person doing it, as well as for observers. However, if one stays with it, praising becomes natural. *The teacher must take the role of an actor playing at being a "fun teacher" until he or she becomes one.*

To Make It Work–Use Behavior-Specific Praise. Dr. Haim Ginott, author of *Between Parent and Child,* has pointed out that often a child does not react to what we consider praise. Take a child who has been repeatedly told he is stupid and who has failed often. He is not likely to be overwhelmed with joy by a teacher telling him, "You are smart." The praise statement doesn't fit with his own experience. On the other hand, if this same child has been working hard for twenty minutes to complete ten long division problems and he gets them all done correctly, he might believe this: "I saw you working hard on your arithmetic for twenty minutes. I've checked every problem and every one is right. And you know, your writing is really neat and clear." This *describes* what the student did and shows appreciation by the detailed attention given to the student's work or behavior. Ginott says it is usually better to make praise *descriptive* rather than *evaluative. Describe—don't judge.* Praise specific behavior.

There is much to be said for this viewpoint. The less you know about a child, the more likely it is that descriptive praise will be effective and evaluative praise will miss the mark. However, it is also possible to make phrases such as "good," "great," and "that's clever" effective for children by initially accompanying such phrases with descriptive statements.

"Jimmy watched carefully throughout the whole lesson. That's paying attention well."

"Mary is sitting up straight with her hands on her desk, ready to listen. She's going to be a good listener."

"Aaron, you kept at that one for a long time and you finally got it. That's good working. When we work hard, we learn."

By repeatedly providing explicit examples of good working, good listening, good talking, good responding, and good thinking, we teach the children what we mean by such praise statements. Later, the statements "good listening," "clever answer," and "that's what I call smart" are not empty phrases.

Using Activity Reinforcers

Next to praise, reinforcing activities are the most readily available motivating tool the teacher has. Yet, so often the teacher just gives away these potential reinforcers without using them to help motivate students. In using activity reinforcers, the first step is to build a chronological list containing possible reinforcing events that are scheduled to occur during the day. This list will prompt the use of these events to help teach. Figure 3.1 shows a list made by one teacher.

In using the events on your "scheduled activities list," have the children earn a privilege by doing good work or improving behavior. Say, "Toni finished her paper first. She can help me collect the papers." Or, "Jeff, you really improved in your arithmetic group today. You can choose the game for recess." Or, "Class, you have all completed your reading assignments five minutes early. That means we get an extra long recess today." Rather than just following a routine automatically, use the fun things coming up to promote social and academic learning.

Going to Recess, Lunch, or Home. Students are usually excited just before a fun activity. Going to recess, going to lunch, and going home often lead to considerable excitement and horsing around. The good manager recognizes from the start that these are times when the teacher has a lot of reinforcement power and can use it to teach desired behavior. A rowdy class should not be dismissed just because the teacher would like to get rid of all the noise. The consequences for noise and confusion could be partial loss of recess, a delay in lunch, or a delay in getting out to go home.

Playing Teacher. In small group instruction, playing teacher can be used to reinforce good work. Special reinforcers like this are especially helpful for working on repetitive tasks, such as learning arithmetic facts or sounds. "If you do a good job in working all these problems on your sheet, you can be teacher and write a problem on the board." Along the way, reminders are given, "Oh, I think John is going to be a teacher. He's really working . . . and so is Tommy. Look at him go . . . We're going to have a lot of teachers today."

Some other items on a scheduled activity reinforcer list might include:

- Running errands
- Being excused from a test
- Taking care of class pets
- Choosing where to sit
- Telling a joke to the class
- Being in a skit
- Supervising a group outside of class
- Competing with another class
- Having the lesson outdoors
- Being called on to answer questions
- Special holiday events and parties

Special Events. The last item on the above list deserves additional discussion. Our society provides many occasions for reinforcing social behavior,

Time	Period	Reinforcing Activities
9:00	Opening Exercises	Lead the salute "Show and tell"
9:15	Reading groups	Pass out seat work Play teacher Read to the group Read for another student Collect papers
10:15	Recess	Go to recess first Go to recess early Choose games at recess Be group leader
10:40	Arithmetic	Help teacher hand out papers Help another student Extra page of "special problems" Collect papers
11:20	Music	Lead the class in a song Extra time for music
11:40	Lunch	Go to lunch first
12:15	Spelling-Writing	Help teacher Team competition on spelling Get to do "toughies"
12:45	Special Events	Go to a movie, TV, assembly, field trip
1:25	Social Studies	Reports to the class Filmstrip
2:05	Gym	Go to gym first Earn extra gym time
2:40	Free time-study time	Use play material during study time
3:15	Go home	Go home first Go home early

Figure 3.1 *A scheduled activity-reinforcer list*

but often they are not used as contingencies. Throughout the seasons, the teacher can use holidays as a time for children to earn special reinforcing events. Halloween, Thanksgiving, Christmas, Valentine's Day, and Easter are some of the fun holidays for children. The teacher can use the activities, plays, and parties surrounding these events as consequences for improved behavior. For example, one teacher had her first graders work to get their names on a list to send to Santa Claus. As a general rule, the teacher should not exclude any child from an event that all children in the class are entitled to, regardless of special requirements.

However, special things the teacher might do with her own class can be set up so that they are special consequences for good work.

Other Ways to Be Reinforcing

Having good teaching material that has been pretested and demonstrated to work will ensure that students will be more successful and thus reinforced for learning. The best classroom management program in the world is good instruction.

Both actors and teachers have in common the need to get and hold the attention of their audience. Teachers could learn a few tricks from actors on creating drama and suspense. Variation in pacing, rhythm, loudness, and pauses are essential aspects of dramatic presentations. Challenging the students, "This is a tough one," or "I'll bet that rule won't work with this problem," can be effective. When it is necessary to drill to increase student proficiency (such as with number facts or sounds), consider ways of making a race or a game to add excitement. If the students are getting quite good on some tasks, try deliberately making mistakes. If the students don't pick it up, say "I really fooled you on that one. Do you really think that 9 plus 2 equals 7?" When they do catch the error, they will take pride in their smartness. They are also learning to trust their own judgment and not just depend on the teacher as an authority.

PROCEDURE 2. USE DIFFERENTIAL REINFORCEMENT TO TEACH DISCRIMINATIONS

Chapter 2 noted that the basic model of operant behavior is an $S \rightarrow R \rightarrow S$ model. A preceding stimulus, called a discriminative stimulus or S^d, sets the occasion in which an operant response is likely to be followed by a reinforcing stimulus or the avoidance of punishment. Basically, discriminative stimuli tell you ***when to do what***. The degree to which humans depend on them in our everyday behavior is not always obvious. But think about the simple process of getting from one place to another in your own house. Suppose you were blindfolded. What would you do without visual cues (S^d's) to guide your movements? You would probably bump into things or reach out to feel your way. Humans are very dependent on a series of visual stimuli to let us know when to stop or when to reach out and open the door—in short, when to do what.

Humans learn about movement in space by experiencing consequences: punishment in the form of bumps and falls or reinforcement from getting where we want to go. We are *differentially reinforced* for the way we read cues that tell us how to move safely. There are two aspects to differential reinforcement. Let S^R stand for a reinforcing consequence. Let S^P stand for a punishing consequence. Let EXT stand for no consequence or an extinction condition. Now consider this example; there are two discriminative stimuli ($S^d{}_1$ and $S^d{}_2$) and two responses (R_1 and R_2).

$S^d{}_1$ Door closed	→ R_1 Reach out and open	→ S^R Get into room
	↘ R_2 Walk into door	→ S^P Bang head
$S^d{}_2$ Door open	→ R_1 Reach out to open	→ EXT
	↘ R_2 Walk through door	→ S^R Get into room

The two aspects of differential reinforcement are:

Appropriate responses are reinforced. In the presence of $S^d{}_1$, R_1 is reinforced.

Inappropriate responses are not reinforced. In the presence of $S^d{}_2$, R_1 is not reinforced. R_2 is not reinforced in the presence of S_1.

We learn which response to make in the presence of which stimulus. In the classroom, the teacher encourages this process by reinforcing acceptable or right responses. If the teacher says, "Take out your spelling books," and Mary does so, the teacher might say, "I'm glad you're ready to work, Mary." If Mary heads for the door, however, the teacher would have to say, "Get back in your seat." Teaching children to abide by rules, follow instructions, and know what to do next all involve teaching them to respond to discriminative stimuli.

Concept Learning

Differential reinforcement of discriminations is also central to concept learning (Chapter 14 is devoted to this topic). Concept learning is a multiple-discrimination process where we learn to make a common response to the central features of a concept and ignore irrelevant features. For example, students can learn to call triangles, squares, and circles *closed geometric figures.* They share the common properties of being regular closed figures. Each example, however could have irrelevant features such as size, color of line, or location.

Discriminating Related Sets

Another important application of the discrimination learning principle is in learning about *sets* of related symbols, concepts, and responses. Suppose you are teaching sounds in beginning reading. You have taught the group to say "shshsh" to the symbol **sh,** but then you find that they say "shshsh" to **ch** and **th,** which share the feature **h.** To get more precise discriminative control, you have to go back to differential reinforcement to get the right sound to occur to these three related symbols. Another common problem in reading is learning to tell the difference between words that are very similar. The little *th* words, such as *the, then, them, this,* and *those,* are often confused. Word-pairs like *rob-robe, can-cane, con-cone, lit-lite,* etc. present discrimination problems. As you will see, good curriculum design should anticipate where discrimination problems are likely to occur and prepare for them by prescribing the critical practice they require.

Two Classroom Illustrations

The following two examples illustrate first how discriminative stimuli can be very important to a pleasant classroom atmosphere, and the potential role of tests as S^d's for studying. *See how many different S^d's you can identify in the first example.*

Setting up a Kindergarten for Instruction. The teacher in this kindergarten was attempting to prepare her students to work on their own for periods long enough to permit her to teach reading and math, at first in small groups, and then on an individualized basis. She divided her children into four groups and assigned them color names (reds, greens, blues, and purples). The classroom was divided into four study areas, each with a table for six children. There was a music area with a rug where all the children could sit together, and an area by a blackboard where a group could come to work with the teacher.

Adjacent to each work area were materials and supplies for a particular kind of fun activity. One table had the clay-modeling materials and some individual games. Another had a record player with headsets for eight children and picture books. One was a painting table with art supplies. The fourth table had coloring books, cut-and-paste supplies, and puzzles.

The teacher began the year by asssigning the same simple task (coloring) to all the children, while she supervised. When the routines of getting set up, working, and cleaning up were established, she assigned two tasks at once. "This morning, children, after you complete your worksheets (coloring and cut-and-paste), you may start a second activity on your own, using the materials on the shelves near your group's table." She walked around the room telling the whole class what the options were for each group. "Each day of the week you will get a chance to move to a different activity area. Everyone will have a chance to do everything each week."

Name tags, color-coded by group, were on appropriate tables when the children came in. When the groups shifted areas each day, the children only had to look for their colors and their names to know where to sit. Frantic questions such as, "Where do I go?" were eliminated from the beginning by good planning.

The next step was to introduce a work activity relating to reading or arithmetic, before the fun activity. Since the children could now go through two activities on their own with little supervision, the teacher could begin to teach small groups in reading and math in the period from 9:15 to 10:45. The children were motivated to complete their work assignments by the availability of fun activities, as well as by the teacher's praise. The teacher also set up an interesting way of encouraging the children to clean up or finish their second tasks without a lot of pressure or confusion. At 10:45, she would put on a record at the music area. The first child with his tasks completed, cleaned up, and put away could come and sit in the group leader's chair. The other children came when ready and sat on the floor to play imitation games directed by the group leader. The children had five minutes to clean up before the formal music period started. The whole operation was so smooth that it ran itself. These children were working in an environment that was teaching them good work habits in an enjoyable way. The teacher's job seemed to an observer to require little effort. She put her effort into planning and structuring her classroom rather than into correcting mistakes after they happened.

The next step was to individualize the activities in the work period. Folders were prepared containing the materials and instructions for each child. There was a place to pick them up and turn them in when completed. When the children wanted the teacher's help, they stood up a little red tent that was kept in their folders, rather than waving their arms in the air for several minutes.

Tests as Discriminative Stimuli for Studying. High school and college teachers alike try to promote daily study behavior so that the students will keep up with the lectures and not be faced with last-minute cramming. Research literature supports the value of evenly spaced study periods for retaining information.

Investigators at Southern Illinois University studied the effects of daily, weekly, and three-week tests on study behavior. Volunteer students participated in a special section in which they would get most of their instruction through readings and programed material. The dependent variable was the number of minutes spent each day in the "reading center." The independent variable was testing on a daily, weekly, or three-week basis.

All students received a course outline describing the requirements, and especially emphasizing that course grades would be based on the accumulation of quiz points. The students were free to use the study area from 3 P.M. to 6 P.M., Monday through Thursday. Study behavior was recorded by observers. Tests were given Tuesday through Friday in the daily test condition and on Friday in the other conditions.

With daily testing, the students studied regularly, about sixty minutes a day. With weekly testing, studying was irregular early in the week and increased as Friday approached. With three-week testing, daily study behavior was very low (average of twenty minutes) right after a test, and gradually increased to a peak (nearly two hours) just before the test.

In planning an instructional program, the wise teacher will consider ways in which a quiz schedule can be used to promote regular studying (Mawhinney, Bostow, Laws, Blumenfeld, & Hopkins, 1971).

SUMMARY

- Reinforcers can be divided into unconditioned and conditioned forms. Unconditioned forms "come with the baby." Conditioned forms of reinforcers are learned by being repeatedly followed by effective reinforcers. We teach children to respond to praise by pairing it with food, warmth, and other reinforcers.

- Three groups of reinforcers important to the teacher are social reinforcers, token reinforcers, and activity reinforcers.
  (a) *Social reinforcers* involve the teacher's behavior—words of praise, attention, smiles, nearness.
  (b) *Token reinforcers* are things such as money, poker chips, points, and gold stars that can be exchanged for other reinforcers.
  (c) *Activity reinforcers* are activities children like to participate in when given a chance. These might include running, games, art activities, singing, eating, recesses, going home.

- The Premack principle states that any behavior a person will readily engage in can be used to reinforce behavior that a person will not readily engage in. You simply require that the less-preferred activity be performed before the more-preferred activity is allowed. The more-preferred behavior is contingent on the less-preferred behavior.

  The general procedure for using reinforcers is to make the reinforcer contingent on the occurrence of the desired response. If the correct behavior occurs, the reinforcer is given; if the correct behavior does not occur, the reinforcer is not given.

- Because of our common genetic and learning histories, you can usually judge accurately what will be reinforcing for students. By using the Premack principle and carefully observing what students prefer to do when given a choice, you can make even better decisions. Finally, remember that students can often tell you what they would like to work for.

- In learning to use social and activity reinforcers, you may need to practice, as an actor would, learning new behavior. A good procedure for practicing is to:
  (a) Specify a setting

(b) Specify what you are trying to learn to do better (for example, use behavior specific praise)
(c) Tape record your performance
(d) Critique it
(e) Record it again. You could also practice with a friend and take turns being teacher and student.

- In using praise, describe the behavior you like. Be factual, not judgmental.

- It is important in motivating students to contingently use the activity reinforcers available to you. Set it up so that the fun activities are used to strengthen good work. Special activities such as going home, to lunch, or to recess can also be used to carefully teach appropriate group behavior at such times.

- Think about how to make teaching more fun. Being more dramatic and challenging is one approach. You can also make games out of drill or deliberately make mistakes. The possible ways in which teaching can be made fun as well as productive are limited only by your imagination.

CHAPTER

4

APPLICATIONS OF PRINCIPLES: STRENGTHENING BEHAVIOR, PART 2

This chapter examines three additional procedures that can be useful in teaching to strengthen behavior: *prompting, shaping,* and *chaining.*

PROCEDURE 3. GET BEHAVIOR GOING IN A NEW SITUATION USING A PROMPT

There are two general classes of prompts: (1) *stimulus-prompts,* designed to get the student to *attend* to critical differences between stimuli, and (2) *response-prompts,* designed to get a specific response to occur under a particular situation.[1] A stimulus-prompt might place a bar over "long" vowels to help the beginning reader discriminate words like *mop* and *mōpe* or *kit* and kīte. Stimulus-prompts (S-prompts) are mostly useful in the design of curricular sequences where there are difficult discriminations to make. Response-prompts (R-prompts) are useful in almost any active teaching situation.

R-prompts are nothing more than discriminative stimuli (S^{d}'s) to which the student can already respond. Suppose you present this task:

	Teacher	*Student*	*Teacher*
	S^d ——————→	*R* ——→	*S (Consequence)*
STEP 1.	(Test) Points to *m*. "What sound is this?"	"aaaaaa"	"No."
STEP 2.	(Prompt) Points to *m* "This sound is 'mmmmmm'." "What sound is this?"	"mmmmm"	"Yes, 'mmmmm'." "Good"
STEP 3.	(Test) Points to *m*. "What sound?"	"mmmmm"	"Yes, 'mmmmm'." "Good"

[1]Note that Skinner (1957) calls an S-prompt a *prompt* and an R-prompt a *prime.*

You should recognize the $S^d \rightarrow R \rightarrow S$ sequence from Chapter 3.

In step 1, the example is presented and the student cannot do it.

So in step 2, the teacher *prompts* the correct answer ("The sound is 'mmmmmmm.' "). Since the student does not respond to the visual *m,* and the teacher knows the student can imitate, the teacher models the response (gives an auditory stimulus that the student can imitate) to get the response to occur in the presence of visual *m.* Once this occurs, it can be strengthened through reinforcement.

In step 3, the teacher tests to see if the student can respond without prompting before going on.

A note on terminology. This text uses the term *task* to refer to an $S^d \rightarrow R$ sequence the teacher is trying to get the student to learn. A task always has two parts: An S^d part ("under this condition") and an R part ("do this"). Thus, the *task stimulus* is the S^d part of the task, and the *task response* is the R part of the task.

Ways of Prompting

There are several different ways in which we get behavior going in a new situation. The following are some of the more common kinds of R-prompts.

Models. The most common type of R-prompt is giving a model response that the student is to imitate: "This is *m.* Say mmmmmm," or, "Watch me do it. Now, you do it." Because most children have already learned to imitate most sounds and actions by the time they come to school, imitation can be a powerful tool for getting responses to occur under the right stimulus conditions.

Verbal Instructions. Instructions are also frequently used as R-prompts. If the student has learned appropriate verbal signals for responses, the teacher can use them to get responses going. For example, "Around the tree, around the tree, makes a three" can be used to prompt the response of writing the number 3. Rules such as "*i* before *e* except after *c*" are also instructions that can be used as prompts.

Nonverbal Instructions. To prompt a place (location) response, simply point where you want the student to respond. If the task is "Put your name in the upper right-hand corner," point to the place where the response is to be made. A number of nonverbal instructions are used by choir directors to keep the group together. Directors pace their choirs' response and control their loudness by arm and hand signals. The teacher can do the same when working with small groups. A foot tap may be used to keep a group counting together.

Physical Prompting. Use of physical prompting to get responses going might involve taking a student's hand to help him or her draw a three, or closing a student's lips to get "mmmm." The student is given a demonstration using his or her own body rather than a model to be imitated.

Added Cues. A cue can also be added to help differentiate similar responses. If the students cannot differentiate a forward 3 from a backward 3 in writing, and they are right-handed, have them place their thumb on the paper and write 3 so that the three points of the 3 touch their left thumb. In teaching students to write, one could start with having them trace letters or numbers, then trace dotted lines, then copy a model, and finally write from dictation. Cues are added to help get the different writing responses going.

S-prompts are mostly of the added cue variety.

Using Prompts Effectively

Fading. Prompts should be faded as soon as possible. *Fading* involves the gradual withdrawal of prompts. A progression of intermediate steps is devised and the teacher moves step-by-step in the progression until the prompts are no longer required. The following examples illustrate some fading progressions (the first three involve S-prompts):

Example 1:

man → **man** → **man** - - - - - →

The boldness of the arrow that cues left-to-right reading of sounds is gradually faded.

Example 2:

"Listen to me count. Tell me what I count to. One, two, three, four, FIIIIVE!"

"Listen to me count. Tell me what I count to. One, two, three, Foooour!"

"Listen to me count. Tell me what I count to. One, two, three, four, five, Siiix!"

"Listen to me count. Tell me what I count to. One, two, three, four, fiive!"

"Listen to me count. Tell me what I count to. One, two, three."

By gradually reducing the loudness and the length of the final number, the teacher fades the prompt.

Example 3: The prompt for a silent *e* is faded:

kīte **kīt**e **kīte**

Example 4:

In physical prompting of a written response, the teacher gradually uses less pressure in moving the student's hand as the student begins to move it more correctly.

Example 5:

Fading an imitative prompt can be accomplished by giving less and less of the behavior to be imitated. The teacher might use these steps: (1) say the whole word the child is trying to read; (2) say just the first two sounds; (3) say just the first sound; and (4) just make the lip movements without the sound.

Example 6:

Prompts that involve pointing or tapping of the feet are faded by gradually reducing the action.

Example 7:

The prompts in a writing program might have the visual supports for forming letters slowly withdrawn. (See Figure 4.1)

Use the Weakest Possible Prompt. In choosing a prompt, consider the progression by which it will be faded and start as close to the end of the progression as you can and still get the appropriate response.

Figure 4.1 *Prompts and fades in a cursive writing program*

The Task Stimulus Precedes the Prompt. Never present a prompt unless the task stimulus is present or, for auditory stimuli, unless the task stimulus has just been given. Suppose the teacher says, "Here's that funny letter again" (the prompt) and then shows the letter *h*. The student doesn't have to look at *h;* the student can just respond to the "funny letter" cue. If the letter *h* is shown first, then the teacher says, "Oh, this is that funny letter," the student is more likely to attend to *h* before the response is prompted. The correct response is therefore more likely to become linked to *h,* and the need for the prompt in the future is reduced.

Do Not Detract Attention from the Task Stimulus. Suppose the task is to teach color concepts. The teacher presents an instance of blue and asks, "Is this ball blue?" The teacher prompts "yes" by nodding, which calls attention away from the task stimulus. It is an ineffective prompt because it leads the students to look at the teacher instead of the blue ball. A more effective prompt would be to give the answer first: "This ball is blue. What color is this ball?"

Some prompts actually direct attention to the task stimulus. For example, a voice inflection can emphasize the critical word to be attended to, as in the following: "We're going to count to *five.* What are we going to count to?"

Examples of Ineffective Prompting. Ineffective prompts do not ensure that the student will attend to the task stimulus while making the required response. The following illustrate some common errors:

1. A question is asked with an inflection to prompt "yes" or "no." The students can answer "yes" or "no" correctly without knowing what was asked.

2. The teacher says, "Oh, you know that word. I just told you on the last page." The student thinks of the word given on the last page and does not have to sound out the word.

3. The teacher says, "I'll bet you can think of that word if I tell you it's an animal that says 'Quack, quack.' " Again, the student does not have to read the word to answer.

4. The comprehension skill being taught is *main idea.* After three examples, a workbook exercise has a little man up in the left-hand corner of the page says, "Pssst. Hey kids, look in the first sentence." Again, the spurious prompt makes it unnecessary to read the example and try to figure out what *main idea* is.

PROCEDURE 4. WHEN PROMPTING WILL NOT WORK, SHAPE NEW BEHAVIOR FROM EXISTING BEHAVIOR

A Woman Learns to Shed Her Clothing

Ted Ayllon (1963) reports a study of a woman who had been hospitalized for nine years as psychotic. She was overweight and constantly stole food; she hoarded towels in her room; and she wore excessive amounts of clothing. She might wear six or seven dresses at one time, with several pairs of stockings or several sweaters. This behavior led others to treat her as unusual, to say the least.

Ayllon eliminated the food stealing by having a nurse remove the woman from the dining room without eating, if she did steal. She stole only six times in the next sixty weeks, and her weight dropped from 250 to 180 pounds. He eliminated the towel hoarding by bringing the patient more and more towels, as many as six hundred a week (Ayllon had to hoard the hospital's supply). She soon got tired of folding and stacking towels and begged for no more. She started removing them from her room on her own. She just had too much of a good thing: she was satiated.

The procedure used to eliminate wearing too much clothing is of special interest in this chapter. The patient's body weight was determined regularly, and she was required to step on a scale before entering the dining room. Initially she could enter only if she weighed under her body weight plus twenty-three pounds. This number was chosen since she usually wore twenty-five pounds of extra clothing. If the patient's weight exceeded the requirement, the nurse would say, "Sorry, you weigh too much. You'll have to weigh less." If the patient did not meet the requirement, she would miss that meal. At times the patient would remove clothing right then to meet the requirement and get to eat. Sometimes she removed more than was needed to meet the requirement. If this occurred, the weight required was lowered for the next meal. Over an eleven-week period, the weight requirement was gradually lowered to a normal three pounds of clothing. When the patient started dressing normally, she also began to participate in social events at the hospital. The patient's parents took her home for a visit for the first time in nine years.

Shaping Procedures

When the response you want is not in the student's repertoire or when you have no way to prompt the response, it is necessary to use shaping procedures. In *shaping,* reinforcement and extinction are skillfully used together to build new behavior. There are two essential aspects of shaping:

1. *Differential reinforcement.* In the context of shaping, differential reinforcement means that the responses that meet a certain criterion are reinforced, while those that do not meet the criterion are extinguished (not reinforced).

2. *Shifting Criterion for reinforcement.* The response criterion to be reinforced is gradually changed in the direction of the behavior you want the learner to end up with (target behavior).

In the case just presented, the patient was reinforced with food if her weight was below a given amount. She was *not* reinforced with food if her weight was above a given amount. *Differential reinforcement* was used. In addition, the requirement or criterion for reinforcement was slowly changed to lead the patient to wear less and less clothing. There was a *shifting criterion* for reinforcement, approaching a target behavior of wearing a normal amount of clothing.

It is also possible to shape misbehavior. If teachers or parents attend to students primarily when they are misbehaving and do not give appropriate reinforcement for cooperative and on-task behavior, the amount of misbehavior is likely to increase, even when the attention given amounts to scolding.

How to Shape

In shaping, the teacher goes through the following steps:

Steps to Take	**Example**
1. Define the target behavior.	**1.** I want Jimmy to do 20 addition problems in 20 minutes without coming to me.
2. Decide what behavior to build from.	**2.** Jimmy will now do 1 problem in two minutes with me there to help him.
3. Establish a reinforcer.	**3.** He will earn points on a card. For every 25 points he earns, he gets to choose one game at recess.
4. Outline the program of steps to get to the target behavior.	**4.** Choose a set of problems that Jimmy can do.

4.1 Jimmy is given a paper with 1 problem on it. I help him do it.

4.2 Jimmy is given a paper with 1 problem on it. "Now you do this one by yourself and I'll come check it."

4.3 A paper with 2 problems is given. "Do these and raise your hand when you have finished. I'll come and check them."

4.4 A paper with 5 problems is given. "Do these and raise your hand."

4.5 A paper with 10 problems is given. "Let me know when you have finished."

4.6 A paper with 15 problems is given. "Let me know when you have finished."

4.7 A paper with 20 problems is given. The time Jimmy takes to complete them is recorded.

4.8 A paper with 20 problems is given. "If you finish in less than *X* minutes you will get a 5-point bonus." *X* is one minute less than the time measured in step 4.7.

4.9 Continue step 4.8 until papers are regularly completed in less than twenty minutes, slowly lowering the time requirement. (This program is carried out over several days.)

5. Start training with your first criterion for reinforcement.	**5.** Jimmy is given step 4.1 and immediately reinforced.
6. Decide when to shift a new criterion for reinforcement. (Stay with each new requirement no longer than is necessary to meet the criterion.)	**6.** Move right on to step 4.2 because step 4.1 was done easily.
7. If the criterion is not met, return briefly to an earlier step or add a new step in between and try again.	**7.** When Jimmy went from 5 to 10 problems, he failed to finish them without help. He returned to 5 problems and then went to 8 problems.
8. Repeat steps 6 and 7 until the target behavior is achieved.	**8.** Jimmy learned to work 20 problems in under twenty minutes.

In shaping, the teacher has to know where he or she is going, what steps to take to get there, and when to go ahead or back, according to the performance of the student. The dilemma faced in shaping is that if the teacher stays too long at one step, time is lost and behavior is strengthened at an undesired level. If the teacher moves on too quickly, the teacher may lose the student when the criterion for reinforcement is not met.

Some Responses That Usually Require Shaping

Working longer, working faster, paying attention, and staying in one's seat are examples of behavior for which shaping is commonly used.

Speech problems often require careful shaping to get the proper sounds going. To teach a student to say "ssss" rather than "thththth" when he or she encounters *s,* the speech teacher might have the student practice saying "ssss" with the teeth closed. The student is reinforced each time the sound is made with the teeth closed, and not reinforced if the teeth are open. Once the student is making regular "ssss" sounds in isolation, the teacher begins to reinforce "ssss" in words, and then in conversational speech.

A teacher might use shaping to get a quiet student to talk more or to talk louder. The program might start with questions or situations that you know the student will respond to and gradually move to general classroom discussion.

Most programs used to teach manuscript or cursive writing involve some shaping. The student usually starts by writing larger letters and then learns to write smaller ones. The criteria are slowly increased. In a program developed by Skinner and Krakower (1968) (illustrated in Figure 4.1), a special pen and chemically treated paper were used to give the student immediate differential reinforcement. If the student made a correct line, it came out gray. If the line was incorrect, it came out yellow. The width of the band that would produce a gray line (correct) was made narrower later in the program; thus the criterion for reinforcement was changed by narrowing the area that was considered a correct response.

Gym skills and many athletic skills are developed best through a shaping process. One first-grader in a rural school that places emphasis on basketball spent most of his gym periods trying to shoot baskets. *He made two all year.* You have never seen such an unhappy child. The whole experience was punishing, to say the least, and quite pointless. Simply by switching from a ten-foot-high basket and a regular basketball to a seven-foot-high basket and a volleyball, some real training could have taken place. Also, the child would have become enthusiastic about the sport instead of sick of it.

Throwing a ball, catching a ball, batting, jumping, and running for speed or distance are all skills that can be taught either in ways that ensure success and enthusiasm or in ways that produce punishment and disillusionment. The key to such training is shaping. Differentially reinforce success according to an increasingly harder requirement, but never go to a harder requirement until there is success at an easier one.

When Shaping Is Needed

Shaping is a terribly inefficient process compared with prompting. If the teacher had to shape every new response, the children would end up pretty dumb. Therefore, the first rule is this: *Shaping is used when there are no prompts that can be used to get the target behavior going.*

It is not possible to tell a student, "Sit and work hard for an hour and I'll give you a special treat," and get him or her to do it, if in the past the student has never worked at any one thing for more than two minutes.

If Ayllon had insisted that the woman wearing twenty-five pounds of clothing remove all the excess before she could eat, she might have eventually done so; but he probably would have had to battle with her and deprive her of food for some time. The hospital staff might have considered this cruel and inhumane. It is also possible that the behavior change might not have been accomplished at all. Shaping is often the gentle and reasonable way to teach new behavior with a minimum of emotional distress.

There is another important rule that applies to shaping. Shaping is concerned with establishing motor skills. *Do not use shaping in teaching discriminations.* If the student says "rob" for "robe" in reading, you have to correct the mistake, not accept it as an approximation. Discrimination responses are right or wrong. If you reinforce a wrong discrimination response, you set up the need for "unteaching" what you have reinforced. Any task always has a stimulus side and a response side. Shaping is only used to work on the response side.

In most classroom applications of shaping, instructions are used along with shaping. Classroom rules can prompt desired behavior. When the teacher reinforces working longer, working faster, paying better attention, writing more clearly, writing more cleverly, sitting longer, or whatever, she should relate the behavior being reinforced to the rules for good classroom behavior.

HIS SHAPING PROGRAM BEGAN WITH SMALL JUMPS. AT EACH TRIAL, HE HAS TO STAY UP LONGER FOR A REINFORCEMENT.

PROCEDURE 5. BUILD LONGER SEQUENCES OF BEHAVIOR USING PROMPTING AND REINFORCEMENT TO CHAIN THE BEHAVIORS TOGETHER

Behavior Chains

Most activities in school consist of sequences, or chains, of behavior. Going to recess can be broken down into the component behaviors of getting up from the desk, going to the coat rack, putting on a coat, lining up at the door, walking down the hall, and going out to the playground. Writing a theme usually involves reading in a topic area, making an outline, writing sentence after sentence, and editing the product. In a chain, simple behaviors under the control of discriminative stimuli are joined into a sequence of behavior. The whole sequence is reinforced at its completion. Formally, the $S \rightarrow R \rightarrow S$ model of operant behavior can be extended into a model that looks like this:

${S^d}_3 \rightarrow$	$R_3 \rightarrow$	${S^d}_2 \rightarrow$	$R_2 \rightarrow$	${S^d}_1 \rightarrow$	$R_1 \rightarrow$	S^R
"Group three, get ready for reading."	Bob takes out his book.	The book in hand is a cue to get up and go to reading corner.	Bob goes to reading corner.	The chairs in the reading corner cue sitting.	Bob sits.	"I can see Bob's ready for reading."

There are two important questions we can ask about a behavior chain: What reinforces R_3 and R_2? And how does one go about establishing a chain?

The Reinforcers in a Chain. In Chapter 2 you saw that learned reinforcers (or conditioned reinforcers) can be established by following a neutral stimulus with a reinforcing stimulus. $S^d{}_1$ precedes S^R and so, with repeated pairing, it is likely to become a conditioned reinforcer. Similarly, $S^d{}_2$ would also become a conditioned reinforcer if repeatedly paired with $S^d{}_1$. Thus you can see that each S^d in a behavior chain tends to acquire a conditioned reinforcing function for the response that precedes it and a discriminative function for response that follows it.

Establishing Behavior Chains. The most common method of establishing a behavior chain in the classroom is to first prompt each step in the chain and then fade the prompts. For example, the chain for going to the reading group could have initially consisted of three separate instructions. The teacher would first ask group three to "Get our your reading books. Good, everyone has a book," followed by, "Now walk quietly to the reading corner." And finally, the teacher might say, "Let's all sit in our chairs. You got ready for reading very quickly. I like that." After several repetitions, it would be unnecessary to say more than, "Group three get ready for reading," because they now know what to do.

Cushion Activities. In Chapter 3 you saw how a kindergarten teacher used a variety of S^d's as prompts for keeping the classroom organized and working so that she could take one group for reading instruction. By building in systematic prompts for what to do next, chains are established so that the completion of one activity becomes the cue for the next.

A useful extension of chaining the completion of one task to the start of the next is the concept of *cushion activities.* Not all students complete a seatwork assignment in the same time. By always assigning a cushion activity option when you make a seatwork assignment, much troublesome behavior can be avoided. And if the cushion activities are fun, they will tend to reinforce faster completion of the seatwork (recognize the Premack principle operating here?). The basic procedure is to say, 'When the __________ assignment is completed and checked, you may __________ ." While the options will vary with the age of your students, here are some possibilities:

New and interesting books	Learning resource center
Music listening station	Time with teacher
Pocket radio with earphone	Study with a friend
Games of all sorts	Use microcomputer
Puppets	Puzzles
Art materials	Teaching machines
Models	Tape recorder
Construction materials	Video games

Habit Chains and Problem-Solving Chains. Habit chains are often considered "rote" (unintelligent) behavior and contrasted with intelligent problem-solving routines (which are also chains). It is interesting to note that the "dumb" habit chain is built by the same process as some of our most intelligent behavior. In each case, each step in the chain is cued one at a time. As a habit chain—like brushing your teeth, getting dressed, or driving to school—becomes habitual or automatic, the external cues drop out (or are dropped out) and the completion of one response provides (internally) the stimuli to cue the next step. Think about what happens when you learn to type. At first each letter is cued by looking at the placement on a chart or the keyboard. Before too long you are typing words and phrases without thinking about where the letters are. When a sequence of behavior is repeatedly reinforced, it tends to become a functional unit. *Bits* of behavior are converted into ***chunks***. Habits are very economical when it comes to effort and demands for attention.

Problem-solving routines are chains of behavior used to solve problems with known solutions. These are discussed in more detail in Chapter 15. Consider the following routine for solving problems of this type A + B = □. The steps of the routine might be as follows:

1. Place as many lines under the first number (A) as are in the set the number stands for.

2. Place as many lines under the second number (B) as the number stands for.

3. Count all the lines to find the total when the two numbers are added together.

4. Place the total in the box.

In a particular example such as 4 + 3 = □
Step 1 involves making 4 lines,
Step 2 involves making 3 lines,
Step 3 involves counting all the lines,
Step 4 involves putting the number 7 in the box.

After prompted practice with five or six problems using these rules, any problem of this type would likely be solved. The set of rules in the rule chain teaches a problem-solving strategy appropriate to a particular class of problems. The "habit structure" learned is the sequence of general rules, which can then control a wide variety of particular response chains producing solutions to problems not solved before.

In both kinds of chains, S^d's come to control response in a particular sequence. In the habit chain, the external S^d control drops out, while in a problem-solving chain it does not.

SUMMARY

There are two kinds of prompts—*stimulus-prompts* (S-prompts) and *response prompts* (R-prompts). S-prompts are added cues used to facilitate difficult discriminations. R-prompts are S^d's the student can already respond to which are used to get the response to occur to a new stimulus.

R-prompts can be verbal and nonverbal instructions, added cues, models for imitation, or physically taking the student through the motions.

Fading involves the gradual withdrawal of prompts. It can consist of reducing the intensity of a stimulus, reducing or increasing the size of a visual stimulus, presenting less and less of a response to be imitated, and so forth. Any way in which a prompting stimulus can be made less discriminable in a given teaching context can constitute fading. Prompts should be faded as soon as possible so that the student does not become dependent on the prompt rather than learning to respond to the task stimulus.

Tasks specify a stimulus condition under which a response is to be made. Thus, a task stimulus is a stimulus the teacher wants to become an S^d for the student, and a task response is the response the student is to make (after instruction) to the task stimulus.

In using prompts, you should always present the task stimulus first, otherwise, the student need not attend to it to get the response. Do not use prompts that take attention away from the task stimulus. Prompts embedded in the task stimulus are usually more effective than those dissociated from it. There are many faulty or spurious uses of prompts in current teaching programs. Faulty prompting (in teaching and in workbooks) can fool you into thinking the students are learning something when they are only responding to the prompt.

Shaping is a process that involves *differential reinforcement* and a *shifting criterion* for reinforcement. Differential reinforcement refers to reinforcing responses that meet current criteria and not reinforcing (extinguishing) other responses. A shifting criterion for reinforcement means that the responses to be reinforced are gradually changed to approach the target behavior.

The steps involved in shaping are to define your target behavior, decide what behavior you are going to build from, select a reinforcer, outline a program to achieve your target behavior, begin training on the program requirements, shift to a new requirement when the first one occurs with regularity, return to an earlier requirement if failure is encountered, and progress through your program until the target behavior is achieved.

Although shaping is inefficient, it is required to get behavior going when instructions, imitation, and other prompts cannot produce the target behavior.

Shaping is used for response learning, not for discrimination learning. It can be helpful in building on-task behavior, studying time, athletic skills, singing, writing, speech, and so forth. Prompting is the preferred technique; it is much more efficient than shaping.

Behavior chains consist of sequences of behavior interconnected by discriminative stimuli. The chains are held together because each S^d also becomes a conditioned reinforcer. The same stimulus in between responses in a chain functions to reinforce the preceding response and cue the response that follows it. The same stimulus has two functions, but each is with respect to different responses. (Be sure to figure this one out!)

To establish a behavior chain, each step is initially prompted. Then the prompts are gradually faded as the completion of one part of the chain provides the cues for the next part.

A consistent daily schedule in the classrooms establishes chains so that completion of one activity provides cues to get ready for the next. When you are dealing with seatwork assignments that might take variable amounts of time to complete, assign a *cushion activity* to be worked on when the first task is done. If this is a fun activity, it will reinforce the seatwork and keep the students occupied.

Habit chains and *problem-solving chains* are built by the same process of prompting each step in the chain. However, when prompts are faded in the habit chain, stimuli associated with the completion of one component automatically cue the next. A new functional response is formed by integrating the components. With problem-solving chains, the process is similar, except that completion of each step produces information (stimuli) that varies from problem to problem and thereby controls variable responding. Many teachers tend to think of the habit chain as rigid and the problem-solving chain as flexible, but they really have a lot in common in terms of how they are initially learned.

CHAPTER

5

APPLICATIONS OF PRINCIPLES: WEAKENING BEHAVIOR

This chapter examines three principles for dealing with problem behavior in the classroom. Since use of reinforcers was found to be central to all procedures for strengthening behavior, it may come as a surprise that *use of reinforcers is also central to procedures for weakening behavior.* But before you look into this paradox, you need to examine the most common practice used by teachers and parents in attempting to eliminate problem behavior, namely, *criticism*—which presents a paradox of its own to unravel. You will also examine more closely punishment that involves presenting aversive stimuli to see why it is usually *not the method of choice,* despite such adages as "Spare the rod and spoil the child."

SPARE THE ROD AND SPOIL THE CHILD.

THE CRITICISM TRAP

The More the Teacher Says "Sit Down," the More They Stand Up

It was 9:20 A.M. The team-taught first grade had forty-eight students in it. Two rooms were available for the class, with a movable divider between them. The students's desks were grouped into six tables of eight students each. They had been assigned work to do at their seats, while the two young teachers taught reading in small groups. Two observers entered the room, sat down, and for the next twenty minutes they recorded the number of students out of their seats during each ten-second period. The observers also recorded how often the teachers told the students to sit down, or to get back to their seats. During the first six days of observation about three first graders were out of their seats every ten seconds. The teachers would say "sit down" about seven times in a twenty-minute period (see Figure 5.1).

Then some very strange events began to occur. The teachers were asked to tell the students to sit down more often. During the next twelve days, the teachers said "sit down" 27.5 times each twenty minutes. The ***students stood up more***—on an average of 4.5 times in ten seconds.

The sequence was tried again. For the next eight days, the teachers went back to saying "sit down" only 7 times in twenty minutes. Out-of-seat behavior declined to an average of 3 times every ten seconds. Again the teachers were asked to tell the students to sit down more often (28 times in twenty minutes). Again the students stood up more—4 times every ten seconds.

Finally the teachers were asked to quit telling the first graders to sit down, but rather to praise sitting and working. They did this, and fewer than two students stood every ten seconds, the least standing observed.

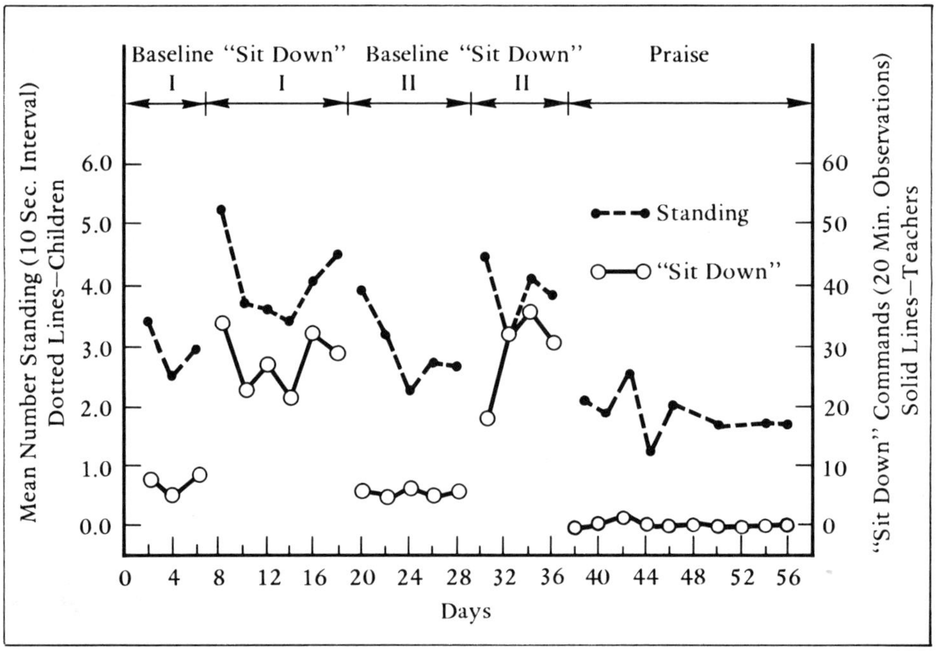

Figure 5.1 *Standing up as a function of "sit down" commands and praise (Data points are averages of each two days.)*

What can be going on? How do we explain such happenings? There is one further perplexing piece of information. The students actually *did sit down when asked by the teacher to do so;* the result wasn't just due to a few students standing a lot.

Consider the following:

STUDENT	R_1 (Stands up) →	S (Hears "Sit down") →	R_2 (Sits)
TEACHER	S_1 (Sees student stand) →	R (Says "Sit down") →	S_2 (Sees student sit)

Hearing the teacher say "Sit down" *followed* the student standing up. The more the teacher said "Sit down" the more the students stood up; and the less the teacher said "Sit down" the less the students stood up. Hearing the teacher say "Sit down" *must have been a reinforcing stimulus* for R_1 (student stands up).

But hearing the teacher say "Sit down" had another effect on R_2 (sitting). The first graders did sit down when told to, so S (hears "Sit down") must have also been a discriminative stimulus (S^d) for R_2 (student sits).

What a beautiful trap! The teacher's response, "Sit down," is followed by S_2 (sees student sit). The teacher is reinforced for saying "Sit down." It worked! But that was only the immediate effect. The effect on standing might have been missed altogether by the teacher if careful observations had not been made. Her words were in fact having exactly the opposite effect on standing from what she desired.

A Caution. Do not conclude that an effect like this will always be found. If the teacher had praised sitting and working a lot (behavior incompatible with standing), saying "sit down" would not likely have had a reinforcing effect. But in the absence of praise and other reinforcers for working and sitting, the behavior most reinforced by the teacher's attention was standing (Madsen, Becker, Thomas, Koser, and Plager, 1968).

Another Example of the Criticism Trap

One study took a good class and made it into a bad one for a few weeks by having the teacher no longer praise the class. When the teacher no longer praised the students, off-task behavior increased from 8.7 percent to 25.5 percent. The teacher criticized off-task behavior and did not praise on-task behavior. When the teacher was asked to increase her criticism from 5 times in 20 minutes to 16 times in 20 minutes, the class showed even more off-task behavior. Off-task behavior increased to an average of 31.2 percent, and on some days was over 50 percent. *Attention to the off-task behavior increased its occurrence when no praise was given for working.* Introduction of praise back into the classroom restored good working behavior (Thomas, Becker, and Armstrong, 1968).

Imagine the situation of the teacher who primarily disciplines by scolding rather than praising. Students misbehave, the teacher catches them and scolds them, and they stop for the time being. *Scolding and criticizing seem to work. The teacher is reinforced for scolding and is likely to do it again.* The undesirable behavior will increase, and then it will be necessary to scold more. It is a vicious circle. Only by seeing clearly what is going on can the teacher avoid this trap and behave in ways that will produce the desired long-range effects.

In the criticism trap, the teacher (or parent) reinforces the very behavior he or she is trying to eliminate. The following two examples illustrate a related trap where teacher attention maintains making mistakes. This might be called the "being too helpful trap."

The Case of the Poor Speller

Michael was eleven years old. He was of average intelligence, but had been placed in a residential treatment center because of his behavior problems. During his English class, his teacher noted that whenever Michael was called on to spell a word that had been previously studied, he would pause, make a distorted face, and mumble letters not related to the word. The teacher would then ask him to sound out the word and, after considerable time and attention, the correct spelling would come out. The teacher began to suspect that her attention might be maintaining the poor spelling.

The teacher decided to test this idea . After Michael had turned in a spelling test with muddled combinations of barely legible letters, the teacher sent him to the blackboard. She told him that she was going to give him a test. "I will read a word and you will write it correctly on the board." The teacher gave a word. Michael mispelled it more than ten times while the teacher sat at her desk ignoring him (busy reading papers). Michael would misspell a word and look to the teacher, but she would not respond. He would erase it and "try" again. Sometimes he would say, "I can't remember it." After ten minutes, Michael spelled the first word correctly. His teacher said, "Good, now we can go on." A second word was followed by a similar scene. As they painfully worked through ten words, the time Michael took to get to a correct spelling decreased. At the end the teacher wrote an A on his spelling chart and asked him to help her color some Easter baskets. In a month's time with consistent reinforcement for good spelling, instead of bad, Michael's bizzare spelling disappeared. Michael had been given real help (Zimmerman & Zimmerman, 1962).

The Digit Reverser

Bob was an eight-year-old enrolled in a Basic Skills class. He was considered one of the better students by his teacher. But nearly every time he added numbers producing a two-digit sum, he would reverse the numerals. For example, he would write 31 as the sum of 5 and 8. Because of this *behavior,* Bob received several neurological and eye examinations. He was also given lots of extra help by several teachers. The problem remained.

A check of Bob's skills showed he could discriminate 31 from 13, 24 from 42, and so on. In fact, he would point out reversals on his paper if the teacher missed them. On several occasions he was seen erasing a correct answer and replacing it with a reversal. An experiment was undertaken to see what was going on.

Sets of twenty problems yielding two-digit sums were made up for each day. They involved the same kind of work, but with different examples. Over four weeks' time, each possible sum was used seven times. Problems with sums having identical digits (11, 22), and with sums of 10 were not used.

During the study, Bob raised his hand when he had completed the twenty problems and his teacher would then check the answers. For seven days (baseline), the teacher marked *C* if an answer was right and *X* if it was wrong. For wrong answers, the teacher would say, "This one is incorrect. You see, you reversed the numbers in the answer." Bob was then taken through each problem he missed and "helped" to get the right answer with the aid of counters and number lines. For these first seven days, Bob made *18 to 20 errors each day.*

For the next seven days, Bob's teacher simply maked all answers *C*. No comments were made nor help given with wrong answers. For right answers, the teacher might give Bob a pat on the back, a smile, and say, "This one is *very* good." For the first three days under this condition, Bob's errors remained near 20. Then for the next four days they *dropped to 5, 1, 4, and 0.*

There could be little question that the teacher had been caught in the "being helpful" trap (Hasazi & Hasazi, 1972).

A CLOSER LOOK AT PUNISHMENT

As noted in Chapter 2, stimulus events that follow a behavior and weaken its future probability of occurring are called *punishing stimuli.* There are two types. One involves presenting stimulus events generally known as painful or aversive. These include loud noises, excessive heat and cold, various odors, excessive pressure on the body, intense light in the eyes, electric shock, and so on. The second type of punishment involves taking away or cutting off reinforcers. *Response cost* procedures, such as fines or loss of privileges, involve taking away reinforcers. *Time out* involves cutting off reinforcers and access to them. The use of punishing stimuli is called *punishment*.

As you know, neutral stimuli, when followed by reinforcing events, develop reinforcing properties. They become conditioned reinforcers. In a similar way, when neutral stimuli are followed by punishing events, they develop punishing properties—that is, they weaken responses that they follow. They become *conditioned punishers*.

Is Punishment Effective?

Some teachers have been told that they should not use punishment because it does not work and that it produces only temporary suppression of behavior, not real change. But current research shows that punishment is very effective. There are many stimulus events that can be shown to weaken behavior. The belief that punishment is ineffective arises from misinterpretation of early research. In early studies, the rate of punished behavior decreased during the period of punishment (temporary suppression), but increased to the prepunishment rate after the punishment was removed. Now suppose the effects of reinforcement followed the same logic. As long as a behavior is reinforced, it is maintained at a high rate. When the reinforcement is removed, the rate eventually returns to is prereinforcement level (extinction). By this logic, behavior followed by reinforcement is temporarily enhanced, but it is not really changed. The fact of the matter is that operant behavior is a function of consequences. As the consequences change, so does the behavior. But this does not mean consequences are not effective. The question becomes one of learning how to use consequences to maintain behaviors over time.

Azrin and Holz's (1966) review of punishment research shows that punishment has an effect on behavior opposite from reinforcement. Most of the principles of reinforcement are readily transferable to the analysis of punishment, except the goal is weakening, rather than strengthening, behavior. For example, punishment is more effective when it is intense or given in greater quantity, as is reinforcement. Also, punishment is more effective when it is given immediately.

Is Use of Punishment Immoral?

Probably no area of behavioral psychology has generated more emotion, confusion, and misunderstanding than the topic of punishment. Some people believe that any use of punishment under any circumstances is immoral. Some believe it is all right to punish children severely as long as you do not slap them in the face. Some equate any form of isolation procedure with prison, regardless of benefits to the child. Some believe the word *punishment* should be eliminated from the English language, as if that would somehow make people more loving.

But consider this example: For three years a child has been kept in a strait jacket whenever unattended (nighttime, for example) to prevent him from gouging his flesh and cutting an artery. Now suppose that by applying a mild electric shock (no more painful than a hypodermic needle) every time the child begins to gouge himself, this behavior could be eliminated in three days. Which is the moral thing to do—to use punishment to eliminate a behavior that completely restricts this child's possibilities for normal development, or to cuddle him and be kind to him each time he begins to hurt himself?

When the long-term effects of using punishment are far more beneficial than not using it, the moral person will do what is best for the child and use punishment. It would be immoral *not* to do everything possible to help children learn what is necessary in order to live freely in our society. There are few mothers of two year olds who question the use of punishment when it keeps their child from being hurt or killed by automobiles, knives, gas, or fire. Punishment in itself is not immoral, even though it may be used in ways that are harmful to children or adults.

There is no question that it is possible to use punishment to produce strong and lasting effects on behavior. *However, that does not mean it should be used.* Other matters need to be considered in deciding when and where to use punishment.

Why Is Punishment Usually to Be Avoided?

The use of aversive stimuli as punishers is usually to be avoided, not because they do not work, but because of undesired side effects. Parents and teachers want to teach children to come to them for help in solving problems. This goal is inconsistent with the major side effect of using aversive stimuli to weaken behavior: *people learn to avoid and escape sources of punishment.*

A number of names have been used to describe the avoidance and escape behaviors *taught to children* through punishment at home and at school. Here are a few of them:

Name	*Avoidance or Escape Behavior*
Cheating	Avoiding punishment for being wrong
Truancy	Avoiding or escaping the many punishments that go with school failure, poor teaching, and punitive administrations
Lying	Avoiding the punishment that follows doing something wrong
Sneaking	Avoiding being caught misbehaving
Hiding	Avoiding being caught
Murdering	Escaping from a punishing person by destroying him

Another reason for avoiding the use of physical punishment is that it shows a child how to be aggressive to others (provides a model for aggression). Children imitate what they see adults doing. Children whose parents are aggressive in the use of punishment are more aggressive with other children.

In summary, the initial examination of punishment-related procedures shows that "misbehavior" can be maintained by the critical attention teachers and parents give, and that while aversive punishment is effective, it has undesirable side effects. A final consideration before turning to effective procedures for weakening behavior is the fact that *the behavior that teachers want to weaken exists because it is reinforced.* If teachers just relied on punishment to weaken a behavior, when they stopped punishing the behavior it would probably return. Teachers need a way around that problem.

EFFECTIVE PROCEDURES FOR WEAKENING BEHAVIOR

Effective procedures for weaking behavior must do the following:

1. Minimize the need for punishment in the future.

2. Prevent avoidance and escape from responsible adults.

3. Not provide a model of aggressive behavior.

Consider the following case history.

Mother Changes Peter (and Mother)

Peter was a four year old boy. His mother was having great difficulty managing him and sought help. Peter often kicked objects or people, removed or tore his clothing, spoke rudely to people, hurt his younger sister, made various threats, hit himself, and was easily angered. He demanded constant attention. He had been seen at a clinic and was found to have poor verbal skills. He was said to be very active and possibly brain-damaged.

Peter's behavior was observed in the home an hour a day for sixteen days. During an hour Peter showed from 25 to 112 instances of behavior objectionable to his mother. When he misbehaved, his mother would often attend to him and try to explain why he should not do what he had done. At times she would try to interest him in some new activity by offering him toys or food. She would sometimes punish Peter by taking away a toy or misused object, but he was usually able to persuade her to return the item almost immediately. Occasionally he was placed on a chair for short periods of time as a punishment. Tantrum behavior usually followed such discipline. His mother responded with additional arguments, attempting to persuade him to stop.

Peter's behavior was changed by the following procedure. An observer in the home would cue his mother by raising one, two, or three fingers. One finger was raised when Peter showed an objectionable behavior. This meant she was to tell him to stop what he was doing (*a warning signal*). If he did not stop, two fingers were raised. This meant she was to immediately place him in his room and shut the door (*time out*). He had to stay there until he was quiet for a short period. If he was playing in a nice way, three fingers were raised. This meant she was to go to him, give him attention, praise him, and be physically affectionate (*reinforcement*).

Peter's objectionable behavior dropped to near zero within a few days. Follow-up observations showed a continuing good interaction between him and his mother and an absence of objectionable behavior. He was receiving more affection from his mother and approaching her in more affectionate ways. She was much more sure of herself, provided clear consequences for his behavior, and no longer gave in after starting a correction procedure (Hawkins, Peterson, Schweid, & Bijou, 1966).

Peter's mother learned that by following his good behavior with attention and affection, and by consistently giving a mild punishment (time out) for objectionable behavior when a warning failed, his behavior changed dramatically. His mother was taught how to teach him to behave in a friendlier and more cooperative way. She learned that she had to consistently respond with positive reactions to behavior she wanted to strengthen.

Clearly Peter's mother had learned some effective procedures for weakening Peter's objectionable behavior. The beginning of this chapter included an apparent paradox: Effective procedures for weakening undesired behavior focus on the use of reinforcers, just as procedures for strengthening behavior do. You are now ready to examine that statement.

Procedure 1. Reinforce Behavior Incompatible with the Behavior to Be Weakened.

The first and foremost strategy for dealing with problem behavior is to reinforce incompatible behavior. While you will go on to other procedures involving *withholding* of reinforcement, these other principles are likely to be ineffective unless combined with this reinforcement princple.

Incompatible behaviors are behaviors that cannot (or are difficult to) be performed at the same time as objectionable behaviors. Out-of-seat behavior is not compatible with in-seat behavior. Hitting is incompatible with writing an essay. Peter's mother reinforced a variety of cooperative behaviors that were incompatible with Peter's "objectionable" behaviors. By reinforcing incompatible behavior, the problem behavior has to occur less. Thus, the future need for punishment is reduced. Also, since this is a positive approach to the problem, the student it likely to stay oriented toward adults who are reinforcing, rather than avoiding or escaping from them.

Procedure 2. Do Not Reinforce the Problem Behavior; Put it on Extinction

You have seen that in many situations, the main reinforcer for problem behavior is attention from adults. You may suspect this is how Peter's problems were shaped up by his mother. If he was playing nicely, he was left alone and his mother got on to other chores. If he made a fuss, mom showed up to criticize him. You may also suspect that the same thing happened in Mrs. E.'s class discussed in Chapter 2. And you have seen it demonstrated that negative attention was the reinforcer in the "Sit Down Commands" study and the study of a "good" class that was turned temporarily into a "bad" class.

One way to put problem behavior on extinction is to "ignore" it. Do not give it attention (unless someone is getting hurt). Several studies have shown that if peer attention is reinforcing the problem behavior, it is effective to have the class "help out" in the change procedure. The teacher explains how the class can help the child with problem behavior (say tantrums) by minding their own business when the problem behavior occurs. If a preset criterion for reduction in the targeted behavior occurs, the whole class shares a treat or a special event.

It should be noted that when a behavior is no longer followed by customary reinforcement, it at first tends to get worse before extinction sets in. This phenomenon is the technical description of what "frustration" is all about. If you are used to getting your pay check on Friday, and it is delayed for some reason, you are likely to get upset. If Johnny is used to getting cookies and milk after school and mom says "No" because he has not been finishing dinner, she can expect frustration. The point is this: When extinction is used, expect things to get worse at first, but stick to your guns; it will get better. As you will see in Chapter 6, if a behavior has been intermittently reinforced (unpredictably), it will take more time for extinction to occur. That is one reason for "sticking to your guns" when an extinction procedure is used. If you give in "when it gets worse," you end up with a more difficult problem.

Although extinction may not produce behavior change as rapidly as can be produced using response cost or time out (procedure 3, next), it can have durable effects in reducing irritating behaviors such as pencil tapping, asking irrelevant questions, "smart talk," and getting out of the seat. These behaviors are often maintained by teacher attention. However, a much more effective approach is to combine procedures 1 and 2, so that incompatible behaviors are being reinforced while the problem behavior is being extinguished.

Procedure 3. If Punishment Is Needed, Use a Punishment Involving Withdrawal of Reinforcers, Preferably Response Cost

Instead of spanking Peter, which might drive him away from her and model aggressive behavior, Peter's mother used *time out* as the punishment. Time out is time out from reinforcement, in this case mother's attention. To earn the reinforcers back, Peter had to be quiet in the time out area for a few minutes. Then he could be with mother again. Taking away mother's attention had the effect of keeping Peter oriented toward mother. A spanking would tend to drive him away.

In general, withdrawal of reinforcers is an effective form of punishment *as long as there are clear-cut steps provided for earning the reinforcers back.* Consider the following case study:

The Case of Claire

Claire was a bright sixteen year old who was about to be expelled from high school for delinquency (truancy, poor grades, and incorrigibility at home). At the time help was sought, Claire was staying at home but threatening to run away. There was no father in the home. Her mother had taken away (as punishment) all money, use of the telephone, and dating privileges.

The treatment plan worked out with Claire and her mother was as follows: one note from school each day (signifying attendance at all classes) earned Claire telephone privileges for that day; four notes during the week earned one weekend date; five notes earned two dates. This plan worked beyond belief, even though Claire's mother was very skeptical at first. When Claire was simply punished by loss of privileges, she showed no improvement. It was not until a definite way to earn the privileges back was provided (by showing responsible behavior) that a change became evident (Thorne, Tharp & Wetzel, 1967).

Peter earned back his mother's attention by being quiet for five minutes. Claire earned back telephone and dating privileges by attending school regularly. Claire's plan worked so well that the notes were eliminated within a few months with no loss of attendance.

The case of Claire clearly shows that for response cost to really be effective, it must be combined with *reinforcement of incompatible behavior.* The combination of procedures 1 and 3 can be a truly strong behavior-change procedure.

Time out versus response cost. Time out is often the method of choice for young children showing aggressive and tantrum behavior at home. The research literature suggests that both methods are effective. However, for the typical school setting, the advantage has to go to response-cost procedures. The reasons are: (1) they can be implemented without taking the student away from learning tasks, and (2) they are less likely to be misunderstood by parents, administrators, or the press. In fact, it is strongly recommended that time out (in the form of a special room) not be used by teachers except under the supervision of a psychologist, and with fully informed consent.

Isolation Is Not Time Out

One is likely to associate time out with isolating a child from other people for a while. But isolation is not necessarily time out, nor is time out necessarily isolation. As noted before, time out refers to *time out from positive reinforcement.* If the classroom is not reinforcing, taking the child out of it cannot be a time-out punishment. In fact, placing a child in the hall or sending him to the principal may be reinforcing if special attention is given or peer status is enhanced. For the autistic child, isolation may be reinforcing. *Isolation is not time out. Time out consists of cutting off the possibility of all reinforcement for a period of time.* This may be done *in* the classroom with a chair in the corner, as long as the rest of the class is trained to ignore the child being punished. Time out might consist of taking away the child's programed reader for the rest of the reading period, because he was looking up the answers and writing them in. Just sitting with nothing to do for twenty minutes while everyone else is learning can be a time-out punishment.

Additional Rules For the Effective Use of Punishment

1. The punishment should be *immediate.* Take away the points, free time, or start time out when the punishable behavior begins.

2. *Use a warning signal.* Peter's mother used "Stop that" as the warning signal. If followed by punishment (in this case time out), it can become a conditioned punisher and thus can reduce the future need for more complicated punishment.

3. *Use only one warning.* The first time a punishable behavior occurs, give a warning. The next time, back up your warning signal with a response cost or time out.

4. *Stay calm and use soft reprimands.* To teach responsible behavior, show responsible behavior. Several studies by O'Leary and colleagues (such as O'Leary and Becker, 1968; O'Leary, Kaufman, Kass, and Drabman, 1970) have shown soft reprimands to be much more effective than loud ones.

5. *Be consistent.* Be sure the undesired behavior is not reinforced on an intermittent schedule.

SUMMARY

This chapter examined the criticism trap, the problems with using presentation of aversive stimuli as punishment, and effective ways to weaken troublesome behavior.

The criticism trap research shows that attention to inappropriate behavior can function as a reinforcer and can strengthen the very behavior you are trying to get rid of. Furthermore, the criticizer can be reinforced by the person being criticized because the short-term effect of the criticism may be a stopping of the criticized behavior. However, the longer-term effect can be an actual increase in the behavior. Teachers and parents need to become aware of this possible effect of attention to inappropriate behavior. A similar process was noted in studies of students whose error-making was found to be controlled by the teacher attention it produced.

It is quite clear that *punishment* can be very effective in weakening behavior and that there are times (rare) when it may be the method of choice. However, punishment that uses aversive stimuli is usually to be avoided because it leads to avoidance and escape behavior, such as lying, cheating, and truancy (as well as related fears and anger). Also, it provides a model of aggressive behavior, teaching children to be aggressive.

Effective procedures for weakening behavior must reduce the future need to use punishment, prevent avoidance and escape from responsible adults, and not provide an aggressive model. This can be accomplished by ***reinforcing incompatible behavior*** as the primary method for weakening behavior, along with extinction or use of response cost or time out if the undesired behavior occurs.

When privileges are taken away as a punishment (a response cost procedure), be sure to specify ways they can be earned back (earning them back is used to reinforce incompatible behavior). For use in school, response cost (loss of privileges, free time, points, and so on) is to be preferred over time out because it is less likely to interfere with learning time and is likely to be more acceptable to parents and administrators.

Additional rules for making punishment effective are: (1) make it immediate, (2) use a warning signal, (3) use only one warning, (4) stay calm, and (5) be consistent.

CHAPTER

6

APPLICATION OF PRINCIPLES: MAINTENANCE OF BEHAVIOR

Behavior that is not reinforced tends to undergo extinction. What are the ways in which this can be minimized or prevented? The generalization and maintenance of behavior over time, during changing stimulus conditions, and under changing conditions of reinforcement is a major goal of much instruction. Procedures that produce generalized learning of concepts, operations, and problem-solving strategies will be the central topic of later chapters on cognitive skills. The focus of this chapter is on those procedures that are useful in maintaining behavior over time and under changing conditions of stimulus control (S^d's) and reinforcement.

THE EFFECTS OF SCHEDULES OF REINFORCEMENT

Careful experimental work has documented the properties of different schedules of reinforcement (Ferster and Skinner, 1957). These studies have demonstrated the effects on behavior of various schedules of reinforcement and what happens when reinforcement is terminated (extinction). These findings are summarized here.

Continuous Reinforcement

When every response is reinforced, a continuous schedule is in effect. Continuous schedules have the advantage of getting new learning to occur quickly. However, if reinforcement stops, extinction is likely to take place rapidly.

Intermittent Reinforcement

When only some responses are reinforced, the schedule is said to be intermittent. Intermittent schedules are defined on the basis of whether the schedule focuses on the number of responses (ratio schedules) or on the passage of time (interval schedules), and on whether the schedule is predictable (fixed) or unpredictable (variable). This two-way classification leads to four types of intermittent schedules. Table 6.1 summarizes the properties of each.

Fixed-Ratio Schedules. In a fixed-ratio schedule, reinforcers are given for every *X* responses. An FR-5 schedule means that after every five responses, a reinforcer is given. Such schedules are common in industry and go under the name *piecework:* A set number of completed tasks is worth so much money. The teacher might use a fixed-ratio schedule with seatwork assignments. Each ten exercises completed correctly in the programed reader is worth one point. Each five arithmetic problems completed correctly is worth a minute of recess. Fixed-ratio schedules produce high rates of response while they are in effect. After terminating a fixed-ratio schedule, extinction follows less quickly than with continuous reinforcement, but more quickly than with variable reinforcement.

Fixed-Interval Schedules. On this schedule, reinforcers are given for the first response to occur after *X* minutes (or seconds or hours) have passed. But there are problems. If reinforcement occurs only at regular intervals, the student will learn to discriminate when it pays off to work and when it does not. Right after reinforcement, the student learns to take it easy until the next time. Chapter 3 discussed a study by Mawhinney et al. that compared the effects of daily, weekly, and three-week testing intervals. For the longest interval between tests, studying was lowest right after a test and gradually increased as time for the next test approached.

On a fixed-interval schedule, the teacher tells the class, "Today, I am going to check you every ten minutes to see if everyone is working. If when I check, everyone is working, you will earn one minute of recess." With this approach, the students get busy just before each ten-minute check by the teacher.

On the other hand, it is possible to give reinforcers on a fixed-interval

Table 6-1 Four kinds of intermittent reinforcement schedules *(after Walker & Buckley, 1974, p. 24)*

Name Schedule	*Definition of Schedule*	*Effects on Behavior*	
		Schedule in Effect	*Schedule Terminated (Extinction)*
Fixed Ratio (FR)	Reinforcer is given after each X responses.	High response rate	Irregular burst of responding. More responses than in continuous reinforcement, less than in variable ratio.
Fixed Interval (FI)	Reinforcer is given for first response to occur after each X minutes.	Stops working after reinforcement. Works hard just prior to time for next reinforcement.	Slow gradual decrease in responding.
Variable Ratio (VR)	Reinforcer is given after X responses on the average.	Very high response rates. The higher the ratio the higher the rate.	Very resistant to extinction. Maximum number of responses before extinction.
Variable Interval (VI)	Reinforcer is given for first response after each X minutes, on the average.	Steady rate of responding.	Very resistant to extinction. Maximum time to extinction.

basis for convenience, but to set the criterion for reinforcement so that it works like a continuous schedule. The teacher simply states the rules and says, "For each ten minutes that no one violates the rules, the whole class will earn two minutes of recess. If a violation occurs, the ten-minute period starts over." The reinforcer is given for good behavior *over the whole period,* not just for the time immediately before the reinforcer is due. This type of schedule is best called a *duration* schedule rather than an interval schedule.

Variable-Ratio Schedules. Variable-ratio schedules give reinforcement for every *X* responses *on the average.* For example, a VR-5 schedule might reinforce after one response, then after four, then after seven, then two, then nine, and so forth. The range varies from one to ten, but would average five. Variable-ratio schedules lead to high steady response rates while they are in effect, and they are very resistant to extinction; that is, the behavior continues a long time after reinforcement is stopped. Most games of chance operate on variable-ratio schedules. The gambler who persists at a slot machine hour after hour even though he is losing shows the powerful control exerted by variable-ratio schedules. Winning a little every once in a while can keep a lot of behavior going. When persistence is the goal, variable-ratio schedules may help achieve it.

Variable-Interval Schedules. These schedules give reinforcement for the first response after *X* minutes *on the average.* For example, a VI-5 schedule might reinforce a response after one minute or after seven minutes. The range of times might be from one to ten minutes and average five. Variable-interval schedules (like variable-ratio schedules) produce high rates of responding when the schedule is in effect and high resistance to extinction. They are very useful for reinforcing behaviors such as time on-task.

IMPLICATIONS OF SCHEDULES RESEARCH FOR MAINTENANCE

Procedure 1. To Get New Behavior Going, Use a Schedule Closer to Continuous Reinforcement. To Keep Behavior Going, Gradually Shift to an Intermittent (Unpredictable) Schedule of Reinforcement

Note that if you suddenly shift from reinforcing nearly every response to reinforcing every 100th response, the student would likely quit long before making 100 responses. A gradual shift is necessary to prevent extinction from occurring. The following examples illustrate right and wrong ways to maintain student performance.

The Wrong Way. The class has been assigned a task the teacher knows they can do. She walks around the room to check their work and answer questions. Jeff just sits and looks in the air until the teacher comes near; then he turns to his work and seems busy. The teacher praises him for working. When she passes, he returns to his daydreaming. The same pattern is repeated frequently. Jeff is being trained to work only when the teacher is near. Jeff is reinforced each time he works (continuous reinforcement), but he does not work continuously. Jeff does what is reinforced: works when the teacher is near. A clear signal is provided (the teacher's approach) as to *when* working is likely to be reinforced.

The Right Way. A colored card with fifty squares on it is placed on Jeff's desk. When the card is filled, Jeff gets to choose the game for the next recess. The

I'M GOING TO SWEAR OFF AS SOON AS I FIGURE OUT THE SCHEDULE

teacher has a kitchen timer (which makes a soft *ding* when it goes off) on her desk. She also has a little card with the following numbers on it: 30″, 2′, 1′, 20″, 4′, 1″, and so forth. Jeff is instructed that the teacher will check to see if he is working each time the bell dings. If Jeff is working, the teacher will nod and Jeff can put a mark on his card (teacher also keeps score at her desk when she resets the timer). The timer is set according to the numbers given above. Unpredictable intermittent reinforcement is given. Jeff can't predict when reinforcement is coming. To keep from losing points, he has to keep working. Slowly the time intervals are increased. Then the bell is eliminated, with the teacher checking now and then on her own. After Jeff has learned to complete his tasks, the points are dropped, and the teacher only gives praise and occasional privileges for good work. *Predictable reinforcement* will lead to working (or paying attention) only when reinforcement is likely to occur. *Variable reinforcement* will lead to steady working or persistent behavior.[*]

SELF-MANAGEMENT

Procedure 2. Use of Self-Management Procedures as a Promising Approach to Maintaining Behavior under Changing Reinforcement Conditions

When we contrast children and adults, it becomes evident that in general, adults have somehow learned to go longer periods without direct and immediate reinforcement for their efforts; that they are able to work for long-delayed, often symbolic, and certainly not obvious reinforcers; that they do a lot self-management of their food intake, sexual desires, money, and other desires by making plans, talking to themselves, evaluating what they do, and so forth. While the direct application of the principles of operant behavior is obviously important in teaching younger children, and continues to underlie what we do as adults, clearly a variety of self-management skills (cognitive skills) and learned motivational processes are operating. These processes seem quite important to the issue of how to maintain behavior over time in the absence of direct reinforcement.

The experimental study of self-management processes is very young.

Two reviews of the literature (O'Leary and Dubey, 1979; Rosenbaum and Drabman, 1979) have examined the effects of self-instructions, self-assessment, self-evaluation, self-reinforcement, and related procedures. Treatment procedures called *cognitive-behavior modification* (Mahoney, 1974; Meichenbaum, 1977) and *social learning theory* (Bandura, 1977) are largely devoted to studying and applying self-management procedures. This section examines this literature and its implications for teachers. A consistent theme running through the literature is that students do not learn to manage their behavior in responsible ways unless they are taught to do so through the models they are presented with and the direct instruction they receive.

Self-Instructions. Our verbal behavior (including talking to ourselves) can be used to provide prompts or S^d's to ourselves to assist what we do. We say rules to ourselves, "Look both ways before crossing the street"; we prompt each member in chains of behaviors, "Do this, then this, then this"; we talk to ourselves as we write a sentence. Training in self-instructions has been shown to facilitate performance in a wide variety of situations, as long as: (1) the students have the skills needed to execute the instructions, (2) they have been reinforced for following self-instructions, and (3) following the instructions leads to reinforcement. Making plans, as in planning an outline for a book and each of its chapters, is a very important form of self-instruction. After analyzing what is to be covered, a set of S^d's (the outlines) are prepared to guide future action. Plans are discriminative stimuli we construct for ourselves or others.

Self-Recording of Behavior. By recording your own behavior, you can sometimes change it, since the feedback can both remind you of what you are trying to change and reinforce you if it changes. The research literature suggests that junior high and high school students can be trained to use self-recording to help control their own behavior. For example, Broden, Hall, and Mitts (1971) found that an eighth grade girl in history class increased her study behavior when provided with slips to record how much she studied each day. Similarly, an eighth grade boy decreased his talk-outs when provided with slips to record them each day. However, after a return to baseline, a second period of recording talk-outs was not as effective. The authors suggest that self-recording procedures should be combined with social reinforcement to be most effective.

Gottman and McFall (1972), in a study using potential high school dropouts, found an increase in classroom participation when students self-recorded their participation and a decrease when they recorded nonparticipation. With two elementary school problem children, Lovitt (1973) found sharp decreases in inappropriate behavior when their behavior was self-recorded. Ballard and Glynn (1975) found that they had to add self-reinforcement to self-recording to get changes in writing skills with third graders.

Other studies suggest that children are not naturally accurate observers of their own behavior. Fixsen, Phillips, and Wolf (1972) found, with boys in Achievement Place (a group home for adolescent delinquents), that it was necessary to train them for observing their own behavior and to give points for concurrence with another observer, before accurate self-observations occurred. Even then, however, just doing self-reports did not significantly improve room-cleaning behaviors.

In their review, O'Leary and Dubey (1979) conclude that self-recording procedures by themselves are not too effective with problem children, but can be effective with students already motivated to do well. Self-recording appears not to add much to an already effective reward system.

Self-Reinforcement. The study of self-reinforcement can only reasonably occur when self-evaluations can be compared to some criterion (Bandura, 1976). A variety of studies show self-reinforcement to be as effective as external reinforcement. The following are a few examples.

In history lessons with ninth grade girls, Glynn (1970) found that test score accuracy was as high with self-determined token rewards as with experimenter-determined rewards. Also, each of these token reward procedures was better than two control procedures using no tokens or random tokens.

In another study, Glynn, Thomas, and Shee (1973) studied the effects of self-management procedures with a group of second graders. After a training program in which the class could earn points if they were all on-task when checked by the teacher (on a random schdule), the program was turned over to the students. A tape recorder played intermittent beeps every one to five minutes. If the children were on-task when the beep occurred, they recorded a check mark. Checks could later be used for self-administered free time. This self-recorded and self-administered system was very effective in maintaining on-task behavior. With a somewhat different procedure, Bolstad and Johnson (1972) also showed that control of an initially externally managed token system could be turned over to the students without a loss in on-task behavior.

With fifth graders, Farnum, Brigham, and Johnson (1977) found that students consistently completed more work when they could determine the rewards. They preferred being in control of the situation and worked harder. Other studies have supported a facilitating effect of being able to choose your own contingencies (Brigham and Bushell, 1973; Brigham and Sherman, 1973; Brigham and Stoerzinger, 1976).

Several classroom studies have suggested that students will select more lenient standards for themselves when given the chance under self-reinforcement conditions (Felixbod and O'Leary, 1973, 1974). Better performance has usually been associated with the use of more stringent standards. When more stringent standards were prompted and reinforced with praise, Brownell et al. (1977) found that those in a prompted group used the prompt and performed better on academic tasks than those in a nonprompted group.

Self-reinforcement procedures and self-choice of reinforcers apparently do work, at least within the constraints of classroom expectations and social reinforcement conditions.

A Self-Control Program. Meichenbaum and Goodman (1971) developed a training strategy for second graders who were called hyperactive. They were taught to follow these steps in approaching new tasks:

- Define the task.
- Verbalize a strategy for doing it.
- Evaluate their performance.
- Praise themselves when they do well.

These procedures were taught through a series of faded support steps. First, an adult modeled the steps of a task, while talking aloud about what he was doing. Next, the child performed the same task while being verbally guided by the adult. Next, the child did the task verbally guiding his or her own performance. Then, the task was repeated using a whisper, and finally, with covert self-instructions.

The measures used in training and to evaluate the treatment were a series of conceptual and perceptual tasks commonly used to assess impulsivity (Matching Familiar Figures, Porteus Maze Test, and so forth). The test outcomes supported the training, but effects on two measures of classroom behavior did not show positive outcomes. These results have been replicated. Again, no effects measurable in the classroom were found. The problem most likely lies in the programing. The students were less impulsive on the tasks they were trained on, but they were not trained on classroom tasks. The potential for this kind of training has still to be demonstrated.

Goal Setting. A self-management procedure (with teacher guidance) recommended for use with secondary students by Sprick (1985) (see also Chapter 8) is goal setting. When a problem is identified, the teacher meets with the student and asks the student to participate in setting some goals that would help overcome the problem. They fill out an agreement form together, specifying some goals and how they will evaluate progress toward those goals. Some short-term goals might be getting assignments in on time, or raising a grade, getting along with other students. Longer-term goals might be getting a good job, completing high school, going to college, getting a part-time job, or earning a scholarship. With long-term goals it is necessary to specify a series of shorter-term goals that would facilitate reaching the long-term goal. While only anecdotal evidence is available for the effectiveness of such procedures (without specifying special reinforcers), there is every reason to believe that the satisfaction of reaching goals you have set for yourself and the social reinforcement that may go with it from a teacher can be an effective self-management strategy.

Experiments in Self-Government. Achievement Place has been used to experimentally study which forms of social design (governments) most readily teach delinquent youngsters to become responsible adults. At Achievement Place a semi-self-government system is used whereby the boys can vote to establish many of their own rules, monitor their own compliance, and conduct "trials" when violations occur. The boys participated more in the discussion of a violation when they had complete reponsibility for setting the consequence of the "trial" than if the teaching parents set the consequence (Fixsen, et al., 1973). On the other hand, another study showed that the boys called fewer "trials" than the teaching parents did. A third study examined the various aspects of the management of routine household tasks (Phillips, Phillips, Wolf, and Fixsen, 1973). The best system involved a peer-elected manager who had the authority to both give and take away points, depending on whether or not the other boys were meeting their obligations.

The Role of External Control. In their review of the self-control research in classrooms, Rosenbaum and Drabman (1979) raise the question of how much continuing external control is actually still present in the studies reviewed. They conclude that all of the studies have "included external variables prior to or concurrent with the introduction of self-control training." For self-control truly to be operative, the person must believe that he or she could cheat if desired and reward himself or herself without fear of external consequences. In true self-control, the person has full control of the available reinforcers and places contingencies on one's self for their use.

The kinds of external controls present in these studies included:

- Prior training under external control before shifting to self-control. This would set up S^d's to maintain an influence after the shift.

- Requiring students to match self-ratings with those of an observer.
- Praising appropriate and ignoring inappropriate behavior.
- Limiting the range of points that could be self-awarded.
- Setting rules for the application of self-rewards.
- Modeling desired performance.
- Cueing desired performance.

Rosenbaum and Drabman conclude that to date what has been shown is at best "a weak form of self-control." These are not unimportant demonstrations, however. It is likely that very few of us are ever completely free from external reinforcers, however distant or however secondary (conditioned). Even the Trappist monk who has forsaken all earthly rewards is likely controlled by an externally generated belief system supported by others of the faith. What these studies do show is that it is possible through training to gradually enhance the self-control capabilities of each of us in the face of temptation. As we mature, we learn to avoid the traps of immediate reinforcers (excessive eating, smoking, drinking, drugs, sex, winning, and overpowering others) in favor of delayed, but potentially more valuable reinforcers for not only ourselves but those we share life with.

ENTRY INTO NATURAL CONTINGENCIES OF REINFORCEMENT

Procedure 3. Maintain Behavior by Planning for Entries into "Natural" Contingencies of Reinforcement

Baer and Wolf (1970) demonstrated another approach to maintenance with a preschool boy who showed low rates of peer interaction. They primed the situation by prompting and reinforcing his play on a jungle gym. Before too long, the play interactions with others took over and the boy maintained social interactions with the other children. In the area of social skills training, one would expect that providing a shy student with initiating and interacting skills would eventually lead to behavior that would keep itself going. The same kind of "natural entry" can occur in learning to play an instrument or in learning to read. The initial learning can be difficult and should be externally motivated by a teacher, if sufficient skill is to be developed to allow the student to get reinforcement from the activity itself (playing a song or reading a novel).

The power of natural contingencies of reinforcement was brought home to me strongly by my son when he was four years old. We were in a restaurant and he had to go to the bathroom. I said I would go with him as I had in the past. He told me he would do it himself. "I can read 'men' I'll get the right place." I let him go, but tagged behind to observe him without his knowing it. When he got to the two bathroom doors (men and women), he sounded men, "mmmmmmeeeeeennnnn," said it fast, "men" and proudly went through the proper door. Reading skills had given him new control over his own reinforcers. He had been learning to read at preschool and had learned enough sounds to deal with that problem.

CHANGING REINFORCER SYSTEMS

Suppose you are using a special reinforcer system, such as a token or point system backed up by special prizes, and you want to "get off of it." This could happen because your class is now running smoothly and you want to prepare the students to function on more "normal" reinforcers such as praise, grades, and special activities. The need to shift might also occur if you are operating a special class and need to prepare the students for a mainstreamed setting.

Procedure 4. Change from a Special Reinforcement System Back to Typical Classroom Reinforcers by Gradually Changing Cues and Reinforcers in the Special Setting to Make Them More Like Those in Regular Classes

When sudden shifts are made in the prompting and reinforcing stimuli that control behavior, your class can end up in chaos. A rapid decrease in the level of reinforcement in a setting produces a contrast effect such that the lower level of reinforcers may actually operate as punishers. This can be obviated by slowly making the special class more like the regular class. Praise is maintained, but made more unpredictable. The points or tokens that can be earned each day are reduced, say 5 percent every few days. And they are only given out at the end of the day, instead of after each work period. Activity reinforcers are kept, but "store items" are faded from the "reinforcer menu." Eventually, the students are working for praise, grades, pride in their accomplishments, and an occasional special activity planned by the teacher. Throughout a fade-out procedure, really let the students know how pleased you are with their progress. "You have really learned to work on your own, without the point system. You should be proud of yourselves!" Walker and Buckley (1974) have demonstrated the effectiveness of this fading approach with aggressive elementary school students being prepared to return to a regular class from a special token-reinforcement classroom. (Chapter 7 discusses more on token systems.)

KEEP REINFORCEMENT GOING IN CHANGING SETTINGS

You may diligently try all of the procedures discussed for maintaining appropriate school behavior under changing S^{d}'s and reinforcers and still find trouble. Walker, Mattson, and Buckley (1971) faced this problem with the aggressive boys they were returning to regular classrooms. Even after gradually fading out the token system, and with the students' improved academic skills and attitudes, the returning students did not behave as well in their old classrooms as in the special classes. For example, for one group of five:

Before treatment appropriate behavior .... 39 percent
During treatment appropriate behavior .... 90 percent
Follow-up appropriate behavior .... 66 percent

The teachers had trouble providing academic materials these students could be successful with. They also used low levels of social reinforcement.

A month prior to the return of the next group of aggressive students to their former teachers, the teachers were asked to participate in a special program of training in classroom management using procedures similar to those covered so far in this book (Walker, Fiegenbaum, & Hops, 1971). The teacher's grade in this special course (college credit was given) was dependent on how well their target students maintained appropriate classroom behavior after returning. The results for this group were:

Before treatment appropriate behavior	34 percent
During treatment appropriate behavior	95 percent
Follow-up appropriate behavior	87 percent

The classroom observations produced other interesting findings. A comparison of the five teachers' behavior before training and after training showed these results:

	Before Training	After Training
Attends to total behavior	11.2 percent	14.2 percent
Attends to appropriate behavior	5.6 percent	13.1 percent
Attends to inappropriate behavior	5.4 percent	2.1 percent

Initially the teachers divided their time between appropriate and inappropriate behavior. After training they focused on appropriate behavior.

These same students were followed up in the next academic year. No attempts were made to work with their new teachers on maintenance. The students averaged 80 percent appropriate behavior. A control group who had received a similar treatment, but whose teachers were not trained in behavior principles, showed only 64 percent appropriate behavior during next year follow-up. The teacher training procedure thus proved very successful in maintaining the gains after the token program ended.

Procedure 5. In Changing Conditions of Cues and Reinforcers, if Maintenance of Newly Established Appropriate Behavior Is Not Found, Consider Training the Staff Running the New Conditions in Appropriate Classroom Management Procedures

SUMMARY

We have examined a range of procedures that can assist in the maintenance of behavior under changing S^{d}'s and reinforcers, including the relative absence of reinforcers. Behavior that is not reinforced tends to undergo extinction. Maintenance procedures are used under conditions where such extinction is more likely.

Studies of reinforcement schedules show:

- *Continuous schedules* (or nearly so) are most effective in getting new behavior started, but lead to extinction most rapidly when they are withdrawn. In a continuous schedule, every correct response is reinforced.

- *Variable schedules* lead to good response rates when they are operating and are very resistant to extinction when they are withdrawn. The "thinner" the schedule, the more the resistance to extinction. Gamblers may be trapped by such schedules, losing money, but can not quit. In a variable schedule, reinforcement is given now and then in an unpredictable fashion.

- *Gradually shifting* from a high rate of reinforcement to a variable schedule will help maintain the behavior and prevent extinction.

- Beware of *fixed-interval schedules,* such as those usually set up for study behavior by the use of widely separated test schedules. Such schedules lead to bursts of behavior just before it is time for the "reinforcer" to occur. Reinforcing being on-task for a fixed period of time (a *duration* schedule) is a relatively simple, but effective, procedure for teachers to use.

Direct instruction in *self-management skills,* including self-instructions, self-recording of behavior, self-evaluation, self-reinforcement, and goal setting, offer considerable promise for improving the longer-term maintenance of behavior. While there is no magic here—external reinforcers, however distant or secondary, remain the ultimate controllers—we can be taught to be better controllers of our own behaviors.

Another way to ensure the maintenance of behavior is to be sure that what is taught will have practical use in everyday life or future learning in the classroom. That is, provide for entry into *"natural"* (that is, readily available) *contingencies of reinforcement.* Some social skills, for example, will be fostered by the interactions with others they facilitate. Learning to says sounds will be maintained by the word reading they facilitate. A basic rule in designing instructional programs is to only teach concepts and skills that will be used later on by the students on their own or as components of more complex skills. Also, many skills we learn lead to activities that can provide reinforcement both inherently and from external sources (such as musical skills).

When changing student environments in ways that change normal cues and reduce directly available reinforcers (in mainstreaming or eliminating a token reinforcement system), stage the changes in slow steps (shape the changes) to maintain appropriate behavior. You can tell if you are moving too fast if off-task and disruptive behavior increase. Also be sure to praise the group for "doing more on their own" with less special help.

When all else fails as you change settings, perhaps the problem is too much punishment (through failure), too much attention to misbehavior (reinforcing it), and too little reinforcing support for desirable behavior by the teacher. It may be necessary to provide classroom management training for the receiving teacher.

CHAPTER

7

SPECIAL REINFORCEMENT SYSTEMS

Sometimes the usual approaches to classroom management based on rules, social and activity reinforcers, and grades do not work for whole classes or for some members. If students are not responsive to the typical methods used to motivate them, it is possible to strengthen the reinforcement system until the students have learned to work more effectively in the learning setting. This chapter explores token reinforcement systems, contracts, and point-grading systems. In the next chapter, we will have further occasion to return to specialized applications of these systems.

TOKEN REINFORCEMENT SYSTEMS

Token reinforcement systems are one practical way to introduce stronger reinforcers for a classroom, a group, or a single student. They also can be used by parents at home. In a token reinforcement system, points or something tangible, like poker chips, are given as the immediate reinforcer. Later, these are exchanged for fun activities, play materials, food, and so on. Token systems have been very successful where other approaches have failed. While they are not the method of first choice, if more typical reinforcers will not work, tokens may work. The following two examples show the power of special reinforcers.

An After-School Program for Potential Dropouts

Wolf, Giles, and Hall (1968) studied sixteen pupils from two elementary schools located in a low-income district of Kansas City. The students worked in a remedial teaching program during the summer and after school hours during the regular school year. Comparisons were made with a group that went to the regular school and did not take part in a remedial program.

The token reinforcement system used was somewhat like a trading stamp plan. The students had cards marked off into squares. The cards were checked by an instructor whenever a student had earned a point. Each checked square was a token. When a student first joined the program, points were given for each problem worked correctly. As the student did better, the amount and difficulty of the work required to earn points increased. The number of points given to a student for a particular bit of work was determined by the instructor alone or by bargaining with the student.

Filled pages of points could be exchanged for a variety of goods and events, such as the circus, swimming, the zoo, daily snacks, candy, soap, novelties, or long-range goals such as clothes or secondhand bicycles. A number of other contingencies were provided for in the program. In some instances, favorite subjects or popular activities could be attempted only after completion of work in less-favored areas. A bonus was given for attendance. Improvement in grades in the regular classroom led to a party after each grading period for all students who had improved. The students also received bonus points for reports of good behavior from their regular class teacher.

During each of the preceding two years the median gain by the remedial groups on an achievement test had been .6 year. The gain during the year of the remedial program for the token group was 1.5 years. Comments by the regular-school teachers suggest that the remedial program benefited the regular school classroom as well. Not only were the program students helped, but their increased participation and changed attitudes increased the achievement of other students in the classroom.

An In-School Program for an Adjustment Class

Most early studies of token programs have used at least one adult to monitor every four or five children. O'Leary and Becker (1967) successfully devised a token program that could be used by one teacher with a class of seventeen. The students had been placed in a special class because they exhibited behavior problems and were behind in classwork—nine year olds working at a beginning first grade level. Also, they were from disadvantaged homes.

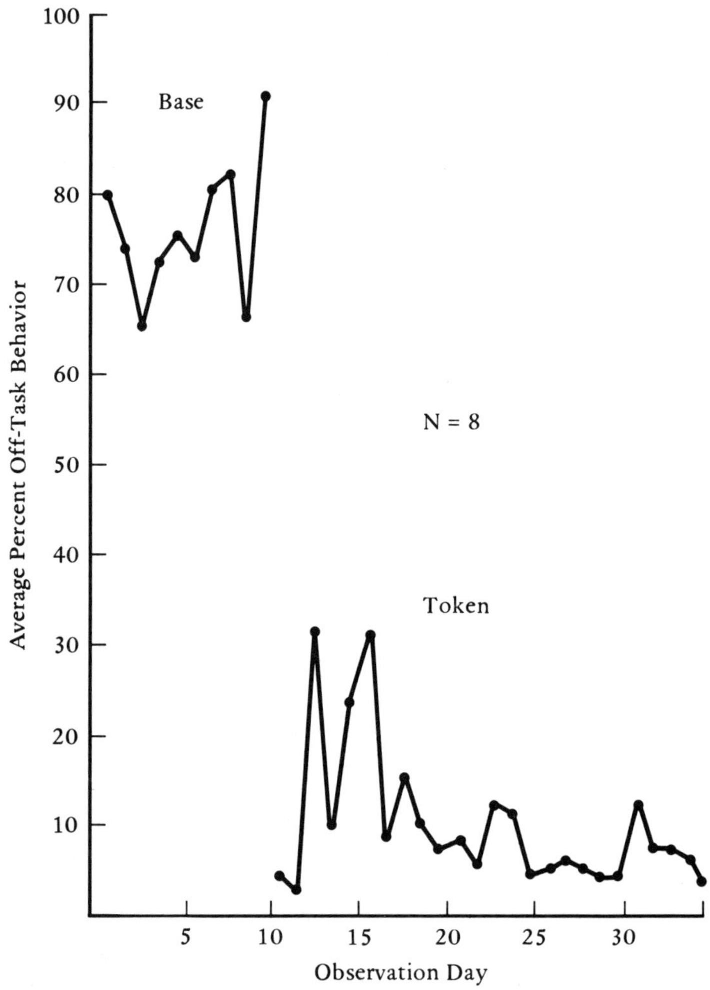

Figure 7-1 *Average percent off-task behavior during base and token periods for eight children*

For practical reasons, behavior was observed for only eight of the seventeen students. They averaged 76 percent off-task behavior before the token system was started. This included being out of their seats, talking out of turn, making noises with objects, talking to peers when it was not permitted, turning away from their work, and other behavior that did not involve paying attention to the teacher or working at a school task. The teacher had a most difficult time carrying out any procedure that might be considered teaching. She would usually leave the classroom worn out.

The token program was put into effect from 12:30 to 2:00 P.M. each day. On the first day, the class rules were placed on the blackboard, and the token procedures explained to the children. Small ten-cent notebooks were taped to each student's desk. The students were told that they would receive points in their notebooks every fifteen minutes. For each of these periods they could get from 1 to 10 points. A mark of 10 meant that they were following the rules very well, while a mark of 1 indicated that they were not doing their tasks. After a few days, point were given for each thirty-minute period.

The points could be traded for small prizes, such as candy, comics, perfume, and kites. The variety of items increased the chances that at least one of the items would be a reinforcer for each student.

At first, the tokens were traded in at the end of the token period. Step by step, the students were required to work up to four days before trading points, and the points required for a prize were increased.

The results are summarized in Figure 7.1. During baseline, the students averaged 76 percent off-task behavior. This dropped to 10 percent during the token period. It was now possible to begin to teach. They quickly learned to respond to the teacher's praise, which was paired with the giving of points. The class became the best-behaved class in the school. The students learned to tolerate delays in trading tokens for prizes. Reports indicated that they also behaved better in other classroom activities in which points were not given, and during music and library sessions. The rewards for the eight-week program cost $80.76. Rewards appear to be less expensive for school districts than psychologists!

"Why, That's Bribery."

The use of rewards for learning is often interpreted as bribery. But bribery is

LEARNING SHOULD BE FOR ITS OWN SAKE. PAY KIDS TO LEARN AND THEY'LL NEVER BE GOOD STUDENTS.

basically different from token reinforcement; tokens are ***earned*** rewards for good work and measurable improvement according to rules. Reinforcing consequences can be used to teach responsible behavior if the appropriate differential reinforcement procedures are followed.

Another concern of teachers is that, if toys and earned free time are used, the students will not discover learning for its own sake. This is just not the case. Conditioned reinforcers are established by following neutral stimuli with known reinforcers. If learning activities are followed by reinforcers, they will become conditioned reinforcers; then learning can take place for its own sake. To make the transition, it is only necessary to use appropriate procedures to fade out the special reinforcement system.

A Caution

Never use a stronger motivational system than you need to get the job done. If praise and grades will do the job, stay with it. If a token system is necessary, try first backing it up with free time or other activities. When you need stronger reinforcers, use them. Then, fade them out using the procedures suggested in Chapter 6. Token systems are most often used in special classes.

Designing Token Systems

There are six steps in the design of a token system:

1. Specify the behaviors that earn tokens.
2. Develop a menu of backup reinforcers.
3. Set prices and wages.
4. Decide on the tokens.
5. Establish operating procedures.
6. Set up a record system.

Each of these steps will be discussed in turn.

Step 1. Specify the Behaviors That Earn Tokens. When the behaviors that earn tokens are specified, the teacher knows when to give tokens, and the students know what to work for. The specification process has two stages. First, decide what general areas of behavior need stronger reinforcement; then, get down to specifics appropriate to each student.

Your general areas might include:

Study behaviors	*Social behaviors*
working on-task *X* minutes	cooperating
checking own work	interacting with others
using teaching machines appropriately	asking questions
using references	relating experiences
doing homework	

Academic behaviors

reading	writing
arithmetic	spelling
language	social studies
	science

The specifics you choose will depend on what your students need to learn. Most academic tasks can be treated as countable behaviors, and some kind of ratio schedule can be used. For example, "For each ten arithmetic problems completed, checked, and corrected, you can earn 1 token." Or, "Complete the five-page story, answer the questions, and do the checkout with the aide to earn 2 tokens."

Most social and study skills can be handled by requiring an interval of performance according to some criterion, (a duration schedule). "For each ten minutes of working on-task without an unexcused interruption, you can earn 1 token." Another method is to use a variable-interval checking procedure. A timer is set to go off at variable times ranging from one to twelve minutes (later, from ten to thirty). The students are checked when the timer goes off and awarded a token if they are working, being cooperative, and so on.

In specifying behaviors that earn tokens, *be sure to specify quality as well as quantity*—so many tokens for so many right reponses or corrected responses. If your concern is with study skills and academic performance, place a contingency on each. Research shows that if just paying attention is reinforced, there is no necessary academic improvement, and vice versa. Best results are obtained when both attending and academic performance earn tokens.

Gradually increase your behavioral requirements. If the students can work for only thirty seconds at a time, start there; but when this criterion is met, move to sixty seconds on-task to earn 1 token. Later the students might work for ten minutes for 3 tokens. In a similar way, initially you might give a token for each item completed correctly in a programed reader. Later, a token might be given for correct completion of a page, or five pages.

At the beginning, define your requirements so that lots of reinforcers can be given immediately. Later, the requirements for reinforcement might cover a day or a week.

Be sure to reinforce improvement! Set your requirements so that all students have a chance to "win" if they follow the rules.

It is often convenient to write out daily assignments for each student. Let the students keep these sheets in work folders to remind them what they are to do and to allow them to monitor their own progress.

Step 2. Develop a Menu of Backup Reinforcers. Consider three classes of backup reinforcers: activities, food, and play materials. Any of the activity reinforcers considered in Chapter 3 can be assigned point values and placed on the menu. It is possible also to equip a special activities area or room and charge tokens (or points) for so much time there. In addition to activities, a menu might include store items:

Food

Gum	Chocolate kisses	Apples
Candied cereal	Cookies	Raisins
Peanuts	Candied popcorn	Jelly beans
Ice cream	Lemon drops	Lollipops
Candy bars	Marshmallows	Soft drinks

Play Materials

Makeup kits	Musical instruments
Toy animals	Paper
Boats	Mechanical toys
Cars	Dolls
Blocks	Kites
Badges	Costumes
Marbles	Balls
Jump ropes	Puzzles
Gliders	Comic books
Model airplane kits	Balloons
Picture books	Playing cards
Painting sets	Games of all sorts
Crayons	Bean bags
Coloring books	Yo-yos
Records	Play dough
Colored chalk	Noisemakers (whistles)
Clay	

Menu Ideas for Older Students. (1) Buy tickets for skating, bowling, or athletic events, and have students earn these. (Very often one can get them donated.) (2) Make a certain level of performance in the token program prerequisite for a work-study job. (3) Write a contract at school in which the parents provide the reinforcers at home, based on tokens earned. (4) Use tokens that can be spent in a school store or lunchroom.

Involve the students. Let students have a part in setting up the menu. Ask them what they would like to have on it. Try to find special and unique ideas for the menu, now and then. Change the menu weekly by adding and subtracting some items. Use only ten to fifteen items at a time.

Step 3. Set Prices and Wages. With behaviors identified and reinforcers selected, prices and wages must be established to relate the two through tokens. The first task is to set the hourly wage. With elementary students, ten cents an hour is adequate. With junior high students, twenty cents an hour will do the job. With high school students, you may need to go as high as forty cents an hour.

In setting prices, begin by setting store items at retail price. Activities are priced in relation to the hourly wage. School-time activities (free time, recess, activity center) are priced at the hourly wage for each five minutes. Out-of-school activities are priced at the hourly wage for each twenty minutes.

Next, you have to decide how many tokens you need to give the average student per hour. This depends in part on how many different behaviors you want to reinforce and the stage in training. Go over your list of behavior objectives and see what would be reasonable. If you need to give out 5 tokens per hour, and the hourly wage is ten cents, then 1 token equals two cents. If you need to give out 10 tokens per hour, and the hourly wage is ten cents, then 1 token equals one cent. Thus, by figuring out the tokens needed per hour, you are able finally to put prices on your menu in terms of number of tokens required for each item. Your menu might look like this if the hourly wage is twenty cents or twenty tokens.

Reinforcer Menu

Activities	*Price in Tokens*	*Store items*	*Price in Tokens*
20 minutes in activity center	80	Two lines of bowling	150
Go home 30 minutes early	120	Candy bar	35
Go on picnic (2 hours)	120	Model car	200
15-minute game period	60	School emblem	50
5 minutes extra recess	20	Soft drink	35

Adjustments. Follow the law of supply and demand in making adjustments over time. Increase the prices of popular items, and reduce the prices of slow-moving items. Gradually make it harder to earn tokens by requiring more work for fewer tokens.

Response Cost. Once a token system is operating well, it is possible to charge for misbehaviors. Tell the students that certain undesired behaviors will cost 2 or 5 tokens each time they occur. The students will have to decide if they want to spend their tokens in this way or some other way.

Step 4. Decide on the Tokens. Select a token that is readily given, handy, and will cause a minimum of interference with the student's ongoing behavior.

Possible Tokens

Marks on the blackboard	Plastic chips that go on a ring
Marks on a paper or card on the child's desk	Poker chips
Gold stars	Pennies
Numbers on a paper	A counter with a light flash or buzzer
Marks on a ladder with 50 steps	Tickets
Marbles in a jar	Punches on a card

Step 5. Establish Operating Procedures. At the start with young children, establish the value of the tokens by handing out one to each child and then requiring the children to use the tokens to get some treat. After a couple of pairings like this, they will get the idea. With older students, instruction alone may be all that is necessary.

When giving out tokens, tell the students what they have done to earn them. Focus on their behavior, not the tokens. In fact, it is a good practice to talk about the tokens as little as possible.

When giving tokens for academic work, be sure the work is checked and corrected *before* the tokens are given.

Initially the exchange can occur daily, but with older students, weekly is enough. Use the exchange to let the students know they are improving and doing a good job. The evidence is there in the tokens or points they have earned. This is also a good time for the teacher to reevaluate the procedures to see what is not working for which students. If students have not earned tokens, there is something wrong with the system, not the students.

Step 6. Set Up a Record System. To monitor and evaluate your system you need a record of the points (tokens) earned and spent each day. This can get complicated for a large class unless you restrict the behaviors that earn tokens to a few that can be readily monitored. One might begin the year focusing on social and study skills important to a functioning classroom. When these goals are achieved, keep them going with a group contingency—tokens for each hour or half day the group as a whole is working well. Individual contingencies can then be shifted to academic skills and tokens awarded in a student folder as tasks are checked out. The same folder could be used to record tokens spent on a separate sheet. Then once a week, folders are collected and points earned and spent are summarized to allow you to evaluate if the system is working.

Informal Token Systems

It is often necessary to devise more effective reinforcement systems for single students in the classroom. Here are some procedures that have worked.

1. Jimmy hit other students and did not complete class assignments. The teacher worked out a procedure with his mother so that Jimmy took a note home each day he worked hard and was cooperative. With a note Jimmy could watch TV for a specified period that evening. Without a note he could not.

2. Aaron was a fourth grade boy from a deprived background. He would not get down to work in class, preferring to dawdle or play with his friends. It was often reported that he hit younger children coming to and from school. Aaron earned check marks on the board, one check for every ten minutes of good working behavior. If he earned ten checks, he could spend thirty minutes in the kindergarten supervising the younger boys in the use of carpentry tools. The younger children could use the tools only when he was there, so they appreciated his coming. Aaron learned to work in the classroom, and work cooperatively with younger children.

3. In one school, the problem of how to manage the students' rowdiness, fighting, and running when leaving school was solved by training the patrol boys to pass out colored chips to students who were well-behaved. The class with the most chips each week got a pennant for its door.

4. Jack earned an *X* on the board for each half day he did not fight in class. Initially, four *X*'s earned a party for the whole class, and Jack became the means of a treat for everyone. Later he worked for ten *X*'s, and so forth.

5. Kenny was sent to see the social worker every time he had a tantrum or fought in class. Tantrums and fighting seemed to increase. After a discussion, the teacher and the social worker decided that Kenny would have to earn time with the social worker by showing progressively improved classroom behavior. Tantrums and fighting decreased rapidly.

Teachers have asked if setting up a system for one student does not lead to other students misbehaving to get a reward. This has not been seen. Usually a simple explanation that Jimmy needs special help is enough. If there were a problem, however, the system can be arranged (as it was for Jack) so that the special student earns a treat for the whole class. Then all are motivated to help the target student do better. The reinforcement system must be suited to the student and the situation.

CONTRACTS AND POINT-GRADING SYSTEMS

Contracts and point-grading systems are specialized token system that specify what the student is to do to earn specified consequences. Contracts may be formally signed by the students, the teacher, and/or the parents. They may also be agreed upon but not signed. Contracts can be very useful for the remedial teacher or learning-center teacher to keep track of the progress of individual students and small groups. They can also be used by teachers, school psychologists, or school counselors to set up contracts between teachers and students, backed up by reinforcers and moral support from parents. Point-grading systems are especially useful for departmentalized teachers who deal with different groups of students every 45 to 50 minutes. In this case, the teacher simply hands out on the first day of class a listing of the course requirements, the points that can be earned for each requirement, and how many points are needed for A, B, C, and so on. In the rest of this chapter we will discuss the properties of such systems and give some examples.

Contracts

There are five steps to designing a contract:

1. Specify the behavior to be reinforced.
2. Specify the privileges or rewards to be earned.
3. Specify the sanctions (if any other than loss of reinforcers) for failure to live up to the contract.
4. Specify a time for completion.
5. Specify a monitoring method.

It is also possible to add a bonus clause for going beyond the stated requirements.

A Learning-Center Contract. Figure 7.2 shows a contract from the Corrective Reading Program (Engelmann et al., 1978) that is designed for the poor reader in grades four to twelve. The students come for daily lessons in the learning center and are taught in groups of five to eight. The lesson involves a teacher presentation of new word-attack skills (ten minutes), group reading designed to give practice on the skills being taught, and individual checkouts on the reading. Charts are provided to show graphically each student's progress and to keep track of points. Contracts are renegotiated each two weeks. A teacher's manual provides detailed guidelines for implementing the point-contract system.

To work efficiently, the learning center must have sequentially programed materials and placement testing so students can begin at a level they are ready for. Then the teacher can negotiate a contract with the student for the week or month, depending on individual needs.

Reading Contract
Lessons 11-30

FOR THE STUDENT

I want to learn to read better. I can earn points for working hard. I will try to earn as many points as I can each day.

I can earn points in the following ways:

A. Word-attack skills
I will read the words on the chalkboard and on my worksheets. I can earn 0 to 3 points for this part of the lesson.

B. Group reading

If the group makes	*I will earn*
0 errors	10 points
1-4 errors	5 points
5-7 errors	3 points
8-10 errors	2 points
11-12 errors	1 point

If the group makes more than twelve errors, we will read the story again in order to earn points.

C. Individual checkouts

1. First reading
   - 0 errors—7 points
   - 1 error —5 points
   - 2-3 errors—3 points
   - 4-5 errors—1 point
2. Second reading
   - 0 errors—5 points
   - 1-2 errors—3 points
   - 3-4 errors—1 point

On timed checkouts I can earn more points.

D. Bonus points
The teacher will tell me if I can earn bonus points.

I will record the points I earn each day on my Point Chart and on my Daily Point Summary Chart.

I can trade the points I earn each week for

____

My teacher will explain how the system works.

FOR THE TEACHER

I will teach at least one lesson each day. I will teach as well as I can. I will give you the points listed in the contract. You will get the most points by following the rules, beating the error limit for each story, and showing improvement in reading.

____
Teacher's signature

____
Student's signature

____
Date

Figure 7-2 *A sample reading contract*

Less formal contracts than that shown in Figure 7.2 can be written. For example:

For successfully completing ______________________,

Johnny can earn ______________________. This agreement is to be

completed by __________ (date). "Successful completion" means

(specify consequence) ______________________.

Signed ______(student)______

Signed ______(teacher)______

Date ______________________

The Home-School Contract. Counselors have tried a variety of agreements in which school performance and attendance is reinforced by parents at home (remember Claire who was about to be expelled from school?). One procedure is called *the daily report card* (Bailey, Wolf, and Phillips, 1970). The teacher, parent, and student work out an agreement that if the student performs appropriately in what has been a problem area, she or he will get a note from the teacher that day. So many "good reports" and the parent provides for a specified treat or privilege.

MacDonald, Gallimore, and MacDonald (1970) used a contracting procedure in Honolulu to increase daily attendance by students who were chronically truant. Specially trained attendance officers made "deals" so students could earn after-school and weekend privileges at home by attending school. One "deal" used time visiting a girlfriend as the reinforcer. The contracts were very successful in increasing attendance.

Point-Grading Systems

A point-grading system has these minimum components (you will learn about some additional components in Chapter 9):

- Clearly defined course objectives.
- Specifications of activities to reach objectives and the points that can be earned for each activity.
- A monitoring system that shows teacher and student progress being made toward the objectives.
- Specification of point criteria to be used in grading.

The most important part of a point-grading system is letting the students know specifically what they are expected to learn and having materials and procedures that will make that learning possible if reasonable student effort is exerted. A number of successful approaches have used programed materials, computer-assisted instruction, and traditional textbooks. (These will be examined more carefully in Chapter 12.) To make a body of information and procedures accessible to students, the course is broken down into units. Performance goals for each unit are specified. Then, a teaching mechanism is determined (programed text, computer-assisted instruction, textbook with study questions and exercises, small-group discussion, lectures followed by exercises and questions, and so on). Finally, a test is given for mastery of the objective.

Research has shown that use of study questions, making grades contingent on the number of points earned, and setting high criteria all contribute to better grades (Semb, Hopkins, & Hursh, 1973; Johnston & O'Neill, 1973). Setting the criterion for passing a unit test at 95 percent correct will lead to better performance than setting a lower criterion, such as 80 percent correct.

The point-grading system shown in Figure 7.3 is set up on the assumption that students may use part of some classes for study or taking checkouts. The checkouts could be handled through a computer, which could then monitor the records rather easily. The specifics would have to vary by subject area. You could also incorporate homework assignments into the point system. In a skills class, such as physical education or home economics, the point-system might specify the skills to be mastered. The important point is that the students know what you expect and what they need to learn to do well in your class. You will see some more specialized point-grading systems in the next chapter.

A Point-Grading System

Your grade in this course will be based on the number of points that you earn. Points can be earned by meeting the following requirements:

1. Pass 12 unit checkouts at 90% correct criterion.	10 points each (Checkouts may be retaken without penalty.)
2. Complete a term project:____________ ______________________	Up to 50 points (see grading criteria on separate handout.)
3. Midterm quiz. Date____________	Up to 50 points.
4. Final exam. Date____________	Up to 70 points.
TOTAL POINTS POSSIBLE	290

Grading
A requires 261 points.
B requires 232 points.
C requires 203 points.
There is no course credit if you earn less than 203 points.

Figure 7-3 *A sample point-grading system*

SUMMARY

Strong reinforcer systems are sometimes needed for poorly motivated students. When this is the case, a token or point system should be considered. Token systems have proved themselves highly effective in reducing problem behavior and in increasing academic learning. Keep in mind, however, this caution: Do not use it if you do not need it.

In designing a token system, the first step is to specify the behaviors that earn tokens. Chart your general goals, then get down to specifics appropriate for each student.

1. Specify quality as well as quantity.

2. Gradually increase your behavioral requirements so the students work for longer periods without reinforcement.

3. Focus on reinforcing improvement.

4. Consider writing out daily assignments for each student where appropriate.

The next step is to build a reinforcer menu. Consider special activities and games, foods, and play materials. With older students you might write a contract at school with reinforcers provided by parents.

In setting prices and wages, decide on an hourly wage. Then set prices so that at first store items are priced at the retail price, each five minutes of an in-school activity costs the hourly wage, and each twenty minutes of an out-of-school activity costs the hourly wage. To specify prices in tokens rather than cents, you need to decide how many reinforcers you should give in an hour to do the job for your class. Once this is decided, the rest falls out by simple arithmetic. Adjustments can be made to your price schedule according to the law of supply and demand. Also, gradually increase the work requirements for earning tokens. "Charging" for infrequent unacceptable behaviors (a response cost procedure) can be considered after a token system is established.

The tokens should be handy, readily given, and noninterfering. Points, electrical counters, and plastic chips may be useful, depending on the setting. When giving out tokens for academic work, require a work-check and corrections *before* the tokens are given. The exchange should be planned to show the students how they are coming along and how pleased you are. Charts and records simplify the management of a token system and let both you and the students know where things stand.

Informal token systems may be devised for a single student or a small group. A number of illustrations of such systems were given.

Contracts and point-grading systems are specialized token-reinforcement systems. Contracts are especially useful in learning centers and in writing agreements where the reinforcers are delivered by parents. Point-grading systems are especially useful for secondary teachers.

To design a contract:

- Specify the behavior to be reinforced.
- Specify the privileges or rewards to be earned.
- Specify the sanctions (if any other than loss of reinforcers) for failure to live up to the contract.
- Specify a time for completion.
- Specify a monitoring method.

To design a point-grading system:

- Clearly define course objectives.
- Specify the activities to reach objectives and the points that can be earned for each activity.

- Build a monitoring system that shows teacher and student progress being made toward the objectives.

- Specify the kind of point-criteria to be used in grading.

A point-grading system can only be effective if there is a clearly outlined program of instruction and procedures for accomplishing it. Teaching materials should be broken down into units, have a specified teaching mechanism, and specified mastery checkouts for each unit. The research literature supports the efficacy of using study questions, contingent grades, and high performance criteria.

As noted in the last chapter, care must be taken in fading out special reinforcement systems, if that is a goal. Step-by-step the special features of the system should be removed while maintaining appropriate social reinforcement for good work. If the students are to be returned to a regular class after being in a special setting, it may be necessary to provide training for the receiving teacher in good reinforcement procedures. Without such training, your efforts may be wasted.

CHAPTER

8

PLANNING FOR THE START OF SCHOOL

So far in this text, we have studied basic principles and looked at the procedures important for their application generally to strengthen, weaken, and maintain behavior, and to situations where special reinforcers are needed. This chapter examines ideas for the application of general procedures to planning for a new school year.

ELEMENTARY LEVEL

The best classroom managers prevent problems before they occur (Brophy & Evertson, 1976). The best way to do this is through planning. What are the rules? How am I going to teach them? What are the consequences for following them or not following them? How am I going to deliver good instructions to 25 to 30 students in a way that will keep them motivated? Teachers who are successful in producing better academic outcomes with their students use procedures that allow more effective learning time for their students. Where students are failing, one typically finds too much wasted time—the teacher is not ready, too much time is devoted to "discipline," transitions from one activity to another go on endlessly, students do not know what to do next, and so forth. This chapter describes and illustrates strategies that can enhance classroom learning time. First you will look at procedures for elementary classrooms, where the students are with the same teacher most of the day, and then for older students in departmentalized classes.

While the focus of this chapter is on positive planning strategies, keep in mind that the start of school may not always work as well as you have planned. Unexpected students may show up, classes may have to be recombined, the books may come late. The idea is to do your best given the circumstances you have to live with. Also, the chapter focuses planning on the individual classroom. You may have to coordinate your planning with others where there is multiple responsibility for a group of students.

Organizing Space

Classrooms differ physically in many ways, serve different kinds of students, and have different goals, so there is no single best way to set up the space in a classroom. There are, however, a number of things to think about in planning your space.[1]

Student Desks. Separate desks into rows facing the blackboard, not the windows. This will help you get around when you need to and minimize students interfering with each other when they should be attending to you or working on their own.

Teacher's Desk. This desk should go in a corner facing the students. If there is an aide, use the diagonally opposite corner for the aide's desk.

Group Teaching Station. Set up a group teaching station in one of the other corners, with the student chairs facing the corner and the teacher's chair facing the class. This will allow you to monitor the class, while working with a group and to provide appropriate social reinforcement or instructions when needed. If you have an aide, then partitions could be used to separate the group at the teaching station from the rest of the class.

Materials and Self-correction Station. In the front center of the class, place a medium-sized table and a few chairs. Materials to be passed out or turned in are stacked here, along with correction keys to use when self-correction of exercises is appropriate.

Computer Stations. Some schools have computers in the classroom and others have them grouped in a special room. Where you place them depends on their number and use. If full-class demonstrations are going to be used, then they should be up front. For individual use, it would be best to have them in carrells toward the back of the room.

Bulletin Board. The bulletin board should be visible to the students and have space for classroom rules and student progress charts.

Cooperative Activities. When your classroom goals involve students working together on projects, peer tutoring, or whatever, have the students reorganize their chairs appropriately for these activities.

Organizing Time

Some General Rules. Following are general rules for planning daily routines:

Prepare cushion activities. Not all children finish a task in the same amount of time. Allow for this by including a cushion activity between tasks assigned to a group. In making an assignment, assign a secondary activity that is permitted when the first task is completed. This is especially effective if the second activity is also a reinforcing activity, thus making use of the Premack principle. For example: "When you finish your workbook exercises and check your answers at the checkout table, you may get one of the games from the activity corner." "When you finish your worksheet and turn it in, you can paint."

[1]The author is indebted to Paine, Radicchi, Rosellini, Deutchman, & Darch for several of the ideas in the first half of this chapter that are taken from their excellent book *Structuring Your Classroom for Academic Success,* Champaign, Ill.: Research Press, 1983.

Use prompts. Planning should provide for *systematic prompts or reminders* for what each student should do next. Lists on the blackboard, verbal reminders, individual folders, checkout stations, and turn-in boxes assist in the process.

Use consistent routines. Planning should provide for day-to-day *consistency in routines.* This reduces the need for all sorts of reminders as the completion of one task becomes the cue for what to do next. Sequences of tasks become chained together. If the teacher haphazardly moves from one activity to the next on impulse, it becomes very difficult for the students to learn good work habits. Of course, it holds students' interest if you break the routine now and then as a surprise.

Change the pace. Planning should provide for periodic *changes of pace.* Quiet work might be followed by talking or singing. Serious material might be followed by an active, fun game. Sitting might be followed by running or some other more vigorous activity. Often, just a minute or two of a vigorous activity is all that is needed to ready a group for more serious work again.

Have a written daily plan. Figure 3.1 (see page 29) presented a daily schedule to illustrate ideas for the use of the Premack principle throughout the day. Later in this chapter (Figure 8.2), a schedule for the first day of class is illustrated, where the concern is with teaching rules for various classroom activities. While daily plans may change throughout the year, and even the week, a formal written plan provides a good guide (S^d's again!) for the teacher.

Transition Times. Transitions from one activity to another occur about 10 times a day. As Paine et al. (1983) point out, it is common for a class to take five to twenty minutes in a transition. If eight minutes were spent for each transition, eighty minutes a day is lost. This is 20 percent of a school day, meaning one entire day a week is lost! It is also equivalent to wasting one school year out of every five. Paine et al. point out that one third grade teacher was able to cut transitions to about thirty seconds each, thereby saving over an hour a day for instruction.

To get short transition times, the teacher first *must be prepared* by having all necessary materials ready ahead of time. Second, the teacher needs to monitor the transitions and teach the students the rules to be followed at transition time. The following rules are presented by Paine et al. (1983, p. 85).

> "*First,* move quietly.
>
> *Second,* put your books away and get what you need for the next activity.
>
> *Third,* move your chairs quietly. (In some classes with small-group instruction, students carry their desk chairs to the group for seating there.)
>
> *Fourth,* keep your hands and your feet to yourself."

Students are taught the importance of making quick transitions and the rules to follow by using procedures like those described later in the discussion about organizing your students.

Planning for Materials. Much time can be lost if needed materials are not ready when needed and if efficient procedures are not used in handing them out and collecting them. If the teacher hands out and collects each paper, much time is lost. If each student picks up or turns in his or her own paper, there is chaos. If each student at the head of a row "takes one and hands the others back," there can be much talking, poking, and dropping of papers. Paine et al. (1983) recommend that all students be taught how to be helpers in handing out and collecting papers, and that two "paper monitors" be selected when needed.

The rules during passing and collecting of materials are: "No talking," "No touching," "Monitors work quickly," and "Monitors stay in their own zone." Again, the procedures should be explicitly taught to the class.

Organizing the Students

The following is an excerpt from an article entitled "Classroom Management: Strategies for Beginning the Year," by Randall Sprick (1983). The article describes five procedures that the teacher can use during the first week of school to help establish classroom rules and get off to a good start.

Teaching Rules

1. Establish and Discuss Classroom Rules. Classroom rules should be established prior to conducting any classroom activities. Rules are best discussed immediately after the teacher has introduced himself or herself on the first day of school. An early introduction of classroom rules means that students will have a clear understanding of the teacher's expectations. This reduces the need for students to experiment and reduces the need for teacher reprimands. It also allows the teacher to begin developing positive interactions with the students. From the first day, students will learn that they can easily get the teacher's attention by following the rules.

Classroom rules should be stated as positive expectations. Avoid the "don'ts." A rule that states, "Cooperate with other people in the class," implies that the teacher expects cooperation. "Don't hit other people," implies that the teacher expects hitting. Below is a sample set of positively stated rules.

- Always do your best work.
- Cooperate with others.
- During independent work times, stay in your seat and work quietly by yourself.
- Raise your hand if you need help or have something to say.

After stating the rules, the teacher should give specific information about what each rule communicates. When talking about cooperation, the teacher should provide different situations that might occur and have students identify and discuss examples of cooperating and failing to cooperate. This type of exercise requires students to think of the classroom rules in terms of their own behavior. The teacher will be teaching students how to take responsibility for themselves.

2. Discuss How the Rules Relate to Each Newly Introduced Classroom Activity. For the first two to three days of school, discuss how the classroom rules relate to the specific expectations you have for each activity. Following are examples of the types of discussions a teacher might have.

- We are going to be passing out your science and social studies books. In a moment, I will ask volunteers to pass out the books. I will only call on four people who remember the rule about quietly raising their hands. Others of you will get a turn to help out later today or sometime this week. If you do not get called on, you can help out by following the rule about cooperating. Raise your hand if you can tell me how you can cooperate if you are not called on to pass out books.

  If no one complains about not being called on that will be a great example of cooperating. You will be showing me how mature you are. While the four people are passing out books, the rest of us will be having a discussion on ____________. How can you follow our rules during the discussion?

  Yes, listening quietly to others will be showing cooperation. Raising your hand and waiting for your turn will also show us that you understand our rules. If you raise your hand and wait for your turn, it will be easier to make sure that everyone gets a turn to participate. All of the things you have mentioned will help us have a fun and interesting discussion.

- During the next half hour, you will do a math paper. You need to follow the rule about doing your best because the problems on this paper will help me decide where we should begin in the math book.

  What is the rule about independent work?

  Yes, it says that you should stay in your seat and work quietly by yourself. What should you do if you need help? Yes, you need to remember to raise your hand if you have something to say or if you need help. Who can tell me what you should do if you break your pencil? Should you get up to sharpen it? (No, the rule says to stay in your seat.) How can you get permission to sharpen your pencil?

  These discussions may seem to waste a lot of teaching time; however, the time will be well worth it.

3. Provide Positive Feedback to Students. Once rules are understood, it is critical for the teacher to provide positive feedback and attention to students who are trying to meet expectations. Feedback should be descriptive, and should periodically relate back to the classroom rules. Following are some examples.

- Thank you for quietly raising your hand.

- Everyone in the class listened while I was explaining the social studies assignment. That is cooperation!

- For the last five minutes, every person in the class has been quietly working on the math paper. It is nice to see that all of you are doing your best.

4. Give Feedback at the Close of Each Activity. During the first several days of school, end each activity by telling students how they did. Did they meet your expectations? If not, let them know what they should have done differently. Do not single out individuals. The teacher will want to avoid giving attention to students who misbehave.

5. Use Positive Practice to Teach Critical Classroom Behaviors. Positive practice means that students actually practice routine daily activities until they can complete them efficiently.

The first step in positive practice is for the teacher to state his or her expectations for the activity. If students fail to perform as expected, have them try the activity again. Continue this procedure until students demonstrate that they can perform the task as required. The teacher should not be punitive during the procedure. The teacher's manner should simply communicate that the task needs to be completed in a certain way. The students will practice until they have demonstrated mastery. As soon as the task is performed according to the teacher's expectations, give praise and then move on to the next task.

You may need different rules for different activities during the day. Figure 8.1 shows some possible rules for different activities developed by Jane Dougall, a teacher in Eugene, Oregon (1983).

Activity	*Rules*
Seatwork	Stay in your desk. Work quietly. Raise your hand if you need help.
Instructional groups	Listen when the teacher is talking. (Talk only on your turn.) Watch the teacher (book or board) Try your hardest.
Activity	Listen when someone else is talking. Raise your hand if you want to talk.
Recess	Line up quietly. Walk outside. Play cooperatively.
Lunch	Line up quietly. Walk in the hall. Talk quietly to the room.
Activities outside the classroom	Walk quietly to the room. Follow that teacher's rules.

Figure 8-1 *Rules for different activities*

Figure 8.2 shows a schedule for the first day developed by Jane Dougall that includes the time for teaching rules for different activities. With younger children, she might take ten minutes to have the children practice repeating and following the rules. With older students, the rules are posted in the room and reviewed daily during the first week or so.

First Day Attitudes

Remember that the first day objectives should also be to show the students that you like them and to get to know their names, as well as helping them to learn about classroom rules and routines. Keep a surprise tucked up your sleeve for later in the day, such as passing out their first books, a visit by a pet, a small party, a new game, a movie, or maybe a computer demonstration. Try to have something they can take home with them that encourages them to tell mother and father about their first day.

8:15- 8:30	Students arrive.*
8:30- 8:45	Introduce Myself. Teach rules for seatwork (testing).
8:45- 9:10	Testing—large group*
9:10- 9:15	Teach rules for going to P.E.
9:15- 9:45	Students go to P.E.
9:45- 9:50	Review rules for seatwork (testing)
9:50-10:10	Testing—large group
10:10-10:15	Teach rules for going to recess
10:15-10:30	Recess
10:30-10:35	Review rules for seatwork
10:35-11:00	Individual testing*
11:00-11:15	Reinforcing Activity or seatwork page*
11:15-11:30	Get acquainted activity (specify which one)
11:30-11:45	Teach rules for going to lunch. Wash for lunch.
11:45-12:30	Lunch & recess
12:30-12:35	Review rules for seatwork (testing)
12:35- 1:00	Testing*
1:00- 1:05	Teach rules for large group instruction.
1:05- 1:25	Social Studies lesson*
1:25- 1:30	Review recess rules
1:30- 1:45	Recess
1:45- 1:50	Review rules for going to another classroom.
1:50- 2:15	All school assembly
2:15- 2:30	Review day's events. Remind students of rules.
2:30	Dismiss
*Indicates where materials should be listed	

Figure 8-2 *First day schedule*

Requests for Help. Raising hands or coming to the teacher for help can disrupt the student's ongoing work and other students. A simple way to get around this problem during seatwork is to have each student make a "help me" card out of construction paper. The card is folded and kept in a folder containing extra exercise sheets the student can work on while waiting for help. When help is needed, the card is taken out and placed on the desk like a tent where it is visible to the teacher.

Correcting Papers. Another way to organize the students is to teach them how to correct their own papers. Not only does the teacher save much valuable time, but the students get more immediate feedback on their work, learn to take responsibility, and learn to monitor and evaluate their own work. Set up a checking station with special correcting pens, scoring keys, and turn-in boxes. Rules for using the correcting station are posted and taught. At first, use of the station is introduced for just one activity. Others can be added after this has been mastered.

Rules for the checking station might include:

- One person at a time.

- No other pens or pencils may be brought here.
- No talking.
- Circle errors.
- Return to your seat to correct errors.
- Recheck errors.
- Turn in papers.

It is possible to set up several stations so that more than one student can correct at the same time. The teacher or aide monitors use of the stations and spot checks in an unpredictable fashion to be sure the students find all errors. Be sure to reinforce those who follow the rules and those who find all the errors (Paine et al., 1983).

When Problems Occur. If after teaching the rules, the rules are violated, a mild punishment procedure can be used as a backup. Inform the students of the procedure to be followed *before* you need to use it.

Step 1. On first occurrence, calmly and quietly give a warning and state the behavior you expect of the student. Remember that quiet reprimands are more effective than loud reprimands.

Step 2. If the violation occurs a second time, place the student's name on the board and take away some privilege. You might require staying after school for ten minutes and doing extra work, losing five minutes of recess—whatever is likely to be effective for this student.

Step 3. For a third violation, step 2 procedures are repeated with longer consequences, and a parent is telephoned.

Remember to focus on the positive and to reinforce appropriate behavior when you see it.

PLANNING AT THE SECONDARY LEVEL

As students get older, the principles governing behavior do not change. Problem behavior still occurs because it is modeled and reinforced, and good teaching is still the best cure. Peer influences become stronger, students may become overly sensitive to some kinds of praise from teachers (especially in front of peers), and there is more self-management of behavior. However, for many students there are still problems in getting motivated about school, especially if they have not done well in school in the past, and there are all of the problems of growing up—sexual changes, learning to be an adult while still part child. Teachers must be friends, "on-call" counselors, advisors in life planning, limit setters, and interpreters of social reality. The demands on teachers can be taxing as well as fulfilling.

In looking at planning at the secondary level, consider a recent book by Randall Sprick[2] (1985). Sprick is a former high school teacher who returned for his doctorate in education and now spends much of his time training teachers in use of effective teaching systems and motivational procedures. His book is a "how to" book, full of explicit details on setting up effective grading and

[2]R. S. Sprick, *Discipline in the Secondary Classroom: A Problem-by-Problem Survival Guide.* By the Center for Applied Research in Education, Inc. Englewood Cliffs, N.J.: Prentice-Hall, 1985.

motivational systems. It also provides "solutions" to some 42 problems commonly faced by secondary teachers—from swearing to extortion.

In the past 25 years, serious problems have arisen in public schools, especially in the larger systems. Violence, vandalism, drugs, and alcohol are common problems. In the 1960s, as educators focused more on student freedom of choice, on student rights, and on keeping everyone in school as long as possible, standards of excellence and student responsibilities were sacrificed (as reported by the Committee on the Judiciary, United States Senate, 1975). Chapter 22 looks in depth at one school district's response to these growing problems. The remainder of this chapter will examine planning steps an individual teacher can take to make secondary teaching more effective.

An Effective Grading System

With 100 to 180 students to teach, supervise, inspire, motivate, and monitor each day, careful planning is required. Effective grading systems are built around point systems of the type introduced in Chapter 7. The goal is to provide the student with a plan showing how participation and effort can lead to a good outcome in your course. We have all taken courses where the exams related to only a small part of the material covered, and there was no way to guess ahead of the exam what was important to learn. Under such circumstances, there is little motivation to study. You cannot know where you are going.

The following steps can be used to establish an effective grading system (Sprick, 1985):

Clearly Define Your Course Objectives. As pointed out in Chapter 7, the first requirement for any point-grading system is to have clearly defined objectives. Evaluation becomes capricious and directed study becomes impossible without them. With clear objectives, grading can be based on the degree to which the objectives are mastered (not on some arbitrary "normal curve"). Objectives can be defined for the student by study questions, examples of problems, or lists of skills (say, in spelling or punctuation).

Relate Course Activities to the Objectives. In lecturing, begin by framing the objectives dealt with in the lecture. Similarly, projects and assignments (when not obvious) should be introduced by tying them to objectives. Finally, tests should clearly focus on finding out whether the objectives have been mastered. Remedial work should be planned for those objectives which have not been met. The effectiveness of grades in motivating students is increased when daily effort can be related to progress toward a good grade.

Base a Percentage of the Final Grade on Daily Participation and Effort. This is truly an important contribution by Sprick to educators' thinking about effective motivation at the secondary level. Most grades in high school (like college) are based on projects and exams. Whether you come to class on time—or at all—and actively participate on a daily basis is not considered. Sprick recommends basing from 5 to 50 percent of the grade on daily participation and effort. The amount depends on the type of course and the students. Typical basic courses in math, science, and English might allocate 20 percent of the grade to participation. Chorus might allocate over 50 percent, a physical education course might allocate 30 to 50 percent, while an advanced course in computers might allocate only 5 percent. The issues are: (1) how central active participation is to course objectives, and (2) how necessary it is to motivate the students to attend class and expend the effort daily. On the latter point, with a basic math course for low-performing seventh graders, 30 percent of the grade might be devoted to participation and effort to help the students to make progress on a daily basis.

In some districts there is a policy that prohibits deducting points from a grade for misbehavior. However, this proposal simply makes effective and appropriate participation a part of the course requirements.

Set Up a Monitoring System. Teachers need an efficient way to keep track of daily participation for up to 180 students. Sprick proposes a Weekly Record Sheet (see Figure 8.3), which can also be used to record attendance, tardiness, and turning in homework assignments. A master form can be made (he provides a model from which a master can be made) with your codes filled in once, a copy made for each class, names filled in, and then copies made for the weeks of the term for each class.

The recording form can be kept on a clipboard or in a notebook. Turning in assignments and attendance can be checked as students enter the classroom. Tardiness (T), disruptive behavior (D), and excellent work (E) can be noted during class or shortly thereafter. In relating points to level of performance, Sprick recommends that 80 percent be allocated for an average performance. Thus, if 20 points a week were possible, 16 points would define an average performance. To add up the weekly totals on Friday for the data in Figure 8.3, you would start with a base of 16 for Donna Agner and add 2 points for excellence on Tuesday. Dana Kuntzmann failed to earn 8 points for attendance Monday and Tuesday, so his point total for the week is 16 minus 8 equals 8. While it takes a little practice to get use to the system, it is very efficient and takes less than five minutes to do totals on Friday. When special points are awarded (such as for outstanding work) or deducted (for example, if a student failed to earn points for following class rules), students should be made aware of the fact as soon as it is appropriate to do so. On Friday, the names can be covered with student numbers (one list is good all term) and a copy (or the original) posted.

In using this system, you need to decide for each class what defines average performance (attends class, follows rules and directions, is prepared for class, on-task most of the time), what defines excellence (100 percent on-task, contributes to discussion, asks relevant questions) and cooperation (assists other students when asked), how bonus points can be earned (peer tutoring, significant improvement in behavior), and how points are not earned (misses class, does not follow rules). In the example illustrated in Figure 8.3, Russ Deane had two excused absences, but these were made up by completing two extra assignments (Bonus +4). An *unexcused absence* cannot be made up.

Determine the Points that Can be Earned for Academic Tasks. Now you need to consider the points to be given for homework assignments, unit quizzes, projects or term papers, and final exam (if there is one). For a woodworking class, points might be assigned for written and performance tests on use of specified power tools, knowledge of woods, and for specified projects.

Once you have an idea of what the total points are and how they are distributed, you can establish the weekly participation and effort points as a percentage of this total. Slight adjustments must then be made so that you deal only with whole numbers. Sprick (1985) provides explicit instructions on how to do this computation.

Make a Student Grading-record Form. To encourage students to keep

WEEKLY RECORD SHEET

Date Sept. 14-18 Reminders________

Class period 4

STUDENT	MON.	TUES.	WED.	THUR.	FRI.	TOTAL
Agner, Donna		✓ E			✓	18
Amato, Lee		✓			✓	16
Anderson, Dan	O	✓		T-2	✓	13
Baumbaugh, Gary		–	O		✓ E	16
Buckee, Cheryl		✓ O			✓	15
Carpenter, Dustin	OOO	✓			✓	13
Crossett, Gelia		✓			✓ E	18
Deane, Russ		A (B+4)	A (B+4)		✓	16
Dorns, Jan	E	✓		O	✓	17
Edwards, Lanny		✓ O			✓	15
Felch, Yvvette		✓			✓	16
Franklin, Laver		✓			✓ E	18
Godon, Randi	A (B+4)	✓ O	E		✓	17
Green, Christopher		✓			✓	16
Hammon, Matthew	E	✓			✓	18
Johnson, Charlene		✓			✓	16
Jones, Jesse		✓ C		O	✓	17
Kemp, Lonnie		✓	O		✓ O	14
Kuntzmann, Dana	UA	UA			✓	8
MacKight, Todd		✓			✓	16
Mezick, Chanya		✓ O			– O	13
Nelson, Wendy	C	✓			✓	18
Owen, Travis		✓			✓	16
Potesta, Sam		✓	E		✓	18
Quince, Bonnie		✓			✓	16
Robinson, Eddie	D	✓		E	✓	17
Schmidling, Ruth		–	A		✓	11
Semolke, Gail		✓			A	12
Sumida, Marilyn	O	✓			✓	15
Taylor, Danny		✓	E		✓	18
Timmons, Jay	E	✓		C	✓	20
Vande Veer, Steve		✓ OO			✓	14
West, Shaun		✓			✓	16

CODE:					
EXCELLENT WORK = E	+2	OFF TASK = 0	−1	ABSENT = A	
COOPERATIVE = C	+2	DISRUPTIVE = D	−1	UNEXCUSED ABSENCE = UA	−4
BONUS POINTS = B		LATE WORK —	−1	TARDY = T−	−2

Figure 8-3 *Weekly record sheet. (From the book* Discipline in the Secondary Classroom, *by Randall S. Sprick, PhD. © 1985 by the Center for Applied Research in Education, Inc. Published by Prentice-Hall Inc. Englewood Cliffs, NJ. 07632)*

track of their grade progress, prepare a form to be used by each student to keep track of his or her points:

- List each activity that can earn points with a blank to be filled.
- Indicate in parentheses the possible points that can be earned.
- Have blanks for subtotals by activity (homework, projects, quizzes) and the total.
- Show the possible points that can be earned by subtotal and total.
- Indicate how point criteria relate to letter grades.

Teach Students the System. As a part of the first day of class, provide the students with handouts on Participation and Effort Points and a Grading-Record Form. Use these to help teach students about the system and how it works.

Setting Expectations for Student Behavior

An important part of planning is deciding what you expect of students for various types of class activities. When do you permit talking? How loud? How do behavior expectations vary from lecture time to group projects, to discussions, to tests? If you make clear your rules for various activities, the students will not have to keep "testing the limits" to find out how far they can go. Out of this analysis comes your classroom rules. For example, the four general rules presented in discussing rules for an elementary classroom in the article by Randall Sprick work at the secondary level, too:

1. Always do your best work.
2. Cooperate with others.
3. During independent work times stay in your seat and work quietly by yourself.
4. Raise your hand if you need help or have something to say.

Your rules should be posted where they can be seen. If you wish, the students can help formulate and revise the rules. Since these rules are broadly defined, you will need to point out examples of following or not following of the rules as the occasion arises and through discussion. The important point is to let the students know what you expect of them. You will have other rules about specific activities, such as turning in assignments, which may or may not be posted.

Using Social Reinforcement

Some of the same rules apply in using teacher attention and praise to motivate good work as at the elementary level. Praise is made *contingent* on good work and it *describes* what the student did that you like. Avoid "flowery" praise and evaluative praise (see Chapter 3). With peer relations relatively more important than adult-child relations, it is important to be more matter-of-fact in giving positive comments about something you like and to keep praise relatively private. For some students, you may have to place your comments on a note or a paper being returned. Brief conferences before or after class or during seatwork can also be used to maintain privacy. Sprick recommends giving positive feedback *to groups* when that is appropriate, for example:

"I am pleased with the improvements that I am seeing on spelling tests. Those of you who have made a commitment to our new study routine are doing much better on your tests. It is really paying off." (Sprick, 1985).

Sprick makes another valuable suggestion for secondary teachers. He notes that many teachers have a habit of waiting for a response after making a praise statement. This can be a problem for the student who feels pressured to say "Thank you" or some equivalent and yet does not want to be accused by peers of "brown nosing." The way around this is: *Do not pause after describing something you like,* just go on to the next point immediately.

Secondary students want and need praise and attention just like the rest of us. You just have to be a little more sophisticated about how you go about it. Often, the unexpected can be used as an attention getter and a reinforcer. Consider the following example:

One high school teacher came into his first social science class, set a tape recorder on the desk, and turned it on without saying one word. It played the number one popular song. When the song was over he said, "Now that I have your attention . . ." and immediately started into a series of short stories about some dramatic changes in people and systems. He indicated to the students that by understanding the principles underlying those dramatic changes, they could change their whole lives, gaining new knowledge to use in working on the problems of people and society. He ended the class five minutes early, allowing no class participation. . . . "I will see you tomorrow. You may prepare for that by doing your first assignment tonight. Assignment sheets may be picked up on the way out." The class was nearly speechless. They left quietly and thoughtfully. They looked forward to class the next day.

Periodically, this teacher would come up with a new surprise. Jokes were tucked into his quizzes. He found good movies that told a real message. "Music to take exams by" was introduced to the school. Fun examples that were personally relevant were built into lectures and discussion. As a joke, he attached a piece of candy to each of the first exams he handed back. The strange thing was that the teacher found himself spending more and more time developing good presentation material and surprises, because he was reinforced by a vitally appreciative reaction from his students.

Setting Limits and Consequences

Setting limits on nonnegotiable behavior is another important part of your planning process. The checklist provided in Figure 8.4 (Sprick, 1985) gives a good starting place for your planning. With answers to the questions posed and a copy of the school discipline policy, you are ready to set rules for your room.

Typically, school policy will cover fighting and defiance of a teacher's authority and specify that the student be sent to the office for action. You need to let students know that you will enforce these conduct rules. You also need to let them know the potential consequences for violating the classroom rules in other ways, such as talking during lectures, swearing, talking back, not doing their work, late assignments, and tardiness. The most effective consequences available to you are:

- Quiet reprimands.
- Parental contacts.
- Discussion and contracting with a student targeting a behavior to be improved.

- Time out within the classroom.

- Loss of free time (response cost).

CHECKLIST FOR TEACHERS NEW TO A BUILDING

If you are a first year teacher or an experienced teacher new to a particular school, use the list of questions below as a guide for finding out critical information regarding school policies. You should be able to answer all the questions below before the students arrive for the first day of school.

- ☐ Do you have a copy of the school discipline policy?
- ☐ Are you expected to discuss these policies with students?
- ☐ What are the procedures for referring a student to the office for misbehavior?
- ☐ What behaviors do the administrators feel should be referred to the office as opposed to handled in the classroom?
- ☐ Do the administrators have expectations regarding student behavior in your classroom?
- ☐ To what extent are you expected to monitor the halls and restrooms?
- ☐ What are you expected to do if a student you do not know is misbehaving in the halls or in the restrooms?
- ☐ What sort of records are you expected to keep regarding student behavior, attendance, tardiness, etc.
- ☐ What are the procedures for allowing students to use the library or computer center during class time?
- ☐ What are you expected to do regarding parental contacts?
- ☐ What behaviors are unacceptable to you and what are the consequences for inappropriate behavior?

Figure 8-4 *An important checklist for teachers new to a building. (From the book* Discipline in the Secondary Classroom, *by Randall S. Sprick, PhD. ©1985 by the Center for Applied Research in Education, Inc. Published by Prentice-Hall Inc. Englewood Cliffs, NJ. 07632)*

The points not earned within a participation and effort plan will also tend to function as punishment for absences, tardiness, disruptive behavior, and off-task behavior.

Quiet reprimands (as well as just ignoring attention-seeking behavior) can be effective with most secondary students. As with praise, you may have to wait for the right time to get privacy or use a note.

For *parental contacts* to be effective, parents need to be willing to cooperate with you and support school policy. Home-school contracts and daily report cards on improved behavior can also be effective where there is parental cooperation. However, if the parents refuse to cooperate or get very punitive with the student, other methods need to be found.

In *discussing a problem* with one or more students, find a neutral time when all involved are calm. Explain how you see the problem and ask the students to give their view of it. Establish what led up to the problem and what actually went on. Then explore other ways similar situations could be dealt with. Let the students know there are alternative ways of dealing with the problem. A behavior improvement plan might be written out and signed by students and teacher, with a date set to evaluate progress.

Time out in the classroom can be effective with students who do not want to be singled out from the group. A desk is placed a few yards away from the rest of the desks and the student must stay there for five minutes showing acceptable behavior or for the rest of the period. If a student refuses to take this punishment, that is defiance, and she or he is sent to the principal's office.

A *response cost* procedure, which Sprick calls "owing time," can be used when students waste time. Depending on bus schedules, and so on, this can be applied before or after school, or before lunch. A few minutes lost before lunch can mean a longer wait in the cafeteria line. Many students would like to avoid that.

Establishing Classroom Routines

As in the elementary school, routines build-in automatic prompts. Sprick suggests two possible routines, and of course there are many more. One routine might provide for lecture for the first half of class, followed by the students completing assignments related to the lecture that are due by the end of class. Another routine might assign homework on Mondays and Thursdays, with homework assigned on Monday due Thursday and that assigned on Thursday due on Monday. This allows students to plan a work schedule as well as more readily remember when things are due.

Assignments can be made on a handout each week or by using a special area of the board for this purpose. The students would be prompted by this to check the board on Mondays and Thursdays.

A routine for collecting assignments is also important. As discussed earlier, the weekly record sheet can be used to record assignments turned in on time. When the teacher expects assignments on time and monitors this, it is more likely to happen.

The First Day of Class

As in elementary schools, what happens on the first day can set the classroom atmosphere for the rest of the semester. You need to communicate that you are there to help them, that the class can be fun, and that you have high expectations for good work and appropriate mature behavior.

Be prepared to get students working with you as soon as you have taken attendance, discussed the handouts on rules and grading system, and your homework procedures. These beginning activities should not take more than ten minutes if you are prepared.

As new activities are begun, let the students know your expectations and how well they are doing; at the end give feedback on how well they did (or did not) meet your expectations.

SUMMARY

Problem prevention is best achieved through planning before hand. At the *elementary level,* there twenty to thirty-five students are with one teacher most of the day, one needs to prepare the organization of space, time, and the students.

The organization of space is aimed at minimizing interferences and maximizing ease of organized use of the classroom. You need to consider the placement of desks, teaching stations, materials, and so forth.

Some general rules for organizing time are the use of cushion activities (applying the Premack principle) to provide systematic prompts for what to do next, to establish consistent routines, to provide for changes of pace, and to have a written plan you can refer to if needed. Planning for transitions is vital to the good use of learning time. Teach your students how to change activities quickly, with a minimum of disruption. Materials should be ready ahead of time and student helpers trained to distribute them.

Organizing the students is probably most central to setting up a classroom in which optimal learning can occur. The steps to follow in teaching your classroom rules are:

- Establish and discuss rules.
- Discuss how the rules relate to each new activity.
- Provide positive feedback to those students following the rules. Tell them exactly what they are doing that is an example of following a rule.
- Give feedback at the close of each activity.
- Use positive practice on teaching how to follow the rules. (If students fail to get it right the first time, have them go through it again.)

Very likely you will have to work on different rules for different kinds of activities. Your approach the first day is very critical. Take the time to teach your students what you expect of them and how to do it for each new activity. Make a plan and follow it.

You can save a lot of time by devising efficient ways for students to request help and correct their papers.

Finally, you may need to plan for backup procedures to be used if the rules are not followed. Quiet warnings, loss of free time, and parent contacts can be effective as well as humane.

Planning at the *secondary level* requires some different strategies because you have so many more students to work with for shorter periods, and because the students are growing up. They are less adult-oriented and more peer-oriented. They may be sensitive to teacher praise in front of peers. And, while capable of more self-management, some have been "turned off" by failure and require a structured system to keep them on-task long enough to succeed.

A key to teacher happiness and sanity at the secondary level is to plan an effective grading system. To devise an effective grading system:

- Clearly define your course objectives.
- Relate course activities to the objectives.
- Base a percentage of the final grade on daily participation and effort.
- Set up a monitoring system.
- Determine the points that can be earned for different academic tasks.
- Make a student grading-record form.
- Teach students the system.

To put the performance and effort part of the grading system into effect, you need to set expectations for student behavior. For the different kinds of activities that can go on in your class, you need to specify your standards and rules. General rules should be posted and examples of following and not following them discussed as the occasions arise.

Using social reinforcement to motivate students should be contingent and descriptive (as at the elementary level), but relatively private, aimed more to groups where appropriate, and very matter-of-fact. Do not pause after praising a student.

Consequences for not following the rules consist first of the "points not earned" in the participation-and-effort system. The following can also be effective consequences:

- Quiet reprimands.
- Parental contacts.
- Discussion and contracting.
- In class time out.
- Owing time (response cost).

Again, the systems and expectations you set up the first day of class and following routines for class and homework activities can be great aids to being an effective teacher.

CHAPTER

9

APPLICATION OF PRINCIPLES IN PHYSICAL EDUCATION, COACHING, AND MUSIC EDUCATION

HISTORICAL NOTES

The first study using behavior analysis procedures in coaching was by Rushall and Pettinger in 1969. It examined the effects of various reinforcers on the skill development of swimmers. The first study using a physical education class was Young's dissertation at Ohio State in 1973. He examined the effects of behavior games to enhance both socially appropriate behavior and motor skills (Siedentop & Taggart, 1984). From the mid-sixties on, there have been a number of studies using contingent music as a reinforcer (and/or loss of music as a punisher), but the first reports suggesting that reinforcement procedures might be very appropriate in music education did not occur until 1971 (Cotter & Spradlin, 1971; Greer, Randall, & Timberlake, 1971; Madsen, 1971).

Some important recent references in these areas are:

- A book by Martin and Hrycaïko (1983) summarizing the behavioral analysis work on coaching.
- A chapter by Siedentop and Taggart (1984) summarizing the literature on applications to physical education and health-fitness.
- A review paper by Donahue, Gillis, and King (1980) summarizing behavioral research studies in sport and physical education.
- A book by Madsen, Greer, and Madsen (1975) covering research on music learning.
- A book by Greer (1980) summarizing behaviorally derived music-teaching practices.

PHYSICAL EDUCATION

Rushall (1981) observed the behavior of coaches for different sports (basketball, volleyball, swimming) and for physical education teachers (45 of them). The data on physical education classes point to some problems. He first assessed the percentage of time spent in physical activity and found this was only 10 to 20 percent for the typical class. Teachers used a nearly equal number of positive and negative statements and they occurred in about 5 percent of the ten-second observational intervals. Teachers typically spent 25 to 35 percent of the class time directing, explaining, and informing. They spent about 40 percent of the time observing and monitoring. The low percentage of physical activity and the relatively high ratio of negative comments (four positives are recommended for each negative for good interactions) imply there were problems in teaching physical education. Also, the fact that the teachers spent more than twice as much time observing and monitoring as the students did engaged in physical activity, suggests that a lot of students were *doing nothing* a good deal of the time.

Dodds (1976) points out that "One need only to observe a secondary physical education class to find ample evidence that students do not learn to love or find joy in movement. One sees nonparticipating students lounging on bleachers, students dressing late and leaving early, students misusing equipment, and students openly expressing their distaste for physical education by comments, gestures, or grimaces" Dodds believes that physical education teachers must make more effort to make class time fun. He recommends that teachers plan events to include more activities that students prefer and to basically use the kinds of procedures recommended in earlier chapters of this text.

It should be apparent that the various procedures for strengthening, weakening, and maintaining behavior discussed up to now have much relevance for physical education. Also, the procedures presented in the last chapter for planning at the secondary level (effective grading systems, clear expectations, and setting appropriate limits) can be applied directly to physical education classes at all levels. Physical education occurs in larger spaces and has much more ongoing action. This leads to a stronger need for effective management procedures. There is also a need for "teaching skills"—the use of prompting, shaping, chaining, discrimination training, praise, specific feedback, and so on.

Most of the research currently available has been done in the areas of fitness and coaching. However, some work has been done in physical education classes. For example, Mohlam, Wade, and Collins (cited in Fox, Copeland, Harris, Rieth, and Hall, 1973) set up a contingency to increase on-time behavior for a boys' high school gym class. If all the boys were on time, they would have to repeat an exercise only 10 times. If anyone was late, they would do the same exercise 50 times. On-time behavior increased from 60 percent to 95 percent.

Rolider (1978) sought to increase peer encouragement of each other in a college basketball class. Three conditions were studied. In one, the teacher presented a *positive model,* making many positive statements to players. An *instructions* intervention stressed the importance of encouraging each other for skill development. In a grade-incentive system, additional points could be earned toward a grade for encouraging peers. All three conditions increased rates of peer praise. The grade incentive was the most effective—more than doubling the rate.

Young (1973) measured skill development of second graders in the physical education class when a free-play period was used as the reinforcer. The number of skills performed increased from baseline (that is, observation made before the experimental change) to the experimental condition and remained high when the reinforcer was withdrawn (reversal condition).

There are problems in applying a more systematic technology to physical education skill development. There is no consensus about the outcome measures that are important. There are no standardized measures of outcome either, except in the area of fitness. There is no agreement on what constitutes a good performance, except where the performance directly produces the outcome (bowling, archery, putting). This makes the definition and measurement of critical behaviors difficult at times. As you will see in examining research on coaching, progress is being made in these critical analyses, but there is a long way to go.

While the application of behavioral principles to physical education is a young field, it is clear that those entering this field need careful training in the use of praise, the importance of good models, the use of peer encouragement, and the procedures for training new skills.

HEALTH FITNESS

There has long been evidence that overweight children become overweight adults (Abraham and Nordsieck, 1960; Crisp, Douglas, Ross, and Stonehills, 1970; U.S. Public Health Service, 1966). It is becoming clearer that increased susceptibility to heart disease and high blood pressure is related to physical fitness in childhood as well as adulthood (Gilliam, Katch, Thorland, & Weltman, 1977; Lauer, Connor, Leaverton, Reiter, & Clarke, 1975). Physical fitness is becoming a growing concern of physical education. A variety of behavioral approaches have been tested with adults to reduce obesity and help in exercise maintenance (for example, Harris & Bruner, 1971; Mann, 1972; Stuart, 1971; Stuart and Davis, 1972). Use of charting, progressive goals, a variety of self-management procedures, and various incentives are readily available to physical educators.

A study by Taggard (1980) extended the work on contracting with parents to fitness training with children. Physical educators trained each set of parents of 11 low-fitness, elementary-aged children in the use behavioral contracting to improve their child's fitness. It was assumed on the basis of other work that increased activity level would improve fitness. So the dependent variable was based on duration and the kind of out-of-school activity engaged in. Using prior research relating caloric expenditure to type of activity, activity points could be earned each day. After a baseline, the treatment phase set a criterion for the next week that was about 10 percent above the baseline. If the target was met or exceeded, a new higher target was set for the following week. This shaping strategy helped to gradually improve performance as fitness improved. If the target was not met, the contracted reinforcer was lost for that week and the target for next week was set near the actual performance for the prior week. The intervention in this study lasted for 11 to 13 weeks. Over this time the average increase (over baseline) in activity points was 100 percent. It is not known whether parents kept the procedure going following the study.

Aragona, Cassady, and Drabman (1975) set up a response cost contract with parents whereby they would lose money they had deposited with the experimenters if their overweight girls (aged 5 to 11) did not meet a weekly criterion for weight loss. Parents were trained to use one of two procedures. There were five girls in each procedure and 5 in a no-treatment group. Each week, parents in both treatment groups could lose money if the parents did not attend the weekly meeting, the parents did not fill out charts and graphs, and/or their child did not reach criterion. One treatment group also used a variety of reinforcement procedures for the girls. The reinforcers were negotiated at the weekly meetings and were earned through daily exercise performances.

At the end of the 12-week treatment, the experimental groups had lost significantly more than the no treatment control group. At an eight-week follow-up, some of the lost weight had been regained, but the response-cost-with-reinforcement group was still significantly below the control group. After 31 weeks, there were no differences. Obviously, it is very important to build-in maintenance procedures in studies like these.

Wysocki, Hall, Iwata, and Riordan (1979) used behavioral contracts with college students to help them manage participation in an aerobics exercise program. They deposited items of personal value with the teacher, which they could earn back by earning "aerobic points" and observing and recording the exercise of others in the program. Aerobic points were assigned to different activities and durations according to charts established by Cooper (1970).

Seven of the eight subjects increased their aerobic points each week for the six-to-eight-week duration of the contracts. A year later, seven of the eight reported they were earning weekly aerobic points that were still above their baselines. Learning to monitor others probably helped them in continuing the self-monitoring after the experiment.

Exercising to get fit or keep fit is not always that much fun. In fact, for the overweight (as well as others), it can be painful. The use of behavioral contracting, charting, special incentives, and maintenance procedures offer a promising technology for helping students to develop better fitness.

COACHING

Some very exciting developments are taking place in the application of behavioral methods to coaching. As noted in the beginning of this chapter, a major summary of this work is provided in Martin and Hrycaiko (1983). This book is strongly recommended to those who plan to go into coaching. In addition to outlining major strategies, they show applications to football, golf, swimming, tennis, little league coaching, hockey, gymnastics, volleyball, basketball, karate, and cross country ski racing. In addition, they cover changing the coaches' behavior, life-fitness programs, self-management, and mental preparation of the athlete using systematic relaxation training, imagery, and other cognitive-behavioral therapy procedures. The next section summarizes some of their ideas and research findings.

A Model of Effective Behavioral Coaching

According to Martin and Hrycaiko (1983), to be effective a behavioral coach needs to do the following:

Specify Performance Objectives. What do you expect of your athletes? (Sounds like the first step in effective planning for teaching, right?) For a competitive sport, this might consist of requirements for practice and requirements for competition.

Expected behaviors at practice:

Attend each session.
Listen to instructions.
Practice techniques as instructed.
Apply good technique in endurance training.
Keep your practice going (without stopping a lot).
Practice as if in competition.
Practice relaxation and imagery techniques (for use prior to competition).

Expected behaviors at competiton:

Use relaxation and imagery to prepare.
Work to show performance improvement.

Support the team.
Show good sportsmanship (shake hands with losers or winners, keep control, show respect for others, and so on).

In the area of skill training it is necessary to get more specific about exactly what is good execution and what is not. Game statistics do not tell you who has mastered what skills. You need to get specific enough to say whether any component of a complex behavior chain is adequate or not. Martin and Hrycaiko illustrate this point with five pictures of swimmers showing each phase of the backstroke. For each picture, there is a set of two to five actions to be checked. With a chart based on the checklist, the coach can rate a sequence of strokes during training and provide feedback to the swimmer. Koop and Martin (1983) evaluated the use of error analyses of this sort in coaching beginning swimmers in the three basic strokes. They found reductions in error rates from near 100 percent during baseline to under 10 percent with error feedback during the experimental period. Martin and Hrycaiko also illustrate the three components of drive block by an offensive lineman and the component behaviors to be checked in each phase. A study in this area will be discussed later in this chapter.

Learn to Maintain as Well as Develop Behavior. You should be well aware of this distinction by now, but you might need a prompt to remember it in the context of coaching. Just because you get some new behavior going, that does not mean that it will continue on its own. Many coaches blame the kids for "dumb plays." They criticize when they should be teaching and using procedures to maintain behavior (public posting of performance, self-monitoring, contracting, and so forth).

Have Athletes Work Against Their Personal Best. Having winning as a goal is not always the best way to go. Athletes cannot always control who will win, but they can work to improve their performance. By setting multiple goals and keeping data on them while working toward the goals, more successes will be experienced and athletes will have stronger motivation to practice.

Base Procedure on Those Demonstrated to be Effective. The effective coach does not fly by the seat of her or his pants. The coach uses the science of behavior and data on performance of team members to make decisions. Circular explanations are avoided—"We lost because they had a lucky day." Focus on the real variables that can affect athletic performance. For example, use *clear instructions* to get better stimulus control over the athlete's behavior. Do not just tell the backfield defense on a football team to "Watch the quarterback." Tell them what to watch. "Watch where he is looking. Watch for an arm cock. He has to look where he is going to throw, and he can't throw until his arm is cocked." Explicit instructions that can be used to guide an athlete's behavior are important to effective coaching.

Monitor Your own Performance as a Coach. Video tape your training session and review it. Develop a checklist to remind you of the critical things you need to do to train, motivate, and monitor the team. Are you giving positive feedback for improvement? Ask this and other behavior-related questions.

Seek Social Validation. Is what you are teaching what your "clients" want to learn? Is your approach acceptable to your team? Are parents and others satisfied with what you have done? Such feedback can help you improve and be responsive to the needs of others.

The use of procedures demonstrated to be effective will be discussed in more detail in the rest of this section.

Use of Reinforcement

Obviously the principle of reinforcement is central to all good teaching, including coaching. In working with youths and adolescents, let them know when they have done a good job. Praise from the coach of the same sex is not the problem that it might be in an English class, with a mixed-sex group, and a female teacher praising a boy in front of his peers. Dishing out verbal punishment for a poor performance is not going to help. It is only likely to upset the athlete and make it harder to do better. When mistakes are made, focus on how to do it the "right way." Demonstrate, guide, and encourage. "Do it this way, and you'll get it. The important thing is to keep trying." With a positive approach, you show your players that you respect them as individuals; with good demonstrations and instructions, you earn their respect as a teacher.

Just as we earlier surveyed the types of reinforcers available to the regular classroom teacher, the coach needs to make a similar survey. "What can I use to motivate different players?" Beyond positive attention and praise, consider how to effectively use the following possible reinforcers:

- Improving times, scores, and so on. Post them; chart them; talk about them.
- Improving skills that may not show in times or scores. Give frequent feedback on improvement in component skills.
- Getting public attention in newspapers, on TV, on radio. Be sure the news gets out.
- Getting awards.
- Getting to travel with the team.
- Getting playing time or participation time, in practice and in competition.

In talking with athletes, remind them about some of the good things that hard work can produce. And, when special goals are reached, call them to the attention of the group and individuals.

One study of the effects of using reinforcers in swimming training was carried out by Cracklen and Martin (1983). They had eight to thirteen year old swimmers earn the opportunity to participate in relay races at the end of practice by: (1) improving the frequency of racing turns made in practice, and (2) reducing the number of stops made when doing a practice set (such as four 100-yard backstroke sprints). This reinforcer produced a dramatic drop in the inappropriate practice behaviors.

Attendance Boards and Program Boards

McKenzie and Rushall (1974) developed a board that permitted a group of 16 year olds on a swim team to self-record their attendance. A large waterproof board was constructed on which the swimmers could check each attendance at practice. There was also space for each swimmer's best consecutive record and current attendance record. When a student was absent, all of his or her check marks were erased and she or he started over on a new "string." Use of the board reduced absences by 45 percent. Part way through the study, coming late or leaving early led to a failure to earn an attendance check that day. Under this condition, late arrivals dropped 63 percent and early leaving stopped entirely. The attendance board proved to be very motivating. The team was very enthusiastic about the use of the board. After 11 months, the record attendance was over 130 consecutive days.

In another study with 8 boys and girls aged 9 to 16, McKenzie and Rushall used 3 × 2 feet "program boards" to cue swimmers about what to do next in their training program. Transparent pockets at the top of the boards could receive "work-unit" cards that specified an activity (such as, do four 100-yard freestyle sprints). The training could be altered from session to session by changing cards. A row at the top also indicated cumulative laps swum after completion of each task on the board. Students made check marks under the appropriate work-unit card beside their name when they completed a work unit. They could then look to find out what was up next. See Figure 9.1 (from Rushall, 1975a).

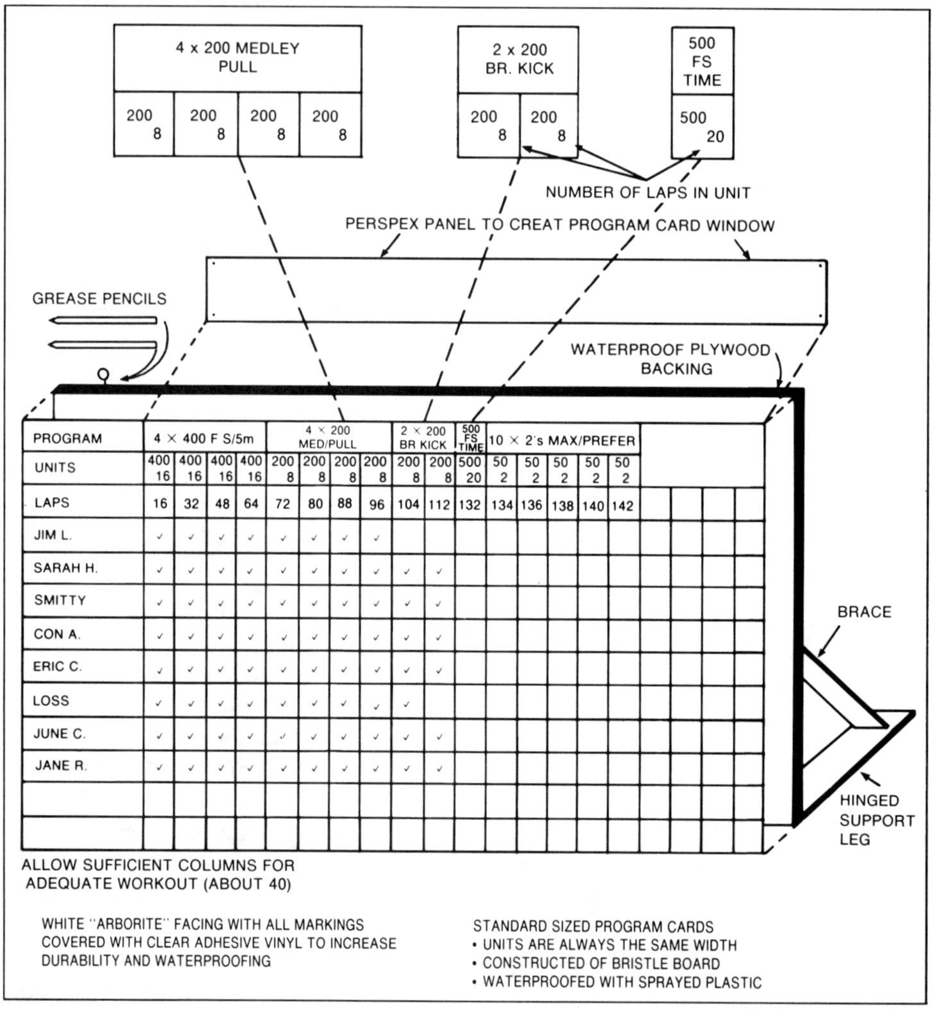

Figure 9-1 *A suggested structure for program boards and program unit cards. (From B. S. Rushall. A motivational device for swimmers,* Swimming Technique; *11:103-106, 1975)*

This study went through a baseline condition (with the usual coaching procedures) and then one using the program board. Each condition was repeated a second time. The number of laps per minute swum increased by 23.9 percent for the four boys and by 30.6 percent for the four girls. This is an averaage increase of 619 yards per session for each swimmer. With the program boards, the swimmers were totally self-directed. They knew what they were supposed to do and did it. They no longer had to gather in groups and wait for instructions. Also, the coaches were more readily available for coaching, not just managing.

Feedback Devices

Another approach to better monitoring of practice is through the use of mechanical and electronic feedback devices. Although I have seen no evidence that this is effective, a machine was built for teaching golf that would keep the head, hips, and the swing plane of the back swing in their proper positions throughout the swing. The idea was to physically prompt the feel for the proper movements. Automatic timers are available for practicing slalom racing in skiing; they could be used in many sports. Video taping football and basketball games and practices provides feedback for coaches and players alike. Video is being used more and more in teaching golf.

Rushall (1975b) reports a device that was used to shape how to scull a boat while keeping it level. (In sculling, an oar is placed in a notch at the rear of a boat and the boat is propelled forward by moving the oar back and forth while changing the pitch of the oar.) The special device sounded a buzzer when the boat reached a certain tilt. This tells the sculler that his or her balance is off. Over training session, the angle of tilt that sets off the buzzer is reduced. The effect is to shape more precise sculling balance. This reduced the need for coaching time and reduced learning time.

Careful Analysis of Performance Requirements

Komaki and Barnett (1977) studied the effects of breaking football plays down into their component parts with a football team of nine and ten year olds. While one might question whether nine and ten year olds should be playing football, the study does illustrate the careful analysis of complex skills into their component parts.

Three different plays that were frequently run were each broken down into a series (chain) of five stages, and then each stage was carefully described in behavioral terms. Training was provided to the offensive backfield and center. The three plays are shown in Figure 9.2. Table 9.1 describes the action for play A.

The team had one game and three practices each week. Three different plays were selected by the coach. All ran off the wishbone set. The plays were introduced one at a time. First, the option play was taught by the new method, then the power sweep, and then the off-tackle counter. The detailed descriptions specified exactly under what stimulus conditions (S^d's) what was to be done. Checklists were used to evaluate execution of the plays. Observations were made for 7 games and 17 practice sessions.

At the start of the season, each player received a play book with diagrams to commit to memory (about 30 plays). About half of each practice was spent on scrimmage, where plays were practiced. The backs would go through the plays and the coach would offer suggestions from the sidelines. This typical procedure was used during the baseline phase of the experiment. In the experimental phase, the detailed descriptions were used. Each step was explained, demonstrations were given, and the backs walked through the play by themselves. Praise was given for good performances.

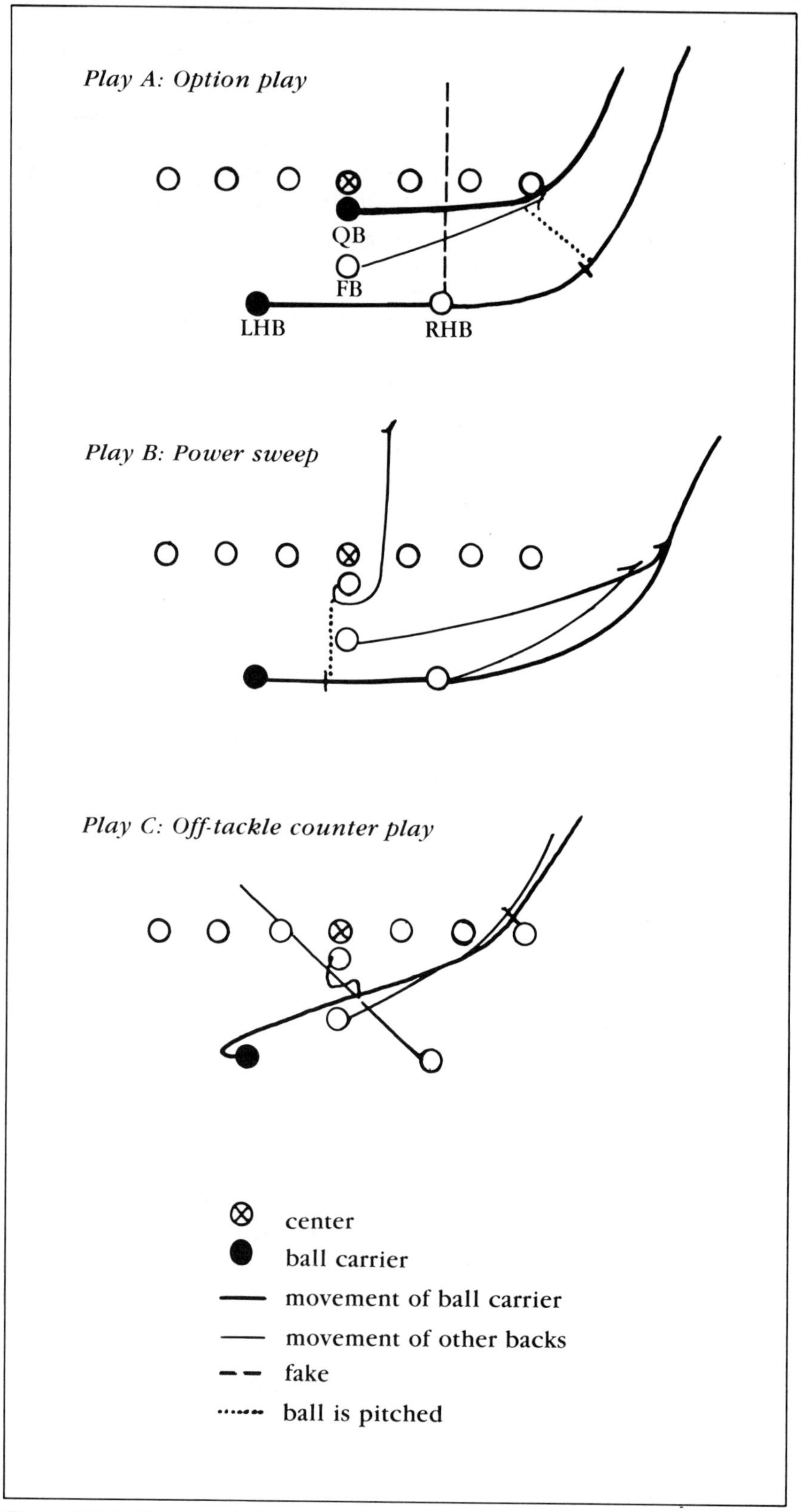

Figure 9-2 *A diagram of plays A (option play), B (power sweep), and C (off-tackle counter play).*

Table 9-1 Descriptions of stages for play A, option play

1. QB—Center Exchange

On the correct count, the center "snaps the ball," i.e., raises the ball between his legs and quickly places the ball in the hands of the quarterback (QB). The QB should have the ball firmly in his hands.

2. QB-RHB Fake

With the ball in his hands, the QB moves quickly down the line as the right halfback (RHB) goes toward the middle of the line. The QB fakes a hand-off to the RHB, i.e., places the ball in the RHB's hands. As the RHB bends over and runs low appearing to have the ball, the QB pulls the ball back and continues going down the line.

3. FB Blocks End

The fullback (FB) sprints toward the defensive right end, watching his position. Depending on the depth of the end, the FB either blocks or passes him by. If the end penetrates three yards (2.7 m) beyond the line of scrimmage, the FB passes him by and turns upfield to block another defensive player. If the end penetrates less than three yards, the FB blocks him away from the QB and drives him out of the area of play.

4. QB Decision to Pitch or Keep

After the QB-RHB fake, the QB continues moving down the line, watching the defensive right end. If the end has been passed by the FB, the QB keeps the ball and turns upfield. If the end has been blocked by the FB, the QB pitches, i.e., tosses, the ball to the [left half back] LHB and turns upfield to block.

5. QB Action

Whatever decision is made, the backs should proceed as described. If the QB decides to keep the ball, he should quickly turn upfield following on the heels of his blockers. The LHB should turn upfield trailing the QB. If the QB decides to pitch, he should pitch the ball to the LHB slightly in front of him and chest high. The LHB should be positioned to the right of and behind the QB, keeping his eyes on the QB. Once the LHB catches the ball, he should turn upfield following his blockers.

The percentage of stages correctly executed increased from 61.7 percent to 81.5 percent for play A, from 54.4 percent to 82 percent for play B, and from 65.5 percent to 79.8 percent for play C. In baseline, plays were executed perfectly (all 5 stages correct) only 2 times out of 84. During the experiment, perfect plays increased to 22 out of 89. The quarterback showed a dramatic increase in correctly deciding when to "keep" and when to "pitch" on the option play.

The coach had difficulty at first in analyzing the components of some of the plays. Once this had been accomplished, however, he was in a better position to instruct his players. The players found the checklists intriguing and held many discussions over the fine points.

Allison and Ayllon (1980) applied a similar systematic behavioral approach to coaching in teaching blocking by football linemen; in teaching of backward walkovers, front handsprings, and reverse kips in gymnastics; and the forehand, backhand, and serve in tennis. The correct action for each skill was first carefully described in all its components, so that reliable judgments could be made by observers about their execution. After a baseline of typical coaching (which the research report describes for each sport), the following five-step procedure was used as the experimental procedure for each study:

1. The athlete was instructed by the coach on how to execute the performance and the athlete would try it.

2. If the task was executed correctly, the coach allowed it to proceed and reinforced the athlete.

3. If the coach saw an error, the coach blew a whistle or said "freeze," "don't move," or a similar signal. The athlete had been instructed to stop and hold that position (when that was possible). The freeze position was held while the coach described the incorrect position ("Your feet are too close together; you can't get any power in a block that way.").

4. Next, the coach modeled the correct procedure.

5. Finally, the athlete imitated the model while the coach described what was now being done right.

With behavioral coaching, the correctness of blocks made by five players (aged 11 and 12) was ten times better than in baseline, increasing on the average from under 10 percent correct to 50 to 70 percent correct. A similar effectiveness of behavioral coaching was found with six teenaged gymnasts, and in tennis with 12 college students. The freeze procedure drew negative comments from the football players, suggesting it was a little embarrassing. Also, it was hard for gymnasts to hold some positions. However, the tennis players thought it really helped them learn the strokes. All three coaches were impressed with the behavioral coaching procedures and said they would continue to use them. The football coach thought it should become an "integral part" of teaching the basics.

Using More Telling Statistics

Heward (1978) applied a reinforcement procedure to a barnstorming baseball team—the Indianapolis Clowns, who were once members of the Negro American Baseball League. The manager posted a sign in the dugout at midseason telling the team he was starting a new program, "Hit for Meal Money." The team members could earn a pot of $10 a week, $5 for first place, $3 for second place, and $2 for third. Players were to be rated for their efficiency average (EA), a new statistic. Hits, runs, RBI's, walks, sacrifices, and hit by pitched ball all counted as single points for the EA. Total points were divided by total times at bat to get the EA.

Under this reinforcement condition, EA increased from .681 to .831, and runs scored increased from 5.21 to 7.36 per game. Perhaps, it was not surprising that the number of hit batters increased from .179 per game to .357. This seems too much to be produced by a $10 reinforcer! Other variables were likely operating. The team liked the statistic. To think of your EA as .800 instead of having a batting average of .250 would be a good feeling. The EA statistic better reflected the contributions of team members toward winning a game. Also, there seemed to be *a lot of side-betting going on among team members* that added to the "action." After the EA game was terminated, the players themselves kept calculating EA's and posting them in the dugout.

The study suggests that it might be beneficial to think about different ways of producing statistics that might have more reinforcement value for the players. The data on "hit by pitched ball" suggests that this should probably be taken out of the statistic, since that is something a coach would not want to encourage. One might also think about additional points for extra base hits, or, alternatively, two points for scoring a run instead of one. The critical question is: "What point system would best reflect a player's offensive contributions to the team?" This question is not too different that posed in Chapter 8 on how to design an effective grading system.

Applications of Cognitive-Behavior Modification

A number of sports psychologists have been working with athletes to help them control what they think about before and during competition as a means of improving performance. Martin and Hrycaiko (1983) report five such studies covering applications to a football kicker (Titley, 1976), karate performance (Weinberg, Seabourne, & Jackson, 1981), golf (Kirschenbaum & Bale, 1978), cross country ski racing (Gravel, Lemieux, & Ladouceur, 1980), and tennis (Desiderato & Miller 1979).

For years, behavioral psychologists have been helping clients get control of fears, anxieties, angers, and inappropriate sexual feelings. The general procedure used is called *systematic desensitization.* The client is first taught deep relaxation through a systematic tensing, holding, and relaxing of groups of muscles, one group at a time (Bernstein & Borkovec, 1973). Then, a shortcut way to get into deep relaxation by counting to ten while inhaling and exhaling deeply is taught. While in deep relaxation, the therapist has the client visualize events that are step-by-step closer to the events that lead to the unwanted effect. It is believed that this process can countercondition the emotions and lead the client to be relaxed in formerly taxing situations. The success of these procedures has been documented, particularly with the milder phobias.

The application of visuo-motor behavioral rehearsal in sports psychology draws on the systematic desensitization technology. Many athletes perform well in practice, but not in competition. The situations are different: Much more is at stake in competition, and excess tension can interfere with a performance. By *imagining* going through all the critical procedures (hitting a drive, kicking a field goal, making karate moves, sinking free throws) while deeply relaxed, the players find it is possible to transfer the relaxed feelings to the competition setting. The psychologist describes the critical settings; the athlete imagines she or he is there performing. Once relaxation procedures have been learned and critical settings defined and imagined, the athlete can continue practice on his or her own, including using this as a part of pregame warmup.

Besides assisting in a more relaxed performance, the visuo-motor ideation can help build habits related to performance itself—"When in this situation, I make these moves. In that situation, I make those moves." The parts of a complex sequence can also be rehearsed mentally.

In the studies just mentioned, a place kicker learned to relax and tune out the stadium noise while focusing on kicking the ball. An amateur tennis player learned not to "tense-out" when playing critical deuce points that could save or win a game. Karate students showed less anxiety. Cross country, competition skiers learned to ruminate less about negative things—self-depreciation, failure, pain, bad weather, family, money, and so on—and to focus energies on skiing stronger and better.

The study with golfers taught deep relaxation procedures that could be used to relieve tension. This study also used other cognitive-behavioral self-management procedures. A planning checklist was used before each shot. Jack Nicklaus' (1974) imagining procedure for the flight of the ball and the swing were also used before each shot. Positive self-recording was used after each hole, and positive self-instructions (to help think about what the player does right) were used when needed to help manage anxiety. While the data from this study had some weaknesses, it supported the potential usefulness of this self-management approach to better golf.

A Misapplication?

O'Brien and Simek (1978) report a training method for golf that they claim is superior to the "traditional" method for teaching golf. This study is cited in some detail because it illustrates a point very important to teachers—the need for a careful analysis of what is to be taught. (Chapters 13 to 18 deal with this issue in more detail.)

In their "behavioral analysis" of golf, O'Brien and Simek state that the reinforcer for golf is "putting the ball in the hole" and then they proceed to use a backward-chaining procedure developed for teaching nonverbal animals. In backward chaining, you start with the behavior closest to the reinforcer, cue it, and reinforce it when it occurs. For example, a pigeon is shaped to peck at a red light to get food. The red light eventually becomes a conditioned reinforcer, as well as an S^d for pecking, because it is followed repeatedly by food. The red light can now be used to shape a new response, such as turning. When the green light is on, if the bird pecks it gets no food; but if the bird turns, the red light is turned on. Now it can be pecked to get food. Now the experimenter has a two-element chain. A third element could be added by using the green light as the reinforcer.

This was the logic used by O'Brien and Simek. They taught golf by starting on the green with a putter, progressively putting longer and longer putts, and using a mastery criterion at each stage before going for a longer shot. Eventually, they got back to the tee shot. Eight ninety-minute lessons were given over a six-week period.

The control group was taught by beginning on the tee and progressively working toward the hole. The usual techniques of modeling, verbal instructions, and feedback were used with both groups. There were six novice golfers in each of the groups. The results showed a difference favoring the "backward chaining, mastery learning group" that was not significant. Another study with twelve additional subjects did produce significant results. The backward chaining group was seventeen strokes better (on the average) on a test round after training. They also hit more precise shots when members of the group were placed at specific test distances.

There are several problems with this study. First, few professionals teach golf starting with the drive, and I have never seen one start on the tee. They usually start with a middle iron on a driving range. Thus, the control group of O'Brien and Simek was not a model of the "traditional teaching of golf." Second, it is seriously doubtful that "getting the ball in the hole" is the main reinforcer for a novice learning golf. Reinforcement can occur on any well-hit ball. A good shot "feels" better and goes straighter, farther, or more on target. A more likely explanation for their positive results is giving more putting practice, the use of mastery procedures before going to more difficult shots, and building the swing off of shorter clubs before using longer clubs.

The third issue, however, is the important lesson for teachers. No analysis was made of the fundamental skill involved in golf, namely, *the swing*. The swing is the central operation involved in all strokes, including the putt. O'Brien and Simek take a procedure that is useful in animal training and blindly apply it to a complex sport. Careful *analysis* of what is to be taught is the most important first step. As noted, the problems of analysis will be discussed later. (If you are interested in golf, the best analysis of the swing I have found is by Carl Lohren *One Move to Better Golf,* Signet, 1975).

There is clearly a growing body of evidence about effective procedures that can be used to improve coaching. Next is a brief examination of some applications of behavioral-cognitive strategies to music education.

MUSIC EDUCATION

The research and model practices in music education discussed in this section are taken largely from the excellent book by Greer (1980). This book is a valuable resource for music educators.

As Greer (1980) points out, one broad goal of music education in public schools is to increase the intrinsic aesthetic value (reinforcing value) of music, especially for styles and forms not covered by the mass media. This goal is an affective goal that can contribute to the student's personal capability for gaining a lifetime of enjoyment from music. However, before many aspects of music can become "self-reinforcing," the student has to develop skills in analysis and performance.

Behavioral approaches to musical education begin with the planning of goals and assessing progress toward these goals with monitoring and charting systems. An emphasis is placed on the use of positive reinforcement, point-grading systems, and special reinforcers. Music education covers a broad range of activities from preschool to post-graduate work. Settings can cover general music appreciation classes, ensembles (chorus, marching band, concert bands, and so on), and studio lessons. Contents range from the performance of music, to analysis and appreciation, to composition and improvisation. At the core of this broad range of work are the principles for strengthening and maintaining behavior this book has been discussing—discrimination training, modeling, prompting, fading, chaining, and shaping. Of course, basic competence as a musician is also fundamental for the music teacher.

A Key-Counting Music Behavior

Counting may seem antithetical to the artistic temperament, but in the area of music, teaching is also changing behavior. Assessing these changes is important to good teaching. One can measure student progress with tests that leave a permanent record in classes for music appreciation and theory. But when it comes to performance, an event in time, there is no permanent record unless you make a special effort to capture it through observation, perhaps assisted by video or audio tapes.

The general procedures for observing and counting behavior can be applied to music performance. As music unfolds in time, there are a large number of features of a student's performance that might be counted. How many notes are on (off) pitch? How many measures have correct rhythm or dynamics? It is impossible to do accurate assessment of all aspects of a performance at once. However, it is possible to focus on one or two key features at a time, and with recording equipment, focus on other features at replay if that is considered important. Where events can be counted, the *percent right* becomes a performance measure. Other measurements have to do with the *duration* of events. The stability of tempo, note length, and so forth can be assessed in terms of durations, but especially important is the duration of practice.

For good group management, it is also important to assess *preparation behaviors*. How much time is wasted getting an ensemble *all* ready to follow the conductor's lead? Forty students waiting two minutes for one or two slow pokes is a loss of 80 personal minutes. How many critical, nagging comments have directors spoken trying to get everyone ready? Preparation behaviors are important and include: (1) following rules for appropriate behavior (being ready on time, with instrument, and warmed up when band conductor takes the podium two minutes after the late bell), and (2) performance preparation behaviors (proper sitting, instrument held correctly, attending to conductor, and so forth).

Effective Teaching-Grading Systems

Several behavioral psychologists working in music education have adapted the Personalized System of Instruction (PSI) developed by Fred Keller (see Chapter 12) to music education (Greer, 1980; Madsen, Greer, & Madsen, 1975). The systems have most of the features of the effective grading systems discussed in Chapter 8, but add to them strategies for *individualized* skill development in music and a reinforcing backup menu made up of *activities designed to enrich the music curriculum.*

A Program for an Elementary Music Class. Greer (1980) describes a PSI program for an elementary music class. A point system was established that could be used to determine a student's course grade and citizenship grade (combined or separately, depending on school policy). The core of program, however, was the development of learning modules that constituted a sequence the students could work through themselves and then take checkouts monitored by students who already had passed that module. Students earned points for passing a module and for serving as checkers. Modules covered listening activities, appreciation, and identification skills. There were modules for performance activities, such as singing on pitch, sight reading, and playing chords on an autoharp. And, there were modules for composition and improvisation.

Students could also earn points for following the rules, for tutoring a fellow student, and giving tests. The points earned led to a grade, but they *also could be spent.* Some of the activities they could "pay" for were taking an instrument home, performing in a class recital, attending concerts, being teacher's assistant (keeping records, developing tests), joining various music groups (chorus, percussion group, recorder class), and taking tapes home. The backup reinforcers generally led to further development of musical skills and appreciation.

Secondary Ensemble Groups. In the appendix to his book, Greer (1980) provides copies of teacher-generated point systems for a junior high school concert band, for a marching band, and for a high school chorus. At this level, in most cases the students recorded their own points when told to do so by a section leader, the director, or a peer test-monitor. Practice times were built around a sequence of specific learning objectives with checkouts required when the student was ready. A home practice assignment might be taped (when the student believed she or he had reached criterion) and checked out during a practice period at school. Records were kept of time spent in practice. In chorus, objectives might initially focus on reading music. Exercises using tapes could be helpful in learning intervals, phrasing, and expression. Exercises for a range of ability levels would be prepared. Tapes could also be used to teach one-finger piano skills to help students learn *to sing accurate intervals* and *to read new music.*

After initial skills were developed in fingering, note reading, voice control, and so on, a primary teaching procedure was very much like one used throughout the teaching of basic skills—model, lead, and test. Band members (as a group in rehearsal, or individually when tutoring) who could do the sequence played it, had the learner do it with them, and later had the learner do it on his or her own. The evidence suggests that peers can be very effective tutors for musical skills.

Figures 9.3 through 9.6 describe a point system for a high school chorus (from Greer, 1980). Greer also provided four additional pages on which students could keep records of points earned and spent.

April 14, 1977

Memo to: All Choir members
From: The Director
Re: New Point system

Next week we will be starting with a new point system, which we will be trying on an experimental basis for the remainder of the school year. I am hopeful that the new system will improve our rehearsals and our performances.

The system is based on giving points or credits, not on taking them away. Choir members will be rewarded for doing right things rather than punished for doing wrong things. There are only two possible instances which can cause points to be subtracted: dishonesty, and unexcused absence from performances.

Credits earned will serve three purposes: 1) they can be *spent* for various activities, privileges, etc.; 2) the average number earned will determine who can have various other privileges; and 3) they will be used to determine your grade.

There will no doubt need to be many adjustments in the system as we go along, and I would welcome your suggestions and comments. All changes will be made by majority vote of the officers, and will be announced in advance.

Save-harmless. Any Choir member who feels this system has resulted in his getting a lower grade may take a quarterly exam as in the past. You will receive the higher of the two grades.

Figure 9-3 *A credit system for a high school chorus*

HOW TO EARN CREDITS

Points Possible	I. Daily Grade Credits—In Rehearsal
10/day	1. **On time.** You must be standing in place when conductor steps on podium one minute after the late bell rings.
5/day	2. **Pen or pencil.** You must have a pencil or pen with you when the rehearsal begins.
5/day	3. **Music.** You must have your folder with you when the rehearsal begins.
up to 10/day	4. **Attention.** When the conductor steps on the podium, you must within five seconds stop talking, stand with music, and look at conductor.
up to 10/day	5. **Listening for instructions.** When conductor stops rehearsal, you must stop singing immediately, look at conductor, and listen for instructions.
up to 40/day	6. **On task during rehearsal.** a. When your section is singing, you should be singing *and* looking at the music or the conductor. b. When your section is not singing, you should be standing, looking at music or conductor, and listening to rehearsal. c. When conductor sits on podium, you should be sitting and listening for announcements, questions, etc. d. When conductor is off the podium, you may relax and talk to your friends.
up to 10/day	7. **Posture.** Stand with entire weight distributed between two feet. Neck vertebrae should be as far from the floor as possible without strain. While singing, music should be held so conductor appears just above the top of the music.
up to 10/day	8. **Marking music.** Mark music as instructed.
5-25	9. **Performance bonus.** For outstanding musicianship in rehearsal—awarded by conductor.
100/day =	Total Daily Grade Credits Possible (excluding Performance Bonus).

II. Quiz and Exam Grade Credits—In Rehearsal

80-100 each	1. Quizzes (written).	Must achieve 80% for credit.
400-500 each	2. Exams (sung).	

III. Performance Grade Credits (per concert)

500	1. **Attendance.**	
	Pre-arranged, excused absence:	250
	Excused absence, no notice:	0
	Unexcused absence:	−500
up to 500	2. **Quality of performance.** Determined by conductor, officers, and section leaders after the performance. Awarded to all who perform in concert.	

IV. Make-up Credits—Outside Rehearsal

These credits can be used to make up credits lost because of legitimate absences. Points earned cannot exceed points lost due to absence.

Credits	Activity
10-50	1. Take a 15-minute make-up lesson or tutoring session on the Choir music from another Choir member. (credits awarded by student teacher)
10-50	2. Rent a cassette of your part and spend 15 minutes practice time at home.
80-100	3. Complete an optional self-instruction program.

* * * * * * * *

V. Spendable Credits—Outside Rehearsal

(Do not affect grade.)

Credits	Activity
20-50	1. Audition for a solo.
100-200	2. Audition for Madrigal.
100-300	3. Perform all All-State solo.
80-100	4. Optional self-instruction programs. (not used for make-up) Must achieve 80% for credit.
10-50	5. Give 15-minute lesson or tutoring session on Choir music or on any instrument. (Credits awarded by pupil).
50-100	6. Make cassette tape of your part for use by other Choir members.
50-200	7. Serve as accompanist for All-State solo.
30/½-hr.	8. Work as librarian/bookkeeper/clerk/audio technician/etc. (outside of rehearsal).
50/hr.	9. Help in fund-raising activities.
50-100	10. Perform in student recital (including accompanists).
100/½-hr.	11. Tutor Choir members in other subjects, hobbies, outside skills, etc.
?	12. Other suggestions?

Figure 9-4 *How to earn credits*

PRIVILEGES EARNED BY MAINTENANCE OF CREDITS

TO BE ELIGIBLE TO . . .	AVERAGE DAILY CREDITS NEEDED:
1. Remain in Choir next quarter.	50 per rehearsal
2. Perform in concerts or recitals.	55 per rehearsal
3. Go on tour or field trips.	60 per rehearsal
4. Audition for solos or Madrigal.	70 per rehearsal
5. Be selected as Section Leader or Asst.	80 per rehearsal
6. Run for office.	90 per rehearsal
7. Buy excuse from rehearsal.	95 per rehearsal

HOW TO SPEND CREDITS

(All must be arranged *at least* 24 hours in advance.)

1. Conduct Choir in rehearsal. (1000/min.)
2. Permission to be late or leave early (50/min.)
3. Rent record overnight. (200)
4. Rent tape recorder overnight. (300)
5. Rent cassette tape of your part for home practice or make-up: overnight. (100)
6. Take a 15-minute lesson from another Choir member on an instrument. (100)
7. Permission to be in Choir room for practicing during free time. (200/period)
8. Check out music not in folder. (25/night; 100/week)
9. Excuse from rehearsal with full grade credit. (2000 plus see above.)
10. Additional tutoring or lessons from other Choir member in preparation for quizzes or exams. (not used for make-up) —50/¼-hr.
11. Conduct Choir in performance. (10,000 plus approval of conductor plus concurrent enrollment in or successful completion of Conducting Class)
12. Get tutoring from another Choir member in an academic subject or get lessons in a hobby, skill, etc. (200/½-hr.)
13. Rent conductor's after-school time (when available) for non-musical endeavors such as chess, bridge, backgammon, ping-pong, golf, etc. (1000/½-hr.) NO CHARGE IF I LOSE.
14. What other privileges, experiences, etc. would you like to buy? All offers will be considered.

Figure 9-5 *Privileges earned by maintenance of credits*

OBSERVATION FORM FOR CHOIR EXAMS

Student________________ Piece________________

Observer________________ Date________________

Criterion________%

1. **Rhythm:** each note held correct value.
2. **Pitch:** each note correct and in tune.
3. **Diction:** vowels accurate and clear; consonants articulated clearly.
4. **Dynamics:** follow markings in score.
5. **Breathing:** breathe where marked or at commas in the text.

To be counted correct, each item must be correct.

Follow the score, and mark in the box below every time you hear an incorrect beat.

Incorrect Beats

Total Beats in Piece ________
Minus Total Incorrect ________
Total Correct Beats: ________

$$\text{Learning Ratio} = \frac{\text{Total Correct}}{\text{Total Beats}} = \_\_\_\_\_\_$$

Grade for this exam =
L.R. × 500 = ______ Enter on TALLY SHEET. (No credit unless L. R. ≥ criterion.)

Figure 9-6 *Observation form for choir exams*

A Note on Art Education

Art teachers may feel they have been neglected in this chapter. The intention is not to neglect art education, but systematic behavioral approaches in this area have not been found in the literature. It should be obvious that artistic skills have a hierarchical structure that can be built through systematic direct instruction. A model for art education similar to that just described would seem very appropriate, with the student attacking the learning of advanced skills only after the basics are mastered. Creative aspects of art (as in music) are also dependent on having a solid base in colors, perspective, art materials, manual skills, analysis of the work of others, and so forth. There is much in art education that would benefit from a more systematic approach.

SUMMARY

Behavioral approaches are being systematically examined in physical education, coaching, and music education. This chapter examined some of the effective procedures and the research supporting them in these special settings. In part, this chapter *reviewed* procedures found to be effective in regular classrooms by showing their applications in new settings. Also, this chapter was intended to help the student expecting to teach in physical education or music education to see more specifically the applications to his or her field.

The observation of physical education classes indicate that they have management problems. There seems to be too much talking by teachers and not enough physical activity. There is student resistance and boredom. While it is clear that behavioral principles offer much promise for more effective physical education, more research is needed to help establish a consensus on goals and to demonstrate effective procedures.

The evidence shows that contracting, charting, monitoring, gradually increasing goals, and special incentives can be quite helpful in improving fitness through exercise and diet. Those who are overweight and who underexercise can be helped to establish more healthy routines.

The research on coaching is showing that coaches' behavior can be systematically changed using behavioral principles and that there are systematic procedures available to coaches that can make them more effective. The effective coach:

- Specifies performance objectives for players.
- Knows how to maintain performance as well as develop it.
- Has athletes compete against their personal best.
- Bases his or her procedures on those demonstrated through research to be effective.
- Monitors her or his own performance as a coach.
- And, seeks social validation for his or her efforts.

Some of the more promising procedures being demonstrated by research are:

- *The use of positive reinforcement rather than criticism* to change the behavior of athletes. Focus on what you want your players to learn and show them how to get there. Let them know when they do it right. Keep in mind the variety of reinforcers especially important to athletes (posted times, improvement, getting to travel).
- *The use of attendance boards and program boards.*
- *The use of mechanical and electronic feedback devices.*
- *Careful analysis of performance requirements* so that one can better let athletes know what to do.
- *Developing statistics that better reflect performance.*

- *Use of such cognitive-behavior therapy strategies* as deep relaxation, systematic desensitization, visuo-motor behavioral rehearsal, self-monitoring, and others.

Behavioral approaches in music education have centered around the development of Personalized Systems of Instruction (PSI), where objectives are defined, instructional modules constructed, measurements of effective performance on modules constructed. A variety of point systems have been constructed for various music settings that let students know what is expected of them and tell them of their progress. Special procedures for measuring musical performance with behavior observations have been devised. The use of peer checkers and tutors has been shown to be very valuable. The use of backup reinforcer menus that consist solely of music-related activities helps enrich student learning about music.

When you examine the problems in music education at the lower skill levels (general music courses, introductory chorus or band) the major problem seems to be how to handle large groups who have quite variable skill levels. Setting up systems that permit students to progress at their own rates, with peer help, with special incentives, and a clear structure that lets them know what to do next seems like a very promising solution. Obviously, as music itself becomes reinforcing, through listening, through performance, through composing, the need for an elaborate prompting and monitoring system is greatly diminished. That is as it should be.

CHAPTER

10

COGNITIVE-MOTIVATIONAL PROCESSES IN THE CLASSROOM

Up to this point, this text has focused on behavioral principles useful to the teacher in relation to individuals. It has pushed into some aspects of cognitive psychology that are readily understood in behavioral terms (planning, goal setting, self-management), but has avoided looking at the individual from an internal frame of reference. This chapter will examine some concepts from cognitive psychology that may have relevance to student motivation.

MOTIVATION

The topic of motivation in psychology covers a broad range of literature, ranging from the study of genetic and physiological bases, to neural mechanisms, to "psychogenic needs." So far this text has taken a pragmatic view of the problem and dealt with motivation as a problem in identifying what is reinforcing for a given individual (including the avoidance and escape from aversive stimuli). You have learned about various unconditioned and conditioned sources of reinforcers, as well as the importance of intermittent schedules of reinforcement in developing persistent behavior. Persistence is an important characteristic of the motivated person. Finally, you have learned that growing up involves learning to respond to longer-term goals (reinforcers) through the mediation of self-management procedures and other cognitive processes.

This approach to motivational processes has grown out of the analysis of the behavior of individual organisms. This work started with the study of naivé animals in simple situations (Skinner, 1938). Since the early 1950s, these principles have been gradually extended to help teachers understand more about complex human behavior (Honig and Staddon, 1977; Catania and Brigham, 1978; Heward, Heron, Hill, and Trap-Porter, 1984).

Another approach to psychology started by studying human adults and attempting to formulate why they do what they do. Often this occurred in a context of psychotherapy. Given adult humans, with unknown learning histories, the approach taken by many researchers was to make a catalog of recurrent behaviors and call them "needs" or motives. Henry A. Murray's catalog of needs is probably the best known. His list of inferred needs was derived, in part, from the analysis of stories made up in response to semiambiguous pictures (the Thematic Apperception Test, or TAT). The needs inferred from thematic verbal productions appear to be residues of prior reinforcement and punishment histories. The story themes may also be a product of recent emotional arousal, incidental stimuli, and so on. Murray identified some twenty "psychogenic" or learned needs such as achievement, affiliation, sex, and the need to understand. Murray recognized that learned needs changed over time and varied with environmental forces, which he called *presses.*

A Need Hierarchy

Abraham Maslow's *need hierarchy* expresses some interesting relations among types of needs. He believed that those needs lower in the hierarchy (more basic) had to be satisfied before those higher up would become important. Thus, the strength of needs at a higher level depended on the relative satisfaction of needs at a lower level. Figure 10.1 shows his hierarchy (Maslow, 1954).

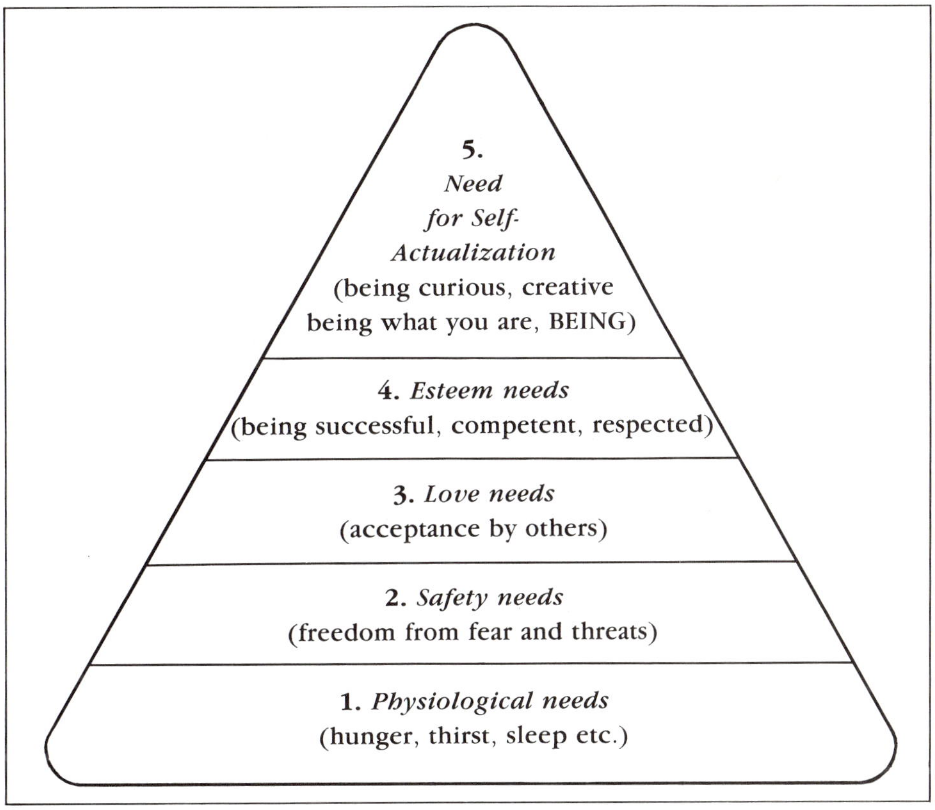

Figure 10-1 *A representation of Maslow's need hierarchy*

In behavioral terms, physiological needs would relate to unconditioned reinforcers. Safety needs would be based on the avoidance and escape from punishing consequences. Love needs and some aspects of esteem needs would relate to social reinforcers (attention, touch, kind words, and so on) and emotional conditioning. Being successful and competent can be related to social reinforcers, token reinforcers (grades, money), and a host of other reinforcers that success and competence can command.

The behavioral psychologist has no ready translation for a need for self-actualization. The behaviorist can understand processes that promote curiosity and creativity, but self-actualization as described by Maslow (1968) is an internal phenomenological state that some very special people are said to reach some of the time. It is a total absorption in the experience of the moment, whether that be interacting with another, viewing a piece of art, or viewing a pretty countryside. Most of the "neurotics" in the world are motivated by deficiency motivations (deprivation, fear, anxiety). We assume this is motivation derived from being poorly treated by others (or stated differently, experiencing much punishment and threat of punishment). The self-actualizer has either grown in a more positive environment or has somehow grown beyond the effects of a punishing environment, and is motivated by "gentle forces that spring from within." We must return to Pirsig's *Zen and the Art of Motorcycle Maintenance,* as discussed in Chapter 1, for understanding here. Maslow is trying to describe an existential experience (see *Toward the Psychology of Being,* 1968) in talking about self-actualizing people. For the empirical behaviorist to deal with this on other than a personal basis, the behaviorist would have to know more about the learning histories and current environmental events that could consistently produce reports of such states. The observations of the great humanistic psychologists, such as Abraham Maslow and Carl Rogers (1969), very likely contain important truths about the development of persons to their fullest. Researchers just do not know enough yet to convert this promise into practically useful information.

COGNITIVE MOTIVATION

Cognitive theories of motivation focus on: (1) motivation that appears to be inherent in certain cognitive states (such as the perception of incongruity, novelty, or dissonance), (2) purposeful behavior, and (3) motivation as affected by beliefs, expectancies, and interpretations of causes (attributions).

Discrepancy Motivational Effects

There is little question that small discrepancies between what is known and what is perceived (incongruity, novelty) can serve to attract attention and reinforce attending behavior (Hunt, 1961; Berlyne, 1960; Helson, 1964). Small discrepancies from expectation draw attention, support play in children, and are responded to as positive. Large discrepancies from expectation (as in a disfigured face) can be frightening. Settings or experiences containing no discrepancies tend to be "boring." Similarly, Festinger's work on cognitive dissonance (1957) implies that conflicting cognitions (attitudes, beliefs, opinions) create tension (dissonance) that motivates action aimed at reducing the dissonance. Piaget's (1952) concept of *disequilibrium* provides another way of talking about cognitive states that can be motivating. These discrepancy notions imply that programing new learning in small steps or raising questions that point to inconsistencies in a student's production can facilitate motivation. On the other hand, instructional sequences involving large discrepancies from expectation should be avoided.

It should be noted, however, that these motivational processes based on discrepancies are relatively "mild forces," and they provide *no specific* guides about what to do to design cognitive learning sequences that would be more motivating, because the size of discrepancies cannot be defined independently of students' response to a situation. One must empirically test a given sequence to see if it motivates and teaches efficiently.

Goal-Directed Behavior

The motivational aspects of goal-directed behavior (making a plan and following it) can be understood behaviorally in terms of the effects of prior reinforcement, the conditioned reinforcers "inherent" in behavior chains, and other discriminative and motivating aspects of self-management procedures (Miller, Galanter, and Pribram, 1960; Bandura, 1971; Mahoney, 1974). I agree these are cognitive processes, but I do not believe that they require any unusual or new principles to account for them. As noted earlier, while purposeful explanations for goal-directed behavior must be false—because causes cannot come after their effects but must precede them—anticipations and expectations (as residual effects of prior learning) need not be circular.

Expectations

It is the area of beliefs, expectations, and interpretation of causes (attributions) that the research on cognitive variables adds to our knowledge of motivational processes in ways that might be of value to teachers.

Expectations are the inferences or predictions we make about events, given what we "know." In 1922, not too long after intelligence tests were introduced into the United States in the form of the Stanford-Binet test (Terman, 1916) and the Army Alpha test (Yoakum and Yerkes, 1920), the political commentator Walter Lippmann initiated a debate with Lewis Terman on the potential dangers of the tests. In the following quote, Lippmann (as reported in Block & Dworkin 1976, p. 26) questioned the assumption made by Terman of a genetically based fixed intelligence quotient (IQ).

> Without offering any data on all that occurs between conception and the age of kindergarten, they announce on the basis of what they have got out of a few thousand questionnaires that they are measuring the hereditary mental endowment of human beings. Obviously, this is not a conclusion obtained by research. It is a conclusion planted by the will to believe (Block and Dworkin, 1976, p. 26).

While Lippmann saw the possible value of the tests in the better grouping of students for instruction by mental age rather than chronological age, he also saw the potential dangers for misuse of the tests by unsophisticated school administrators. Lippmann continues:

> I do not mean to say that the intelligence test is certain to be abused. I do mean to say it lends itself so easily to abuse that the temptation will be enormous. Suppose you have a school in which there are fifty ten-year-old children in the seventh grade and fifty eleven-year-olds in the eighth. In each class you find children who would jump ahead if they could and others who lag behind. You then re-grade them according to mental age. Some of the ten-year-olds go into the eighth grade, and some of the elevens into the seventh grade. That is an improvement. But if you are satisfied to leave the matter there, you are doing a grave injustice to the retarded children and ultimately to the community in which they are going to live. You cannot, in other words, be satisfied to put retarded eleven-year-olds and average ten-year-olds together. The retarded eleven-year-olds need something besides proper classification according to mental age. They need special analysis and special training to overcome their retardation. The leading intelligence testers recognize this, of course. But the danger of the intelligence tests is that in a wholesome system of education, the less sophisticated or the more prejudiced will stop when they have classified and forget that their duty is to educate. They will grade the retarded child instead of fighting the causes of his backwardness. For the whole drift of the propaganda based on intelligence testing is to treat people with low intelligence quotients as congenitally and hopelessly inferior. (Lippmann, as reported by Block and Dworkin 1976, p. 18).

This phenomenal prophecy by Lippmann from 1922 came true in the decades that followed this debate. The tests did in fact come to be used to place students into tracks where prophecies were fulfilled. Some students went to special education, some to vocational education, some to college preparatory programs. It was nearly 50 years later in 1971 that legal action was taken in the Federal District Court for Washington, D.C. (*Hobson* v. *Hansen*) to declare tracking students on the basis of IQ tests unconstitutional because it led to self-fulfilling prophecies or expectations. In a *self-fulfilling prophecy,* the prediction (say of low ability to learn in school) leads to actions (teach less to those low on the test) that ensure that the prophecy will come true.

Because IQ tests placed a higher percentage of black than white students into special education classes (where less was expected of them and less taught), a California court (in *Larry P.* v. *Riles,* filed in 1971) held that IQ tests could not be used in such placements. By 1984 that ruling had been upheld through a federal appeals court. However, an Illinois court (*Pace v. the Chicago Board of Education*) drew a contrary opinion—that the tests were not biased and could be used for placement. Both courts agreed that special education placement was ineffective.

A "60 Minutes" TV production (1975) presented the case of a Chicano professor in his thirties who had been placed in a class for retarded students when he was quite young. He could not read English and so could not pass the group test. He thought the special placement might get him the skills he needed, but most of the time the special class played physical-skill games. The students were not thought to be very teachable. It was not until he was in the Navy that he was able to really develop the skills he needed. When he was admitted to college, it was "conditionally." Four years later, he graduated with honors, with the conditional admission still on his record. He eventually earned a Ph.D. Expectations do influence actions.

In the classroom, expectations can function as S^d's about students that can influence how much the teacher is motivated to teach some students. Rosenthal and Jacobson (1968) provided teachers with false information about their students' capabilities. In this way they experimentally varied teacher expectations. The findings were interpreted as supporting an effect of expectations on IQ gains. While interpretation of their findings were marred by design flaws, Elashoff and Snow, (1971) more carefully controlled studies do support the reality of the self-fulfilling prophecy. Many investigators, using a variety of approaches, have shown teacher expectations to influence student behavior in self-fulfilling ways (Braun, 1976; Brophy & Good, 1974; Dusek, 1975).

So far this text has tried to create the expectation that *with appropriate use of behavioral principles, teachers can be effective in motivating all students.* Because a student comes from a deprived home does not mean she or he cannot be motivated to learn. Later, in considering research on instructional methods and mastery learning, the text will attempt to create the expectation that *all students can learn if they are taught appropriately.* There is nothing wrong with expectations; we all have them, and we would have them even if we did not want them. Problems arise when old beliefs continue long after they have been demonstrated to be untrue. IQ can predict *level* of performance on achievement tests, *but not how much students can gain from one year to the next* (Gersten, Becker, Heiry, & White, 1984). This issue will be discussed further in Chapter 20. Low-income students can be motivated and taught effectively (Becker & Carnine, 1980). Special education students can learn much more than they have been given credit for (Lockery and Maggs, 1982; Maggs and Morath, 1976). It is important that teachers develop an *awareness* of how they might be biasing the opportunities of their students by working harder with, expecting more from, and giving more positive attention to the higher-level performers, the girls, or whatever. This is a situation where tape recording part of a class day might provide useful data to improve teaching behavior.

Achievement Motivation

There is an extensive literature on achievement motivation (or need achievement) growing out of the work of Atkinson and McClelland (1948). Their work used measures developed out of Henry Murray's procedures for using story responses to the Thematic Apperception Test (TAT) to assess motives. In their 1948 study, they tested the effects of 1, 4, and 16 hours of food deprivation on the content of TAT stories using the same subjects in each condition. The study showed greater hunger to be reflected in stories after greater deprivation. These results gave them some confidence that achievement motivation could be measured by a similar procedure. Four cards (2 from the TAT and 2 new ones) that drew a high proportion of achievement-related themes were used in the earliest studies (McClelland, 1951). Stories were written around four questions: What is happening? What has led up to this situation? What is being thought? What will happen? This early study showed that achievement-related arousal conditions led to higher need achievement scores, and that subjects with high need achievement produced more solutions to scrambled words over a five-minute period and solved more addition problems in five minutes.

Since this early work, there have been many studies showing interesting relations between need achievement measures and various performances. For example, those higher in need achievement are more likely to remember interrupted tasks than completed tasks (Atkinson, 1955), are likely to complete interrupted tasks more often than uninterrupted tasks (Heckhausen, 1967), complete more total tasks, and complete more tasks correctly (Wendt, 1955).

These studies were carried out on groups, and the reliability of the assessment of need achievement was relatively low ($r = .4$ to .7), so that their usefulness in making predictions about individual students is not high.[1]

One outcome of this work was the development of the concepts of "hope of success" and "fear of failure." In achievement settings, some individuals seem to be more motivated by hope and some more by fear. These differences appear to be related to histories of reinforcement for achievement versus achieving to avoid punishment. Mahone (1960) found that those who were more motivated by success than failure had more realistic vocational aspirations than those more motivated by fear of failure. Weiner (1972) found that those who were more success-motivated decreased effort after success and increased it after failure. Those who were more failure-motivated decreased effort after failure and increased it after success. These differences could be important for teachers. Again, however, because of measurement problems, need achievement measures on students are not available to teachers. An examination of what can be done will be made a little later in this chapter.

Locus of Control

The concept *locus of control* was developed by Rotter (1954) to refer to an external versus internal orientation in accounting for ("explaining") one's successes and failures. Luck, or the power of someone else, is used by "externals" to explain successes and failures. Hard work and skill (or the relative lack thereof) are used by "internals." Crandall, Katkovsky, and Crandall (1965)

[1]The Pearson correlation coefficient (r) is discussed in Chapter 19, and reliability is discussed in Chapter 27. For now, note that r is a measure of relationship between two measures. Reliability is the degree of relationship between two measures of the same thing. For individual predictions to be very accurate, r's of at least .85 are desirable.

developed a measure of locus of control for use with children. They found that internals had better achievement in grades 3 to 5. Messer (1972) found higher grades and achievement scores for internals matched for IQ's with externals. Coleman et al. (1966) found that black children were more apt to attribute success to luck than white children, but that blacks who believed success was due to hard work (internals) had higher achievement scores in reading than those who believed in luck. (For a review of the literature of locus of control, see Fanelli, 1977.) Again, these studies and others like them appear to have important implications for teachers that we will come back to.

Attribution Theory[2]

Weiner (1972, 1974, 1977) has evolved an attribution theory from the work on achievement motivation and locus of control. *Attributions* are inferences about the causes of our behavior. The theory deals with the perceived causes of success and failure. Four main causes are involved: ability, effort, task difficulty, and luck. In approaching an achievement-related task, the first decision is to *analyze the task*. Does it require ability, effort, coping with difficult procedures, or luck? The causal attribution is made and the probability of success or failure is estimated. This then leads to a hope of success or fear of failure that can affect *task motivation*. Achievement-related behavior occurs, followed by success or failure. This again leads to *causal judgments* of what led to the success or failure (ability, effort, luck, or task difficulty). These judgments affect whether one feels good or bad about the outcome and also affect future achievement expectancies. From a cognitive point of view, motivation is strongly affected by what the student thinks is going on relative to the variables in the theory.

Weiner (1979) states that students high in achievement motivation:

- Prefer tasks where the outcomes can be said to be under their control.
- Believe that hard work pays off in success.
- Readily pick up cues on the importance of effort.

Thus, when students believe that failure is due to low ability or task difficulty (regardless of what is true) they are less likely to put out effort than when failure is attributed to lack of effort or bad luck.

Self-Esteem in the Classroom

Another concept that often enters into discussions about cognitive motivation in education is self-esteem or self-concept in school settings. The term *self-concept* refers to attitudes about self. An *attitude* is a belief referring to how one feels about some object or event (or classes of these). Human beings do not have a singular self-concept, although for some, its components can add up to a *general* positive or negative feeling about self. As Shavelson, Hubner, and Stanton (1976) point out, we can have attitudes about ourselves as students, and these can vary by content areas. We can have attitudes about our physical self and these can vary for appearance, athletic skills, dancing, and so on. And, we can have attitudes

[2]Bandura's (1977) self-efficacy theory also presents an integration of need achievement and locus of control research that has many features in common with Weiner's attribution theory. Bandura's theory differs in that it is a more comprehensive treatment of cognitive-behavioral phenomena.

about our social self that can vary in the areas of friendships, dating, status in social groups, etc.

High self-esteem in school settings has obvious relationships to positive achievement motivation (hope of success) and internal locus of control ("I can do it if I try"). Anticipation of failure and low self-esteem about academic tasks are synonymous terms. Many studies have reported positive relationships between positive school self-concepts and school success after controlling for IQ (such as Brookover, Paterson, & Thomas, 1962; Brookover, Erickson, & Joiner, 1967. For reviews, see Purkey, 1970; Rubin, Dorle, & Sandidge, 1977; Scheirer & Kraut, 1979; Hansford & Hatti, 1982).

A positive self-concept is certainly an important educational goal in itself (Bloom, 1977) and this is one reason for the focus on positive reinforcement rather than punishment in this text. However, some researchers have assumed that poor self-esteem is the cause of poor learning in school (such as the supporters of open education; see Maccoby & Zellner, 1970.) Thus, if a student increases self-esteem, better learning will take care of itself. It is my opinion (which is supported by the current evidence) that the causal relation goes *primarily* in the other direction—that competence promotes confidence (Kifer, 1975; Calsyn & Kenny, 1977; Scheirer & Kraut, 1979). This conclusion is also supported by data from the Follow Through study (Becker & Carnine, 1980; Stebbins, St. Pierre, Proper, Anderson, & Cerva, 1977). This long-term, nationwide study of economically disadvantaged children in kindergarten through third grade showed that only the models with the most effective learning gains (and using positive behavior management procedures)—the Oregon Direct Instruction Model and the Kansas Behavior Analysis Model—were significantly higher than comparison groups on measures of self-esteem (Coopersmith, 1967) and locus of control (Crandall, Katkowsky, and Crandall, 1965). The model that advocated the building of self-esteem as a *primary goal* of the program—Open Education—did more poorly than their comparison groups on both achievement and self-esteem measures.

We measure positive attitudes through verbal statements about "goodness" and liking, through observing choices, and through other approach behaviors. Positive attitudes are quite obviously the product of reinforcers and positive emotional conditioning. A similar process can be described for negative attitudes. Attitudes are not *causes* of learning (at least initially), they are a *result* of encounters with reinforcers and punishers. They can also be learned through observations and stories told by others. Once established, however, they could be thought of as the current "representatives" of the earlier causes and serve as mediators influencing whether a student tends to approach a challenging learning task or tends to avoid it (Kagan & Moss, 1962; Shavelson & Bolus, 1982; West, Fish, & Stevens, 1980). The data on attitude change suggests that changes in behavior (for example, getting reinforced for improving skills) more readily lead to changes in attitudes than the converse. Bandura (1969) writes, ". . .the relative superiority of a behaviorally oriented approach stems from the fact that a basic change in behavior provides an objective and genuine basis by which one feels self-respect, self-confidence, and dignity." Thus, if the concern is to improve self-esteem, the most effective approach is probably to provide the conditions to make students competent and reinforce them for good performances.

Teaching Success Striving and Self-Esteem. Self-confidence and self-esteem are attitudes toward one's own capabilities and one's self. Students learn these attitudes through experiences that show them that they are capable or not, likable or not in different settings and for different activities. It is likely that all learning experience teaches students something related to their feelings of confidence and self-esteem. It is important that the teacher recognize and take advantage of this. For example, in teaching students to sound out the word *man* (or any other task for that matter), the teacher could present the task, get an individual or group response, and give a simple confirmation. On the other hand, the teacher might have the group "sound it out," "say it fast," and then say "Good work! You are really reading!" With active, positive responding, the students are given examples of the attitudes "school work is fun," "the teacher is nice," "I am likable," and "I am capable." These are important attitudes to learn along with reading.

If teaching material is presented in ways that make it less likely that the students will learn it, there is a higher probability that negative attitudes will be transmitted. For example, the teacher holds up a car and says, "This is red. What is this?" The child answers, "Car." The teacher says "*Look at it.* Is it red?" The child shrugs and looks down. The teacher may not have intended this outcome, but it provided a failure example. A clearer presentation would have first have been sure the object name was known, and then said, "This car is red. What *color* is this car?"

There are a number of important elements in teaching procedures that help develop students who like school and themselves. First, the students must receive praise and other demonstrations that they are capable, successful, smart, and so forth.

Second, the model the teacher presents is also very important. This model, itself, must be an instance of "I can do it," "I can succeed if I work hard," "I am smart," and "learning is fun." The teacher tries to show through behavior what she or he wants the students to learn.

Third, it is essential to have a suitable academic program—one in which the students can succeed with low error rate. The program should provide frequent demonstrations that the students are smart and capable. It should also teach the skills required for living successfully in a technological society. Without a basic competency in language arts, science, mathematics, physical skills, and interpersonal skills, it is highly unlikely that any sense of competence or esteem established in school will last for long outside the classroom. There is good reason to believe, in fact, that academic failure is a major cause of low self-esteem in our society. The unproductive use of punishment is the second major cause.

Two specific attitudes can be taught systematically as a part of a program for promoting self-esteem and success striving. These attitudes are, "persistence pay offs" and "I know when I'm right." The procedures presented are modeled after those used by Engelmann within the DISTAR programs.

Teaching Persistence ("Hard Work Leads to Success"). In many new learning situations the students have to stay with a task long enough to accomplish it. The students need to learn the rule, "If I keep trying, I will succeed."

The program for teaching persistence requires *reinforcing success trials following error trials* on new learning tasks. A rule is learned about persistence that can be transferred to other new learning tasks. This rule becomes a self-management aid. The procedures are as follows:

1. When a student is having difficulty on a new task, focus on reinforcing working hard. "Tommy's working hard. You watch, he's going to catch on. If you work hard, you'll get it." Reinforcement is given for working in the face of failure. "He'll learn this. He's a smart boy." Introduce the same routine if another student makes fun of the student having difficulty. "Wait a minute. He's working hard. And he's going to show you. He'll get this stuff."

2. In the early stages of training persistence on difficult tasks, be sure

other tasks at which the student can succeed are also provided. Avoid too much failure early in the program, because a student might quit before he or she succeeds. When the student successfully fulfills the task requirements, the requirements are increased. Also, in the early stages, give praise and attention for working hard frequently, then gradually make it more intermittent.

3. When the student demonstrates mastery of the skill, relate his or her performance to the rule. "What did I tell you? I told you she would get it. She kept working hard and she got it." "If you work hard, you'll get it." Reinforce persistence by making a fuss over a new accomplishment.

Teaching Confidence in One's Own Judgment. This program begins with simple fooler games. The teacher indicates that she or he is going to "catch" the students unless they are careful.

1. The teacher announces that she or he will do something: "I'm going to name animals. Listen: tiger, elephant, dog, table, horse—" If the students do not react, act gleeful. "I tricked you. Lisa thinks that a table is an animal. Tyrone thinks that a table is an animal. That's silly." When the students catch the teacher's mistake, the confidence routine is presented: "Good thinking. Karl knew what was right, and I couldn't fool him by saying something else."

2. As the students become familiar with a variety of fooler games, begin to introduce foolers out of context. Be careful not to introduce foolers in presenting new tasks. The students have to be able to trust the teacher there. However, after the students have mastered a basic skill, such as adding, the teacher might ask, "What's six plus two? Yes, eight." The teacher then writes on the board $6 + 2 = 9$. If the students do not catch the mistake, the teacher acts amused. If they do catch it, the confidence routine is presented: "You knew what was right. I couldn't fool you."

Note that these tasks are also good for training attention. If a student fails the task because of not attending, the teacher can point to the importance of attending: "If you don't watch and listen, I'll catch you every time."

3. After the students have begun to work with foolers, the teacher can introduce a variation. "I'm going try to teach you something that is really hard, and you might not be able to get it. I'm probably the only one who can do it." The teacher then presents a new task that will probably be learned with little difficulty. The teacher acts surprised. "How did you do that? I thought I could catch you, but I couldn't. You learned this the right way. You're too smart for me." This routine demonstrates to the students that if they attack new learning situations right away, they will succeed, even beyond the expectations of the teacher.

For a fooler program to succeed, the material must be carefully sequenced so that the students are successful enough times for them to become confident about their ability.

Other Self-Esteem Procedures. Perhaps now it can be recognized that much of Part I of this text "Classroom Management" has centered on procedures likely to be effective in promoting self-esteem in the classroom and striving for academic success. Use of behavior-specific praise (telling students what they did that was so great), the Premack principle, goal setting and contracting with older students, effective-grading systems, charting progress, shifting to intermittent reinforcement, and so forth—these are all methods designed to teach students that they are successful, that hard work pays off, and that they are liked.

Intrinsic-Extrinsic Motivation

This chapter closes with a brief examination of issues related to intrinsic and extrinsic motivation. When behavior is maintained without apparent reinforcement from the outside, it has been spoken of as being "intrinsically" motivated.[3] Research on intrinsic motivation is frequently cited by educational psychologists as evidence *against* using consequences such as token reinforcers, since in some studies the effectiveness of intrinsic reinforcers was reduced following the use of extrinsic reforcers.

Some researchers view the intrinsic-extrinsic distinction as a problem in the attribution of causes. If the person believes (truly or not) that he or she is doing something "because I want to" (that is, because of intrinsic motivation), the person is presumed to work harder at it than if the person thinks he or she is being "manipulated" by outside forces. The early work in this area was carried out by Deci (1971, 1972a, 1972b, 1975). Most of Deci's work used college psychology students as subjects and three-dimensional puzzles as the task. The puzzles were selected because they had "intrinsic" interest for many students.

In a 1975 review of the research in this area, Notz concluded that "the arousal of extrinsic motivation may occur at the expense of intrinsic motivation," but it is quite unclear under just what conditions this might occur. In a more recent review covering the extensive research in this area of the last decade, Morgan (1984) points out that there is still no single explanation for the findings, nor is it clear that they have implications for classroom practices. There does appear to be a weakening in the choice of undertaking an activity (that you would originally choose to do) after it has been associated with the promise of a reward. It appears that the originally preferred task is devalued. It is as if we have a rule that "Gee, if they're going to pay me to do that, it can't be much fun." Morgan concludes that "rewards can have either undermining or enhancing effects depending on the circumstances." Positive outcomes are found when the reward serves as a symbol of success, or in the case of praise, when it clearly informs the learner of what he or she did well. Decrement effects appear to occur when rewards are given for tasks that are already perceived as fun to do. Also, Staw, Calder, Hess, and Sandeland (1980) found that when there was a norm (expectation) of payment for participating in experiments, there was no decrement induced by payment. When there was no such norm for payment, task satisfaction was lowered by being paid to do it.

Staw et al. (1980) point out that the inhibitory effects of payment for "work" are most likely to occur when payment is "inappropriately applied," that is, where there are strong norms against payment. But where norms for payment exist or are built, money rewards can increase task satisfaction.

Chapter 7 recommended that teachers use not any stronger reinforcers than are needed to get the job done. To do so may create problems in shifting to less strong reinforcers. This advice is consistent with Staw's advice not to violate "norm" expectations. Also relevant here is the experimental work demonstrating reinforcer contrast effects. For example, you might agree to work for five dollars an hour, but after making ten dollars an hour, you would be less likely to work for five. An incentive that is perfectly adequate under some conditions will be less effective if it follows a higher level incentive.

SUMMARY

The study of human adults has led to a variety of systems for describing their motives (or the kinds of activities they find reinforcing or punishing). This

[3]Note that empirical behavior theory does not have a concept of intrinsic reinforcers. Events attributed to intrinsic reinforcers are typically explained by appeal to conditioned reinforcers, novelty effects, and so forth). However, Skinner (1957) did recognize a kind of "automatic reinforcement" to account for some of the effects of music and art on behavior.

chapter began by considering Maslow's need hierarchy, which proposes that after more basic needs become satisfied, other needs relating to competence, success, curiosity, creativity, and self-actualization tend to emerge. While most of the needs described in Maslow's hierarchy have parallels in behavior theory in terms of what is reinforcing to a person, there is no ready translation of the existential experience described as self-actualization. This does not mean these ideas are not important, only that they are not yet tied to objective events that might be used to teach people to be self-actualizers.

The focus of this chapter was on cognitive-motivational processes. It examined motivational processes relating to discrepant and novel cognitive states; to goal-directed behavior; to beliefs, expectancies, and attributions; and to what has been called "intrinsic" motivation.

Rather than summarize this somewhat complex exploration into what some behaviorists consider to be an alien land, this summary will list the potential implications of cognitive-motivational processes for teachers.

Discrepancy Motivational Effects

The unexpected can be used as an attention getter.

Posing problems (that set up dissonance or disequilibrium) in the beliefs held by students can motivate thinking toward resolutions. In lecturing, creating plots that describe conflicting viewpoints and holding back the solutions until the lesson has been fully developed can increase student interest and attention.

Building new learning in small steps appears to be consistent with potential reinforcing effects of events that are slightly different from what is known. However, only an empirical test can determine if your guess about "small steps" was right or not.

Goal-Directed Behavior

The active teaching of planning processes to help guide longer-term actions can greatly facilitate those actions. Helping students to set goals and subgoals can provide S^{d}'s to guide more effective behavior. (Since these ideas are covered in earlier chapters, they were only briefly mentioned here.)

Expectations

The belief in a fixed intelligence has led educators to fail to provide appropriate teaching for those with lower IQ's and produced a self-fulfilling prophecy. The debate between Lewis Terman and Walter Lippmann in the 1920s was used to present this problem. Teachers do not really know what can be taught to whom until they try teaching with the best technology available. The current evidence suggests that all children can be taught. Many of the discriminatory practices by schools against minority groups can be traced to educators' false beliefs, which are self-fulfilling. Several courts have sided with the minority plaintiffs on these issues.

There are other teacher expectations about the sexes, what students in general can learn, minorities, and so on that can have similar biasing effects on students' opportunities in life.

Achievement Motivation, Locus of Control, and Attribution Theory

Some students have learned that if they work hard, they can be successful—they are motivated to achieve. Others believe that their personal effort does not count for much and that chance or outside forces determine whether or not they will be successful (external locus of control). Those in the first group are more likely to have positive self-concepts about their functioning in the classroom than those in the second. Teachers can promote positive striving by students: (1) by ensuring student success through the use of effective teaching methods, (2) by using lots of positives to let students know they are improving, (3) by reinforcing *persistence* in the face of a difficult task, and (4) by teaching students to rely on their own judgment through the use of fooler games.

Self-esteem (high self-concept) is correlated with success in school. Some have believed that just by improving self-esteem in poor students one could improve their school success. The evidence implies, however, that a better strategy is to provide successful learning with lots of verbal reinforcement. In this way the student learns that she or he is successful and what she or he can do is valued. If the goal is to improve students' self-concepts, systematically apply in a positive way the principles covered so far in this text.

The chapter briefly examined research from which it has been argued that the use of tangible rewards with students can be detrimental to their intrinsic motivation. While the research in this area has produced inconsistent results, an appropriate conclusion for teachers is to not use a stronger reinforcer than is needed (because then teachers may have to work out the transition problems later), but to not be afraid to use what is needed to get poorly motivated students learning in school.

CHAPTER

11

GROUP PROCESSES IN THE CLASSROOM

People all live as a part of many groups—family, friends, social organizations, part of a city or town, our country, and so on. So too do the members of a classroom. People all live in groups within groups. Social psychologists have been studying group processes and dynamics since the early work of Kurt Lewin (Lewin, Lippitt, and White, 1939) on group climates. So far this text has focused on the teacher as a leader of individuals in a group (the class) and the variables by which individuals are influenced. Obviously, many of these discussions or recommendations could have been *phrased* in terms of the effects on group processes. Chapter 8, "Planning for the Start of School," covered many group-related processes (group rules, use of peer helpers, promoting group participation through the grading systems, and so forth). That chapter could have stressed the importance of the use of positive reinforcement (as opposed to punishment) in promoting group cohesiveness. An example of how to train cooperative group processes was given in discussing the use of peer tutors and checkers to facilitate band instruction. This chapter looks more closely at the actions teachers can take to reduce conflict and to facilitate group learning, group cohesiveness, group discussion, group problem solving, and group products.

In developing this chapter, I am greatly indebted to Richard and Patricia Schmuck (1983) and to Meredith and Joyce Gall (1976) whose works in this area were valuable resources. The Schmucks' book, *Group Processes in the Classroom,* is a text suitable for use by teachers in training that contains many "how to" ideas for group processes, as well as an extensive review of the research in this area. The Galls' chapter on "The Discussion Method" is an excellent research review and contains many practical implications for teachers. Those who wish to pursue this area further will find these works excellent resources.

THE GOALS OF GROUP ACTIVITIES IN THE CLASSROOM

Group activity goals can be divided into two types—those that are oriented toward the accomplishment of some *task* and those that are oriented to the *social and emotional* outcomes for the group.

Task Oriented Goals

Subject-matter Mastery. Group discussions and other group procedures can be used to help achieve basic learning objectives. Gage and Berliner (1979) suggest that it is useful to distinguish between ***high-consensus fields*** and ***low-consensus*** fields in deciding when to use the discussion method. In high-consensus fields (such as mathematics and the natural sciences), there is considerable agreement on what should be taught, and efficiently structured courses suitable to learning from texts, lectures, and exercises have been developed. In low-consensus fields, such as social science, history, literature, and music appreciation, there is much less agreement on the goals of instruction. The use of discussion methods and readings permits an examination of alternative theories, values, and personal conclusions. Even though there is no research on which subject matter areas are best taught through the discussion method (Gall and Gall, 1976), it is certainly clear that in practice, teachers tend to use lectures more in the high-consensus fields and discussion more in the low-consensus fields.

Group procedures other than discussion are also important in facilitating subject-matter learning. Some examples are: cooperative learning in groups, peer tutoring, and project groups.

Developing Cognitive and Language Skills. Discussion methods have been found useful in teaching problem-solving skills and critical thinking. The ***discovery method*** for analyzing problem examples and discovering rules and principles was built around the discussion method. Students in groups also get oral practice in thinking "on their feet" and verbally expressing their ideas. The facilitation of oral expression skills is another important goal of group discussion.

Developing Democratic-process Skills. Group processes can be used to teach a variety of skills related to democratic process, such as respect for minority views, majority or consensus decision making, listening to others' views, withholding judgment until the facts are in, cooperating with others, expressing personal opinions, filling a leadership gap, and compromising (or not compromising).

Social-Emotional Goals

Changing Attitudes. We live in a world of controversies, biases, and emotions. Group interactions in discussion, role-playing, simulation, and so on can be helpful in learning to see another's point of view and in bringing reason into the picture. There are many issues confronting present society that our youth need to examine carefully, ranging from nuclear missiles and atomic energy to the feminist revolution and women's rights.

Motivating and Developing Group Cohesiveness. In a cohesive group, the members support each other. Whether this is good or bad for an effective classroom can depend on the group norms or the expectations of the teacher and the students. The question for the teacher is, "How do I develop a group *esprit* that will facilitate classroom learning?"

GROUP DYNAMICS RESEARCH

First you will examine some of the research on group processes that provides guidelines for structuring your choices in selecting or developing model-group-process procedures. Group dynamics has been an experimental field within social psychology since the pioneering work of Lewin (Lewin et al., 1939). Lewin left Germany to escape Hitler and was vitally interested in action research that had implications for society.

Effects of Group Size

In terms of member satisfaction, Hare (1962) claims that the optimal size for a discussion group is five members. Keeping an odd number also helps to prevent deadlocks on group decisions. The preference for smaller groups probably results from the increased opportunity for participation (Gall and Gall, 1976). While there are some data to support Hare's conclusion, it is not clear that larger groups could not be effective, given adequate training in group processes. Effectively working with groups of five in a class of thirty to forty requires careful planning and management.

Group Heterogeneity

Most of the research on group heterogeneity is with college and military groups. This research suggests that where there is high similarity (low heterogeneity) of attitudes, there is higher group cohesiveness. But studies of group performance tend to find heterogeneous groups more effective, although not without exceptions. A study of attitude change with high school students by Mitnick and McGinnies (1958) found use of discussion with homogeneous groups did not change the attitudes of highly racially prejudiced students. In this experiment, there were two conditions—film only, and film with discussion. Half of the *groups* under each condition rated high in prejudice and half rated low. The low-prejudice students were changed most by film with discussion. The high-prejudice students were changed most by film only. In discussion, the high-prejudice students tended to express their negative attitudes toward blacks, rather than discuss the prejudice issues raised in the film. The low-prejudice students discussed the prejudice issues directly. While this study does not prove the case, it seems that placing high-prejudice students in groups with low-prejudice students would create a better chance of attitude change, since the issues would more likely be discussed.

It appears that groups with a breadth of attitudes and skills are more likely to profit from group discussion, although the evidence is not strong, and good leadership might override homogeneous composition.

Group Cohesiveness

A cohesive classroom is made up of students who like each other and take care of each other. In summarizing the literature on cohesiveness, Gall and Gall (1976) conclude that cohesive groups: (1) have higher maintenance of membership and group participation, (2) have members who communicate more with each other, and (3) feel more positive about each other. These relationships seem to be little more than the characteristics that *define* cohesiveness. However, there are other findings. Wright (1943) examined group responses to frustration and found that more cohesive play groups were more cooperative when placed in a frustrating situation than less cohesive groups. Both Back (1951) and Dittes and Kelley (1956) found that when they experimentally increased cohesiveness, interactions increased among group members.

Whether group cohesiveness facilitates or hinders academic performance depends on the norm expectations of the group A cohesive group that did not have positive academic norms could hinder academic performance (Schmuck & Schmuck, 1983). They could reinforce peer interactions that teachers would consider off-task behavior. On the other hand, a group that supported the learning of its members could be a definite asset. Lewis and St. John (1974) contribute some evidence on this issue. They studied 154 black sixth graders in twenty-two classrooms that were mostly white. A rise in the achievement of blacks was found where: (1) the classroom norm expectation valued achievement, and (2) blacks were accepted into the peer group.

Back's (1951) study, mentioned previously, suggests that groups can be cohesive in different ways. Two-person groups were selected to work together because they had expressed a liking for each other, or they had common interests in the task, or because they were attracted to the group because of the prestige it gave its members. All three experimental groups worked more effectively on tasks than noncohesive groups.

There are also some studies that suggest that high cohesiveness leads to greater resistance to attitude change (Gerard, 1954) and a greater likelihood of rejecting a member who does not share the majority norm view (Emerson, 1954; Schachter, 1951).

It would appear that facilitating the liking of group members for each other can have quite positive effects on classroom learning if at the same time the group members value learning and they have the skills to help promote it.

Effects of Communication Patterns

A number of studies in group dynmamics have experimented with the effects of different communication structure. A *controlled structure* might be shaped like a wheel with spokes where all communications among group members had to go through the hub. (See Figure 11.1). The person at the hub could directly communicate with any member, but the others could only go to the hub. An *open system* would permit each member to communicate with all others. A *circle structure* would permit communication with those next to you, and a *chain* would give two-way communication to members in the middle, but not those at the end.

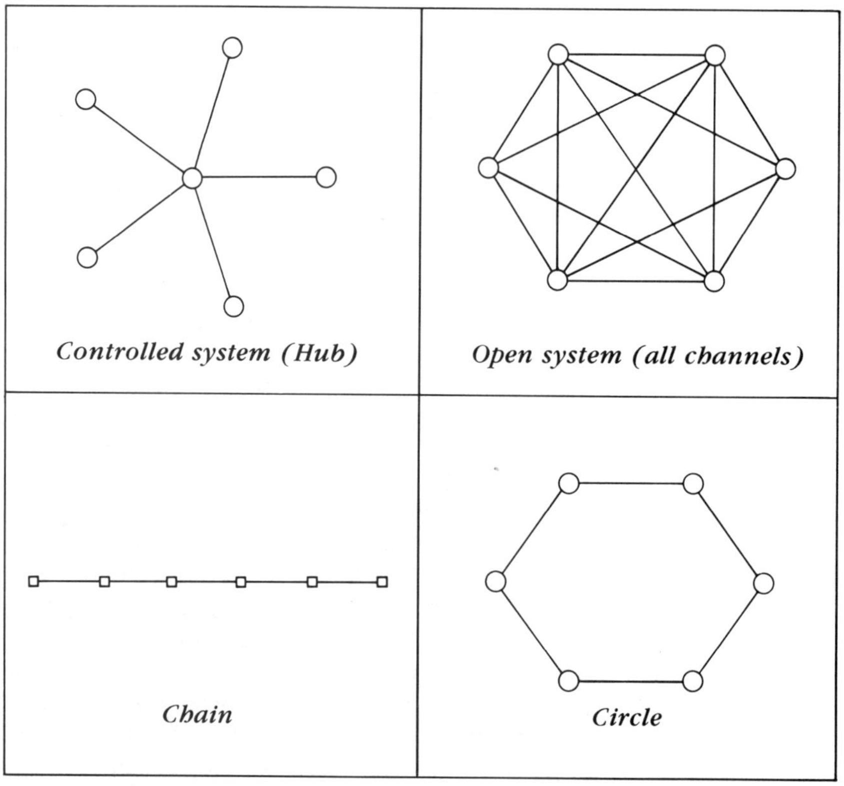

Figure 11-1 *Experimental group communication patterns.*

Studying structures of this sort, Leavitt (1951) found that there was greater efficiency in problem solving that required communications in hub-like structures; but when errors were made, the errors persisted longer. Also, the group members were more dissatisfied. Group members were most comfortable with and corrected errors more readily in the less efficient circle pattern. Leavitt did not include an open system.

These ideas on communication channels were applied to classroom structures by Sommer (1967). He compared a lecture-style seating arrangement with an open seminar. In the lecture classrooms, students in the front-center of the class participated more than those at the sides or the rear. Direct visual contact between teacher and students was assumed to be the critical variable. Visual contact was available to all in the seminar.

Where discussion is the goal, seating arrangements that foster eye contact and open communication are likely to be more effective. In teacher-directed instruction, the more traditional lecture setup may hold attention better, although the teacher may have to give some thought to who sits where.

Leadership Styles

The topic of leadership styles has embedded in it a value issue—the assumption by many that student-directed activity is better than teacher-directed activity. Because this value issue is fundamental to decisions about group processes, you will explore it in some detail.

The philosopher John Dewey (1930) believed that schools should prepare students to be functioning members of a democratic society by modeling democratic *processes* in the way schools operate. Schools should be structured democratically, so that individuals learn to work together in cooperative ways, interact and debate issues, and constructively deal with conflict. In Dewey's view, schools should be as concerned with the interpersonal aspects of school living and values as with academic achievement. The free-school movement of the 1960s and early 1970s was one of many expressions of this philosophy. The English Infant School movement (open education) was another (see Brown & Precious, 1968). They were reactions against the demeaning atmospheres found in schools where students are not treated with respect.

One problem in pursuing Dewey's philosophical goals is that students need to learn *basic competencies,* which may be best taught through adult-directed methods. For example, the results of the Follow Through experiment (discussed in detail in Chapter 12) showed that the teacher-directed Direct Instruction Model was most effective in improving the academic performance of disadvantaged children, whereas Open Education and other child-centered approaches did more poorly than traditional classrooms. Another problem is that students need to *learn* democratic values and actions involving personal responsibility and respecting the rights of others. These do not just develop automatically. Freedom without responsibility is chaos and possibly tyranny. Consider the following example.

The Colorado Springs Free School

By C. L. Salzberg

The Colorado Springs Community School was begun in 1969 by a group of parents as an alternative to the local public school system. From the outset it was developed along the free school model. Children ranged in age from five to fourteen years old. Classes were voluntary for the children. Teachers, for the most part, tried to help the children organize activities by providing guidance, materials, and explanations when they were requested. Children had free run of the school and the surrounding area. There were very frequent field trips to local places of interest as well as more prolonged trips for camping. Children were not coerced into participating in any activities. They were encouraged to express their thoughts and feelings. Over the course of the year academic work became less and less frequent. The best efforts of a dedicated staff with a low student-teacher ratio were not sufficient to generate very much skill oriented behavior. Even more discouraging was the development of inconsiderate, rude, and abusive social behavior of the children toward one another and toward the adults. Children showed little respect for one another's rights to privacy, to work undisturbed, to their own property, or to be free from physical abuse. On occasion group meetings were held where these issues were discussed. The children would agree that many social and property abuses were undesirable for everyone concerned. However, these verbal statements had no effect on their subsequent actions. The school had become a place where nothing and no one was safe from destruction, even the building itself. Complete freedom from adult constraints had produced an environment where none of the children were free, even from fear for their own physical well-being.

We cannot be sure about the extent to which our experience applies to other free schools. However, it would not be surprising if the above factors have something to do with why so many free schools fail in a short time.

In planning for the next year the staff and some of the parents at the Community School began to rethink the issue of freedom within the school. First, it became evident that freedom is not a global entity. In fact, there seemed to be innumerable potential freedoms within a school environment. There were the host of freedoms associated with access to materials, activities, and areas, both within the school and within the community at large. Then there were the more personal freedoms such as the freedom of movement, of speech, of self-expression. There were freedoms associated with scheduling one's own activities, in one's own time, in a place of one's own choosing. There were also many freedoms which could be stated negatively: the freedom to leave a project momentarily without returning to find it destroyed or missing; the freedom to pursue a task without constant disruption; the freedom not to be continually abused or intimidated by fellow students as well as by adults. The list of potential freedoms seemed boundless.

Second, specific freedoms could be maintained only so long as they were accompanied by associated responsible behaviors. The Community School used many resources outside the school. However, when some of our children abused those resources we stood in danger of becoming less welcome guests. There have been many people who volunteered to conduct interesting projects at the school. However, when volunteers were verbally or otherwise abused they were less likely to volunteer their services in the future. When the destruction of property became rampant it was no longer possible to give children free access to equipment and materials. Thus, the abusive and destructive behavior of the children was eroding the freedoms within the Community School, and it was doing it in a way more certain than adult authority could ever do.

Another consideration was that all the children at the school were losing freedoms because of the irresponsible behavior of a minority of students. Even more frustrating was that the younger children were beginning to emulate the most aggressive, abusive, authoritarian behavior of their older peers. It seemed that the adults had relinquished their authority to the most aggressive children who were in turn shaping all the children to become progressively more insensitive toward each other.

The question that came sharply to focus from these discussions was how could a school develop and maintain the kind of responsible behaviors that would allow freedoms within the school to be maximized for all children. In the past we gave our children a school environment with a maximum of freedom from adult authority and assumed that their actions would rise to meet the occasion. They didn't. The opposite effect occurred, and the result was a hostile, unproductive atmosphere. Therefore, we decided to try the opposite strategy.

That is, we could award specific freedoms to individual children only as they began to demonstrate the appropriate responsible behavior.

Before attempting to put this new strategy to use on a school-wide basis we decided to try it first in a more limited way. The children had no previous systematic instruction in mathematics and their skills in this area were correspondingly limited. Therefore, we decided to examine the effect of making math class time available for students to use as free time dependent on their maintaining satisfactory rates in the acquisition of mathematics skills. . . .

When the freedom to leave class was made contingent on finishing one page of math their rate of work (problems/minute) almost doubled. A procedure in which children recorded their own progress in math on special charts generated much interest but little change in their rates of math progress. A third procedure in which students were required to pass a quiz each week in order to leave class early almost doubled the rate of work. Students in the older group were subsequently permitted to elect a condition in which they did not have to attend class at all if they passed two quizzes per week. Sixty percent of the older students elected to try this procedure. Their rate of work once again doubled. Those students were progressing at four times the normative rate of their public-school-age peers. With the onset of the last two conditions, students began to take initiative for their own academic progress. They began to come to class early to get a fast start. Students also began to voluntarily take some work home. They were beginning to demonstrate behavior that the teachers would call *responsible* (Salzberg, 1972).

Learning to be responsible involves learning to be motivated by longer-term goals, learning self-management strategies, and developing an enlightened self-interest that is reflected in a concern for the rights of others. Thus, in examining leadership processes in the classroom, two intertwined issues must be kept in mind:

1. A technical concern with how group processes can be used to facilitate both the academic and social-emotional goals of schools.

2. A humanistic concern, as expressed by Dewey, that children learn democratic values and actions through the kind of school environments they live in.

Authoritarian verses Democratic Leadership: Some Background Ideas and Research. The pediatricians Aldrich and Aldrich (1941) wrote a book called *Babies Are Human Beings*. The book was designed to help those learning about young children to understand that all infants are different, that they very early are self-directed in different ways, that they have feelings and needs like the rest of us, and that it helps to try to see things from *their perspective*. Children are human beings. They like to have choices and have their views respected.

When one examines the literature on personality development in children (Becker, 1964), there is one correlation that stands out above all others. Parents who are warm, positive, loving, democratic, and so on, have children who are adjusted, intelligent, and outgoing. Parents who are hostile, power-assertive, authoritarian, punitive, and so on, have children who are aggressive and difficult to control (when accompanied by lax or inconsistent discipline) or withdrawn (when accompanied by strict controls). These negative outcomes probably reflect the long-term effects of using shouting and physical punishment to try to "teach" children to behave. Power-assertive parents model aggressive ways and instill anger, fear, and avoidance behavior. Democratic parents provide positive models, direct-verbal guidance about what to do (we call that *teaching*), and reinforce their children for their successes. These studies of parental "leadership styles" have some relevance for understanding of effective teacher leadership styles and give support to Dewey's concern for democratic school processes. While teachers rarely use physical punishment these days, they still can use commands and threats, exclusion, and other power-assertive methods; and they can get angry.

The classic study of group leadership styles by Lewin et al. (1939) is relevant to this issue. In this study, two leadership types were studied in the operation of boys clubs engaged in hobby activities. Some group leaders used an authoritarian approach and some a democratic approach. Because some of the "democratic leaders" failed to exercise much leadership and did not provide their boys with the training to lead themselves, a third group was designated *laissez-faire* after the study got under way (White & Lippitt, 1960).

The autocratic leaders made all group decisions, set project goals, and told the boys in detail how to complete them. They were bosses. They could threaten and reward, but did not let the boys help make decisions on their own. The democratic leaders asked the boys to choose among alternatives, let them know what materials they could work with, and used their expertise in a consultive role when help was needed. The laissez-faire leaders sort of let the boys go their own way, providing little guidance, structure, or technical help.

The "climates" in the three types of groups were quite different. The boys in the autocratic groups produced more "work," but its quality was poorer. In group interpersonal relations, boys in the autocratic groups were more hostile, competitive, and dependent on the leader. The boys in the democratic groups were more open, friendly, and independent of their leaders. In the laissez-faire groups the boys were frustrated, disorganized, and unproductive. The distribution of leadership in the democratic group facilitated better group cohesiveness, as well as better products. Leadership style appears to be important to group accomplishments, as well as social-emotional satisfaction.

Kounin and Gump (1958) evaluated how teachers disciplined students in the classroom using several hundred video taped samples. They found that when teachers were coersive ("Stop that, Bill") there was a resultant current of activity through the peer group that they called the "ripple effect." As we have pointed out in discussing the criticism trap, critical attention to inappropriate behavior can often be reinforcing and increase the very behavior the teacher is trying to reduce. Kounin and Gump found that harsh and critical approaches to problem behavior would stop them temporarily, but the students subsequently became more disruptive. Other observations showed that behavior-specific criticisms ("Take your hands off Jack's book and work on your arithmetic problems") were more likely to be effective. This is analogous to the findings that behavior-specific praise is more effective than "general praise" (Horton, 1975). The studies of reprimands by O'Leary (O'Leary & Becker, 1968; O'Leary et al., 1970) mentioned earlier are also relevant here. O'Leary found that *soft* reprimands (as private as possible) were more effective than *loud* reprimands. The soft-private reprimand does not come across as angry power-assertion, but as concern that the student do better.

Teacher-Directed versus Student-Directed Activities. The social psychology literature has focused on authoritarian versus democratic leadership styles. In this context, one can find several studies to support the Lewin et al. (1939) result that a collaborative-democratic approach fosters a positive and cohesive peer group (such as Anderson, 1970; Withall, 1951). However, reviews by Stern (1962) and McKeachie (1963) suggest that *authoritarian,* teacher-centered leadership is better in transmitting facts and concepts, or at least equal to student-centered approaches. The Follow Through results (Becker and Carnine, 1981; Stebbins et al., 1976, 1977) apparently conflict with these findings. Direct Instruction students showed more significant outcomes in *both academic performance* and measures of *classroom self-esteem* by the end of third grade than did students in child-centered approaches.

These different conclusions are confounded by differences in subject matter and age of students (for example, McKeachie's findings were based on college undergraduates and Abt's on third graders). But another problem that interferes with talking about what is going on here is the use of value-loaded terms like authoritarian and democratic (the bad Hitlers and the good Americans). While hostile power-assertion by individuals and governments is frequently a critical social concern, the equating of teacher-directed activities with power-assertive, authoritarian ways *is not necessarily a correct description of what is happening*. There is no reason that a teacher cannot be a positive, fun-oriented, loving person, *and* actively direct student learning in areas where this is the most effective way to do so. The teacher is an authority (but does not have to be authoritarian). Being in authority is an appropriate role for parents and teachers (Baumrind, 1971). After all, teachers and parents do have the ultimate responsibility for the young and older students in their care.

Affective goals and academic goals in education do not have to be met at the same time, although this is possible in some areas. If the concern is with teaching the group how to learn to work together toward a common goal, then the teacher should provide a democratic role-model, be a facilitator, and serve as a source of advice and expertise. If the concern is with transmitting new information, concepts, rules, and problem-solving strategies in an efficient way, well-designed teacher-directed activities may be most effective for initial teaching, and group procedures may be helpful in teaching broader applications. As students see that *they* gain in power (self-efficacy) through knowledge that is effectively and positively transmitted, they are willing to let the expert be their leader. Again, we must be aware of false dichotomies that can trip up our reasoning.

Robert Benjamin (1981) describes a black ghetto school on the north side of Houston (Wesley School) where in 1975 some 40 percent of the sixth graders could not read at all. Three years after a new principal, Thaddeus Lott, introduced Direct Instruction (DISTAR and related programs), third graders were reading everything placed in front of them. Lorraine Killion, a third grade teacher, stayed with her class through fourth and fifth grades to show what could be done (personal communication). They became "Killion's kids" (with their own T-shirts proclaiming the fact). They won the Houston citywide class attendance award, they astounded medical students at the Houston Medical Center with their knowledge of the muscles and bones of the body and bodily functions (taught through their reading program). They loved school and their teacher and at the end of fifth grade every student who had been in the program for five years qualified on reading and math tests for the Houston gifted program. This is quite a contrast to the effects of the program that preceded Direct Instruction at Wesley school. Teacher-directed instruction is not automatically detrimental to student social-emotional development, and student-directed learning is not automatically beneficial. Much depends on how one goes about it.

In summary, the research findings suggest that discussion methods can be effective in promoting many cognitive and attitudinal goals. The research is not clear on whether discussion methods are better than teacher-directed instruction in many areas, largely because the research has not been precise enough in instructional methodology or group-process methodology to know if current findings are due to method differences or to implementation differences.

However, it remains very apparent that many educational goals involve learning: (1) to work in groups to reach common objectives, (2) to interact and communicate with others, and so forth. These are best practiced in group-interaction settings. This fact alone is enough to justify our interest in group processes.

DEVELOPING GROUP-PROCESS SKILLS

Classroom groups, even in the same grades, are likely to differ in their group skills. Table 11.1 (from Schmuck and Schmuck, 1983, p. 64) summarizes some stages in group process development and important questions to ask for each stage.

Table 11-1 Important questions about group development
(Schmuch & Schmuch, 1983, p. 64)

Stage 1: Facilitating Psychological Membership	*Stage 2: Establishing Shared Influence*	*Stage 3: Pursuing Academic Goals*	*Stage 4: Recognizing Conditions of Self-Renewal*
Are there procedures to get to know everyone?	→	→	→
Is it all right for students to express their fears, concerns, and ideas?	→	→	→
Do students and the teacher listen to one another?	Can the group assess its own functioning?	→	→
Do students interact with a variety of classmates?	Can leadership be shared and rotated?	Are individual differences respected?	→
Is there sensitivity to and appreciation of the different needs and styles of others?	Are new and different ideas listened to and evaluated?	Can the group set some long-range goals?	→
	Are conflicts openly recognized and discussed?	Can students set learning goals for themselves?	Can the group evaluate its own effectiveness?
	Are the skills of all members being used?	Can problems be specified and resolved?	Can the group solve its own problems?
		Can conflict be used creatively?	Can individuals evaluate themselves and set goals for personal improvement?

The Schmucks recommend that the teacher first assess how the class members feel about various group interactions by presenting a set of descriptors to be rated, such as, "It is good to help others with their school work, except on tests." "Quite a few students often go against the teacher." Students rate the descriptors for how they think and for their perception of how many others in the class think the same way (Schmuck & Schmuck, 1983). This gives the teacher an idea about cooperative attitudes, sex-group patterns, and student-teacher attitudes. The Schmucks also describe an observation form that can be used during a group activity each day, early on in the school year. Two student observers (different each day) record examples of "who listened," "who talked," "who gave an idea," and their overall positive or negative reaction to the group. After the observation the class receives a report and discusses ways in which group participation might be improved. This provides training for the observers in discriminating various group processes and also provides feedback to the class.

The various stages of group development shown in Table 11.1 will be examined in sequence.

Stage 1. Facilitating Psychological Membership

The first job is to get students to know more about each other. Members of the class are allowed to freely circulate, and the teacher prompts them with interaction ideas. Students might be asked to, "Find someone they think they have something in common with and talk a few minutes about it"; or "Talk to someone you don't know and learn something about her or him"; or "Find someone you'd like to work with and discuss why."

To facilitate *expressing feelings,* the Schmucks (1983) recommend the game, "Where do I belong?". While milling around in an open area, the teacher asks the students to form groups of four. The teacher does not talk or give any more guidance, but when necessary uses hand signals if a group has more than four members. The rule is that no more than four can be in a group. After the groups are formed, they are asked to tell (in their groups) how they felt about the process. Did they feel excluded? Were they attracted or repelled by some groups? What led them to feel accepted or rejected? Next, the whole class works together to develop a list of actions that meant acceptance and actions that meant rejection, and perhaps, a list of how it felt when they thought they were rejected. Then, ways in which new members might be helped to be accepted in the group are discussed.

Building a biography book is another way to get to know others. Each student is expected to write a biography on another. The class as a group plans an outline of questions to be asked, students are paired off, interviews are conducted, and biographies prepared. They are placed in a book. The Schmucks report that one teacher used the books for supplemental reading in groups each day. It would also be possible to have authors give oral reports (perhaps five a day over a week) and allow questions.

Obviously, there are many creative ways to help students to get to know each other and at the same time for you to get to know them. The key is to let your students know this is important to you by allowing time for it.

Stage 2. Establishing Shared Influence

The concern here is sharing between students, as well as between teacher and students. After having set up a topic for discussion, the teacher fosters listening and communication skills by having a student paraphrase what the previous speaker said. The teacher follows the same rule, and sometimes asks for additional students to give their paraphrase. One way of preventing a few students from dominating discussion and making students conscious of the right of all to participate is to hand out 2 or 3 tokens (poker chips) to each student. When a student makes a contribution to the discussion, she or he gives up a token. When her or his tokens are gone, the student might be allowed to comment on the group process, but not make other content contributions.

Another way to get more participation is to break up into small groups ("buzz groups") for 3 to 5 minutes to discuss some controversial issue that students might feel hesitant about discussing in a large group. A group reporter could then present a summary to the class at the termination of the small groups. A final procedure suggested by the Schmucks for getting participation by all in a large group is called "fishbowl." A small group meets in the middle of a circle formed by the rest of the class. Extra chairs are provided in the center so that members of the outer circle can join the small group when they have something to contribute.

Stage 3. Pursuing Academic Goals

There are a variety of ways to pursue academic goals, such as discussion groups, project groups, cooperative-learning groups, peer tutoring, and ensembles.

Discussion Groups. Discussion groups are especially popular at the secondary level in the "low-consensus" fields, but this does not mean they are not appropriate for elementary students. They certainly are. The following paragraphs describe a typical procedure for setting up a discussion group:

- *Assign a reading or activity* (text, library, newspaper, TV show, movie, tape recording, or other source) covering the topic for discussion. Provide a set of study questions that will focus the discussion. (Other questions can be brought in, of course, but this provides a common ground for discussion.) The range of topics will depend on the subject area and level, but they can range from environmental issues, to pros and cons on presidential candidates, to the causes of the Civil War, to the nature of light or gravity, to analysis of a literary or musical work.

- *Assume the role of moderator* at the time set aside for the discussion. If an agenda has not been set through study questions, then the first step is to establish one. When the discussion is focused on an assignment, the teacher's role is to *orient the group* to the task. "For the next 45 minutes, we are going to discuss the pros and cons of the Republican and Democratic candidates for president. The study questions are on the board. Would anyone like to add other questions? . . . All right, let's consider the first question, 'What are the major problems the next president is likely to be facing?' " During the discussion the teacher may take notes and from time to time make *summarizing statements.* This provides feedback to the students of what the teacher heard being said. The teacher may also make *procedural statements* such as, "We have 15 minutes left. How would you like to spend it? Should we move to the next question?" The teacher also notes illogical arguments and inaccurate facts. These reactions should be shared briefly in a matter-of-fact manner with the group. Other moderator functions might include taking a *survey* to see if a consensus has been reached if the group is trying to make a decision; noting students who are not participating much and trying to draw them in; *giving positive comments* to the group when it is appropriate; and commenting on progress, digressions, and so forth. Finally, there are some *debriefing* questions to be asked. "What did (didn't) you like about today's discussion?"

Try to avoid leading questions and giving your position on the issue early in the discussion. You may decide not to express your opinion at all or to bring it in later where this is appropriate (perhaps through pointed questions).

Project Groups and Cooperative-learning Groups. In a project group, a group of four to eight members is assigned or selects an end product they are to achieve through cooperative action. The project might involve presenting a skit to the class dramatizing some historical event. This could require library research, script writing, costume making, designing a set and backdrop, and acting. It might be producing a class newsletter. This might involve delimiting the news areas that might be covered, making assignments to reporters, writing stories, typing, editing, layout, and printing. Group projects can be developed for many areas of the curriculum—bookmaking, play writing, redoing a classic experiment in physics or chemistry, construction projects, or cooking.

In a cooperative-learning group, the group is assigned or selects an area of knowledge to synthesize and report on it (for each other). The group must divide up the work and make a plan of action. Eventually, each member helps other groups' members understand what they have learned. The goal is to reduce the individual effort needed to study and research an area of knowledge and at the same time make studying a more social, cooperative activity. These kinds of groups are probably more likely to be used in the low-consensus areas, where a variety of sources might need to be consulted to formulate a comprehensive picture of the state of knowledge in the area.

For project and cooperative groups, it is helpful, initially, for the teacher to provide the group with an overall *strategy* of action. The group then works out the details of plan and the teacher reviews the plan for groups new to the process before work begins. For experienced groups, the teacher is available as a consultant on request. The groups might be given a strategy something like this (compare Sharan and Hertz-Lazarowitz, 1981):

1. Clearly define your goal(s). (Sound familiar?)

2. Define subgoals that can be undertaken by individual group members or pairs of students.

3. Make a specific plan of action. This should include assignments and timelines (times when the group needs to meet to review progress and perhaps make changes).

4. Complete the plan.

5. Evaluate the adequacy of the group process and the product.

Peer Tutoring. Peer tutoring has been found to have benefits for the tutor as well "the tutee." Academic learning gains have been found to occur for the tutor and the tutee, and the tutor has an opportunity to experience a leadership role. Greenwood, Delquardi, and Hall (1984) and others (see Ellson, 1976) have emphasized that in one-on-one teaching (as tutoring is), there is a great opportunity to: (1) individualize instruction, (2) provide many more opportunities to make relevant academic responses, and (3) give immediate feedback (corrections, reinforcement) to students. The research by Greenwood et al., has demonstrated the academic value of peer tutoring in reading and spelling.

The procedures used by Greenwood et al., involve the teacher training all class members in a tutoring procedure. The program and procedures are briefly described, and then *demonstrated* by the teacher and a student who has been briefed on the procedures. Care is taken to show how errors are corrected and how points are awarded by the tutor. The students go through a practice on tabulating points and reporting them. The next day the procedures are reviewed and the students pair up and try out the procedures. The teacher circulates and checks out the tutors. During actual tutoring sessions, the teacher sets up the pairs (or allows students to choose partners), times the session, lets tutor and tutee know when to switch roles (5 to 15 minutes, depending on the task), monitors, helps as needed, and tabulates and posts points earned by each student.

How the task is set up, whether a point system is used, length of sessions, and method of recording progress will vary. However, it is important to establish a specified set of procedures for the students to follow and to train them with it. It is also a good idea to seek student feedback on how it is going. They may have some good ideas for making the procedures more effective.

Ensembles. As noted in Chapter 9, performing groups (ensembles) in music (bands, orchestras, choruses) can be organized so that peers can help tutor each other and record data on each other's progress. Keep in mind that such procedures might also be appropriate for other kinds of performing groups, such as dance groups, theatrical groups, and athletic teams. Practicing lines in theater or steps in dance can be set up as a peer-tutoring activity or a section-leader activity.

Role Playing and Simulations. When simulations involve only people, they are fundamentally role playing. (Of course, human computer simulations are beginning to deal with issues of ecology, diet and health, the economy, international relations, and so on). Role playing is a technique that has been used as a part of psychotherapy. It has many potential applications in schools, especially when the goal is to understand both sides of a problem involving value conflicts in a multivalue society. It can be useful in teaching "empathy" and in teaching conflict-resolution strategies. Some common issues for role playing might involve: the relevance of homework or a particular required course, current or past political issues, breaking the law, issues of school rules, race issues, and sexism issues. In addition to focusing on value conflicts, role playing is useful in improving communication among class members and developing personal communication skills.

Setting up a role playing sequence requires: (1) selecting an issue; (2) describing the roles of the participants and the audience, being careful to outline the issues on each side; (3) carrying out the action; (4) having the audience discuss what happened; (5) deciding how it might have been handled better; (6) replaying the action; and (7) discussing the personal relevance of what was learned.

Stage 4. Self-Renewal

As a group matures in its ability to work cohesively, you should look for new goals and procedures. It may be time to simplify a point system or eliminate it all together. It may be time for students to be more self-directed in some areas. From time to time, the teacher should seek group feedback on how things are going, what the members like and do not like about the process in place, and what their suggestions are for making the class a better place for learning to occur.

DEALING WITH CONFLICT

Conflicts have to do with incompatible activities (Deutsch, 1973). Within the individual, the old adage "You can't have your cake and eat it, too" expresses one kind of conflict. Between individuals, conflict arises when what one person wants to do is blocked, resisted, or punished by another. Conflict can also exist between incompatible values and ideas: One spouse believes in God and the other does not, and they can't leave it at that. Each one tries to convince the other that she or he is right.

No one can go through life without facing conflicts. That is another fact of life. So it is important to learn how to understand conflicts and how to resolve or otherwise deal with them. Group interactions in the classroom provide examples of conflict and opportunities for teachers to help their students learn to deal with them. A conflict can have a "productive outcome" if both parties feel they gained from the outcome (Deutsch, 1973). Destructive outcomes occur when someone (or both) lose, and animosity is generated.

Types of Conflict

Schmuck and Schmuck (1983) distinguish three types of conflicts between individuals—conceptual conflicts, goal conflicts, and procedural conflicts.

Conceptual Conflicts are diagreements over facts, theories, and opinions. People interpret the same situation in different ways. Do you view human action from the inside (cognitive theory) or from the outside (behavior theory)? Should women stay in the home and be mothers or have the same freedom of activities as men? Is abortion murder or an important option for women? Did we evolve through evolution or were we created? Conflicts between members of close-knit peer groups (in-group versus out-group) are conceptual conflicts. Conflicts over grading criteria can be conceptual conflicts. Conflicts of this sort often motivate heated interchanges and can often be used to facilitate learning, if they are not allowed to get out of hand.

Goal Conflicts are disagreements over the value of various options for action. Mom wants Jim to study; Jim wants to watch TV. Mary wants to drive; dad thinks she is too young to drive. Bill's teacher is concerned with academic performance; Bill is more interested in his friends. As the Schmucks point out, when student goals and teacher goals are in conflict, the responsibility falls on the teacher to find ways to encourage (reinforce) students to work toward the teacher's goals (assuming they are in the student's best long-term interest). Carefully specified course objectives (which the students are aware of) and a system of monitoring progress toward those objectives can help keep students and teacher working toward the same goals. Many of the value conflicts mentioned in the discussion of role playing are goal conflicts.

Procedural Conflicts involve disagreements on how to reach a goal. They are usually the easiest to solve. Procedural conflicts often arise in the classroom when the rules are not clearly spelled out ahead of time by the teacher or in joint planning with the students. Homework is not turned in or is turned in a day late by some students and the teacher marks a −10 in the grade book. The students argue that it is unfair. "You didn't tell us you would penalize us if it was late." Procedural conflicts can arise in planning a course of action for a group project.

Solutions

Often, just classifying what kind of conflict you are dealing with will take you a long way toward a solution. When dealing with a conceptual conflict, the solution requires looking together for more information. In a goal conflict, you can decide to agree, agree to disagree, or compromise on some in-between goal. In a procedural conflict, an attempt is made to assess the effects of the alternative procedures. An agreement is sought to try one way and see how it works. The issue is re-evaluated later.

Conflicts can also be purely personal. Because of the way two people interact, they can decide they do not like each other. One tries to dominate or make a fool of the other, and the other retaliates. The solution to interpersonal conflict is not always easy. If the combatants do not have to interact, they can just part company. If they do have to interact, they need to try to talk it through or get the help of a mediator. In the classroom, the teacher is often the mediator. Marriage counselors are often put in the mediator position, helping to sort out goal aspects of conflicts from the emotion. Often *restructuring* what appears to be an emotional conflict ("The way she is, I just don't like her." "He is just a mean person! I can't stand him.") into a goal conflict ("You would like to have sex more often with her, and she would like you to spend more time talking to her.") can lead to effective solutions.

Group norms can also play a role in conflicts. If the norm is a competitive one, conflict is more likely to arise than if it is a cooperative one. As we mentioned in discussing coaching goals, competing against a personal goal can lead to more success (and less conflict). In the classroom, grading against a standard (rather than a normal curve) and encouraging cooperative learning can also help to reduce conflict (Deutsch, 1973).

SUMMARY

The classroom is a group and the literature on group processes has some valuable ideas for the teacher to consider in working toward learning goals that involve academic skills; communication processes; democratic processes; and students' feelings and attitudes about themselves, each other, and their teacher.

The research on group dynamics suggests that small groups (of four to eight members) are more satisfying to group members. Task oriented groups are more effective when their members have different skills to contribute and differing viewpoints (heterogeneous groups). Cohesiveness among class members can be an asset to the teacher if the group norms are consistent with the teacher's goals. Cohesive groups interact with each other more in positive ways, are more likely to exclude members with differing views and show greater resistance to attitude change. The structure of communication patterns in a group have effects on what transpires. In lecture classrooms, those in best eye contact with the teacher (front and center seats) participate more. Where discussion is the goal, a circular-seminar format that maximizes eye contact of members with each other leads to the most interaction.

Classroom leadership styles have ranged from student-centered and student-directed approaches, to teacher as a democratic leader, to teacher-directed (and sometimes teacher-dominated) interactions. For student-directed learning to work, the students must have first learned how to responsibly manage their own behavior toward well-chosen goals. It is important to recognize that the teacher is the educational leader in the classroom and must seek to use his or her behavior in ways that best help to reach the learning goals. This may at times be accomplished through organizing group processes so that students assist each other or work toward common goals. At other times, teacher-directed (authoritative, not authoritarian) learning may be the method of choice. Studies of leadership style show that "democratic climates" foster more friendly, open interactions than "authoritarian" or "laissez-faire" climates.

Discussion methods can be used to promote a variety of cognitive and affective goals. They are not necessarily better for all instruction, but they certainly have an important role to fill in teaching students to work together toward group goals, to interact and communicate effectively, to evaluate conflicting theories and information, and so on.

It is important to recognize that the development of an effective group involves stages; it is a building process. The members first need to learn to know each other better and to feel comfortable communicating feelings. Then, a feeling of shared influence among members (including the teacher) needs to be established, and the teacher fosters listening and communication skills (including paraphrasing), uses procedures that prevent dominance of the group by a few members, and uses buzz groups. Then, procedures for pursuing academic goals and group self-renewal can be introduced.

Group methods for pursuing academic goals involve discussion groups, project groups, cooperative-learning groups, peer tutoring, cooperative procedures for use by performing arts groups, and role playing.

Effective discussion groups usually first cover a common reading and study questions. Then a discussion is held, with the teacher serving as moderator. The teacher orients the group to the topic, makes summary statements, and provides suggestions to keep the group moving toward its goals. At the end, the teacher leads a debriefing that evaluates progress.

In setting up project groups and cooperative-learning groups, the teacher (initially) needs to help the group develop a working strategy, such as: (1) define goals; (2) define subgoals for different individuals or pairs of individuals; (3) make a plan that includes individual assignments, timelines, and plans for group review; (4) complete the plan; and (5) evaluate the product and the process.

In using peer tutoring, it is important to train tutors in appropriate procedures. Peer tutoring has much promise for better individualization of instruction.

Role playing is especially useful in teaching students about conflicting values and in learning to taken another's point of view. A seven-step strategy for "staging" a role play was discussed.

In teaching about and dealing with conflicts, it helps to recognize three kinds of conflicts—conceptual conflicts, goal conflicts, and procedural conflicts. Conceptual conflicts deal with questions of fact or information and can be solved by getting more information. Goal conflicts deal with differing values and are more difficult to solve. The choices are to compromise, agree to disagree, or decide to agree. Procedural conflicts are usually easier to solve by agreeing to try one way and evaluate it. If it does not work out, another approach is tried next time.

Personal conflicts involve not liking someone else (for whatever reason). They can sometimes be solved through discussion, through converting personal conflicts to one of the three types of conflicts just mentioned, or through use of a mediator or counselor. Competitive group norms encourage conflict. Developing more cooperative group norms can help to reduce conflict.

PART II

THE DESIGN OF QUALITY INSTRUCTION

Part II of this text concerns how to design quality instruction to teach concepts, rules, and other intellectual skills. The information in these seven chapters is not found in most other educational psychology texts. Some of it is difficult, because many new concepts are involved. However, your *Workbook* is designed to help you come to grips with this new learning. The material in these chapters is important in helping teachers to understand good textbook design when they see it. These chapters are also important in helping one develop effective teaching strategies.

Chapter 12 opens with an analysis of several mastery-learning models of instruction that have grown out of research on *effective teaching practices*—practices found to produce better student learning. Mastery-learning models have a number of common features that are consistent with the behavior theory principles you have been studying. They are aimed at getting the student engaged in meaningful learning and keeping both teacher and student informed about what is being (or not being) learned. The major deficiency of many of these models is that even though they produce better learning compared with traditional teaching methods, they often fail to present quality instructional sequences—sequences designed to be efficient and to provide for generalized applications of what is taught.

Chapter 13 addresses issues that underlie a *theory of instruction.* To design instruction that teaches efficiently and provides for generalization, it is necessary to add to our analysis of behavior (represented by mastery-learning models) an analysis of *knowledge types* and an analysis of the *communication sequences* used to teach students knowledge of a given type. Chapter 13 examines the structure of types of knowledge. Chapters 14 through 17 examine more promising approaches to ways of designing the communications to teach different kinds of knowledge.

Finally, Part II closes with an examination of problem-solving strategies and related metacognitive processes. What do we know about teaching skills for dealing with problems when we do not know the answer?

The ideas in these chapters are very important for teachers. They can help you understand better why some approaches to teaching work and others do not. While it will take some effort for you to achieve mastery of these chapters, the effort is likely to pay off in the future.

If you are preparing for special subject areas such as art, physical education, and music, you may not believe at first that these chapters are relevant to you. The examples in these chapters are derived from teaching cognitive skills. Keep in mind that there are cognitive skills involved in music, understanding football strategies, and evaluating art. The principles to be presented have direct applications to *all* areas of learning, even though good analyses of those applications may have not yet been made. Maybe some of you will be the ones to bridge the gap.

CHAPTER

12

MASTERY-LEARNING-BASED MODELS OF INSTRUCTION—THE BASIC STRUCTURE OF EFFECTIVE TEACHING

Until about ten years ago, most reviews of research on teaching methods had concluded that as long as the relevant content was covered, one method was as good as another. However, improved research designs in the past decade have consistently shown that a pattern of teaching practices that Rosenshine (1976, 1980) labeled "direct instruction" leads to better student outcomes in reading and math (Stebbins, et al, 1977; Anderson, Evertson, & Brophy, 1979; Becker & Carnine, 1980; Bloom, 1984; Brophy & Evertson, 1974, 1976; Fisher, Filby, Marilave, Cahen, Dishow, Moore, & Berliner, 1978; Good, 1979; Rosenshine, 1976, Stallings & Kaskowitz, 1974; Stallings, Needles, & Stayrock, 1979; and many others). Better gains are found for elementary and secondary students where the teacher is an active planner and leader of instructional activities, where the teacher paces instruction rapidly, requires frequent student responding, provides feedback and corrections, and uses teacher-directed rather than individual or self-directed activities. These findings are interpreted as procedures that foster more *academic engaged time* and *mastery learning*. Rosenshine also calls this basic model a demonstration-practice-feedback approach.

Note: This research does not mean there is not a role for group discussion, cooperative-group learning, tutoring, seatwork activities, self-directed learning, and other learning formats. The comparative research has not ruled out "good models" of these activities, and logically, there is no reason these activities could not be structured to be effective. It is possible to make almost any method work for some learning goals, if you understand what the critical variables are. However, it may be that some methods still are more effective for the majority of goals.

From Chapter 2 on you have been learning a model of teaching derived from behavioral research on learning processes. The simplest form of this was the S → R → S model for operant learning. In the presence of a task stimulus (S^d), get an appropriate task response to occur (R) (usually by providing a model), and provide reinforcement (S^r) (or a correction if the desired response did not occur). Chapters 3 to 6 elaborated on this model in discussing a variety of strategies for strengthening, weakening, and maintaining behavior. In discussing special reinforcement systems (Chapter 7), other components were added to a model of good teaching: specifying your goals, specifying your rules, and setting up monitoring and recording systems. Chapter 8 looked at organizational strategies at both the elementary and secondary levels for dealing with total classrooms in ways that would teach group rules, let the students know what was expected of them, keep track of progress, keep motivation going, and have the students provide you with help in working together. Chapter 9 extended these basic teaching ideas to physical education, coaching, and music education. This chapter examines a number of highly related, mastery-learning models of instruction that share many properties with the behavioral model we have been developing.

FEATURES COMMON TO MASTERY-LEARNING MODELS

The following features are common to most (but not all) of these models:

1. Objectives are specified, along with subobjectives grouped in small units for instruction.
2. Preskills are tested to ensure that placement is appropriate.
3. Procedures are developed to motivate and engage the student in active learning. These include reinforcement for working hard, for improvement, and for success.
4. Attempts are made to develop "quality instruction" that teaches the targeted objectives effectively and efficiently.
5. Differential time is allowed for different students to reach mastery.
6. Ungraded, frequent testing is provided to monitor progress during early learning and provide feedback to the student.
7. Corrective-remedial procedures are provided if an approach fails.
8. Adequate practice to mastery of subskills is provided.
9. There is testing for longer-term mastery of objectives.

EARLY APPROACHES

In the 1920s two approaches to mastery learning programs were developed in the Chicago area. Carleton Washburne (1922) developed what came to be called the Winnetka Plan, and Henry C. Morrison (1926) at the University of Chicago Laboratory School developed what came to be called the Morrison method. In each approach there was:

- A definition of educational objectives.
- Instruction organized around well-defined units.
- Complete mastery of each unit before progressing to the next.
- An ungraded, diagnostic-progress test at the end of each unit. This provided feedback to the students on what remediation was need.

- Supplemental instruction as needed.
- Allowance for the time necessary to meet mastery.

SKINNER'S FIRST TEACHING MACHINE

The Morrison method faded sometime in the 1930s, and little can be identified as a mastery learning strategy until the development of programed instruction by B. F. Skinner (1954). After a visit to his daughter's fourth grade math class on November 11, 1953, he went home and constructed his first "teaching machine" to teach math facts (Vargis, 1984).[1] Like many of us who have spent time in elementary classrooms, Skinner was appalled by the active learning that *was not* taking place. His first machine permitted students to proceed at their own rate. It presented problems, and the student answered. Then, using a slider device, the student found out immediately if she or he was right and was corrected when wrong. This was a simple drill and practice device, but it opened up several decades of extensive work in programed instruction and the use of teaching machines.

Programed learning was based on the assumption that any complex discrimination or skill could be broken down into simpler component tasks that could be taught in small steps, building up the more complex behavior with a high rate of success at each step. If the task were analyzed properly, potentially any student could be brought to mastery of it. The "machines" (some were programed textbooks) were the ideal, patient "tutor" if they were programed to: (1) teach efficiently, (2) anticipate where mistakes would be made, and (3) provide appropriate corrections. They were also the "ideal" mastery learning teacher. Right responses were reinforced and errors immediately corrected.

The promise of programed instruction was so great in the 1960s that two major efforts were made to build full elementary curricula in reading and math, and one in science. These were the University of Pittsburgh's Individually Prescribed Instruction (IPI) developed by Robert Glaser (1967), and Stanford's computer-assisted instruction (CAI) developed by Richard Atkinson (1968) and Patrick Suppes (1966).

INDIVIDUALLY PRESCRIBED INSTRUCTION

IPI uses team teaching, nongraded classrooms, programed instruction, and systematic testing. The curriculum material is sequentially ordered into tracks of skills (called a *continuum of objectives*) that build upon one another. Figure 12.1 shows the gross structure of the levels (like grade levels, but ungraded), and the different tracks within the first four levels. Figure 12.2 shows a few sequences of tasks within levels C and D math (from Eichelberger, 1975).

Placement tests (general screening) and pretests (diagnostic for precise placement) determine what lessons should be worked on or skipped. If the student passes a short curriculum-embedded test (CET), she or he can take the posttest. The student must pass the posttest at an 85 percent score before moving on. Students work on their own much of the time, but help is available from teachers and aides when needed. The process followed by teachers and aides is illustrated in Figure 12.3 (Eichelberger, 1975). Follow the numbers around the circle to see the process.

As step 2 in Figure 12.3 suggests, IPI uses a variety of instructional tasks. These include thousands of worksheets, records or audio tapes, programed

[1]The first teaching machine was invented by Sidney L. Pressey in 1926. The device was designed to give tests and to facilitate scoring, but it turned out to teach as well.

Progress Summary
Follow Through 1974–75

IPI MATH
(new)
Levels A–D

- \- Completed last year
- X Placement tested out of
- M Worked in *and* mastered
- P Pre-tested out of
- • Currently working

District *Happytown*
Building *Lowel*
Teacher *Brown*
Grade *1* Room *12*
Date *October 20*

Name	Level A							Level B											Level C												Level D									
	NPI	NPII	ASI	ASII	Fr	Mon	Time	NP	ASI	ASII	Mult	Div	Fr	Mon	Time	SoM	Geom	App	NPI	NPII	ASI	ASII	Mult	Div	Fr	Mon	Time	SoM	Geom	App	NP	AS	Mult	Div	Fr	Mon	Time	SoM	Geom	App
Mark	X	X	X	M	X	M	X	X	M	X	•																													
Julie	X	X	M	X	M	M	•	•																																
Wes	X	X	X	X	X	X	X	X	X	X	X	M	X	X	X	M	M	M	M	•																				
John	X	P	X	P	M	M	X	M	•																															
Angie	X	X	X	M	X	X	M	M	M	M	M	•																												
Linda	X	X	X	M	X	M	M	X	M	X	M	M	M	M	•																									
Jeff	X	X	X	P	M	M	M	•																																
Ken	X	M	M	M	X	M	•																																	
Jill	M	M	M	M	•																																			

NP	Numeration/Place Value	Mult	Multiplication
AS	Addition/Subtraction	Div	Division
Fr	Fractions	SoM	Systems of Measurement
Mon	Money	Geom	Geometry
Time	Time	App	Applications

Figure 12-1 *Completed Progress Summary*

level C	level D
Numeration	
1. Reads, writes numerals 1-200. Sequence from any starting point. 2. Supplies number 1 more, or less, or in between—1 to 200. 3. Skip counts 2's, 5's, 10's to 200.	1. Reads, writes to 1,000. Any point. 2. Skip counts, by 3's, 4's from any point. 3. (a) Identifies and reads decimal fractions to hundredths. (b) Converts decimal numbers to fractions and other forms. (c) Fills in missing single decimals.
Place Value	
1. Identifies place value of the units, 10's, 100's, to 200. Indicates >, <. 2. Writes numbers, columns 100's, 10's, units.	1. Identifies units, 10's, 100's, 1000's. Uses >, <. Writes number before, after to 1,000. 2. Writes numerals, expanded notation, to 1,000. Regroups, renames.

	3. Uses number families, bridging, to work addition, subtraction problems. 4. (a) Gives place value of decimal fractions in fractional or other form. (b) Makes place value chart.
Addition	
1. Use of associative principle. 2. Adds 2 numbers—sum of 20. 3. Sums of 2 or 3 numbers, no carrying. 4. Uses $>$, $<$, $=$. Equations, 2 step, combining add-subtract. 5. Works column addition—3 or more addends, sums to 20.	1. Demonstrates mastery, sums thru 20. 2. Does column addition—no carrying. 3. Finds missing addends—3 single digits. 4. Uses words, sum, addend—labels part. 5. Adds, carrying to 10's using 2 digit numerals, 2 or more addends. 6. Adds, carrying to 10's, 100's, using 3 digit numerals, 2 or more addends. 7. Adds, carry 10's 100's, using 3 digit numerals, 2 or more addends. 8. Finds sums, column addition. Using 2 or more addends of 1 digit.
Subtraction	
1. Subt. problems—numbers to 18. 2. Subt. 2 digit—no borrowing. 3. Finds missing addend—2 single digits.	1. Mastery subtraction facts, numbers to 20. 2. Subtraction no borrowing—3 or more digits. 3. Subtraction borrowing 10's place—2 digits. 4. Subtraction borrowing 10's, 100's—3 digits. 5. Subtraction borrowing 10's, 100's—3 digits.

Figure 12-2 Mathematics continuum for IPI

readers (McGraw-Hill Sullivan Readers), filmstrips combined with audio tapes, tutoring, and small-group instruction. Individual student folders are used for making daily assignments, to provide the worksheets for the day, and to chart individual progress. This is a most valuable tool for teacher and student in keeping track of progress.

The heart of IPI is its continuum of objectives and the tests built around them. Its greatest weakness (as I experienced it through the early 1970s) was its heavy dependence on worksheets from traditional workbooks, which really just tested or gave practice, but did not teach. With disadvantaged students using early forms of IPI, it was often necessary to devise small-group, teacher-directed instruction for each new skill. This was less necessary with middle-class

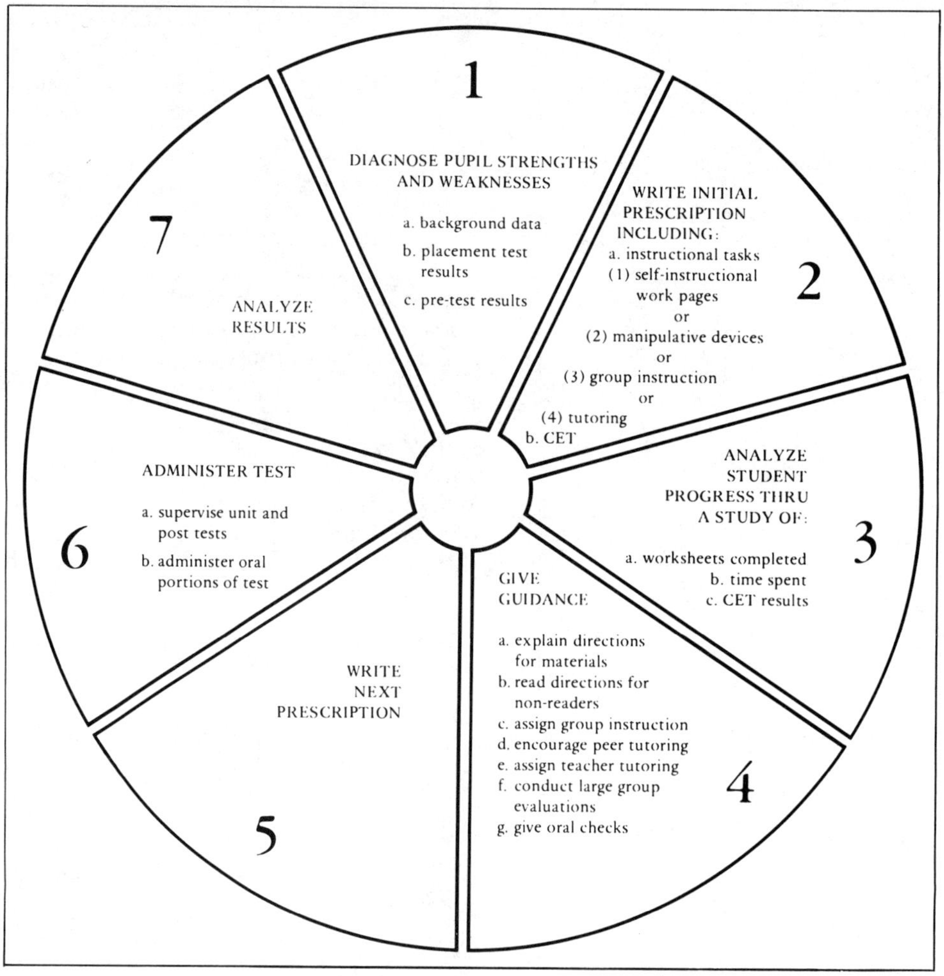

Figure 12-3 *Teacher functions for Individually Prescribed Instruction*

students. The model also did not provide sufficient practice in ***oral communication skills*** for lower-performing students.

The strength of the IPI is in its mastery-learning framework and its hierarchical structure (learn basic skills to master, as demonstrated by a test, before going on to more complex tasks that use those skills). This allows the teacher to know "who is learning what," so that corrective action can be taken where needed. The individualization allows the faster learners to progress into new learning without being limited by a "grade-level" text, and slower learners to work to mastery.

Later versions of IPI incorporated Computer Management of Instruction. This reduced the clerical time needed.

COMPUTER-ASSISTED INSTRUCTION[2]

Computer-assisted instruction (CAI) is the most elaborate example of mastery learning based on programed instruction and teaching machines. In CAI, the student communicates with a computer that keeps careful records of the student's responses to each step in the program and makes decisions on what to teach next. The Stanford Tutorial System, built under the direction of Suppes in

[2]Obviously, the microcomputer revolution is drastically changing the nature of CAI; Chapter 28 discusses the impact of the microcomputer as a teaching medium.

math and Atkinson in reading, is an example of a quite advanced system. The goals of the programs were to teach all phases of beginning reading and math skills (Atkinson, 1968). The student station consisted of a television monitor, a film projector system, a keyboard, an earphone set, and a light pen that could be used to make responses to questions on the monitor screen. A later, cheaper model used only a keyboard and an audio headset (Atkinson, 1974). The heart of the system was an IBM mainframe computer. As many as 2,000 students a day in different parts of the country could use the computer for reading and math lessons through telephone line connections.

Most students found the programs fun. After the student logged in, the computer picked up instruction from where the student left off last time. Light arrows and recorded audio messages were used to prompt attention to critical features on the screen. A standard signal was used to let the student know the teacher (computer) wanted a response. For every "frame" of instruction, a student response was required and evaluated. When an error occurred, a branch program provided a correction. Correct responses were reinforced by words from the audio unit such as "great," "fantastic," and "good." The computer can be a good reinforcer and is very patient with mistakes.

Evaluation of student progress and remediation reaches a potentially ideal form with CAI. The record keeping and testing feature of CAI is most valuable. It has the ultimate long-term potential for delivering mastery learning to most students, especially if coupled with a videodisc system (see Chapter 28).

The cost of the *revised* (low-cost) Stanford system for teaching reading (getting the student to grade level by the end of third grade) was about 55 cents per student per day (10 years ago), or $291 for three years of daily lessons running 15 to 30 minutes each. Using the low-cost system, Fletcher and Atkinson (1972) compared 44 matched pairs of first graders. Those taught with 8 to 10 minutes of CAI reading per day for five months, scored five months ahead of the control group in reading achievement. They were still 4.9 months higher a year later, even though they had no more CAI. Vinsonhaler and Bass (1972) in a review covering some 10,000 students in many different experiments concluded that augmenting traditional instruction with CAI improves performance on achievement tests.

KELLER'S PERSONALIZED SYSTEM OF INSTRUCTION (PSI)

This mastery learning system was first introduced in 1964 by Fred Keller at the University of Brasilia (1968). Keller had just retired from Columbia University and was facing the problem of teaching introductory psychology to classes where many students had a very limited range of verbal skills, especially in English. Since 1964, there have been many research studies on PSI, and some PSI instruction occurs in many universities and secondary schools. PSI is a more elaborate version of the Morrison Method with a few special twists.

- The course is broken down into small units (perhaps by chapters if the text is suitable for this).
- Objectives for each unit (questions to be answered) are provided in advance.
- When the student thinks he or she is ready to take a test on a unit, a "readiness" test (there are four test forms for each unit) is given which takes about ten to fifteen minutes of writing. Proctors (students who have previously passed the course) immediately grade the paper with the student watching. If there are too many wrong answers, the

student is advised to study some more. If there are only two or three errors, the proctor will ask the student to defend his or her answers orally. The system is aimed at showing understanding of principles and not just memorizing some statements in the text. If the student passes, he or she is congratulated and is given the questions for the next unit.

- A final examination is given covering the course (to ensure review and integration), which counts 25 percent of the grade. The other 75 percent is allocated according to the number of units completed.
- Lectures and demonstrations are scheduled occasionally, but the student must be at a certain course level to attend specified lectures. The lectures are not required and do not count toward a grade. Keller used them as reinforcers for making so much progress by a certain time. (He was a very exciting lecturer.)
- Class periods are typically used for studying and taking checkouts.

This method has been quite successful. A key feature of the Keller method is the requirement of considerable written and oral responses. This ensures that the student can talk about and write about what he or she is learning in his or her own words. Several studies support the value of using proctors. Farmer, Lachter, Blaustein, and Cole (1972) varied the number of units proctored and found better performance on the final exam when more units were proctored, and the students made faster progress through the course. Another study has shown that if the performance criterion on unit tests is set higher, the student performance is higher (Johnston and O'Neill, 1973). When grades are made contingent on level of performance, performance is higher (Semb, Hopkins, and Hursh, 1973). Bostow and O'Connor (1973) found that requiring the student to redo a unit if performance was below 90 percent increased the group performance by one-half of a letter grade.

In various comparison studies of the Keller method at the college level, most of the PSI groups outperform traditional lecture method. Block and Burns (1976) found that in 21 of 24 comparisons, PSI students did better, and in 17 of the 24 the difference was statistically significant. In a review of reviews, Johnson and Ruskin (1977) reported that most studies favored PSI. Robin (1976) reported that the average size of the effect was 9 percent, or one letter grade, favoring PSI.

One outstanding study by Thompson (1980) failed to verify that PSI students perform better than a well-designed lecture-discussion program in freshman calculus at the Air Force Academy. Both approaches were equally effective on a wide range of measures. Thompson notes that more than 85 percent of the PSI studies have been conducted on courses in the social sciences, and only 15 percent involved math and math-related subjects. In this study, the lecture discussion program was well-designed and taught by outstanding instructors whose main basis for promotion was excellence in teaching (not research). Thompson concluded that his findings do not imply that PSI approaches are not good, but that its superiority in other research is probably due to the relative weakness in the way traditional lecture-discussion courses are presented in many institutions of higher learning.

PRECISION TEACHING

Precision Teaching was developed as a mastery-learning model by Ogden Lindsley (1971; Kunzelmann, 1970). Lindsley was a student of B. F. Skinner's. The heart of Precision Teaching is the use of procedures for the daily measurement of improvement on some target behaviors. Most often a rate measures is taken (responses per minute) and the students chart their daily progress on their own graphs. If the behavior requires an oral response, the teacher, aide, or another student will time a thirty-second or one-minute performance each day when the student is ready. If the measure involves a written response, then a group might be tested at the same time. A key to Precision Teaching is learning to state learning objectives in terms of observable behaviors (pinpointing). Next, a way of measuring the rate of pinpointed behavior must be found, and finally, a charting procedure established. Assuming that key teaching goals have been identified by the measurement procedures, teacher and students get daily feedback on their progress. This feedback motivates both students and teachers.

According to Lindsley (1984), research and writing about Precision Teaching appears to be fading, having peaked about 1975. One problem has been the need for teachers to develop their own sets of objectives. Unless Precision Teaching is tied in with a systematic curriculum, it is likely to flounder. Another problem is that many in the field have overemphasized the virtue of rate measures, when in much new learning (as Lindsley notes) accuracy is more important at first. Rate becomes important after accuracy is good, and you want to speed up the use of basic skills for use in more complex tasks. Rate measures are also inappropriate as tests of concept learning and logical processes. However, a key procedure in Precision Teaching—the daily charting of progress by students—can be used by any teacher for key skills. Most kindergarten and first grade students can be taught to read graphs and chart their own progress. Students find this very reinforcing.

BLOOM'S MASTERY LEARNING

Bloom's Mastery-Learning strategy (Bloom, 1976; Block, 1971) was derived in part from John Carroll's (1963) model of school learning (1963) and is clearly supported by the related models described in this chapter. Carroll (1963) proposed that if aptitude for learning was distributed following the bell-shaped, normal curve,[3] and all students were given exactly the same instruction (in terms of time and quality), the amount learned would be normally distributed. On the other hand, if the quality and time for instruction were adapted to the entry skills and other characteristics of each learner, the majority of students would achieve subject mastery (see Figure 12.4).

Carroll's ideas imply that the customary assumption that the intelligence quotient (IQ) determines "who can learn what" may be wrong. Bloom set out to build a model for instruction that might prove that to be the case.

Mastery Learning (ML) has these features:

- A specific set of objectives is defined.
- The subject matter is broken into smaller learning units (about two weeks of instruction each).
- Unit objectives are defined.

[3]See the bell-shaped distribution on the left side of Figure 12.4. The normal curve is discussed in more detail in Chapter 20.

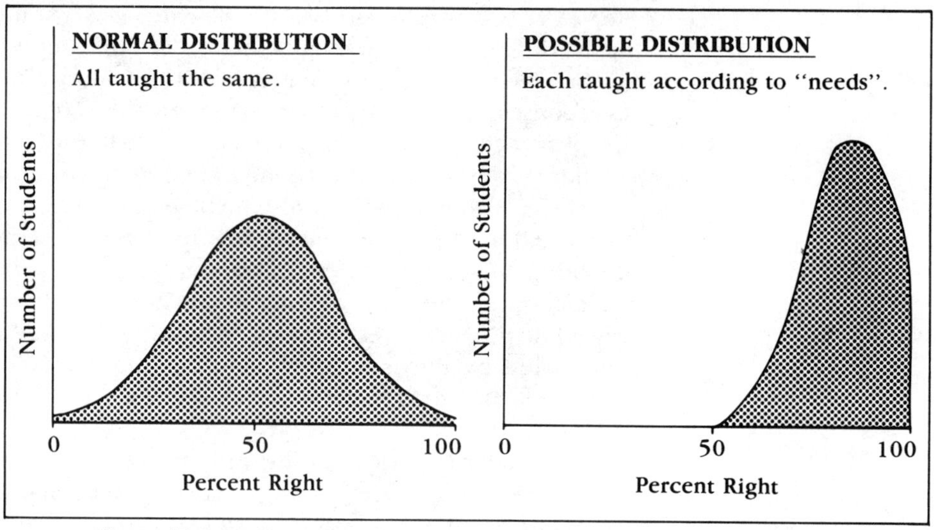

Figure 12-4 *An illustration of Carroll's assumptions*

- The instructor teaches the units using typical group methods, but gives tests of the objectives and provides feedback/correction information to the students. The feedback tests are not graded. Quality instruction is sought: (1) through the clarity of the logical analyses of what is to be taught and its sequencing, (2) by increasing the active participation and practice by students, and (3) by providing effective reinforcers for students.

- Supplemental instruction is given when needed to help each student reach mastery. The correctives used include small-group study sessions, one-on-one tutoring, reteaching, and use of other materials (texts, workbooks, programed instruction, games, and audiovisuals).

Mastery Learning comes in many forms in its different applications around the country and the world. In some applications, teachers work from prepared scripts to directly guide instruction. Mastery Learning differs from traditional teaching in that: (1) learning time is ideally based on the task—what it requires—not the time available today, (2) the initial testing and feedback provide a kind of "private tutoring," (3) normal-curve grading is thrown out, and (4) the teacher must address student failures and help reverse them.

Bloom (1984) accepts a standard of quality to shoot for in ML that can be accomplished by a "well-trained" tutor. Recent data by two of Bloom's doctoral candidates at the University of Chicago (Anania, 1982; Burke, 1984) suggest that tutoring produces learning outcomes that are at the 98th percentile relative to the regular class (from Bloom, 1984). Mastery Learning, as defined by Bloom, achieves results that are at the 84th percentile relative to the regular class in many subject areas (Bloom, 1984).

In the past several years, Bloom (1984) has been trying to find ways to get ML from the 84th percentile to the 98th percentile by adding other procedures to the approach. One strategy (Leyton, 1983) was to *enhance* the student's *prerequisite skills,* prior to beginning each Mastery Learning unit. For example, students going into Algebra 2 or French 2 would review the material from Algebra 1 and French 1 that teachers considered most essential. This took about three to four hours. This enhancement procedure led to performance at the 95th percentile rather than the 84th percentile. These results suggest that *testing prerequisites* and *preteaching* these skills looks like a promising procedure, especially for sequentially dependent courses.

In another study, Tenenbaum (1982) showed that adding better instruction to ML in the form of "enhanced cues," greater student participation (responding), and more reinforcement led to performance at the 96th percentile of the comparison group in sixth grade science and ninth grade algebra. Also Burke's (1983) work suggests that use of tutoring and ML will lead to performance at the 98th percentile compared to conventional teaching.

Kim (1969 as reported in Block, 1971) studied ML strategies in Korea where there is only one teacher for every 70 students. The study examined the learning of a unit on geometric figures by 272 seventh graders. Half used ML procedures and half regular instruction. The ML students had tests for each subunit that they corrected themselves. Those scoring less than 80 percent were given forty to fifty frames of programed instruction to take home and study. Review questions were also provided. In the experimental group, 74 percent reached the 80 percent criterion, while only 40 percent of the control group reached mastery. For those with IQ's below 93, 50 percent of the ML students reached mastery and only 8 percent of the controls. For those with IQ's of 93 or above, 95 percent of the ML students reached mastery and 64 percent of the controls. Nearly as many ML students with low IQ's (50 percent) reached mastery as high IQ students in the control group (64 percent).

Block and Burns (1976) in reviewing the 17 best designed studies comparing ML with traditional methods found that ML students scored higher 89 percent of the time, and significantly higher 61 percent of the time. Retention scores were nearly always higher for ML.

DIRECT INSTRUCTION

A final mastery-learning approach is Direct Instruction (DI) as developed by Siegfried Engelmann, Douglas Carnine, myself, and a host of others working under their direction. In one definition, DI is 43 commercially available sequences of programed scripts, designed by Engelmann, which teachers can follow in working with groups (see Appendix A for a list of these programs). Most of the programs provide for a full school year of daily lessons (taking twenty-five to forty minutes) that have been tested to ensure that they work. In DISTAR (direct instructional system for teaching and remediation), there are now two levels each of reading, language, and arithmetic. *Reading Mastery* has 6 levels. *Corrective Reading* has 3 levels of *decoding* and three levels of *comprehension*. Math Modules consists of nine programs for upper elementary and junior high students. *Spelling Mastery* has five levels and *Corrective Spelling Through Morphographs* is a single program for use in grades four through twelve. Finally, there are six other programs dealing with cursive writing, expressive writing, facts, using library books, and a program for parents to teach their children to read at home. These 43 programs (with proper training in their use) provide the basis for the dissemination of proven mastery learning strategies.

Direct Instruction is best known for the DISTAR programs, which were the instructional core of the University of Oregon Direct Instruction Model in the national experiment called Follow Through. Follow Through took children coming out of Head Start through three or four grades of school. In his 1981 book, *Making Schools Work,* Robert Benjamin devotes a chapter to Bloom's Mastery Learning and then turns to DISTAR:

> But DISTAR works. It consistently has delivered what other programs usually just promise. Even more convincingly than mastery

> learning (to which it is related in some ways), it has provided powerful proof that virtually all children can learn. In the largest, most expensive, most ambitious social experiment ever conducted in the United States—in which nine different instructional programs representing the major educational theories of the 1970s were pitted against each other to find out what works best with low-income children—DISTAR far and away comes out on top. It was the only program that showed it could bring poor children up to the average achievement levels of their middle-class peers with some regularity—the previously unattainable educational goal of the 'War on Poverty.'
>
> DISTAR takes the mystery out of teaching kids to read; in the process, it reveals many of the underlying flaws of traditional instruction. Rife with clear cues as to what it is to be learned, intensive student participation, positive reinforcement of the lessons, and immediate feedback from the teacher, DISTAR carries Benjamin Bloom's principles of high-quality instruction to their ultimate, systematic conclusion: programmed direct instruction. It leaves nothing to chance. Every action by the teacher—verbal and nonverbal—is specifically outlined; every student response is similarly choreographed. Everywhere it is taught the same way: in small groups, with students and teachers face-to-face in touching range, and with only a flip chart, storybooks, or worksheets between them (Benjamin, 1981, p. 71-72).

Figure 12.5 illustrates a page of script taken from *Mastery Reading I* (Engelmann and Bruner, 1983). Different typefaces are used for what the teacher says and what the teacher does. The task stimuli the students are to respond to (in this case the words the students sound out) are also included in the teacher's books.

The central, visible features of DI instruction are small-group instruction, with frequent responding by the students, as teachers and aides follow scripts in an active, participation oriented classroom. Other strategies are also used, but most new learning starts this way.

Underlying the visible features of DI is a procedural structure built around the rule "Teach more in less time." Procedures are favored that reduce wasted time and hasten the teaching of given objectives. Some procedures help to *increase student contact time* with adults (aides, small-group teaching, tight scheduling). Some procedures help to *increase the effective use of that time* (scripted presentations, pretested lessons, general-case programing strategies, teacher training on program-relevant skills, and monitoring with criterion-referenced tests).

At the core of the model are a set of principles and assumptions that provide the basis for specific program details. Direct Instruction appeals to modern behavior theory for principles to guide teaching strategies and to set constraints in the design of a program. Most distinctive in DI, however, is a focus on *logical analysis of knowledge sets* and *teaching examples.* These aspects of Direct Instruction's underlying curriculum theory will be the topics of subsequent chapters.

The historical foundations for the development of DI as an educational approach lie in the studies of Carl Bereiter and Siegfried Engelmann at the University of Illinois in the early 1960s. Their empirical approach to problems of instruction were later merged with behavioral analysis through contact with Douglas Carnine and myself. Today Direct Instruction stands as a systematic approach to the design and delivery of a range of programs for building cognitive skills.

In a 1984 review I cited 78 references to research on the effectiveness of Direct Instruction. In the National Follow Through Project, there were up to 9,000 students a year in the Oregon Direct Instruction Model from 1968 on (some continued through 1985). The students entering in 1970 and 1971 were evaluated each year, and upon completing third grade in a national evaluation (and those entering from 1968 to 1973 were evaluated by the DI Model research team). As noted in the quote from Benjamin, DI was the only model to raise students from under the 20th percentile on entry to national median (50th percentile) at the end of third grade in Math, Spelling, and Language on the Metropolitan Achievement Test. On Total Reading (comprehension and vocabulary), these students reached the 41st percentile (Becker & Carnine, 1980; Becker, Engelmann, Carnine, & Maggs, 1982; Stebbins et al., 1977). On oral reading decoding skills, the DI Follow Through students scored at the 82nd percentile (grade level 5.2) on the Wide Range Achievement Test at the end of third grade (Becker & Carnine, 1980).

An analysis of achievement gains by IQ levels of the children shows that lower-IQ students start lower in reading and math and end up lower, but *GAIN AS MUCH* on almost every measure (Gersten, Becker, Heiry, and White, 1984). Lower-IQ children can be taught. Bloom's assumption that IQ may have little to do with "who can be taught what" gained strong support.

Follow-up studies in fifth and sixth grade showed that the DI students were significantly better in reading and math on 50 percent of the comparisons made, but there was some loss against national norms (in reading comprehension and math, but not decoding), probably due to the inadequacies of the programs after the children left Follow Through (Becker and Gersten, 1982).

The researchers have recently examined the first high school graduates (18 year olds) in several communities. Results show that there were fewer retentions, fewer dropouts, and more high school graduates among the DI Follow Through students than non-Follow Through comparison students (Gersten, 1982; Gersten and Carnine, 1983, 1984; Gersten and Keating, 1983; White and Gersten, 1983a, 1983b).

In preschool studies in which four and five year old students were taught DISTAR Reading, Language, and Arithmetic for two school years half-day, disadvantaged children scored at the 2.6 grade level in reading decoding skills, and 2.5 in math (Wide Range Achievement Test) on entry to first grade, and showed an increase of about 30 IQ points (Engelmann, 1970). Middle class children under a similar schedule, but with less intensive teaching, showed a similar level of performance in reading and math (Anderson, 1971). Low-income preschoolers attending a *full-year, full-day* program in Alabama for two years scored 3.8 grade levels on the Wide Range in Reading on entry to first grade (above the 98th percentile). This is truly an example of mastery learning that seriously questions the notion of "reading readiness" (Weisberg, 1984).

In Australia, Maggs and Morath (1976) randomly assigned 28 moderately and severely retarded children to a DISTAR Language I group (along with behavioral reinforcement strategies) or to a Peabody Language group (P-level) (augmented by the teacher as needed). Instruction took place one hour a day over two calendar years. The DISTAR group greatly outscored the Peabody group on five comprehension measures. On the Stanford-Binet IQ test, the DISTAR group gained 22.5 months in mental age in 24 months, while the Peabody group gained 7.5 months. The DISTAR group progressed at ***nearly a normal rate*** (which would be a month in mental age for each calendar month).

There are a host of other studies with bilingual students, with bright middle-class students, and all sorts of special groups showing the successful use of DISTAR programs. There are also many studies with the corrective programs

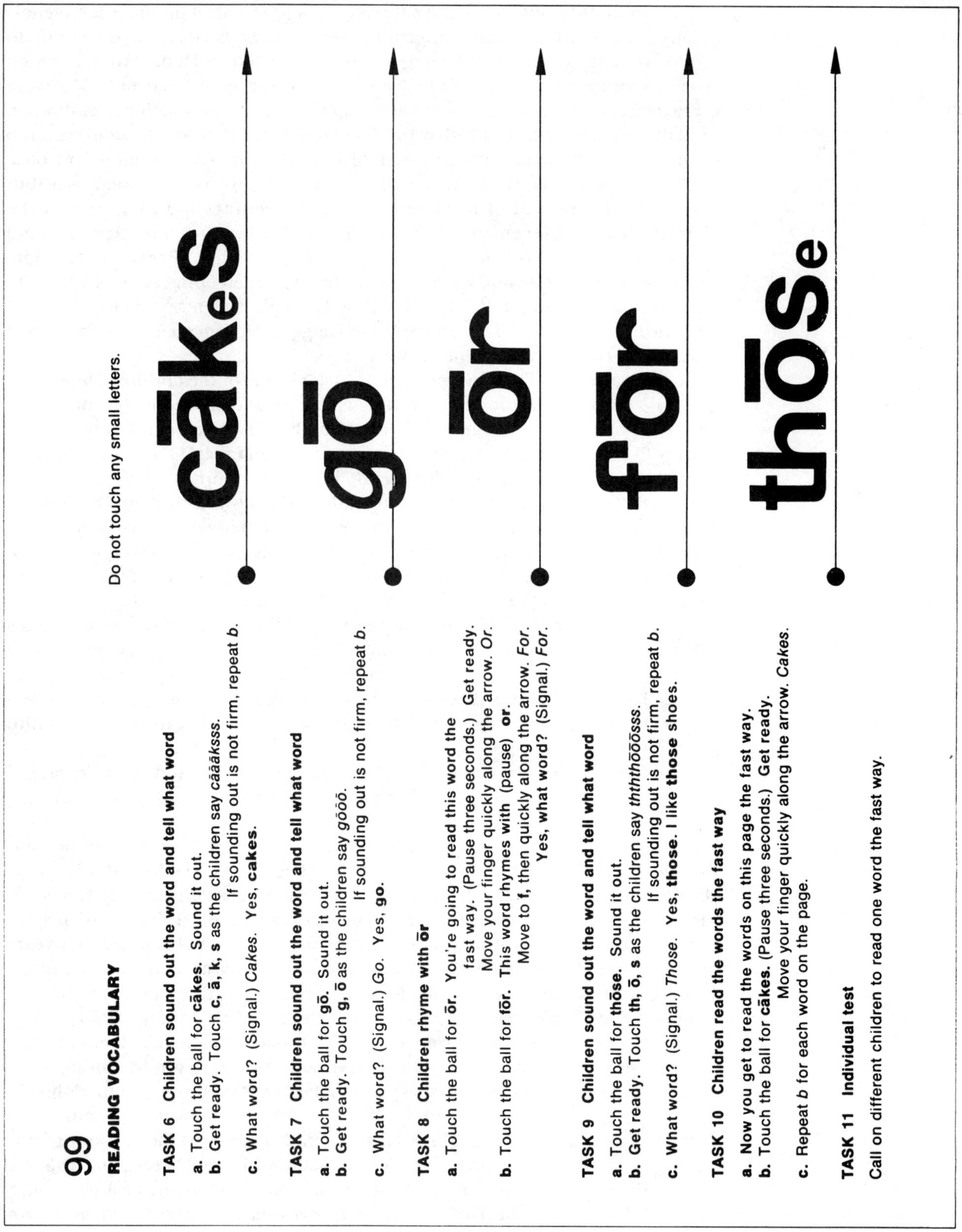

99

READING VOCABULARY

TASK 6 Children sound out the word and tell what word

a. Touch the ball for **cākes.** Sound it out.
b. Get ready. Touch **c, ā, k, s** as the children say *cāāāksss.*
If sounding out is not firm, repeat *b.*
c. What word? (Signal.) *Cakes.* Yes, **cakes.**

TASK 7 Children sound out the word and tell what word

a. Touch the ball for **gō.** Sound it out.
b. Get ready. Touch **g, ō** as the children say *gōōō.*
If sounding out is not firm, repeat *b.*
c. What word? (Signal.) *Go.* Yes, **go.**

TASK 8 Children rhyme with ōr

a. Touch the ball for **ōr.** You're going to read this word the fast way. (Pause three seconds.) Get ready. Move your finger quickly along the arrow. *Or.*
b. Touch the ball for **fōr.** This word rhymes with (pause) **or.**
Move to **f,** then quickly along the arrow. *For.*
Yes, what word? (Signal.) *For.*

TASK 9 Children sound out the word and tell what word

a. Touch the ball for **thōse.** Sound it out.
b. Get ready. Touch **th, ō, s** as the children say *thththōōōsss.*
If sounding out is not firm, repeat *b.*
c. What word? (Signal.) *Those.* Yes, **those.** I like **those** shoes.

TASK 10 Children read the words the fast way

a. Now you get to read the words on this page the fast way.
b. Touch the ball for **cākes.** (Pause three seconds.) Get ready.
Move your finger quickly along the arrow. *Cakes.*
c. Repeat *b* for each word on the page.

TASK 11 Individual test

Call on different children to read one word the fast way.

Do not touch any small letters.

cākes

gō

ōr

fōr

thōse

Figure 12-5 *Sample from a DISTAR Reading Lesson*

(From Reading Mastery 1, DISTAR® Reading I, p. 265 by Siegfried Engelmann and Elaine C. Bruner. Copyright© Science Research Associates. Reprinted by permission of the publisher.)

in reading and spelling that typically show an average of 2 months gain for each month of instruction. (See my 1984 review for fuller details.)

The hardest task we faced in Follow Through was building reading comprehension skills (see Becker, 1977). We believe this was because of the vocabulary-learning load faced by children growing up in homes where the adult caretakers were not well-educated. In homes with reasonably educated parents, children are constantly learning new words. This is less likely to occur in homes of the disadvantaged. Much school learning *assumes* knowledge of vocabulary. These data and the vocabulary issue are discussed in later chapters on reading and home variables in school learning.

SUMMARY

This chapter examined a variety of approaches to instruction that focus on assessment of learning progress during the process of learning and provide feedback to the student and additional instruction where needed. The similarities among these mastery approaches are many. If you examine the features common to most mastery-learning approaches, you can find that they all deal with the following features *(numbered as they were at the start of this chapter):*

1. Stated objectives.

2. Assessment of entry skills.

5. Differential time to mastery for different students.

6. Frequent testing and feedback.

7. Correction procedures.

8. Adequate practice to mastery of subskills.

The different approaches vary in their strategies for features 3, 4, and 9. Each of these will be examined in turn.

3. Procedures to motivate and engage students in active learning. All mastery-learning models have procedures to engage the student in active responding. Of the group, only IPI has not directly recommended reinforcement procedures to enhance motivation ("the student learns at his or her own rate"). However, there is no reason a point-reinforcement system could not easily be added to IPI to enhance learning rates for slow learners.

4. Attempts to develop "quality instruction." The mastery-learning models probably differ most on this feature. Definitions of "quality instruction" are for the most part either lacking or vague. Precision teaching has no "teaching system." It is a testing system with the teaching left up to the teacher. While many attempts have been made to formally sequence objectives in Precision Teaching, for the most part teaching method is up to the teacher. The rate measure and daily charting continue to be valuable contributions of Precision Teaching. IPI recommends many teaching strategies and formats and provides some tapes, programed readers, and so on, but for the most part, the teachers and aides carry the burden of figuring out what to do when the prescribed materials fail. If you were to set up criteria for "quality instruction" that included that it be *effective* and *efficient* (leading to generalizable skills and knowledge wherever possible), then you would have to conclude that early forms of programed instruction would not meet such criteria (just as much of the currently available software for microcomputers provides only practice and testing, without effective mechanisms of instruction). The Keller system assumes that teachers have good textbooks that can teach if approached with study questions, and so on. There is no doubt that textbooks can work, but can teachers do better?

Bloom expresses concern about quality instruction and believes that by following the guidelines from his own work (Bloom, Engelhart, Furst, Hill, and Krathwohl, 1956) and Gagné's (1965, 1970, 1977) on the analysis of knowledge forms that quality instruction can be devised (this issue will be addressed in the next chapter). With good logical analyses, programs can be sequenced more effectively, relationships made more explicit, and generalizations communicated. This is a step in the right direction. But as you will see, Bloom just did not go far enough to provide specific principles to guide the design of the details in developing teaching materials. For the most part the details of instruction are left up to the teacher in Bloom's method, although some programed scripts have been constructed.

Direct Instruction, on the other hand, has worked from the start with explicitly programed materials that have been designed using careful, logical analysis of the domain to be taught and of the examples used for each step along the way. It is unique in its pretesting for effectiveness as programs are being developed, and its explicitness. The developments in the next few chapters should help you to learn about that uniqueness.

9. Testing for long-term mastery. This feature of mastery-learning programs is found in most of the models presented except Precision Teaching. However, there are definite differences in the explicitness of how or why long-term mastery testing is done. The fundamental issue is the fact that if new learning is related in some way to old learning, it may interfere with the old learning (retroactive inhibition). Long-term mastery testing is a check on whether this is occurring or not. In Direct Instruction, explicit programing is planned for to ensure that where such interference is possible, it is eliminated through discrimination practice. For example, a student may learn a set of procedures to solve addition problems. Then a set of procedures for solving subtraction problems is introduced. It is very likely that if given addition problems mixed with subtraction problems, there would be confusion on when to use which strategy, unless careful instruction is provided on the critical discriminations. "You have to decide first whether you are supposed to add or subtract." Later on, multiplication and division problems have to be discriminated from addition and subtraction, as well as from each other.

The review of mastery learning approaches in this chapter has laid a foundation for an understanding of the features of effective instruction. You are now in a better position to consider the one area where most mastery models (as well as all other nonmastery-learning options) seem to fail most often—"quality teaching." As you will see in Chapter 13, the key to understanding effective and efficient instruction in cognitive processes is a merger of behavioral analysis with logical analysis.

CHAPTER

13

THE STRUCTURE OF COGNITIVE KNOWLEDGE

The last chapter identified nine features of behavior-theory-based mastery learning models of instruction. This chapter begins an expansion of procedure 4, *Attempts to develop "quality instruction."* Figure 13.1 summarizes this expansion as a preview.

From Mastery Learning and Behavior Theory	*From Theories of Instructional Design*
1. State objectives. 2. Assess entry skills. 3. Engage the students. 4. Develop quality instruction. 5. Allow differential time to mastery for different students. 6. Test and give feedback often. 7. Provide corretion procedures. 8. Provide adequate practice to insure mastery of subskills. 9. Test for long-term mastery.	4a. Begin with an analysis of *types of knowledge*. (1) Identify samenesses. (2) Identify kinds of knowledge that can be taught with the same strategy. 4b. (1) *Sequence* concepts, rules, etc. used in major and minor objectives. (2) *Sequence* examples used in specific concepts, rules, and problem-solving routines.

Figure 13-1 *Summary of a mastery learning model with an expansion focusing on the design of quality instruction*

While each of the nine features of mastery learning listed in Figure 13.1 is important to the overall quality of instruction, the analysis in the last chapter suggests that what is so often missing, or left to the teacher to figure out, in mastery-learning approaches are the quality teaching demonstrations (point 4); it is this aspect of quality that this chapter addresses.

Quality instruction requires the teacher to know what is to be taught, how it ties in with related materials being (or to be) taught, how component skills can be put together into more complex problem-solving skills, and how individual examples can be efficiently sequenced to teach a generalization. Quality instruction can only occur where there has been a careful analysis of what is to be taught, in what sequence, and with what procedures. This analysis is a most important and largely neglected aspect of education. If you look at more traditional classrooms and at textbooks commonly used in such classrooms, it is even more difficult to find examples of quality instruction than in mastery-learning classrooms. The following three examples will help to *illustrate the discrepancy* between what is and what could be.

SOME CURRENT PROBLEMS IN INSTRUCTION

The first example is concerned only with the question, "Do teachers provide instruction?" It omits the question of quality. The heart of instruction is a demonstration of what is to be learned, in small steps, using specific examples, and checking to see if the students understand. While this should be obvious, Durkin (1978–79) found that this rarely occurs in teaching reading comprehension. Durkin defined *comprehension instruction* as teacher-directed instruction aimed at helping students to understand the meaning of more than a single word. Asking students questions and telling them if their answers were right or wrong was called *testing,* not *instruction.* Observations of 24 fourth grade teachers during reading periods for nearly 5,000 minutes (200 per teacher) revealed *instruction* to occur less than one percent of the time. In a follow-up study, Durkin (1980–81) examined reading texts for elementary students and found that they did not provide explicit demonstrations of how to give answers to questions relating to comprehension.

A study by Engelmann (1982) leads to a similar conclusion and adds other important evidence. The study examined the teaching of reading comprehension skills in grades four, five, and six. The study analyzed how four textbook series taught the concept of *main idea* and a number of other concepts such as *cause-effect* and *fact versus fiction.* Researchers also video taped 17 teachers presenting two ten-minute lessons each and interviewed the teachers on adequacy of the teaching materials, and they tested the students on what explicitly was supposed to have been taught.

The analysis of the *program materials* (Ginn; Scott, Foresman; Houghton Mifflin; and Holt, Rinehart & Winston) showed some interesting outcomes. Only 14 percent of the examples of main idea were considered to have been taught (using a very liberal definition of "taught"). For each set of examples presented, there was an average of four possible misinterpretations (that is, the main idea might be presented in the *first sentence only* in all three examples). Forty-nine percent of the workbook examples were inappropriately prompted (for example, a picture of a little man up in the corner of the page says "Pssst kid! Look in the first sentence."). Where the main idea is located has nothing to do with the critical features of the concept *main idea,* so this kind of prompting does nothing to help learn about the concept. The average number of days between examples was 62 (which is not the way to foster concept learning). Only 14 percent of the workbook examples occurred on the same day as the topic (main idea) was discussed by the teacher (thus not producing effective independent practice). Over three years, only 22 examples were presented (where 50 to 80 might be needed). Corrections were specified for *no* examples.

The programs would seem to be incapable of teaching the average student. Do the teachers improve them? For the primary part of the lesson, the teachers did not deviate from the text lesson. The teacher presentations required too few student responses and most tasks requiring responses were presented to individuals (84 percent) rather than groups. Teachers gave the answer to 34 percent of the tasks. They praised 46 percent of the correct responses, but in only 2 percent of the cases was behavior-specific praise used. Students made wrong responses 27 percent of the time and these were corrected only 37 percent of the time. In responding to mistakes, teachers added questions of their own, 48 percent of which were judged to be irrelevant or misleading.

Criterion-referenced tests were constructed to measure what was specifically "taught." Using a 90 percent correct criterion, only 12 percent of the students reached it. Using a 75 percent criterion, only 30 percent reached it. Using a 50 percent criterion, only 55 percent reached it. Multiplying the criterion by the percent reaching it, one must conclude that only about 25 percent of the information being "taught" was transmitted. This is a far cry from the goals (and possibilities) of mastery learning.

The conclusion was clear. The teachers were no better than their programs, which were very inadequate for teaching basic reading comprehension skills.

Consider a third example. In 1955, Rudolf Flesch published a book called *Why Johnny Can't Read.* In 1981, he published a sequel called *Why Johnny Still Can't Read.* Flesch's basic message is this: The field of reading is broken down into two camps. One group believes that teachers should focus from the beginning on meaning, prompting with pictures, encouraging guessing, and not worrying about teaching children to crack the reading code (through phonics). This group teaches *sight* words with the kind of redundancy you might recall from the Dick and Jane series. The second group also believes very much in the importance of comprehension, but they believe that *decoding* (converting the written letters into a spoken word you are likely to be familiar with) is an absolutely essential preskill to comprehension (and it can be taught efficiently). If the sentence says "The house is on the corner" and you read "The horse is on the corner," there is no way you will understand what is being communicated.

Flesch believes that the problem with the sight-word approach (which controls about 80 percent of the textbook market) is that a high percentage of children fail to learn to decode with that method. Yet, since 1911, there have been 124 studies that have shown the phonic approach to be superior to the sight-word method (see *Learning to Read: The Great Debate* by Jeanne Chall, 1967; see also an update by Chall, 1983, and the report of a national commission *Becoming a Nation of Readers,* Anderson, Hiebert, Scott, and Wilkinson, 1985). No studies have shown the sight method to be superior. Flesch (1982) gives this quote from the 1978 teachers' manuals for seventh and eighth grades for the program published by Houghton Mifflin.

> An Important Statement Regarding the Decoding of Words Strange Only in Printed Form . . .
>
> Some students have not yet learned how to decode easily and quickly the printed form of the language into the oral form with which they are thoroughly familiar. . . They are probably not sufficiently aware that any specific reading passage consists of letter symbols in a sort of secret code. . . . They almost certainly lack mastery of a reliable strategy for decoding printed language. . . . For those students . . . provide the necessary instruction recommended on pages 445–458. (From *Family Circle, 11/1/79, p. 44)*

In plain English this means that many seventh and eighth graders who were taught by the sight method do not know how to read. The exercises suggested to correct this problem, eight years too late, are totally inadequate, relying on guessing from context cues and still failing to teach phonics.

The estimates of reading failures due to lack of decoding skills range from 20 percent to 25 percent for middle-class students and 40 percent to 50 percent for more disadvantaged ones. Barbara Bateman wrote in a chapter on learning disabilities (Haring and Bateman, 1977) that an estimated 95 percent of middle-class students labeled "learning disabled" are a product of poor initial teaching of reading. They were not taught to crack the code.

It is not the intent here to deny the importance of comprehension and vocabulary knowledge to reading (later chapters will have more to say on this); the point is simply that schools are currently failing to teach decoding skills, which can readily be taught and are essential prerequisites for reading comprehension.

The point of these examples is to bring home the fact that in a lot of classrooms *quality instruction is not occurring* in very important basic skills, and as you might suspect in other areas as well.

BRUNER'S CONTRIBUTION

In *Toward a Theory of Instruction,* Jerome Bruner (1966) set forth and illustrated some general properties a theory of instruction should contain. He first distinguished a theory of instruction from learning theory in this way: a theory of instruction *prescribes* efficient procedures for transmitting types of knowledge. A theory of learning *describes* how learning naturally takes place. The *design* of instruction is clearly behavioral engineering. The four general properties of a theory of instruction delineated by Bruner were:

1. *Predisposition.* The theory should be concerned with student current skill levels and motivation to learn.

2. *Structure of Knowledge.* The theory should be concerned with how a body of knowledge should be structured for efficient, economical teaching.

3. *Sequence.* The theory should have rules for effectively sequencing tasks used in teaching.

4. *Reinforcement.* The theory should specify the shifting of reinforcers from more extrinsic to more intrinsic.

Bruner illustrates some structures and sequencing ideas in his work, but he did not undertake a comprehensive analysis. He did, however, provide three characteristics of knowledge structures, two of which could serve as useful criteria in evaluating alternative structurings. He described knowledge structures in terms of their mode, economy, and power. *Mode* refers to how knowledge is represented, whether: (a) with concrete objects and events, (b) with representational image or graphs, or (c) with mathematical or verbal symbols. For example, the concept of *seriation* might be taught with a sets of objects to be ordered, with pictures of objects to be ordered, or the verbal and mathematical descriptions of objects to be ordered. By *economy,* Bruner meant the simplicity by which a knowledge set could be represented. For example, the Pythagorean theorem for the relationships among the sides of a right triangle ($A^2 + B^2 = C^2$) represents economically the properties of a lot of specific triangles. By *power* Bruner meant basically the generality of the structures for covering lots of applications. Learning the problem-solving skills to decode phonically is much more powerful than learning to decode by the sight method. One analysis of words leads to almost no generality (sight method); the other analysis leads to extensive generality. Similarly, the principles of behavior have power because they can be applied to child-rearing, teaching, economics, world politics, and so forth. The criteria of *economy* and *power* become important in evaluating different approaches to the analysis of knowledge.

The remainder of this chapter examines the gross architecture of knowledge and skills with a focus on types of cognitive knowledge.

COGNITIVE KNOWLEDGE FORMS

Taxonomies of knowledge have been constructed to cover cognitive, affective, and motor areas. At this point, the concern is with taxonomies related to the analysis of cognitive knowledge.

Bloom's Six Levels of Cognitive Skills

Bloom et al. (1956) developed an extensive taxonomy of cognitive knowledge objectives based on six main categories: knowledge, comprehension, application, analysis, synthesis, and evaluation.

Level 1, Knowledge. The emphasis of this level is on the *recall* of facts, whether very specific ("What is the date of Lincoln's birthday?") or very general ("What is the rule about the movement of gasses?").

Level 2, Comprehension. The emphasis here is on meaning, intent, or relationships in communications. The learner shows that she or he has received what was communicated and can use it. "Explain the causes of . . .?" "Why was Mary mad at Jane?" "How much is three times four?" "Give three examples of *vehicles.*"

Level 3, Application. This level involves the use of principles, rules, and other generalizations in particular situations. Examples might be: "Use phonic rules to sound out new regular-sound words"; Solve for the unknown in this equation"; "Solve this word problem"; "Given the specific gravities, predict whether a given object will float or sink in some fluid."

Level 4, Analysis. Here the process involves breaking a complex communication, set of facts, or other multifaceted process down into its parts, showing the relationships and organization of the parts where appropriate. "Describe the plot of this short story." "What are the prerequisite skills for solving an algebra addition problem with sums under 21?" "How are oranges and bananas the same and how are they different?" "What are the essential parts of a news story?"

Level 5, Synthesis. At this level, learners put together elements to form a whole that was not clearly there before. Examples might include: "Write a short story"; "Design a way to get electric power out of this river"; "Find a rule that covers all of these examples"; "What is the main idea of this story?"

Level 6, Evaluation. At this stage, learners make judgments about the degree to which different products or actions satisfy specified criteria. "Write a critique of this movie." "Evaluate the adequacy of our school's government." "Argue the case for or against abortion." "Critique these works of art."

Levels 4, 5, and 6 of this taxonomy are built around key "mental operations," that is, how the learner *acts on* the communications, rather than on the structure of the communications themselves. As indicated in Figure 13.1, what is needed instead is a taxonomy of knowledge that: (1) identifies kinds of knowledge that can be taught with *similar strategies* (that is, a taxonomy that can serve as a basis for an *economical* theory of instruction) and (2) identifies how different pieces of knowledge share *samenesses* to provide the basis for *powerful* generality, rather than isolated bits and pieces. These goals require *logical analysis of knowledge itself,* rather than of thinking processes, as Bloom has done.

Gagné's Types of Learning

Since the early 1960s, Robert Gagné has been publishing research on the analyses of knowledge structures. His book, *The Conditions of Learning* (1965, 1970, 1977) represent a landmark in progress toward a structural analysis of knowledge in ways that can facilitate cognitive instruction. His book with Leslie Briggs, *Principles of Instructional Design* (Gagné and Briggs, 1974, 1979) explores issues in designing instructional systems. In developing principles for the design of instruction, Gagné (1970) first distinguishes eight "kinds of learning." Types two to eight provide a basis for a taxonomy of cognitive knowledge forms:

> In brief, the varieties of learning that can currently be distinguished are as follows:
>
> Type 1: *Signal Learning.* The individual learns to make a general, diffuse response to a signal. This is the classical conditioned response of Pavlov (1927). [It is also Skinner's (1938) respondent conditioning, where a conditioned stimulus comes to control a respondent.]
>
> Type 2: *Stimulus-Response Learning.* The learner acquires a precise response to a discriminated stimulus. What is learned is a connection (Thorndike, 1898) or a discriminated operant (Skinner, 1938), sometimes called an instrumental response (Kimble, 1961).
>
> Type 3: *Chaining.* What is acquired is a chain of two or more stimulus-response connections. The conditions for such learning have been described by Skinner (1938) and others, notably Gilbert (1962).
>
> Type 4: *Verbal Association.* Verbal association is the learning of chains that are verbal. Basically, the conditions resemble those for other (motor) chains. However, the presence of language in the human being makes this a special type because internal links may be selected from the individual's previously learned repertoire of language (see Underwood, 1964).
>
> Type 5: *Discrimination Learning.* The individual learns to make *n* different identifying responses to as many different stimuli, which may resemble each other in physical appearance to a greater or lesser degree. Although the learning of each stimulus-response connection is a simple type 2 occurrence, the connections tend to interfere with each other's retention (Postman, 1961).
>
> Type 6: *Concept Learning.* The learner acquires a capability of making a common response to a class of stimuli that may differ from each other widely in physical appearance. He is asked to make a response that identifies an entire class of objects or events (see Kendler, 1964). Other concepts are acquired *by definition,* and consequently have the formal characteristics of rules.
>
> Type 7: *Rule Learning.* In simplest terms, a rule is a chain of two or more concepts. It functions to control behavior in the manner suggested by a verbalized rule of the form 'If A, then B,' where A and B

> are previously learned concepts. However, it must be carefully distinguished from the mere verbal sequence, 'If A, then B,' which, of course, may also be learned as type 4.
>
> Type 8: *Problem Solving.* Problem solving is a kind of learning that requires the internal events usually called thinking. Two or more previously acquired rules are somehow combined to produce a new capability that can be shown to depend on a 'higher-order' rule. (Gagné, 1970, pp. 63–64).

One problem with Gagné's analysis is the use of the term "types of learning." Chapter 2 identified four basic stimulus functions by which all learning processes could be understood. In terms of basic stimulus functions, *signal learning* clearly deals with respondent conditioning and *is* a type of learning. Gagné's *problem solving* refers to *unknown* processes that go on "inside the head" when the student faces a problem for the first time. These processes probably do not involve a new kind of learning, and refer to mental operations rather than a type of knowledge. Gagné's types 2 to 7 all involve discrimination learning, and types 3, 4, and 5 also involve prompting, shaping, and differential reinforcement as necessary to build chains. So six of these "types of learning" can be derived from three basic stimulus functions (reinforcing, punishing, and discriminative), and an extinction procedure.

Excluding signal learning and problem solving, Gagné is basically describing different products of learning, or *types of knowledge* or *types of tasks* to be learned, not different learning processes. Some of the above problems are dealt with in Gagné and Briggs (1977) where "What is to be learned?" (such as knowledge and skills) is broken down into: (1) intellectual skills, (2) cognitive strategies, (3) information (facts, verbal chains), (4) motor skills, and (5) attitudes. Types 5 to 8 are viewed as intellectual skills, and type 4 as information or facts. These five *cognitive* knowledge forms are discussed further later.

Important aspects of this analysis by Gagné are summarized in Figure 13.2 (after Gagné and Briggs, 1977, p. 62). This figure illustrates the hierarchical dependency of different types of knowledge and provides the basis for

Simple Forms: *DISCRIMINATIONS*

↓

which are required as prerequisites for

↓

CONCRETE CONCEPTS

↓

which are required as prerequisites for

↓

RULES AND DEFINED CONCEPTS

↓

which are required as prerequisites for

↓

Complex Forms: *PROBLEM SOLVING STRATEGIES (HIGHER-ORDER RULES)*

Figure 13-2 *Levels of complexity in intellectual skills.*

some principles for the analysis of more complex tasks into their simpler components, which can be taught prior to their use in the more complex tasks. This provides one basis for sequencing principles. Gagné and Briggs' *information* (facts) could also be inserted into this hierarchy at the same level as rules and defined concepts (as is done in Engelmann and Carnine's analysis, to be presented later). Facts, like rules, involve combining two or more concepts into a more complex verbal chain.

Figure 13.3 illustrates the hierarchical structure of knowledge forms in ordering numbers (Gagné, 1965). Starting at the bottom are some very basic

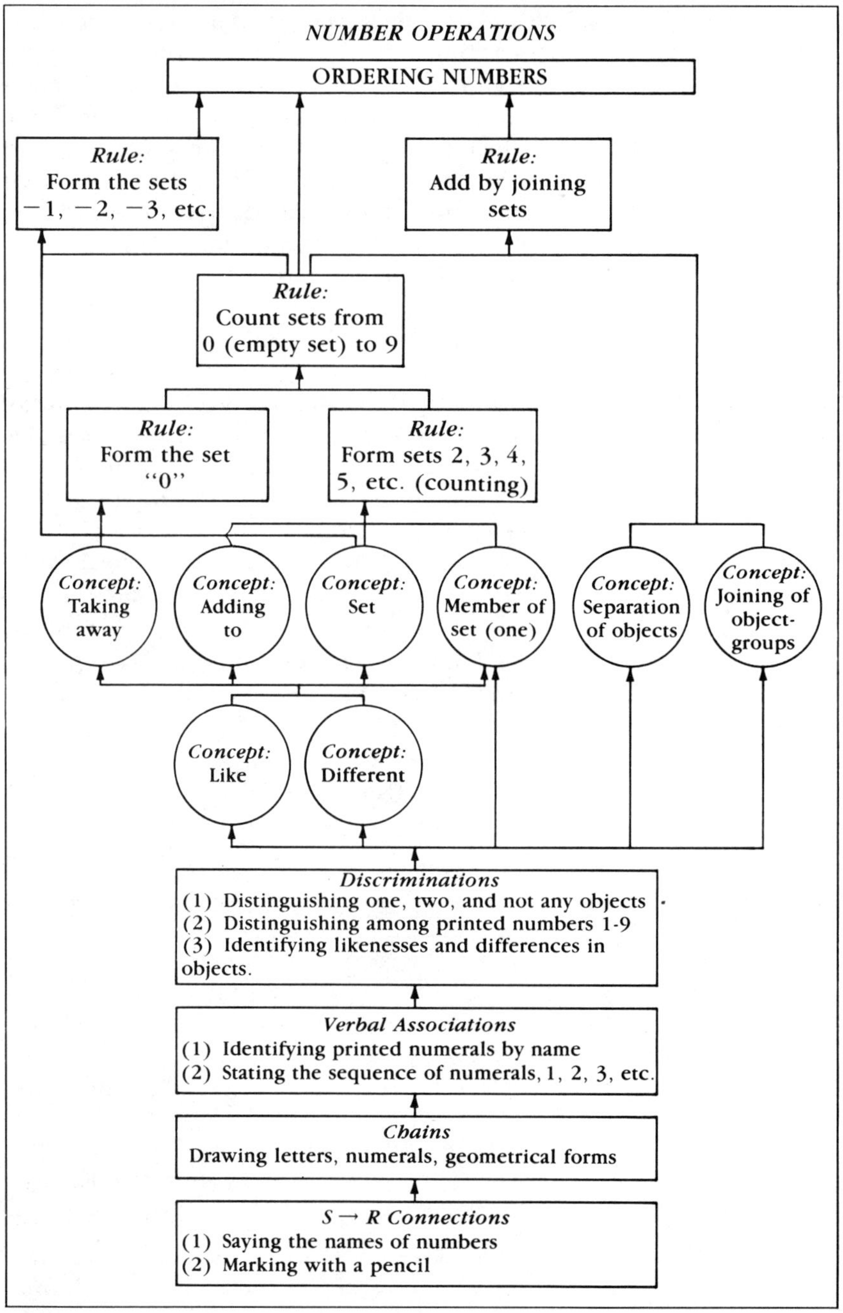

Figure 13-3 *A learning structure for number operations (Source: From* The Conditions of Learning *by Robert M. Gagné. Copyright © 1965 by Holt, Rinehart and Winston, Inc. Reprinted by permission of Holt, Rinehart and Winston, Inc.)*

skills assumed by the skills above them. The hierarchy builds to *concepts* and *rules,* and eventually to *problem-solving skills* (such as being able to order numbers).

Tiemann and Markle's "Types of Learning"

Tiemann and Markle (1983) present a rather elaborate analysis of what they call "types of learning," which is illustrated as Figure 13.4. The emotional substrate to all learning is recognized, and operant learning is divided into psychomotor, simple cognitive, and complex cognitive types. As in the case of Gagné, you could argue that they are dealing with types of knowledge and skills, or types of learning products, rather than different ways in which students learn.

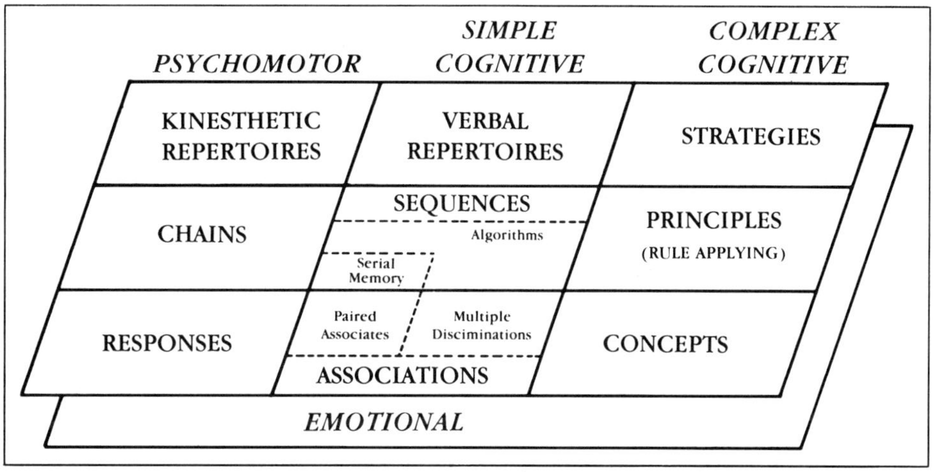

Figure 13-4 *Diagram of the types of learning*

A comparison with Gagné's types of learning is of interest. Gagné's type 1 is listed as emotional. His type 2 is covered as associations. His type 3 as chains. His type 4 as verbal sequences. His type 5 as multiple discriminations; and his types 6, 7, and 8 as concepts, principles, and strategies, respectively. In addition, Tiemann and Markle include:

- Paired associates as a special case of associations.
- Serial memory (for instance, memorizing the alphabet) as a special case of sequences.
- Algorithms as a subcase of sequences.
- Response learning.
- Kinesthetic repertoires (as a football player or golfer might have).

The addition of response systems (psychomotor) does not concern us, nor do the addition of paired associates and serial learning, since they mean little to the teacher and add nothing new. However, the classification of algorithms (or problem-solving chains, as they were called in Chapter 4) is absent from Gagné's analysis and has obvious importance for the teacher. When we have known solutions to problems, they can be taught as a set of procedures to follow, as is done for many kinds of math problems.

This analysis does much to support Gagné's position and adds to it.

However, it does not show some of the hierarchical dependencies among cognitive knowledge forms as well as Gagné does nor as Engelmann and Carnine do in the following section. A strong contribution from Tiemann and Markle is in providing the student with a clever mix of text and programed instruction to help teach the student about the design of instruction (see also Markle, 1983).

Engelmann and Carnine's Cognitive Knowledge Forms

As suggested by Bruner and by the summary in Figure 13.1, the design of instruction for cognitive learning requires three analyses. Siegfried Engelmann and Douglas Carnine make this explicit, as shown in Figure 13.5. (from Engelmann & Carnine, 1982).

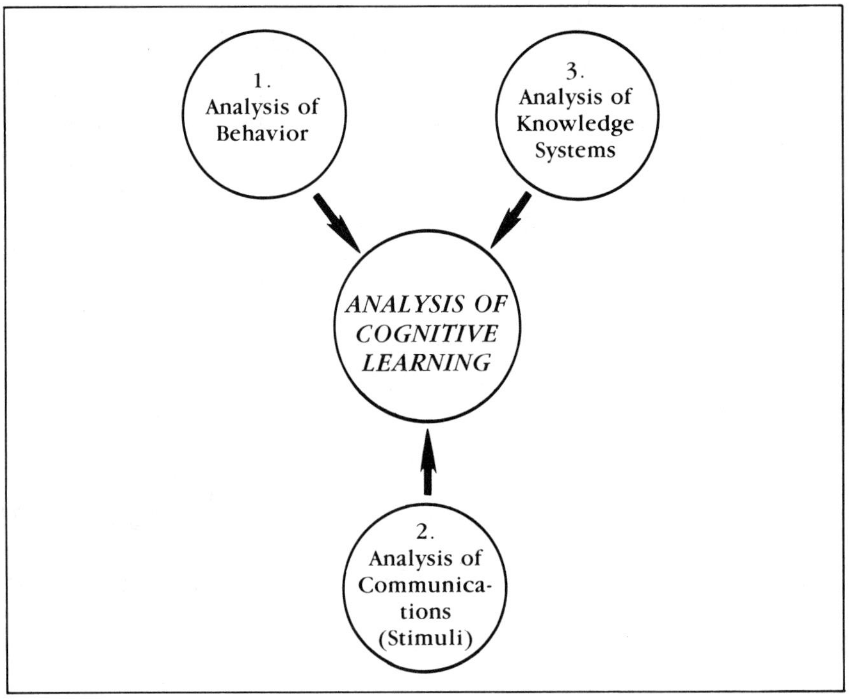

Figure 13-5 *Three analyses in the analysis of cognitive learning.*

The analysis of behavior seeks empirically-based principles that provide the basis for teaching any task: How to motivate and get attention, how to present examples, how to secure student responses, how to reinforce and correct student response. This part of their analysis can be summarized as the *mastery-learning model.* The analysis of communications seeks principles for the logical design of teaching sequences so that they will effectively transmit knowledge, preventing the learning of: (1) misrules, (2) overgeneralization to inappropriate examples, or (3) undergeneralization. This analysis focuses on the ways in which sets of stimuli are the *same* and how they are *different* (that is, what discriminations must be taught). The analysis of knowledge systems is concerned with identifying sameness across apparently different pieces of knowledge. This provides a basis for teaching as broad a general case as possible and strategies for teaching different kinds of knowledge structures.

The analysis of the structure of knowledge forms underlies Engelmann and Carnine's (1982) *Theory of Instruction.* Figure 13.6 summarizes their taxonomy. This analysis, in our view, has the most direct implications for the design of instruction of any system created so far, and for this reason it is used to structure the next four chapters.

A. BASIC FORMS (sensory-feature concepts)
   1. Comparatives (single-dimension concepts)
   2. Non-comparatives (single-dimension concepts)
   3. Nouns (multiple-dimension concepts)
B. JOINING FORMS (relations between sensory-feature concepts)
   1. Logical transformations
   2. Correlated feature relationships (facts)
      a. Name a concrete example .... give a feature
      b. Label a set .... give a feature
      c. Given a concept .... give a synonym
      d. Given a class .... tie to a higher-order class
C. COMPLEX FORMS
   1. Communications about events (fact systems)
   2. Cognitive problem-solving routines (chains)

Figure 13-6 *Engelmann and Carnine's taxonomy of cognitive knowledge forms*

Engelmann and Carnine distinguish three major cognitive knowledge forms: basic forms (or sensory feature concepts), joining forms that relate basic forms logically or empirically, and complex forms, that include problem-solving routines (Tiemann and Markle's algorithms) and communications about events (that is, sets of related facts).

Basic forms are subdivided into single-dimension (or single-feature) concepts and multiple-feature concepts. The latter are nouns or objects *(ball, tree, Martha)* and the former are comparatives *(hotter, steeper, bigger),* object properties *(red, rough)* and object relations *(under, inside of).* Very similar strategies can be used to teach *all* single-dimension concepts through the presentation of examples. Nouns, on the other hand, require a slightly different strategy because of their multiple features and the broad range of their negative examples.

Joining forms include *logical* transformations and *empirical* facts that relate basic forms. Given that the student knows singular nouns *(ball, house, cup),* a transformation rule can be applied to cover plural forms ("This is one ball," "These are two balls."). Transformations take several forms. In some cases (as in the singular-plural example), a small change in the example (one ball to two balls) leads to a small change in the response. In others, such as the logical relations of number sequences, a small change in the example can change the response totally. These differences imply different teaching requirements. Facts can take four logical forms (see Figure 13.6). All facts name at least two concepts to be discriminated, such as "hotter objects—expand," "ducks—fly south in the winter." Some symbolic facts imply transformations, for example, "The first digit of a two-digit number tells how many 10's you have." Once again, differences in the substructures of classes of facts imply differences in teaching programs.

Problem-solving routines differ greatly in their structures, but a common strategy can be used in designing such routines. In a condensed form the steps are:

1. Specify the range of examples for which the routine will work.
2. Make up a *descriptive rule* that tells exactly what the learner must do to attack every example within that range. (The same rule must hold for all examples.)
3. Design a task that tests each component discrimination mentioned in the descriptive rule.

4. Construct a chain composed of the tasks that test the component skills or the "steps" in the routine. (Engelmann & Carnine, 1982, p. 195).

(*Note:* In devising a problem-solving routine, you start with the range of examples you want to be able to deal with. The specific examples define the range of generality of the routine.)

A simple example of this can be found in teaching fractions.

1. For fractions, the examples include fractions greater than 1, less than 1, and equal to 1, within the learner's counting range. (Many current textbooks start out with fractions all less than 1 and have the potential for teaching the misrule that fractions only deal with values less than 1.)

2. The descriptive rule is "The bottom number tells us how many parts in one whole and the top number tells us how many parts we have."

3. A model for the interpretation of fractions would be a series of circles (representing "wholes") to be divided into parts and filled in to illustrate the fraction.

4. The steps to be followed in doing this task would be the routine.

Another type of complex forms (see Figure 13.6) is communications about events, or sets of facts. Whether we are talking about historical events, kinds of clouds, or the human circulatory system, we are dealing with sets of facts that can be related in some way. Because of the memory demands imposed by learning lots of facts, it is typically helpful to use visual representations of sets of related facts and to provide a lot of practice. Examples of teaching strategies will be illustrated later.

SOME COMPARISONS

A comparison of the cognitive portions of the taxonomies of Gagné and Briggs, Tiemann and Markle, and Engelmann and Carnine shows many similarities and a few important differences. A comparison with Bloom's six levels of cognitive operations is less fruitful because, as noted, it is not based on an analysis of knowledge. However, Bloom's level 1 is clearly dealing with the facts or information in the other systems, and his level 3 deals with rules.

Gagné and Briggs, and Tiemann and Markle make a distinction between *discrimination learning* and *concept learning.* Discrimination learning is said to occur when the student can tell whether two symbols, figures, or objects are the same or different, such as △ and □ ("different"), or △ and △ ("same"). Concept learning is said to occur when sets of triangles and squares, for example, can be correctly labeled, even though they vary in size, color, positions, and so on. Engelmann and Carnine see no need for such a distinction, since the process involved is the same (discrimination learning). Discrimination learning is just a *less generalized form* of a concept that must occur in the earlier stages of learning any concept. For Gagné and Briggs, concept learning involves learning to respond to a class of objects, relationships, or events as a whole. The *samenesses* that define the concept are seen to lie in some mediating responses in the brain (Gagné, 1970). For Engelmann and Carnine, and Tiemann and

Markle, the *samenesses* that define basic concepts can be found in the examples of the concepts themselves, although the logical operation called "interpolation" can also enter into the definition of sameness. (Detailed discussion of these issues will be reserved for the next chapter.)

Other differences with instructional implications are the recognition by Engelmann and Carnine of:

1. Three classes of basic concepts that have different teaching implications.

2. The recognition of logical and empirical joining forms—that is, transformations and facts with different teaching implications.

3. The recognition of *fact systems* when looking at complex forms.

Engelmann and Carnine do not include problem-solving strategies, since by definition, these involve problems for which solutions are not known. Since Engelmann is concerned only with a theory of *instruction,* his focus is on problems for which solutions are known and can be taught. It would be consistent with Engelmann and Carnine's goals to teach the kinds of problem-solving *strategies* covered by Gagné and Briggs and Tiemann and Markle; however, they have not done so.

SUMMARY

After relating where the text is going (toward a theory of instruction) to where you have been (looking at the properties of mastery-learning systems), this chapter discussed three examples of current problems in instruction that illustrated the need for better quality instruction. Durkin's work showed that elementary teachers do very little instruction in comprehension skills, and that their textbooks do little to help. In looking at the teaching of reading comprehension in grades four, five, and six, Engelmann and Steely concluded that the textbooks are not well-designed to teach comprehension skills, that teachers do not improve on the textbooks, and that at best the students comprehend about 25 percent of the material being taught. The chapter also looked at the high failure rate in learning reading decoding skills. Rudolf Flesch sees the problem as due to most schools using nongeneralizing sight-word methods when in fact the research overwhelmingly favors phonic decoding systems. The issues of quality instructional design are not trivial ones. Current reading systems are creating high failure rates that are totally unnecessary.

In the search to understand how to design quality instruction, the chapter defined some requirements for a theory of instruction. In his analysis of instructional theory, Bruner stressed the importance of analyzing the structure of knowledge and of finding efficient sequences in designing instructional programs. He also proposed the criteria of economy and power to evaluate different analyses. Economy refers to the simplicity with which a knowledge set can be represented. Power refers to range of potential application (generality) of a given analysis.

Three major attempts to build functional structural analyses of knowledge types were reviewed. These kinds of analysis are important in understanding how to take complex knowledge forms and break them down into simpler component skills for instruction. These analyses are also important in the design of instruction in deciding how to sequence the chunks of knowledge to be taught. In Engelmann and Carnine's analysis, basic concepts are joined together into logical transformation rules and empirical facts. Sets of rules and facts are joined together in building complex forms that may be problem-solving routines or fact systems. Some of the similarities and differences in the analyses developed by Gagné and Briggs, Tiemann and Markle, and Engelmann and Carnine were discussed.

Now you will turn to some of the issues involved in designing instruction that teaches generalized skills and that efficiently sequences the examples used in teaching.

CHAPTER

14

BASIC CONCEPTS—SAMENESSES PROVIDE THE BASIS FOR GENERALIZATION

The idea that samenesses in *examples* provide the basis for responding to members of a concept class in the same way (generalization) has been around a long time, but usually hidden within the concept of "similarity" which implies both samenesses and differences (Osgood, 1953). Also, samenesses within *types of knowledge* provide the potential for using the same teaching strategies for examples of the same type of knowledge. Could all single-dimension basic concepts be taught using the same strategy? Could a slight variation be introduced to deal with comparatives *(warmer, steeper, faster)* versus non-comparatives (*under, red, penetrate*)? How do the teaching requirements change when you consider nouns (object concepts) that have multiple features and many, many negative instances? These questions will be answered later in this chapter; but first it is necessary to explore the nature of concepts and build up some rules about teaching basic concepts.[1]

THE NATURE OF BASIC CONCEPTS

A concept can be defined by the stimulus properties common to concept instances and not common to not-instances (Engelmann, 1969). Imagine a finite set of objects that have different colors. To make it easier to imagine, just use red, orange, and yellow colored balls, all two inches in diameter. However, the balls range across different values of red, orange, and yellow. Now, the task is to teach a young child to say "Yes" when members of the appropriate class are pointed to and the question is asked, "Is this ball orange?" When asked if red or yellow balls are *orange,* the child should say, "No." You can probably teach this task with relatively few trials, as illustrated in Table 14.1.

The sequence in Table 14.1 illustrates a procedure for discriminating the essential properties of *orange* from the essential properties of two color groups that are *not-orange.* The range of values of *orange* demonstrated by the examples become discriminative stimuli (S^ds) for the concept *orange.* The range of values illustrated for *not-orange* become the discriminative stimuli for *not-orange.*

So initially, concept learning is a process of discriminating the essential

[1]Most of the basic ideas for concept teaching in this chapter come from Engelmann and Carnine (1982).

Table 14-1 The beginning of a concept teaching sequence

Demonstration	*Teacher Wording*
1. Hold up a yellow ball.	"This ball is not orange."
2. Hold up a red ball (close to orange).	"This ball is not orange."
3. Hold up an orange ball (close to red).	"This ball is orange."
4. Hold up an orange ball (medium value).	"This ball is orange."
5. Hold up an orange ball (close to yellow).	"This ball is orange."
6. Hold up a yellow ball.	"Is this ball orange?"
(Test with five more randomly chosen examples.)	

properties of the concept from the essential properties of the not-concept(s). Note that in the Teacher Wording in Table 14.1, the concept *ball* appears. This implies that the teacher knows that the child already has learned this concept. Also note that some concepts have a *range of positive values* and a *range of negative values.* If the teacher consistently uses a presentation procedure that shows the range of positive values, the student will learn that other values of *orange* that fall within the range are also examples of *orange.* This is an abstraction process based on a logical operation called *interpolation.* A related logical operation called *extrapolation* allows the student to infer for the range of negative values that examples more different from *orange* than those used to teach it are also *not-orange.* (You will return to these two operations shortly.)

So far your student has learned some essential properties of *orange,* but to fully develop the concept, you would have to teach other *not-orange* colors, *and* present as examples objects that differ in their *irrelevant features.* The objects would differ in shape, size, material, texture, and so on. In the *initial teaching examples,* the only properties that made a difference were differences in color. Once these discriminations are learned, you show the student that the *objects* that are orange can change and are still examples of *orange* (that is, they were not restricted to two-inch balls). This makes concept learning a *multiple-discrimination problem.* The multiple discriminations are:

1. *Between positive and negative instances, it is necessary to discriminate between the relevant characteristics of each.* For example, to learn about the concept *orange,* it is necessary to learn to discriminate not-orange colors from orange colors.

2. *Within positive and negative instances, it is necessary to discriminate relevant characteristics from irrelevant characteristics.* For example, a positive instance of *orange* might be shaped like a truck (irrelevant), made of wood (irrelevant), and sitting on a table (irrelevant). Colors have to be discriminated from shapes, materials, positions, and other properties of objects. Within a negative instance of *orange* (say, a blue sweater) it is also necessary to discriminate the color property from the other properties to determine that it is a negative instance.

Let S+ stand for the discriminative stimuli that define positive examples of a concept. Let S− stand for the discriminative features that define negative examples *in the same coordinate class as S+* (such as other colors, if S+ is *orange*). If S+ is *90 degree angles,* S− would be examples of *all angles greater than or less than 90 degrees.* If S+ is an example of the comparative *steeper,* S− would be examples of *just as steep* or *less steep.* If S+ was the vehicle class *cars,* S− might be examples of *bicycles, trucks, trains,* and *busses.*

Let Si stand for *irrelevant features* of either positive or negative concept instances. Irrelevant features can vary without changing a concept. Piaget called Si features *variants* and the S+ features the *invariants.*

The two aspects of this multiple discrimination problem can be illustrated as follows:

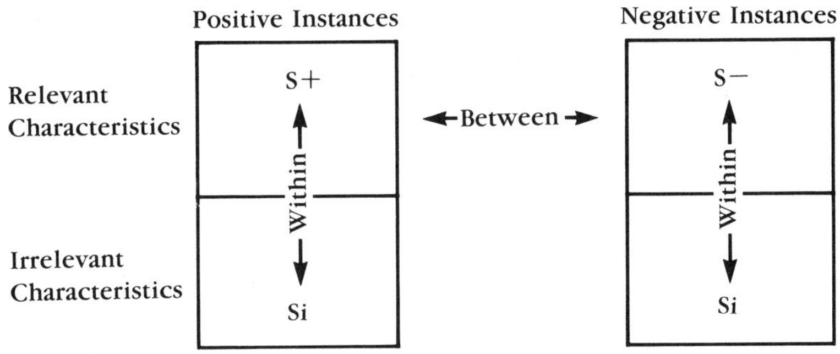

Note: S+, S−, and Si may be a single characteristic or a *set* of characteristics.

Thus, you can see that a concept cannot be taught without teaching a lot of discriminations from other concepts. Many concepts must be taught even to teach a very simple concept like *orange.*

A Note on a Common Confusion

A number of writers maintain that learning a concept involves generalization within the concept class and discrimination between classes of concepts. With the recognition that some concepts have a range of values and the introduction of the principle of interpolation, it would seem that there may be some truth to the generalization-discrimination notion. However, it is false on two counts. First, most writers in referring to "generalizations within a concept class" imply "generalization" across changing irrelevant characteristics. This text has argued that such "generalization" is clearly a discrimination process between relevant and irrelevant characteristics within a concept instance. Second, if the writers are referring to "generalization" across a range of values for positive concept instances, this too is a discrimination learning process. The limits of the range are discriminated and the intervening possibilities are filled in using the logic of interpolation.

GENERAL CASES

When the relevant features (S+) of concept instances have been discriminated from the relevant features of not-instances (S−) and from irrelevant features (Si), the student has learned a general case. After a general case has been learned, the student can respond correctly to the other members of the general class that were not used in instruction. This is illustrated by the following diagram:

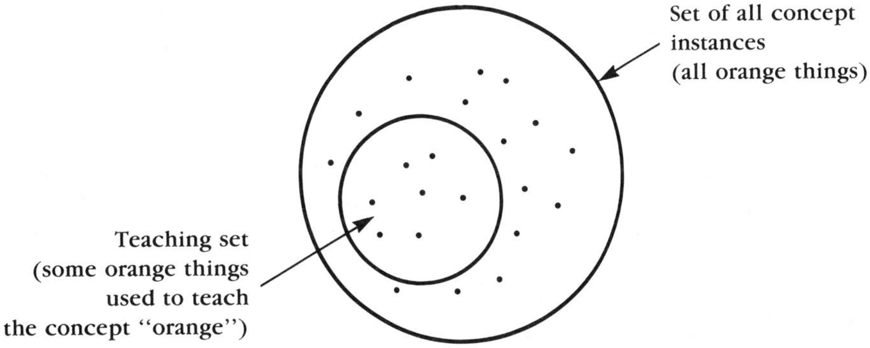

Examples of general cases besides concepts are motor operations, transformational rules, scientific principles (generalizable facts), problem-solving routines, and problem-solving strategies.

SOME RULES FOR TEACHING BASIC CONCEPTS

Imagine that I am holding in my right hand, out in front of me over a table, a blue, cylindrical, plastic pen, six inches long. I say, "This is an example of *ryenit.* What is *ryenit?*"

Now take a few seconds and jot down what concepts you think *ryenit* could be an example of.[2]

Rule 1. It is impossible to teach a concept with a single example, since any instance of a concept must be an instance of many concepts. *Thus, we need a set of positive examples.*

Rule 2. We want the teaching sequence to produce a generalization, so that new examples not used in the teaching will be responded to correctly. *Thus, there must be a structural basis for this generalization in the sameness of our positive examples.*

Now suppose I show you a pirate's sword, a butcher knife, a scalpel (that a surgeon might use), a razor blade, and a saw. They are a set of positive examples of *chot.* What might *chot* be? Take a few moments and write down as many possibilities as you can.[3]

There was a structural basis for *sameness* in these examples, but there was obviously *more than one sameness.* This can lead to learning a misrule (responding to a feature that is not the intended S+).

Rule 3. It is impossible to teach a concept using only positive examples, since a group of concept instances can be instances of many concepts. *Thus, we also need a set of negative examples.*

Suppose I added to the above set a monkey wrench and said, "This is not *chot.*" This negative example would rule out *things made of metal, tools, handtools, objects, man-made objects,* and *things made of steel.* It gave you a lot of information about what *chot* was not. If the negative example had been a flower, it would not have ruled out any of the alternative concepts, except *object* (the class of all examples that are matter).

Rule 4. A sameness that occurs in both positive and negative examples rules out a possible interpretation. *Thus, you can minimize the number of examples needed by using a common* setup *for the initial teaching of a concept, so that the positive and negative examples share the greatest possible number of irrelevant features.*

The earlier example that used two-inch colored balls to teach the concept *orange* illustrated the use of a common setup for initial teaching. *Orange* had nothing to do with shape or size, since both positive and negative examples were the same in these respects. The only thing that changed in going from a positive to a negative example, or visa versa, was the color.

Rule 5. To show the limits of a concept, use the difference principle: *Juxtapose (place side by side, or one after the other) examples that are minimally different and give them different labels (such as "orange," "not-orange").*

Rule 5 (the difference principle) assumes the students have been taught the logical operation extrapolation. *Extrapolation* occurs when after being shown the boundaries of a concept by using minimally different examples,

[2]It could be an example of a *writing instrument, blue, cylindrical, something held in the right hand, over, something made of plastic,* and the list could go on and on.

[3]*Chot* might be *things made of metal, cutting instruments, tools, handtools, objects, man-made objects, things made of steel,* and so on.

examples more different are treated as not-instances. Consider the following illustration:

X X	Y P P
S+	S−

In this illustration, the *X*'s show the range of S+ and the *Y* the beginning of S− (*Y* is minimally different from some *X*). If the student can extrapolate, values more different from *X* than *Y*, such as *P*, will also be called *Y*. This logical operation can be taught, through a series of examples that follow the rule: "If the examples I show you are more different from the *X* than the not-*X*'s demonstrated, they are also not-*X*."

Now suppose that all of the examples of *orange* had the exact same hue, and all of the examples of *yellow* and *red* were also the same hue. Under these conditions it is very likely that a restricted concept of *orange* would have been learned, and that reddish-orange balls and yellowish-orange balls might not be called "orange." Appropriate generalization to the full range of a concept class can be obtained by using the following principle.

Rule 6. To show a range of positive features, such as orange or cutting tools, sample that range using the sameness principle: *Juxtapose positive examples that are as different as possible (within the context of the* setup*) and indicate that they are the same.*[4]

Rule 6 assumes that the students have been taught the logical operation called interpolation, as illustrated in our example of orange. *Interpolation* occurs when after being shown a range of examples, the student responds to new examples within that range as concept instances. Consider the following:

X	*P*	*X*	*P*	*X*
		S+		

The *X*'s represent the range of S+ values for the concept orange. Interpolation occurs if after presenting the three *X* examples, the student also calls the *P* examples "orange." Interpolation can be taught by presenting a series of ranges for different concepts, and reinforcing students for following this rule: "If the examples I show you after demonstrating a range are within that range, they are also members of that concept class."

Rule 7. After teaching a concept, test with new examples to see if it has been learned.

Rule 8. Finally, vary the setup to show what is irrelevant and thereby expand the range of applications.

APPLYING THE RULES TO TEACH SINGLE-DIMENSION CONCEPTS

An eleven-step sequence that can be used to teach and test almost any single-dimension basic concept will be illustrated. The teacher first designs the setup

[4]Tennyson, Wolley, and Merrill (1972) use the sameness and difference principles in presenting sets of items to be discriminated as positive or negative examples in teaching a concept or rule. In presenting two positive instances, they make them as different as possible (a divergent pair). In presenting a positive and a negative pair, they make them as similar as possible (a matched pair). For example, the rule is, "When there is an *e* on the end of a one-syllable, consonant-vowel-consonant word, the vowel says its name."

DIVERGENT PAIRS: cope–kite or made–cute

MATCHED PAIRS: cope–cop or cope–copy

for presenting *all eleven* examples. For example, to teach the concept *over,* the setup might be a table and a ball. The teacher would use a real table and ball and just move the ball in going from example to example. The diagrams that follow are representations that illustrate the steps and the moves the teacher would make. Notice that the first six steps are the same as were used for teaching *orange* earlier.

The first two examples are two negatives, with the 2nd example designed to be *minimally different* from example 3.

EXAMPLE — TEACHER WORDING

1.  "The ball is not over."

2. 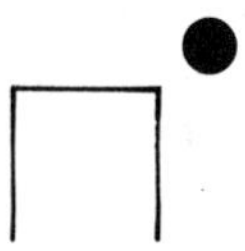 "The ball is not over."

Next, the teacher shows three positives that illustrate the possible range of positive examples, ending with a positive that is *minimally different* from the negative shown in example 6.

3. 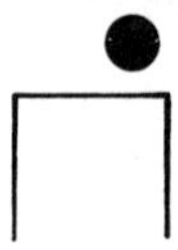 "The ball is over."

4. 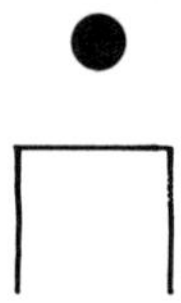 "The ball is over."

5. 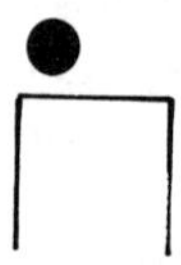 "The ball is over."

Next, the teacher shows six random positive and negative examples (except that the first one is minimally different from example 5) and tests the students.

6.  "Is the ball over?"

7.  "Is the ball over?"

8. 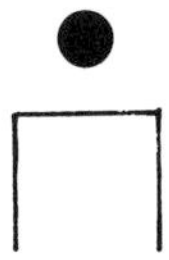 "Is the ball over?"

9.  "Is the ball over?"

10. 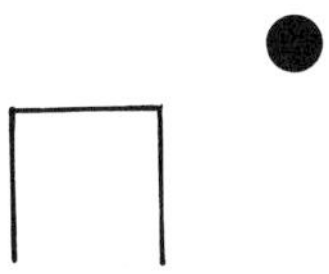 "Is the ball over?"

11. 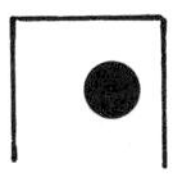 "Is the ball over?"

Finally, the teacher changes the setup and varies the irrelevant features. The teacher takes a variety of objects and asks, for example: "Is the ball over the chair?" "Is the pen over the table?" "Is the cup over the saucer?"

This strategy can be applied to a wide number of single-dimension concepts, both comparatives (such as *taller, farther*) and noncomparatives (such as *between* and *rough*). In the case of comparatives, however, the teacher gives a ***starting point*** to compare the first example with (see Figure 14.1); otherwise, the logic of the sequence is the same. In interpreting Figure 14.1, imagine you are actually watching the teacher's hand as it moves from example to example. It is the ***comparison*** with the previous example that defines each new example.

A sequence starting with negatives (as illustrated) is not essential. A teacher might start with three positives and then two negatives and produce a similar result. However, for single-dimension concepts, the negative-first approach is more likely to isolate the positive features ***on the first positive example*** and reduce the possibility of learning a misrule (responding to a feature that is not S+).

Continuous Conversion

An additional important principle in presenting examples for initial teaching is: ***Where possible, directly change positive examples into negative examples, and vice versa.*** In the eleven-step sequence just shown, a negative example of *over* would be converted to a positive example by a simple movement. Since everything is kept the same except the position (difference principle); this helps the learner focus on the critical features of *over*. Similarly, in showing the range of S+ (steps 3, 4, and 5), the continuous conversion examples show how much change can take place and still be S+ (sameness principle).

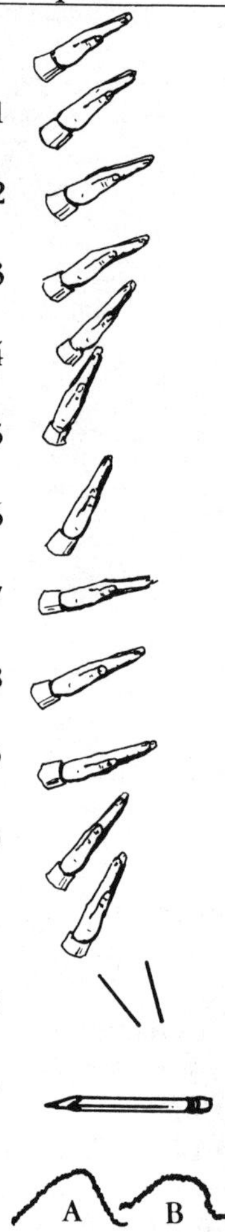

Example	Teacher Wording
	Watch my hand, I'll tell you if it gets steeper.
1	It didn't get steeper.
2	It didn't get steeper.
3	It got steeper.
4	It got steeper.
5	It got steeper.
6	Did it get steeper?
7	Did it get steeper?
8	Did it get steeper?
9	Did it get steeper?
10	Did it get steeper?
11	Did it get steeper?
12	Touch the line that is steeper.
13	Hold up a pencil so that it is steeper than this pencil.
14	Which hill is steeper? Hill A or Hill B?

Figure 14-1 *An 11-step sequence for teaching a comparative concept*

Noun Concepts

A modified strategy is required in teaching ***noun*** concepts. Since nouns have many features, there are no precise minimum differences between instances and not-instances. Also, because there are so many possible negative examples, the teacher is constrained to using negative examples that are in the student's repertoire. Furthermore, by presenting positive instances first, there will likely be a quicker focus on at least some of the many essential features. Since the names of the negatives have already been taught, they are used in identifying examples. The sequence might start with three or four positive examples and then negatives interspersed with positives. For example, in teaching ***truck,*** you might present a semitrailer, a van, and a pickup; and then start testing ("What's this?") with a train, a bus, a flatbed truck, a car, and a van.

In teaching noun concepts, Tiemann and Markle (1983) recommend identifying a ***minimum rational set.*** A minimum rational set includes: (1) a set of critical attributes, (2) a close-in nonexample for each critical attribute, and (3) variable attributes. Since for many nouns (especially manufactured things), S+ has ***variable attributes*** as well as critical attributes, it is necessary to identify these attributes and their variations so that the range of positive examples can be properly sampled. For example, for the concept *chair,* the analysis might go as follows (after Tiemann and Markle, 1983):

Variable Attributes:

1. Number of legs: 4, 3, 2, 1, 0
2. Arms: present, absent
3. Size of back: high, medium, low
4. Nature of feet: rockers, wheels, ornate, none, etc.
5. Upholstery: no, yes (range of types)
6. Planes: flat, curved

Critical Attributes:	*Close-in Nonexamples:*
1. Supports the back	Stool
2. Single-person seat	Loveseat
3. Supports sitting position	Beach lounge seat

In selecting positive examples, the teacher tries to make each example represent as many variable features as possible. For example, a Scandinavian "Egg" chair might show a chair with one leg, arms present, high back, round base, cushion upholstery on seat, and curved planes. Other examples would be selected to show additional variable properties.

Very likely, Engelmann would approach teaching the concept *chair* by focusing on the critical attributes and abstracting a function rule such as: "A chair is a seat with a back that holds one person in a sitting position." The rule could be used to examine any example for its "chairness."

GENERAL-CASE SETS VERSUS SETS COMPOSED OF INDEPENDENT MEMBERS

In classifying teaching objectives, *general-case* objectives (as defined earlier) are to be contrasted with sets made up of *independent members.* (These will be called IM sets to ease communications.) When IM sets are being taught, it is often called "rote learning." In IM sets each and every set member must be taught (Becker & Engelmann, 1976). In learning sounds to be used in the routine called *decoding* in reading, the learning of one sound helps very little in learning another (although there may be some savings in the ability to follow directions more readily on members added to the set later). Being able to say "aaaaaah" to the sound *a* does not help in learning to say "buh" to the sound *b.*

Sounds form an IM set, and instances of the concept *orange* form a general case set. But consider the illustration in Figure 14.2.

Each member of the IM set has all the features of a concept. S+ has a range of values that can be found in the many, many instances that form a class of symbols called "aaaah." Other sounds in the set define the S− examples. And, both positive and negative examples have many irrelevant features (Si). To learn to identify a sound is to learn a concept. To learn a set of related concepts requires multiple-discrimination learning. It would appear that these are not two different "kinds of learning" or "kinds of knowledge" (rote learning and concept learning), but rather sets of related concepts and the set members.

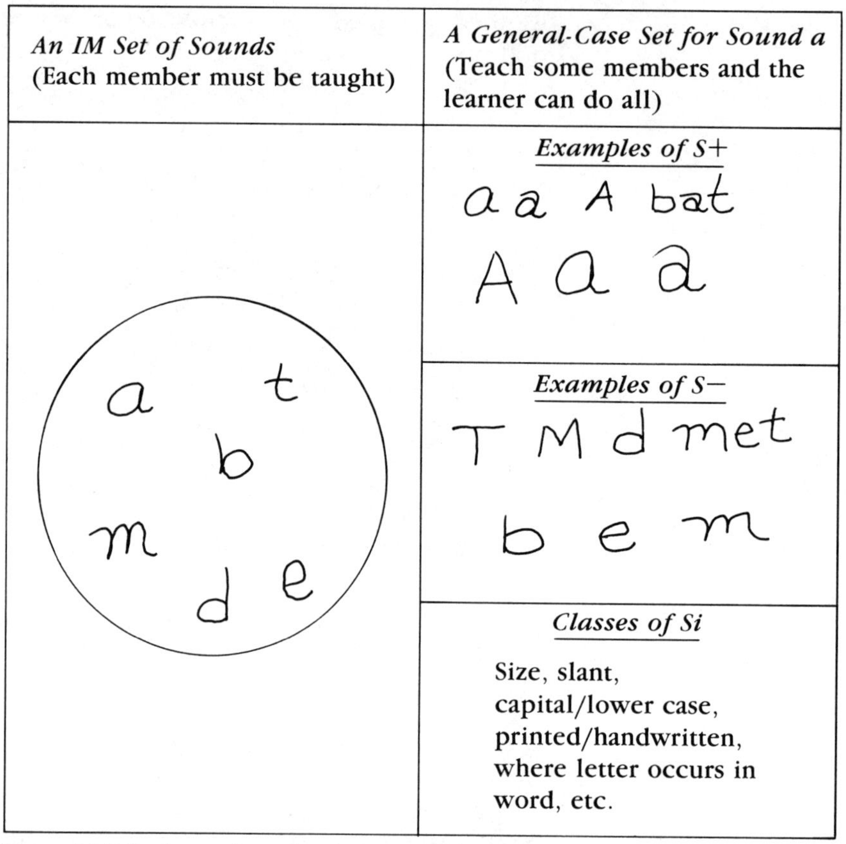

Figure 14-2 *Each member of an independent member (IM) set may be a general case*

Now consider the illustration in Figure 14.3.

Again you can see the same structure. When concepts are grouped into a related set, teaching *each member* involves general-case teaching, but *each member of the set has to be taught* if it is going to be learned (thus, sets of concepts are IM sets.)[5] When it comes to instructional requirements, sets of symbols (words, sounds, numbers) have the same status as basic concepts.

TEACHING SETS OF RELATED CONCEPTS

Learning does not occur in isolation from other learning. If a student learns an addition strategy, it must be discriminated from a subtraction strategy. If a student learns to say the sound for the letter *m,* it must be discriminated from the symbol and sound for the letter *n.* The concept *on* has to be discriminated from *over,* the concept *pony* from *horse* or *dog.* All knowledge and skills that students learn share some properties with other things they learn. These samenesses provide a basis for overgeneralization of a concept to inappropriate instances. For example, the common features of the letter *b* and *d* can lead to one being called the other, if care is not taken in designing the instruction. To take into account the features *common* to two or more concepts, you need to add a new class of stimuli to your multiple-discrimination model of concept instances. Let Sc stand for the features common to both positive and negative instances that are not irrelevant. Both elephants and people are warm blooded. The characteristic cannot be arbitrarily replaced by cold-bloodedness.

[5]In the chapter on problem-solving routines, you will see that some kinds of knowledge can be taught as a general-case set or an IM set, depending on the teaching strategy.

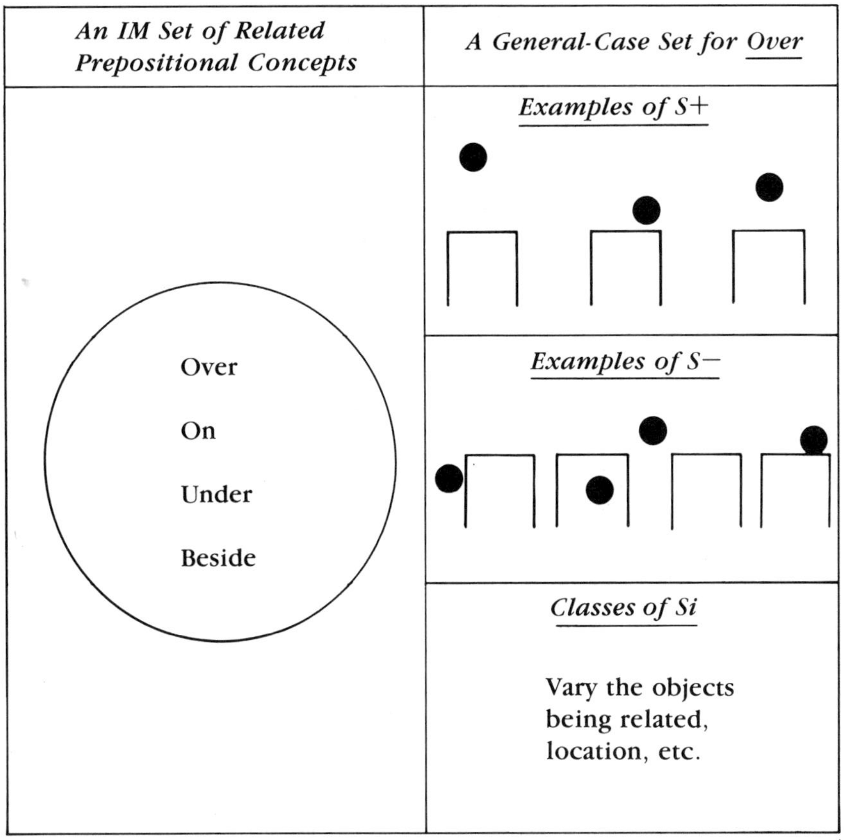

Figure 14-3 *Related sets of concepts also have an IM and a general-case aspect*

S+ and S− are mutually exclusive feature sets, although there are "gray areas" for most concepts. If red is S+, all other colors are S−. If dogs are S+, all other kinds of pets or all other kinds of mammals are S−. If you know it is S−, you know it is not S+.

Positive Instances
S+
Sc
Si

Negative Instances
S−
Sc
Si

Sc features may be present in both positive and negative examples. There are two varieties of common characteristics for multiple feature concepts. If S+ is defined by three features for chair:

1. Has a back

2. Holds one person

3. In a sitting position

S+ is all of these features. A ***couch*** or a ***stool*** would share two of the features. In these cases, Sc is part of an S+ set at a ***collateral*** feature level. The second variety of Sc involves features of ***higher-order*** concepts. Couches and chairs are all in the class furniture. Red and orange are both colors. These Sc characteristics provide the basis for forming higher-order concepts where all lower-order class instances are included in the higher-order class also.

Figure 14.4 illustrates a hierarchy based on object concepts (nouns). Only some of the subsets are shown in the figure. For example, it shows a subset for mammals, but not its coordinate concepts (birds, fish, and so on). Similarly, the figure shows a subset for dogs, but not for man, zebras, and elephants.

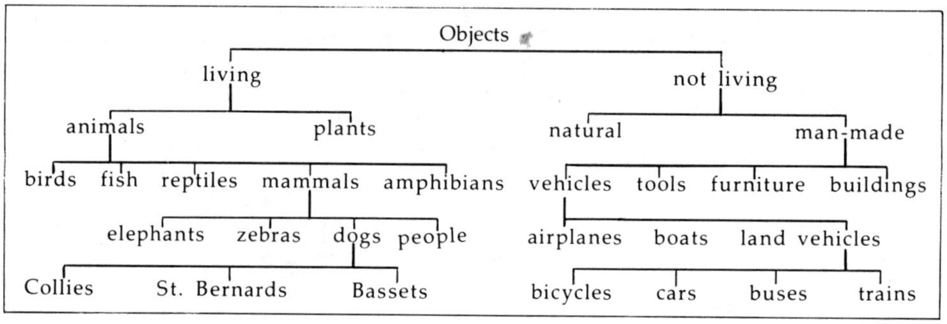

Figure 14-4 *A concept hierarchy based on objects*

In teaching hierarchically ordered concepts where the goal includes teaching the hierarchy, *teach at two levels at once.* For example, if you are teaching varieties of mammals, first distinguish mammals from not-mammals, and then teach the subgroupings of mammals: "This mammal is an elephant." "This mammal is a person." This shows the student directly how different concepts are related to each other. It also helps the student to learn that an instance of one concept can be an instance of another.

The Bases for Errors

Concepts are learned through the discrimination of members of related sets of concepts. Errors are most likely to occur in this learning when:

1. There are many common characteristics (Sc) shared by the instances of two concepts.

2. There are few differences in concept features (S+ versus S− differences).

3. There has been little previous discrimination training.

Consider the letters **a** and **d**. They share the characteristics (Sc) of being letters and being formed in the same manner. They differ only in the length of the stem. If the difference in the stem length is small, we can predict a greater difficulty in discriminating *a* from *d* than if the difference were large. Also, you can predict that these two letters are more likely to be confused with each other than either would be with the letter *s*. A program designer could reduce the possibility of errors by exaggerating the difference in stem length or by making the *a* this way: **a**; and the *d* this way: **d**. This eliminates some of the common characteristics (Sc). A programmer could also focus on directly training the difference to be learned.

With knowledge of factors that control errors, you can prepare programs in which errors are reduced or eliminated. In order to do this, it is first necessary to specify the set of related concepts (including symbols) to be taught and analyze them *pair-by-pair* for *samenesses* (Sc) and *differences* (S+ versus S−). Such a process is illustrated in Figure 14.5. This figure shows examples of five concepts from the set *closed geometric figures.* The S+ features of each concept are listed, with the same letter being used to define features common (Sc) to more than one concept. The numbers show how many *differences* exist (S+ versus S−) for each pair. For example, square and triangle have two differences, the number of sides and the size of the angles. They also have two samenesses, straight sides and equal sides.

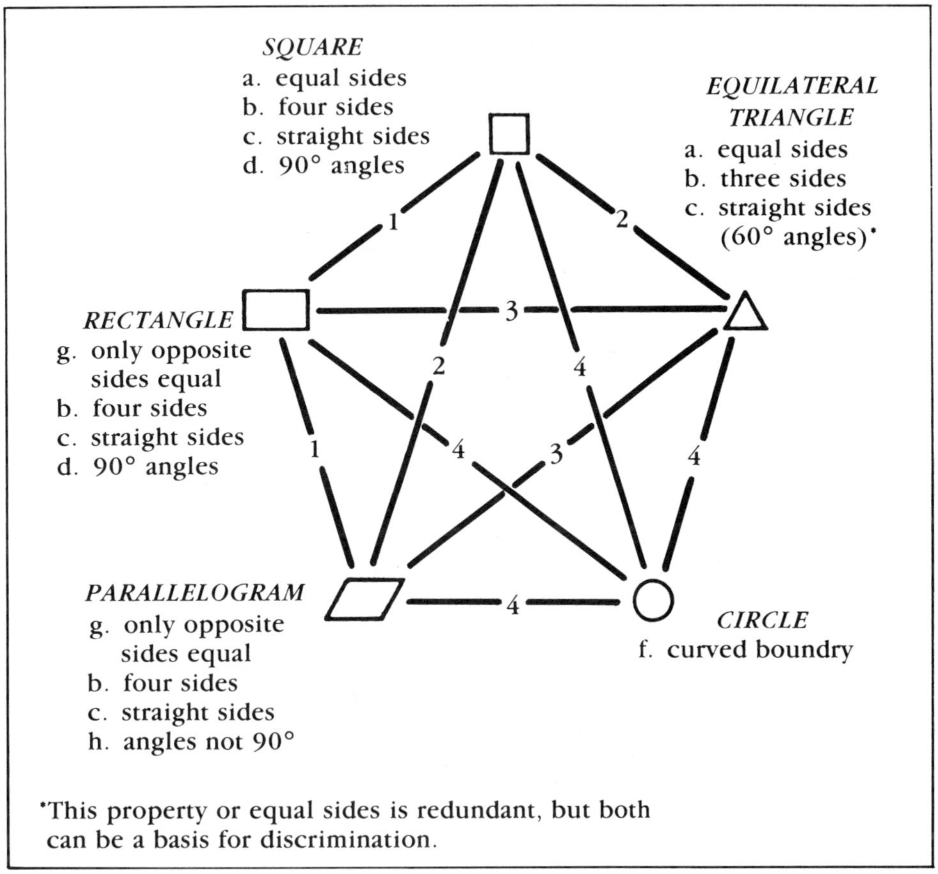

Figure 14-5 *A set of related concepts and their essential properties. Numbers on connecting lines indicate the number of ways in which two concepts can be discriminated.*

Where concepts differ in many ways, only a sampling of the ways in which they differ need to be taught. Where there are few differences, each of the differences may need to be taught. For the examples in Figure 14.5, more attention would be given to discriminating *squares* from *rectangles* and *rectangles* from *parallelograms* than any of these from *circle.*

In the classical verbal learning literature, the errors that occur in teaching sets of related concepts are discussed using the concepts of *proactive* and *retroactive inhibition* (Hilgard, 1951)—the effects of prior learning on new learning (proactive) and new learning on prior learning (retroactive). However, by viewing the problem logically in terms of sameness and differences (pair-by-pair), the instructional designer can predict where such "interference" will occur. In this view, there is no inhibition process going on, simply a failure to provide appropriate *discrimination training.*

Cumulative Programing

A major goal of carefully designed instruction is to attempt (wherever possible) to teach one thing at a time. When it comes to sets of related concepts (including symbols), the goal of teaching one thing at a time is most readily achieved by following a procedure that has been called cumulative programing. In *cumulative programing,* you begin by teaching two members of the set, then add in a new member after the master criterion has been reached, continuing the process until the set has been taught. For the example in Figure 14.5, you might begin by teaching the discrimination of *square* from *circle,* then add *equilateral triangle,* and bring the three concepts to criterion. Next add *parallelogram,* and finally *rectangle.* In teaching the identification of numbers to chimpanzees, Ferster and Hammer (1966) compared a cumulative programing procedure with one that brought each possible pair to criterion, one after the other. The cumulative approach led to good general-case learning. Numbers could be discriminated when presented in any order. The second approach failed to produce the ability to discriminate among members of the set when they were presented in a random order. Using a related procedure, Neef, Iwata, and Page (1980) showed that interspersing known spelling words among new ones led to better acquisition and retention of new words than when just new words were presented. The students also preferred the interspersal method.

Cumulative programing allows the achievement of at least three goals. First, easier items can be taught first to get the student going with a new topic. Second, the aspects of multiple-feature concepts (noun concepts) such as *square* can be taught incrementally, as new members are added to the set requiring new discriminations.

(As an exercise, take the ordering given previously for cumulatively teaching five geometric figures and use the features listed in Figure 14.5. Write down what new discrimination[s] would have to be learned as each new member is added to the set.)

The third goal that can be achieved with careful analysis and cumulative programing is separating the introduction of highly similar concepts (those that have many samenesses and few differences) as far as possible in time. Introducing highly similar tasks close together (such as saying the sounds for *d* and *b* or *m* and *n*) is more likely to lead to greater confusion between the sounds than if they are separated as far as possible in time and in the number of sounds introduced in between them (Gibson, Pick, and Asser, 1962). A common example of confusion in most of our learning histories is derived from the fact that *stalactite* and *stalagmite* were introduced in the same paragraph one day in ninth grade science. You know one goes up and one goes down, but which is which? (Or try: *abcissa* and *ordinate* or the symbols < and >.) Keep in mind that tasks used to teach concepts may be confused because of similarities in their response properties as well as the stimulus properties.

Finally, another potential benefit of using cumulative programing can be inferred from the study by Neef et al. (1980). The students preferred the interspersal method more most likely because it provided for some "right responses" (reinforcement?) while working on difficult new concepts.

There are many other related issues that influence the design of tasks and sequencing strategies. They include how to program *practice* and *review* to ensure discrimination among potentially confusible members of a set and how to use *prompts* to reduce similarities that are potentially troublesome (for example what has been called "long-e" could be written like this: ē, and "short-e" like this: e.).

Some Important Concept Sets

Probably the most important set of concepts people ever learn is *words.* This set undoubtedly has many important subsets, some of which have been discussed in this chapter. But the point here for "related sets" is to show a mapping of the several sets involved learning a language. Consider Figure 14.6.

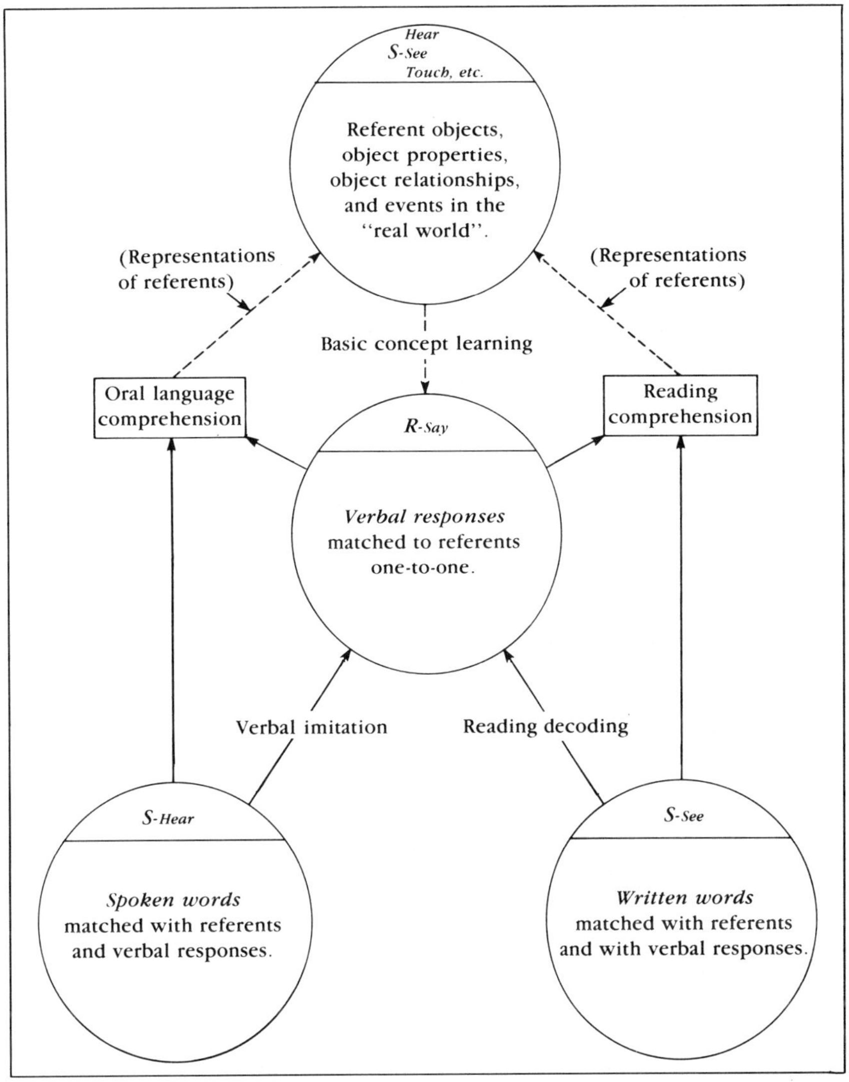

Figure 14-6 *A mapping of sets of related stimuli and responses important for intelligent behavior*

Figure 14.6 illustrates how three stimulus sets (the instances for basic concepts, the names you hear for them, and the written words that refer to them) relate to the verbal responses students learn to make. Basic concept learning is learning to make a culturally appropriate response for each referent concept (including symbols people have created). Oral language comprehension ties the words students hear to some representation of the concepts or direct examples. Reading comprehension ties the words students see to some representation of the concepts. Just repeating what you hear someone else say is simple imitation if the referent for the word is not known. Similarly, decoding in reading can be simply "word calling" if the referent is not known. It becomes a part of reading comprehension when the referent is known. If you were to add a set of written responses to the figure, you could also represent the process of taking dictation (hear-write) or copying script (read-write).

SUMMARY

In concept learning (and in other general-case learning), samenesses shared by members of a concept class (and not other classes) provide the basis for learning a generalization. Basic concepts can only fully be defined in relation to a finite set of concepts that a given concept is to be discriminated from. Concept learning is a multiple-discrimination problem. *Between* positive and negative instances, it is necessary to discriminate the relevant characteristics of each type of instance (S+ versus S− differences). *Within* positive or negative instances, it is necessary to discriminate relevant features from irrelevant features (S+ from Si, or S− from Si). A general case has been learned when, after instruction on some examples from a set, the student can respond correctly to any example in the set.

Some rules for teaching basic concepts are:

1. There should be a *set* of positive examples.

2. There must be a *structural basis* for a generalization in the samenesses of the positive examples.

3. There should also be a *set* of negative examples.

4. In initial teaching, the number of examples needed can be reduced by using a common *setup* in which the positive and negative examples share the greatest possible number of irrelevant features.

5. Use the *minimum difference principle* to show the limits of a concept. Juxtapose positive and negative examples that are minimally different from each other.

6. Use the *sameness principle* to show the range of positive examples. Juxtapose positive examples that are as different as possible (within the limits of the setup) and indicate that they are the same.

7. After teaching a concept, *test* with novel positive and negative examples to see if the concept has been learned.

8. Finally, *vary the setup* to show what is irrelevant and thus expand the range of application.

If the students have been taught the logical operations of interpolation and extrapolation, fewer examples are needed than if these operations have not been taught. In interpolation, the student knows that any examples falling within the range of positives demonstrated by the teacher are also positive. In extrapolation, the student knows that any negatives more different than those illustrated by the teacher are also negatives. The use of continuous conversion in going from positive to negative examples (or vice versa) or to show a range of positives more clearly isolates the critical discriminations for the learner. Everything is kept the same in going from example to example except the critical feature.

An eleven-step sequence following these principles that can be used to teach any single-dimension basic concept was illustrated. Five examples are used as teaching examples, and six for testing. Two negatives are followed by three positives, a minimally different negative, and then five randomly ordered examples are presented. Minimal differences are used in going from examples 2 to 3 and 5 to 6. Examples 3, 4, and 5 are used to show the range of the positives. The setup is varied after presenting the 11 teaching and testing examples to expand the range of application by showing what features are irrelevant to the concept.

Teaching objectives that form general cases were contrasted with those where every member of the set must be taught (called independent-member or IM sets). Sets of concepts (including symbols) form IM sets, but each concept (or symbol) within the set can become a general case. Later, in discussing problem-solving routines, you will see that whether one is dealing with a general or IM (rote) case can depend on the teaching strategy.

Sets of related concepts share common features (Sc). Errors in learning related sets of concepts are most likely to occur where two members of a set share many common features (Sc) and have few differences (S+ versus S− differences), and where there has not been prior discrimination training about the differences. The program designer can use pair-by-pair analysis of sets of related concepts to determine where errors are most likely to occur and to design the instruction to reduce the possibility of errors. Where concepts differ in many ways, only a sampling of the differences needs to be taught. Where there are few differences, each of the differences may need to be taught.

Cumulative programing is used to teach sets of related concepts. In cumulative programing, two concepts are discriminated from each other first, then a third is added and the set is brought to criterion. New members are added until the set has been taught. Cumulative programing also allows the teacher to begin with easier set members, to slowly expand the definitions of multiple-featured concepts, and to widely separate highly similar members.

This chapter concluded by mapping some of the important subsets involved in learning a language.

You should note that not all teachers are expected to become competent educational designers, but they should know how to recognize well-designed and poorly-designed programs and how to use good presentation methods.

CHAPTER

15

JOINING FORMS AND COMPLEX FORMS

JOINING FORMS

Basic concepts can be related either *logically* or *empirically*. Sets of basic concepts can be joined logically by transformation rules which provide a basis for generalizing from some examples to a fuller set. When concepts are joined empirically, the resulting fact statements can range from very specific facts (such as "There is a fly on your refrigerator door.") to very generalizable facts called *rules* and *principles* (for example, "*i* before *e* except after *c*." "Solids melt when heated."). Fact statements also provide the basis for expanding vocabulary through verbal definitions of new words using known words. Some rules and principles become the *steps* in problems-solving routines. As in the last chapter, the analyses to be presented draw heavily from Engelmann and Carnine's *Theory of Instruction* (1982).

Transformations

Transformational rules cover many aspects of learning including the rules of grammar, operations like rhyming, and the structural properties of number systems. Transformations permit generalization to new examples, because they follow the same rule as the teaching examples. The rule need not be verbal. If the rule is: "subject before predicate" and you start with these subjects: *Mary, He, She, Bill;* and these predicates: *ate the cake, threw the ball, opened the door;* it is possible to generate 12 sentences of the form *Mary* (subject) *threw the ball* (predicate). You simply replace the subject or predicate (or both) to create new examples of the rule.

To identify tranformations, look for: (a) tasks where changes in the elements would lead to many examples of the same form, (b) where different verbal responses are produced by different examples, and (c) where the responses share a sameness (such as subject before predicate). These features of transformations imply a teaching structure that uses the same wording with each example, requires different responses for each example, and a teaching presentation that shows *what is the same about all examples,* as well as *how changes in examples relate to changes in responses* (Engelmann and Carnine, 1982). Figure 15.1 illustrates a single transformation sequence for teaching the rule "Make both sides of an equation equal."

Example					*Teacher Wording*	
1.	15=				My turn. What makes the other side equal? Fifteen.	
2.	16=				My turn. What m akes the other side equal? Sixteen.	
3.	61=	**C**			Your turn. What makes the other side equal?	
4.	6=				What makes the other side equal?	
5.	5=				What makes the other side equal?	
6.	5J=			**B**	What makes the other side equal?	**A**
7.	27M=				What makes the other side equal?	
8.	9=		**E**		What makes the other side equal?	
9.	K=				What makes the other side equal?	
10.	23=				What makes the other side equal?	
11.	0=	**D**			What makes the other side equal?	
12.	R=				What makes the other side equal?	
13.	C+1=				What makes the other side equal?	
14.	12=				What makes the other side equal?	

Figure 15-1 *Transformation sequence for the rule "Make both sides of an equation equal"*

The *A* bracket shows that the same teacher wording is used for each example. The *B* bracket shows a common setup. The examples begin by showing (progressively) minimal differences in positive examples by changing only one part of an example at a time (*C* bracket). In Figure 15.1, 15 is changed to 16 (a difference based on counting), 16 is changed into 61 (a difference based on order of digits), 61 is changed into 6 (a difference based on the number of digits), and so forth. After showing minimal differences, the examples 7 to 14 show the range of sameness by using greatly differing examples and treating them in the same way (*D* bracket). Finally, the *E* bracket shows test examples. There are no negatives in a transformation sequence.

Subtypes. An important concept in the analysis of examples to be taught with the same strategy (such as transformation rules and problem-solving routines) is the analysis of *subtypes*. In teaching past tense, irregulars like *eat* (*ate*), *fly* (*flew*), *run* (*ran*), and *sit* (*sat*) are likely to lead to errors like "eated," "flied," and "runned." These kind of intelligent overgeneralizations are common with young children who have learned a past-tense rule, but not its exceptions. Subtypes are groups of examples that have the same irregular features. Subtypes require additional learning not covered by the main routine. They call for separate treatment to help the student learn special discriminations and responses. In teaching reading by sounds, irregulars like *was* ("wuz") and *is* ("iz") need special attention. However, special prompts can sometimes be used to allow subtypes like *cope* (versus *cop*) to become regular. For example, in *DISTAR Reading,* increased regularity is achieved for initial teaching by making silent letters smaller and by using a bar over the key vowel when the vowel "says its name."

In making a subtype analysis, Engelmann and Carnine (1982) recommend that you begin with a small set of examples that differ greatly from each other. They present an analysis of the set of two-digit numbers (10 to 99). Starting with 52, 17, and 90, the analyst asks, "How are they different?" Where a difference is found, the question becomes "How many other members of the set share this difference?" For example, the name for 90 refers to the tens digit only. So 10, 20, 30, and so on share this difference. The number 17 says the unit digit first, and the name for the tens digit is distorted. These properties are shared by 14, 15, 16, 18, and 19. With 13, the units digit is pronounced first, and both the units and the tens digit are distorted. The numbers 11 and 12 are truly irregulars. If the numbers from 11 to 19 were to be regular, we would say "one-one, one-two, one-three," and so forth. The names for 20, 30, and 50 are also distorted. We don't say "*two*ty", "*three*ty", or "*five*ty", but we do say "*four*ty", "*six*ty", and "*seven*ty".

Subtypes are brought into an instructional program after the regulars in the set have been taught. For example, in teaching numerical expansion ("Seventy-six equals seventy plus six"), a transformation program similar to that in Figure 15.1 would be used to teach the regular forms, and then the subtypes would be added one at a time. The reader seeking more detail is referred to Engelmann and Carnine (1982, Chapter 8).

(Go to Concept Practice 15A in your *Workbook* before continuing.)

Facts, Rules, and Principles

Engelmann and Carnine (1982) call the type of joining form that deals with facts, rules, and principles the *correlated-features form*. They involve statements about things that happen together. When dealing with a rule or principle about things that occur together, the learner is able to *infer* from observations of some stimulus features that other things or events also occur.

> The joining involves two discriminations. One is shown; the other is not. The learner is asked to predict the status of the *unobserved discrimination* from the observed discrimination.
>
> The communication of correlated-features is the transition between the immediately observable features of examples and the completely symbolized representation of events presented in facts (verbal statements). The correlated-features communication is most appropriate for teaching science rules, spelling rules, unfamiliar words that have familiar meanings, and similar applications. (Engelmann & Carnine, 1982, p.93).

Facts can be thought of as having two parts. The first part (1) names some thing or event and the second part (2) links the thing or event to other features. This is a fact: (1) Professional football linemen (2) are very heavy. If you know someone is a professional football lineman, you could infer that he would be quite heavy without seeing or weighing him. This is a fact: (1) Ice (2) melts above 32 degrees Fahrenheit. If we know something is ice, we can predict that it will melt if we raise the temperature above 32 degrees. This is a fact: (1) *Above* (2) is another word for *over*. If we know the meaning of *over*, but not *above*, we can infer the meaning for *above*. This is a fact: (1) If a verb ends in *y*, (2) change the *y* to *i* before adding *ed* (as with *carry, carried*).

Choice of Sequencing Procedures. The second part of a fact statement determines what kind of sequencing to use in teaching the fact. Some facts imply a transformation. For example, the fact: "The bottom part of a fraction tells us how many parts in each whole" implies a transformation. Each different bottom number would lead to a different number of parts in a whole. For example, the number of parts each whole is divided into is determined by the "bottom parts" of these fractions:

$\frac{3}{4}$ $\frac{8}{5}$ $\frac{1}{3}$

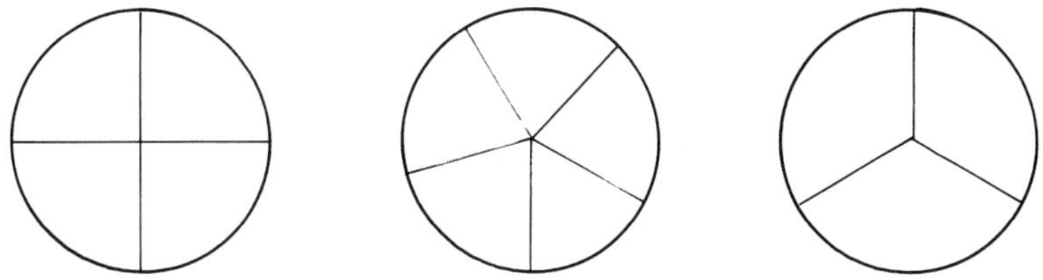

Transformations can occur only when the first part of the fact has a *symbolic* referent, as in the rule about fractions just illustrated. But not all such symbolic referents imply transformations. The example using ***above*** and ***over*** had a symbolic referent (the word ***above***), but did not have the properties of a transformation (changing responses to changing stimuli, with a sameness in format). If something is *above,* the only response we can infer is that it is *over.*

If the second part of a fact statement implies a transformation, follow the sequencing procedures for teaching a transformation (use positive examples only, use the same wording, demonstrate sameness, relate the change in examples to the change in response, start with minimal differences, show the range of examples, and test).

If the second part does not imply a transformation, follow the eleven-step procedure for teaching a *single-dimension concept* (demonstrate with two negatives and three positives that show the range, test with six more examples, show minimum differences in going from examples 2 to 3 and 5 to 6).

Teacher Wording. In teaching facts, the Teacher Wording asks two questions. The first question asks for the inference about what is not shown. The second question asks the reason for the conclusion.

Suppose the fact is: Ice melts above 32 degrees Fahrenheit.[1] You could present examples of ice being placed in a heating-cooling chamber with the temperature set above 32 degrees and below 32 degrees and ask, "What will happen to this ice?" After the student responds, you could ask, "How do you know?"

Example	***Teacher Wording***	***Response***
Ice is placed in a 35-degree chamber.	What will happen to this ice?	It will melt.
	How do you know?	The temperature is above 32 degrees.
Ice is placed in a 31-degree chamber.	What will happen to this ice?	It will not melt.
	How do you know?	The temperature is not above 32 degrees.

[1]This is true only if you use distilled water.

The fact is used to predict the outcome. With the right kind of equipment, the conclusion can then be tested by observing the outcome. For most students, examples that were representation of the relation of ice to heat could be used. This would allow examples to be juxtaposed rapidly to teach the rule. For example, just the verbal statements given under the Example column could be used. Following a single-dimension sequence, a sequence like that presented in Figure 15.2 might be used.

Temperature of Chamber Ice is Placed in	*Teacher Wording*
	I'm going to tell you whether this ice will melt when placed in the chamber.
1. 25 degrees	It won't melt. How do I know? Because the temperature was not above 32 degrees.
2. 32 degrees	It won't melt. How do I know? Because the temperature was not above 32 degrees.
3. 33 degrees	It will melt. How do I know? Because the temperature is above 32 degrees.
4. 35 degrees	Your turn. Will the ice melt? How do you know?
5. 33 degrees	Will the ice melt? How do you know?
	(Continue with 5 or 6 randomly sequenced examples.)

Figure 15-2 *An example of a single-dimension sequence for teaching a fact*

This sequence uses fewer teaching examples, because the learner at this level would be more sophisticated. If the student makes repeated mistakes in using the rule, eliminate the question "How do you know?" temporarily so you can go from example to example more quickly. When this is successful, test with the two-question format again.

For teaching use of equivalent meanings (synonyms), Engelmann and Carnine (1982, p.99) recommend this procedure:

"I'll say things one way. You say them another, using the word *above.*"

Listen: "The light is over the table. Say it another way." (The light is *above* the table.)

Listen: "My hand is over this book. Say it another way."

Fact Sequences Involving Transformations. Figure 15.3 illustrates a sequence involving a transformation. The sequence follows the same rules outlined for the single-transformation sequence in Figure 15.1. The differences are that fewer teaching examples are used (assuming more sophisticated learners) and two questions are used instead of one to ensure understanding. Note that the symbols D and R are used in four of the examples so that students do not learn that the rule applies only to numbers and get lost in the future when they encounter algebra.

Example	Wording
	I'm going to show fractions that equal one, but part of each fraction is missing.
1. $\frac{12D}{\square} = 1$	My turn to say the fraction that equals one: 12D over 12D. How do I know 12D over 12D equals one? Because the top and bottom are the same.
2. $\frac{12}{\square} = 1$	My turn again: What fraction equals one? 12 over 12. How do I know it equals one? Because the top and bottom are the same.
3. $\frac{2}{\square} = 1$	Your turn: Say the fraction that equals one. How do you know?
4. $\frac{\square}{2} = 1$	Say the fraction that equals one. How do you know?
5. $\frac{\square}{17} = 1$	Say the fraction that equals one. How do you know?
6. $\frac{\square}{3+R} = 1$	Say the fraction that equals one. How do you know?
7. $\frac{100R}{\square} = 1$	Say the fraction that equals one. How do you know?
8. $\frac{\square}{2/3} = 1$	Say the fraction that equals one. How do you know?
9. $\frac{5R/7}{\square} = 1$	Say the fraction that equals one. How do you know?

Figure 15-3 *A transformation sequence*

Transformation sequences can be used for many rules in arithmetic, spelling, reading decoding, and language comprehension. Figures 15.4 and 15.5 give two additional illustrations. Figure 15.4 illustrates a transformation involving a revaluing rule in arithmetic, while Figure 15.5 illustrates a sequence for beginning the teaching the final-e rule in reading decoding.

Example	*Wording*
1. $5=5$	Here's the equation we start with. I'll make changes. I'll tell you if each change means that we have to change the other side of the equation.
2. $4+1=5$	What do we have to do with the other side? Nothing. Why? Because we didn't revalue the side.
3. $4+1+\underline{1}=5$	My turn again: What do we have to do with the other side? Add one. Why? Because we added one to this side.
4. $4+1+\underline{1-1}=5$	My turn again: What do we have to do with the other side? Nothing. Why? Because we didn't revalue this side.
5. $4+1+\underline{1-1-1}=5$	Your turn: What do we have to do with the other side? Why?
6. $6-1=5$	What do we have to do with the other side? Why?
7. $6-2=5$	What do we have to do with the other side? Why?
8. $5\times3=5$	What do we have to do with the other side? Why?
9. $5+2=5$	What do we have to do with the other side? Why?
10. $5\times1=5$	What do we have to do with the other side? Why?

Figure 15-4 *A revolving transformation*

Example	*Wording*
	For some words below the vowel is /ā/. For the others it is /ă/.
1. ate	My turn. What is the vowel in the word? /ā/. How do I know? Because the word ends with **v c** and **e.**
2. at	My turn: What is the vowel in this word? /ă/. How do I know? Because the word does not end with **v c** and e.
3. rat	Your turn: What's the vowel in this word? How do you know?
4. rate	What's the vowel in this word? How do you know?
5. rafte	What's the vowel in this word? How do you know?
6. rafe	What's the vowel in this word? How do you know?
7. safe	What's the vowel in this word? How do you know?
8. stand	What's the vowel in this word? How do you know?
9. ale	What's the vowel in this word? How do you know?
10. Stane	What's the vowel in this word? How do you know?
11. malte	What's the vowel in this word? How do you know?

Figure 15-5 *A "long-short" vowel transformation*

(Go to Concept Practice 15B in your *Workbook* before continuing.)

COMPLEX FORMS

Complex forms join together facts into systems of related facts and join together rules into problem-solving routines.

Fact Systems

A high percentage of learning that goes on in schools after grade three is concerned with teaching facts—the teaching of history, the geography of our country and the world, the structure of governments, varieties of weather and clouds, animal and plant families, and so on. Organizing related facts into a system for teaching can be very useful in showing the relationships among the facts. Fact systems call for a variety of different responses about the features of the system. Juxtaposed items rarely deal with the same response dimension. As a result, much more practice is required to produce mastery.

There are two basic approaches to describing a system of related facts to a student. Teachers could write paragraphs of text that describe the facts and their relationships (or lecture on them), perhaps accompanied by some pictures (or audiovisuals). In this case the student is attempting to master some verbal chains, but how the chains become organized in memory (if they do) is pretty much left to chance. A second approach is to use teacher-directed instruction, along with visual-spatial displays of the facts and how they are related. Both laboratory and applied research has supported the conclusion that when there are *both* auditory and visual inputs of the same information, retention of the information is approximately doubled (Sprick, 1979; Darsh and Carnine, 1981). For this reason, Engelmann, Davis, and Davis (1982, 1983) have designed Direct Instruction programs to teach fact systems.

The programs have these features:

- Charts are designed to represent a set of facts, and a script is written to teach the words and relationships represented in the charts.
- After presenting the chart information, the teacher introduces a blank chart with the words removed, but the spatial configuration is still represented.
- Groups of students then practice by playing a game. They role dice and take turns answering questions depending on the number (from one to twelve) on the dice using a blank chart. The answers to the questions usually involve filling in the wording on the chart. Points are earned on scoring charts kept by a monitor (rotating students).

These three steps parallel the steps in concept teaching: Go from initial teaching to testing for learning, followed by expanded applications and practice.

Where appropriate, charts are designed so that they can be expanded by adding new information later. For example, early teaching about the weights of metals might begin with just five examples covering the range from lead to aluminum, and a later chart might interpolate five new members. In a very real sense, the charts help to build organized memory systems. If the early charts are used to cover the gross features of a set of facts, later charts can then be used to fill in the details on subsystems.

Figures 15.6 and 15.7 illustrate two charts.

Fact systems charts can be based on combinations of natural and created structures (as in the Teeth illustration), representations of such stuctures (such as an engine design cutaway to show internal workings), or charts can be created to show the relationships sets of facts not naturally prestructured (as in the factories chart) Engelmann and Carnine (1982) provide a number of guidelines for designing charts and suggestions for avoiding inappropriate prompting.

(Go to Concept Practice 15C in your *Workbook* before continuing.)

Problem-Solving Routines

When a set of related problems can be solved by learning one generalized overall routine for dealing with all the problems, there is a great saving in teaching time. As noted in the last chapter, a general case is to be contrasted with a linear set, wherein each and every set member must be taught. Now for many skills, whether the student learns a rote skill or a general case *depends on the teaching method*. For example, as noted in Chapter 13, about 80 percent of the reading

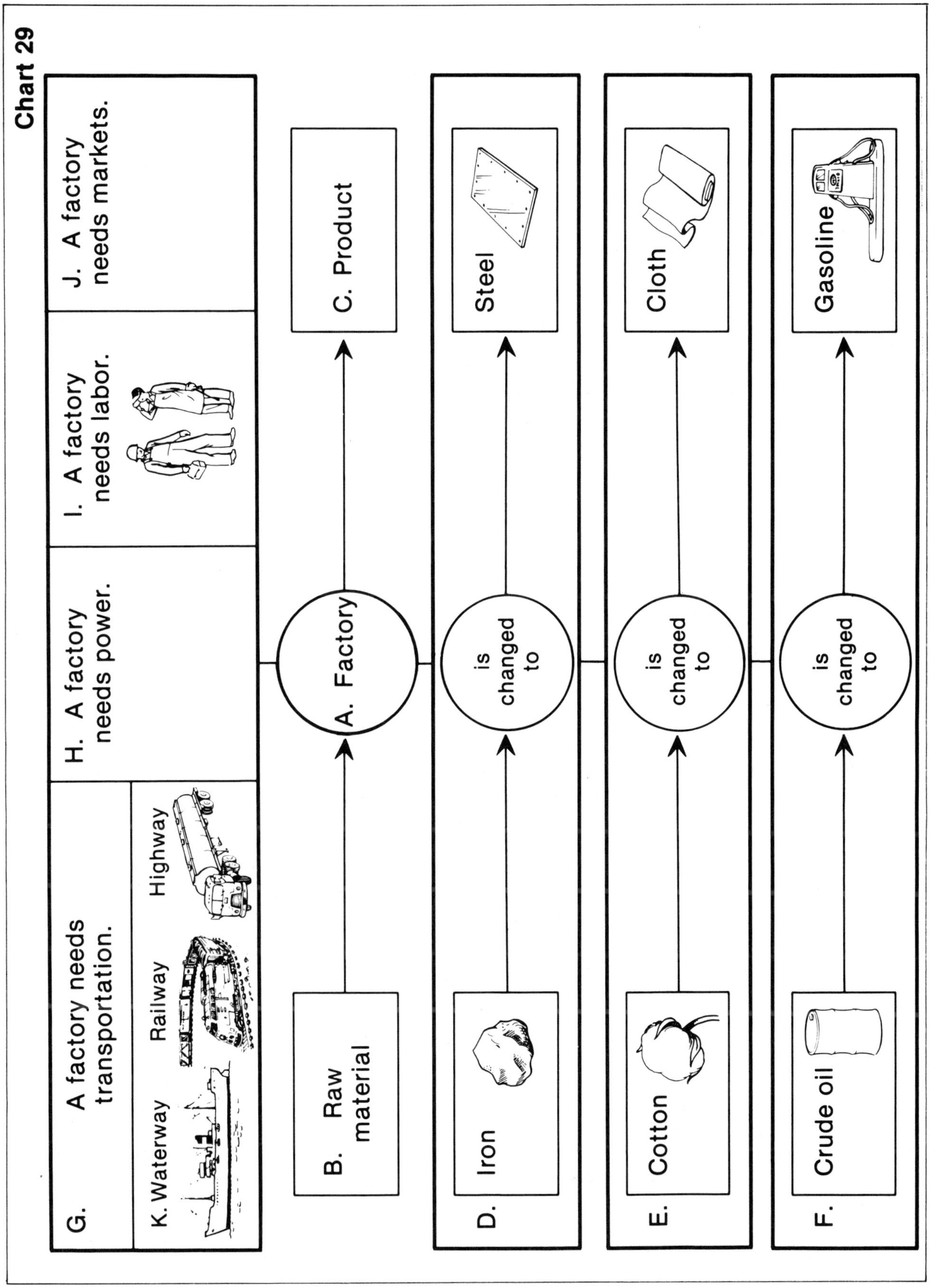

Figure 15-6 *A fact chart for factories*

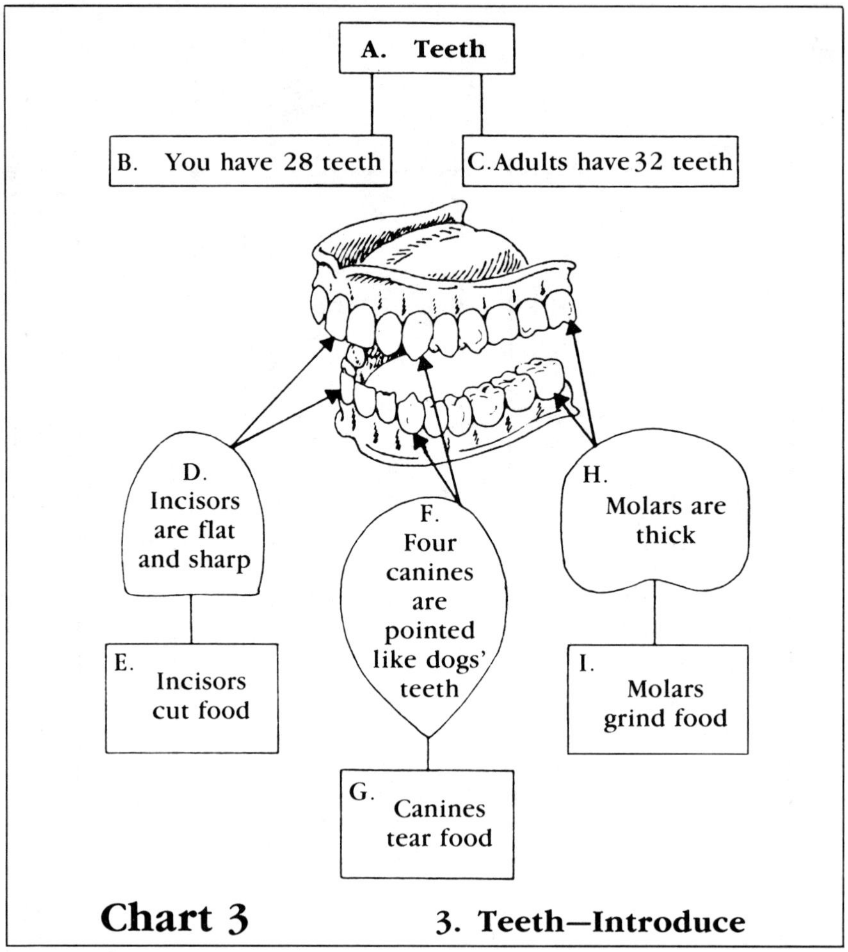

Figure 15-7 *Fact chart 3: Teeth introduction*

textbooks in the United States teach beginning reading by the sight-word method (Flesch, 1981). This is a rote (linear) method. Learning one word does not help a student with others. *DISTAR Reading* and a few others, on the other hand, use a systematic phonic method. This involves a general-case problem-solving routine for decoding words. The students are taught 40 sounds, blending skills (say the sounds slowly and hook them together), and say-it-fast skills. With these skills, they can read any of more than 10,000 regular-sound words. In the same time as it might take to teach basic phonic skills, one might be able to teach 80 to 100 sight words. But the student who learned the sight words would only know the words taught. There is no generalization inherent in the method. If you recall the data on reading presented in Chapter 12, the low-income DI Follow Through children who learned this problem-solving approach to decoding completed third grade with reading skills at the 5.2 grade level. DI Follow Through students were more than a year ahead of *average children* and two years ahead of typical disadvantaged children in decoding skills. That result was a product of general-case teaching.

Consider another example from math. You can teach beginning addition as a set of facts:

$$\begin{array}{rl} 5 & \\ +3 & \text{STIMULUS} \\ \hline 8 & \text{RESPONSE} \end{array}$$

or you can teach addition as a generalizable problem-solving skill—making the early learning more fun because new problems can be solved. (Later on, games are used to provide practice on the facts that need to be memorized so they can be readily used in multiplication and division.)

To teach problem-solving routines for addition, first teach these component preskills:

1. Equality rule: "As many as I have on this side of the equal sign, I have to have on the other side."

2. Symbol identification of numbers.

3. Counting-to-a-number up to 20.

4. Making sets of lines for numbers, using counting-to-a-number as the strategy.

If the component skills are pretaught as basic concepts or joining forms, it is easier to demonstrate the critical discriminations that the student must learn than is possible within a longer problem-solving routine. With the component skills pretaught, you are ready for the problem-solving routine.

(Show) 5 + 3 = □	
Teacher	**Learner**
1. Read it.	Five plus three equals how many.
2. Which side do we start counting on?	(Points to left side.)
3. Why?	Because there is an unknown on this side.
4. What does this tell us to do? (Points to 5)	Make 5 lines.
5. Do it.	5 + 3 = □ /////
6. What does this tell us to do? (Points to 3)	Make 3 lines.
7. Do it.	5 + 3 = □ ///// ///
8. How many on this side of the equal?	Eight.
9. So how many must go on the other side?	Eight.
10. Do it.	(Learner makes lines and writes the answer.) 5 + 3 = [8] ///// /// ////////
11. Read the problem and the answer.	Five plus three equals eight.

Figure 15-8 *A problem-solving routine for addition problems adapted from DISTAR Arithmetic*

Figure 15.8 shows a problem-solving routine for regular addition problems with sums up to 20 (the restriction made earlier in specifying a counting preskill). After teaching five to eight problems using this strategy, the students should be able to do the rest of the problems the first time they are presented. Later on, they will ***drill*** on addition facts, but even then they would have a strategy for testing whether a given fact answer is correct or not.

The same component skills used to solve regular addition problems can be applied to algebra addition problems and subtraction problems. The initial analysis of the range of related examples ***planned for this range of application.*** Algebra addition problems[2] take this form:

$$5 + \square = 8$$

To solve these kinds of problems the student needs one new component skill, namely, counting from a number to a number. "We are going to count from five to eight, get it going, Fiiiiive, 6, 7, 8." (Students make three lines under the box as they count). "How many did we plus?" "Three." "So what's the answer?" "Three." This skill also gives the students a fast way to do regular addition problems—count from the first number as many as the second number stands for.

Figures 15.9 and 15.10 illustrate the application of a similar strategy to

(Show) $5 - 3 = \square$

Teacher	**Learner**
1. Read it.	Five minus three equals how many?
2. (Touches under 5.) What does this tell us?	Start with five.
3. Do it.	(Learner makes 5 lines: $5 - 3 = \square$) /////
4. (Points to −3.) What does this tell us?	Minus three.
5. Do it.	(Learner crosses out 3 lines: $5 - 3 = \square$) +++//
6. (Points to equal sign.) What does this tell us?	We must have the same number on both sides.
7. What number is that?	Two.
8. Make the sides equal.	(Learner makes lines and writes answer: $5 - 3 = \boxed{2}$) +++// //
9. Read the problem and the answer.	Five minus three equals two.

Figure 15-9 *A subtraction routine from DISTAR Arithmetic*

[2]Mathematicians usually consider this a subtraction problem in which the "counting on" solution method is used.

(Show) 3 − 5 = □	
Teacher	**Learner**
1. Read it.	Three minus five equals how many?
2. (Touch under 3.) What does this tell us?	Start with three.
3. Do it.	(Learner makes three lines: 3 − 5 = □) ///
4. (Points to −5.) What does this tell us?	Minus five.
5. Do it.	(Learner "crosses out" 5 lines: 3 − 5 = □) ///--
6. (Points to equal sign.) What does this tell us?	We must have the same number on both sides.
7. What number is that?	Minus two.
8. Make the sides equal.	(Learner makes lines and writes answer: 3 − 5 = [-2]) ///-- --
9. Read the problem and the answer.	Three minus five equals minus two.

Figure 15-10 *A subtraction routine with negative numbers from DISTAR Arithmetic*

the solution of subtraction problems, including negative numbers. To solve these classes of problems, you then need only to teach that the minus sign means "take away" and how to minus count by making little minus signs to cross out plus counters.

Basic Design Procedures. As pointed out in Chapter 13, a common strategy can be used in designing problem-solving routines. Engelmann and Carnine's (1982) steps are:

1. Specify the range of examples for which the routine will work.
2. Make up a descriptive rule that tells exactly what the learner must do to attack every example within that range. (The same rule must hold for all examples.)
3. Design a task that tests each component discrimination mentioned in the descriptive rule.
4. Construct a chain composed of the tasks that test the component skills or the "steps" in the routine.

One goal in the analysis of knowledge is to find common structures across broad sets of problems, so that common strategies can be used to solve them. The addition and subtraction strategies just presented and the problems shown in Figure 15.11 illustrate this idea. Each of the problems in Figure 15.11 can be solved within a common generalized strategy. All of the needed subskills are not shown, just the general idea.

1. Four cows eat 3 tons of hay. How many cows would be needed to eat 5 tons?
2. Jim typed 7 pages in 4 hours. How many pages did he type per hour?
3. What is the speed of a plane that covers 50 kilometres in 8 minutes?
4. It takes 4 workers 7 hours to paint 5 houses. How many houses can 5 workers paint in 9 hours?
5. 3B = 7. What is B equal to?
6. 5 percent of what number equals 7?

Figure 15-11 *Sample story problems*

In systematic steps, the students are taught to convert each problem to an equivalent fraction statement, which they then solve for the unknown. They are first taught how to change any number into any other number. "I want to change 3 into 5."

$$3\,(\qquad) = 5$$

"I don't know how to change 3 into 5, but I know how to change three into 1, so if I have 1 on this side, I can multiply by 5 to make the sides equal."

$$3\left(\frac{1}{3}\cdot\frac{5}{1}\right) = 5 \qquad\qquad 3\left(\frac{5}{3}\right) = 5$$

Next, an equivalent fraction strategy is taught to solve the problems:

1. In the first problem, we are talking about cows and tons. So these are noted first. Then, the equation is completed.

$$\frac{\text{COWS}}{\text{TONS}}\ \frac{4}{3}\ \begin{matrix}\rightarrow\\ \rightarrow\end{matrix}\ = \frac{\square}{5}$$

Arrows point toward the unknown.
The student starts the solution on the bottom because there is no unknown there.

$$3\left(\frac{5}{3}\right) = 5$$

"If I multiply by 5/3 on the bottom of the equation to change 3 into 5, I must do the same to the top so as not to revalue the equation."

$$4\left(\frac{5}{3}\right) = \frac{20}{3} \qquad \text{Gives the answer.}$$

2. The pages per hour problem uses the same strategy, except we teach the *per* means per "one" something. So:

$$\frac{\text{PAGES}}{\text{HOURS}} \quad \frac{7}{4} \quad \begin{matrix}\longrightarrow \\ \longrightarrow\end{matrix} = \frac{\square}{1}$$

Problems with *per* form a subtype.

3. By learning to identify the *rate unit* in problem 3 (kilometers per one minute), it can be written as:

$$\frac{\text{K}}{\text{M}} \quad \frac{50}{8} \quad \begin{matrix}\longrightarrow \\ \longrightarrow\end{matrix} = \frac{\square}{1}$$

4. By learning to identify the ***product*** of the work in problem 4, it is solved. The product (houses) goes on top, the work (hours × workers) on the bottom (or vice versa).

$$\frac{\text{Houses}}{\text{Hours} \times \text{Workers}} \quad \frac{5}{4 \times 7} \quad \begin{matrix}\longrightarrow \\ \longrightarrow\end{matrix} = \frac{\square}{5 \times 9}$$

5. To do problem 5, the student simply learns that the B is the same as the parentheses.

$$3B = 7 \text{ is the same as } 3(\qquad) = 7$$

6. Finally, the percent problem is solved by knowing that 5 percent of something is five-hundredths $\left(\frac{5}{100}\right)$ of something. So:

$$\frac{5}{100}A = 7 \quad \text{or} \quad \frac{5}{100}(\qquad) = 7$$

Overgeneralization. The example using equivalent fractions just completed was intended to show how to prevent undergeneralization by making a careful analysis of related kinds of problems. As illustrated earlier with past-tense verbs (eat, eated; go, goed) and the teen numbers, overgeneralization can intelligently occur because irregular subtypes violate the rule. Special attention in the form of discrimination practice must be given to such subtypes to show the limits of the generalization. Most often overgeneralization occurs because discrimination practice has not been provided on similar, but yet different, kinds of problems.

Misrules. Probably the most common type of error found in traditional instruction is based on misrules, in which student behavior is controlled by some irrelevent features common to an early teaching set. Consider the following examples:

$$\begin{array}{r} 24 \\ -18 \\ \hline 14 \end{array} \qquad \begin{array}{r} 32 \\ -27 \\ \hline 15 \end{array} \qquad \begin{array}{r} 55 \\ -39 \\ \hline 24 \end{array}$$

In these examples, the student is subtracting the smaller number from the larger one, instead of the bottom from the top. This could have been learned as a misrule because all earlier examples did not involve revaluing, so that the smaller number was always subtracted from the larger one. Careful instruction is needed to introduce the new type of problems to prevent the possible misrule. Consider the following:

```
 4     7     9
 9     6     3
 7     4     4
--    --    --
13    13    12
```

In these examples, the student had always in the past only added two digits. When three were presented, the student just added the first two. Again, preparation is required when new problem types are introduced to prevent a misapplication of prior learning in a limited setting.

Additional Principles. Some additional principles involved in designing problem-solving routines are:

1. Teach component skills before presenting them in the problem-solving routine.

2. Make all steps overt at first. Later on fade the steps so that they become covert.

3. Present examples first in a simplified context, later use more complex contexts.

The next two chapters illustrate the application of these and other principles for designing problem-solving routines. It is important to note that the single most important difference between Engelmann's approach and that taken by other curriculum designers is that Engelmann starts with a full range of *examples* of the specific problems the student is to respond to and analyzes how they are the *same* and how they are *different* in designing a generalized approach to teaching them. Other curriculum designers begin with statements of objectives and then analyze them for components and prerequisites, often neglecting to see how different objectives relate to each other and not examining the range of possible tasks that might be performed with the same routine.

(Go to Concept Practice 15D and then return to the Summary.)

SUMMARY

This chapter examined how basic forms can be joined logically through transformation rules and empirically through statements of fact. It also examined how facts can be joined into fact systems and various rules can be chained together to form problem-solving routines. A major goal of this chapter was to show how the more complex knowledge forms relate to basic forms and to each other. This analysis provides an explicit basis for helping the future teacher to analyze more complex forms into the components they are built from. Another goal of this chapter was to further demonstrate the different teaching strategies appropriate for different forms of knowledge.

Transformation rules provides a logical basis for generalizations in the study of grammar, mathematical systems, and so forth. Transformation sequences use only positive examples. The sequences begin with progressive minimum differences (changing one aspect of an example at a time). These are followed by greatly differing examples that show the full range of application. In the analysis of examples, the instructional designer looks carefully for subtypes and irregulars that do not follow the main rule, but that need to be included in the full teaching goal.

Correlated feature forms (of which the fact statement is the most common example) also join together basic forms. These forms are common in the rules of science, spelling rules, and learning new words for old concepts. The first part of a fact names some thing or event. The second part links the first part to other features. If the second part of a fact involves a transformation, a transformation sequence is used to teach the fact. If the second part does not involve a transformation, the 11-step procedure for teaching a single-dimension concept is followed. However, the teacher's wording is modified in teaching a fact. The student is asked to predict what will happen given an example of rule and then to explain why the prediction was made. In teaching equivalent meanings (synonyms) for words, the teacher makes a statement using the known word and asks the student to "Say it another way."

Fact systems attempt to show through a combination of visual and verbal presentations how a set of facts is interrelated. By using a procedure of teach, test, and then apply and practice in a game format, it is possible to overcome some of the discrimination and memorization problems common to learning facts.

Problem-solving routines, when designed to teach a broad general case, can produce great savings in learning time over rote drill-and-practice approaches. The design of a routine begins by specifying the range of examples the routine will cover. A descriptive rule that will work for each example is developed. Tasks are designed to teach each component concept in the descriptive rule. Finally, a problem-solving sequence (chain of steps) is built from these component tasks. Several illustrations of planning for the "range of application," developing descriptive rules, analysis of components, and the development of the routine were examined.

Some causes of overgeneralization (failure to discriminate a not-instance) and the learning of misrules (responding to an irrelevant feature) were further examined.

Additional principles to consider in designing a problem-solving routine are: (1) teach component skills in isolation first, (2) make all steps initially overt, and (3) start with a simplified context that is later expanded.

CHAPTER

16

APPLICATIONS TO MATHEMATICS

In *Theory of Instruction,* Engelmann and Carnine (1982) go beyond the basic ideas presented in the last three chapters to describe strategies for the design of complete programs. Because of the fundamental importance of mathematics and reading skills, however, this chapter will illustrate program design ideas by examining applications in these areas. Two major works *Direct Instruction Mathematics* (Silbert, Carnine, & Stein, 1981) and *Direct Instruction Reading* (Carnine & Silbert, 1979) provide the source materials for these illustrations. The goals of this chapter and the next are to provide you with a basic understanding of the logic of program design and possibly to motivate some of you to look further into these two textbooks.

PROGRAM DESIGN PRINCIPLES

Instructional design has the goal of producing efficient teaching sequences that will lead students to make appropriate generalizations across the widest possible range of applications. It involves engineering the details of instruction to ensure that learning will take place. It involves teaching critical discriminations that will prevent inappropriate overgeneralization. It involves building systematically from simple tasks the student can perform to complex tasks you wish to teach. In teaching cognitive routines, instructional design involves making *all steps overt* at first, so that the teacher has a basis for correcting mistakes, and then gradually fading out the overt steps until problems can be done covertly (by thinking). When tasks occur within closely related sets (as they usually do), instructional design involves cumulatively building sets of related skills to criterion and being sure to provide adequate practice on older set members that might be confused with newer set members. The cumulative building of sets of related members also applies to routines as well as concepts. After teaching solutions to addition problems, when subtraction problems are introduced cumulative review is planned for to teach the necessary discrimination of the two classes of related problems. When multiplication and division problems are added later, they too become mixed in for discrimination practice after being "firmed up" in isolation.

As in any engineering problem, a teacher can always do a better job. There is never just one best solution, but some may be better than others as judged by efficiency, generality, and student gains. The major steps in the design of a program are:

1. Specify objectives.
2. Devise problem-solving strategies.
3. Determine necessary preskills.
4. Sequence skills.
5. Select a teaching procedure.
6. Design formats.
7. Select examples.
8. Provide practice and review. (From *Direct Instruction Mathematics*, by J. Silbert, D. Carnine, and M. Stein. Copyrighted © 1981 by Charles E. Merrill, Columbus, Ohio. Reproduced with permission of Charles E. Merrill and Douglas Carnine.)

Specifying Objectives

Ask yourself what generalizable tasks the students should be able to perform after instruction. For example, "The student will add any two-digit numbers with sums under 1,000." It is also important to specify a mastery level and perhaps a rate criterion (for example, complete ten problems per minute with a 90 percent accuracy).

Devising Problem-Solving Strategies

Where possible to do so, the goal of good design is to give the student a *general strategy* for solving a given type of problem. Chapters 14 and 15 have illustrated this point several times. Recall the ratio-equation strategy for solving story problems involving rates, work, percents, and so on. Recall also that in the solution for the addition and subtraction problems illustrated in the last chapter, the problem-solving strategy taught was a counting strategy (counting to a number or counting from a number to a number).

Determining the Preskills and Component Skills

For the addition problems of the form 5 + 3 = □, the preskills consist of symbol identification, equality rule, a rule for the side to start counting on, counting to a number, and making line sets to represent what a number stands for. To solve the problem, "What is 35 percent of 82?" the student must set up the problem like this

$$\begin{array}{r} 85 \\ \underline{.35} \\ 425 \\ \underline{255} \\ 29.75 \end{array}$$

and use preskills to convert a percent to a decimal equivalent, multiply two-digit numbers, and place the decimal point in the product.

Sequencing the Skills

The three rules important in sequencing skills should sound familiar by now:

- Teach the preskills for a given strategy before teaching the strategy. For example, the equality rule should be taught in isolation before being incorporated in an addition routine.

- Teach easy skills before more difficult skills. Subtraction problems involving borrowing (renaming) are more difficult than those without borrowing. Borrowing problems with zeros (402 − 78) are more difficult than those without. Reading the numbers 11, 12, 13, and 15 is more difficult than 23 or 46 because they violate the general rule "Say the tens number and then the ones number." But they are also more difficult than 14 and 16, because the name of the ones unit is distorted. We say "four-teen" and "six-teen," but not "two-teen" or "five-teen."

- Separate in time those concepts, skills, and operations likely to be confused. The symbols 6 and 9 are the same if rotated. This sameness could lead to confusion. Counting by fours and counting by sixes both share the numbers 12, 24, and 36. This could be confusing if the two series are taught at the same time.

Selecting a Teaching Procedure

In mathematics, tasks can involve *motor chains* (counting to a number, drawing the numeral 9), *basic concepts* (identifying instances of the numeral 9, the equality sign, operation signs), *transformations* (plus-one series, plus-two series), *rules* (equality rule, the side-to-start-counting-on rule), and *problem-solving routines.*

Motor chains are taught through these steps: *model, lead, test,* and *delayed test.* The teacher demonstrates, practices with the students to prompt the steps of the chain, and then fades out the help so that the students do it on their own. After some intervening activity, the delayed test is performed. If students fail, the teacher returns to guided practice.

You have already considered the initial teaching of basic concepts through examples. An additional consideration, however, is the way in which new members of a related set are "programed in." The basic steps are to: (1) model the correct response, (2) provide an alternating test using previously learned set members, and then (3) provide a delayed test after several intervening examples have been presented. If you are teaching symbol identification and the students have learned 4, 9, 2, and you are introducing 7, the pattern might go like this: *7,* 4, *7,* 9, *7,* 2, then *7,* 9, 2, *7,* 2, 4, *7,* 4, 2, 9, *7,* and so on. The delayed test would follow working on a different kind of task.

The teaching of transformations and other rules follows the guidelines discussed in Chapter 15, and the teaching of problem-solving routines uses modeling, guided practice, and test procedures. Questions by the teacher prompt when to apply each (previously taught) component skill. Throughout guided practice the teacher's help fades until the students perform on their own in independent workbook activities.

Designing Formats

A *format* is a framework, a set of specific steps, for doing problems of a given type. Once a format is designed, any example can be "plugged into" it. Formats

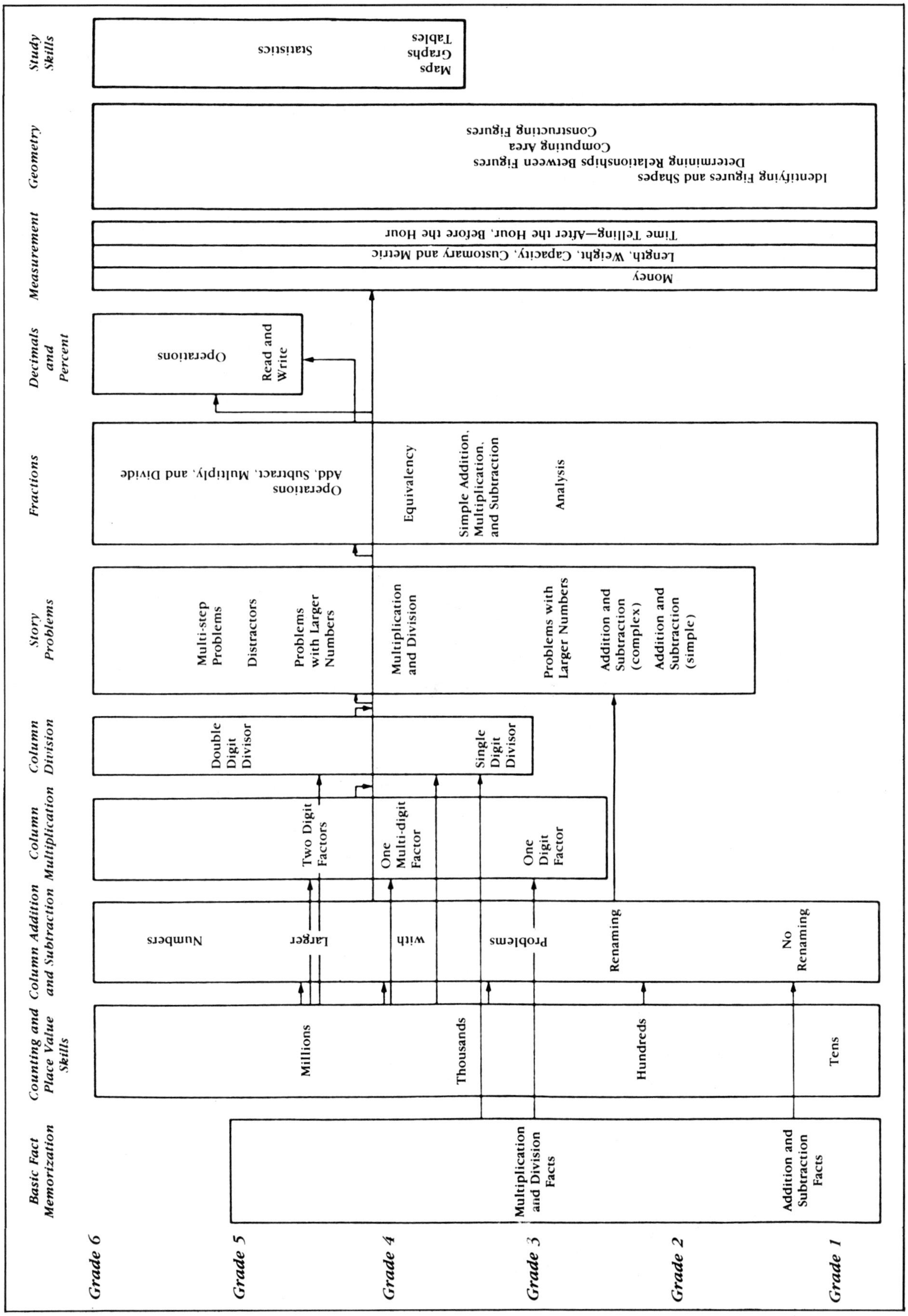

Figure 16-1 *Skill hierarchy for elementary mathematics instruction. (From* Direct Instruction Mathematics, *by J. Silbert, D. Carnine, and M. Stein. Copyright © 1981 by Charles E. Merrill, Columbus, Ohio. Reproduced with permission of Charles E. Merrill and Douglas Carnine.)*

must be designed carefully to avoid words the students do not know and other confusions. The text by Silbert, Carnine, and Stein is unique in providing the teacher with formats for teaching the major mathematical skills and concepts taught at the elementary and intermediate levels. Examples of these formats will be illustrated later in this chapter.

Selecting Examples

There are two general guidelines for selecting examples. First, be sure that the current (or a previously covered) strategy will work with the examples. If students are just learning a renaming strategy for subtraction, a problem such as 504 − 89 would be inappropriate because of the zero. Additional steps would need to be taught to cover this kind of problem, because it is necessary to rename the hundreds' place as well as the tens' place. The second guideline is (after the initial teaching in isolation) to intermix previously taught related problem types, so that the student learns to discriminate when to use each strategy.

Providing Practice Until Mastery

Initial practice is massed until students reach mastery. Then systematic review (distributed over time) is provided to get consolidation and discrimination from related skills.

Most current commercial programs available to teachers do not provide for adequate practice to achieve mastery and fail to provide exercises for discriminating related types of problems. Another major deficiency of current math texts is the failure to provide step-by-step procedures to assist teachers in providing instruction on story problems. You will look at some strategies for story problems later. Silbert et al. (1981) provide teachers with explicit guidelines for analyzing and adjusting commercial math programs for their deficiencies. These authors also provide placement tests appropriate for entry levels and the grades through six.

SCOPE AND SEQUENCE

Figure 16.1 shows a mapping of elementary mathematics skills by types of skills and grade levels. The arrows show the interdependencies.

Figure 16.2 shows a more detailed breakdown of skills for beginning instruction. Note that the skills are grouped by the type of knowledge represented, that is, counting chains, symbols (concepts), operations, rules (language), and facts.

Figures 16.3, 16.4, and 16.5 give three examples of the kind of detailed skill hierarchy analysis that is necessary before you can begin to actually design programs. Study the sequential dependencies carefully.

These skill hierarchies help to show how various skills are interrelated and what needs to be taught before what. Types of tasks are also grouped according to their teaching requirements.

PROGRAMING INSTRUCTION

Detailed formats for teaching three classes of skills will be used to illustrate some programing strategies in mathematics. The first format shows how many preskills are combined into a problem-solving routine for solving addition problems the *slow way,* (see Figure 16.6). (A less detailed, related format was illustrated in Chapter 5, so it should be familiar to you. After examining the major features of this format, you will examine a format for *addition the fast way* to show part of the transition that occurs in going from overt steps to covert steps in teacher-guided problem solving.

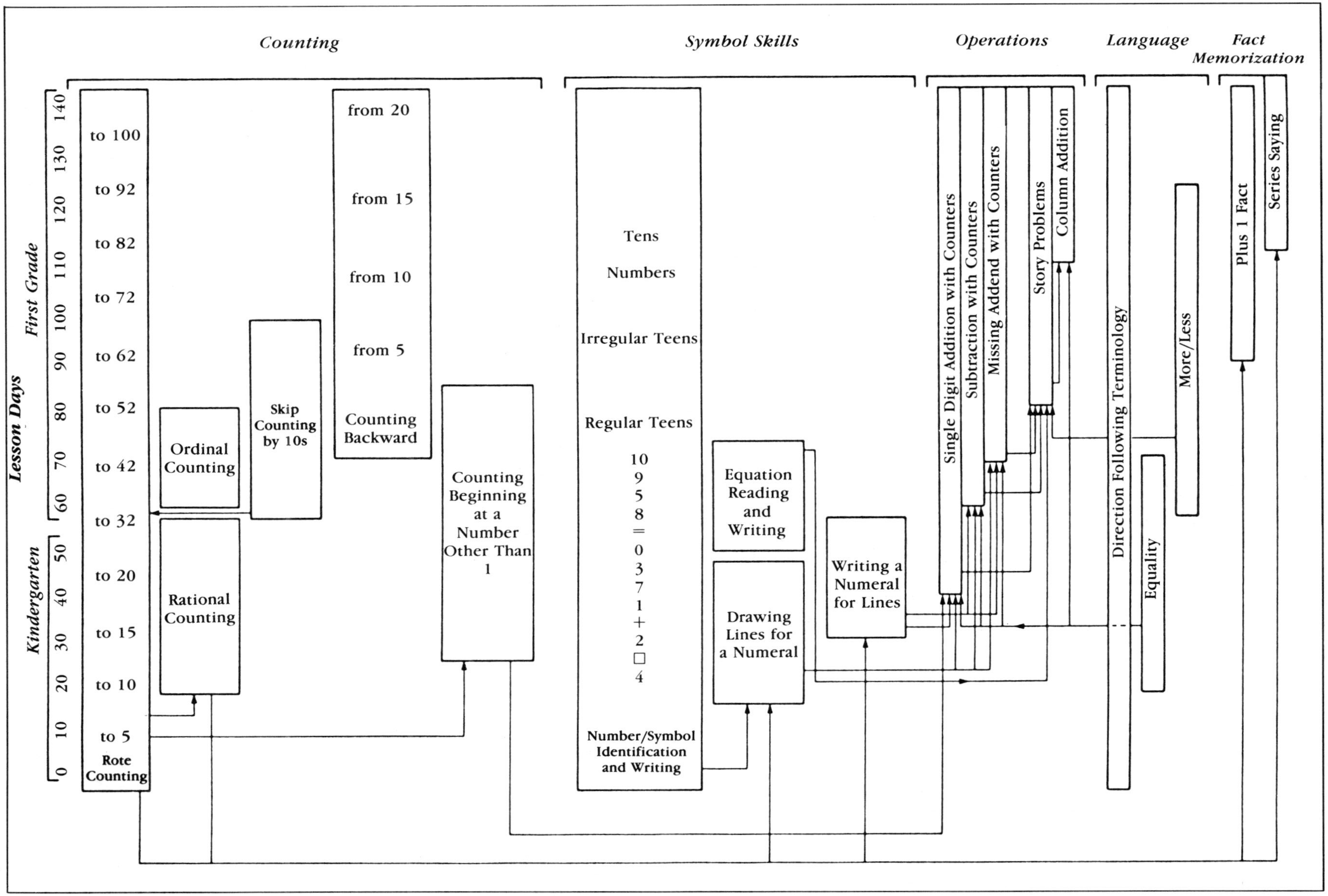

Figure 16-2 *Skill hierarchy for beginning mathematics instruction (kindergarten and first grade). (From* Direct Instruction Mathematics, *by J. Silbert, D. Carnine, and M. Stein. Copyright © 1981 by Charles E. Merrill, Columbus, Ohio. Reproduced with permission of Charles E. Merrill and Douglas Carnine.)*

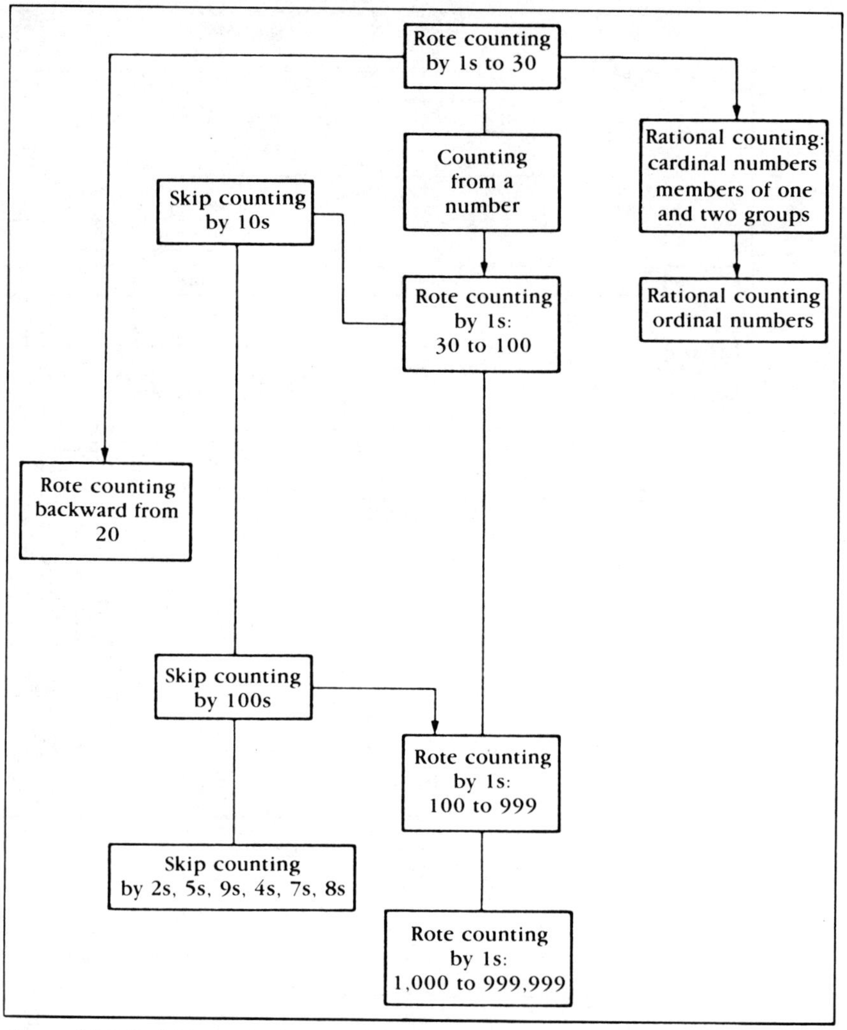

Figure 16-3 *Skill hierarchy for counting. (From* Direct Instruction Mathematics, *by J. Silbert, D. Carnine, and M. Stein. Copyright © 1981 by Charles E. Merrill, Columbus, Ohio. Reproduced with permission of Charles E. Merrill and Douglas Carnine.)*

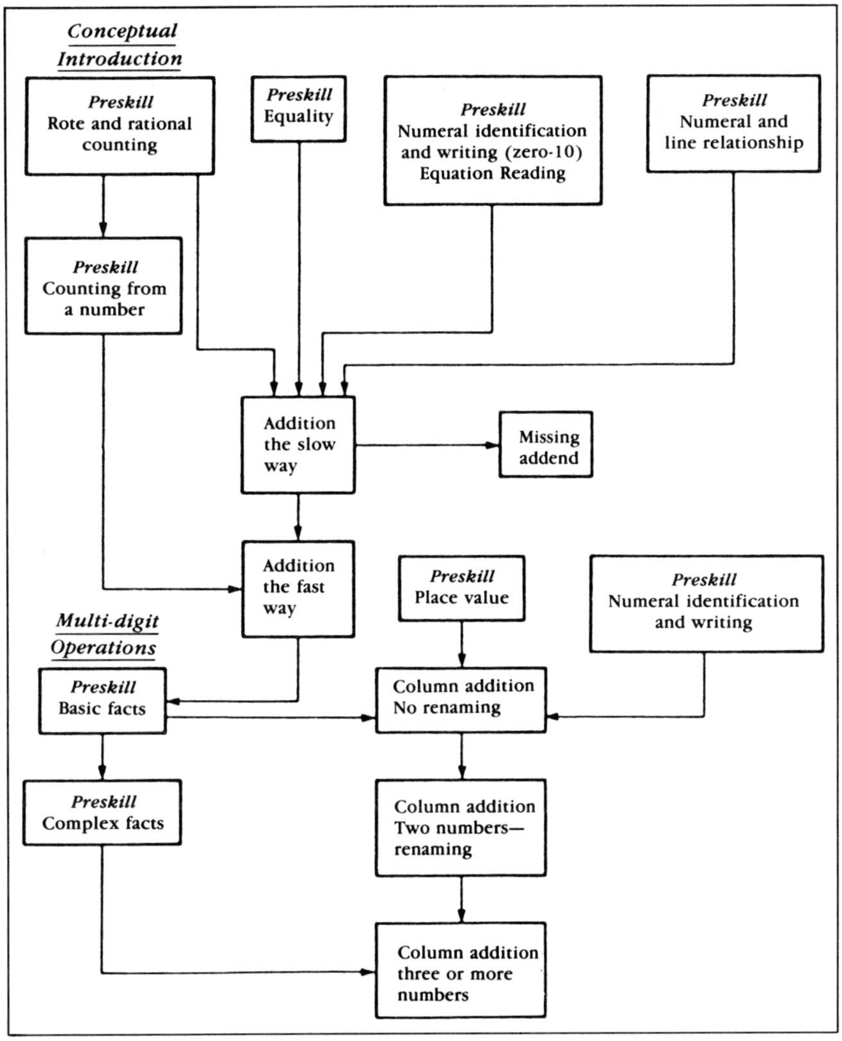

Figure 16-4 *Skill hierarchy for addition. (From* Direct Instruction Mathematics, *by J. Silbert, D. Carnine, and M. Stein. Copyright © 1981 by Charles E. Merrill, Columbus, Ohio. Reproduced with permission of Charles E. Merrill and Douglas Carnine.)*

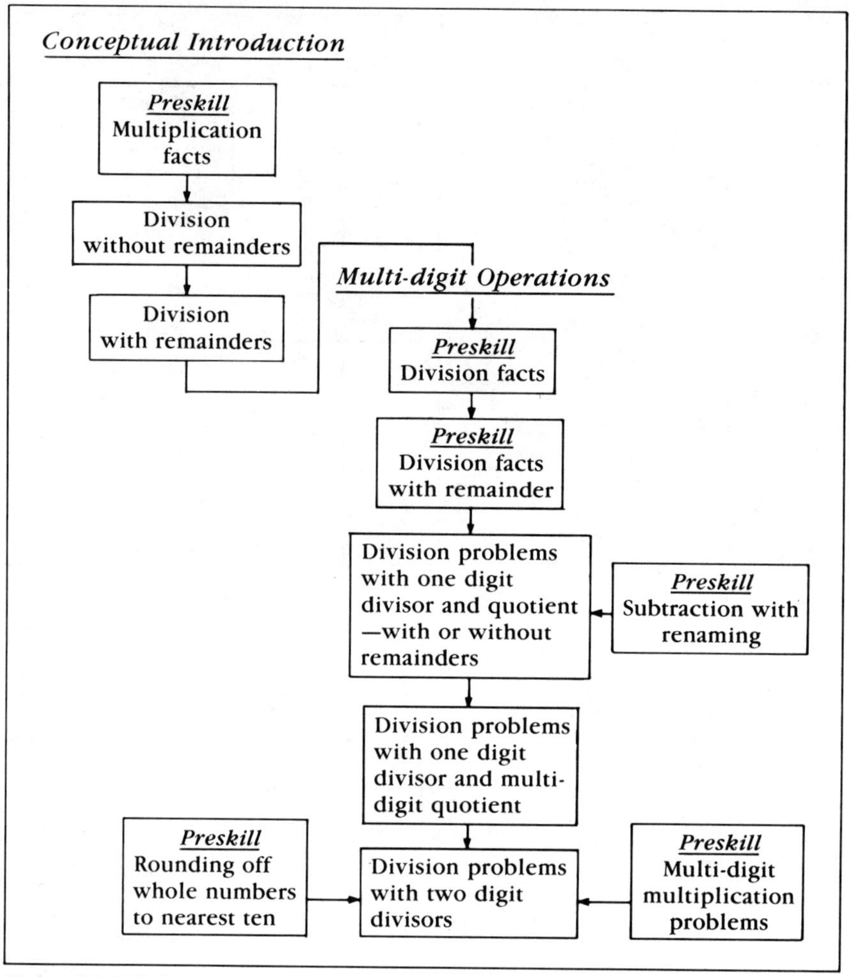

Figure 16-5 *Skill hierarchy for division. (From* Direct Instruction Mathematics, *by J. Silbert, D. Carnine, and M. Stein. Copyright © 1981 by Charles E. Merrill, Columbus, Ohio. Reproduced with permission of Charles E. Merrill and Douglas Carnine.)*

Take time to carefully read through the format for addition the slow way. This format represents the first one the students will learn to actually solve problems. Note the overall structure:

- There is a plan for teaching with various degrees of teacher direction over eight or more days.

- The format has four parts:
  A. Structured board presentation.
  B. Structured worksheet problems.
  C. Less-structured worksheet problems.
  D. Supervised practice problems (not shown).

- In Part A, the teacher carefully guides the students through the solution. In Part B, the students are guided through worksheet problems using a less prompted format. In Parts C and D, guidance is further reduced.

- Procedures for correcting errors are specified.

Figure 16.7 shows a format for addition the fast way that is used as a transition to working the problems mentally without making any lines. Notice how much shorter this format is than the first one. Many more problems can be completed in the same time now. Again, notice the plan for "staging in" over several days the various parts of the format.

A final example of a format is taken from long division using a short-form algorithm for estimating the quotient by rounding to the nearest tens unit. Read through the format in Figure 16.8 and see if you can detect preskills that would have to be taught before this format could be successful. Note that this algorithm sometimes produces estimates of the quotient that are too large ($16\overline{)\,60}$), too small ($38\overline{)\,193}$), and greater than 9 ($74\overline{)\,725}$). The students should be taught to check for these possibilities.

Day	Part A	Part B	Part C	Part D
	Structured Board Presentation Problems	Structured Worksheet Problems	Less Structured Worksheet Problems	Supervised Practice Problems
1	3			
2-3	1	3		
4-5		2	3	
6-7			4	4
8-till accurate				8-10

PART A: Structured Board Presentation

TEACHER	***STUDENTS***
Write on board: 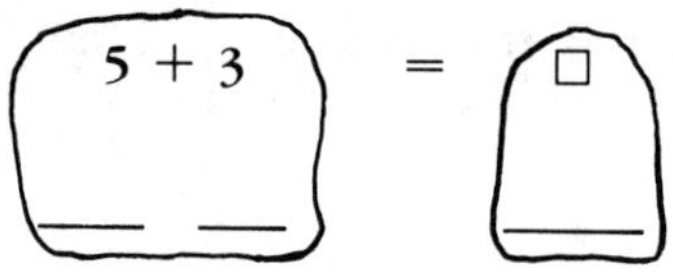	
1. "READ THE PROBLEM."	"5 + 3 = how many?"
2. Point to the equal sign. "WHAT IS THIS?"	"Equal"
3. "LISTEN TO THE EQUAL RULE: WE MUST END WITH THE SAME NUMBER ON THIS SIDE OF THE EQUAL (circle 5 + 3) AND ON THE OTHER SIDE" (circle box).	
4. Point to 5. "HOW MANY IN THE FIRST GROUP?"	"5"
"I'll DRAW FIVE LINES UNDER THE 5. COUNT AS I DRAW THE LINES." Draw five lines.	"1,2,3,4,5"
5. Point to + 3. "THIS SAYS PLUS THREE. PLUS TELLS US TO DRAW MORE LINES, SO I DRAW THREE MORE LINES UNDER THE 3. COUNT AS I DRAW THE LINES." Draw three lines.	"1,2,3"
6. "WE'VE DRAWN ALL THE LINES ON THIS SIDE. LET'S COUNT AND SEE WHAT WE END WITH. COUNT AS I TOUCH THE LINES." Touch lines.	"1,2,3,4,5,6,7,8"
"WHAT NUMBER DID WE END WITH?"	"8"
"WE MUST END WITH THE SAME NUMBER ON THIS SIDE AND THE OTHER SIDE."	
7. Point to 5 + 3. "WE ENDED WITH 8 ON THIS SIDE. SO WHAT NUMBER MUST WE END WITH ON THE OTHER SIDE?"	8
"I'LL DRAW THE LINES. YOU COUNT AND TELL ME WHEN TO STOP." Draw lines under box.	"1,2,3,4,5,6,7,8,stop"
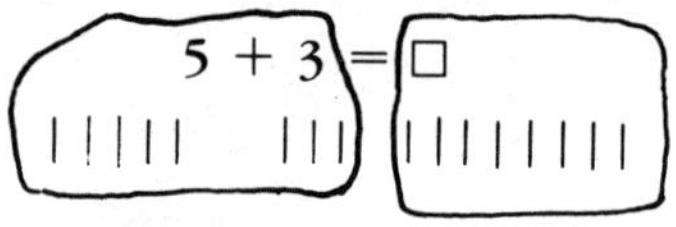	
TO CORRECT: If children don't say stop after 8, keep drawing lines, then say, "WE MADE A MISTAKE. YOU HAVE TO TELL ME TO STOP." Repeat step 6.	

Figure 16-6 *Format for teaching addition the slow way* *(continued on next page)*

TEACHER	***STUDENTS***
8. "THE LINES UNDER A BOX TELL WHAT NUMERAL GOES IN THE BOX. HOW MANY LINES ARE UNDER THE BOX?"	"8"
"SO WHAT NUMBER GOES IN THE BOX?"	"8"
Write 8 in the box. "WHAT DOES 5 + 3 EQUAL?"	"8"
9. "SAY THE WHOLE STATEMENT."	"5 + 3 = 8"
10. Repeat steps 1-9 until students can answer with no errors. Repeat steps 1-10 with several problems.	

PART B: Structured Worksheet

TEACHER	***STUDENTS***
Sample Worksheet Items:	

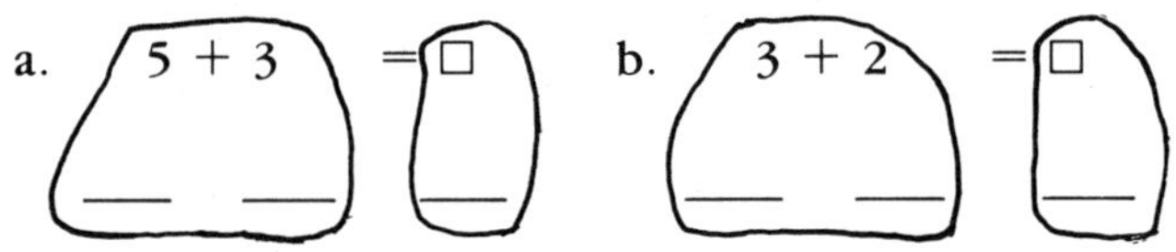

TEACHER	***STUDENTS***
1. "TOUCH PROBLEM a."	
2. "READ THE PROBLEM AS I CLAP. GET READY." Clap at 1 second intervals.	"5 + 3 = how many?"
3. "HOW MANY IN THE FIRST GROUP?"	"5"
"MAKE THE LINES."	Students draw five lines.
4. "THE NEXT PART OF THE PROBLEM SAYS PLUS 3. WHAT DO YOU DO WHEN YOU PLUS 3?"	"Make three more lines."
5. "MAKE THE LINES UNDER THE 3."	Students draw three lines.
6. "LET'S COUNT ALL THE LINES ON THAT SIDE. PUT YOUR FINGER OVER THE FIRST LINE." Check. "TOUCH AND COUNT THE LINES AS I CLAP." Clap one clap per second.	"1,2,3,4,5,6,7,8"
7. "HOW MANY LINES DID WE END WITH?"	"8"
8. "SO, HOW MANY MUST WE END WITH ON THE OTHER SIDE OF THE EQUAL?"	'8"
9. "MAKE THE LINES AND WRITE THE NUMERAL."	
10. "WHAT DOES 5 + 3 EQUAL?"	"8"
11. "SAY THE STATEMENT."	"5 + 3 = 8"
Repeat steps 1-11 with remaining problems.	

PART C: Less Structured Worksheet

Give students worksheets with problems.	
1. "TOUCH PROBLEM a."	
2. "READ THE PROBLEM."	"6 + 3 = how many?"
3. "FIRST YOU MAKE SIX LINES, THEN YOU PLUS 3. HOW DO YOU PLUS 3?"	"Make three more lines."
4. "MAKE THE SIDES EQUAL AND FILL IN THE MISSING NUMERAL." Check.	
5. "WHAT DOES 6 + 3 EQUAL?"	"9"
6. "SAY THE STATEMENT."	"6 + 3 = 9"
Repeat steps 1-5 with remaining problems.	

Figure 16-6 *Format for teaching addition the slow way. (From* Direct Instruction Mathematics, *by J. Silbert, D. Carnine, and M. Stein. Copyright © 1981 by Charles E. Merrill, Columbus, Ohio. Reproduced with permission of Charles E. Merrill and Douglas Carnine.)*

Day	*Part A* Structured Board Presentation Problems	*Part B* Structured Worksheet Problems	*Part C* Less Structured Worksheet Problems	*Part D* Supervised Practice Problems	*Part E* Independent Practice
1	*3*	*2*			
2	*1*	*3*			
3-4		*2*	*3*		
5			*4*	*4*	
6-till accurate				*8-10*	*6-10*
Till fluent					

PART A: Structured Board Presentation ***TEACHER***	***STUDENTS***
Write on board: 5 + 3 = □	
1. I'LL TOUCH AND YOU READ."	"5 + 3 = how many?"
2. "WE'RE GOING TO WORK THIS PROBLEM A FAST WAY. WE DRAW LINES UNDER THE NUMBER AFTER THE PLUS." Point to + 3. "WHAT DOES THIS SAY?"	"+3"
"SO HOW MANY LINES ARE WE GOING TO DRAW?"	"3"
"I'LL MAKE THE LINES." Draw three lines under the 3.	
3. "WATCH ME COUNT THE FAST WAY. "Touch 5 and then each line. "FIIIIVVVE, SIX, SEVEN, EIGHT. NOW IT'S YOUR TURN TO COUNT THE FAST WAY. HOW MANY ARE IN THE FIRST GROUP?"	"5"
"GET IT GOING . . . COUNT." Touch 5 for 2 seconds then touch each line.	"5555, 6,7,8"
4. "HOW MANY DID WE END WITH ON THIS SIDE?"	"8"
"SO HOW MANY MUST WE END WITH ON THE OTHER SIDE?"	"8"
I'LL WRITE AN 8 IN THE BOX." Write 8 in the box.	"8"
5. "READ THE WHOLE STATEMENT."	"5 + 3 = 8"
Repeat steps 1-5 with 7 + 4, 9 + 5.	

Figure 16-7 *Format for teaching addition the fast way (continued on next page)*

PART B: Structured Worksheet

TEACHER	STUDENTS
4 + 2 = □	
1. Point to 4 + 2 = □. "TOUCH THIS PROBLEM ON YOUR WORKSHEET" Pause. "READ THE PROBLEM OUT LOUD. GET READY." Clap for each symbol.	"4 + 2 equals how many?
2. "LET'S WORK THIS PROBLEM THE FAST WAY. TOUCH THE NUMERAL AFTER THE PLUS." Pause. "HOW MANY LINES ARE YOU GOING TO PLUS?"	"2"
"MAKE THE LINES UNDER THE 2." Check.	
3. "TOUCH THE 4 AND GET READY TO COUNT THE FAST WAY. FOUR. GET IT GOING." Clap as students touch and count. "COUNT"	"ffoouurrr,5,6"
TO CORRECT: Teacher models. "MY TURN. . . . "If necessary, moves student's finger as he counts.	
4. "HOW MANY DID YOU END WITH ON THE SIDE YOU STARTED WITH?"	"6"
"HOW MANY MUST YOU END WITH ON THE SIDE WITH THE BOX?"	"6"
"YES, 6 EQUALS 6. WHAT NUMERAL WILL YOU WRITE IN THE BOX?"	"6"
"DO IT."	
5. "READ THE WHOLE STATEMENT."	"4 + 2 = 6

PART C: Less Structured Worksheet

TEACHER	STUDENTS
1. Read problem and determine side. "EVERYBODY, READ PROBLEM ONE ON YOUR WORKSHEET. GET READY." Clap for each symbol.	"4 + 3 = how many?"
2. Work problem. "NOW YOU'RE READY TO PLUS LINES AND COUNT THE FAST WAY. WHAT ARE YOU GOING TO DO?"	Plus the lines and count the fast way."
"DO IT." Check students as they work.	
3. "READ THE WHOLE STATEMENT."	"4 + 3 = 7"

Figure 16-7 *Format for teaching addition the fast way. (From* Direct Instruction Mathematics, *by J. Silbert, D. Carnine, and M. Stein. Copyright © 1981 by Charles E. Merrill, Columbus, Ohio. Reproduced with permission of Charles E. Merrill and Douglas Carnine.)*

TEACHER	*STUDENTS*
1. "READ PROBLEM a."	"37 goes into 1586"
2. "UNDERLINE THE PART TO WORK FIRST."	37)<u>158</u>6
3. "READ THE FIRST PART."	37 goes into 158"
4. "ESTIMATE THE QUOTIENT AS TENS UNITS."	37 is converted to 4 10s 158 is converted to 16 10s 4 goes into 16 four times
5. "PLACE ESTIMATED QUOTIENT ABOVE LAST UNDERLINED DIGIT, THEN MULTIPLY AND SUBTRACT."	4 37)<u>158</u>6 <u>148</u> 10
6. "COMPARE THE DIFFERENCE AND DIVISOR TO SEE IF QUOTIENT IS CORRECT. BRING DOWN THE NEXT NUMBER IN DIVIDEND."	4 37)<u>158</u>6 <u>148</u> 106
7. "READ THE NEW PROBLEM."	37 goes into 106
8. "ESTIMATE THE QUOTIENT FOR THE NEXT PROBLEM."	37 is converted to 4 10s 106 is converted to 11 10s 4 goes into 11 two times
9. "PLACE ESTIMATED QUOTIENT ABOVE THE LAST DIGIT BROUGHT DOWN, THEN MULTIPLY AND SUBTRACT."	42 37)<u>158</u>6 <u>148</u> 106 <u>74</u> 32
10. "COMPARE DIFFERENCE AND DIVISOR TO SEE IF QUOTIENT IS CORRECT."	

Figure 16-8 *Short-form algorithm—two digit divisors. (From* Direct Instruction Mathematics, *by J. Silbert, D. Carnine, and M. Stein. Copyright © 1981 by Charles E. Merrill, Columbus, Ohio. Reproduced with permission of Charles E. Merrill and Douglas Carnine.)*

Story Problems

The importance of analysis of problem types for instruction is made quite clear in the area of story problems, where such analysis is missing in most commercial programs. Figure 16.9 and Table 16.1 present a skill hierarchy for story problems and examples of the many subclasses.

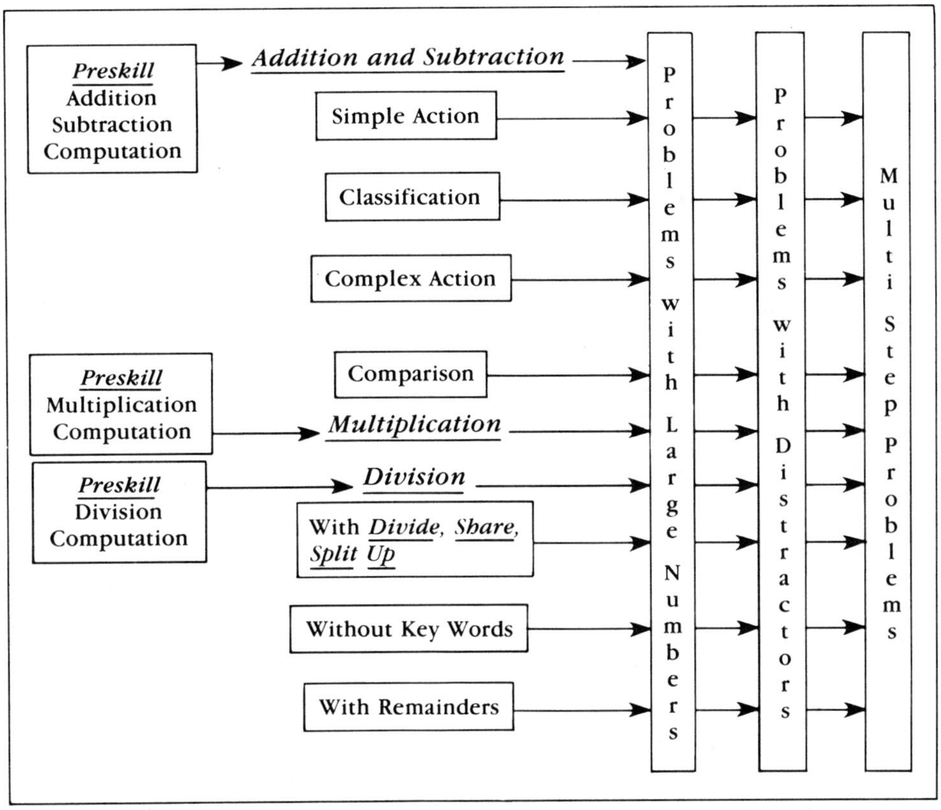

Figure 16-9 *Skill-hierarchy for story problems. (From* Direct Instruction Mathematics, *by J. Silbert, D. Carnine, and M. Stein. Copyright © 1981 by Charles E. Merrill, Columbus, Ohio. Reproduced with permission of Charles E. Merrill and Douglas Carnine.)*

***Table 16-1* Instructional sequence and assessment chart for story problems.** *(From* Direct Instruction Mathematics, *by J. Silbert, D. Carnine, and M. Stein. Copyright © 1981 by Charles E. Merrill, Columbus, Ohio. Reproduced with permission of Charles E. Merrill and Douglas Carnine.)*

Grade Level	*Problem Type*	*Performance Indicator*
1	Addition/subtraction simple action problems with phrase-by-phrase translation.	Bill had 7 apples. He got 3 more from the store. How many apples does he have in all?
		Lisa had 5 apples. She bought 3 more. How many does she have now?
		Carlos had 7 apples. He gave 3 to his sister. How many does he have left?
1-2a	Addition/subtraction classification problems.	Eight men are in the store. Three women are in the store. How many people are in the store?
		Eight people are in the store. Three are women. How many are men?
		Ramona had 4 hats; 3 of the hats are blue. How many hats are not blue?
2b	Addition/subtraction complex action problems.	Jill sold 5 hats in the morning. She sold 2 hats in the afternoon. How many hats did she sell?
		Leroy had 9 seashells after looking on the beach all day. If he had 3 in the morning, how many more did he find in the afternoon?
		Sarah needs 15 points to get a prize. She has got 5 points so far. How many more points does she need?
2c	Addition/subtraction comparison problems.	Bill is 7 years old. Alice is 5 years old. How much older is Bill?
		Hole A is 5 feet deep. Hole B is 7 feet deeper than Hole A. How deep is Hole B?
		Hole A is 5 feet deep. Hole B is 7 feet deep. How much deeper is Hole B?
2d	Multi-step problems: add three numbers.	Bill ran 5 miles on Monday, 3 miles on Tuesday, and 4 miles on Wednesday. How many miles did he run altogether?
3a	Multiplication problems with word *each* or *every*.	Bill has 4 boxes. In each box there are 6 pencils. How many pencils does Bill have?
		Tammy jogs 5 miles every day. How far will she jog in 3 days?
3b	Multiplication problems without the word *each* or *every*.	The ABC Company makes pens. They put 6 pens in a box. How many pens are in 3 boxes?
		Sarah collects marbles and puts them in bottles. She puts 7 marbles in a bottle. She has 3 bottles of marbles. How many marbles does she have in the bottles?

Table 16.1 Instructional sequence and assessment chart for story problems (Continued)

Grade Level	Problem Type	Performance Indicator
3c	Division problems containing the words *divide, split up,* or *share equally.*	There are 20 students. The teacher wants to divide them into 4 equal groups. How many students will be in each group?
		A mother wants to divide a pie among her children. The pie has 18 pieces. There are 9 children. How many pieces should she give to each child?
		There are 30 pencils in a box. Mr. Adams wants to split them up into 6 equal groups. How many pencils will be in each group?
3d	Addition/subtraction problems with larger numbers.	Bill ran 214 miles in January and 158 miles in February. How many more miles did he run in January?
		There are 153 students in the school. If there are 61 girls in the school, how many boys are there?
		Forty-seven new students came into our school. Before there were 125 students. How many students in the school now?
3e	Multiplication problems with large numbers.	There are 35 students in every class. There are 5 classes in the school. How many students in the school?
		Jean worked 2 days. If she makes $16 a day, how much did she make?
		Alex plants 15 roses every year. How many roses will he plant in 5 years?
3f	Division problems: no key word given.	Manuel earns $8 a day. How many days will it take him to earn $24?
		Rosa runs 2 miles a day. How many days will it take her to run 8 miles?
		Ann saved $3 a week. She had $12. How many weeks did she save?
3g	Division problems with remainders.	There are 22 students. The teacher wants to divide them into 4 equal groups. How many students will be in each group?
		A mother wants to divide a pie equally among her children. The pie has 19 pieces. There are 9 children. How many pieces should she give to each child?
3h	Addition/subtraction problems with distractors.	There are 20 blue pencils, 5 red pencils and 16 yellow pens in a bag. How many pencils are in the bag?
		Bill weighed 120 pounds. He ran 6 miles. Now he weighs 117 pounds. How much did he lose?
		Bill had 12 hats; 5 hats were old. He gave away 3 old hats. How many hats does he have left?

Table 16.1 Instructional sequence and assessment chart for story problems (Continued)

Grade Level	*Problem Type*	*Performance Indicator*
4a	Division problems with larger numbers.	Jill has 215 pencils. She wants to make bundles with 5 pencils in each bundle. How many bundles can she make?
4b	Division and multiplication problems with larger numbers (two digit divisor or multi-digit factors).	Sarah wants to save $385. If she puts $35 in the bank each month, how many months will it take her to save the $385?
		A factory produces 325 cars a day. How many cars will it produce in 25 days?
		A pound of apples cost 60¢. How much will 20 pounds of apples cost?
4c	Multi-step problems: three numbers; the sum of two numbers is subtracted from third number.	Julie sold 12 pencils in the morning. Ann sold 15 in the afternoon. How many more must they sell before they've sold 50 altogether?
		Timmy weighed 84 pounds. He lost 4 pounds in May and 7 pounds in June. How much did he weigh at the end of June?
		Jean sold 10 pens in the morning. She began with 18. If she sells 2 more, how many will she have left?
4d	Three numbers: two quantities are. multiplied; the product is added or subtracted from third number.	Tom has 3 pens in each pocket. He has 5 pockets. Ann has 16 pens. Who has more pens? How many more?
		Ann has $7. If she works 4 hours and earns $3 each hour, how many dollars will she have at the end of the day?
4e	Three numbers: two quantities are added; the sum is divided or multiplied.	There are 10 boys and 20 girls in the class. Each row can sit 5 students. How many rows will there be?
		Jill earns $2 every morning and $4 every afternoon. How much will she earn in 6 days?
5a	Four numbers: two sets of quantities are multiplied; the product of each is added.	Pam ran 5 miles a day for 3 days, and 6 miles a day for 2 days. How many miles did she run altogether?
		Tammy bought 3 cakes and 2 drinks. A cake cost 10¢. A drink cost 15¢. How much did Tammy spend?
5b	Five numbers: two sets of quantities are multiplied; the product of each is added; the sum is subtracted or added to a given quantity.	Bill needs $30. He worked 5 hours on Monday for $2 an hour. He worked 2 hours on Tuesday for $3 an hour. How much more money does he need?
		Bill weighed 135 pounds in May. He gained 3 pounds each month for the next 2 months. Then he gained 5 pounds each month for the next 3 months. How much does he weigh now?

With a careful classification of problem subtypes, strategies can be developed for teaching the students how to deal with them. For example, addition and subtraction problems can have literal translations to equation form or be complex.

Literal example: Bill had 7 apples and got 3 more.

Complex example: Sandy had 9 seashells after looking on the beach all day. If she found 3 in the afternoon, how many did she find in the morning?

In the following example, the word *more,* which is usually associated with adding, implies subtraction.

Sarah needs 15 points to get a prize. She has got 5 points so far. How many more points does she need?

Some problems require *classification* and some involve *comparison.*

Comparison: Bill is 7 years old. Alice is 5. How much older is Bill?

Classification: There are 8 men in the store and 3 women. How many people are in the store?

In looking for strategies to teach problem solving skills, one useful approach has been to teach about *number families* such as 3, 5, and 8. These can be used to produce the following equations:

$$3 + 5 = 8;\ 5 + 3 = 8;\ 8 - 5 = 3;\ 8 - 3 = 5$$

By teaching students to recognize related members of a family, it is possible to tie addition and subtraction story problems together. The students are taught that two of the three numbers in a family are given in a problem, and the students' job is to find the third. For classification and comparison problems like those just given, the student is taught that the rule: "If one of the numbers stated is *the big number in a family,* the problem calls for subtraction to find the other small number. On the other hand, if the big number is not given, addition is called for—adding the two small numbers will give the big number": If 6 boys and 5 girls went on a hike, how many children went on the hike?

The kinds of analyses presented by Silbert, Carnine, and Stein (1981), which grew out of their work with Engelmann, offer much promise for improving the quality of education in mathematics through the design of more effect teaching strategies.

SUMMARY

Program design principles were illustrated in this chapter, with examples from elementary mathematics. The major steps in the design of a program are to:

1. Specify objectives in terms of the types of tasks the students will be able to perform after instruction.

2. Devise a problem-solving strategy for each class of tasks.

3. Analyze the preskills assumed by any class of problems.

4. Sequence the skills so that: (a) preskills are taught before they are needed as part of a problem-solving strategy, (b) easier skills are taught before more difficult skills, (c) problems or examples likely to be confused with each other are separated in time.

5. Select a teaching procedure. Motor chains are taught through the steps: model, lead, test, and delayed test. Basic concepts are taught

through examples. The eleven-step sequence presented in Chapter 14 is used for single-dimension concepts and modified as necessary for nouns. In building a set of related concepts, after the initial teaching of a new member, the new member is added to the related set in a pattern that looks like this (D is the new member; A, B, and C are the old members):

D A *D* B *D* C *D* B A *D* C B *D* A C B *D*

In teaching transformations, facts, and problem-solving routines, the principles illustrated in Chapter 15 are used.

6. Design formats to provide a general strategy for solving problems of a given type.

7. Select examples that fit the format. After initial teaching, related problems are intermixed to provide appropriate discrimination of when to use each strategy.

8. Provide practice until mastery is reached.

Scope and sequence charts are used to summarize teaching objectives and to show the relationships among skills, subskills, and preskills. The chapter described a variety of skill hierarchies, along with a number of detailed teaching formats. The formats showed how students are gradually brought to independent work following the initial teacher-directed activities. Also, formats are shortened as skill develops so that (where appropriate) eventually the student performs the task covertly (thinking) rather than overtly.

Varieties of story problems were presented to show the importance of *analysis* of types and subtypes of problems in designing effective instruction.

CHAPTER

17

APPLICATIONS TO READING

The design of instruction for reading is probably one of the most complicated tasks a program designer could undertake. Reading with comprehension has two major components: (1) decoding the letters into some familiar-sounding word, and (2) using oral language comprehension to provide meaning. Both components have complexities to them, but the comprehension component is by far the most complex, covering almost anything you could imagine would belong in a knowledge base.

Table 17-1 A direct instruction model for comprehension. *(From* Direct Instruction Reading, *by D. Carnine and J. Silbert. Copyright © 1979 by Charles E. Merrill, Columbus, Ohio. Reproduced with permission of the publisher and Douglas Carnine.)*

	Decoding	*Comprehension*
Units	letter features, letters, letter combinations, syllables, words, phrases	words, phrases, sentences, paragraphs, passages
Skills	sounding out, sight reading, breaking larger words into parts	literal, inference, sequencing, summarization, simplifying syntactic and semantic complexities, critical reading, and study skills
Knowledge Base	oral language, familiarity with words, syntax, semantic constraints	syntax, semantics, facts, logic, schema

Table 17.1 (from Carnine and Silbert, 1979) provides a gross mapping of many of the skills involved in an analysis of reading. Note that the size of the *units* dealt with grows larger as mastery of smaller components develops (the functional chains get longer). Note that the skills listed under comprehension could be defined and mapped (as to goals and preskills) in thousands of different ways. The components of the knowledge base under comprehension is most complex. *Syntax* covers the rules of grammar. In reading, knowledge of these rules helps the student to correct errors by constraining possible interpretations

in decoding. *Semantics* involves vocabulary or word meanings. Consistency in meaning also serves to constrain possible interpretations in decoding. Nagy and Anderson (1984) estimate that there are 54,000 to 88,500 distinct *word families* in school texts (through ninth grade) for which students might have to learn up to 110,000 distinct meanings. This fact, coupled with the fact that the direct teaching of more than 400 new words to mastery a year (Nagy and Anderson, 1984) would be difficult at best, suggests that if students are not learning vocabulary through sources other than school, problems are likely. This fact is one of the reasons why children from homes with poorly educated (or non-English-speaking) parents are likely to have trouble in school (Becker, 1977).

Returning to Table 17.1, *facts* and *logical rules* can span all knowledge content areas and depend on vocabulary knowledge (concepts) as preskills. Finally, *schema* are basically sets of interrelated facts (fact systems) that permit inferences to be drawn.

DECODING

Decoding is an essential preskill for comprehension, the main goal of a reading program. Figure 17.1 (from Carnine and Silbert, 1979) lists some of the skills taught in a systematic phonics approach to beginning reading. The most effective decoding programs teach some form of systematic phonics as a strategy for attacking new words. An analysis of the letter-sound correspondences in different words reveals many irregular subtypes. This has led some to say that English is so phonetically irregular that it precludes a generalizable phonics approach. Engelmann and Bruner (1974, p. 12) solved this problem in the DISTAR reading program by devising a modified alphabet for the initial teaching of reading that greatly reduces the number of irregular subtypes. This alphabet is illustrated in Figure 17.2.[1] A sample DISTAR story is illustrated in Figure 17.3. Note that the story does not use capital letters except for I. Capitals are not needed for decoding and only serve to confuse the beginning reader.

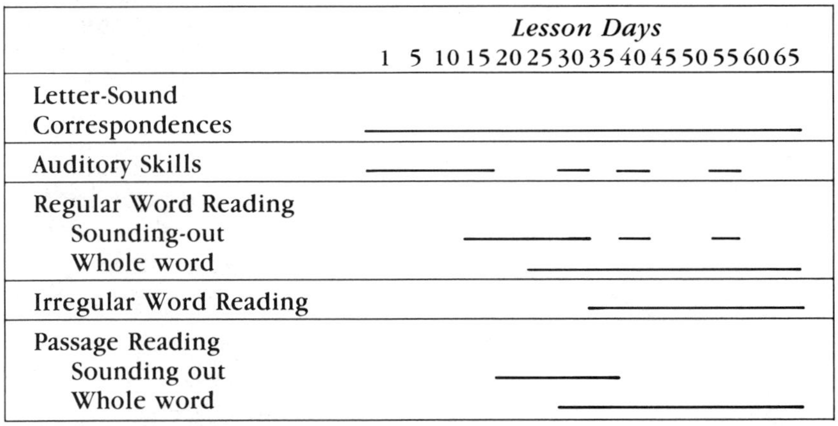

Figure 17-1 *Scope and sequence, beginning reading stage, decoding skills. (From* Direct Instruction Reading, *by D. Carnine and J. Silbert. Copyright © 1979 by Charles E. Merrill, Columbus, Ohio. Reproduced with permission of the publisher and Douglas Carnine.)*

[1]Engelmann originally tried the Initial Teaching Alphabet (ITA) that was developed in England; it has even greater regularity than DISTAR. However, he abandoned it because the transition was too difficult from ITA to standard English.

Figure 17-2 *Sounds from revised DISTAR Reading 1*

A major source of difficulty is the vowels that change their sounds (*hat–hate, pet–Pete, kit–kite, pop–pope, cut–cute*). This was cured by placing a bar over the sound when it says its name. Other irregulars were eliminated by introducing combined letters (*th, sh, ch, wh, qu, oo, er, ing*) as single sounds. The student is cued that she or he is dealing with a combined form because the letters touch each other, or for *ing* there is line over the letters. By making silent letters smaller and later letting them get bigger, the student is prompted not to say them (for example, the *a* in *bread,* the *e* in *cute.* Note that the silent *e* in *cute* is the equivalent of a "long-vowel" mark over the *u.*) Finally, to avoid confusion of similar letters, such as *d* and *b,* they have been constructed not to be mirror images. In constructing a reading program without this special alphabet, the programer has to be much more careful about the choice of examples, so that regular words are used most of the time in the early teaching of sounding-out skills and the irregulars are introduced in families where possible.

STORY 23

spot

this is a stōry of a dog nāmed spot. spot did not hēar well. the other dāy shē went to a stōre to get some bōnes. the man in the stōre said, "it is a fīne dāy."

"what did you sāy?" spot asked.

tell spot what the man said.

the man got some bōnes fōr spot. hē said, "pāy mē a dīme fōr thēse bōnes."

spot asked, "what did you sāy?"

tell spot what the man said.

spot did not hēar the man and the man was getting mad at spot. the man said, "give mē a dīme fōr thēse bōnes."

spot asked, "what did you sāy?"

Figure 17-3 *A story using the DISTAR alphabet (continued on next page.)*

tell spot what the man said.

spot said, "it is tīme fōr mē to lēave. sō I will pāy you a dīme fōr the bōnes and I will gō hōme."

sō spot gāve the man a dīme. then shē took the bōnes hōme and had a fīne mēal of bōnes.

the end

Figure 17-3 *A story using the DISTAR alphabet*

(From Reading Mastery 1, DISTAR® Reading II, Storybook 1, by Siegfried Engelmann and Elaine C. Bruner. Copyright© Science Research Associates. 1983, 1975, 1969 Reprinted by permission of the publisher.)

To sound out a word, it is very important to hold one sound and move to the next without pausing. Try sounding this out without pausing between the sounds: *sssssaaaaaaaammmmmm.* Now pause between the sounds: *sss aaa mmm.* If you do not pause between the sounds, you can speed up the word and get *sam.* With pausing between the sound, you just get the sounds *s a m.* This blending requirement requires teaching of the auditory skill of listening to a word said slowly (without stops between the sounds) and then saying it fast. This provides a model of how to blend and training in sound discriminations. It also helps later in spelling by sounds.

The blending requirement forces a distinction between continuous sounds *(s, m, a, i, e,* and so on) and stop sounds *(b, t, k, c, p,* and so forth), because stop sounds are difficult to blend. After blending is well along, stop sounds are introduced first at the end of words (where it is okay to stop) and later at the beginning of words by using a rhyming prompt (such as "Read these words: *man, fan, ran,* so this must be: *can"*). High-frequency irregulars, such as *was (wuz)* and *is (iz),* are introduced in a special format. Lists of the most frequently needed irregulars are available. The students eventually learn to sound out the word without pausing and to "say it fast." Whole-word reading follows, with sounding out being used as the strategy for dealing with new words.

More advanced decoding skills involve the teaching of minor sounds of *c* and *g* and certain letter combinations like *ail (pail), all (ball),* and *ight (night).* Also, there is the structural analysis of prefixes and suffixes, breaking longer words into syllables, the *y* to *i* rule, the doubling the final consonant rule, the final-e rule, and the introduction of more irregulars. Finally, there is a focus on the progressive acceleration of reading speed through the use of timed tests. As they also did for mathematics, Carnine and Silbert (1979) provide the teacher with formats and lists of examples for teaching most decoding skills.

COMPREHENSION

The analysis of comprehension into generalizable sets of related tasks has only just begun. There is no analysis available today that is even as close as the Model T is to a modern car. The nature of the problem is one of both size and structure. John Carroll (1971), in his review of comprehension research, estimated that vocabulary is 80 percent of comprehension. The other 20 percent has to do with rules of syntax, logic, evaluation, and so forth. The latter are mostly generalized forms that can be used across a broad range of applications and are quite teachable. Vocabulary, however, is another problem. In examining comprehension, some of the logical skills and rules involved in reading comprehension are described first; then, the vocabulary problem is examined in more detail.

Comprehension Skills

There have been reasonable analyses of the logical skills important to comprehension, although there is also much to be learned. At the very beginning levels, such basic oral comprehension skills as statement repetition, following directions, and answering questions are vital. Unless the student can hold a statement in memory long enough to repeat it, it is unlikely that she or he will be able to show comprehension by answering questions about it. Comprehension of oral directions is obviously important for any classroom activity. And, oral practice in how to answer *who, what, where, when, how,* and *why* questions sets the stage for comprehension questions during reading activities. Teaching young children the logic of making *comparisons* for samenesses and differences is also quite basic.

At a slightly more advanced level, the students read passages and answer questions about what they have read (literal comprehension). They may also be asked to make inferences about feelings and attitudes. They need to learn to summarize what they have read, to sequence events, to use dictionaries when they encounter unknown words, to make inferences (including analogies), and to critically evaluate what they are reading for value and truth. The latter skills include identifying conclusions, discriminating evidence from opinion, determining how much the author can be trusted, identifying faulty arguments, and identifying invalid conclusions.

To become independent learners who can learn from reading, students need a host of study skills: How to locate information in books, how to locate books in learning resource centers, how to approach a reading assignment efficiently to meet a variety of learning objectives, and more. Carnine and Silbert (1979) provide guidelines for teaching most of these kinds of skills. Two examples are illustrated in Figures 17.4 and 17.5.

Teacher	*Students*
1. **"An argument may be faulty because it is based on tradition or because it is based on an improper generalization."**	
2. **"What does an argument based on tradition say?** (signal)	Something should be a certain way because it has always been that way."
3. **"What does an argument based on improper generalization say?"** (signal)	"That because a part has a certain characteristic the whole thing must have that characteristic."
4. **"I'll say some arguments that are faulty. You tell me why the argument is faulty, because of tradition or because of improper generalization."**	
a. **"Tomas can spell very well. I bet he is the smartest student in the class. Why is that argument faulty?"**	It is based on improper generalization."
b. **"New York had the first good subway system. Its subway system must be the best. Why is that argument faulty?"**	"It is based on tradition."
c. **"Mr. Ricardo has lived on this street since 1970. He'll never move. Why is that argument faulty?"**	"It is based on tradition."
d. **"That restaurant serves delicious pies. It is the best restaurant in town. Why is that argument faulty?"**	"It is based on improper generalization."

Figure 17-4 *Discrimination format. (From* Direct Instruction Reading, *by D. Carnine and J. Silbert. Copyright © 1979 by Charles E. Merrill, Columbus, Ohio. Reproduced with permission of the publisher and Douglas Carnine.)*

Teacher	Students
1. **"Sometimes an author makes a conclusion that is based on a faulty argument."**	
2. **"One type of faulty argument is called tradition. A conclusion based on tradition says that something should be a certain way because it has always been that way. What does a conclusion based on tradition say?"** (signal)	"That something should be a certain way because it has always been that way"
3. **"Here is an example. Mr. Rotter said our family has always bought Brand X shoes and should keep buying Brand X shoes. The conclusion that we should continue doing something just because we have done it in the past is based on the faulty argument of tradition."**	
4. **"Listen to this argument: Mr. Jones said the Yankees are a sure bet to win this year since they won last year. Do you agree with Mr. Jones' conclusion?** (signal)	"No"
"Why not?" Teacher calls on individual students; accepts reasonable answers. **"Right, his conclusion was based on tradition. Just because something has been done a certain way in the past doesn't mean that is the way it should be done."**	
5. **"Listen to this argument. Mrs. Spencer told her daughter, 'When I was a young girl, my mother had me come home at 9 P.M. from a date. So, when you go out, you should be home at 9 P.M.' Do you agree with Mrs. Spencer's conclusion?"** (signal)	"No"
"Why not?" Teacher calls on individual students; accepts reasonable answers. **"Right, the conclusion was based on tradition."**	

Figure 17-5 *Format for identifying invalid conclusions based on tradition. (From* Direct Instruction Reading, *by D. Carnine and J. Silbert. Copyright © 1979 by Charles E. Merrill, Columbus, Ohio. Reproduced with permission of the publisher and Douglas Carnine.)*

The Vocabulary Problem

The size of the vocabulary used in schools, even if restricted to through ninth grade, is vast and not well-defined. As indicated earlier, Nagy and Anderson (1984) estimated that there are 54,000 to 88,500 word families built around a base word. Figure 17.6 provides an example of a base-word family). The lower

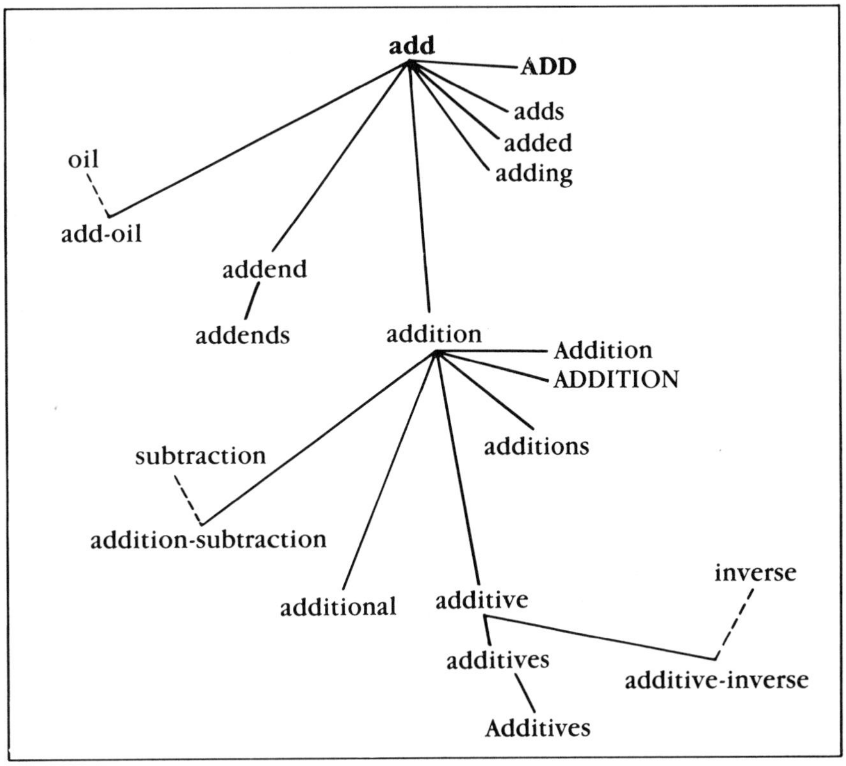

Figure 17-6 *Relationships among words*

figure is based on the assumption that obscurely related meanings of family members might be helpful (such as deriving the meaning of *condescend* from *descend*). The upper figure (88,500) treats obscurely related words as base words. For each base word, Nagy and Anderson estimate there are (on the average) 6.2 or 3.8 family members (depending on whether the lower figure or higher figure given above is used to determine base words). For these family members, the meanings for 2.6 or 1.6 are "transparent" derivatives (on the average). For example, *cleverly* or *cleverness* is readily derived from knowing the meaning of *clever* and generalizable meaning of the suffixes *-ly* and *-ness.* In addition, for each base word there are 1.9 or 1.2 regular comparatives, superlatives, and inflections (that is, change of case, gender, number, tense, person, and voice). There are also a small number of irregular inflections, truncations, and abbreviations to consider. Beyond this there are some 90,000 proper nouns in school English.

Schools have generally treated vocabulary as an independent-member set. Each new word is taught (if at all) in relative isolation from other words. Considering the estimates produced by Nagy and Anderson, it is little wonder that there has been no systematic analytic approach to building vocabulary. But the problem is not quite as bad as it would appear from these figures. Of the 88,500 base words, only 6703 (7.6 percent occur more than once in a million printed words in school texts. That means the student would have to read 2,000 to 3,000 pages of text to encounter a rare word once. Of the 90,000 proper nouns, Nagy and Anderson estimate that only 1,000 would need to be remembered in a knowledge base—names of geographical terms, government bodies, floral and fauna, and so forth.)

Becker, Dixon, and Anderson-Inman (1980) did an analysis of vocabulary with the goal of finding generalizable structurings of word forms and word meanings. The semantic part of the analysis has not been completed because of financial constraints. However, the word-form analysis and the analysis of the number of root words (base words) provides useful information in evaluating the magnitude of the task facing educators. They started with the vocabulary in the *Teacher's Word Book of 30,000 Words* (Thorndike and Lorge, 1944). This was a compilation of the 30,000 most frequent words in print. They added more than 4,500 words from school texts and more recent compilations of word listings (Harris-Jacobson, 1972; Carroll, Davies, and Richman, 1971). They deleted from the initial analysis some 8,700 words in the Thorndike-Lorge list. Deleted and placed in special lists to be considered later were proper nouns (3,879), technical words (1,857), nongenerative flora and fauna (653), hyphenated words (549), two-word compounds (353), foreign words (332), out-of-date words (272), alternate spellings (189), archaic words (170), abbreviations (170), religious words (120), slang words (75), interjections (67), and disparaging words (51). These specific counts are listed so you can see where adjustments to estimates come from.

Of first interest is the number of root words found. A *root word* was defined as the smallest word from which other words could be derived. In analyzing 25,782 words, 8,109 root words were found. This figure is in the same ballpark as Nagy and Anderson's 6,700 base words with frequency of over one in a million words of text. Now add to this 1,000 proper nouns, 1,000 technical words, and about 1,500 words from the rest of the deletions and assume that over half of these would be considered root words. You would need to add about 2,000 words to the 8,100 as the core of a vocabulary knowledge base. This is a far cry from the 88,500 words with which this discussion opened. The issue of how students can learn to deal with those low-frequency words is explored later.

As suggested earlier, however, this still implies a horrendous teaching job, if schools were to undertake the job of systematically teaching a core vocabulary. As things stand now, Dupuy (1974) has shown that basic-word vocabulary continually grows through the school years, but there is as much spread *within* grades from grade 4 to grade 12 as there is *between* average vocabulary knowledge for grades 4 and 12 (about a 5,000 basic-word difference). See Figure 17.7. To interpret this figure in terms of vocabulary size, multiply the Basic Word Vocabulary Test Score (BWVT Score) by 100. The teacher is faced with a difficult job teaching against this vast variability of base knowledge.

While there are a lot of words out there with different meanings, it is not clear that they involve that many different *concepts*. In the late 1920s and early 1930s, Ogden (1932) developed what he called *Basic English* as an aid to international communication. It is composed of only 850 words and has been used to successfully translate *Robinson Crusoe* and the *Bible*. Siegfried Engelmann was asked to analyze this list to determine those words that were best taught by examples (basic concept teaching) rather than with other words. Approximately 350 words were identified that could serve as a core vocabulary to use in defining other unknown words from known words (assuming these core words were taught first). These core words, incidentally, overlap completely the vocabulary taught in DISTAR Language I and II, an analysis Engelmann had completed 14 years earlier without knowledge of Ogden's Basic English. Children from middle-class homes usually come to school knowing this core; those from less-privileged homes often do not.

The semantic analysis took two steps beyond that just described before funds ran out. An attempt was made to define, (using the core words) in full-usage statements, the most common meaning of the 8,100 root words. On the first run, 1,800 acceptable definitions were developed. This fact shows the approach was likely a workable one. In the middle of a second iteration the project was stopped. The ultimate goal was to build a set of grade-level-based guides for the increase in vocabulary that could be used for program develop-

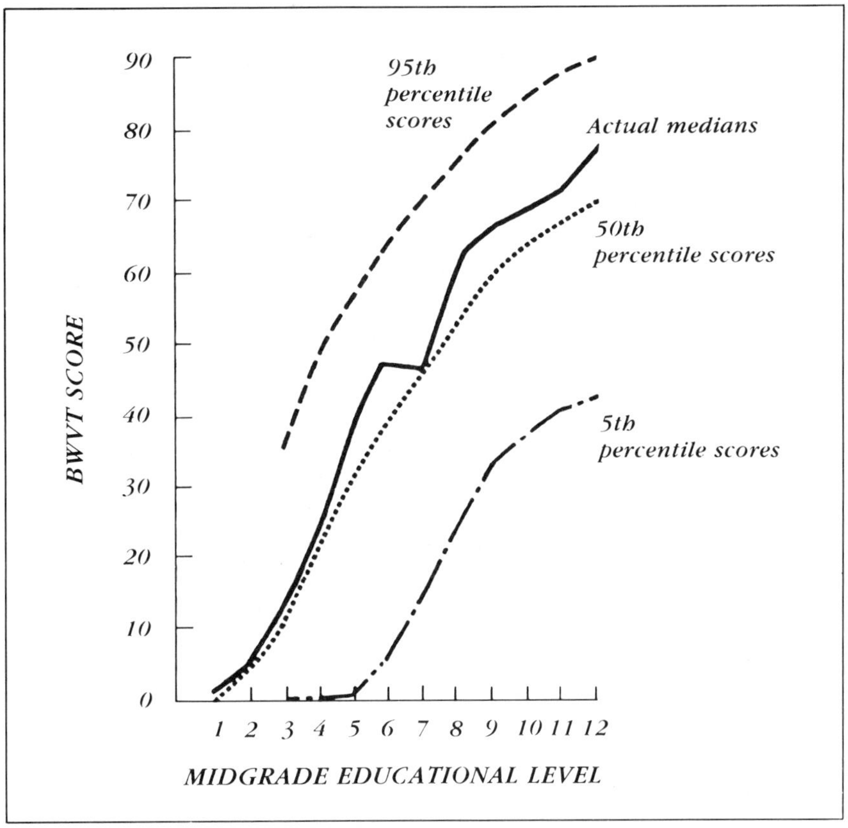

Figure 17-7 Basic word vocabulary growth pattern of children by educational level

ment and as a guide for textbook writers. It might also provide the basis for a set of dictionaries where unknown words could usually be defined in terms of words taught at earlier levels.

The other step that was begun but not completed was to look at the meanings of the 800 highest-frequency root words and affixes to see what potential there was for using their meanings to generate the meaning of compound words. This is analogous to the kind of transfer that has been reported to occur from learning Latin and applying it to understanding English. For example, *port* is the modern form of the Latin word that means "to carry." So to *import* means "to carry in." The goal is to find generalizable families of words or word parts to reduce the total amount of instruction required in teaching vocabulary.

One analysis of the 26,000 words that was completed was the form analysis or the morphographic analysis (Becker et al., 1980). This task was directed by Robert Dixon, author of several spelling programs based on morphographs (see Appendix A). Dixon defined a morphograph as an irreducible unit of meaning in written English. The researchers asked how many such forms existed in the 26,000 word lexicon we were working with. The process of analysis took several cycles. All the rules were not known at the start. We had to collect sets of related examples and make judgments about the most efficient way to relate the parts. Then the analysis would have to be rechecked to see what else changed as a function of what was learned. As a design problem, there were of course alternative possibilities, and different researchers might make different judgments.

This analysis showed that the 26,000 words were made up of 6,531 different morphographs. Approximately 3,000 occurred in only one or two words. Approximately 2,000 occurred in three to five words, leaving approximately 1,500 in six or more words. About 800 of these occurred in ten or more words. It was estimated that the 800 high frequency morphographs could be used to *generate more than 12,000 words.* In *Corrective Spelling through Morphographs,* Dixon and Engelmann (1979), found that with 580 roots, 72 affixes, and 5 rules for combining morphographs, students could potentially spell more than 10,000 words. This is the kind of generative analysis needed if teachers are to effectively teach the English language. Figure 17.8 provides an illustration of morphographs.

Prefixes	*Root Words*	*Suffixes*
dis	arm	able
un	chain	er
re	cover	ing
	port	ed
With these 11 morphographs, over 75 words can be constructed such as the following:		
uncovered	recoverable	recovered
unarm	disarm	disarming
chainable	rechained	chaining
report	portable	reporter

Figure 17-8 An example of morphographs and some of the words that can be made from them

Vocabulary Teaching Formats

Formats for teaching basic concepts were described in Chapter 14. Formats for teaching vocabulary through synonyms and definitions follow the strategies for teaching facts and rules. Figures 17.9 and 17.10 show two such formats from Carnine and Silbert (1979). Note the questions asked to be sure the students have understanding and are not just parroting back what they are told.

Learning vocabulary from context is also important. Without context, students would have a difficult time dealing with those 80,000 rarely encountered words. Figure 17.11 shows a format aimed at teaching students to find out what new words mean on their own (eventually). The teaching a dictionary skills is also important in this regard.

CLOSING COMMENTS

A few of the following comments and suggestions might be useful in approaching reading instruction.

Some self-taught readers (usually quite bright) come to school with good *silent* reading skills, but may still be poor *oral* readers and thus go undetected. If this is suspected, you might ask a child to read a passage silently and then ask questions about it.

A 1985 report of The Commission on Reading entitled *Becoming a Nation of Readers* (Anderson, Hiebert, Scott, & Wilkinson, 1985) strongly supports parents teaching reading skills at home, keeping parents involved with a school reading program to reinforce more home reading, teaching reading skills in kindergarten (not "readiness" skills), using systematic phonics to teach decoding, and using some of the direct instruction skills illustrated in this chapter to teach comprehension. They also suggest that extensive reading in itself may help to deal with those 80,000 low-frequency vocabulary words encountered in schoolbooks. This report is a must for members of reading text

Teacher	Students
1. Teacher states the new word and the equivalent, familiar word and then tests. a. **"Here is a new word. Sturdy. Sturdy means strong."** b. **"What does sturdy mean?"** (signal)	"strong"
2. Teacher presents positive and negative examples until the students make six consecutive correct responses. Examples are not repeated in the same order. a. **"Tom leaned against a pole. The pole fell over. Was the pole sturdy?"** (signal)	"No"
b. **"Tom leaned against another pole. The pole didn't move. Was the pole sturdy?"** (signal)	"Yes"
c. **"A house didn't shake at all in a high windstorm. Was the house sturdy?"** (signal)	"Yes"
d. **"A different house fell down when the wind started blowing. Was the house sturdy?"** (signal) Note: The teacher can also provide practice by asking the students to generate examples. **"Tell me about something that is sturdy."**	"No"
3. Teacher reviews new word and other words until students answer all questions correctly. a. **"Is it mild out today? How do you know?"** b. **"Is that bench sturdy? How do you know?"** c. **"Is my desk tidy? How do you know?"**	

Figure 17-9 *Format for synonym teaching. (From* Direct Instruction Reading, *by D. Carnine and J. Silbert. Copyright © 1979 by Charles E. Merrill, Columbus, Ohio. Reproduced with permission of the publisher and Douglas Carnine.)*

selection committees. It is available (as of January, 1986) by sending a check or money order for $4.50 to:

Becoming a Nation of Readers
P.O. Box 2774
Station A
Champaign, Illinois, 61820-8774

For explicit guidelines for "fixing up" a basal reading program you may be "stuck" with, see Carnine and Silbert (1979). This text has provided the basis for most of the analyses presented in this chapter and can be very helpful.

Finally, remember that research-based knowledge of the teaching of reading is expanding rapidly these days. Keep watching for good ideas.

Teacher	Students
1. Teacher states the new word and its definition and has students say definition. a. **"An exit is a door that leads out of a building."** b. **"What is an exit?"** (signal)	 "A door that leads out of a building."
2. Teacher presents positive and negative examples. a. Teacher holds up a picture or points to a closet door. **"Is this an exit?"** **"How do you know?"**	 "No" "It doesn't lead out of the building."
b. Teacher holds up a picture of a movie theater, points to door, **"Is this an exit?"** **"How do you know?"**	"Yes" "It leads out of the building."
c. Teacher continues presenting examples until the students answer five consecutive questions correctly.	
3. Teacher reviews words recently introduced. a. Teacher holds up picture of barracks. **"What is this?"** **"How do you know?"**	 "A barracks" "It's a building full of bunk beds."
b. Teacher holds up picture of an exit. **"Is this an exit? How do you know?"** etc.	

Figure 17-10 *Format for teaching vocabulary with definitions. (From* Direct Instruction Reading, *by D. Carnine and J. Silbert. Copyright © 1979 by Charles E. Merrill, Columbus, Ohio. Reproduced with permission of the publisher and Douglas Carnine.)*

SUMMARY

Designing reading instruction is probably one of the most complex tasks an instructional designer could undertake. Even decoding skills, which are infinitely easier to teach than the vocabulary base that underlies reading comprehension, has many irregularities associated with it. As reading skills build, the size of units (length of the verbal chains) being dealt with expands from letters to phases in decoding, and from words to passages in comprehension. The skills involved in both decoding and comprehension are so extensive that they have yet to be fully analyzed, although there are acceptable solutions to the design of decoding programs.

A key to the design of the initial teaching of decoding was the development of a modified alphabet that helped reduce the number of irregular words the young learner had to master. As noted several times earlier in this text, the decoding strategies developed by Engelmann have enabled thousands of disadvantaged children to decode on the Wide Range Achievement Test at an average of 5.2 grade equivalents by the end of third grade. The DISTAR modified alphabet uses a variety of prompts to help reduce apparent samenesses and permit the student to discriminate more readily when a given response was appropriate. The

Teacher	Students
An advanced exercise might include four to six passages such as this one: When the first men came to our country, they saw a dark, living cloud of birds. The cloud was so huge that it almost eclipsed the sun. When this happened, men could hardly see what was happening.	
1. Students read first passage and identify unknown word.	
a. **"Read the passage."**	
b. **"A new word is underlined, what word is that?"** (signal)	"Eclipsed"
2. Teacher calls on a student to find synonym or definition.	
a. **"Who can find the words that tell what happened when the birds eclipsed the sun?"** (signal)	"The men could hardly see."
b. **"Because of the eclipse of the sun, the men could hardly see. What do you think an eclipse does to the sun?"** (signal)	"Covers it up."
3. Students say the sentence substituting the meaning of the new word.	
a. **"Read the sentence with *eclipse* in it."** (signal)	"The cloud was so huge that it almost eclipsed the sun."
b. **"Now tell me what that sentence means. Don't use the word *eclipse*."** (signal)	"The cloud was so big that it covered up the sun."
4. Teacher repeats steps 1-3 with remaining passages.	

Figure 17-11 *Format for teaching vocabulary through context. (From* Direct Instruction Reading, *by D. Carnine and J. Silbert. Copyright © 1979 by Charles E. Merrill, Columbus, Ohio. Reproduced with permission of the publisher and Douglas Carnine.)*

prompts are eventually faded and students master the traditional letter forms. There are still many irregular word families to be taught and many outright irregular words that have to be learned as sight words, but their number has been greatly reduced by Engelmann's procedures. Another important strategy used in teaching decoding was the development of blending procedures that allow the student to say a word correctly after sounding it out slowly (by not stopping between sounds).

The analysis of comprehension skills into generalizable sets of related tasks is in its infancy. Because of the extensive quantity of potential skills and concepts involved (since it could conceivably include all knowledge), an exhaustive analysis is next to impossible in dealing with a living, changing language. However, progress is being made in the identification of the most important skills for inclusion in a reading program. For example, at a beginning level, if students do not have such basic oral comprehension skills as statement repetition, following directions, and answering questions, the students must be taught them before they can progress in reading. Examples of higher-level skills include logical rules for detecting faulty arguments, the discrimination of fact from opinion, and self-monitoring study skills.

The major knowledge base underlying reading comprehension is vocabulary. Carroll has estimated that vocabulary amounts to 80 percent of the knowledge involved. Nagy and Anderson have estimated that the written English in school texts contain 88,500 word families (each built around a base word) with 110,000 distinct meanings. In addition, there are 90,000 proper nouns. However, only 6,700 of the base words occur more frequently than once in a million words of text, and only 1,000 of the proper nouns are important enough to memorize. Becker et al. analyzed 26,000 of the most frequent words in print and found 8,100 base words. They estimate that the average high school senior would need to know about 10,000 core words (8,100 base words, plus technical words, proper nouns, and abbreviations and contractions). Based on the work in Basic English, it is very likely that the number of different concepts underlying this core vocabulary is much smaller than 8,000 to 10,000. There is a critical need for further analysis in this area to provide a plan for building vocabulary through the school years. It is currently a most haphazard process, mostly being left to incidental learning. As a result, students from less stimulating environments are handicapped unnecessarily. Needless to say, even if a full and appropriate task analysis were completed in this area, it would still be unclear whether there is enough school time (even using microcomputers) to teach a full vocabulary to underprivileged students. Dupuy's data on the range of variation in vocabulary knowledge within grades poses enormous problems for teachers in communicating with the lower performers.

In terms of word forms, the analysis of morphographs has led to highly generative spelling programs and offers the promise of developing some generative programs in word meanings by teaching the meanings of morphographs that occur most frequently in words.

To deal with the problem pointed out by Nagy and Anderson, the presence of some 80,000 low-frequency words in school texts, students need to learn a variety of skills ranging from use of the dictionary to making inferences from context. Fortunately, most students acquire these skills in some form by fifth grade, and they can be improved by carefully directed teaching. A series of examples of formats from Carnine and Silbert's reading text for teaching vocabulary were presented.

The chapter closed with some comments on silent readers, the conclusions of a National Commission on Reading, where to get a guideline for fixing up a basal reader that does not cover many essential skills, and the possible importance of keeping up with research on reading.

CHAPTER

18

PROBLEM-SOLVING STRATEGIES AND RELATED METACOGNITIVE SKILLS

Chapters 15, 16, and 17 examined some problem-solving *routines* and their structure in elementary reading and mathematics programs. Problem-solving routines are sets of rules for solving problems with acceptable known solutions. Problem-solving *strategies,* on the other hand, are generalized procedures for approaching classes of problems you have not solved before (Gagné, 1970). Problem solving is still a poorly developed field of knowledge. Teachers do not know all there is to know to teach others to become effective problem solvers. However, much has been learned that can provide us with a useful beginning approach to this important area. A field called *artificial intelligence* (Simon, 1969; Winston, 1984), has in recent years contributed much to our understanding of important classes of problems. Researchers in this field attempt to build problem-solving programs to make computers "intelligent."

Closely related to problem-solving strategies are the processes called *metacognitive.* These processes refer to knowledge of your own thinking activities and products, including such things as knowing when you are right, being able to predict how well you will do, estimating task difficulty, planning, and study skills (Flavell, 1976; Brown, 1978). Metacognition is concerned with self-management behaviors (Skinner, 1957) as first discussed in Chapter 6. The question is, "Are there generalized strategies that can be used in managing your attempts to solve problems?" It would seem that there should be.

THE NATURE OF PROBLEMS

Some years ago a psychologist named Wolfgang Kohler (1925) gave this problem to an ape named Sultan: If he could join two bamboo sticks together to make a longer stick, he could use the sticks to reach a banana and pull it into his cage.

At first Sultan just sat. Then he picked up the two bamboo sticks and began playing with them. He happened to get them into the right position for joining them. He pushed the thinner stick into the opening of the thicker one. He then jumped up, ran to the side of the cage and drew the banana to him with the double stick. Kohler considered this an example of *insight.*

To Kohler, insight meant learning with an understanding of the structure of the problem. Even with his "most intelligent" ape (Sultan) such understanding often came very slowly. For many chimps, Kohler had to prompt and shape the elements of the solution strategy before the chimps were able to solve the stick problem or other problems that involved using boxes to get to bananas tied to the top of their cage. Once successful in solving the problem, the chimp could usually repeat the solution. Kohler interpreted their actions as "thinking through" the possibilities and then testing one that might work. As Hilgard and Bower (1975) note, this work focusing on the intelligence of apes helped to counteract the "somewhat sterile behaviorism" of the 1920s.

Some years later, Birch (1945) did an experiment following up Kohler's informal research. Birch showed that unless apes had prior experience using sticks as extensions of their arms in poking, raking, prying, and similar operations, they did not solve the problem. The solution to the problem involved two sequential operations: (1) putting two sticks together; (2) reaching with the stick to draw in the banana. The problem took some time to solve, because the apes had to learn by trial and error to join the sticks. This had not been previously taught. If training in the joining operation had been given, the problem would have been simply a combination of previously taught operations. The teaching for this problem involves: (1) training in joining sticks to make them longer, and (2) training in reaching with sticks (in one piece) to pull in objects.

Much of the experimental work on problem-solving by psychologists has involved "invention" problems such as Kohler's did. In summarizing work by Duncker (1945), Wertheimer (1959), Maier (1970), and Luchins and Luchins, (1970), Resnick and Glaser (1976) point out that in all of the problem solutions, the learner was able to use *component skills in his or her repertoire to do something new.* A procedure has to be invented by assembling component behaviors in a way that would reach a specified goal. The tasks found on intelligence tests illustrate some of the operations involved in problem solving: comparing, searching, counting, eliminating alternatives, orienting in space (directions), and transforming. The steps involved in the solution to a problem are what Gagné (1970) has called *intellectual skills*—concepts, rules, and rule sets. Gagné (1968) likens these skills to the subroutines in a computer program, which when called up (signaled), can be used to operate on a variety of information inputs and recombined into a variety of problem solutions. The essence of problem solving is developing *procedures to assemble actions in an appropriate order* (Resnick and Glaser, 1976). These might range from random searching to hypothesizing and testing. It would appear that good problem solvers learn when certain strategies are more likely to pay off than others.

CLASSES OF PROBLEMS

Problems can take many forms. A lot of problems involve searches. *Finding routes* to a goal, *designing* something new (a machine or a better recipe for apple pie), *game strategies* (chess, checkers), *finding lost objects*—all involve search strategies. The problem solver has to examine the consequences of many possible alternatives before making a choice. Other problems require *discovering and/or using rules,* as in finding the rule in this number series (192837 . . .) or solving a geometric theorem. *Understanding* what you read can be thought of as a problem (and it often is). *Learning* itself can pose problems when you have to figure out how to learn what you need to pass a test on your own or when you attempt to induce a concept or rule from examples. The strategies you use can be very critical to your success.

Analysis Strategies and Solution Strategies

It is conceivable that one could have a variety of problem-solving operations in one's repertoire and not know when to use them. Detecting when particular solution strategies are likely to work involves skills in *problem analysis.* What kind of a problem is it? Is it a fact problem or a judgment problem? What is known and not known? Training in analyzing the nature of problems is the key to teaching problem-solving behavior. Without problem-analysis skills, solution strategies are useless. You would not know when to do what. Analysis strategies lead to cues that indicate which solution strategies will be more fruitful.

It is at this point in instruction that the so-called "discovery method" becomes useful. A problem example is presented and the student makes some guesses (hypotheses) as to the nature of the problem. He is gaining practice in problem analysis. A series of examples may eventually lead to the conclusion that this is an X-type problem and the answer is such and such. Now a new class of problems is introduced through new examples. A different analysis is required, a different solution is implied. After experience with multiple sets of different kinds of problems, the student may have sufficient inductive experience to begin instruction in rules for problem analysis. The process becomes one that Shulman (1968) has called "guided discovery." The discovery process is programmed to provide the needed inductive experience with problem classes. Then, more formal rule learning about such classes and related solution strategies can be provided.

The logic of the approach proposed in this text can be best communicated through demonstration and example. You will first look at the notion of classes of problems and then see how this analysis can relate to possible solution strategies.

Fact versus Judgment Problems

Theoretically, all problems can be divided into fact problems and judgment problems. A fact problem has a specific answer. "What is the diameter of the moon?" "What comes next in this series: 12y34y56y?" "Where did I lose my wallet?" Judgment problems have many solutions that differ in value. For example, most problems in engineering, architecture, or creative writing involve some fixed criteria (minimum standards), but they also involve judgments about which criteria are more important (relative weighing of criteria) and about characteristics that are not specifiable in criterion terms, such as beauty. With judgment problems, people may disagree about the value of different solutions.

Whenever you are faced with a problem, the initial analysis should be concerned with whether the answer is a fact or a judgment. The next step is to determine what is known and what is not known.

Givens

Problems differ in what is given and what is not given (required for solution). The following groupings cover the majority of tasks used to define intelligent behavior. Most of the examples are adaptations of the Stanford-Binet (Form LM) items.

1. *Concept words are given. The task is to identify or compare characteristics.*

Problem Class	*Example*
Vocabulary	"What is a lemon?"
Analogies	"Equity is an asset, a mortgage is a *(liability)*."
Essential differences	"What is the difference between concepts and operations?"

2. *The concept or rule is not given. The task is to find the concept or rule.*

(a) *Instances are given (induction):*

Problem Class	*Example*
Problem situation	"Jim saw an animal in the woods, and he tried to take it home, but it got away. His parents burned his clothes when he got home. Why?"
Induction	A paper is folded once and a hole cut. Then a paper is folded twice and a hole cut. Then three times, and so on. "Give me a rule so I can know how many holes there will be?"

(b) A concept class is given, find an instance:

Problem Class	*Example*
Twenty questions	"By asking questions that can be answered yes or no, find out what I am thinking of."

3. *The goal response is given. The task is to identify the route to the goal.*

Problem Class	*Example*
Ingenuity	"Use a 4-pint can and a 7-pint can to bring back exactly 3 pints of water."
Mazes	"Show me how to take the boy to school the shortest way."

4. *The goal response is not given. The task is to use your knowledge of concepts and rules to produce the answer.*

Problem Class	*Example*
Arithmetic problems	"If a man earns $100 a month and spends $75, how long will it take him to save $400?"
Paper cutting	"Draw how a paper that has been folded and cut will look when it is unfolded."

5. *The criteria for goal response are given. The task is to use your knowledge of operations to construct an acceptable product.*

Problem Class	*Example*
Planning a search	"Something has been lost in this given area. Show how you would search to find it."
Sentence building	"Make up a sentence that has in it the words, *sled, snow* and *cold.*"

PROBLEM-SOLVING STRATEGIES

Rules for problem solving specify possible strategies for different classes of problems. The first step is to classify the problem. Is it a fact problem or a judgment problem? What is given and what is not given? The next step is to identify possible solution strategies.

Fact Problems

Fact problems require finding the answer. There are many, many classes of fact problems where different information is given and different solution strategies are required. The following examples illustrate some major classes of fact problems.

Concept identification. Instances are given. Consider the following concept-identification task. The set of possible concepts is restricted to groups of three geometric figures, each of which is a circle, triangle, or square. Concept instances and not-instances can vary in the type of figure found in any of the three positions. The problem is to find out, from as few instances as possible, what concept this is an example of:

Select instances one at a time from the following list. After each selection, check the key below to find out if you have picked an instance or not-instance of this concept. Try to figure out the concept as you go along.

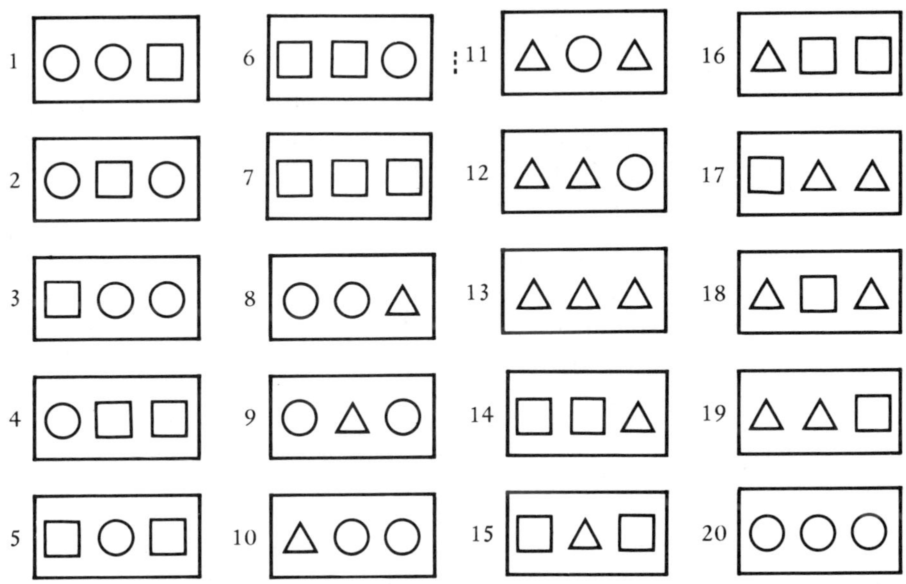

1. –
2. –
3. –
4. –
5. –
6. –
7. –
8. +
9. –
10. –
11. +
12. –
13. +
14. +
15. –
16. –
17. +
18. +
19. –
20. –

21 ○ □ △	23 △ ○ □	25 □ △ ○
22 □ ○ △	24 △ □ ○	26 ○ △ □

21. +	23. –	25. –
22. +	24. –	26. –

The smart way to go about it is to select instances that change only one characteristic at a time (Bruner, Goodnow, & Austin, 1956). This will tell you what is essential to instances and not-instances of the concept. For example:

Instances Selected		
○ △ △	(+)	1. You started with this.
17. □ △ △	(+)	2. Circle in position 1 is not important.
21. ○ □ △	(+)	3. Triangle in position 2 is not important.
26. ○ △ □	(–)	4. Triangle in position 3 is essential.
9. ○ △ ○	(–)	5. Circle in position three is not important. (This eliminates the possibility that the concept is triangle *or* circle in position three.)

Since nothing else is common to all three instances, the concept must be "triangle (only) in position three."

Note carefully the problem-solving strategy: change only one thing at a time to identify the critical elements and to eliminate alternatives systematically. This is another example of the minimum-difference principle. When concept instances are given, identification is most quickly accomplished by the systematic testing of alternatives. This can be done experimentally by changing things one at at time, or observationally by examining a series of instances and not-instances to see what characteristics are shared by the instances.

Concept identification. Instances are given, but there are many possibilities. If there are a large number of possibilities and only a few essential characteristics in a given concept instance, then a combination of deductive and inductive procedures should be considered. Suppose the problem is to find the cause of polio (infantile paralysis). Causes are antecedent events. Polio is a disease of the nervous system. Deductively all events that do not influence the nervous system can be eliminated. The causal events must take place inside the body. All food substances regularly used that are not followed by polio can be eliminated. There remains the weak possibility that a given food substance could act in combination with some other causal factor. Microorganisms whose effects are known can be eliminated. At this point, it is necessary to find what remaining events are common to instances of polio and not common to not-instances. Systematic testing of possibilities one at a time is now required.

A concept class is given, find an instance. The problem is the game Twenty Questions: I am thinking of an object class. You have to determine what I am thinking about by asking twenty questions or less that can be answered yes or no. Let's analyze the problem. It is a concept-identification problem. The answer is not given. It is known that there is a specific answer and that the answer is the name of a thing. It is necessary to search to find the answer. Because there are so many things in the world, there is no point to just guessing "Is it a baseball?" or "Is it an orange?" The characteristics of this thing must be determined. A *zeroing-in* strategy is used. Questions are asked that start at the top of the hierarchy of things and work down. Deduction is used when no instances are given.

"Is it living?" "No."
"Is it synthetic?" "Yes."
"Is it larger than a breadbox?" "No."
"Is it found in the home?" "Yes."
"Would most people have one?" "Yes."

Each question eliminates about half of the alternatives until the object is identified.

Even when the question involves the identification of a concept or a stimulus within a small group, the strategy is the same: "I am thinking of a number between 1 and 10."

"Is it greater than 6?" "No."
"Is it greater than 3?" "Yes."
"Is it 4?" "Yes."

The size of the set is not critical. What is critical for this strategy is *the lack of instances and knowledge only of a higher-order set of which the concept is a member.*

Concept-characteristic problems. To teach children to handle analogies, essential similarities and differences, and other problems involving identification of concept characteristics, practice in *comparing, relating,* and *contrasting* is given after teaching the basic concepts. Without knowledge of the basic concepts, these problems cannot be solved. Without the operations of comparing, relating, and contrasting, new problems involving these problems cannot be solved.

Route-to-the-goal problems. *Goal response is given.* If the goal response is given, consider starting from the goal and working the problem backward. Consider this maze:

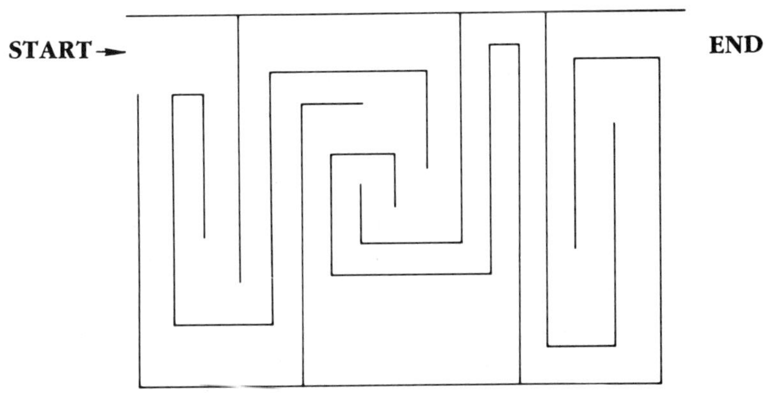

By starting at the end, the solution is readily found with no errors. Even if the task requires drawing a line from the "Start" to the "End," going through the tracing operation mentally from "End" to "Start" will allow most people to solve the maze quickly with no errors.

Similarly, people faced with Sultan's problem could start by defining the solution: "I need something long enough to reach the banana so I can pull it in." Then the search involves how to get or make something long enough.

Consider this problem: The task is to move the coal car on the right to the position of the coal car on the left and the coal car on the left to the position of the coal car on the right, and end up with the engine where it is now.

Rule 1. Only the engine can go through the tunnel.

Rule 2. The engine can hook on to cars from either end. It can move forward or backward on the tracks.

Rule 3. The sidetrack holds two cars.

E = Engine
R = Right Coal Car
L = Left Coal Car

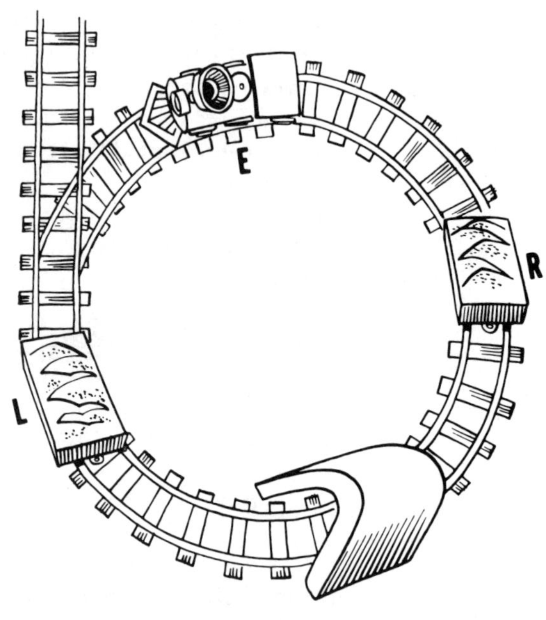

To try this problem, cut out three small pieces of paper and label them E, L, and R. Put your "train cars" on the track and try to solve the problem before going on.

Before looking at the solution, read this.

If you did not solve the problem, take this information and try again. At solution, the cars will be in this order:

R	E	L

To get into this order, the step before the solution must look like this:

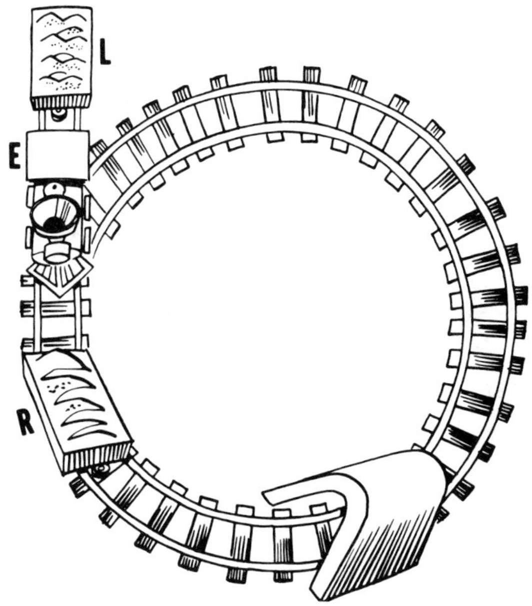

Now try again!

Codes: *R position* is the starting position of R as drawn in the original problem.
L position is the starting position of L.
E position is the starting position of E.
E, L, and R stand for the cars you are moving.

Solution Steps:

1 E puts R in sidetrack.
2 E puts L in E position.
3 E goes through tunnel to R.
4 E takes R to L position.
5 E goes through tunnel to L and takes L to R.
6 E returns through tunnel to R.
7 E moves R and L to sidetrack.
8 E returns R to L position.
9 E goes through tunnel to R and up to L in sidetrack.
10 E takes L out of sidetrack and over to R position.
11 E returns to E position.

This train problem illustrates the importance of looking at the final step (answer) in planning a solution. The final order is R, E, L, and the only way it can get that way is for some step before the final one to show this order also. When the solution is defined as getting the L car into the sidetrack ahead of the engine, the rest of the steps fall into place.

Puzzles are often difficult because the situation is structured to elicit habitual responses that are wrong. Consider this problem: The task is to draw through all nine dots with four straight lines without taking your pencil off the paper and without retracing a line.

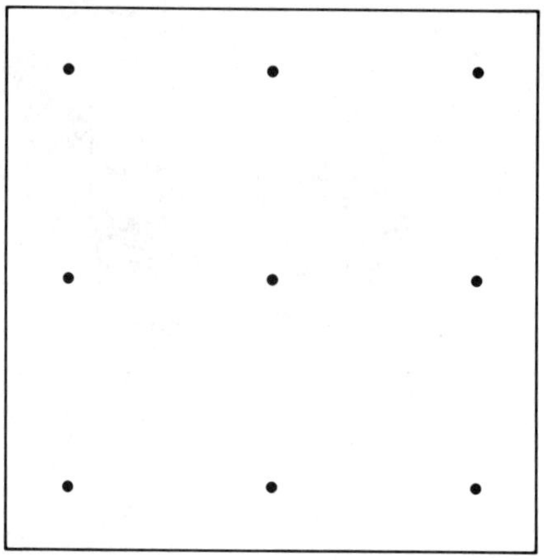

Most people will use old habits in trying to connect the dots. They will try going around the square and then play with the diagonals. Then they are stuck. Here's a hint. The solution involves drawing lines beyond the square containing the nine dots. When stuck with old habits, consider the various ways in which the problem can be transformed. Restate the question. Look at the definition of the problem implicit in your wrong responses and ask yourself if there is a broader definition. Logically, what alternative responses can be made in this situation?

When the problem is to find something that is lost, what to look for is given, but where to look is not. Because learned associations are established forward in time rather than backward, it is best to start the search at the place where the lost item was last known to be and work forward in time, systematically eliminating alternatives.

Goal response is not given. Produce the answer! Many problems test the ability to use a variety of concepts and operations to produce an answer. Many problems of arithmetic or logical reasoning are of this form. Once the problem-solving routines for their solutions have been taught, they can be used in new examples. If the student does not know the solution rules, he or she cannot do problems of this sort. Strategies involving defining the solution, finding the question, or searching for response alternatives are not helpful. What is needed most is direct teaching of sets of prototype problems.

Criteria for goal response are given. Produce the answer. Construction problems involve producing an answer to fixed criteria. Specific concepts and operations must be taught and sequenced, as in learning to write, copy figures, make cookies from a recipe, or construct grammatically correct sentences. Construction problems with fixed criteria are taught directly as rule chains; complex strategies are not required.

Creative Judgment Problems

Judgment problems require strategies for designing creative solutions that might work. An example might be to design a vehicle for landing on the moon. Analysis of this problem would first require a statement of the functions of the vehicle and other fixed requirements. How many persons must it hold? In what kind of terrain must it land? From where must it descend? Where must it go afterward? What kind of communications system is required? What life-support systems are required? Is there a weight limit? What characteristics must the propulsion and control system have? What is the cost limit? Next, a series of trial designs are made. What incompatibilities among priorities are encountered? How can they be solved? How can weight be saved? How can cost be reduced? All initial decisions are kept tentative. Alternatives are sought by systematic review of the possibilities. Finally, alternatives are evaluated according to how well they meet specifications, and a working model is built for further evaluation. After testing, a production model is designed.

Teaching children to analyze a construction problem is quite complex and will not be dealt with here. The point to be made is that this is an important class of problems. The complex skills involved can be taught by systematic assignment of construction tasks along with the teaching of the component concepts and operations. After a large number of tasks have been mastered, the student can be taught more formal steps for analyzing construction problems.

The teaching of the many skills involved in creative designs has not yet been sufficiently analyzed into its component behaviors to permit exposition here. Very likely the component concepts and operations required will vary markedly from one area of activity to another. The component skills required by the design engineer will be quite different from those of the science fiction writer or the composer. One difference between creative design problems and fact or construction problems (which can be solved with problem-solving routines) is that, at any point in the solution, ***the alternative possibilities have to be kept in mind.*** This implies that learning to think of unusual or different alternatives at any point in a problem solution is an important aspect of the creative solutions to design problems. Several studies have looked experimentally at what it takes to produce behavior judged to be more creative in this sense.

In a study with preschool children, Goetz and Baer (1973) gave descriptive social reinforcement for producing different forms in block building. The teacher would show delight and say something like "Oh, that's nice. It's different." The findings demonstrated that when production of different forms was reinforced, the children produced many more "creative" constructions than when no reinforcement was given, or when "same" forms were reinforced.

In a study with fourth, fifth, and sixth graders, Maloney and Hopkins (1973) gave points and backup reinforcers to promote creative writing. Each day the students were given a key word that they were to work into a ten-sentence story. After five days without reinforcement for diversity, the class was divided into two teams to play the "good writing game." On various days the teams earned points by writing stories with more different adjectives, or action verbs, or both of these along with different sentence beginnings. Both teams could win the game if they made enough points. The points could be exchanged for extra recess time and a piece of candy. There were marked increases in the production of different words. Also, independent judges rated the stories more creative when diversity was reinforced.

ARTIFICIAL INTELLIGENCE

In designing computer programs that can solve problems, researchers learn about the details of problem analysis that could serve to guide instruction in problem-solving skills. This is a rapidly growing field with current applications in medical diagnosis (such as the system called INTERNIST by Pople, 1973) industrial design for example, XCON, developed by McDermott in 1982 to configure Digital Equipment Corporation's VAX computers) and many other areas such as military training, the comprehension of oral and written language, and the identification of objects (using programs that can learn concepts and rules).

One of the first programs for problem solving was developed by Newell, Shaw, and Simon (1957; see also Ernst and Newell, 1969). A program called GPS or General Problem Solver was developed to solve route-to-goal problems or "means-end" problems. A key feature of this kind of problem was the comparison of a *current state* with the *goal* and then taking steps to reduce the difference, as is found with a travel problem like getting from Chicago to San Francisco. For problems in this class, GPS would have a *procedure table* based on differences in distance. The procedure table specifies the means to various ends (goals and subgoals). If the distance is over 1,000 miles, it chooses to fly. For distances of 100 to 1,000 miles, a train or car is chosen. For distances of 1 to 100 miles, a car or taxi is used. For distances less than 1 mile, the choice is walking. Since Chicago is more than 1,000 miles from San Francisco, a jet is chosen. The problem now becomes one of getting to the airport, which is 20 miles away. The car is chosen. The problem now becomes one of getting to the car, so walking is chosen. GPS now has you at the airport, and the problem is to get to the airplane. Walking is again the solution. Now you are at the San Francisco airport and wish to get to your aunt's house 10 miles away. Since your car is in Chicago, a taxi is selected. This leaves you at the curb in front of her house and the final leg to the problem solution is walking again. With a general strategy for a class of problem, GPS searches the alternatives reducing differences and setting up subgoals when needed.

A key to designing problem-solving programs according to Winston (1984) is to have a good *representation* of the problem. The representation allows you to describe a class of things. Descriptions use the conventions of the representation to describe specific things or events. This involves problem analysis and the possible solutions. But in designing a computer representation of a problem, the analysis must be very complete. Winston uses the following children's puzzle to illustrate what he means by a good representation:

A farmer has a fox, a goose, and a sack of grain that he wants to get across a river. The boat, however, is so small that he can only take one of his possessions across at a time. Also, he can't leave the goose alone with the grain or the goose will eat it all up. And, he can't leave the fox alone with the goose, or the fox will eat the goose. What should he do?

Figure 18.1 shows a representation of the problem. The farmer, fox, goose, and grain are named. The river is symbolized as WWWW, and at each step of the solution, the four objects are shown on one side of the river or the other. Since there are two places for the four things to be, there are a total of sixteen possibilities (24). But the constraints eliminate six of these:

- Two are eliminated because the farmer can't be on one side and the goose, fox, and grain on the other.

- Two are eliminated because the goose and the fox can't be on the same side without the farmer.

- Two more are eliminated because the goose and the grain can't be on one side with the farmer and fox on the other.

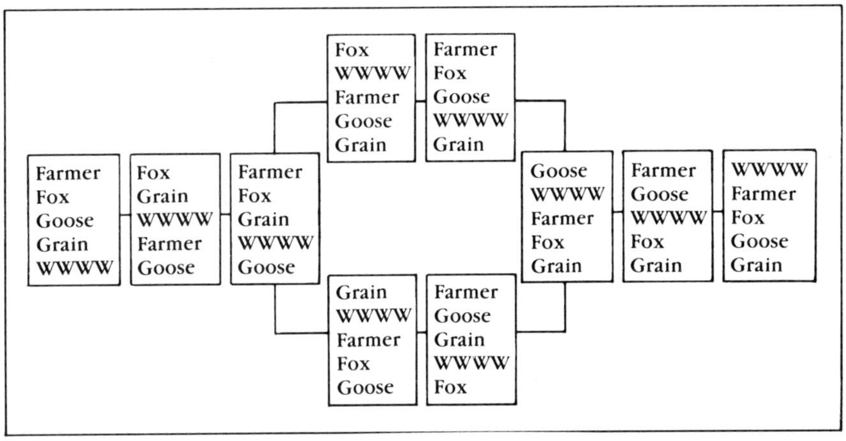

Figure 18-1 *The problem of the farmer, fox, goose, and grain. The farmer must get his fox, goose, and grain across the river, represented by the wavy line, from north to south. His boat will hold only him and one of his three things. Foxes eat geese, and geese eat grain. (From P. H. Winston,* Artificial Intelligence, *© 1984, Addison • Wesley, Reading, Massachusetts, p. 23, Figure 2-1. Reprinted with permission.)*

The ten boxes in Figure 18.1 show the two possible solutions. The representation contains all of the essential information and could be used to describe any problem of this sort.

Simon (1976) describes a computer simulation of how humans solve problems involving pattern sequences such as the following:

ABMCDMEFM

The basic strategy takes this form:

DISCOVER PATTERN
  Detect period
  Determine the rules
  Test the rules
EXTRAPOLATE PATTERN

The subskills needed to solve such patterned sequences are a SAMENESS operator for determining that two letters are the same and a NEXT TO operator for determining what comes next in a sequence such as the alphabet. To handle problems of the form, 162534, a COMPLEMENT operator is needed also. Beyond this, a knowledge-base having to do with whatever is being patterned is needed, but operations for same, next, and complement define the basic skills and allow you to represent rules for patterns in a succinct form.

While much progress has been made in the past two decades in building intelligent machines, and the work has many suggestions for skills needed in problem solving, it is also quite clear that human experts have capabilities that far exceed machines in problem-solving skills, unless the skills involve just number crunching or systematic searches.

METACOGNITIVE PROCESSES WITH CHILDREN

Metacognitive processes (self-management, self-awareness, and so forth) are also relevant to understanding problem-solving behavior. Pellegrino and Schadler (1974) trained fifth graders in the component skills needed to find how big a rectangle is by covering it with blocks. These skills are illustrated in Figure 18.2 as: (1) USE BLOCKS, (2) TEST FOR APPLICABILITY, and (3) TRANSFORM. After training on the component skills, the students were tested for "inventions" (can they put them together to solve a new problem) with the problems shown in the bottom center of the figure. In two previous studies using the same problems, Morris and Resnick (1974) and Mulholland (1974) found invention occurred (correct solutions without help) in less than 50 percent of the cases. Pellegrino and Schadler required their students to "look ahead" when given the invention condition by asking the students "What do you think I want you to do?" Only after the students had given as many goals as they could, were they asked "Tell me how you would find which is bigger?" The students were asked to state a *plan* and tell how it would solve the problem. Under these conditions, 14 of 16 solved the problem. In a comparison group that was asked only to "Find which is bigger?" only 6 of 16 showed invention. In reporting these studies, Resnick and Glaser (1976) conclude that planning ahead might be a valuable metacognitive strategy to use in problem solving. It appears to be generalizable across problems and is obviously teachable.

John Flavell (1976) defined *metacognition* as follows:

> "Metacognition"refers to one's knowledge concerning one's own cognitive processes and products or anything related to them, e.g., the learning-relevant properties of information or data. For example, I am engaging in metacognition (metamemory, metalearning, metattention, metalanguage, or whatever) if I notice that I am having more trouble learning A than B; if it strikes me that I should double-check C before accepting it as a fact; if it occurs to me that I had better scrutinize each and every alternative in any multiple-choice type task situation before deciding which is the best one; if I sense that I had better make a note of D because I may forget it. . . . Metacognition refers, among other things, to the active monitoring and consequent regulation and orchestration of these processes in relation to the cognitive objects on which they bear, usually in the services of some concrete goal or objective (p. 232).

Study Skills

Study skills are an important subset of metacognitive strategies. Knowing what you know and what you do not know can help make self-directed learning more effective. Having a plan for approaching various kinds of new learning can make that learning more efficient. Consider this simple example. Six and eight year olds were asked, after being told a friend's telephone number, if they would prefer to phone right away or get a drink of water first. Ninety-five percent of the third graders indicated they would phone first or at least were aware that there was a potential memory problem. Only 40 percent of the kindergarteners showed such awareness. All of the third graders showed they would do something to help remember it (write down, rehearse, and so forth), but only 40 percent of the kindergarteners had any plan (Kreutzer, Leonard, and Flavell, 1975).

In a memory study with first graders, third graders, and college students, the students had to memorize items on a list. The second time through and subsequently, the students were free to select 50 percent of the items for further study. Third graders and college students followed the strategy of selecting items they had missed. The first graders did not (Masur, McIntyre, & Flavell, 1973). Selection of a good strategy was related to good performance only for college students. However, it is likely that the third graders could not keep the "known"

ROUTINE	*PHYSICAL ARRAY*	*E'S INSTRUCTION*
USE BLOCKS	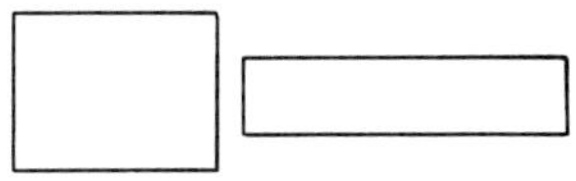	"Find which is bigger."
TEST FOR APPLICABILITY	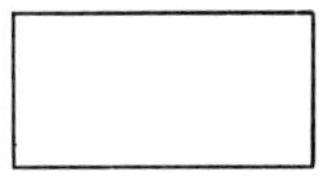 or 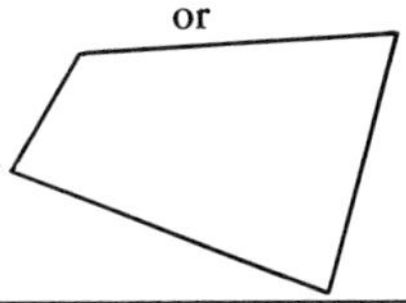	"Does this figure have four right angles?"
TRANSFORM	Various non-rectangular figures presented one at a time. Scissors handed to or pointed out to child. Booklet to paste figures into.	"To make this into a rectangle, you have to cut a part off and paste it on somewhere else. You must use all pieces and have four right angles."
INVENTION	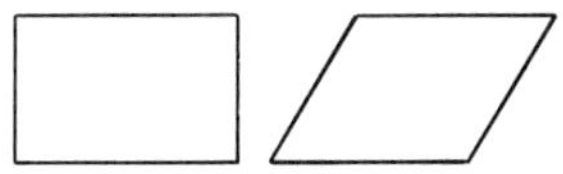 or 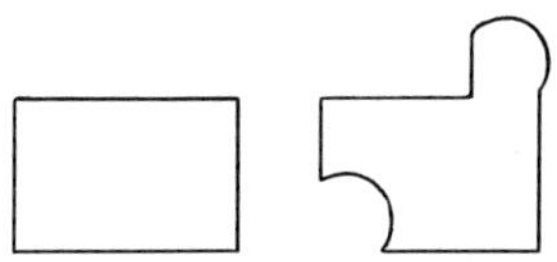	"Find which is bigger."

Figure 18-2 *Summary of stimulus conditions in the Morris experiment (From Resnick,* The Nature of Intelligence, *1976)*

items alive while practicing the unknown items. Attempts to train study skills usually have been effective, with younger children profiting less than older children (Brown, 1978). However, children do not continue to use the study skills after training unless prompted to do so.

Study skills programs have been around for a long time. Robinson's (1946) *SQ3R* strategy is one of the oldest. It is designed to help the student benefit from a reading assignment. The student is told first to ***survey*** the text by reading the chapter headings, italicized words, and similar organizers. From this, the student develops ***questions.*** Then he or she ***reads*** to answer the questions. Next, the student is told to close the book and ***recite***[1] the answer to the question, and then open the book to ***review.*** The procedure is aimed at promoting an active study process through following a plan. But the procedures leave much up to the student to figure out.

Stanton (1968) proposed a modification to Robinson's procedure for studying a reading assignment that uses the steps: (1) preview, (2) question, (3)

[1]Robinson originally used the word *recall* here, but *recite* has been used by others because it leads to a performance.

read, (4) restate in your own words, and (5) delay test yourself. Stanton also points out that you need:

- *Motivation.* Find a way to add some if it isn't there.
- *Concentration.* Get rid of the distractors. Set up a study area that is used only for study. Try to keep the times of study consistent. That too will help concentration.
- *Reaction.* Think about what you are reading, diagram it, restate it, tie it to what you already know.
- *Organization.* Get the big picture of what you are learning.
- *Comprehension.* If you don't understand something, find out about it.
- *Repetition.* Review, test yourself, practice.

Other kinds of study strategies are good note taking, summarizing, and charting or drawing pictures of set of facts.

Sheinker, Sheinker, and Stevens (1983) have recently prepared a training program on Study Strategies that train groups of students in explicit skills for structured skimming, summarizing, note taking, and outlining. For each of these skills, six- to nine-step procedures are outlined, and students are given teacher-directed practice in learning the steps and doing exercises to practice the skills.

SUMMARY

Problem-solving strategies are generalized procedures for approaching new problems. Research on "invention" problems has made it clear that new problems are not solved unless the problem solver has all of the component steps in his or her repertoire. The task is basically one of determining which skills are needed and in what order. It is an *assembly* task.

Because there are many different classes of problems having different solution requirements, skills in problem analysis are as important as solution skills. A first step in analysis is to determine whether you are dealing with a fact problem or a judgment problem. Fact problems have a right answer(s). Judgment problems have solutions that are better or worse than others. Judgment problems usually have multiple criteria defining what is "good," such as cost, beauty, simplicity, and efficiency. Many judgment problems have known solutions found in manuals such as cookbooks. In judgment problems, it is necessary to consider alternative possibilities and operate tentatively until various possible solutions have been produced and evaluated.

A second step in problem analysis is to decide what is known or given and what is not. A variety of problems were examined to show how the structure of the problem determines the potential solution strategies.

The field of artificial intelligence is producing programs that allow computers (and related equipment) to solve various kinds of problems. The analyses going on in this field should help to clarify our understanding of problems and contribute in the future to better training of students in problem-solving strategies.

The close of this chapter, examined briefly the potential role of metacognitive processes in problem solving. Of course, many of the analysis strategies already discussed are metacognitive processes. They just were not looked at in that way. For many problems, making a plan, keeping track of important information on what has been done and what needs to be done can be useful in working out a solution. Studies of these processes with children are beginning to describe the "natural" development of these processes and establish the effectiveness of instruction in the use of metacognitive skills. An important subset of such skills are study skills. Quite a bit is known about how to learn on your own more effectively, but there is still a need for further research on effective study methods.

PART III

DEVELOPMENT AND INDIVIDUAL DIFFERENCES

Part III opens with a diversion from the main theme of this text to discuss five statistical concepts needed as preskills for your future work in this text. These skills will help you to better understand the assessment of intelligence and, later on, achievement tests scores. It is important to take the time to understand these concepts.

Next you will explore the fascinating area of intelligence—what it is, how it is assessed, and the hereditary-environment controversy that has surrounded this concept since the early 1900s. Cognitive development is explored next, after setting the context of the physical development that underlies it. Jean Piaget's comprehensive view of cognitive development is examined, along with a neo-Piagetian viewpoint, attending especially to implications for teachers.

Chapter 22 examines what is involved in personal and social development, with particular attention to how schools, parents, and communities can systematically foster responsibility in addition to intellectual competence. Chapter 23 takes many of the principles learned in Part I of this text and applies them to ways of dealing with the personal-social problems students might have. A variety of personality problems and conduct problems that students might have are examined.

In Chapter 24, the developmental research on differences between the sexes is examined, along with the issues involved in building a society based on equity between the sexes. Throughout history, women have been treated as second-rate citizens. Changes in the laws have helped to bring more equity, but there is still a long way to go. Teachers need to be well-informed on the issues of sex bias and should know how to contribute to its elimination.

Part III closes with an examination of the needs of handicapped students and other special groups, including the gifted. The past 20 years have brought about remarkable changes in special education that all teachers need to be informed about. With mainstreaming the norm, all teachers will more and more need to study special education. Chapter 25 provides an introduction to some of the concepts and issues.

CHAPTER

19

FIVE STATISTICAL CONCEPTS

This chapter digresses from the main objective for Part III of this text—exploring student characteristics important for teachers to understand—and studies some preskills you need to understand before tackling the interpretation of norm-referenced tests, such as IQ tests. You need an understanding of five concepts:

1. Frequency distribution
2. Mean
3. Standard deviation
4. Standard scores
5. Correlation

These concepts will help you to better understand all sorts of test scores besides IQ tests. All of the basic achievement test scores are usually interpreted in terms of one kind of standard score or another. There are exceptions, such as percentiles and grade-equivalent scores, but these are not difficult concepts to grasp. The concepts *mean, standard deviation, standard score,* and *correlation* are also quite important in interpreting research findings relating to teaching.

FREQUENCY DISTRIBUTION

Assume that you have just given two tests to your class. One involves spelling forty irregular words that the students have been learning for the past month. The other consists of fifty problems covering multiplication of two-digit numbers. The number of right answers (the test score) obtained by each student is given in Table 19.1.

A frequency distribution shows graphically how many students received each score. The vertical dimension on the graph shows frequency (how many), and the horizontal dimension shows the scores (in this case, number right). For spelling, the frequency distribution of the scores in Table 19.1 would look like the illustration in Figure 19.1.

Table 19-1 Test scores for a class in spelling and arithmetic

Name	Spelling	Arithmetic
Joe	25	45
Ned	28	42
Julie	25	49
Aaron	22	50
Sharon	32	40
Carlos	23	48
Jessie	25	49
Brenda	28	49
Donna	29	50
Rodney	27	48
Kathy	24	48
Milly	26	50
David	20	50
Gary	26	49
Joanna	27	50
Felix	27	48
Kerry	24	49
Vonda	26	47
Tom	30	49
Helen	26	50

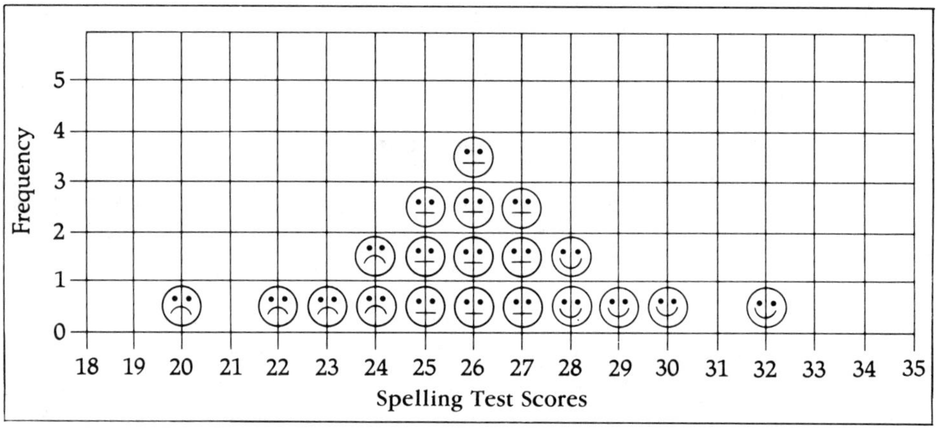

Figure 19-1 Spelling test scores

If three students got a score of 25, then a circle, box, or other mark would be placed on the 25 for each student. If one student got a score of 30, one mark would be placed on the 30.

Use the arithmetic data in Table 19.1 to make a frequency distribution for the students in arithmetic on Figure 19.2. Check your frequency distribution by comparing it to the one given on page 284, Figure 19.6.

A frequency distribution gives a graphic picture of the relative position of scores on a test. It provides a norm-referenced comparison of people. You can now see that Joe is near the middle of the distribution in spelling (25) and on the low side in arithmetic (45). Ned's 28 in spelling now looks like a pretty good score compared to the rest of the class, but his 42 in arithmetic looks like a poor performance compared to the rest of the class.

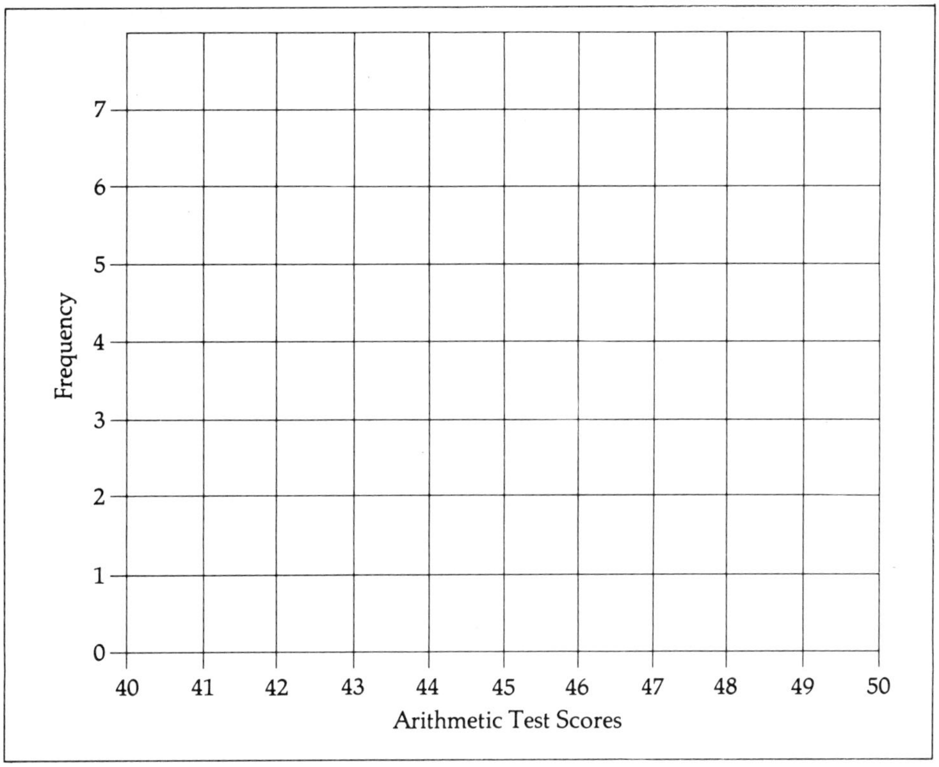

Figure 19-2 *Arithmetic test scores*

Computing the Mean of a Distribution

In talking about scores in a frequency distribution, two measures are particularly useful, especially when you are comparing a large number of students with each other. These are the ***mean*** of the distribution and the ***standard deviation*** of the distribution. The mean (*M*) is the same as an average. All of the scores (*X*s) are summed and then divided by the number of scores (*N*).

$$\text{Mean} = \frac{\text{Sum of scores}}{\text{Number of scores}}$$

$$M = \frac{\text{Sum Xs}}{N}$$

For spelling, the sum of the scores is 520. The number of scores equals 20. So, the mean of the distribution is 26. Find the mean for the distribution of arithmetic scores.

$$\text{Arithmetic Mean} = \frac{\text{Sum of scores}}{\text{Number of scores}} = \_\_\_\_\_\_\_\_\_\_$$

Check your answer by turning to page 284, Figure 19.6.

By computing the means, you can see that the average raw score in spelling was lower than that in arithmetic. To find out whether Joe and Ned did better in spelling than arithmetic, place both distributions on the *same scale*. This can provide you with a basis for comparison. One way to do this is to use the standard deviation as the unit of measurement.

Computing the Standard Deviation of a Distribution

To describe a distribution of scores (frequency distribution), you first find the mean; then you find the *standard deviation.* The standard deviation is the square root of the *variance.* The variance of a distribution is another average. The mean is subtracted from each raw score, these deviations are squared (to get rid of the negatives), and then the sum of the squares is divided by the number of scores (N).

$$\text{Variance } (V) = \frac{\text{Sum } (X - M)^2}{\text{N}}$$

$$\text{Standard Deviation } (SD) = \sqrt{\frac{\text{Sum } (X - M)^2}{N}}$$

The variance of a distribution (and its square root—the standard deviation) gives you a measure of how far the scores spread out from the mean. Examine Figure 19.3. Distribution A has a larger standard deviation than distribution B because the scores spread further from the mean. The standard deviation for distribution A is 2.9 and that for B is 1.9.

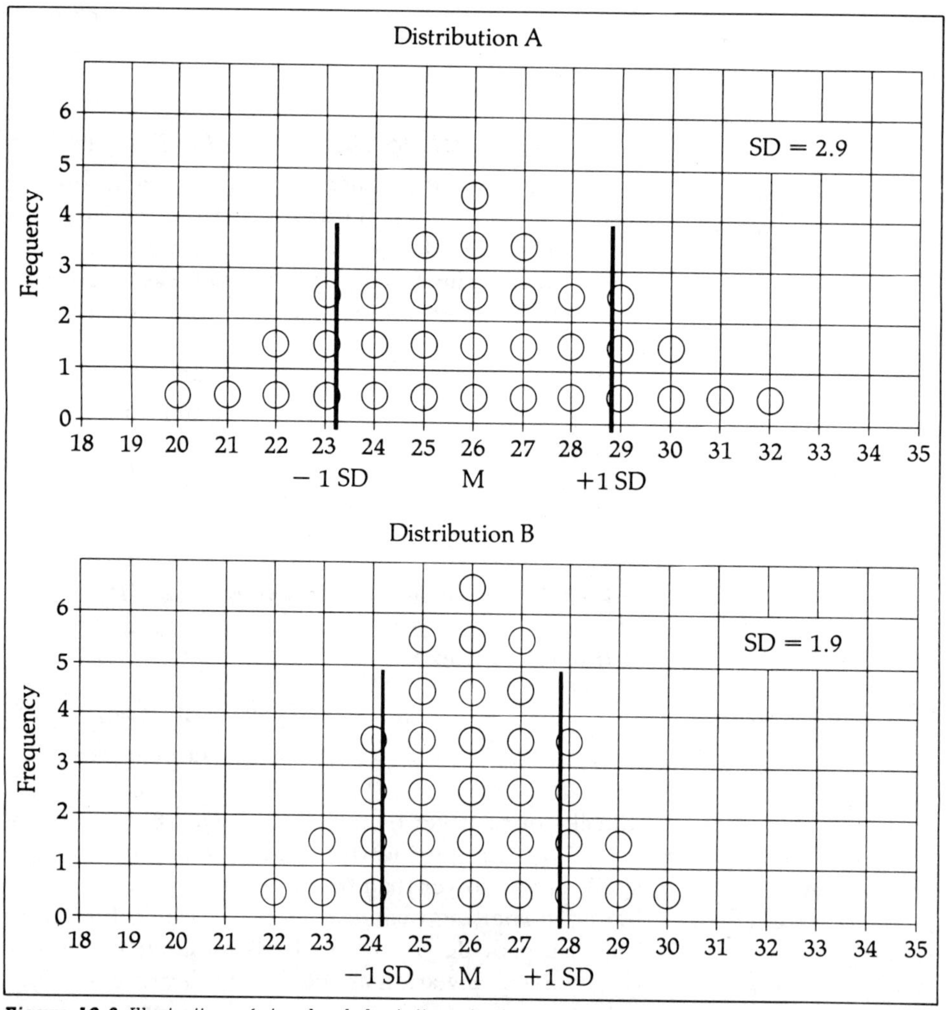

Figure 19-3 *Illustration of standard deviations for two distributions*

If you smooth out the frequency distributions and draw them as curves, you can readily illustrate the standard deviation for a number of distributions (see Figure 19.4). To make the comparisons easier, the mean of each distribution has been kept the same. Distribution A has a standard deviation of 7. It is smaller than the standard deviation for distributions B and C because there are more scores near the mean and fewer scores away from the mean.

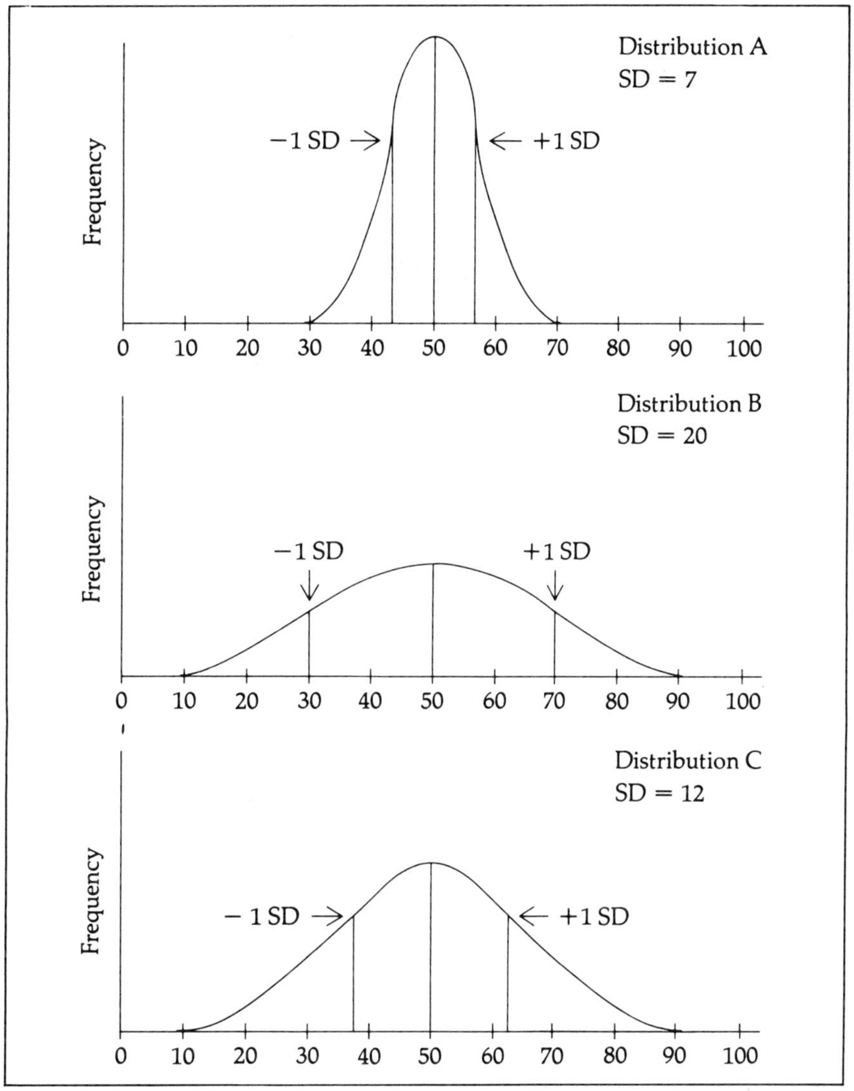

Figure 19-4 *Illustration of standard deviation for three smoothed distribution*

Distribution B has a large standard deviation relative to A and C because there are more extremely high and low scores and relatively fewer scores near the mean. The standard deviation for distribution C is between that of A and B. Each of these figures illustrates that the standard deviation depends on the average spread of the scores from the mean of the distribution. To compute a standard deviation, follow these steps:

Step 1 Subtract the mean from each score $(X - M)$

Step 2 Square the deviations obtained in step 1 $(X - M)^2$

Step 3 Sum the squared deviations Sum $(X - M)^2$

Step 4 Divide by N (the number of students) $\dfrac{\text{Sum } (X - M)^2}{N}$

Step 5 Take the square root of the result $SD = \sqrt{\frac{\text{Sum } (X - M)^2}{N}}$

The deviations from the mean are squared to eliminate the problems of dealing with negative numbers. Squares and square roots can be found by using a calculator. The standard deviation for the spelling scores is calculated in Table 19.2.

Table 19-2 Calculation on the standard deviation for the scores on the spelling test

	Step 1					*Step 2*
Name	*X*	–	*M*	=	*(X – M)*	$(X - M)^2$
Joe	25		−26	=	−1	1
Ned	28		−26	=	+2	4
Julie	25		−26	=	−1	1
Aaron	22		−26	=	−4	16
Sharon	32		−26	=	+6	36
Carlos	23		−26	=	−3	9
Jessie	25		−26	=	−1	1
Brenda	28		−26	=	+2	4
Donna	29		−26	=	+3	9
Rodney	27		−26	=	+1	1
Kathy	24		−26	=	−2	4
Milly	26		−26	=	0	0
David	20		−26	=	−6	36
Gary	26		−26	=	0	0
Joanna	27		−26	=	+1	1
Felix	27		−26	=	+1	1
Kerry	24		−26	=	−2	4
Vonda	26		−26	=	0	0
Tom	30		−26	=	+4	16
Helen	26		−26	=	0	0
						Sum = 144

Step 3: Sum $(X - M)^2 = 144$

Step 4: Sum $\frac{(X - M)^2}{N} = \frac{144}{20} = 7.2$

Step 5: $SD = \sqrt{\frac{\text{Sum } (X - M)^2}{N}} = 7.2 = 2.68$

This calculation was relatively easy because the mean was a whole number (26). Usually this is not the case. For example, if the mean in spelling had been 25.6, then Joe's deviation score $(X - M)$ would have been −.6, Ned's +2.4, Julie's −.6, and Aaron's −3.6. Squaring and adding these numbers would take a little more work.

Many pocket calculators now have standard deviation keys on them. They permit you to simply punch in the scores and push a button to get the standard deviation. Some pocket calculators give an answer using $N - 1$ in the denominator, rather than N. $N - 1$ is used when estimating a ***population*** value from a *sample.* You do not have to be concerned about this, but if you use a calculator (and that is a good idea) be sure to find out which value is being used in the denominator. (For more details on the standard deviation or variance, consult a standard statistics textbook.)

With a mean and a standard deviation, you have two kinds of averages for describing a distribution: the average score in the distribution (M) and a kind of "average deviation" or average spread of scores from the mean of the distribution (SD). These two scores can be used to change the scale of any distribution to a standard score scale that more readily permits comparison of scores from different distributions.

STANDARD SCORES

Now return to the distributions of scores from the spelling and arithmetic tests. On the spelling test, the mean was 26 and the standard deviation was 2.68. On the arithmetic test, the mean was 48 and the standard deviation was 2.65. To convert a raw score (X) to a standard score (SS), subtract the mean (M) from the raw score and divide by the standard deviation (SD).

$$\text{Standard Score } (SS) = \frac{X - M}{SD}$$

Thus, the standard score for a raw score of 26 in spelling is 0, since $X - M = 0$.

Raw scores higher than 26 have positive values, while those lower than 26 have negative values. A raw score of 29 has a standard score equivalent of $(29 - 26)/2.68 = +1.12$. A raw score of 22 has a standard score equivalent of $(22 - 26)/2.68 = -1.49$. Most standard scores will fall in the range between +3 and −3.

To change a standard score back to a raw score, use the following:

$$X = \text{SS} \times SD + M$$

For spelling the raw score equivalent for a standard score of 2 is: $X = 2 \times 2.68 + 26 = 31.36$. The raw score equivalent for a standard score of −1 is: $X = -1 \times 2.68 + 26 = 23.32$. With calculations of this latter sort, you can rescale the distribution of spelling scores as shown in Figure 19.5.

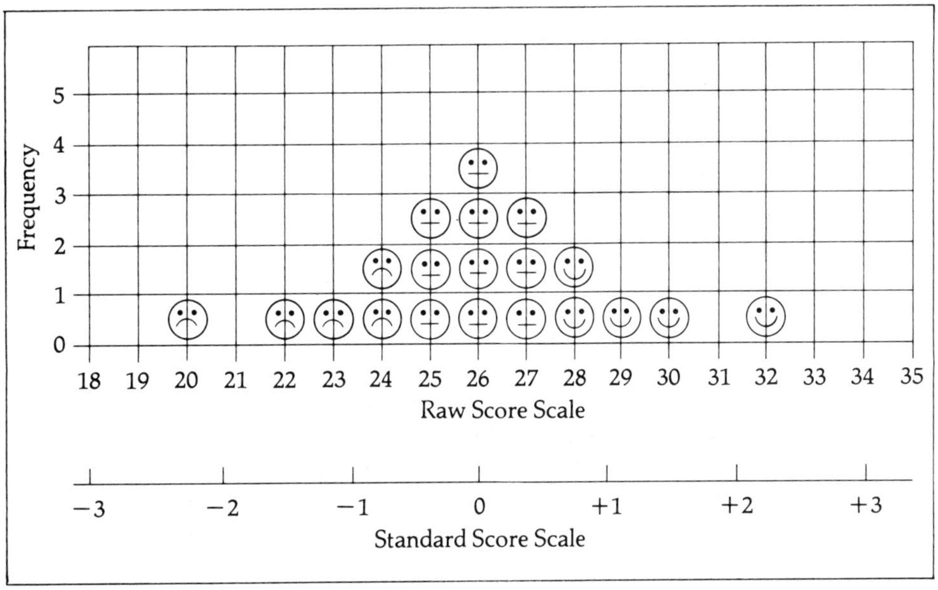

Figure 19-5 *Spelling score distribution on a standard score scale and a raw score scale. The mean of the raw score distribution is 26 and the standard deviation is 2.68.*

Note that all of the scores fall between +3 and −3 on the standard score scale or between +3 and −3 standard deviations (between 17.96 and 34.04) on the raw score distribution. This is usually the case. Note also that the ***standard deviation becomes the unit of measurement*** (the yardstick). On the standard score scale, plus one unit (+1) is 2.68 above the mean (28.68), plus two units (+2) is 2 × 2.68 above the mean (31.36), and plus three units (+3) is 3 × 2.68 above the mean (34.04). Similar properties can be shown for scores below the mean. ***Standard scores are scores expressed in terms of the number of standard deviations they are from the mean.*** The standard deviation is used as the unit of measurement. Standard scores of this type (Mean = 0, standard deviation = 1) are called z-scores.

For arithmetic scores, the rescaling is shown in Figure 19.6.

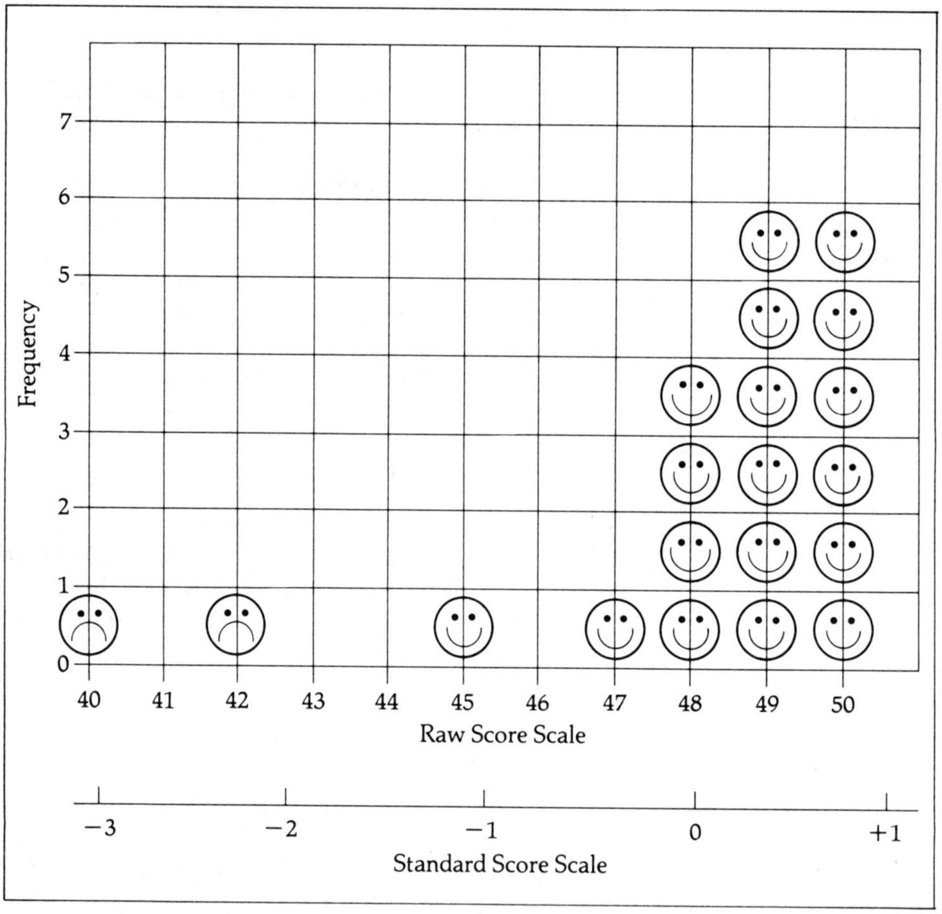

Figure 19-6 *Arithmetic score distribution on a standard score scale and a raw score scale. The mean of the distribution is 48 and the standard deviation is 2.65.*

Because the arithmetic distribution is not symmetrical around the mean, it is not possible to get standard scores even as high as 1.0.

You can use the standard score formula to convert each student's raw score on each test into standard scores. The result is shown in Table 19.3. Each student's score is now expressed as a positive or negative deviation from the mean, and the yardstick for asking "How much is much?" is based on the standard deviation of the distribution rather than on the raw scores. The student's scores are expressed in a form that compares each score ***to the distribution of*** *the scores in the group.* The scores are expressed in relative terms, rather than in absolute raw score units. That is, they are positive or negative relative to the mean, and their size depends on the size of the standard deviation. From Table 19.3, you can now see that Joe did better in spelling (−.37) than arithmetic (−1.13) relative to the group, Ned did much better in spelling (+.75) than arithmetic (−2.26), and Julie did better in arithmetic (+.38) than spelling (−.37) relative to the group.

Table 19-3 Standard scores on the spelling and arithmetic tests for each student

	Spelling		*Arithmetic*	
	Raw Score	*Standard Score*	*Raw Score*	*Standard Score*
Name	*X*	$\frac{X-M}{SD}$	*X*	$\frac{X-M}{SD}$
Joe	25	− .37	45	−1.13
Ned	28	+ .75	42	−2.26
Julie	25	− .37	49	+ .38
Aaron	22	−1.49	50	+ .75
Sharon	32	+2.24	40	−3.02
Carlos	23	−1.12	48	0
Jessie	25	− .37	49	+ .38
Brenda	28	+ .75	49	+ .38
Donna	29	+1.12	50	+ .75
Rodney	27	+ .37	48	0
Kathy	24	− .75	48	0
Milly	26	0	50	+ .75
David	20	−2.24	50	+ .75
Gary	26	0	49	+ .38
Joanna	27	+ .37	50	+ .75
Felix	27	+ .37	48	0
Kerry	24	− .75	49	+ .38
Vonda	26	0	47	− .38
Tom	30	+1.49	49	+ .38
Helen	26	0	50	+ .75

UNDERSTANDING CORRELATION

The concept of correlation provides the key to understanding how norm-referenced tests are built. The concept of correlation underlies the procedures for selecting items in constructing a test and for evaluating tests for their reliability and validity.

The term *correlation* is made up of the terms *co* and *relation.* A correlation is an index of the degree of relationship between two variables. A correlation is a co-relationship. First, look at correlations as expressed in a two-by-two matrix.

Correlations in a Two-by-two Matrix

Suppose you give a spelling test to a class. The test contains two words, *during* and *caution*. The results are as follows:

Student	*during*	*caution*
1	+	+
2	−	−
3	−	+
4	+	+
5	−	−
6	+	−
7	−	−
8	+	+
9	−	−
10	+	+
11	+	+
12	−	−

One question that might interest you as the teacher is, "How does the performance on *during* relate to the performance on *caution*?" Do students who do well on the first word do well on the second?

One way of looking at this question is with a two-by-two matrix like this:

during \ caution	−	+
+	/ (+−)	///// (++)
−	///// (−−)	/ (−+)

Student 1 passed both words, so a mark is placed in the top right quadrant; student 2 failed both, so a mark for him is placed in the lower left quadrant; student 3 failed *during* and passed *caution* so a mark is placed in the lower right quadrant, and so on. When most of the cases fall in the + + and − − quandrants, as in this example, it implies a high *positive* correlation.

Now consider the following two possible outcomes:

during \ caution	−	+
+	/////	/
−	/	/////

A

during \ caution	−	+
+	///	///
−	///	///

B

In example A, most of the students fall in the + − and − + quadrants. This is an example of a high *negative* relation. In example A, if students passed *during,* they tended to fail *caution,* and if they failed *during,* they tended to pass *caution.* When there is a positive correlation between two measures, a high score on one measure goes with a high score score on the other. When there is a negative correlation, a high score on one measure goes with a low score on the other.

Example B shows no correlation between the outcomes for *during* and *caution.* Half the students who pass *during* pass *caution,* and half fail *caution.* Half the students who fail *during* pass *caution* and half fail. It is possible for two measures to be correlated positively, negatively, or to have no correlation. Positive and negative correlations can vary in degree.

The Joint Frequency Distribution

Now, consider the case where the scores on two measures are not simply pass-fail, but can vary over a range of possibilities. Suppose the two measures are IQ and grade-point average (GPA).

Student	*IQ*	*GPA*	*Student*	*IQ*	*GPA*
One	125	3.8	Six	120	3.0
Two	100	2.5	Seven	90	2.3
Three	88	2.0	Eight	130	4.0
Four	115	3.0	Nine	110	2.8
Five	95	2.3	Ten	105	2.6

You can plot these scores on a joint-frequency distribution (or scatter diagram) as shown in Figure 19.7.

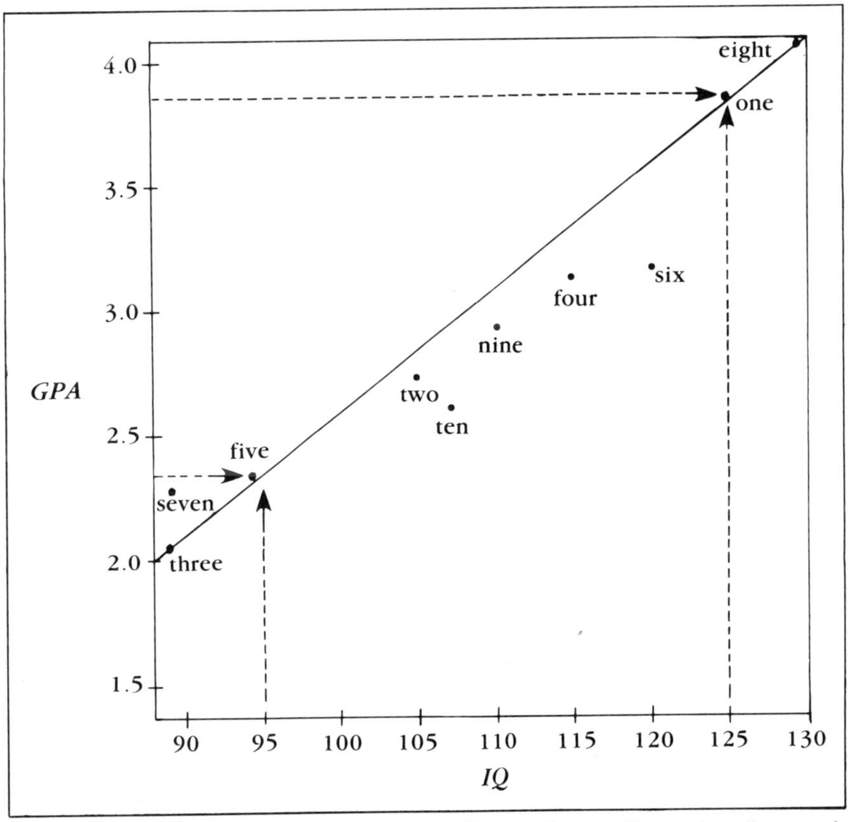

Figure 19-7 *A Joint Frequency Distribution (The numbers written out on the graph above are student identification numbers)*

Student One scored 125 on the IQ test and had a 3.8 grade-point average. A dot is made to represent him where 125 and 3.8 intersect on the graph. Similarly, Student Five had an IQ of 95 and a GPA of 2.3. A dot to represent her is made at the intersection of 95 and 2.3. Usually, in making a joint frequency distribution student numbers are not included as was done in Figure 19.7. It was done here to show explicity how each dot got where it is. Drawing a line through the dots helps to show the relationship. These data show that the higher the IQ, the higher the GPA, and vice versa. They show a high positive correlation.

Now, consider Figure 19.8. This figure is the same as 19.7 except that the student numbers were eliminated and a line was drawn at the mean for each

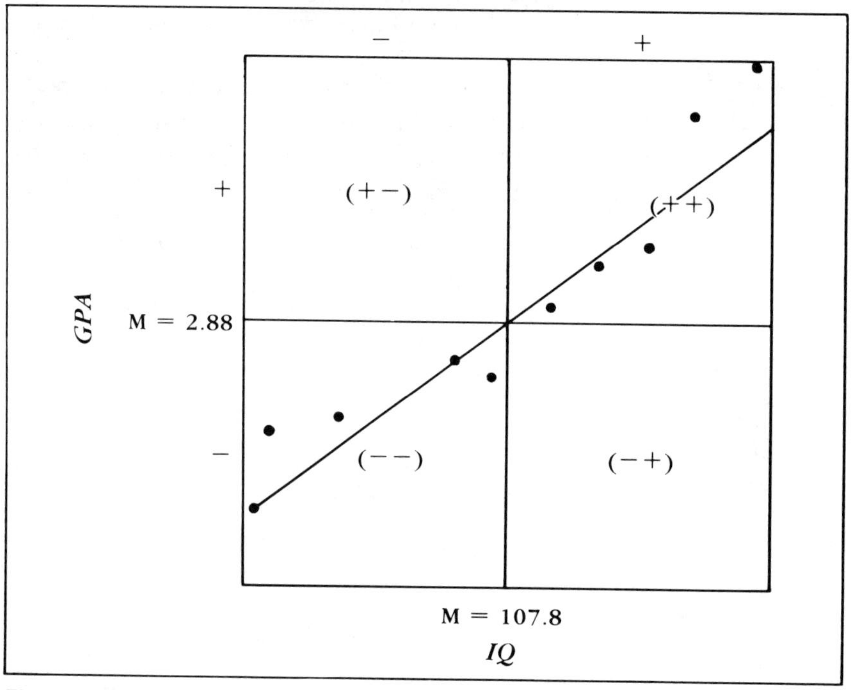

Figure 19-8 *A Joint Frequency Distribution Divided Into Quadrants*

measure. Scores above the mean are called +'s, and those below the mean −'s. Count how many students fall into each of the four quadrants produced by the lines through the means. The results would look as follows:

		IQ −	IQ +
GPA	+	0	5
	−	5	0

Thus, the two-by-two matrix first used to illustrate positive, negative, and zero relations can be seen to be special cases of joint frequency distributions where the scores were forced into only two categories.

Predictability

Another way of thinking about a correlation is in terms of the degree to which you can predict one variable from another. Suppose the relationship between IQ and GPA for a given school is as follows:

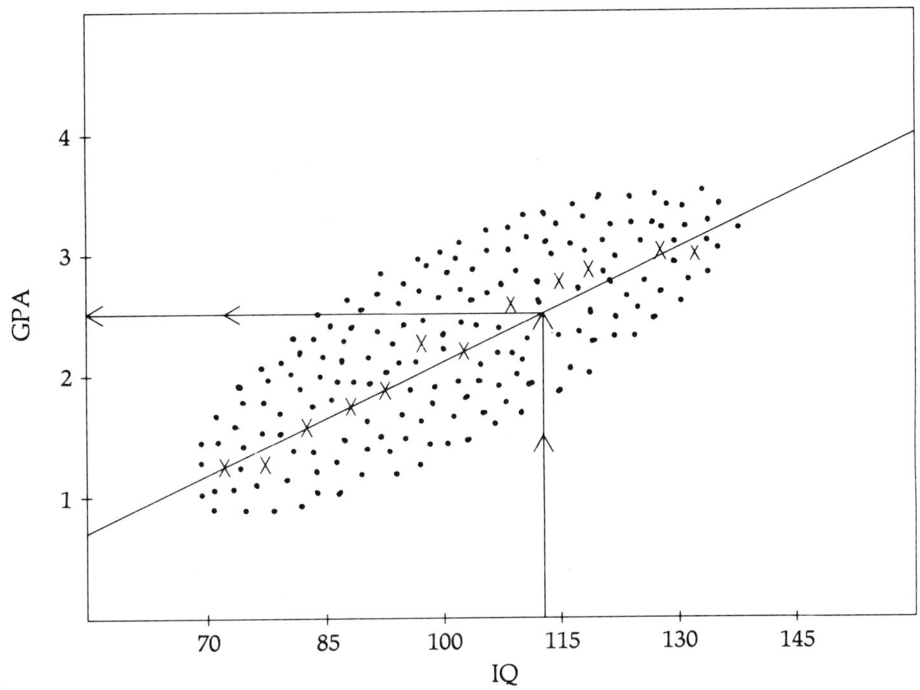

The *X*'s represent the mean GPA for each grouping of 5 IQ points. For example, the first *X* on the left is the average GPA for all students with IQ's from 70 to 74. It is the mean of the scores in that vertical column. The sloping line that runs approximately through the *X*'s is a best-fit line to the averages represented by the *X*'s. If you know a student's IQ to be 114, you can predict his or her GPA by proceeding vertically from 114 to the sloping line and from there going horizontally to 2.50. This gives the predicted GPA for an IQ of 114. An important point to note is that the higher the correlation, the better the prediction. The more the data scatter away from the best-fit prediction line, the more error is likely in the prediction. In looking at a scatter plot, it is useful to think of the length of the scatter along the best-fit prediction line in relation to the average scatter from this line. High correlations have small scatter relative to the length of the best-fit prediction line when both measures are expressed in standard deviation units. For low correlations, the length of the average scatter approximates the length of the best-fit prediction line. For example:

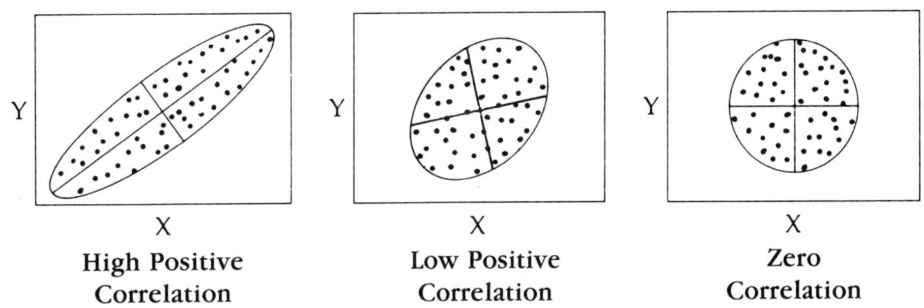

The size of a correlation is also directly related to the slope of the prediction line when both variables are expressed in standard deviation units (z-scores). As the slope approaches 45 degrees, the correlation increases to its maximum value of 1. As the slope approaches zero, the correlation approaches zero. Correlations are often used in predicting future performances based on current performances. In the example given, IQ was used to predict GPA. A battery of tests is used by the U.S. Air Force to predict success in flight training. Predictive validity is an important property of tests that the correlation coefficient helps us to summarize.

The Pearson Correlation Coefficient

So far you have learned about correlations in terms of two-by-two matricies and the shape of joint-frequency distributions or scatter plots. Most of the basic understandings required for interpreting correlations can be derived from such analyses. However, a more technical understanding of measures of correlation is useful in understanding the basic tenets of test theory.

The most frequently used index of the degree of relation between two variables is the Pearson correlation coefficient, which has been given the symbol r. Karl Pearson, an English statistician, invented r. The Pearson r is defined as:

$$r = \frac{\text{Sum } z_X \cdot z_Y}{N}$$

where the z-scores are the standard scores for x and y. This formula can be interpreted as follows: Given a set of scores on two variables (X and Y) for N persons, r is obtained by multiplying each z_X times its pairmate z_Y, summing these products, and then averaging them by dividing by the number of cases (N). Thus, r is the mean of the z-score products. The Pearson r can take on values from $+1$ to -1. A correlation of $+1$ is a perfect positive correlation. A correlation of -1 is a perfect negative correlation. A zero correlation indicates no relationship.

Computing r from z-Scores

Table 19.4 shows the computation of r using z-scores. X and Y stand for raw scores on two variables for 10 students.

Table 19-4 Computation of r using z-scores

X	Y	z_X	z_Y	$z_X z_Y$
30	15	1.65	1.70	2.8050
27	13	1.23	1.21	1.4883
24	12	.82	.97	.7954
21	8	.41	.00	.0000
20	9	.27	.24	.0648
16	7	− .27	− .24	.0648
14	6	− .55	− .49	.2695
12	5	− .82	− .73	.5986
9	4	−1.23	− .97	1.1931
7	1	−1.51	−1.70	2.5670
$M_X = 18$	$M_Y = 8$			$\text{Sum } z_X \cdot z_Y = 9.8465$
$SD_X = 7.29$	$SD_Y = 4.12$			

$$r = \frac{\text{Sum } z_X z_Y}{N} = \frac{9.8465}{10} = .98$$

The mean and the standard deviation of X and Y are computed first so that z-scores can be computed. Then r is computed as the mean of the products of z_X and z_Y. The r for the variables in Table 19.4 is .98. This is a very high positive correlation. Figures 19.9 and 19.10 show scatter diagrams for the data in Table 19.4. Figure 19.9 plots the raw scores and Figure 19.10 plots the z-scores. The raw score scatter plot confirms that the relationship is very high and positive. The z-score scatter plot shows that all of the scores fall in the + + and − − quadrants. This is often the case for a high positive correlation. Two positives multiplied together make a positive and two negatives multiplied together make a positive. So, when most scores fall in the + + and − − quadrant, a positive sum is produced. When most scores fall in the + − and − + quadrants, negative products are produced leading to a negative correlation. Finally, if some of the scores fall in quadrants that produce positive products and some in the quadrants that produce negative products, they would cancel each other out and produce a low or zero correlation. This analysis should provide an understanding of how the correlation coefficient, in ranging from +1 to −1, can provide a summary statement of a relationship shown by a scatter diagram.

Note: You are not expected to be able to compute a correlation coefficient, just to understand how they serve to index the size of a relationship between two variables. You are expected to be able to make frequency distributions and to compute means, standard deviations, and standard scores, given a set of raw scores.

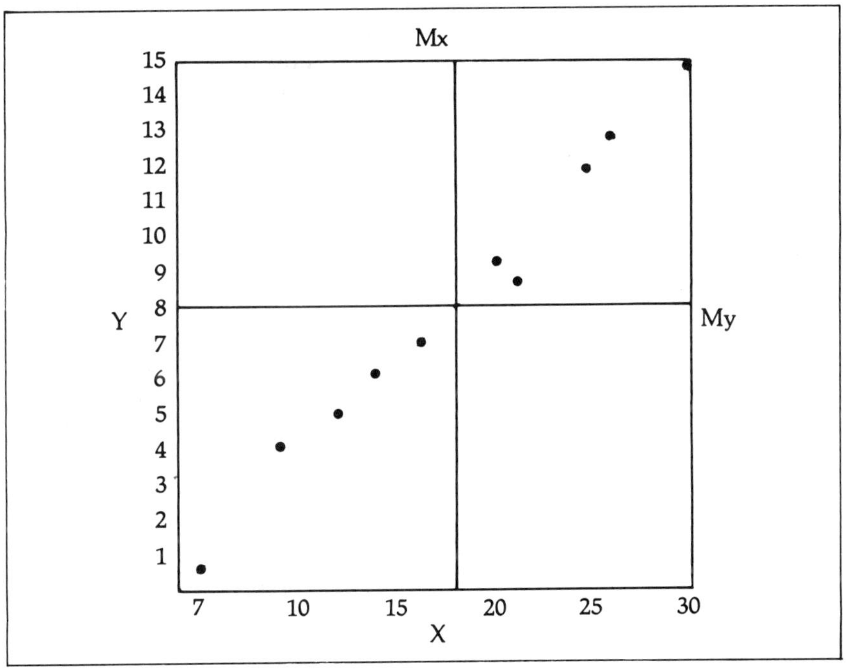

Figure 19-9 *Raw Score Scatter Plot of Data from Table 19.4*

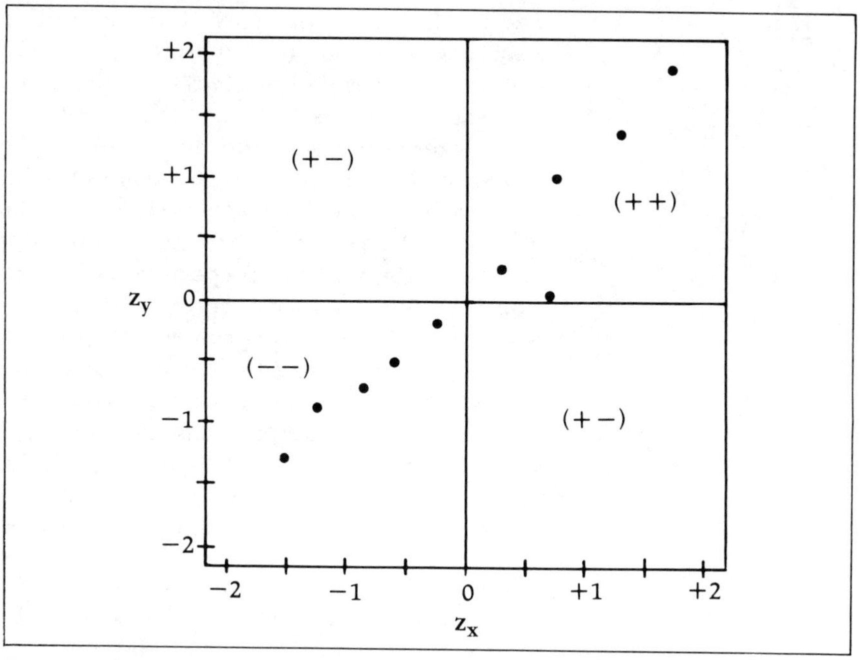

Figure 19-10 *Z-score scatter plot of data from table 19-4*

SUMMARY Five statistical concepts were introduced to prepare you for understanding norm-referenced tests, such as IQ tests and achievement tests. The concepts are also useful in interpreting research findings. A ***frequency distribution*** graphically depicts how many people received what scores on a test. The vertical axis on the graph shows "how many" people, the horizontal axis shows "what scores." Two important statistics for describing the set of scores that make up a frequency distribution are the mean and the standard deviation. The ***mean*** (*M*) is an average. All of the scores (*X*s) are summed and then divided by the number of scores (*N*).

$$M = \frac{\text{Sum } Xs}{N}$$

The ***standard deviation*** (*SD*) is a measure of the degree to which scores in a distribution deviate from the mean. It can be thought of as the "average" of the deviations from the mean, except that the deviations are squared and then the average is later "unsquared" by taking the square root. The standard deviation tells you how far the scores in a distribution spread from the mean on the average.

$$SD = \sqrt{\frac{\text{Sum } (X - M)^2}{N}}$$

← square root
← squared deviations from mean
← taking the average

The mean and the standard deviation of a distribution can be used to convert each score in the distribution to ***standard scores*** (SS). The raw scores are expressed as a deviation from the mean, and then they are divided by the standard deviation. This type of standard score has a mean of 0 and a standard deviation of 1 and is called a z-score.

$$\text{z-score} = \text{SS} = \frac{X - M}{SD}$$

The sign of a standard score tells you immediately whether the score is above or below the mean. Most raw scores will fall between +3 and −3 on a standard score scale. Standard scores provide one frame of reference for comparing scores of individuals within a distribution, and between distributions involving different measurements. You will learn more about standard scores in Chapters 20 and 27.

The concept of *correlation* is important for understanding how norm-referenced tests are constructed and evaluated. In a two-by-two matrix, a high positive correlation exists when most of the cases fall in the + + and − − quadrants. A high negative correlation exists when most of the cases fall in the − + and + − quadrants. No correlation exists when the cases are equally distributed throughout the four quadrants.

When there is a range of scores for two different measures we can plot these scores on a joint-frequency distribution or scatter diagram. It is possible to judge the nature of the correlation from the shape of the scatter diagram. In a high correlation, the data points tend to fall along a line. If the correlation is positive, this line slopes from the bottom left to the top right quadrant. If the correlation is negative, this line slopes from the bottom right to the top left quadrant. Low or zero correlations have scatter plots where the data points spread all over.

The most important index of the degree of relation between two variables is the Pearson correlation coefficient, or *r*. Starting with z-scores, the Pearson *r* is obtained by multiplying each z_X by its pairmate z_Y, summing these products, and taking the average by dividing by *N*.

$$r = \frac{Sum\ z_X \cdot z_Y}{N}$$

When the properties of *r* are examined in z-score form, it is easier to see what it means when *r* takes on positive and negative values. The Pearson *r* is positive when more cases fall in the quadrants which produce positive products (+ + and − −), and r is negative when more of the cases fall in the quadrants which produce negative products (− + and + −). The Pearson *r* can take on values from +1 to −1. A correlation of +1 is a perfect positive correlation. A correlation of −1 is a perfect negative correlation. A zero correlation indicates that two measures are unrelated.

Measures of association can also be computed with dichotomous variables, although the details of how it is done are not important here.

CHAPTER

20

THE NATURE OF INTELLIGENCE AND IMPLICATIONS FOR TEACHING AND LEARNING

WHAT IS INTELLIGENCE?

Modern-day views of intelligence are many and varied, ranging from a strong emphasis on a genetic basis (Jensen, 1973; Herrnstein, 1973) to a focus on IQ tests as cognitive tasks that obviously have a learning history (Carroll, 1976). The discussion of problem-solving strategies in Chapter 18 dealt to a large extent with tasks taken from intelligence tests. Intelligent people are better able to solve problems they have not seen before. Besides genetic and learning-process-based views of intelligence, there are a variety of statistically derived views, based on the correlations of different tests with each other. Most such views hold that there is general positive intercorrelation among cognitive tasks that implies some underlying general intelligence (Spearman, 1927). None of these viewpoints are necessarily incompatible with each other, except in their extreme forms.

Many theorists, after acknowledging a *general factor* (a *factor* is a construct derived from a set of intercorrelations of tests), proceed to break intelligence down into groups of more highly related tasks. For example, Thurstone (1938) identified six groupings (called "group factors") which he named *verbal comprehension, reasoning, spatial relations, numerical ability, word fluency,* and *perceptual speed.* More recently, Guilford (1967) has proposed a matrix of some 120 cognitive abilities made up by the intersection of five operations, six products, and four contents (see Figure 20.1). As Carroll (1976) points out, Guilford's model, while designed to synthesize viewpoints, is too "rigid" to encompass "the structure of intellect" and is not well-enough supported by the facts to be the ultimate model. The question of "What is intelligence?" is explored again toward the end of this chapter after you look into some of the issues.

HOW IS IT MEASURED?

Historical Origins

The development of the intelligence tests was spurred by governmental requirements for compulsory education (Tyler, 1976). Massachusetts, in 1852, was the

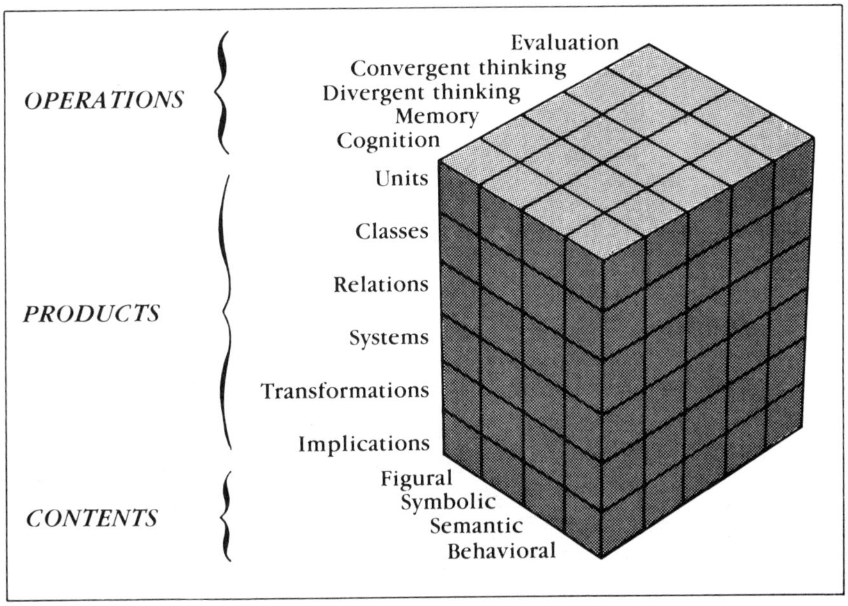

Figure 20-1 *Guildford's model of the three faces of intelligence. (From* The Nature of Intelligence, *by J. P. Guilford. Copyright © 1967 by McGraw-Hill Book Company. Used with permission of McGraw-Hill Book Co.)*

first state in the United States to *require* education. All states had some form of compulsory education by 1918. Alfred Binet, a Frenchman, and his colleague, Henri Simon, were commissioned by the French government in the 1890s to identify children likely to have trouble in school so the children could be given special help. IQ tests, thus, grew out of the problems teachers were having after education became compulsory.

In contrast to previous attempts to assess intellectual potential, Binet and Simon tried out "higher level" cognitive tasks rather than measures of simple sensory-motor skills. They included tests of *memory, imagination, comprehension,* and *attention* and tested a range of children between the ages of three and thirteen. Tests were selected that were not measures of school subject matter, but the tests had to discriminate children rated as "good learners" from those rated as "poor learners" by teachers. If teacher judgment was used as the criterion for test selection, why was a test needed? Tests were needed because human judgment is often *biased* by how pretty or sociable someone is. But if teacher judgment has some validity, then the tests, without a bias, might actually do a better job. The original Binet-Simon test had 58 kinds of tests. They were ordered by "mental levels" so that on the average, items would be passed by a higher percentage of older children than younger children. This provided a crude measurement scale for assessing intelligence.

Making his judgment from the nature of the tests that discriminated better learners from poorer learners, Binet defined *intelligence* as "the tendency to take and maintain a definite direction; the capacity to make adaptations for the purpose of attaining a desired end; and the power of auto-criticism" (Cronbach, 1949, p. 13). One can see in this definition some of the goal-oriented, problem-solving skills and metacognitive skills (auto-criticism) discussed directly and indirectly in Chapters 13 to 18.

The Stanford-Binet

The Binet-Simon tests were adapted for use in the United States by Lewis Terman (1916) at Stanford University. They have gone through several revisions since 1916 (and a new one is in process at this writing). The term *intelligence quotient (IQ)* was adopted by Terman after it was first proposed by the German Clifford Stern. The original IQ was based on a ratio of mental age to chronological age:

$$\text{Intelligence Quotient} = \frac{\text{Mental Age}}{\text{Chronological Age}} \times 100$$

In theory, the test was built so that the average IQ would stay at 100 from age group to age group. Test items were selected and sequenced to produce a year's increase in mental age for a year's increase in chronological age. When test theory became more sophisticated, these ratio scores were abandoned in favor of standard scores.

A careful examination of the Stanford-Binet, which is the name Terman gave to the American version of Binet's test, reveals that for the most part, the test measures whether or not the person being tested has *learned* various concepts, facts, rules, and problem-solving strategies. Test items include assessment of vocabulary, critical differences between concepts, analogies, numerical skills and problems, getting through mazes, logical absurdities, and so forth. It also includes tests of memory and word fluency, tasks that are less obviously measures of learned skills. If intelligent behavior is learned operant behavior, as I believe it is, then teaching (by parents and teachers) should be vitally important in its development. This conclusion does not mean there is not a genetic contribution to intelligence, but only that *opportunity to learn* must be an important variable in how smart students get. The hereditary issue is examined shortly. But first you need to briefly learn about two other sets of tests—the Wechsler scales and group tests.

The Wechsler Scales

The Wechsler scales come in three varieties: the WPPSI for ages four to six and a half, the WISC-R for ages six through sixteen, and the WAIS-R for ages 16 and older. These tests are probably used more than any other *individual* tests. The tests are broken down into a Verbal Scale (leading to a Verbal IQ) and a Performance Scale (leading to a Performance IQ). There are six subtests in the Verbal Scale:

Information—Questions such as "Where is Italy?" or "When is Independence Day?"

Similarities—"How are a jar and a cup alike?"

Arithmetic—"If you had six apples and got seven more, how many would you have altogether?"

Vocabulary—"What does *precocious* mean?"

Comprehension—Answer question involving social judgment and common sense such as "Why is honesty the best policy?"

Digit span—Series of digits are spoken (getting progressively longer) and the task is to repeat them correctly either forward or backwards.

There are five Performance subtests:

Picture Completion—The task is to name the missing parts of a picture, such as a face without an ear.

Picture Arrangement—Order a set of pictures to make a sensible story.

Block Design—With three-dimensional blocks with different colors on each side, duplicate a design from a picture.

Object Assembly—Put together cut up pictures of things such as a face or an animal.

Coding—A key is provided for converting numbers to other symbols. The task is to "code" as many numbers as possible in a fixed time.

The Stanford-Binet did not separate verbal and performance items into separate measures, although it contains a number of performance items, especially at the levels below age six. On the Wechsler, the separation of verbal and performance skills is not clean, since verbal skills are needed to understand the directions for performance tasks, and verbal hypotheses may control much of what one does. While the patterning of subscores sometimes can provide useful information (especially a sizable verbal-performance difference), the significance of differences can be easily overestimated because of problems with measurement errors.

The Slosson

The Slosson Intelligence Test (SIT) is a short form of the Stanford-Binet type test. It uses the items that are easier for an examiner to give and score and takes about 20 minutes.

Group Tests

The individual tests of IQ like the Stanford-Binet and the Wechsler scales are presented orally by a trained examiner and oral responses are permitted. Group tests are restricted to presenting items in paper and pencil form and usually are restricted to multiple-choice, machine-scorable responses. You may have taken the Scholastic Aptitude Test (SAT) of the College Entrance Board, and you may have taken the Cognitive Abilities Test (CAT, Thorndike and Hagen, 1971) for use with school-age students. The SAT has Verbal and Quantitative subscores. The Verbal section includes a lot of vocabulary and reasoning by analogy items. It also examines reading comprehension skills. The Quantitative section involves reasoning skills within a framework of high school geometry and algebra. The CAT has a Verbal score, a Quantitative score, and a Nonverbal score. The verbal test assesses vocabulary, reasoning, and information. The Quantitative test assesses reasoning about numbers (word problems, number series, number concepts). The Nonverbal test assesses analogies using various shapes, spatial relations (pick out a figure that can be made from these two), classification of figures, etc. While three separate scores are reported, the three scores are correlated with each other (implying a general factor).

In using group tests, it is very important that students being tested know the English language. As was pointed out in Chapter 10 while discussing the power of "expectations" and "self-fulfilling prophecies," much mischief has been perpetrated on non-English-reading children and adults in the name of scientific objectivity because of a failure to recognize that the group tests require English reading skills as preskills. It is also very important that students taking the tests be instructed in the test-taking skills needed to respond to the test formats and answer sheets. Most tests provide practice booklets through which such skills may be trained.

INTERPRETING TEST SCORES

The Normal Distribution

In norm-referenced testing, scores are usually expressed in relation to the distribution of scores obtained by some reference group. Standard scores (SS) can be computed to express any given score (X) in relation to the mean (M) and standard deviation (SD) of a reference group's scores.

$$SS = \frac{X-M}{SD}$$

For most tests, the distribution of standard scores tends to be bell-shaped. An idealized form of the bell-shaped distribution known as the *normal curve* is useful in interpreting test scores stated in standard score form. The normal distribution can be thought of as a smoothed frequency distribution generated by making the score intervals very, very small. The area under the normal curve can be divided into portions which sum to one. The proportion of area between any two points on the curve gives the *relative frequency* of persons falling between those two points. Thus, if we know that a given distribution of scores is approximately normal, we can immediately find out the proportion of students falling above or below a given standard score. Multiplying by 100, these proportions become percentages. For example, 2.28 percent of the cases score higher than +2 standard deviations. Conversely, 97.72 percent score below that point.

Note that 99.74 percent of the cases fall between plus or minus 3 standard deviations and only .26 percent fall beyond this point. Because of these relations, a convenient approximation for remembering the percent of cases covered by standard deviation units is this:

Mean to 1 SD	=	34%
1 SD to 2 SD	=	14%
2 SD to 3 SD	=	2%
Mean to 2 SD	=	48%
Mean to 3 SD	=	50%

This approximation can be used, of course, with SD units above or below the mean.

The standard score defined by $\frac{X - M}{SD}$ has been given the special symbol z. It is also known as a z-score.

$$z = \frac{X-M}{SD}$$

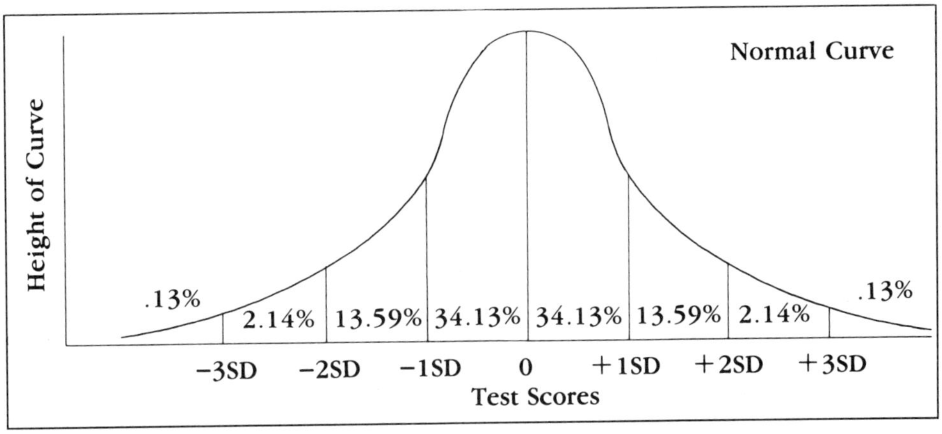

Figure 20-2 *A normal curve*

Transformed Standard Scores

When standard scores are reported for various educational tests, they are usually in a form other than z-scores. Explaining a zero standard score to a parent might be difficult. Also, the negative numbers and decimal points can be a nuisance. Standard scores can be transformed in a variety of ways to make them more convenient. This is done by changing the mean (M) and standard deviation (SD) of the z-score distribution. The general transformation is:

$$\text{Transformed standard score} = z \cdot SD + M$$

where SD is the standard deviation of the transformed distribution and M is the mean of the transformed distribution. To produce transformed standard scores, the z-scores are multiplied by the desired standard deviation of the new distribution and the mean desired for the new distribution is added to each score.

Some common transformed standard scores are given in Table 20.1. IQ's are transformed standard scores with a mean of 100 and a standard deviation usually of 15 (16 for the Stanford-Binet). The subscales on the Wechsler Intelligence Tests are transformed standard scores with a mean of 10 and a standard deviation of 3. Many achievement tests use transformed standard scores with means of 50 and standard deviations of approximately 21. These are called normal curve equivalents or NCEs. The College Board Examination and the Graduate Record Examination use transformed standard scores with a mean of 500 and a standard deviation of 100. The final entry in the Table 20.1 is stanines. Stanines are *standard nines;* they are transformed standard scores with a mean of 5 and a standard deviation of 2. All of the other scores illustrated in Table 20.1 can take on any precise three or four digit value. Stanines are restricted to one digit values from 1 to 9. Figure 20.3 illustrates how the normal curve is divided into stanines. Each stanine covers about one-half of a standard deviation or one-half of a z-score unit. Stanines are relatively easy to explain to parents. Five is average, one is low, and nine is outstanding.

Suppose we wish to convert the following z-scores to standard scores in a distribution with a mean of 100 and a standard deviation of 15:

$$z_1 = -1.5$$
$$z_2 = 0$$
$$z_3 = +2.0$$

Table 20-1 Some common standard scores

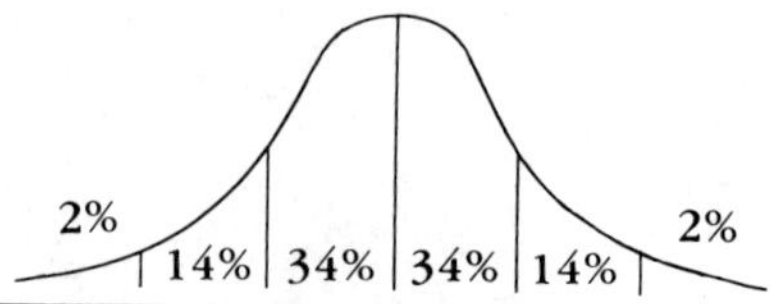

Type of Standard Scores	Mean	Standard Deviation	Standard Scores for SD Units						
z-Scores	0	1	−3	−2	−1	0	+1	+2	+3
IQ Scores	100	15 (or 16)	55	70	85	100	115	130	145
Wechsler IQ Subtest Scores	10	3	1	4	7	10	13	16	19
Many Achievement: Normal Curve Equivalents (NCEs)	50	21	1	7	29	50	71	93	99
College Board and Graduate Record Exam Scores	500	100	200	300	400	500	600	700	800
Stanines	5	2	(1)	1	3	5	7	9	(9)

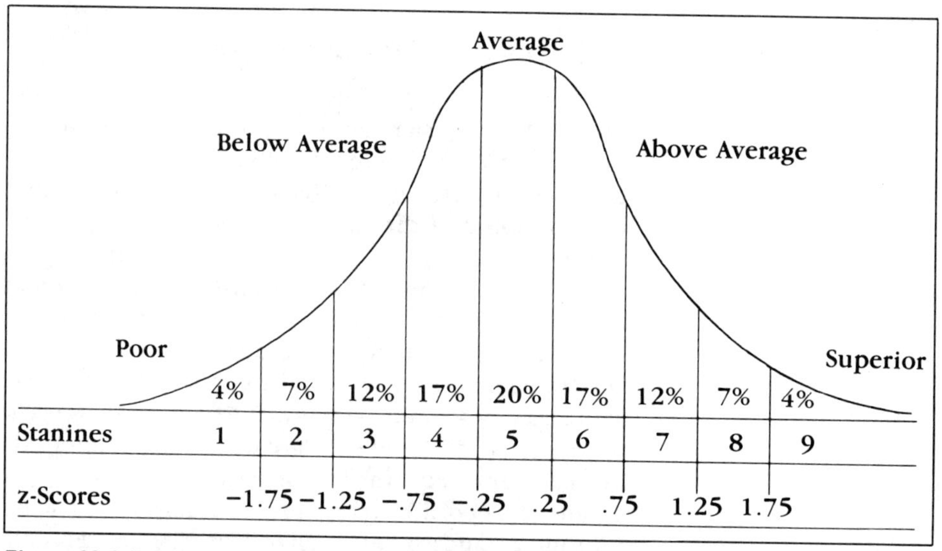

Figure 20-3 *Relations of stanines to the percentage of area under the normal curve and to z-Scores*

This can be accomplished as follows:

$$\text{Transformed } z_1 = -1.5 \times 15 + 100 = 100 - 22.5 = 77.5$$
$$\text{Transformed } z_2 = 0 \times 15 + 100 = 100$$
$$\text{Transformed } z_3 = 2.0 \times 15 + 100 = 30 + 100 = 130$$

Since most scores in a normal distribution fall between plus and minus three standard deviations, most scores for this transformation would fall between 55 and 145. This eliminates negatives and gives an adequate range of scores without decimals. Most IQ scores are expressed in this way—as standard scores with a mean of 100 and a standard deviation of 15.

Suppose a student receives an IQ of 125. What does this mean? You can *estimate* the percent of the population that earns scores at least this high (it gives us the *percentile*). You can see that 50 percent would score under 100. Another 34 percent would score between 100 and 115, and that 14 percent score between 115 and 130. Ten or 11 percent would score between 115 and 125. Adding up the percentages falling at 125 or below we get: 50 + 34 + 11 = 95 percent. This implies that only 5 percent of the population would score IQ's higher than this. Ninety-five is the *percentile* for an IQ of 125. You can estimate a percentile for any standard score (including z-scores) by remembering 34, 14, and 2, and the rough shape of the normal curve, and knowing the mean and standard deviation for the standard score. It is sometimes easier to work with z-scores. For example, an IQ of 130 would have a z-score of +2 (130 is 2 SDs above the mean) and the percentile equivalent would be 50 + 34 + 14, or 98. What is the percentile for an IQ of 85?

Levels of Intelligence

Intelligence test scores are often used to determine levels of brightness and retardation. Theoretically, 50 percent of the people receive scores between 90 and 110. Those above 135 to 140 are called "gifted," those in the range from 125 to 140 are called "bright," and those in the range from 110 to 125, "bright-average." The range from 75 to 90 has typically been referred to as "dull-normal." Persons with scores below 75 are considered retarded (although social behavior factors and self-care also enter into the labeling). Three degrees of retardation have been defined, as follows:

1 *Mildly mentally retarded.* IQ between 50 and 75. This range is equivalent to an adult having a mental age of seven and a half to eleven years. About 2.6 percent of all children born in a given year can be expected to fall in this range.

2 *Moderately mentally retarded.* IQ between 25 and 50. This range is equivalent to an adult having a mental age of three to seven and a half years. About .3 percent of all children born in a given year can be expected to fall in this range.

3 *Severely and profoundly mentally retarded.* IQ between 0 and 25. This range is equivalent to an adult having a mental age of three years or less. About .1 percent of all children born in a given year can be expected to fall in this range.

The distinctions between categories are often arbitrary. Generally, the *severely and profoundly retarded* have severe brain damage and are usually given custodial care in state institutions. They can be trained to some extent, but, with present knowledge, it is unlikely that they can be trained to live independent lives.

Moderately retarded children are said by most experts to require custodial care. As with the profoundly retarded, a high percentage of these children also have physical defects. They are not supposed to be able to learn to read or write, but some have been taught to do so through the effective use of learning principles. Usually, the aim is to teach self-care skills and simple work activities to be carried out under supervision. It is reasonable to expect that with improved training methods, many more children who in the past would have ended up in institutions for the moderately retarded will be educated to live largely self-supporting lives.

The *mildly retarded* group is the largest group and the one for which the most can be done in regard to developing behavior necessary for independent living.

It should be kept in mind that these "levels of intelligence" blur into one another and should not be treated as fixed categories. It should also be recognized that an IQ score is an estimate subject to measurement error and change over time. Now you will examine the hereditary issue.

GENETICS, INTELLIGENCE, AND ACHIEVEMENT

In 1869 Sir Francis Galton published *Hereditary Genius,* wherein he described an association between family membership and outstanding intellectual achievement. These investigations had their root in the work of Galton's cousin Charles Darwin. Galton generally accepted the notion that adult characteristics are determined by heredity. The notion of a genetically fixed intelligence was transmitted to early leaders in American psychology by G. Stanley Hall (Hunt, 1961), whose student Lewis Terman constructed the first American intelligence test. With a measure of intelligence, experimental evidence began to be collected showing IQ's to be quite stable over time, supporting the notion of a fixed ability. In addition, studies of identical twins, fraternal twins, siblings, and unrelated persons produced correlations supporting a strong influence for heredity on the scores. With modern estimation procedures, Jensen (1970) summarizes the data to show that 80 percent of the variance in intelligence can be attributed to heredity. Jensen (1969) goes so far as to suggest that early intervention studies for the disadvantaged could raise IQ no more than a few points because increasing IQ is probably not an attainable goal.

The belief in a genetically fixed intelligence takes on additional implications for education when coupled with data showing correlations in the .80 to .90 range between measures of intelligence and measures of school achievement (Kelley, 1927). The teacher is faced with conceptions (supported by research findings) that suggest that children with poorer genes learn less in school. The obvious solution for the teacher is to expend less energy on the (inferior) children who are doing poorly. One might also be inclined not to search for instructional methods that will work with all children. Fortunately for children and education, the basis for these conclusions can be challenged on many grounds.

Is Intelligence Inherited?

The point has been made that IQ tests, such as the Stanford-Binet, measure learned behavior (operant behavior). Geneticists recognize this fact when they treat intelligence as a *phenotype* (a visible characteristic that includes effects of environmental influences) and not a *genotype* (characteristics that can be traced to specific genes, such as blood type). Jensen and others have attempted to deal with this fact by using an index (heritability index) that attempts to proportion variance in a phenotype to effects of environment and heredity, using empirical evidence and genetic theory. The geneticist Cavalli-Sforza (1970) points out that four types of environmental differences can occur.

1. Within families: age, birth order, and so on.

2. Between families (same social class): teaching methods, number of children, and others.

3. Between social classes: income, educational opportunities, nutrition, and so forth.

4. Between cultures: educational institutions, health practices, and a host of major sources of differences.

The usual heritability index using twins is sensitive only to environmental variations of type 1 above; and these are variations as they exist now, not as they might be. When twins are reared apart, there is a chance to estimate environmental variation due to sources 2 and 3, but these kinds of data are very rare and likely to be biased. No studies have included level 4 environmental variations. The point to note is that the relative contribution of heredity to variation in IQ, as reflected in a heritability index, is an estimation based on data which probably *grossly underestimates* the role of environment. One could easily consider a 50–50 contribution of heredity and environment under existing conditions when cross-cultural variations are considered.

Beyond this, there is a more serious consideration for the teacher. Given that intelligence *is behavior* that is learned, within the constraints imposed by a partially genetically controlled physical structure, the question of the relative contribution of heredity and environment is not the real question for the teacher. The real question is, "How much can be done through instruction to improve intellectual functioning?"

The study of stature offers some information of interest to the teacher. Stature, like intelligence, is based on many different genetic contributions. It is not the effect of a single gene. In the last 70 to 100 years, average stature has shown an increase *on the order of one standard deviation* (Cavalli-Sforza, 1970). There is clear evidence that this effect cannot be attributed to genetic factors. In fact, there is evidence that socioeconomic factors are involved. For example, family size is negatively related to stature. Very likely, better nutrition is behind the increase in height.

In an analogous way, better education has likely produced a general rise in IQ of a similar magnitude during the past seventy years. For example Tuddenham (1948) found that soldiers' IQs (measured by the Army Alpha test) increased by one standard deviation (15 points) from World War I to World War II. As Joe McV. Hunt (1961) and others (such as Hess and Shipman, 1965, 1968; and Strodtbeck, 1965) have documented, environmental experiences can have profound influences in promoting and retarding intelligence. Hess and Shipman demonstrated that middle-class black mothers are better teachers of their children (in an experimental setting), and that the best combination of mother's teaching behavior correlated higher (.64) with child's cognitive skills than did the best combination of mother's IQ, child's IQ, and social class. The parent as teacher is probably a very important variable in the intellectual development of children. The mother's education has been consistently a good predictor of positive child attributes.

Hunt has shown that many children are retarded not because they cannot be taught, but because they *have not* been taught. A little extra training can rapidly change the behavioral development of infants living in a stimulation-deprived environment (Dennis and Najarian, 1957; Sayegh and Dennis, 1965; Skeels, 1966). Most of the existing evidence shows that remarkable changes occur in intellectual development when children are moved from extremely barren to more stimulating environments.

Bereiter and Engelmann (Engelmann, 1970) gave the first strong demonstration of the contribution that good teaching of language, reading, and arithmetic skills could make to the intellectual development of disadvantaged black four and five year olds. They raised the IQs of twelve disadvantaged children an average of twenty-four points with two years of direct instruction. Control children placed in a child-development oriented preschool for two hours a day gained an average of five points in two years (see Figure 20.4).

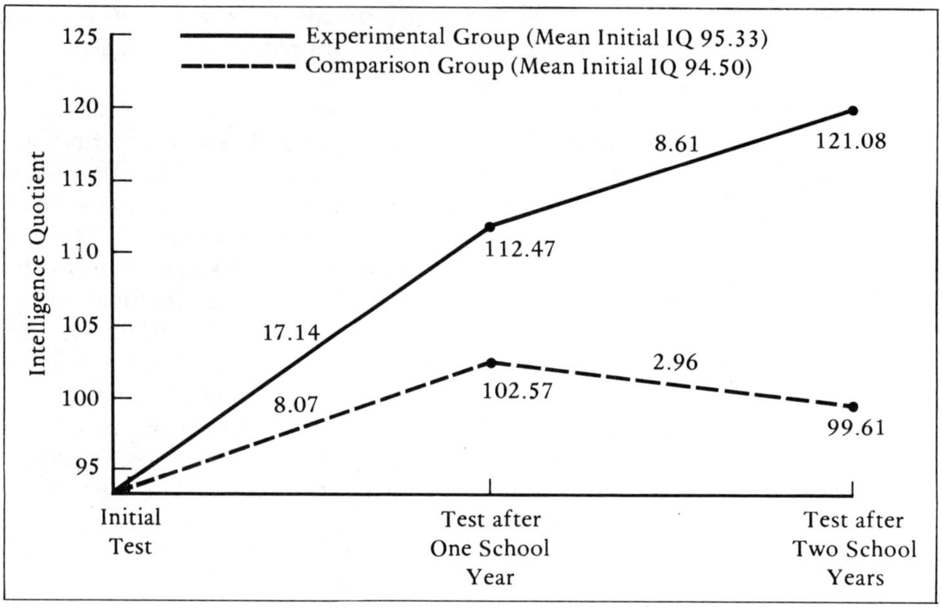

Figure 20-4 *Stanford Binet IQ performance of disadvantaged subjects after one and two years of training*

Heber et al. (1972) selected forty mothers with IQs of less than 75 prior to the birth of a child. At birth the families were assigned to experimental and control groups. The experimental-group mothers received adult education classes and training in vocational skills. The infant intervention program began at three months and was carried out at a child training center, all day, five days a week, until the children were six years old. The program focused on activities designed to enrich intellectual development, including motor skills, cognitive-language skills, and social skills. While the experimental and control groups did not differ on IQ tests at twelve months, they differed by nearly 30 points at three years and maintained this difference through five and a half years (IQs of 125 versus 95).

That the IQs of the control group children are much higher than their mothers' is to be expected because of regression effects (which occur when a group is selected deviant from the mean) and because fathers' IQs were not controlled. But the 30-point IQ difference is remarkable and consistent with other evidence on what can be done with an enriched environment. Heber also reports differences on a variety of other measures of language and conceptual behavior and has produced some remarkable films illustrating the behavioral differences in the groups of children (Heber, 1978).

The children were again followed up at age nine, three years after leaving the special program. Their IQ's then averaged 108 and that of the control group averaged about 80. The drop in IQ may be a function of the lack of continued special support; the cause is not known for sure. But the difference of 28 points three years later is still remarkable.

The Follow Through results for the Direct Instruction Model (summarized in Chapter 12) also strongly support the importance of quality education in improving the intellectual functioning of children from disadvantaged homes.

A study with moderately and severely retarded children carried out at two inpatient schools in New South Wales, Australia (Maggs and Morath, 1976) showed some remarkable gains in mental age as a function of careful instruction. The children ranged in age from six to fourteen and had been institutionalized at least five years. At each school the children were randomly assigned to either a *DISTAR Language I* group using behavioral teaching techniques or to a *Peabody Language Kit* (P-level) group. Instruction was provided for one hour a day over two calendar years. Independent testers (blind to groups) tested the children before and after the two years of instruction. The results are summarized in Table 20.2.

Table 20-2 Mean gain scores on six tests

GROUP	*Basic Concept Inventory*	*Reynell Verbal Comprehension in Mental Age Months*	*Stanford-Binet IQ in Mental Age Months*	*Sereatim (Total Score)*	*Class Inclusion (Total Score)*	*Matrix (Total Score)*
DISTAR GROUPS (N = 14)						
Mean	12.0	17.1	22.5	2.9	2.2	2.1
Standard Deviation	*3.6*	*6.9*	*5.2*	*1.5*	*1.0*	*1.4*
PEABODY GROUPS N = 14)						
Mean	3.1	6.0	7.5	1.1	.6	.4
Standard Deviation	*3.8*	*4.1*	*6.4*	*1.1*	*.8*	*1.0*
Significance of Difference	.01	.01	.01	.01	.01	.01
Omega Squared	60%	57%	47%	41%	31%	28%

The results show the DISTAR group to have done better on all measures of cognitive functioning. The last line in Table 20.2 (Omega Squared) shows the percent of total variance attributable to experimental treatments (remember, variance is what you have before you take its square root to get a standard deviation). These are powerful effects. The IQ gains show that the *DISTAR Language* group gained 22.5 months in 24 months, while the *Peabody Language* group gained only 7.5 months in 24 months. The DISTAR group gained at almost a normal rate. The Peabody group gained at the rate to be expected from those with an average IQ in the low 30's (which is where the children started).

In another Australian study by Booth, Hewitt, Jenkins, & Maggs (1979), 12 moderately retarded children with IQ's averaging about 40 were followed for 5 years. *DISTAR Language I* was started the first year and *Reading I* was added after *Language I* was completed (18 months later). The children were in beginning *Reading III* when tested. While there was no pretest on reading, the children were reading at the early third grade level on posttest. Their mean IQ's had risen from 41.9 to 50.6 ($p < .001$) (Gersten & Maggs, 1982).

These examples support the conclusion that there is much the teacher can do to improve the intellectual skills of lower IQ children.

Is Achievement Different from Intelligence?

In 1927, Truman Kelley pointed out that "the correlation between a good battery achievement test and an intelligence test is found to be very high." About 90 percent of the reliable variance is common, leaving a scant 10 percent that is different. Kelley believed that, for practical purposes, two measures of the same behavior were given different names, and then one was used to "explain" the other. If this is the case, then to say that intelligence is a *cause* of good performance on an achievement test is circular reasoning. One measure of achievement is called intelligence and then used to explain another measure of achievement. Thus, achievement causes achievement.

But is there a difference between an IQ test and an achievement test? Lloyd Humphreys (1974) suggests that there is a difference in the way the tests are built. While both are measures of learned behavior, achievement tests tend to focus on more recent learning, while intelligence tests tend to focus on older learning.

Thus, the high correlations between measures of intelligence and achievement batteries do not imply that intelligence causes achievement. They only show that a measure of *past achievement* is related to *current achievement.*

Can Past Achievement Really Predict Current Achievement?

If you discard the hereditary issue and concern yourself with whether or not future achievement (learning) can be predicted from past achievement (intelligence), you still have a problem. As early as 1939, John Anderson reported that mental age correlated with the general *level* of achievement, but not with year-to-year *gains* in learning. Those who started higher in achievement ended higher in achievement, but did not gain more. The failure to distinguish between measures of levels and of gains is a source of much confusion in the intelligence-achievement issue.

Figure 20.5 shows a hypothetical correlation between a grade-equivalent measure of achievement and mental age. The posttest X's, which are "circled," showed a high positive correlation between the two measures. The

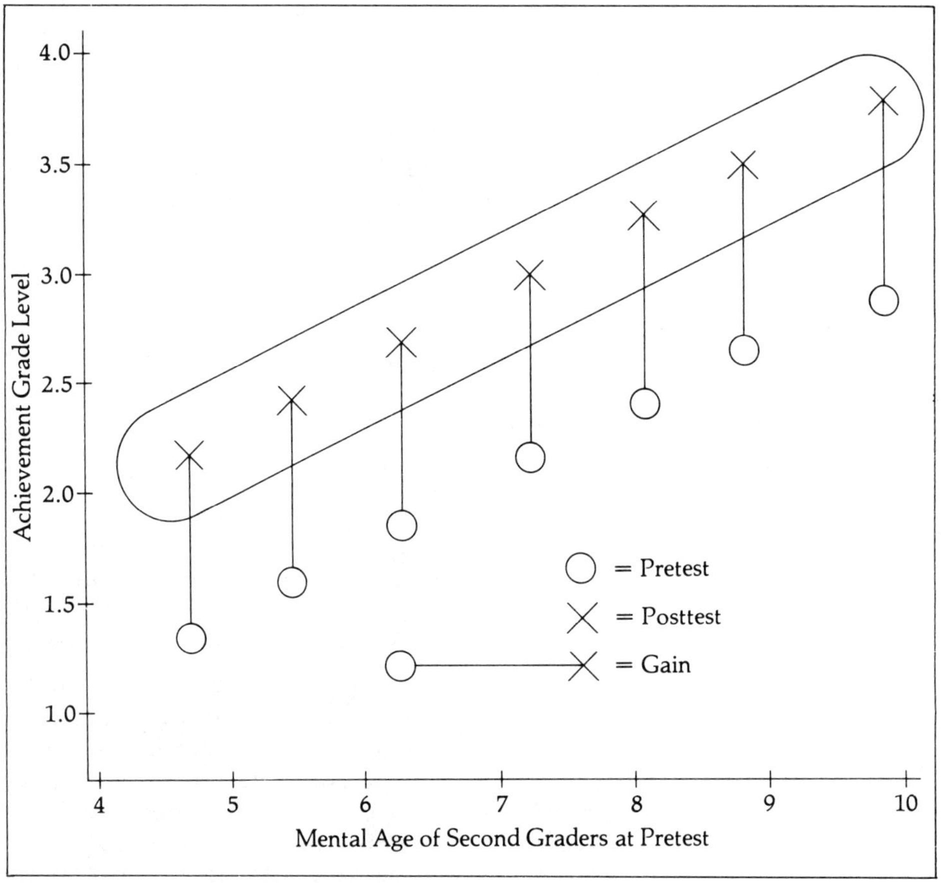

Figure 20-5 *Hypothetical correlation between mental age and achievement for grade-level measures*

pretest achievement measures also correlate highly with mental age, but the gain measures show no relationship to mental age (see Figure 20.6).

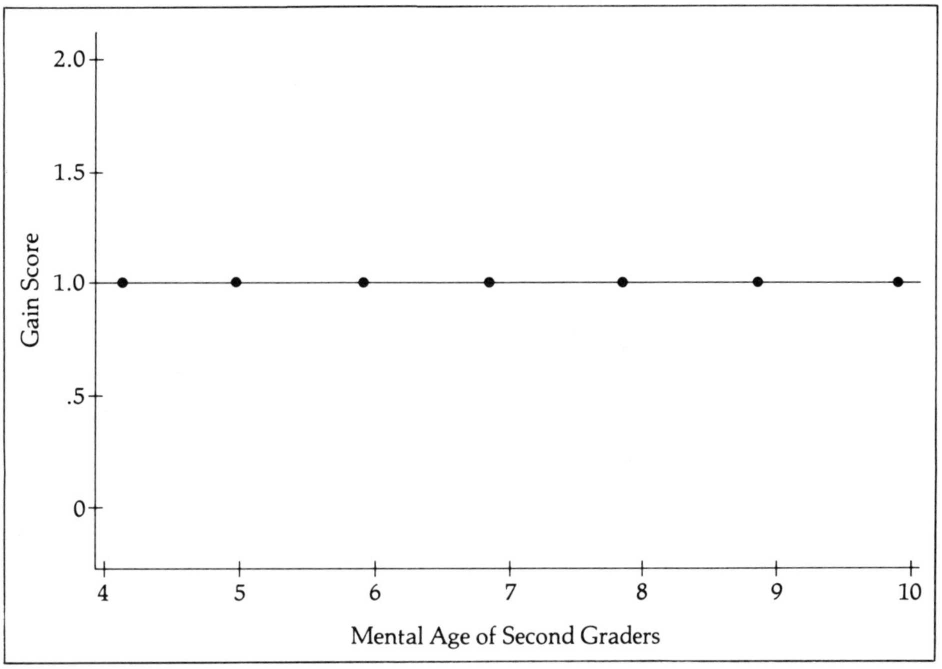

Figure 20-6 *Scatter-plot between mental age and achievement gain scores for the data from Figure 20-5*

To understand this better, consider the following:

1. Mental age is a measure of past achievement (PA) — PA
2. The achievement pretest is a measure of past achievement (PA) — PA
3. The achievement gain is a measure of new learning (NL) — NL
4. The achievement posttest is a measure of past achievement plus new learning — PA + NL

Mental age (1) and achievement pretest (2) will correlate highly because they are largely measures of the same thing (past achievement). Mental age (1) and the gain measure (3) are measuring largely different things and should not correlate highly. However, mental age (1) and the posttest achievement correlate highly. *Correlations reflect what two measures have in common.* Achievement *level* measures are likely to have much more in common with mental age measures than are achievement *gain* measures.

The evidence showing correlations of .80 to .90 between intelligence test scores and achievement test scores have been based on level-type measures rather than gain measures. Because of this, they cannot have much relevance for making judgments on the effects of past achievements on *current instructional progress.* A fresh approach to the problem is needed to understand how prior learning can influence new learning.

Follow Through Data

Gersten, Becker, Heiry, & White (1984) report an analysis of the gains made by Direct Instruction Follow Through students for a range of IQ blocks (see Figures 20.7, 20.8, and 20.9). The data showed almost no contribution to "learning rate" (pretest to posttest gains) for IQ. If IQ were correlated with gains, lower-IQ children would make smaller gains and higher IQ children would make larger gains. This does not happen for Reading on the Wide Range (decoding) or for Mathematics on the Metropolitan Achievement Test (MAT). For Reading Comprehension on the MAT, there is no IQ effect for gains from the end of grade one to the end of grade two (most of the gains are about equal), but there *is* an effect for the gain from the end of grade two to the end of grade three. I believe this effect is due to the fact that the end of third grade test for Reading Comprehension on the Metropolitan uses an uncontrolled, adult-level vocabulary (as found in fourth grade texts). Since vocabulary ***instruction*** in school does not progress gradually to the adult level (but jumps from a carefully controlled vocabulary to an adult vocabulary after third grade), the test at this level is now measuring something not taught at school. Thus, students who score higher on a test of verbal skills (IQ) do better on a test of verbal skills (Reading Comprehension) when the content was not systematically taught in school. (*A caution:* The data may have imposed a ceiling effect on the brighter students'; the program stressed preventing failures and thus teachers may have given more effort to teaching lower performers. Even if this is the case, however, the data are noteworthy in showing what can be done "gainwise" for lower-IQ children.

The notion that the IQ measures the ability to learn is challenged by the cited logical arguments (on level scores and gain scores) and the actual data. In reviewing this issue, Cronbach (1970) concluded that "ability to learn" is not a satisfactory construct. More relevant is the question "Learning what from what instruction?" There are many kinds of learning tasks, having different prerequisite skills, that make the new learning possible or impossible. And, there are many kinds of "instruction." He concludes: "There is a suspicion afoot that education calls for analytic ability just because the materials are capable of being put into meaningful relationships *and* the instructor has either failed to display the relationships or has given an explanation that is hard to follow. Then one has to use his brain!" (Cronbach, 1970).

Cronbach is suggesting that the high-level analytical ability measured by IQ tests may be important for learning in situations where the *teaching is bad,* in addition to situations where untaught vocabulary is required. Under poor teaching conditions, only intelligent students have a chance. Consider one more unbelievable example:

A Comparison of Two Extreme Groups

Linda Meyers completed a study in which the children had to learn to discriminate and name a set of five related concepts. In this study, five children with Down's syndrome who had IQ's in the 30s were compared with five children with IQ's in the 130s. All children were five years old. The Down's syndrome children had been in a special training program during much of the prior year, in which they had been taught to respond to simple instructions and to value tokens as rewards for learning. The "normal" children could already follow instructions and quickly learned to value the tokens that could be exchanged for a prize. Usually, in the comparison of learning rates of normal and retarded children, the ability to follow the directions used in the learning tasks and the motivation in the situation are not controlled. In this study they were both controlled. In addition, prior learning experiences relating to the task itself were

WRAT Reading
Longitudinal Progress by IQ Block for Children in Entering-Kindergarten (EK) Sites (N=692)

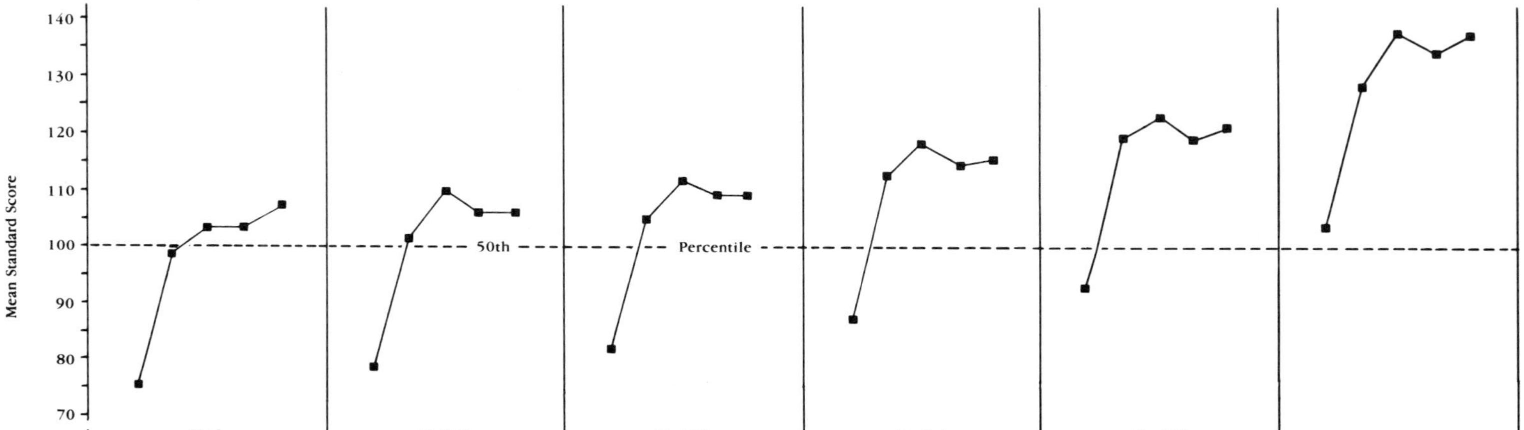

IQ: Under 71 (N=8)	EK	K	1	2	3
Std Score	75	99	104	104	108
S.D.:	15.2	16.3	13.8	13.4	23.0
%ile:	5TH	47TH	61ST	61ST	70TH
GE.	-	k8	1.9	3.1	4.3

IQ: 71-90 (N=108)	EK	K	1	2	3
Std Score	78	101	110	106	106
S.D.:	14.2	15.4	15.9	16.8	18.6
%ile:	7TH	50TH	75TH	66TH	66TH
GE.	-	k9	2.2	3.2	4.1

IQ: 91-100 (N=194)	EK	K	1	2	3
Std Score	82	104	112	108	108
S.D.:	13.3	13.6	15.8	16.8	18.6
%ile:	12TH	63RD	79TH	70TH	70TH
GE.	k0	1.0	2.3	3.4	4.3

IQ: 101-110 (N=214)	EK	K	1	2	3
Std Score	88	112	119	115	116
S.D.:	14.2	16.6	16.8	18.4	18.9
%ile:	21ST	79TH	90TH	84TH	86TH
GE.	k2	1.3	2.7	3.9	5.0

IQ: 111-130 (N=156)	EK	K	1	2	3
Std Score	93	120	124	119	121
S.D.:	14.5	17.1	17	17.8	17.9
%ile:	32ND	90TH	95TH	90TH	92ND
GE.	k4	1.6	2.9	4.2	5.4

IQ: Above 130 (N=18)	EK	K	1	2	3
Std Score	105	130	139	135	139
S.D.:	10.5	13.9	11.1	15.2	15.1
%ile:	63RD	97TH	99TH	99TH	99TH
GE.	k8	2.0	3.8	5.3	7.1

(Grade:[a] EK, K, 1, 2, 3)

[a]All testing performed at end of academic year, except for EK

Figure 20-7 *WRAT Reading, Longitudinal progress by IQ block for children in Entering-Kindergarten (EK) sites (698).*

MAT Total Reading
Longitudinal Progress by IQ Block during 2nd and 3rd Grade for Children in Entering-Kindergarten (EK) Sites[b] N=1, 082)

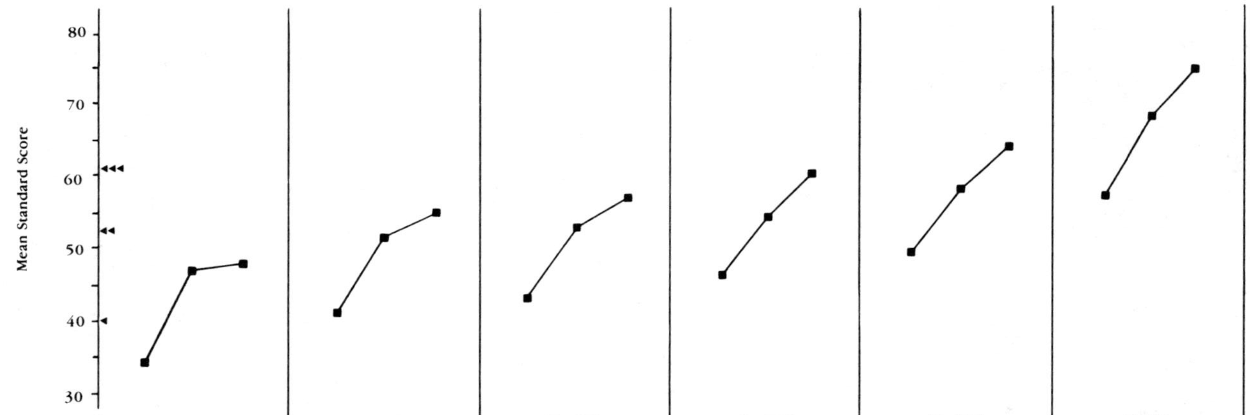

	N=19			N=181			N=271			N=310			N=265			N=36		
Grade:[a]	1	2	3	1	2	3	1	2	3	1	2	3	1	2	3	1	2	3
Std. Score:	33.9	46.6	47.4	40.1	50.6	54.3	43.1	52.7	56.0	46.0	54.5	59.6	49.0	57.1	63.2	55.4	65.1	72.6
SD.:	7.7	7.0	13.1	8.2	6.5	8.4	8.6	7.5	8.6	8.4	8.1	8.5	9.3	8.7	9.6	8.1	9.2	7.7
%ile:	30TH	22ND	11TH	50TH	41ST	29TH	66TH	51ST	34TH	78TH	59TH	44TH	88TH	70TH	58TH	94TH	88TH	81ST
G.E.:	1.6	2.2	2.3	1.9	2.5	2.8	2.0	2.7	3.0	2.2	2.9	3.4	2.4	3.1	3.7	2.9	3.9	4.9
IQ:	Under 71			71-90			91-100			101-110			111-130			Above 131		

[a]All testing was performed at end of academic year

[b]During Grade 3, the highest IQ block gained significantly more than the lowest block (which reflects the verbal content of the SIT and the Total Reading subtest of the Elementary Level MAT)

◂ Grade 1 National Median
◂◂ Grade 2 National Median
◂◂◂ Grade 3 National Median

Figure 20-8 *MAT Total Reading, Longitudinal progress by IQ Block during 2nd and 3rd grade for children in Entering-Kindergarten (EK) sites B (N=1,082).*

MAT Total Mathematics
Longitudinal Progress by IQ Block during 2nd and 3rd Grade for Children in Entering Kindergarten (EK) Sites (N=1,056)

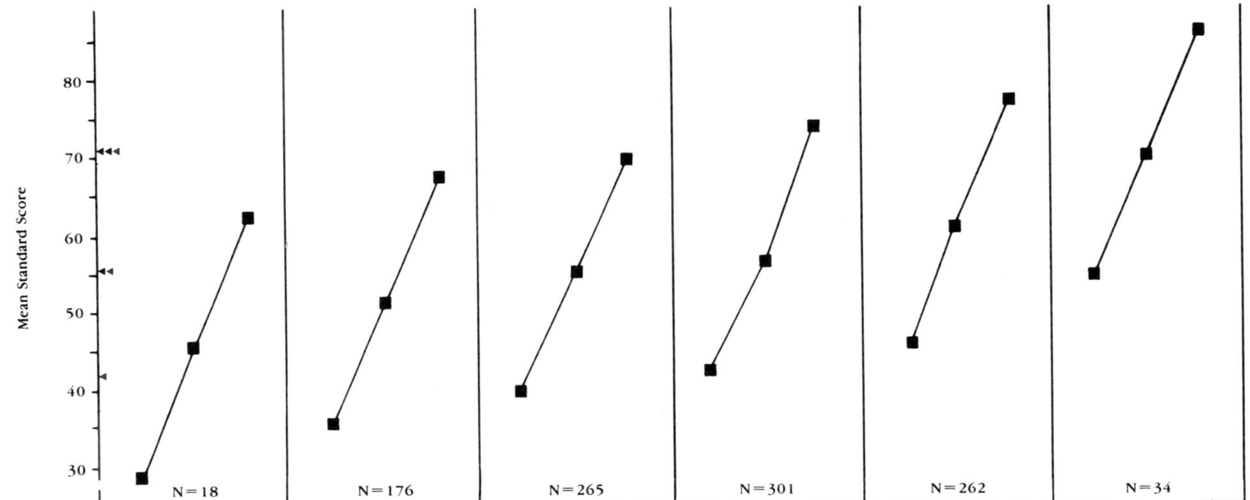

Grade[a]	1	2	3	1	2	3	1	2	3	1	2	3	1	2	3	1	2	3
Std. Score:	29.2	46.1	62.6	35.8	51.4	67.7	40.0	55.2	69.7	42.6	56.9	73.5	45.6	60.2	76.4	54.4	69.2	85.1
S.D.:	7.3	10.1	9.5	8.0	8.5	10.6	9.0	8.2	9.7	9.2	8.8	10.7	10.8	10.0	11.6	10.6	8.5	8.1
%ile:	10TH	10TH	24TH	30TH	22ND	39TH	46TH	38TH	47TH	51ST	50TH	61ST	57TH	63RD	69TH	83RD	84TH	88TH
G.E.:	1.2	2.0	3.2	1.5	2.3	3.5	1.7	2.5	3.7	1.8	2.7	4.0	2.0	3.0	4.3	2.5	3.6	5.3
IQ:	Under 71			71-90			91-100			101-110			111-130			Above 131		

[a]All testing was done at the end of the academic year

◂ Grade 1 National Median
◂◂ Grade 2 National Median
◂◂◂ Grade 3 National Median

Figure 20-9 *MAT Total Mathematics Longitudinal progress by IQ Block during 2nd and 3rd grade for children in Entering-Kindergarten (EK) sites (N=1,056).*

controlled by devising a set of novel figures that were given nonsense names. The tasks were like these:

Task		*Response*
"This is a spreel. What is this?"		"A spreel."
"This spreel is lack. What kind of spreel is this?"		"Lack."
"This spreel is sote. What kind of spreel is this?"		"Sote."

Five tasks were used. The first task was taught to criterion, and then a new one was added. These two were brought to criterion, and then a new one was added. *Cumulative programing* was used until all five were mastered to criterion.

The results showed that it took an average of 22 minutes for *each group* to learn the five concepts. A retention measure one week later showed approximately 75 percent retention by both groups, although there was more variability in retention for the Down's syndrome children than the normals. While based on a small sample, the outcome is entirely consistent with the conclusion that IQ tests do not measure learning rate or learning ability, but only the effects of past learning.

Implications for Teaching and Learning

This wandering trip into the world of IQ's and achievement tests leads to a very simple conclusion. What any person can be taught depends on what he or she has already learned, as well as the methods used in instruction. If the method of instruction is lecture, and the same assignments are given thirty students of highly different backgrounds, it is very likely that some will fail because they lack the preskills assumed by the teacher. In this situation, an IQ test could, in part, predict who would succeed or fail. If the method of instruction systematically builds upon the skills each individual brings to the educational setting and uses good motivating procedures, each student will learn to the degree he or she is effectively taught.

The fact that human beings are products of their genetic histories does not limit what they can learn *or* guarantee that they *will be taught.* Genetic histories probably do have some influence on how well students learn, but since there is no measure of or control over the variables involved, the potential influences currently have no practical implications for the teacher.

The net effect of the arguments considered in this chapter is this conclusion: *The potential power of instruction in increasing intellectual behavior has no known limit.* If you can imagine and even support with data a two-standard-deviation increase today, it seems entirely probable that, in another decade or two, teachers will have the skills and technology to consider another two standard deviations. Through better teaching, there is the promise of a smarter world tomorrow.

SUMMARY

In the beginning of this chapter, three statistically derived views of intelligence were presented: Intelligence as a general factor or dimension (Spearman), intelligence as a set of correlated group factors (Thurstone), and intelligence as a matrix of some 120 cognitive abilities (Guilford). These varied views have had little impact on what teachers do. What has had the greatest potential impact are the *false* propositions that the intelligence quotient (IQ) is *fixed by heredity* and that the IQ *determines what a person can learn.* While genetics (and the integrity of the physical structure that is a person) undoubtedly influence general intelligence, intelligence is best viewed by the teacher as the concepts, facts, rules, and problem-solving skills a student has learned so far in life. The current evidence suggests that what a student can learn is more dependent on whether or not he or she has the preskills assumed by a particular task, rather an IQ score.

IQ tests were developed by Alfred Binet and Henri Simon to help teachers cope with the wide range of capabilities children brought to the classroom after compulsory education became law. The goal was to identify children needing special help. Lewis Terman brought Binet's tests to the United States. As discussed in Chapter 10, Walter Lippmann, in his 1922 debates with Terman, saw much potential danger in the use of IQ tests to "grade" children. The doctrine that the IQ was inherited dominated much of the early thinking of American psychologists. This actually led to the use of the tests to track students into college-preparatory and vocational sequences early in life. Such practices are now viewed as unconstitutional.

When you examine carefully the tests used to measure IQ, it becomes quite clear that you are dealing with learned cognitive skills whose development most assuredly requires critical environmental inputs. This chapter described the general nature of the major individual IQ tests. It also reviewed two major pencil-and-paper or group tests.

To interpret IQ scores, you need to recognize that they are standard scores with a mean of 100 and a standard deviation of 15 (or 16 for the Stanford-Binet). By keeping in mind the nature of the normal distribution underlying the test scores and the percentages 34, 14, and 2, it is possible to closely estimate the percentile for any IQ score. For example, it helps in interpretation to know that an IQ of 125 is 1.66 standard deviations above the mean and is at the 95th percentile. The descriptive labels given to various ranges of IQ from severely retarded to gifted are also sometimes useful in interpretation, as long as they are approached as products of fallible estimates that need to be supplemented by careful examination of students as they actually function in real-life situations.

A variety of studies support the importance of a stimulating, teaching environment in the development of intelligence. Current evidence suggests that with current technologies, IQ can be increased by nearly two standard deviations when sustained effort is applied to build language skills and other cognitive skills.

The presumed causative role of intelligence in school achievement is open to question on several grounds. First, as Kelley did, one can interpret the high correlation between IQ test scores and scores on achievement test batteries as simply two measures of achievement; or with Humphreys, you can note that IQ test items tend to focus on past achievements and achievement test items on more recent achievements. But to say that one measure of achievement *causes* the other is poor logic. You can only say that some measures of achievement are *related* to other measures of achievement.

When you distinguish between measures of *level* of achievement (such as mental age, grade level) and measures of *gain* in achievement (which are a function of current instruction), we find the relation between IQ and achievement gain becomes much smaller or disappears. A level measure combines past learning *and* current learning and, not surprisingly, is related to past learning. A gain measure reflects *only current learning* and shows at best low positive correlations with past learning. Cronbach's review of the relation of IQ to measures of learning (gain) implies that IQ relates to learning gain only when prior learning can be used to advantage in the new learning. A study by Linda

Meyers shows that when the effects of prior learning (including motivation) are controlled, the average rate of learning does not differ for bright and dull students. This conclusion is a far cry from popular belief.

For the present, the conclusion is that the potential power of instruction in increasing intelligent behavior has ***no known limit.*** Through better teaching, people can be smarter. People learn what they are taught.

CHAPTER

21

COGNITIVE DEVELOPMENT

HISTORICAL PERSPECTIVE

Social and scientific concern about the development and care of children is a relatively modern affair. In the early 1800s in the United States, it was not uncommon for five and six year olds to work in factories up to sixteen hours a day. Children were thought of as little adults. Adults worked, why shouldn't the children. We are not too far from the days when the killing of infants was quite common, and child abuse laws have only had some strength to them since Colorado citizens passed their state law in 1963. In 1984, there were still reports of infanticide for girl babies in parts of China, and child abuse is still a critical social issue in the United States. However, our children live in a relatively sheltered and protected world, where they are valued and where scientific study is helping us to better understand how to help foster their development.

DEVELOPMENT—AN OVERVIEW

The scientific field involving the study of development is concerned with the changes that occur from conception to death. Through early phases of human development, behavior becomes more differentiated, adaptive, and integrated or organized. Human development is usually broken down into major subareas such as *physical development, motor skill development, personal-social development,* and *cognitive development.* This chapter and the next focuses on the latter two areas, since they are more important for teachers. But to set the context for the examination of cognitive and personal-social development, you should first become acquainted with a few of the more salient aspects of physical and motor-skill development.

Physical and Motor-Skill Development

Just as social and intellectual development involve the interaction of a *physical person* with an environment, so do physical growth and motor-skill development. In the case of physical growth, the variables of interest are the nutrients we take into our bodies, our health, genes, and time. In the case of motor-skill development, the variables of interest are *physical growth* (called *maturation* when it is not influenced by learning experiences) and *learning.*

The early years. A large number of studies have attempted to separate the roles of learning and maturation in the early development of motor skills. For example, McGraw (1935) gave one identical twin (Johnny) training in grasping, creeping, and walking, but withheld it from the other (Jimmy) until he was 22 months old. The early training made no difference. Later studies of buttoning, climbing, and trike riding showed that early training produced a temporary advantage, but it took much more training effort than later training. In general, maturation of the nerves, muscles, and bones needed for many motor skills must occur before training is very effective. These findings (and many others like them) provide us with a concept of *biological readiness.* (The notion of *reading readiness* is probably derived by analogy from *biological readiness.)* In the early years, if children are given the opportunity to explore and practice motor skills with appropriate play equipment, they are likely to develop quite adequately. Attempting to accelerate motor-skill development with young children is in most cases inappropriate.

The middle years (6-12). Figure 21.1 shows the general pattern of growth expressed as a percentage of 20-year old size (Flake-Hobson, Robinson, & Skeen, 1983, p. 339). The average 6-year old is about 4 feet tall, and by age 12 is nearly 5 feet tall. Girls are usually shorter at 6, equal to boys at 9, and taller by 12. As the chart shows, brain size is 90 percent of adult size by age 5, and 95 percent by age 10.

Puberty and adolescence. Adolescence usually refers to period after the beginning of puberty—the sexual changes associated with adulthood. The social and emotional aspects of this change will be discussed in the next chapter.

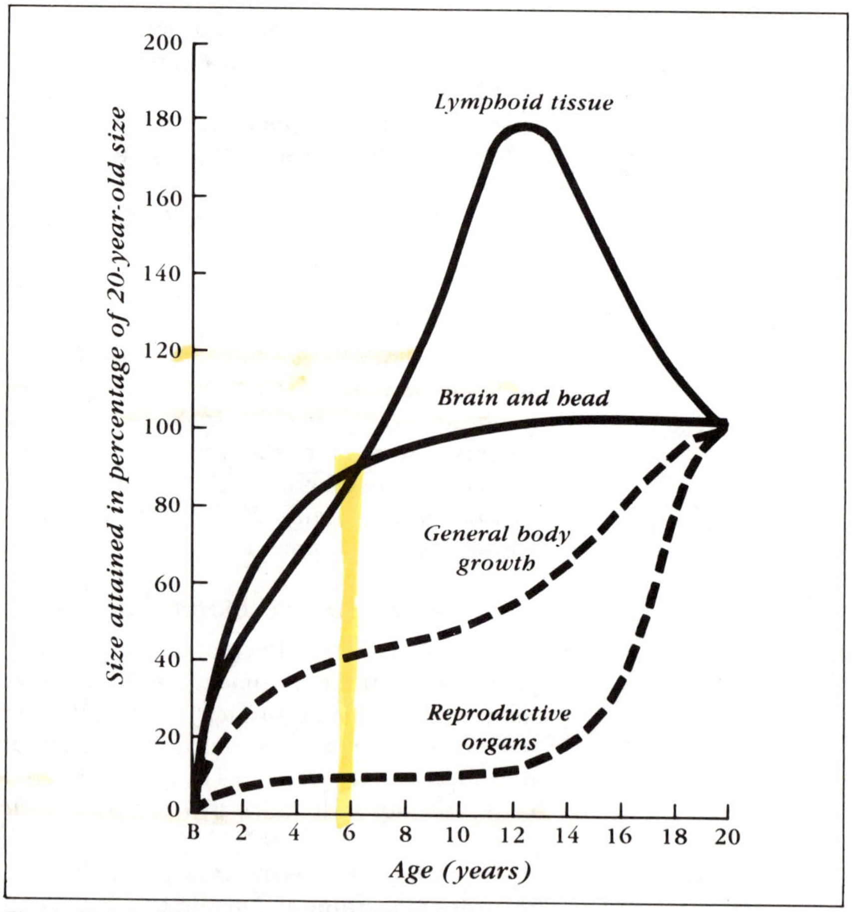

Figure 21-1 *Summary chart of growth and development*

Most of the physical changes in sex characteristics occur between 9 and 16 for girls and between 10 and 17 for boys. There are two major points about these changes: (1) they occur a year or two earlier for girls on the average, and (2) within sex groups the range in age of onset is over two years. Many girls are capable of becoming pregnant by 14, and boys on the average have mature sperm by 15 (range of 11 to 17). A growth spurt occurs preceding and paralleling sexual changes, again with a wide variability in onset. In girls, it can begin in the period from 7½ to 11½ and average 3½ inches per year. In boys, it can begin in the period from 10 to 16 and averages 4 to 5 inches per year. These physical changes can bring quite unsettled times for adolescents and need to be kept in mind in examining cognitive development.

JEAN PIAGET'S THEORY OF COGNITIVE DEVELOPMENT

From the early 1920s until his death in 1980 no other person studied the cognitive processes of children more than Jean Piaget. As a zoologist, Piaget was concerned with the adaptive aspects of intelligence. Life, in his view, is a creative interaction with the environment. In this interaction process, new internal structures are created. As life and new adaptations go on, the structures enlarge and reorganize to better reflect complexities of the world to which one is adapting.

Methods of Investigation

Many of Piaget's formulations about the development of intelligence came from observations of his own children in their early years. Piaget made systematic daily observations of responses to various stimulus conditions, and he "experimentally" varied the conditions to see what led to what (as a behaviorist would do). The following quote is an example of the precision in his descriptions of stimulus and response events:

> *From Observation* 120: At six months one day, Laurent tries to grasp a piece of paper that I offer him. I finally place it on the hood of his bassinet. Laurent begins by stretching out his hands. As soon as the object is placed, he reacts as he always does in the presence of distant objects: he shakes himself, waves his arms, etc. I regulate the situation by removing the paper from the hood for a few seconds in order to move it progressively closer and further away. It is when the paper seems inaccessible to the hand that Laurent shakes himself. After having thus behaved for a moment, he seems to look for the string hanging from the hood with which he had learned to shake various objects. He pulls it harder and harder while staring at the paper. At the moment when the paper is ready to fall from the hood, Laurent lets go of the string and reaches for the paper of which he immediately takes possession. Several subsequent attempts yielded the same result. It goes without saying that it cannot be demonstrated that Laurent pulled the string in order to grasp the paper, but the whole behavior pattern gave me the impression of being performed with this end in view, and of being perfectly coordinated.
>
> *Observation* 121: At age eight months 20 days, Jacqueline tries to grasp the cigarette case which I present to her. I then slide it between the cross strings which attach her dolls to the hood. She tries to reach it directly. Not succeeding, she immediately looks at the strings which are not in her hands and of which she sees only the part in which the cigarette case is entangled. She looks in front of her, grasps the strings,

> pulls and shakes them. The cigarette case falls and she grasps it . . . Second experiment: same reactions but without trying to grasp the object directly (Piaget, 1952 pp. 214-15).

These observations were used to support the hypothesis that the children, at this stage, were discriminating between *means* and *ends*. In the language of Chapter 18, the behavior would be viewed as problem-solving behavior—chaining together several motor operations.

The main method of investigation used by Piaget and his associates is to pose a series of questions or problems covering a conceptual area such as spatial relations, conservation of mass, or the causes of common events, and use probe questions that vary according to the response given. The inquiry is adapted to the child's view of things in a flexible, natural way. This method is called the "clinical method." The following are examples (The numbers in parentheses refer to the children's ages in years and months):

> Here are two children, Raoul and Gerald (4; 6 and 7; 2): "Raoul, have you any brothers?—*Gerald.*—And has Gerald a brother?—*No, only me has a brother.*—Oh, come! Hasn't Gerald got a brother?—*Raoul? . . . No, he hasn't got one.*" Gerald, after giving the same answers in respect to Raoul, hits upon the right solution.
>
> Jacq (7; 6): "Have you any brothers?—*Two* [Paul and Albert].—Has Paul any brothers?—*No.*—You are his brother?—*Yes.*—Then Paul has some brothers?—*No,*" etc. He is then told the solution and seems to understand it. "And has your sister any brothers?—*Two, one brother Paul and one brother Albert* [he leaves himself out again]. An hour later: "Has Albert any brothers?—*One* [Paul].—And Paul?—*One* [Albert].—And your sister?—*Two.*"
>
> Labert (8; 6): "Have you any brothers?—*Arthur.*—Has he got a brother?—*No.*—How many brothers are there in the family?—*Two.*—Have you got any?—*One.*—Has he got any?—*None at all.*—You are his brother?—*Yes.*—Then he has got a brother?—*No.*"
>
> Di (9; 6) one of our 1st type subjects examined three months after the Binet-Simon test: "Have you any brothers?—*One.*—Has he got a brother?—*No.*—You are his brother, aren't you?—*Yes.*—Then he has a brother?—*No.*" (Piaget, 1959 pp. 84-5).

The answers from groups of children at various ages are then analyzed to see how properties of "mental structures" change with age. In this case, many of the examples on the relationship *brother* are consistent with a more general egocentrism (personal frame of reference) in the young child's thinking.

Theoretical Constructs

Through the study of children's thinking processes at many age levels, Piaget formulated a descriptive model of the developmental stages of intelligence from birth to maturity. Basic to his stage theory is the idea that certain kinds of learning require certain kinds of mental structures (strategies, rules, concepts) as prerequisites. In this respect, the theory parallels those of Gagné and Engelmann. There is a critical difference, however: Many in American education interpret the stage limitations implied by Piaget's theory to mean that children cannot learn certain tasks at certain ages, whereas Gagné, Engelmann, and neo-Piagetians (discussed later) would assert that if one could teach the preskills, one could teach the tasks. There is quite a bit of support on the teachability of cognitive operations (Bucher and Schneider, 1973; Engelmann, 1966, 1967; Gelman, 1969; Zimmerman and Rosenthal, 1974). Piaget was not concerned with whether progression in the stages of intellectual development could be accelerated. He called this "the American question."

Processes of change. In his early work as a zoologist, Piaget studied changes in adaptive behavior and physical structure in shellfish that occurred when their environment changed. For example, the movement of clams from quiet water to turbulent water required strong movements of the foot. This led their shells to become wider and shorter.

Piaget generalized this finding and concluded that all species inherit capacities for *adaptation* and *organization*. In adaptation there is a change in behavior. In organization, there is a change in structure to support the adaptation. These same two concepts underpin his theory of cognitive development.

Organizational processes. As humans learn, we naturally organize nets of concepts and skills into *cognitive structures*. Simple initial structures are continually combined with related structures in ways that make them more effective. For example, an infant might be able to look at something or to grasp something, but not do both. Later they become chained together into a functional unit (look and grasp). Note that the processes we described in Chapter 14 for cumulatively teaching sets of related concepts were devised explicitly to foster the kinds of discriminations necessary to produce an organized net of concepts.

The cognitive structures that have been called problem-solving routines, transformations, fact systems, or sets of related concepts, Piaget would call *schemas*. American psychologists now use the term *schemes* to refer to organized systems that underlie thinking. As Piaget has recognized, these *schemes* are like the routines in a computer program for operating on sets of inputs (Piaget, 1953). They are the generators, the testers, other strategies, and production systems in an artificial intelligence program. The following discussion of Piaget's concept of schema is taken from Flavell (1963, p. 54).

> Another characteristic of schemas is hinted at by the phrase "class of similar action sequences" in our initial definition. A schema is a kind of concept, category, or underlying strategy which subsumes a whole collection of distinct but similar action sequences. For example, it is clear that no two grasping sequences are ever going to be alike; a grasping schema—a "concept" of grasping—is nonetheless said to be operative when any such sequence is seen to emerge. Schemas therefore refer to *classes* of total acts, acts which are distinct from one another and yet share common features. Although the terms *schema* and *concept* are not completely interchangeable, Piaget has recognized a certain similarity between them: "The schema, as it appeared to us, constitutes a sort of sensorimotor concept, or more broadly, the motor equivalent of a system of relations and classes" (Piaget, 1952, p. 385).

This particular discussion of schemes is restricted to illustrations of sensorimotor schemes, but as suggested, they can take many forms, from the simple to the complex. As the quotation from Flavell implies, a motor schema is the equivalent of an operant response—that which is common to a set of responses having a common effect on the environment. An operant response class, like a concept class, can be defined by the essential features of the class (Piaget calls these *invariants*). Essential features of related but different classes (for concepts we called these S−) can be specified. And, irrelevant features that can vary can be specified (Piaget calls these the *variants*). The point here is that the basic descriptions of the nature of concepts and of motor operations are nearly identical, whether they come from Piaget, from Skinner, or from Engelmann.

One more point on terminology is necessary. Piaget uses the term *operation* to refer to a *mental operation* such as addition, reversibility, or seriation. There are also important concepts like object permanence and conservation that are a part of mental structures. The point is that mental operations are *concepts* about motor operations. You can use blocks to show that $2 + 4 = 6$ and to reverse the operation and show that $6 - 4 = 2$. The student can be shown examples of the reversing operations without actually having to perform them. This means that it is possible to use concept teaching strategies to teach mental operations. In contrast to the Piagetians, who would favor the concrete "doing," Engelmann has suggested that it would be easier to teach a generalized *seriation* operation with a number of examples and nonexamples, using juxtaposition rules, than to insist that it be taught by physically ordering objects by number, size, and so forth. In any case, the recognition that a mental operation is a concept (a concept of doing something) should help your understanding of Piaget.

Adaptive processes. Piaget ascribes adaptation to the processes of *assimilation* and *accommodation*. Assimilation fits new examples into what we already know (perhaps distorting it in the process). Assimilation is equivalent to perception and understanding in American psychology. If a chimpanzee who had been taught a sign language, signed "chicken" the first time she saw a swan, this would be assimilation. The young child who called men smoking pipes "daddy" (daddy smokes a pipe) is showing assimilation, although the response is not correct. Using a ratio-equation routine to solve "work problems" (as illustrated earlier) is assimilation.

Accommodation. This process occurs when it is necessary to change a scheme to respond appropriately. When a new problem-solving strategy is created out of old component strategies, accommodation has occurred. Accommodation is what most American psychologists mean by learning. A behavior change takes place. Piaget would say that we change our thinking to fit new information. Accommodation can involve fitting new instances into old schemes. The chimpanzee Coco, who was taught a sign language, actually called the swan mentioned in the example above a "swimming chicken." This response had never been made before. Two elements in her vocabulary were combined into a new response. This is analogous to the chimpanzee Sultan solving the banana and stick problem by combining the operations of joining and reaching (in that order).

Critical variables in development. Developmental change is said to be due to: *maturation, activity, social transmission,* and *equilibration*.

- Maturation consists of the preprogramed physical development discussed earlier.

- Activity, which is interaction with the environment, leads to the operation of assimilation and accommodation.

- The social transmission of knowledge, especially language, allows us to benefit from the previous learning of others.

- Equilibration is a cognitive-motivational process set up by a discrepancy in the system that requires accommodation. A disequilibrium is set up when a scheme does not produce a satisfactory result and thus is said to motivate the search for a more effective scheme. (There is a discrepancy between two current states or between a current state and a goal state.)

Consider the following example of equilibration. Engelmann taught subjects to learn to "hear" through tactile vibrations by distributing different frequencies to different places on the arm (going from low to high frequencies). He found that students would master the discrimination of ten to twelve words, and *then it would all break down.* A new word added to an enlarging set would make it impossible to use the *initial coding system* (the cognitive structure for discriminating among the words). For example, one could discriminate "telephone" from "stay" and "bird," but adding "elephant" to the set would no longer allow "the longer one" to serve as the cue for "telephone." In the language of concept learning from Chapter 14, the students were using cues to discriminate words that would no longer work because they were now common to other words. To resolve the conflict, a new coding system was needed (accommodation).

Four Stages of Cognitive Development

Table 21.1 summarizes Piaget's stages of cognitive development. The ages given are crude approximations. The actual stage a given student is in would have to be determined by some kind of testing. This problem will be discussed later.

In the developmental analysis of cognition, Piaget tries to *describe* what a person *can do,* given a certain kind of structuring (which is inferred from observation of behavior in a variety of situations). The varieties of structuring are seen to progress through developmental stages. Development is a continuous process, but stages can be described according to the nature (form) of the thinking structures predominant in a stage. The major stages are called the sensorimotor, the preoperational, the stage of concrete operations, and the stage of formal operations.

The sensorimotor stage (birth to two years). Central to the structure of cognition at this sensorimotor stage is its dependence on external stimulation and overt actions. To *"think" is to act. Cognition and behavior are one.* This earliest period can be broken down into a series of accomplishments that build on one another. The newborn begins dealing with his environment with built-in sensorimotor schemes. When a newborn's lips are stimulated he or she sucks; a touch on the palm leads to closing of the hand; a bright light draws the eyes toward it. As these reflexive schemes become well-practiced, coordinations between them occur. Hearing a sound leads to looking. The eye tries to follow the hand. Then occasionally, an interesting new effect is produced, like the shaking of a rattle, and attention focuses on reproducing the event. The reproduction of these events is said to represent the beginning of intention.

It is often observed that a familiar object is given recognition with a smile or with some part of the motor response used with that object in the past. For example, a six-month old infant might indicate recognition by shaking his hand if a rattle were held in front of him (if he had previously developed a

Table 21-1 Piaget's stages of cognitive development

Stage	*Approximate Age*	*Characteristics*
Sensorimotor	0-2 years	Begins to make use of imitation, memory, and thought. Begins to recognize that objects do not cease to exist when they are hidden. Moves from reflex actions to goal-directed activity.
Peoperational	2-7 years	Gradual language development and ability to think in symbolic form. Able to think operations through logically in one direction. Has difficulties seeing another person's point of view.
Concrete operational	7-11 years	Able to solve concrete (hands-on) problems in logical fashion. Understands laws of conservation and is able to classify and seriate. Understands reversibility.
Formal operational	11-15 years	Able to solve abstract problems in logical fashion. Thinking becomes more scientific. Develops concerns about social issues, identity.

rattle-shaking scheme). At seven months, one might observe only a closing of the fist as a sign of recognition.

Slowly reality is constructed. Objects take on permanence, as can be shown when the child searches for a ball hidden under a blanket. The beginnings of imitation occur. (It is of interest to note that Piaget's examples with Lucienne show a training process. Piaget imitated Lucienne's putting out her tongue, and this led Lucienne to do it again. This same kind of training was used with noises later.) Toward eight or nine months, there is evidence for the differentiation of means and ends. Different schemas are tried as the means to an end. The examples quoted earlier to illustrate Piaget's methods of observation illustrate how Laurent and Jacqueline tried a series of responses to get something held in front of them so it could be grasped and inspected.

Shortly after differentiation of means and ends, barrier problems are solved by using schemes for hitting, pushing, pulling, and so on, to remove a barrier to a goal. During this period, behavior is continually varied to produce novel effects on the environment. There is a beginning of active experimentation to find out what-leads-to-what (like playing with a light switch). This earliest stage ends with the development of mental invention. Schemes for problem solution are first "thought out" and then executed. For example, after looking for possible objects, a stick might be grasped and immediately used to reach a cookie that is otherwise not reachable. (Note that this is a variation on Sultan's problem as discussed earlier.)

By the end of the sensorimotor stage the child *can do* many things like finding hidden objects, making detours in space, and imitating speech sounds, but his intelligence is limited to here-and-now actions for the most part. Thought and behavior are still one.

The preoperational stage (two to seven years). This is a period of massive growth in language skills and understanding the referents of words. Central to the structure of cognition in this period is the differentiation of signifiers and the things they stand for (referents). Piaget distinguishes two kinds of signifiers, signs and symbols. Signs, such as words, have an arbitrary relationship established by convention with their referents. Symbols bear some similarity to the referent. For example, the young boy, playing at being a hunter like daddy, might use a stick to represent his gun. The stick bears some similarities to a gun in that it can be held in the hand, is long, and can be pointed. Symbols can also be mental representations. An example comes from an observation of Lucienne when she was sixteen months of age. Piaget had several times before played with her by hiding a chain in a match box into which Lucienne had learned to put the chain. Lucienne at the time of critical observation could get the chain out by turning the box over if it was open or by using a finger to get the chain out. She had never *opened and closed* the box. At this point she was given the box with a very small opening. She could not get her finger in, and tipping did no good. She then studied the situation and several times in succession opened and shut her mouth, first slightly, and then wider. She appeared to be using a motor symbol for the mental representation. She then used her finger to enlarge the opening and get the chain.

In moving from the sensorimotor stage to operational thought, several things must occur during the preoperational period. There must be a speeding in thought or actions, so more information can be dealt with at once. There must be an expansion of the contents and scope of what can be thought about. And, there must be concern not only with the results of action, but also with understanding the processes by which a result is achieved. This later effect is said to be accomplished through the gradual growth of logico-mathematical operations for thinking about what is going on or might go on. Toward the end of the preoperational stage, the basis for logico-mathematical thinking has been laid in the use of language, but the child is still far from reaching operational thought. This latter point is often illustrated by experiments concerned with the conservation of liquid amount, conservation of quantity, or conservation of weight. In these experiments, a fixed amount of matter is transformed in shape. A liquid might be poured into a taller narrower glass or a fixed weight of clay might be reshaped. Usually, the preoperational child will say that the taller narrower glass contains more water than was in the shorter wider glass, when nothing was added or taken away; or that the longer piece of clay is heavier. The change in height or length has deceived him. He missed the reciprocal change going on in the other dimension. The preoperational child also lacks a test for conservation (for example, "They are the same before and after the change in shape because nothing was added or taken away").

Stage of concrete operations (7 to 11 years). For Piaget, an operation is a *mental action* that usually occurs in a structure with its counteraction—adding goes with its reverse operation subtracting, combining with separating, identity with negation. An operation is said to be *concrete* if it can be used only with concrete referents rather than *hypothetical* referents. In the concrete operational stage, thinking shows many characteristics of mature logic, but it is restricted to dealing with the "real." For example, an eight year old might have no trouble ordering a set of sticks according to height, but might fail to solve the problem, "Bill is shorter than Mike; Bill is taller than John; who is the tallest of the three?"

Stage of formal operations (11 to 15 years and up). Formal operations involve thinking in terms of the formal propositions of symbolic logic and mathematics or in terms of principles of physics. One can deal with the hypothetical. One can deal with operations on operations. For example, the concept of density involves a ratio of weight to volume. A hypothetical object could be made more dense by adding to its weight while keeping volume constant or by subtracting from its volume while keeping its weight constant. But now consider the concept of specific gravity, which involves a ratio of two densities: the density of some matter to the density of water. In this case we have an operation on operations. At this stage, it is possible to generate many possible hypotheses by combining various operations and setting out to test them.

Throughout the development of mind from the sensorimotor stage to the stage of formal operations, there is a parallel change in the orientation of the child to the world. Initially, the viewpoint is *egocentric* (self-centered); and gradually it becomes *objective,* as the child sees the self as an object in the world and learns to view reality from the point of view of others.

Educational Implications

Positive contributions to education from Piaget's work can be summarized in five points. First, the evidence on the ways in which new structures are built in an orderly fashion out of old ones implies a need for a careful analysis of what each child brings to the learning situation. Second, Piaget clearly recognizes that *learning is doing,* especially for the young child. Active responding is important to learning operations, and thinking is to a large extent built out of initially overt operations. Third, there are strong suggestions, *at least by example,* that the development of cognitive structures can be fostered by the teacher's questions and probes that introduce contradictions. This is parallel to the notion of introducing negative instances in the work of Engelmann and others. Fourth, there are implications for the goals and design of curricula. The focus is on instruction to develop productive thinking that has the characteristics of what Piaget calls the operational stage.

Finally, Piaget has made major contributions to the analysis of many areas of knowledge, noting its structurings. He has explored concepts of physical causality, the properties of objects, space, time, mathematical logic, classification of objects, relations among objects, and propositional logic. He has also pursued the study of concepts in moral reasoning, in children's views on human behavior, and in language development. The logical analyses and descriptive material in his work can teach us to think more clearly about the world around us and to see more clearly what we need to teach others. Pertinent references to these major works are: Inhelder and Piaget, 1958; 1964; Piaget, 1954; 1960; 1962a; 1962b; 1963; 1965a; 1965b; 1967; 1970; 1971.

Rohwer, Ammon, and Cramer (1974) have identified five limitations of the Piagetian form of cognitive theory for educational practice. The following points are indebted to their analysis:

1. Cognitive theory takes behavior for granted. There is little said on how one gets from cognition to performance. There is no information given on teaching motor skills (overt operations), such as speech, handwriting, or athletic skills.

2. Noncognitive aspects of motivation tend to be ignored. If the student is not "intrinsically" motivated by the task, cognitive theory is of little help in telling the teacher what to do.

3. The teacher is not given any specifics of behavior to use as guidelines in deciding what to do or expect. The teacher has to clinically explore

each student's performance, make an inference about structure, ***and then decide what to teach next.*** This could be a formidable problem with twenty-five students.

4. The focus on structure of the mind has led to a neglect of analysis of conceptual contents to be taught in ways that could facilitate teachng. While many content areas have been studied, analysis has not focused on teaching implications.

5. Lastly, and most critically, Rohwer points out that cognitive theory has failed to study the environmental variables that bring about changes in cognitive structure. As a consequence there is a lack of teaching prescriptions that would help foster cognitive development. The theory, in focusing on the nature of mental structures, has failed to show the processes that lead to the development of mental structures.

A NEO-PIAGETIAN VIEW

There have been further criticisms and extensions of the educational applications of Piaget's work by a group called neo-Piagetians (Pascual-Leone, 1972; Lefebvre and Pinard, 1972; Case, 1978; among others). We draw our material from Robbie Case's (1978) review. The neo-Piagetian view integrates an information-processing approach to cognitive psychology with Piagetian theory, drawing on the methods of those concerned with designing intelligent systems.

A Developmental Theory of Instruction

As noted, a theory of learning *describes* principles of learning, while a theory of instruction *prescribes* the basis for making sound instructional decisions. Case points out that a similar distinction can be made between a theory of intellectual development (descriptive) and a *developmental theory of instruction* (prescriptive). Piaget's goal was to describe (provide a model of) how thinking processes change from birth to maturity. A developmental theory of instruction would be concerned with optimizing the process of development to achieve specific instructional goals. Assuming that the environment is not already optimal (a safe assumption, since many adults never reach the stage of formal operations), and assuming acquisition of cognitive schemes can be facilitated, what are the necessary steps to take?

For Case the basic steps are to:

1. Do a structural (logical) analysis of what is to be taught so that its operational requirements are known.

2. Do an individual assessment of the general operational level of the students.

3. Plan a curriculum.

There are problems with each of these steps. Consider first the *structural analysis.* In the problem of conservation of liquid quantity, Piaget argues that to understand the concept, the student would have to understand a compensation argument—getting taller was compensated for by getting narrower (see Figure 21.2). Being able to mentally reverse the effect in one direction by considering the effect in the other direction is characteristic of the stage of concrete operations. However, it is not clear that the compensation argument is necessary or how Piaget arrived at his conclusion. The performance by the children gives no indication that they are using a compensation logic. "Thus, even in well-defined areas that clearly require logical reasoning such as science and math, it is not clear how the operational structures that underlie specific tasks should be identified." (Case, 1978, p. 172).

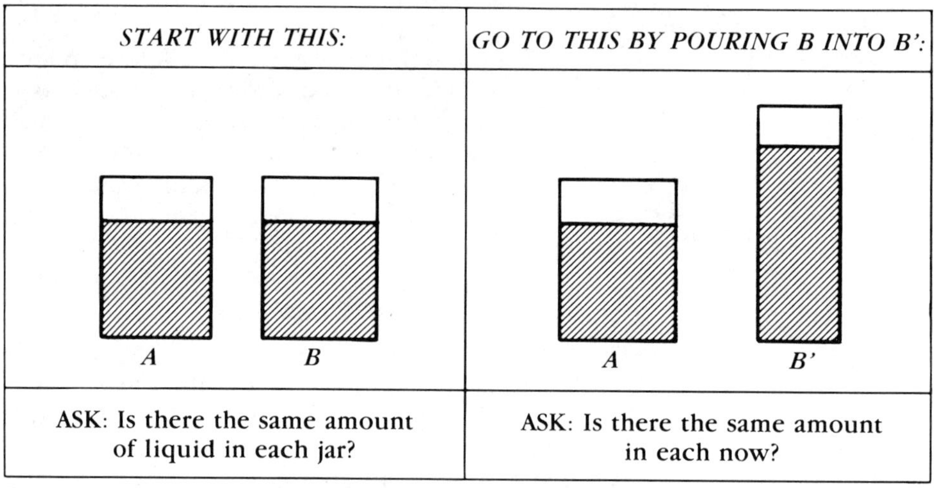

Figure 21-2 *An illustration of conservation of liquid quantity (volume)*

When it comes to ***individual assessment,*** there are problems. Different measures of similar structures correlate very little with each other or not at all. This implies that assessment would have to focus on very specific cognitive structures and not just on the "level" the student is in. "If one looks at Piagetian tests of the ***same*** operational structure, one discovers a problem that is even more serious. Although the correlations between items are much higher, the absolute ***levels of success*** (that is, the percent of students passing) vary widely as a function of the particular test item that is employed. For example, while tests of conservation of number are passed by about the age of six, tests of conservation of weight are not passed until about the age of nine or ten, and tests of conservation of displaced volume are not passed until about the age of eleven" (Case, 1978, p. 173). If a structure is supposedly available by age six, but cannot be used until twelve for some problems, the usefulness of this knowledge is questionable. This poses a serious problem for the educational application of Piaget's ideas.

Assuming the above problems were solved, the problem becomes one of ***designing instruction*** to facilitate moving students to the next level of intellectual functioning. However, the theory is quite vague about the process for transitioning from stage to stage. While Piaget describes some of the substages (within a stage) that students go through in acquiring a concept like conservation, the processes by which the student moves from substage to substage are not known. What needs to be known are the critical characteristics of effective instruction. Are procedures that foster setting up inner conflect for the student (disequilibrium) essential? It would appear not. Direct instruction on the concepts, operations, and rules of concern to Piagetians also has been found to be effective (Bucher and Schneider, 1973; Engelmann, 1965; 1967; Gelman, 1969; Zimmerman and Rosenthal, 1974).

Note that the steps necessary for ***optimizing*** stage transition (with their problems) would also be the steps needed in adapting current curricula to the student's cognitive stage. Case concludes that something more is needed if

Piaget's work is to be relevant to instruction. (Keep in mind that this is the "American question." Piaget's goal was to *describe* the changes occurring over time in intellectual functioning, not to show how to *produce* those changes.)

A Reformulation

Drawing on the work of Pascual-Leone (1969, 1970, 1972, 1976), Piaget's basic notions about schemes and the process of equilibration are redefined using the language of artificial intelligence (Newell and Simon, 1972). All knowledge is stored as schemes. Schemes have two components: the first part specifies the conditions where they apply, and the second part specifies conditions that they generate. For example, a four year old views two beakers that are the same as part of a conservation of liquid quantity problem. The setting condition (1) is an example of two equal things, this generates (2) a conclusion "They are the same." Three classes of schemes are described:

- Figurative schemes—*represent* facts, states, or meanings.
- Operative schemes—*do things* like transform a set of figurative schemes into another set of figurative schemes.
- Executive schemes—serve a *control function,* like problem solving and problem evaluation strategies. These are the metacognitive strategies of Chapter 18.

Table 21.2 shows a model for the operations a student would have to go through to be placed in conflict (disequilibrum) while working on a conservation of liquid quantity problem. The figurative and operative schemes are illustrated. The whole sequence is a model of one executive scheme for approaching such problems (that is, a problem-solving strategy).

"Once the content of intellectual development is characterized as a sequence of executive schemes of increasing power and complexity, it becomes possible to take the sort of model described in [Table 21.2] as a prototype and to provide a general characterization of the equilibration process" (Case, 1978, p.187).

Equilibration is viewed as the activation of a heuristic (investigative) executive scheme to search for a resolution when conclusions have been drawn that conflict with each other. Specific mental steps occur: (1) retrieving from memory figurative schemes, (2) operating on figurative schemes in active memory. The theory states that *operating memory* is limited—that is the number of schemes that can be activated at the same time is limited. If a resolution is found, the steps by which solution was reached are stored as a *new executive scheme* that can be used under similar conditions in the future.

An interesting concept developed by Pascual-Leone (1970) is *M-power.* M-power is operating-memory power, defined as the number of schemes a person can keep active at once. M-power is assumed to increase by .5 units every year from ages three to twelve. At each age active memory is assumed able to hold an executive scheme plus so many units of M. Careful tests of the age progression of M-power have confirmed Pascual-Leone's hypothesis (Burtis, 1974; Case, 1972; Diaz, 1974; Parkinson, 1976; Pascual-Leone, 1970; Toussaint, 1974). M-power influences the complexity of problem-solving strategies that can be used. Moderate correlations (independent of age) have been found between measures of M-power and the complexity of operations required in the solution of Piagetian tasks. If tasks are modified to reduce their memory requirements, children with lower M-power are then able to do them.

Table 21-2 *Detailed model of conflict discovery while applying bidimensional scanning strategy*

Step or Operation	*Specific Schemes*	*Symbol*[a]
1. Note that Beaker B has a taller column of liquid than Beaker A.	(1) Operative scheme taking the perceived difference in vertical projection between two objects as input and generating as output a conclusion as to which is higher.	ψ Height
	(2)[b] Figurative scheme representing the perceived difference in vertical displacement between the two columns.	ϕ Vertical displacement
2. Conclude there is more water in Beaker B.	(1) Operative scheme representing the rule: taller things contain more.	ψ Higher = more
	(2)[b] Figurative scheme representing the fact generated in Step 1, namely, that Beaker B is taller than Beaker A.	ϕ B > A (height)
3. Note that Beaker B is narrower than Beaker A.	(1)[c] Figurative scheme generated in Step 2, representing the conclusion that Beaker B contains more than Beaker A.	ϕ B > A (height)
	(2) Operative scheme taking a perceived horizontal projection difference as input and generating as output a conclusion as to which is wider.	ψ Width
	(3) Figurative scheme representing the horizontal projections of Beaker B and of Beaker A.	ϕ Horizontal displacement
4. Conclude that there is less water in Beaker B.	(1)[c] Figurative scheme generated in Step 2 (B > A)	ϕ B > A
	(2) Operative scheme representing the rule, wider things contain more.	ψ Quantity (width)
	(3)[b] Figurative scheme representing the fact that Beaker B is narrower than Beaker A.	ϕ B < A (width)
5. Note that the two stored conclusions are in conflict.	(1)[b] Figurative scheme generated in Sept 2 (B > A).	ϕ B > A
	(2) Figurative scheme generated in Step 4 (B < A).	ϕ B < A

[a] ψ = operative scheme; ϕ = figurative scheme.
[b] Activated by perceptual input.
[c] Scheme being activated (stored) for subsequent use.

Case (1977a) showed that *programed training* in dealing with conservation problems reduced the M-power requirements of the task. Fifty-seven percent of subjects with M-power of two solved the problems with direct training, while only 13 percent of those with indirect training solved the problems. The indirect training gave problems and feedback on adequacy of judgments. The direct training took students through steps like those in Table 21.2. For subjects with M-power of three, 100 percent solved the problems with direct training. Only 50 percent solved the problems with indirect training. No children with M-powers of one solved the problems.

Bringing the active memory requirements of a task into a developmental analysis of learning processes is undoubtedly an important contribution. Also, the adaptation of the strategies developed in the study of artificial intelligence to the kinds of problems posed by the Piagetians is a nice integration of ideas. However, as you examine the actual instructional design suggestions proposed by Case, there is much to be desired. The procedures for designing problem-solving routines presented in Engelmann and Carnine's *Theory of Instruction* are much more useful and they already are fully developed for a wide variety of important educational content areas. The potential for integrating seemingly divergent approaches to the study of cognitive processes, and their instructional implications shows promise in this work.

SUMMARY

The scientific concern with human developmental processes is a relatively new endeavor. This chapter began with a brief overview of physical and motor-skill development as background for the study of cognitive and personal-social development. Besides health and nutrition, the key concepts in physical and motor-skill development are *maturation* and *learning*. It appears in the years of rapid growth, that there are physical maturation requirements that must be met (biological readiness) before motor-skill learning can become very efficient.

Growth curves show that brain development is 90 percent complete by the age of five, but general body growth has progressed only 40 percent by this age. The maturation of reproductive organs is not complete for girls until about fourteen and for boys, about sixteen. Girls start their growth spurts earlier than boys so that there is a point at around twelve years of age when girls are taller than boys. These are the kind of physical facts that set the context for our study of cognitive development. Our examination of cognitive development focused on Piaget's remarkable works and some reinterpretations by the neo-Piagetians.

Piaget spent 50 years of his life studying development changes in the intellectual functioning of children and young adults. He studied the intellectual development of his own children during their first two years of life. He would pose problems for them and see how they handled them. Most of his studies of the development of various conceptual structures were carried out with groups of children at various ages. From these studies, Piaget formulated a theory of the developmental stages where the higher stages grow out of the base of knowledge built up at lower stages. As Figure 21.1 showed, in the sensorimotor stage, thinking is doing. All thinking begins as overt behavior, which slowly comes to be represented by signs and symbols for actions. In the preoperational stage, there is a differentiation between signifiers and the things signified. Thought and action are separated as language develops, but the child still lacks an understanding of causal processes. In the stage of concrete operations, an understanding of what leads to what is achieved, but is restricted to dealing with the real. Only in the stage of formal operations can the child deal with the hypothetical and perform operations upon operations.

The stages of mental development described by Piaget represent steps taken by the child in approaching the most flexible and mobile forms of mature thinking. Concepts and operations are the key components of mature forms of thinking. Piaget has noted a formal similarity in the structure of concepts and operations. Both involve what is common to a set of events (invariants), and examples of both have irrelevant characteristics (variants).

As humans learn, what they learn is organized into cognitive structures or schemes. Through maturation and experience, these become more complex and better able to represent "reality" efficiently. Adaptation is said to occur through the processes of *assimilation* (perception, understanding) and *accommodation* (a behavioral or cognitive change—learning). The attempt to reduce inner conflict caused by conflicting conclusions is called *equilibration*. This is a form of cognitive motivation (like the discrepancy motivation discussed in Chapter 10). The accommodations that occur when puzzling information is confronted is an important basis for cognitive growth in Piaget's view. While he recognized the importance of the cultural transmission of knowledge by parents and teachers, how this occurs was not an interest of his.

Piaget has described the orderly growth of intellect. He has stressed the importance of active, self-directed learning. There are suggestions that cognitive development can be fostered by helping the child to see paradoxes in his or her conclusions. Piaget has given us a view of operational thinking that has helped to set major goals for curricula in American education. His analysis of concept areas like causality, space, time, mathematical logic, and propositional logic provide rich materials for educators.

However, there are limitations to applying Piaget's ideas to education. Foremost is the fact Piaget's work has been descriptive and not experimental. He was not concerned with fostering development, but with describing it. The kinds of processes you studied earlier in this text are more relevant to producing behavioral or cognitive change.

The neo-Piagetians have been concerned with formulating a developmental theory of instruction that could subsume within it the major descriptive and analytic contributions of Piaget. They see problems in trying to use Piaget's stage theory as a guide to instructional decisions. In the first place, it is not clear how the operational structures of content areas should be identified. Then there are serious problems in deciding what stage a student is in. Different tests give different answers. Also the stages may not be all that important if teaching strategies can be found that could get around a "stage barrier." And finally, as noted above, Piaget was silent on instructional design issues.

The neo-Piagetians, as summarized by Robbie Case, take the language of information-processing theory (and the subspecialty artificial intelligence) as beginning steps in formulating a developmental theory of instruction. Knowledge is stored in schemes (computer routines that can be pulled from memory). Schemes have two parts: a part that specifies where they apply, and a part that specifies what they can do. Figurative schemes represent facts, states, meanings; operative schemes do things; and executive schemes control what goes on. Another way of saying this is that there are schemes based on stimulus events, schemes based on response events (or their mental representations), and schemes that are strategies.

The neo-Piagetians attempt to derive models of executive schemes that parallel intellectual functioning at different stages of development. They attempt to show how, through a reinterpretation of the equilibration process, it is possible to move from stage to stage. Equilibration involves an executive scheme taking over to find a new solution when conflicting conclusions are reached. If a solution is found, a new executive scheme using that solution is formed. The theory is not clear on where these routines come from. What the theory attempts to do is specify *the properties they must have* as a starting point. "How would we design a computer program that could function this way or that?" This designing is another name for building a *model* of mental functioning at various stages.

Pascual-Leone defined M-power as the number of schemes a person can keep active at once. Studies have shown that M-power increases about .5 each year from ages 3 to 12. M-power appears to be a factor in the child's capacity to deal with concrete of formal operations.

The current instructional design attempts of the neo-Piagetians are lacking in fundamentals. Engelmann's design procedures appear far more relevant for designing instruction at this time than do those of the neo-Piagetians.

However, the attempt to build a developmental theory of instruction is intriguing. Whether in the end it will contribute new ideas for instruction, beyond the contributions of Bloom, Gagné, Engelmann remains to be seen.

CHAPTER

22

PERSONAL AND SOCIAL DEVELOPMENT

Describing and understanding the intricate social-learning processes that go on from birth to maturity that help determine who we are as persons is not an easy task. There is a lot of learning and maturation occurring that is difficult to study in systematic ways. Research has shown that the same learning principles operate in fostering personal-social development as in intellectual development. However, the intertwined respondent (emotional) conditioning plays a more important role as the young child develops attachments, preferences, and attitudes—including attitudes about self.

Personality theorists, such as Sigmund Freud and Eric Erikson, have attempted to describe major stages in personal growth from birth to maturity based on the analysis of clients in therapy and through the study of the development of individuals in different societies. Erikson's theory is most commonly reviewed in educational psychology textbooks because it has a "sense of truth" to it, and because it is more socially oriented (and less male-biased) than Freud's theory of psycho-sexual development.

Erikson's stage theory focuses on the different kinds of problems that arise in personal development as children progress from total dependence on others to maturity. It deals with the major social roles children learn to play as they grow up. It deals with the dreams they develop for themselves—the longer-term goals adults work toward in life. Many topics already touched on—such as self-esteem, self-actualization, developing communication skills in groups, dealing with conflict, achievement motivation, attitudes, self-management, problem-solving skills, and so on—are all involved in understanding the development of a personality.

This chapter first briefly examines Erikson's stage theory to give the "big picture," and then looks more closely at issues of most importance to teachers in understanding the great differences in personal characteristics children and young adults bring to school. It will also examine some issues in the development of personal responsibility (moral behavior) and how to deal with common social behavior problems. The next chapter looks more closely at specific ways of dealing with problems in personal and social adjustment.

ERIKSON'S STAGES IN PERSONAL-SOCIAL DEVELOPMENT

While derived in part from Freud's psycho-sexual theory, Erikson's (1963) theory goes beyond to look at the development of individual social competence in a world that is continually expanding for the individual. New crises are encountered at each stage that must be mastered if one is to become a competent, happy, self-actualizing adult. Erikson's stages are summarized in Figure 22.1.

	PERSONALITY DEVELOPMENT
1. Infancy: Trust vs. Mistrust ....>	
2. Early Childhood: Autonomy vs. Shame and Doubt ....>	
3. Preschool Age: Initiative vs. Guilt ....>	
4. Elementary and Middle-School Age: Industry vs. Inferiority ....>	
5. Adolescence: Identity vs. Role Diffusion (confusion) ....>	
6. Young Adulthood: Intimacy vs. Isolation ....>	
7. Adulthood: Generativity vs. Stagnation ....>	
8. Old Age: Integrity vs. Despair ....>	

Figure 22-1 *Erikson's stages of personal-social development*

1. Infancy: Trust versus Mistrust

The infant whose needs are well-cared for with gentle affection develops a bonding to parents through an emotional conditioning process. Living in an environment filled with pain can lead to the learning of broadly generalized fears that provide the basis for not trusting those around you. Ainsworth (1979) has found that infants whose mothers have been more responsive to their needs during the first year are more *securely attached* to their mothers. They are able to use their mothers as a secure base from which to explore the world. These trusting babies are more cooperative with their mothers and less aggressive. When they get older they become more competent and show more sympathy to peers. *Anxiously attached* babies are more aggressive, less cooperative and sympathetic, and less competent. In their first year, mothers of these babies are less reliable in meeting their infants' needs. A favorable ratio of trust to mistrust appears to be a foundation for healthy personality development.

2. Early Childhood: Autonomy versus Shame and Doubt

As children do more things on their own, they: (1) can learn they are *competent,* or, if overprotected and/or thwarted in their efforts, (2) can learn to *doubt* their capabilities. The struggle for autonomy can enter into problems in toilet training and is readily apparent in the phenomenon of "two year old negativism," where children will oppose almost any command from an adult. A healthy sense of autonomy ("I am an individual, too") can derive from a protecting, teaching environment, that continues to let the toddler explore his or her world with a protective adult ready to help when needed.

3. Preschool Age: Initiative versus Guilt

In the period from approximately two to six years, the young child is modeling and practicing more adult-like tasks in play and in being "a helper." Children are learning about adult roles and at the same time about the "don'ts" and "no's" that go with adult responsibility. Sex-role identities and concepts of sex differences develop. Both *modeling* and *differential treatment* by adults and other children contribute to this learning. For example, boys are given a much wider freedom of movement away from home than are girls (Lewis and Weinraub, 1974). In the process of moving away from direct parental supervision, the possibilities for "getting into trouble" arise. Punishment may be used when parents' rules are violated (fighting, stealing, sexual play, and so on) or parents perceive the child to be in danger (from cars, fire, knives, poisons, and so forth). Guilt can arise when the "don'ts" are transgressed and the child perceives that he or she hurt someone. The challenge of this stage is to develop self-directed initiative in balance with learning appropriate social prohibitions—learning to respect the rights of others, learning the rules of the game, and maintaining the affection of friends and the important adults around one.

The rules for effective punishment discussed in Chapter 5 provide a guide to parents or teachers in promoting effective social behavior at this age.

4. Elementary and Middle-School Age: Industry versus Inferiority

In our culture at least, schools become the "work" of children. In schools, children face the crises of working-to-learn in order to become competent or be exposed as failures. The comparisons in hard work and accomplishments are there for all to see, even when they are not emphasized by the teacher. As noted in Chapter 10, effective teaching methods that bring all children along in basic competencies can go far to build self-esteem and minimize feelings of failure and inferiority. A study that followed 450 men for 35 years concluded that the most well-adjusted (and well-paid) adults, with the most satisfying personal relationships, had been good "workers" as children. A danger on the industrious side is expressed by the saying, "All work and no play makes Jack a dull boy." Workaholic adults very likely got their start in the satisfaction of completing a job well as children. While good academic work is very important to success, teachers need to help children develop a balance across activities (social, physical, artistic, and academic). There is also a need to help children realize that they cannot all be the best at everything. Children have different talents and interests and some will excel in one area and some in another.

The early school years are also a period where friendships with peers become more important. Learning "to be a friend" is a valuable set of social skills. Popular students tend to be outgoing, kind, nonaggressive, interested in the needs of others, and not easily upset (Hartup, 1970). Teachers can help to foster friendships in many ways, such as by helping children to initiate conversations to others, helping them to learn about each other as persons, and helping them to support (reinforce) each other.

Again, almost all of the principles developed in this text so far have been aimed at providing a basis for structuring classrooms so that all children can learn that they are competent and liked.

Having a sense of trust, autonomy, initiative, and industry the young adult is ready to face the decisions of adolescence in planning for adulthood.

5. Adolescence: Identity versus Role Diffusion (Confusion)

A sense of personal identity comes with charting a course for your own life. "Who am I?" is answered in part through the question "What do I want to become?" Adolescents search for people and ideas they can have faith in to help chart a life course. The identity crisis is complicated by a rapidly changing body that comes with the growth spurt and sexual maturity. Identity crises deal with such questions as: "Am I lovable?", "Am I a child or adult?", "Do I want to become a parent?", "Can I make it in college?", "How will I earn a living?", "What do I believe?" This period of development is further complicated by the loss of egocentrism (I am the center of the universe) and the perception of the "smallness" of *me* in the world and the smallness of the world in the universe. But then, there can be a beautiful magnificence to this realization also.

Early and late maturers. In Chapter 21 you learned about the wide range of variation in completion of puberty. Early maturation has certain advantages for boys. There is a physical advantage in athletic competition. Early-maturing boys tend to be more popular and become leaders. Later-maturing boys sometimes benefit by focusing on academic successes. For girls, early maturity may be a problem, because the early-maturing girl is likely to be out of step with her friends just when she wants to "be like the rest." Later-maturing girls have the advantages of: (1) taking more time to adjust to the changes going on, and (2) more likely maturing in step with the boys.

With sexual maturity comes increased sexual behavior. Rosen and Hall (1983) report that today about 60 percent of teenagers (unmarried) have sexual relations before they are age nineteen. This may lead to emotional problems for those involved and their friends, as well as the problems pregnancy can create. Teenage pregnancies are a growing problem.

Teachers and counselors can play very important roles in helping adolescents chart their course through troubled waters toward their futures. The failure to solve the crises of adolescence can lead to a prolonged period of dependence on others, a personal sense of confusion, and much worse.

6.–8. Erikson's Later Stages

The crises of adulthood have to do with the quality of interpersonal relations—intimacy-isolation, generativity-stagnation, and integrity-despair. Intimacy refers to how you relate to others (not necessarily sexually), generativity refers to caring for the next generation, and integrity implies a full acceptance of what you are and have been without regrets. These are important aspects of personal development, deserving much more attention than this text can afford to give them.

MORAL DEVELOPMENT

Social Roles and Rules

Much of the learning that goes on in Erikson's stages 3, 4, and 5 is concerned with what sociologists call social roles and societal rules. Socialization involves learning the rules governing the roles appropriate to various positions in society. Rules can be very general so that they apply to nearly all people, such as the rule against killing. Rules can also be general so that they apply to most situations, for example, "Be fair." Some rules apply only to some people—"You have to be over eighteen to drink alcoholic beverages." Rules can be very situational—"You can shout at the football game, but not in church." Some rules are permissive—"Fathers are expected to play with their children, but are not required to do so."

The roles we enter into are sometimes ascribed (imposed) and sometimes achieved (earned). The role of a school-child is ascribed for the six year old. Age and sex roles are also ascribed. You cannot choose to be an age or sex other than what you are (at least, most of us cannot). Achieved roles are chosen and usually earned. Being a doctor, a quarterback, or a teacher are achieved roles. A role is defined by the rules that govern the behavior of the person in the role.

Chapter 24 will look at some findings and issues relating to sex roles. This chapter explores some issues in the learning of rules related to moral development—learning to be a responsible member of society. Being responsible involves learning the rules for various roles (or principles that cut across roles), *as well as being motivated* to follow the rules. A prominent stage conception of the development of moral thought is that developed by Lawrence Kohlberg (1963, 1964). Kohlberg analyses are based on the *reasons* children and young adults give for choices when faced with moral dilemmas.

Kohlberg's Stages of Moral Thought

Using a Piagetian approach, Kohlberg studied stages in the development of thinking about moral issues by presenting students of various ages with a variety of moral dilemmas with themes like these:

- Should Bill tell his father that his brother did something wrong?
- Should a husband steal an expensive drug needed to save the life of his wife?
- A terminally ill patient requests to die because of severe pain. Should the doctor perform a mercy killing?

In his analysis, Kohlberg breaks the development of moral thought into three levels and then describes two stages within each level:

Level 1. Preconventional. The child looks at the pleasure-pain aspect what will happen to him or her.

Stage 1. The child obeys because of a *fear of punishment.*

Stage 2. The child follows a principle of *reciprocity.* "If I do this for him, he'll do that for me."

Level 2. Conventional. Morality based on loyalty to family, group, and nation. Conventional rules are respected.

Stage 3. Good behavior occurs *to please others* or to help others—the "good-girl" or "good-boy."

Stage 4. *Law and order* is valued. There is a need to do one's duty.

Level 3. Postconventional. Moral judgment is based on principles apart from authority or loyalty to the group.

Stage 5. Rules are based on *social agreement* on what is good for the group. Rules can be changed for good reasons.

Stage 6. Moral decisions are based on *self-chosen universal ethical principles* such as justice, equality, the Golden Rule, and the dignity of the individual. (Adapted from Kohlberg, 1975, p. 171).

At Level 1, the child is influenced by what will happen to himself or herself. At Level 2, there is an appeal to laws of church or state. At Level 3, it is the underlying personal values that influence decision making.

The percentage of moral statements classified at each stage for children aged 7, 10, 13, 16 is as follows (Kohlberg, 1964). The 7 year olds give mostly Level 1 interpretations of moral dilemmas. The 10 year olds give about 55 percent Level 1 and 35 percent Level 2 interpretations. The 13 year olds give 25 percent Level 1, 55 percent Level 2, and 15 Level 3 interpretations. Finally, the 16 year olds give 15 percent Level 1, 60 percent Level 2, and 25 percent Level 3. The understanding of moral principles obviously comes slowly. The highest levels probably require the ability to use formal operations and are not reached by many.

Moral behavior appears to develop far ahead of advanced levels of *moral judgment*. Children can learn to act responsibly through modeling and direct tuition long before they have an abstract understanding of moral principles. Actual correlations of level of moral judgment (based on Kohlberg's tests) and moral conduct *based on teachers' ratings* range from .30 to .50 (Kohlberg, 1964).

Classroom Discussions of Moral Dilemmas

Kohlberg (1973, 1975) has built an approach to moral education around the discussion of moral dilemmas. Teachers do not make judgments or state their values, but they foster discussion and help students clarify their ideas. Since there is range of stages in any classroom, exposing lower-stage children to higher-stage reasons can help lower-stage children advance in their thinking. The students also participate in decisions on making classroom rules and determining consequences for violating the rules.

Parent-Child Studies

While teachers all have important roles to play, moral development is to a large extent the responsibility of parents. Studies with parents (Hoffman, 1979) show that children are more likely to adopt parental moral standards if:

- Parents maintain *close affectional relations* with their children. Affection is important because it keeps the child oriented to the parents and, thus, receptive to discipline.

- Parents use *love-oriented* and *inductive* method of discipline. Love-oriented procedures praise examples of moral behavior, use time out, and loss of privileges rather than physical punishment and threats. Inductive discipline involves pointing out how what the child is doing can hurt others (including mom and dad). This kind of reasoning provides verbal cues that can help the child "think of how another feels" in similar situations in the future. Children of parents who use more power-assertive punishment techniques (spanking, scolding, threatening) are more likely to behave only if they are afraid of getting caught rather than because of a concern for others.

- Parents provide models of prosocial moral behavior, and express feelings and talk about empathetic concern for others.

The reader should note that these same recommendations could be derived from the discussion in Chapters 3 to 5 of effective procedures for strengthening and weakening behavior.

Tenth grade students rated low on responsibility by teachers rate their parents as rejecting, neglecting, and unaffectionate. Firm discipline by fathers is related to low responsibility for girls, but lack of firm discipline relates to low responsibility for boys (Bronfenbrenner, 1961). Many studies have shown that girls are more readily socialized than boys (as well as being kept closer to parents). The danger for girls appears to be oversocialization, producing inhibited-passive behavior. The risk is the opposite for boys. Delinquent, noncompliant, and aggressive boys tend to come from homes where parents are hostile, model aggressive behavior, and are lax and neglecting in discipline

(Becker, 1964; Martin, 1975). Highly compliant children tend to come from homes where parents are warm, but restrictive.

RESPONSIBILITY, THE FOURTH R—THE MODESTO PLAN

A personal note. I intended to continue this chapter this day by discussing a program called "Responsibility, the Fourth R". To my surprise, my local newspaper (The Register Guard) featured on the front page an article credited to the *Washington Post* entitled "Report cites school failures—character development 'ignored.' " The article described the conclusions developed by twenty-seven professors and school superintendents on the failing role of schools in fostering moral development in children. The report was edited by Edward Wynne, an education professor at University of Illinois at Chicago, and was titled "Developing Character: Transmitting Knowledge." Among the signers was Urie Bronfenbrenner, the famous developmental psychologist from Cornell who played a major role in the development of Head Start. The coincidence was just too much, I had just referenced Bronfenbrenner in the previous paragraph. I had written the title for this section when I stopped last night. The article reinforced my resolve to write what I had planned to write in this section. I did have doubts, because it sounds like a conservative position, and I am a liberal on social issues. But noting that the signers of the report included both liberals and conservatives, I decided the issue was one that should concern all of us.

The basic message of the report was this:

Many schools have failed to develop important aspect of character such as cooperation, persistence, and moral integrity—aspects of social behavior important to individual success and community well-being. In the past two decades, academic performance has declined and youth have developed serious problems as seen in "soaring rates of teenage suicides, homicides, and out-of-wedlock births."

Among other things, the report recommends that schools provide more emphasis on academic team-competitions (to foster cooperation while striving for *academic* competence), make students more responsible for discipline and school upkeep, foster more community service projects, and use more "ceremonial activities" (assemblies or class festivities) that emphasize important social values.

In the rest of this chapter, I describe a plan for improving student responsibility and academic excellence that has worked.

Learning to be responsible involves learning to avoid immediate reinforcers that can be harmful in favor of reinforcers a person has to work and wait for. It involves learning to understand how a person's behavior affects others and being empathetic for the feelings of others. It also involves learning the potential consequences of violating the rules. A lot of this learning is knowledge learning and a lot of it involves getting more experience working with others in potentially conflicting situations. Most of the procedures for strengthening, weakening, and maintaining behavior discussed earlier can be readily applied to moral education.

In Modesto in 1976, a whole school district of 20,000 students, their administrators, students, and community agencies, set about to become more responsible and to improved social and academic standards through making everyone *accountable* for what was expected of them. The school set up a plan to hold students accountable to certain standards, and the town of Modesto would hold the public schools and *itself* accountable for how the students measured up.

The Modesto story began in 1975 when James Enochs was promoted from high-school principal to assistant superintendent in charge of curriculum. At the time, Modesto was a comfortable, largely middle-class, community surrounded by fruit farms. There were not a lot of "pressing problems" in the schools when Enochs took over. However, Modesto was a rapidly growing community, reaching 150,000 in population by mid-1980. In the recession of the early 1980s, Modesto had over 20 percent unemployed (second highest in the nation). In terms of the percentage of students from welfare homes, Modesto was at the 82nd percentile in comparison to other cities in California. There is a large and increasing number of limited and non-English speaking students. The socioeconomic index for Modesto (based on how people make a living) placed Modesto at the 34th percentile in the state.

James Enochs began his new job by examining what was happening in schools across the country—declining achievement scores, rising conflict, rising truancy, rising vandalism, and declining public support for schools that were not doing their jobs. He strongly suspected these problems would also increase in Modesto. At the center of the problem, as James Enochs analyzed it, was the failure by educators to be professionally responsible. Standards were relaxed in the name of innovation and relevancy. Flexibility of program and student choice were the highest virtues. As Enochs eventually wrote:

> First we relaxed our standards and then abolished them completely. We began to feel guilty and proceeded to pull up our roots and examine them for rot. Homework, honest grading, demanding courses, required courses, earned promotion—up they went and out they went. We leveled the field so that all could pass through without labor or frustration . . . . To be sure we had our share of accomplices . . . pop psychologists who convinced us that grades were responsible for everything from bed-wetting to the military/industrial complex; social engineers who turned schools into battering rams for their latest experiments; and innovation hustlers with hardware, software and a copy of the latest Elementary-Secondary Act funding proposal . . .
>
> But there was an even more appealing element in their siren call, a kind of hidden melody that we could never publicly acknowledge: It was all simply easier that way. If there were no standardized bench marks against which to be measured, there was no accountability. The tough, time-consuming process of monitoring—teachers monitoring students, principals monitoring teachers, superintendents monitoring principals—was lifted from our shoulders. There were fewer decisions to be made, judgments to be weighed, and stands to be taken. *Yes* is always easier to say than *no*. Something called the "affective domain" became the cloak of decency for lazy teachers and administrators. It was easier to make students feel good than to hold them accountable to the rigors of learning (Enochs, 1979, pp. 7-8).

Having identified the problem, Enochs, being the unusual leader he is, set about *doing something about it.* He began with a set of principles that he asked the school board to adopt as school policy. Central to these principles is what Enochs calls "the world's best kept secret—"Children want adults to be adults." Enochs figured if he could not get his principles accepted by the school board, he surely would have difficulty getting the details of his "radical" changes accepted. The principles were (from Enoch's, 1979, pp. 19-24):

1. It is essential that a public institution clearly define itself; to say unequivocally what it believes in and stands for. . . .

2. The development of responsible adults is a task requiring community involvement. It cannot be left solely to the public schools. . . .

3. The principal tasks of the public schools cannot be achieved if a disproportionate amount of time and resources must be given to maintaining order. . . .

4. Parents must consistently support the proposition that students have responsibilities as well as rights, and the schools have an obligation to insist upon both. . . .

5. High performance takes place in a framework of [high] expectations. . . .

6. The full responsibility for learning cannot be transferred from the student to the teacher. . . .

7. There is nothing inherently undemocratic in *requiring* students to do things that are demonstrably beneficial to them. . . .

8. In order for a program to succeed, it must be maintained for a reasonable period of time and be assured of continued support (Enochs, 1979, pp. 19-24).

The board accepted his principles and Enochs set about developing programs to implement them. Even though the current problems in Modesto were most evident at the high schools, programs were developed at every level because it is at the lower levels that the problems get started. Enochs wanted to see every student coming into high school understanding standards and responsibility. Table 22.1 outlines the component programs that Enochs helped develop to implement the eight principles.

Table 22-1 Modesto city schools program components: Academic expectations and the fourth R—Responsibility

I. *Academic Expectations:*
   - A. Basic Skills Program, K-8
   - B. "Help Yourself" Home-School Program, K-8
   - C. High School Specialization Diploma, 9-12
   - D. Competency-Based High School Graduation, 9-12
   - E. "Excellence Is a Community Affair"—Student Recognition Program, K-12
   - F. Title I: Direct Instruction Staff Development Center
   - G. Writing Assessment Program

II. *The Fourth R: Responsibility:*
   - A. Character Education, K-6
   - B. Written Conduct Codes, K-6; 7-12
   - C. Citizenship Accountability, 7-12
   - D. Community Consortium, K-12
   - E. A.C.T.—Active Control of Truancy, K-12
   - F. "Excellence Is a Community Affair"—Student Recognition Program, K-12

Academic Expectations

Many behavior problems in schools begin with academic failure. So any meaningful approach to responsibility training in schools must start with the schools being responsible by ensuring that all students have the opportunity to be academically successful.

Basic skills program, K-8. For each grade, minimum competencies were identified, and stated in terms of specific, testable, knowledge, and skills. Testing occurs at mid-year, and those below grade are required to pass an end-of-year test to be promoted. Exceptions are made only where the teacher provides clear evidence, based on classroom work, that the student knows the skills. On the wall across from James Enochs' desk are thirteen large posters outlining the basic skill requirements that his staff helped to develop.

"Help yourself" home-school program, K-8. This is a required program for students with deficiencies. Daily homework is provided in special packets tailored to the individual student's needs. Parents either provide quiet study time or work with the student and sign off each day that the work was done at home. Parents can receive training at school on how best to help. The packets are prepared and checked by one paraprofessional in each Title 1 school following instructions from each teacher. Non-Title 1 schools sometimes share a paraprofessional among several schools.

High school specialization diploma, 9-12. With parent and counselor guidance, students select one of three high school plans: *academic* (college preparatory), *vocational* (prepares for employment in business or industry), or *general* (for students not ready to decide on either of the first two choices—prepares them to enter community college).

Competency-based high school graduation, 9-12. Criterion-referenced tests are given in English (reading and writing), math, social studies, science, and health. All tests have to be passed to get a diploma. Tests are taken during the junior year. If failed, remedial courses must be taken and the tests retaken.

"Excellence is a community affair"–student recognition program, K-12. Academic achievement is given recognition and awards in cooperation with the community. Separate programs were developed for elementary, junior high, and high school. Business people and professionals sponsor competitions, provide awards and cash prizes for excellence, and serve on panels selecting winners. The prize categories range from creative writing to homemaking skills, as well as grade-point average. A "blue book" is printed listing seniors and their capabilities. This is distributed to local employers.

Title 1: Direct Instruction staff development center. Some federal funds were used to train principals and teachers. Principals are expected to become "curriculum leaders who know good teaching when they see it and tolerate nothing less." Over 250 teachers were trained to use DISTAR in their classes. Enochs believed the Follow Through data and implemented Direct Instruction with lower-performing students. Enochs holds the principals accountable by evaluating them in terms of the performance improvement of the students in their schools.

Writing assessment program. Beginning in fourth grade, writing skills are assessed for minimum competencies at each grade level. Teachers were trained in economical ways of assessing mechanics and content. Teachers file quarterly reports with their principals on the frequency of writing assignments. The principals report to Enochs, who has often taken piles of assignments home to read. Teachers get back comments from Enochs.

The Fourth R: Responsibility

Character education, K-6. This program takes about 30 minutes of class time 3 days a week. The program attempts to emphasize commonly held values such as courage and conviction, generosity and kindness, honesty, tolerance, good use of time and talents, and so forth.

Written conduct codes, K-6, 7-12. These booklets are distributed to all students. Parents are required to sign a note that they have received the booklets. The codes define students rights and responsibilities, acceptable student behavior, and the actions that will be taken for violations. Repeated offenders are expelled so that students do realize there are limits beyond which they are not welcome in the school community.

Citizenship accountability, 7-12. Students receive a quarterly mark for being on time, meeting deadlines, and coming to class on time. If a student receives two or more unsatisfactory marks, student privileges (athletics, student government, school clubs, etc.) are lost until the marks are improved in a future quarter.

Community consortium, K-12. The school district established regular meetings between school administrators and representatives of probation, mental health, welfare, police, juvenile court, and other agencies. The committee seeks to promote cooperation and reduce conflicts between the agencies with the goal of providing more effective services to students in need.

Active control of truancy, (ACT) K-12. This program is designed to make coming to school more enjoyable than being truant. It is a cooperative program between local police, the schools, and merchants. Students found on the streets during morning school hours without a legitimate excuse are brought to a central "drop center" where staff are available to notify the schools and parents. Parents are called and must pick up their child and deliver him or her to school. Operators of soda fountains and amusement parlors agreed to post signs stating that students were not welcome there during school time. Since most truants are left walking the streets, it is easier for the police to do their part. Parents are involved in resolving truancy cases and legal steps are taken if needed to enforce the state laws. Students are expelled for the remainder of the semester if they are truant 8 times. Parents must petition for readmission the following semester. Enochs reports that *students did not want to be expelled* (many claim that expelling students is just giving them what they want). "Our experience is that they plead with us not to expel them." They all petition for readmission and many give up truancy. The community was initially "lukewarm" to the police picking up truants until Enochs demonstrated a significant drop in daytime crime as a result of the program.

"Excellence is a community affair"–student recognition program, K-12. This program is like the one described earlier for academic honors. Recognition and awards are given to students for citizenship, community and school service, for performance in the Character Education Program, and so on. Responsibility is given recognition as well as achievement.

Some Implementation Problems

These programs provide the school system and the community with a system of mutual accountability. They specify what is expected, what happens if students meet the standards or do not, and provide for report systems so all can see what is happening.

In summarizing some of the problems he has had, Enochs notes that implementation has "more phases than the moon":

> First phase: staff cynicism (which increases as you move up the grade levels) and student disbelief that you mean it or have the courage to enforce it (which also increases as you move up the grade levels).
>
> Second phase: business-as-usual until the consequences come crashing down. For example: the first quarter of the citizenship program, forty percent of the students had unsatisfactory citizenship [and lost extra-curricular privileges]. 56 percent of the ninth graders failed the math competency test the first year.
>
> Third phase: panic! We can't retain all those kids. We can't expel all those truants. We can't remove all those fullbacks, song leaders, first trumpeters, commencement participants. It sounds like the Wailing Wall in Jerusalem.
>
> Fourth phase (almost indistinguishable from the third): retribution and retreat. It's easier to junk the program and "can" the assistant superintendent who got us into this mess.
>
> Fifth phase: remind the board of how it was before, their unanimous commitment to the principles (especially the one about leaving it in place despite periodic criticism), and their rhetoric about excellence. Assure them that if they ride it out, the kids will shape up and they'll be heroes. The No Guts, No Glory argument again.
>
> Sixth phase: you get a split vote [but are supported], and the kids get the message that the adults are going to act like adults this time.
>
> Seventh phase: the results begin to change dramatically, the program is no longer an orphan (or the illegitimate offspring of the assistant superintendent), the media start saying nice things, and you get a lot of fat consulting fees for workshops. (Enochs, 1981).

While the students and teachers expressed early doubts, the parents have remained silent but for two events. First, early in the program, 20 athletes lost privileges because of poor citizenship grades. The board stood firm in the face of the protest of the parents. The second protest occurred when 5 percent the first graduating class failed one or more the competency tests twice. This meant that they could not graduate. The board made an exception in this case, allowing them to take the test for a third time (two-thirds still failed).

Some Outcome Data

The most important part of this story can be found in the changes in student performance. Table 22.2 shows some of the statistical outcomes. Within three years, the percent of high school students failing minimum competency in math dropped from 56 percent to 4 percent, in reading from 12 percent to 3 percent and in writing from 21 percent to 7 percent. These are truly remarkable changes. Unsatisfactory marks in citizenship dropped from 40 percent to 20 percent.

Table 22-2 Changes in competencies, citizenship, and truancy before and after introduction of the fourth R at Modesto High School

Minimum Competencies: Percent of Failures			
Year	Math	Reading	Writing
1977-78	56%	12%	21%
1978-79	15%	3%	13%
1979-80	4%	3%	7%
Citizenship: Percent of Unsatisfactories			
1st Quarter			40%
2nd Quarter			35%
3rd Quarter			25%
4th and Subsequent Quarters			18-21%
Truancy: Percent of Unexcused Absences			
1975-75 (before 4th R)			4.5%
1976-77			4.0%
1977-78			3.5%
1978-79			2.5%
1980-81 (5 months)			1.5%
1982-83			1.9%

Table 22-3 Non-academic gain since adoption of academic expectations and the **Fourth R—Responsibility**

	1975-76 (Pre-4th R)	1982-83	Gain or Loss
Vandalism	$75,890.00	*$52,532.55 *(Not adjusted for inflation)	−$23,357.45
	1975-76 (Pre-4th R)	1982-83	Gain or Loss
Average Daily Attendance			
Elementary (K-8)*	97.5%	99.2%	+1.7
High School (9-12)	95.5%	98.1%	+2.6
District (K-12)	96.5%	98.5% *(K-6: 99.43%)	+2.0
Unexcused Absences Lost ADA			
Elementary (K-8)	35,899 days	17,654 days	−19,235
High School (9-12)	60,214 days	25,211 days	−35,003
District (K-12)	97,103 days	42,865 days	−54,238
Dollar Savings ADA			
Elementary (K-8)	19,235 days @ $ 9.54	=	$183,501.90
High School (9-12)	35,003 days @ $11.38	=	398,334.14
District (K-12)			$581,836.04

Table 22-4 Academic gains since adoption of academic expectations and the Fourth R—Responsibility

California Assessment Program (California Norms)	1975-76 (Pre-4th R)	1982-83	Gain or Loss
Grade 3			
Reading	47%ile (A)*	68%ile (A)	+21%
Written Language	Not Tested	66%ile (A)	
Mathematics	Not Tested	76%ile (A)	
Grade 6			
Reading	39%ile (W)	59%ile (A)	+20%
Writing	38%ile (B)	60%ile (A)	+22%
Spelling	40%ile (B)	80%ile (A)	+40%
Mathematics	41%ile (W)	80%ile (A)	+39%
Grade 12			
Reading	47%ile (W)	73%ile (A)	+26%
Writing	46%ile (W)	62%ile (A)	+16%
Spelling	38%ile (B)	78%ile (A)	+40%
Mathematics	44%ile (W)	69%ile (A)	+25%

*Modesto scores are compared with scores of districts in California which, statistically, are like Modesto.

(A) = Above comparison score band
(W) = Within comparison score band
(B) = Below comparison score band

Standardized Achievement Tests:
Comprehensive Test of Basic Skills

Percent of Students at or Above Grade Level

	1975-76 (Pre-4th R)	*1982-83*	*Gain or Loss*
Grade 3			
Reading	56%	83%	+27%
Mathematics	58%	83%	+25%
Grade 4			
Reading	50%	73%	+23%
Mathematics	48%	79%	+31%
Grade 5			
Reading	54%	76%	+22%
Mathematics	50%	83%	+33%
Grade 6			
Reading	52%	78%	+26%
Mathematics	50%	84%	+34%

College Admissions Testing

Scholastic Aptitude Test		1982-83	
Verbal	432	456	+24 points
Mathematics	482	514	+32 points
National Mean			
Verbal		425	
Mathematics		468	

Unexcused absences at the high school dropped from 4.5 percent to 1.9 percent. Table 22.3 shows attendance and vandalism data before and after The Fourth R for all grades. It also shows dollar savings. School districts in California get state monies according to daily attendance figures. The increases in daily attendance for 1982-83 alone meant an additional $581,836. That could buy a lot of books! Table 22.3 also shows the one-year savings in reduced vandalism ($23,357.45). Again, an impressive figure. While all of these figures give evidence to the effectiveness of the program, most impressive are the achievement gains shown in Table 22.4.

Table 22.4 shows statewide and national normative comparisons on achievement tests for reading, writing, spelling, and mathematics. The statewide comparisons also are evaluated relative to other communities similar to Modesto in socioeconomic make up. Before The Fourth R program, Modesto was below other cities like it in spelling and writing, ahead in third grade reading, and equal in other areas. By 1982-83, Modesto was above other districts like it *on all tests.* The percentile gains ranged from 16 to 40. Most of these gains are about one-half standard score unit, which is indeed impressive.

The data for the Comprehensive Test of Basic Skills (CTBS) show similar progress at grades three, four, five, and six in reading and math. In standard score units, the gains average .75 to 1 standard score. Gains of .25 standard score unit were made on the Scholastic Aptitude Test on both verbal and mathematics scores. Data since 1980 shows continued progress, even after raising the standards for both behavior and academics.

The Modesto Plan has much in it that deserves careful thought if you are into planning ways to increase responsible, moral behavior in schools, as well as academic competence. The plan offers a proven solution to the "school failures in character development" bemoaned in my morning newspaper. It is very possible that the academic decline of the past twenty years, as Enochs suggests, were due to educators pushing too much responsibility onto children.

It is possible (as of 1985) to get a menu of booklets developed to support the Fourth R plan. The listing tells what is available and what they cost. One can order parts of the program or all of it. For a listing write to James Enochs, Modesto City Schools, 426 Locust Street, Modesto, CA 95351-2699.

SUMMARY

Personal and social development is a complex process. This chapter looked at one "grand approach" to conceptualizing such development. It also examined how parent behavior enters in, Kohlberg's theory of the development of moral thinking, and the specific plan used by one school district to foster competence and responsibility.

Erikson's stage theory was used to sketch out the kinds of progressive problems humans face in developing from birth to maturity. Briefly, Erikson's stages are:

1. Infancy:	Trust versus Mistrust
2. Early Childhood:	Autonomy versus Shame and Doubt
3. Preschool Age:	Initiative versus Guilt
4. Elementary and Middle-School	Industry versus Inferiority
5. Adolescence:	Identity versus Role Diffusion (confusion)
6. Young Adulthood:	Intimacy versus Isolation
7. Adulthood:	Generativity versus Stagnation
8. Old Age:	Integrity versus Despair

In the early years, good personal-social development is associated with warm care from parents, who remain a secure base from which the young person can venture out to explore the nearby world. Through modeling, differential reinforcement, and other forms of tuition, the young child learns rules and appropriate behavior for his or her expanding social roles and these are practiced in play and through being a "helper" to those who are older. The school years can teach some of the benefits of being a "hard worker." There is also the possibility of learning about failure and inferiority. Learning to be a friend is also an important social task in the early school years.

With adolescence comes the problems of a changing physical form, the development of sexual maturity, and the task of deciding about longer-term life goals. It can be a difficult time for many students. Identity crises can be very real and upsetting. Loves won and lost are very weighty matters. Physical appearance can be an asset or a heavy burden. Early maturing boys seem to have advantages in athletics and in "keeping up with the girls" who tend to mature two years earlier (on the average). Early maturing girls sometimes have problems of being much bigger than their age-mates.

In the adult years, the personal-social issues for Erikson center around the quality of personal relationships, while living a productive life and helping the next generation to develop.

It was noted that much of the learning that goes on in Erikson's stages 3, 4, and 5, is concerned with learning rules and behavior appropriate for the various social roles children are playing and will take on in the future. Critical to what society views as "moral character" is learning to follow rules aimed at protecting the best, long-term interests of the group as well as the individual. Kohlberg's stages of moral thinking is one approach to the analysis of developmental processes in this area.

By studying responses to moral dilemmas, Kohlberg was able to describe the development of moral concepts as progressing through three levels: the preconventional, the conventional, and the postconventional. In the preconventional stage, the point of view is egocentric. One behaves out of fear of punishment or hope of a favor in return. In the conventional stage, one behaves to please others or because law and order is valued. In the postconventional stage, one behaves because society has agreed to rules to protect each other (an enlightened self-interest) or because one believes in some set of universal ethical principles such as truth and justice.

About 55 percent of ten year olds are at preconventional level, about 55 percent of the thirteen year olds are at the conventional level. And, while a quarter of sixteen year olds reach the postconventional level, 60 percent are still at the conventional level. Fortunately, moral behavior develops far ahead of moral judgment. Most children and young adults learn how to act responsibly long before they can verbalize about moral principles.

Studies of parent child-rearing practices have identified child-rearing approaches most likely to be associated with children adopting their parents' moral standards. Children are found to be more mature and responsible when their parents maintain an affectional relationship, provide good models of moral behavior, use disciplinary methods that involve time out and loss of privileges rather than power-assertion, use praise for appropriate behavior, and point out how the misbehavior can hurt others. Where spanking, scolding, and threatening are used to control children, they are likely to behave because they are afraid of getting caught, not because it might hurt others. Delinquent, aggressive boys tend to come from parents who model aggression in their discipline, but are neglecting in their enforcement. Compliant (conventional?) children tend to have warm, restrictive parents.

In the second half of the chapter we examined the way in which one school district developed a systematic approach to building academic excellence and responsibility at the same time. The program developed by James Enochs was aimed as letting students know what responsibilities they had to meet in citizenship and in academics, and the benefits and costs of meeting them or not. Enochs believes that schools went too far in the sixties and early seventies in removing standards and requirements from school programs. Student choice was made the guidepost. The effect was a continual decline in scholarship, and rising conflict, vandalism, and truancy. Professional educators were no longer behaving as professionals and using their best judgment about what was best *in the long run* for their students.

Enochs's program began with eight principles:

1. The schools should say what they stand for.
2. The community has to be involved in moral training.
3. Schools cannot get their tasks done if a lot of time is wasted on maintaining order.
4. Schools and parents, together, need to insist that students have responsibilities as well as rights.
5. High standards promote high performance when backed with appropriate consequences.
6. The student must assume some of the responsibility for learning.
7. Adults should require students to do things that will benefit them.
8. To succeed, a new program must be given a chance over time.

The programs for academic excellence included: A basic skills program (K-8), a "help yourself" home program, choice of three high school diplomas (college preparatory, vocational, junior college preparatory), required passing of five competency tests for graduation, involved the community in reinforcing excellence, brought Direct Instruction in for use with lower performers, and established a writing assessment program. The programs to promote responsibility included: a character education program (K-6), written conduct codes, citizenship grading (7-12) with loss of extracurricular activities for two or more "unsatisfactory" grades, coordination of community resources, a program to control truancy, and community recognition for excellence in citizenship and service.

While many felt the program could not be implemented and would not work, it was and it did. Performance on competency tests rose rapidly, achievement test scores rose .25 to .50 standard deviations. Citizenship grades improved rapidly. Unexcused absences dropped from 4.5 percent to 1.9 percent. The gain in state funds based on attendance in 1982-83 alone was $580,000. Vandalism dropped by 50 percent.

The Modesto Plan for improving academic excellence and student responsibility is highly successful and deserving of your consideration.

CHAPTER

23

UNDERSTANDING SOCIAL BEHAVIOR PROBLEMS

This chapter examines some problems in social behavior problems that are often considered to define a personality (for example, aggressive, withdrawn, anxious). The goal is to illustrate how the learning principles developed in the earlier chapters apply to such problems and to extend your understanding of personal and social development. There are two major classes of social behavior problems—those where the focus of the problem lies external to the person and those where the focus is internal. When the problem is externalized, it is called a *conduct problem* (aggression, truancy, stealing, cheating). When the problem is internalized, it is called a *personality problem* (fears, dependence, withdrawal). Keep in mind, however, that these are just convenient labels for classes of social behavior.

PERSONALITY PROBLEMS

The Learning of Fears

Chapter 2 introduced the distinction between operant and respondent behavior. Ever since then, this text has mostly dealt with operant behavior, although recognizing that the respondents called emotional reactions are likely to be present whenever reinforcing and punishing stimuli are used. Stimuli capable of eliciting respondent behavior—such as a loud noise, being slapped on the face, or food in the mouth—can also be conditioned to neutral stimuli associated with them. Children can learn fears that are realistic (fear of a barking dog who might bite you) or unrealistic (fear of leaving momma to go to school).

John Watson and Rosalie Rayner provided the first demonstration of the conditioning of a fear in an eleven month old infant named Albert (Watson and Rayner, 1920). The first step was to demonstrate that a loud noise (a hammer striking a steel bar near the child's head) produced a fear reaction consisting of jumping or puckering his lips, trembling, and violent crying. They also determined that showing the child a white rat produced no reaction. Next the presentation of the white rat was closely followed by the loud noise. After a couple of pairings, the eight-month-old boy was found to cry in terror and tremble in the presence of the white rat.

In this example, the fearful response of the child to the white rat was conditioned by following the presentation of the white rat with a loud noise. After a few pairings of this sort, the white rat alone came to elicit the fearful response without the loud noise. The child had been taught to be afraid of the white rat. Feelings of love, sexual attraction, appetites, hate, disgust, and sadness may be conditioned in a similar way.

Figure 23.1 reviews the model of respondent conditioning discussed earlier. In stage 1, a neutral stimulus S_1 occurs; then unconditioned stimulus S_2 occurs and elicits the respondent. In stage 2, the formerly neutral stimulus (now the conditioned stimulus) directly elicits the respondent.

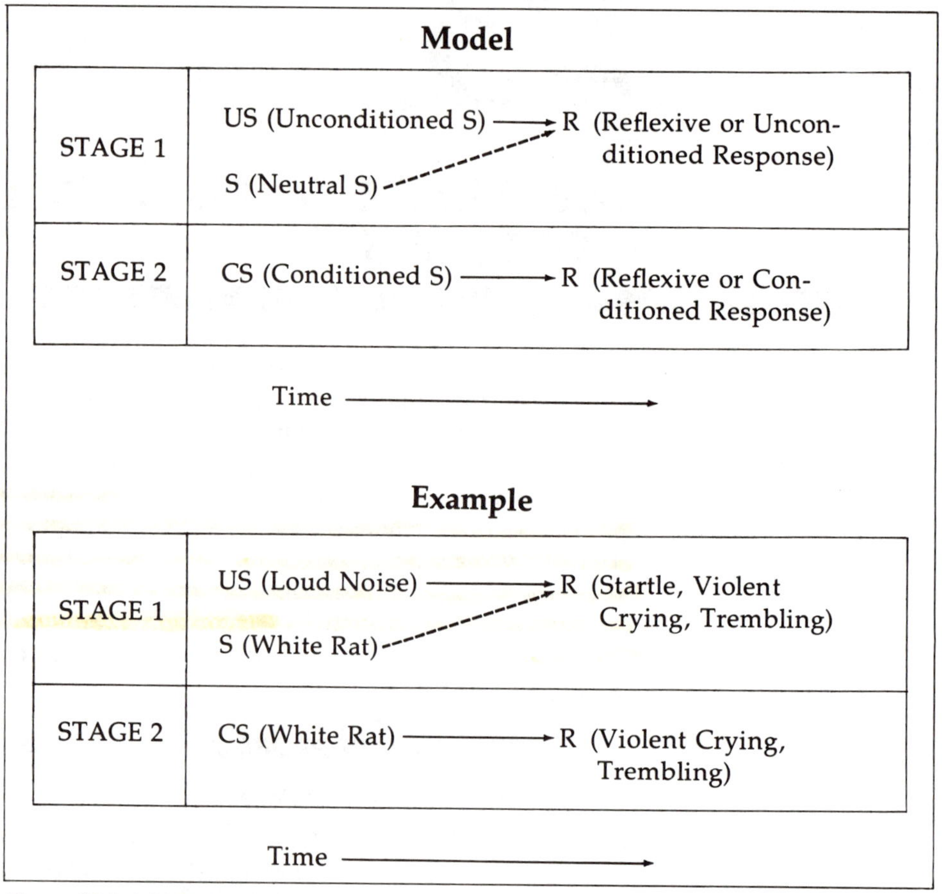

Figure 23-1 *A Model of respondent conditioning*

Ways to Eliminate Fears

Teachers work primarily at strengthening operant behavior. If teaching is carried out in a way that emphasizes reinforcement, success, and competence, there is little need to worry about the affective or emotional development of students. They will be taught positive attitudes and feelings at the same time they are taught learning tasks. The effective use of reinforcers will automatically eliminate negative attitudes and feelings *and* build positive attitudes and feelings. There are times, however, in dealing with emotional problems such as fear, when knowledge of the principles of reflex conditioning can be useful.

Extinction. There are two ways in which the reaction to a conditioned stimulus can be changed. First, one can keep presenting the conditioned stimulus without pairing it with the unconditioned stimulus. The reflex reaction to the conditioned stimulus will slowly weaken. This process is called *extinction.* Note that the conditioned stimulus has to be presented; the mere passage of time is not enough to weaken the reflex reaction. To eliminate the fear of the white rat, the rat would be presented to the child many times, unaccompanied by the loud noise. Eventually, the presence of the rat would not be fearful to the child. The fear would be extinguished.

Extinction is probably the weakest procedure for getting rid of fears because it is possible for the frightened person to avoid attending to the fear-arousing stimulus. The procedures discussed next are more likely to be effective.

Counter-Conditioning. The second way to eliminate a reaction to a conditioned stimulus is to condition an incompatible reaction to the same stimulus. This is called *counter-conditioning.* Mary Jones (1924) described the procedures she found effective with a boy named Peter in eliminating a fear of a rabbit. The two methods of greatest value were showing him a number of other children playing with the rabbit, and gradually bringing the rabbit closer while Peter was being fed. In the first case, the rabbit was paired with the positive reactions of other children. In the second case, the rabbit was paired with an unconditioned stimulus—food. In both cases, a new positive reaction that was incompatible with the fearful reaction was associated with the conditioned stimulus, the rabbit.

For counter-conditioning to be effective, it is important to use procedures that keep the fearful reaction from occurring. In the above example, the rabbit was *gradually* brought closer to Peter. A conditioned stimulus at a distance does not elicit as strong a reaction as one that is close by. When the fear-arousing stimulus is presented in graded steps while positive unconditioned or conditioned stimuli are paired with it, the fearful reactions are less likely to occur, and the new reactions are more likely to be associated with the conditioned fear stimulus.

Reinforcing Approach Behavior. There is a third method for reducing fears that focusses on operant behavior.

If the teacher or parent reinforces closer and closer approaches to the feared stimulus, all the conditions are present for effective counter-conditioning of the fear. In other words, it is possible to change fears by changing the avoidance behavior (operants) that go with them rather than by focusing on the respondents. Avoidance behavior can be changed to approach behavior if the right reinforcement is given at the right time. As avoidance is being changed to approach, the fear is counter-conditioned.

Any problem involving emotional conditioning can usually be more clearly formulated and dealt with in terms of the related operant behavior. The reason for this is that the operant behavior can be observed and can provide clear feedback on the progress of the change program. Often respondents are not visible and, therefore, there is no way of knowing whether they are being changed.

Examples of Problems and Their Solutions

The following are documented case studies that illustrate a variety of change procedures used for fearful, dependent, and withdrawn children.

Karl Overcomes His Fear of School. Many children cry wildly when their mothers leave them at school. Usually, if they are left alone for a few minutes, the crying is quickly extinguished, and other responses take over. In some cases when the conditioning is very strong, or the reinforcement of crying and screaming has been high, other steps are required to eliminate the fearful reactions.

Patterson (1965a) described a procedure to overcome Karl's reluctance to stay at school. Karl was seven when he was brought to the University of Oregon Clinic on referral from the school nurse. In his first few days in first grade, he had shown a reluctance to stay at school. By the second week, he would stay only as long as his mother remained in the room. He had had similar troubles in nursery school and had always tried to accompany his mother when she left for home. Attempts to punish, bribe, and cajole failed to keep him in school.

In the first clinic session Karl did not want to go with the therapist. His teeth chattered; he clenched one fist and had a firm grip on his mother with the other. He was brought to the playroom with his mother. She sat by the door as the therapist set up a doll-play situation in which the doll, Henry, was being taken by his mother to see the doctor. After structuring the situation, the therapist would ask how Henry felt in the doctor's office without his mother, or what Henry was going to do. Karl was given candies if he said Henry was not afraid and showed "big boy" behavior. Mother was soon moved out of the playroom. Other situations were presented, such as Henry's mother leaving him at home while she went to the store, or his mother staying home while Henry walked toward school.

At the end of the first session, Karl's mother was encouraged to praise him for remaining in the playroom. She was also to encourage other independent behavior at home and report on it at the next session. Karl listened to this interchange with interest.

In the next eleven sessions, situations were presented in which Henry was slowly taken closer to school and eventually was staying there. Karl began expressing positive feelings about staying at school. He continued to receive candy. The fear-arousing stimuli were being associated with adult reactions and candy. At the time of session eleven, he made his first actual trip to school with his visiting teacher, who had been helping him at home with his reading. Over the next two weeks, he gradually stayed longer and longer in school, until finally he was staying all day by himself. He was given much praise for his bravery, and he soon announced that he would return to school full time, which he did.

Three months later, a follow-up showed a dramatic improvement in Karl's classroom adjustment—and no fearfulness.

Comments. Karl's fear of leaving his mother was eliminated by reinforcing closer and closer approximations to the desired behavior and verbalized feelings. This use of graded steps is another example of the principle of shaping described in Chapter 4. Note that the process began with imaginary situations involving Henry, a doll. The fear-arousing stimuli were psychologically kept at a distance at first, and then they were slowly brought closer and closer as Karl showed he could handle them.

Dependent Behavior. Karen, age six, would not get up, dress herself, and eat her breakfast in time for school unless her mother was nagging or helping every step of the way. Her mother reinforced her "help me" behavior in part because she thought that was what mothers were for and in part because she was afraid Karen would be late for school.

Since the tasks were ones Karen could do, the problem was handled by: (1) getting Karen an alarm clock and telling her she was responsible for getting ready for school; (2) stopping all nagging; and (3) praising her for her success.

Karen's teacher was informed about what was being done and was asked not to give her extra attention if she came late. Her mother kept records of her progress.

Karen was late for school six times in the first two weeks, but only once in the second two weeks. In the next six weeks, Karen left home a little late about once a week, but hurried to school on time. Her mother was pleased with the change in their relationship. She said, "This is now her problem, not mine. The whole situation is very much improved." Karen was very proud of herself on the days she left for school early, and she received praise for this.

Comments. When the parent or teacher continues to do things for a child after the child could be taught to do them for himself, the child is being reinforced for not growing up, for being dependent on adults. If the teacher views immature behavior as a sign of anxiety, insecurity, or slowed development, and then smothers the child showering such behavior with affection and attention, it is very likely to encourage the behavior.

Regressive Crawling. Francis Harris and colleagues illustrated how teachers inadvertently kept an undesired behavior going because of their misinterpretation of it. Mary was a three year old girl attending nursery school. Mary spent over 80 percent of her morning crawling like a baby. At first, her teachers thought she was showing regression because there was a new baby in her home. They tried to give Mary sympathetic attention, especially when she crawled. They would also suggest activities that required her to stand. None of this helped. When the teachers began to ignore the crawling and to give her constant attention when she was standing, normal behavior became predominant within a week. When the teachers went back to attending crawling, it quickly returned to an 80-percent level. Then, once again, reinforcement of standing and extinction of crawling corrected the situation. Within a week no special attention for standing was required because Mary was engaging in regular nursery school activities. (Harris, Johnston, Kelley, and Wolf, 1964).

An Adult-Oriented Child. Ann was four and from an upper-middle-class family. She reacted freely with adults but did not play with children. She was not withdrawn or frightened. As time went on, she spent more and more time just standing and looking. Often, she retired to a make-believe bed in the play yard to sleep for a few minutes. Less than 15 percent of her time was spent playing with peers. About 40 percent of her time was spent interacting with adults.

A program was devised to encourage more peer interaction. When Ann was alone, she was given no attention by the teacher. If she came to the teacher with another child, attention was given. If she came to the teacher alone, minimal attention was given. When Ann was playing with another child, the teacher would go to them and give them attention and play materials. For example, "You three girls have a cozy house. Here are some more cups, Ann, for your tea party." If Ann began to leave the group while the teacher was there, the teacher turned away from her and attended to the other children. During the six weeks of this program, Ann's playing with other children quickly increased to about 60 percent of the time, and interactions with adults dropped to under 20 percent. Isolated play dropped from about 45 percent to 20 percent of the time. Attention from adults was slowly faded out and the peer play continued on its own (Allen, Hart, Buell, Harris, and Wolf, 1964).

Clingy Behavior. Another frequent classroom problem is the child who has to be by his teacher's side all of the time. Like Ann, such children are adult-oriented, but they are not necessarily as verbal and engaging as Ann. There is a general rule about dependent behavior:

Children who show dependent behavior are reinforced by social reinforcers from adults (attention, affection, praise, nearness). These same

reinforcers can be used to strengthen independent behavior such as playing alone, exploring, playing with peers, learning skills, and working on tasks. The teacher suggests (prompts) small steps toward some independent activity, gives support to help the child take new steps on his own, and reinforces improvement. When the dependent behavior occurs, she appears to be busy with other things. "Big boy" and "big girl" behavior is praised and encouraged.

A Warning. When reinforcement for any behavior is withdrawn, there is initially some emotional upset. A teacher who no longer reinforces "help me" behavior is bound to encounter this. Therefore, you should be prepared to put up with some outbursts without giving in or getting angry. Ignore the behavior, and it will fade out in a short time. The first few outbursts are usually the longest. Stay with your change program and you will succeed.

Withdrawn Behavior. Withdrawal from adults, from peers, or from activities can have several bases. First, withdrawal can represent a fearful avoidance of persons or situations, in which case the procedures described earlier are relevant. Second, withdrawal can be the result of extinction of all behavior in that situation. When this is the case, some priming action is needed to get behavior going that can then be reinforced. Third, withdrawal can be due to not having been taught the appropriate social behavior in the first place. Some children have not been taught how to interact with others. In this case it is necessary to teach the appropriate social behavior.

A Withdrawn Girl. Linda was a nursery school child who was quite withdrawn. She showed little peer interaction or interaction with adults. Adults were not reinforcers for her. One teacher set about making herself Linda's special friend. She spent time with her, gave her things to play with, played with her, talked especially to her, and so forth. This made Linda more adult-oriented, and the teacher became a more effective reinforcer for her. The teacher could now use this new capability to reinforce child-oriented interactions. The steps were slow. The teacher had to set up many of the interactions, such as bringing other children to Linda's play area. The result was a striking change in Linda's interactions with others (Coats, 1969).

Teachers who have switched from criticism to praise to establish good classroom control often report that it is not just the previously misbehaving children who benefit from the change. Formerly quiet children benefit as well, because the teacher now has time to reinforce their steps of progress and to draw them out with various prompts. Withdrawn children need someone to take the time to turn them on.

A Passive Boy. The inactive or passive boy is usually not fun for other boys to play with and is likely to be excluded from play groups. Mark was such a boy in an experimental nursery school. He showed little interaction with his peers.

The teachers decided to reinforce one particular activity to see what effect this might have on peer relations. Climbing on the jungle gym was the target behavior. Before the program was begun, frequency of climbing on anything was less than 5 percent of the time spent in the play yard. Social reinforcement was then given to Mark every time he climbed on the jungle gym. After nine days, Mark spent over 60 percent of his time outside climbing on the jungle gym. His peer interactions changed. He began talking more with peers, and he became a happy and active member of several boys' play groups. By taking a key behavior and working on it, the teachers saw desirable changes in other behavior also (Johnston, Kelley, Harris, and Wolf, 1966).

Older Students and More Severe Problems

The reader preparing for teaching at the secondary level is probably wondering what help these studies of children at the preschool and elementary level might be. The answer is first that each of the studies was based on carefully controlled behavior-change procedures with objective data recording. So we are not just dealing with speculations. It is apparent that these social behavior problems are learned and can be modified by careful use of models, prompting, practice, reinforcement, etc., *and* that the teachers and parents did do something about the problems. Similar approaches can be taken with the self-depreciating student, the apathetic (unmotivated) student, the student who is over-sensitive to criticism, the helpless student, and the anxious student.

As mentioned earlier, Randall Sprick's *The Solution Book* (1981) provides guidelines for applying behavioral strategies to some 100 common behavior problems at the elementary level. Also, Sprick's (1985) *Discipline: A Problem-by Problem Approach in the Secondary Classroom* provides problem solution guidelines for the secondary teacher and includes plans for dealing with threats of suicide, the use of drugs, the unmotivated "passive-resistant" student, and many other problems.

Problems with older students can get quite complex and might require additional professional help from a counselor, psychologist or other mental health specialist. Consider this problem of a girl who does not seem to care about anything.

Ella, a ninth grader, did not complete homework or work in class. She did not ask questions. She just shrugged her shoulders if her teacher asked her a question. She was very unresponsive and withdrawn.

What is wrong? There are many possibilities to be checked out. Has she given up because of repeated failures, poor grades, etc.? Does she have the academic skills to do the work? Is she desparate enough that suicide is a possibility?

Sprick (1985) suggests these steps be taken to investigate the problem (note that I have grossly abbreviated Sprick's recommended procedures):

- Find out if the withdrawal is a recent change. If recent, consider that there could be a suicide risk and get help for her. If not recent, go to the next step.

- Find out if she can do the work. Work with her individually to explore academic problems. Sprick suggests an approach to informal diagnosis focusing first on reading skills. If academic problems are found, remedial help should be sought. If not, go to the next step.

- List the specific behaviors that led you to believe she had a problem. Use this list to try to set up "goal-setting agreement" with the student to be discussed and evaluated weekly. (Each week goals for change in behavior are specified on an agreement form and worked on.)

- Provide the student with feedback on progress.

- If all this fails, consider going to a structured point-reinforcement system.

Some problems are not easy to deal with when working with older students where the prolonged effects of failure may be difficult to overcome. But, we need to be ready to try with reasonable strategies.

CONDUCT PROBLEMS

The term *conduct problem* is a label given to intense, active, unlawful, or immoral behavior. This text has illustrated several conduct problems in earlier chapters—Peter's objectionable behavior, Elmer and Edward's disruptive classroom behavior, and Claire's truancy. In discussing the case of Claire, it was suggested that a variety of conduct problems, such as lying, truancy, and cheating, are the means for avoiding or escaping from punishment, and that a critical part of "treatment" when using a response-cost punishment is to provide a way to earn back lost privileges or other reinforcers.

Conduct problems always involve a payoff for the undesired behavior. The student learns to get a reward, or to avoid and escape from punishment. In the rest of this chapter we will look at more specific causes of and approaches to reducing conduct problems.

Throwing Tantrums

In response to seemingly minor events some children will flop on the floor, pound their arms, legs, or heads, and scream and yell. Some may attack their parents, and others may hold their breath until they turn blue or even pass out. Temper tantrums begin with the minor emotional upsets that go with the loss of reinforcers. Suppose Joe is used to eating various snacks before dinner, and his mother decides to stop this. She says, "No, you must wait for dinner." Joe stamps his feet and cries that he's hungry, and his mother gives in. Imagine this process taking place many times. Mother tries to wait Joe out, but he comes on even stronger. She gives in again. Progressively, Joe is *reinforced* for more intense protest behavior. Intense forms of protest, or tantrums, are taught through withholding reinforcers and then giving in and providing them.

Tantrums are relatively rare in school; but when they do occur, the teacher should know their causes and the procedures to eliminate them. The basic rule is that the teacher should not let tantrums be followed by reinforcers. It is also important to reinforce behavior incompatible with tantrums. In one case, we worked with Diane and eliminated her intense tantrums in three weeks. Her chair was placed in the back of the room. She was told she would be held down by the aide if she began a tantrum. This was done about five times. The other students were told they could earn a treat now and then by paying no attention to Diane's tantrums. And, Diane was told she could earn checkmarks on the board toward a class party for each half-day of good behavior. Diane made great progress and soon became a cooperative member of the class.

The sad part of Diane's story was that she went to a different school the following year. When she tried the same tricks again, she found they paid off. (Note that one should not expect to get generalization to situations a person has *already* learned to discriminate as providing different consequences. That takes explicit retraining.) The staff at the new school felt that she had a deep-seated emotional problem. They had her put on drugs as her behavior got worse and eventually shipped her off to a class for the emotionally disturbed. The teacher who had seen Diane flower socially after her tantrums were eliminated found this outcome most disturbing. No one would listen to her at a case conference held to discuss Diane's behavior. The idea that behavior problems can be caused by reinforcement and punishment had not been accepted widely enough at that time to save Diane.

A standard procedure for eliminating tantrums at home is to isolate the child in a room alone (or with an unresponding adult) until the tantrum is over. Typically, the first tantrum lasts from thirty minutes to two hours. The next tantrum may last only ten to fifteen minutes, and the third may be five minutes or less if no reinforcement for tantruming has occurred in the meantime.

In school, use of time out in a special room can be interpreted as interfering with the student's right to an education. Therefore the least drastic means that might get the job done should be tried first. A response cost procedure might be tried first. If this does not work, try moving the student's chair away from the group, but facing the class. A third step would have the student face the wall. And, only as a last resort should out of room time out be used. The evidence suggests that shorter time outs (two to three minutes) are more effective than longer ones. In the case of tantrums, the student should know he or she can rejoin the group after being quiet for two or three minutes. Remember, too, the importance of reinforcing improvement in behavior.

Zimmerman and Zimmerman (1962) reported a case of tantrum behavior by an eleven year old boy in a residential treatment center. The tantrums usually occurred in the hall when the boy was being brought to class. The result was a crowd of staff members standing around the boy, who was kicking and screaming. The teacher observed this consequence one day and told the attendant to put the boy in the classroom at his desk and leave. The teacher then proceeded to ignore him until he quieted down. After two to three minutes, the boy's crying became quieter, and he looked up. The teacher said she would be ready to work with him when he was ready. He continued crying for another four or five minutes and then indicated he was ready to work. The boy worked cooperatively for the rest of the class period.

When the environment permits it, ignoring the behavior (extinction) is a good approach to eliminating tantrums.

Negativism

Protest behavior ("I won't do it." "No." "I don't want to." "Do we have to?") generally results from students not being managed in a positive way. The behavior continues, because it pays off; that is, the teacher gives attention to the protests and now and then lets the students have their own way.

Negativism can be avoided for the most part by following the suggestions presented earlier on how to reinforce and punish. If the student is intently involved in some activity, do not insist that she or he suddenly leave it. Give a warning before taking any action. One can also avoid negative reactions by giving a student (or a class) a choice of two alternatives: "Would you rather stay an extra five minutes and finish the exercise before recess, or go to recess now and have to finish it when you come back?" "You have a choice, you can line up quietly the first time, or we can try it again."

Often negative reactions are provoked by being too abrupt, too bossy, and too negative in approaching students. If strong negativism has already developed, check to see how much attention you are giving it. Do not be trapped into acting insulted by a disobedient, disrespectful student. Make interactions more positive, and consider ways of increasing the reinforcement for desired behavior.

Fighting—Hitting, Kicking, Biting

All children learn to hit, kick, and bite. They are taught to hit a baseball, kick a football, and bite a steak, but not to use these responses to hurt people (except maybe in self-defense). When they do so, they are likely to be called aggressive.

Traditional views of aggression have focused on weak superegos, guilt feelings, or internal drives. Often these have led to circular explanations. A popular view is that frustration causes aggression (Dollard, Doob, Miller, Mowrer, and Sears, 1939). If frustration is defined as the reaction to absence of an accustomed reinforcer, then the development of tantrums, explained earlier, is consistent with the frustration-aggression view. The intensified reactions that occur when a response is first put on extinction are sometimes viewed as aggressive. However, just withholding reinforcement is not enough to build aggressive behavior. In fact, these intensified reactions disappear if no reinforcement is forthcoming. The critical element in the development of most aggressive behavior is the *reinforcement of more intense response forms when they do occur.*

This point is well illustrated in a study by Walters and Brown. Second grade boys were trained to hit a plastic clown. Some of them were reinforced for hitting hard, and some for hitting softly. Fifteen reinforced turns were given. Later that day the boys were observed playing three games with an untrained second-grade boy. In one game the object was to be the boy standing on a cross when the referee yelled, "Stop." The next game was a period of free play. In the third game, called Scalp, the object was to get a piece of tape from another boy's arm without losing your tape. Observers who knew nothing of the prior training rated the boys for aggressiveness from behind a one-way screen. The boys who had undergone high-intensity training were rated more aggressive than those who had undergone low-intensity training. Results were similar when the training was reversed—that is, when those who were first given low-intensity training were then given high-intensity training, they were rated more aggressive (Walters and Brown, 1964).

In a study by Brown and Elliot, the aggressive behavior of a whole classroom of three- and four-year-old boys was changed dramatically by training the teachers to give attention to cooperative behavior and to ignore aggressive behavior. The changes were quite unexpected by the teachers who were initially skeptical. The effect on two highly aggressive boys was especially dramatic. These two boys became friendlier than the teachers believed possible (Brown and Elliot, 1965).

The procedures for eliminating fighting are these:

1. Be sure the fighting does not pay off. Where possible, do not give attention to the aggressive behavior. Do not let the aggression produce a consequence favorable to the aggressor.

2. If punishment is used, do not be a model of aggression yourself. Use withdrawal of reinforcement as your punishment and provide a way of earning the reinforcers back through cooperative behavior.

3. Reinforce cooperative behavior directly.

4. Use rules and prompts to teach behavior incompatible with fighting.

Verbal Abuse and Swearing

Name calling and swearing can be learned through the model of parents or peers. The behavior is probably reinforced by the upsetting effects it has on others and by the attention it receives. Quite often children say, "I hate you" to their mothers or teachers. If the adult overreacts to such comments by acting hurt or trying to find out what's wrong, the child may well learn to use such comments to get attention.

In general, the first and best approach to verbal aggression is to ignore it. Act as if it did not happen. Give attention only to acceptable verbal behavior.

Martha, a five-year-old girl, was "balky, verbally insulting, occasionally foul-mouthed, and prone to tell disjointed stories about violent accidents." The variables controlling her behavior were systematically studied.

For the first ten days, Martha's teachers maintained their ongoing pattern of responding to her. During this baseline period Martha exhibited very little cooperative behavior with other children (see Figure 23.2). For the next seven days, Martha was showered with praise, attention, and desirable material goods. Some psychologists might have predicted that this "unconditional love" might lead Martha to be more cooperative. It did not. Only in phase 3 of the study, when cooperative behavior was directly followed by attention, praise, and play materials, and her abusive verbal behavior was ignored, did Martha become more cooperative. When reinforcement for cooperation was withdrawn (phase 4), cooperation decreased. When the reinforcement was reinstated (phase 5), cooperative behavior again increased. Just being nice to Martha was not enough to eliminate her verbal aggression. Reinforcement had to be diverted from the aggression and given to incompatible behavior (Hart, Reynolds, Baer, Brawley, and Harris, 1968).

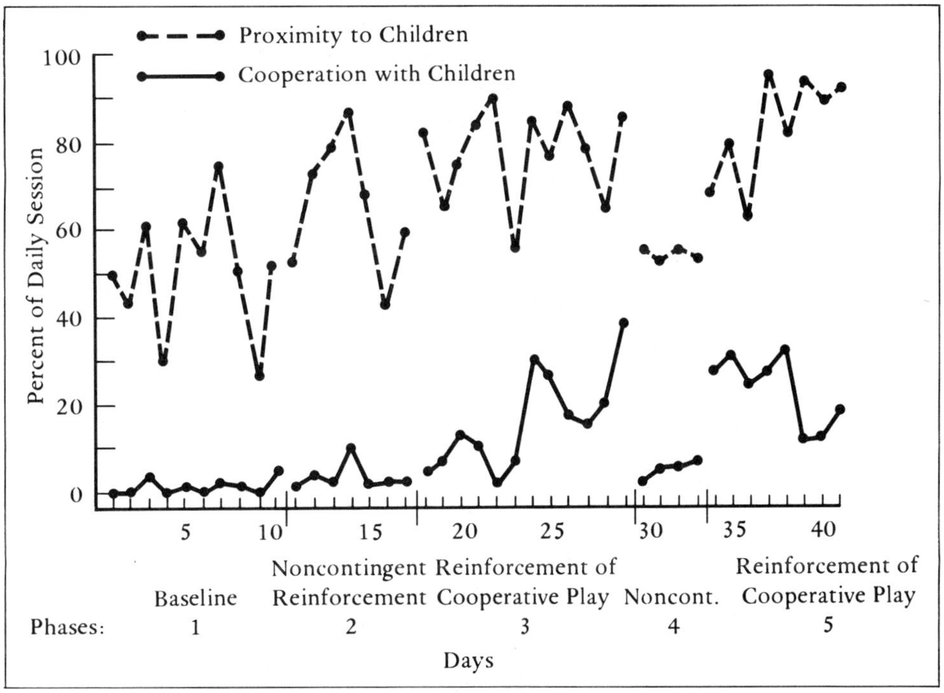

Figure 23-2 *Daily percentages of proximity and cooperative play*

The following suggestions for reducing swearing in class at the secondary level come from Sprick (1985).

- Start by discussing the problem with the class and letting them know that swearing is offensive to many people and those who swear are often considered as not having regard for others. They may lose many opportunities because they are less likely to be chosen as leaders by peers. They are not welcome in some homes. Explain that you are discussing this with them so that they have a chance to improve on their own.

- If there is improvement, let them know you are impressed with their maturity and self-control.

- If swearing does not improve, set a response cost for swearing such as loss of five minutes from lunch or other free time or loss of points in a participation-and-effort grading system.

- Before implementing the response cost, discuss it with the class and explain the consequences. Be specific about what swear words will lead to a penalty (students can help with examples), but indicate that if there is any doubt, the penalty will be imposed.

- Impose penalties as needed, calmly and consistently.

- Reinforce improvement.

Hyperactivity

Hyperactive is a fancy label for a child or adolescent who is always on the go or who does not stay at one task very long. Hyperactive-behavior patterns are sometimes found in children who show evidence of neurological impairment, but this isn't always so; the presence of hyperactivity is *not* a reliable basis for inferring brain dysfunction. Hyperactivity has also been attributed to food allergies, lead poisoning, chemical imbalances, genetics, maternal smoking and drinking during pregnancy, and not having been taught the skills to keep working at a task. The large proportion of students I have worked with who were called hyperactive have simply not been taught to stay with a task long enough to be successful, and many "hyperactive"students are fully capable of quietly watching TV all Saturday morning. However, there is some evidence to support each of the possibilities listed (Feingold, 1975; Ross and Ross, 1976; Satterfield and Cantwell, 1976; Reith, 1977; Fine, 1977). Hyperactivity has been reported to occur in about 5 percent of boys and 1 percent girls (Ross and Ross, 1976).

The stimulant drugs Dexedrine, Ritalin, and Cylert have been commonly used with variable effects. (At the time of this writing, Cylert is more popular with physicians because the others are class II drugs, which require the physician to see the patient at least every thirty days.) Physicians often have to experiment with different levels of the drugs to find out what works with which child. While having a quieting effect in about 70 percent of the cases, they also have unwanted side effects produced by the stimulants (heart rate increase, raised blood pressure, insomnia, nausea, weight loss, and so on) (O'Leary, 1980; Walden and Thompson, 1981). There is some weak evidence that diets free of sugar, artificial flavorings, and food additives are also helpful (Feingold, 1975), but the data are open to alternative interpretations. For example, parents who succeed in getting a child to comply with a strict diet will probably be able to get the child to comply with about anything else.

In comparative studies between reinforcement techniques and drugs, reinforcement techniques have been found to be more effective in reducing hyperactive behavior (Kazdin and Wilson, 1978).

The following example from the work of G. R. Patterson (1965b) is just one of many similar cases in which good reinforcement procedures produced dramatic changes.

Earl had a sad history. In early life he had been treated brutally by his parents and later by his grandparents. He had received a skull fracture when he was less than one year old. At four he had begun suffering from convulsions and motor incoordination. He had been adopted at the age of three, and for the next six years he had kept his new parents pretty busy. Earl was nine and in the second grade when Patterson became involved with him. He was hyperactive and doing poorly in school. In the classroom he was in continual motion. He often played "snowplow" with his desk. In many ways a small terror, he was controllable only when his teacher was present. He was very distractable and did little work. He was quite destructive to the classroom and aggressive toward his peers.

Earl's hyperactive behavior was reduced to a level lower than that of the other boys in the class by using the following procedure. The class was told that Earl had trouble learning because he did not pay attention. An "Earl box" was going to be used to help him. Each time he paid attention to his work for ten seconds, a light on the box on his desk would flash and a counter would move up one. For each flash he would earn candy (or pennies) that would be shared with the whole class at the end of the period. In this way his peers were encouraged not to distract him, and to support his progress. That is just what happened. His classroom behavior and performance improved, and he made new playground friends as well. Four months later Earl's parents indicated that his school behavior was still improved, that he was progressing in reading, and that for the first time other children were coming to his home to play with him.

Stealing, Cheating, Lying, and Other Delinquencies

Stealing, cheating, lying and other forms of delinquency often reflect the inadequacies of our current social system. No new principles are needed to understand why such behavior occurs. It occurs because immediate reinforcement is given and punishment is avoided. One immediate reinforcement for stealing is obvious: The child or adolescent gets something he or she wants. He or she may also receive reinforcement from peers for boldness or bravery. At the same time, our social system often fails to provide direct reinforcement for socially appropriate behavior. When children lack basic necessities, they are likely to learn to steal them. When children fail in school because of inadequate teaching, and when failure is punished, they are likely to learn to cheat. When children are not trained by the use of reinforcers, but are only punished for their misdeeds, they are likely to learn to lie.

As with other conduct problems, the solution is to make sure that the undesirable behavior does not pay off and to reinforce behavior incompatible with that which you wish to extinguish. Token reinforcement systems have been shown to be especially useful with court referred delinquents (Phillips, 1968; Liberman and Ferris, 1974).

This chapter closes with another example from Sprick (1985), this time on vandalism. As suggested in discussing the Modesto Plan, vandalism is more likely to occur when students are not held accountable for their actions and in settings where the effects of prior vandalism are left unrepaired.

Minor vandalism can be handled by having the students repair or clean up the damage. There should be clear consequences. For example, a student who writes on a desk, might have to wash all of the desks. Parents should be notified about the reason their son or daughter has to stay after school to clean up the damage.

More serious damage requires a schoolwide policy and a concerted plan among the faculty to enforce it. For example, a student might be referred to the office and the extent of the damage is assessed by the custodial staff as soon as possible. The student would have to pay for the damage if he or she has a source of income (parents are not allowed to pay for them). If the student has no income, then work with the custodial staff at school (at less than the minimum wage) would earn the credits to pay for the damage. A contract should be written specifying what is required. If an agreement is not reached or kept, then formal charges with the police should be made.

Evidence of vandalism should be removed as soon as possible.

Another approach (along with the above) is to encourage student groups to take on the problem and sponsor "cleanup week," before and after newspaper articles. The aim is to develop a pride in the maintenance of their building.

SUMMARY

Fears are learned through a conditioning process and can be eliminated through the use of extinction procedures, counter-conditioning procedures, or through reinforcing approach behavior. In using extinction, the fear-arousing stimulus is repeatedly presented until fear is no longer aroused. In counter-conditioning, the conditioned stimulus is associated with an incompatible emotional response. A gradual introduction of the feared stimulus is accompanied by something positive (such as food or other children playing with the feared object). In reinforcing approach to the feared objects, small steps closer to the feared object are reinforced.

Fear of school often involves emotional reactions to leaving mother, rather than a fear of school itself. The case of Karl illustrated one approach to eliminating such a fear. He was first reinforced, through doll play, for more grown-up feelings and actions; then, step by step, he was reinforced for going to school and staying there.

The key to understanding dependent behavior such as pleading "help me," acting babyish, and clinging to adults for attention is to recognize that it is maintained by social reinforcers. These same reinforcers can be used to teach independent behavior. When reinforcers are withdrawn from a particular type of behavior, the teacher should anticipate an increase in that behavior at first and some possible emotional outbursts before extinction will occur.

A child's withdrawal from adults, peers, or activities can be due to a conditioned fear, prior extinction of all behavior in that situation, or the failure of someone to teach the appropriate social behavior in the first place. In each case, the solution involves the reinforcement of the desired interactions.

Problems with older students might require help from a counselor or other mental health specialist.

Conduct problems are often more troubling to teachers and school administrators than academic failures. Somebody has misbehaved, and somebody has to do something about it. This chapter has presented many instances of problem behavior in order to demonstrate that it always has a payoff and can be eliminated by changing what is rewarded.

People teach each other how to behave. Groups that have the power to reinforce or punish children (parents, peers, teachers, or school administrators) teach the behavior that is later labeled appropriate or inappropriate. To eliminate problem behavior it is necessary to provide students with what they need in order to live and learn without pain or punishment, and to reinforce behavior that is generally acceptable to the larger social sphere in which the student lives.

Approaches to dealing with tantrums, negativism, fighting, swearing, hyperactivity, stealing, and other delinquencies were examined. Holding students accountable for their actions and developing a school climate among faculty and students that reinforces mature are important in dealing with conduct problems.

CHAPTER

24

SEX DIFFERENCES AND SEX EQUITY

The legal attack on sex bias in education was contained in Title IX of the Education Amendments of 1972. The act states:

> No person shall, on the basis of sex, be exluded from participation in, be denied the benefits of, or be subjected to discrimination under any education program or activity receiving federal financial assistance.

Virtually all 16,000 public school systems and the 2,700 colleges and universities in the United States are covered by this act. The reduction of sex discrimination in athletics is probably the most obvious change in evidence since 1972. There have been many others, but there is still a long way to go if both sex groups are to have equality of opportunity.

There are obvious biological differences between the sexes in weight, size, sexual functions, and so on, that can account for some of the historical differences in sex roles. But the research literature on differential treatment of girls and boys suggest that many of the current differences between the sexes are produced by the way parents, peers, and teachers behave. This being the case, it is important that teachers understand what these differences are, their potentially damaging effects, and what can be done about them.

An examination of the history of "marriage" can give you some idea of where the differential treatment of the sexes came from. As David Mace (1982) points out in his book *Close Companions,* one of the oldest forms of "marriage" was by capture, and for centuries brides have been purchased. Throughout history, men have considered themselves superior to women and have kept women in a submissive role, often treating them as a possession or commodity. The Catholic Church did not decide that women had souls until the Council of Nicene (Nice) in 325 A.D. For more than 2,000 years, churches and states have supported what we now call the "traditional marriage," where there are clearly defined male and female roles. Young people were thoroughly trained for this kind of marriage, where, at least most recently, the husband worked and went to war, and the wife was mother and homemaker. This traditional marriage is in the process of changing today toward a marriage with companionship and equality at its base. Many of the current differences in social behavior and achievement between the sexes can be traced to socialization training aimed at fulfilling the traditional marriage-role expectations.

BIOLOGICAL FACTORS

Research on biological contributions to sex differences, beyond the most obvious features, is most difficult to interpret as Jeanne Block (1981) so nicely illustrates. Suppose you believe that the male hormone, androgen, provides the basis for sex differences in aggressiveness. Studies have shown that female mice become more aggressive if given androgens when young. However, they become more aggressive also if given the female homone, estrogen. Testosterone level (another male hormone) in males has been found related to some forms of aggression, but not others. And then, other studies with monkeys have shown testosterone levels change as their social environment changes. Monkeys low in social dominance showed a rise in testosterone when given access to sexually receptive females. The hormone level dropped when the target monkey was exposed to a group of males who defeated him, and rose again when he was given access to receptive females whom he could dominate and have intercourse with. As Block (1981) concludes, current evidence on endocrine or other biological factors in sex differences is "not compelling."

SEX DIFFERENCES IN PERSONAL-SOCIAL BEHAVIOR

In Block's review of the literature (1983), she reports sex differences in personal-social behavior in seven areas: "aggression, activity, impulsivity, susceptibility to anxiety, achievement-related behaviors, self-concept, and social relationships" (1983, p. 1337). I am indebted to Block's review for the summaries on sex differences in personal-social behavior and the related findings from studies of parents and teachers that follow.

Aggression

Boys are found to be more aggressive than girls from an early age. Boys tend to play rougher, fight, show more antisocial behavior, and are more competitive. They prefer TV shows with more aggressive content. In the animal kingdom, males are also found to be more aggressive than females.

Activity Level

In childhood, boys are more active, as well as more curious, and show more exploratory behavior.

Impulsivity. When impulsivity is defined by difficulty in delaying gratification and over-reacting to frustration, males show more than females. Observational studies show male automobile drivers to be more impulsive than females.

Susceptibility to Anxiety. Girls and women show more anxiety and fear and less confidence than males in problem-solving tasks. Longitudinal studies have shown that women decrease in their personal confidence over the critical years from eighteen to twenty-six. Men, on the other hand show an increase during this period (Nawas, 1971). Related to these findings are those showing females to be more suggestible, acquiescent, and compliant. Studies by Lockheed (1976) and Stake and Stake (1979) show that women can learn to resist group pressures if they are given training in task-related competencies prior to confrontations in mixed sex groups. Such findings suggest that the differences in compliance can be changed.

Achievement Motivation

As Block (1983) indicates, the studies on achievement motivation show "inconsistent and sex-specific results." Males appear to be motivated by challenge and ego-involvement. Females are sometimes hindered by the same involvement. It is as if the need to be successful and the need to be liked conflict with each other (Lois Hoffman, 1972) (or in behavioral terms, social reinforcers are more important to females and reinforcers associated with task completion are more important to males). This interpretation is supported by Caplan's (1979) finding that females show greater achievement when an adult (to be pleased) is present than when such a person is absent. The presence of an adult does not make a difference for males.

Self-Concept

Girls are more likely to show a "helplessness" in achievement-related situations. "Males describe themselves as more powerful, ambitious, energetic, and as perceiving themselves as having more control over external events than females" (Block, 1983, p. 1139). Sears and Odom (reported in Maccoby and Jacklin, 1974) followed up Terman's sample of gifted women who were then in later middle-age. As these gifted women reviewed their lives, they reported feeling that they had missed their opportunities to make something of their lives—the "despair" described by Erikson that goes with an unfulfilled life. This despair was not the typical case for the gifted men who were generally successful.

Social Relationships

Martin Hoffman's (1977) review clearly shows women to have more empathy to the feelings of others. Women are also more likely to develop close relations with other women than men are with other men (Waldrop & Halvorsen, 1975). Females are more likely to seek help and reassurance than males. They are also more interested in babies and show more nurturing behavior when babies are around. They are more oriented to personal relationships.

As suggested earlier, the examination of the context in which boys and girls are reared, gives strong support to the hypothesis that these differences are a function of how adults and peers react differentially to boys and girls. We now turn to that literature.

PARENT-CHILD STUDIES

Block (1979) summarizes findings from six studies where parent self-reports (not direct observations) were used. Both parents report that they stress achievement and competition more for boys than girls. Boys are also more likely to be encouraged to be independent, to control feelings, and to be responsible. Boys are more likely to be punished, and fathers are more power-assertive with sons than daughters, thus providing a model of aggressive behavior. Fathers tend not to accept feminine-role behavior from boys.

Parental relations with daughters involve greater warmth, contact, and trust. "Ladylike" behavior is expected. Mothers restrict and supervise daughters more than sons.

Observational studies indicate that parents respond more contingently (both positively and negatively) to boys than girls (Margolin & Patterson, 1975). This occurs even in response to early vocalizations (Lewis & Freedle, 1973; Parke & Sawin, 1976; Yarrow, 1975). These additional contingent consequences for boys could greatly facilitate early learning. There are other pieces to the picture. Toys for boys have greater variety, providing greater opportunities for invention and problem solving, and are more likely to provide contingent feedback in play. Boys' toys also tend to take boys further way from parents than girls' toys. Girls' toys tend to keep them close to mom imitating mother roles (Fagot, 1978). Differences in cognitive development are potentially a product of these differences in treatment.

Male infants are also more likely to be held and have gross-motor activities stimulated. Boys also generally are given more freedom to explore their environment. Even in the assignment of household chores, boys tend to get the outside jobs and girls the inside jobs.

These general differences are consistent with girls becoming more compliant, adult dependent, and interpersonally oriented than boys. And, they are consistent with boys showing better problem-solving skills, more mastery activity, independence, and task orientation.

The importance of fathers in fostering these sex differences is suggested by observational studies. In a study by Block, Block, & Harrington (1975), the teaching behavior of mothers and fathers were video taped separately and rated. Fathers set higher standards and placed greater emphasis on cognitive achievement for their sons than for their daughters. "With their daughters, fathers focused more on the interpersonal aspects of the teaching situation—encouraging, supporting, joking and playing, and protecting" (Block, 1983, p. 1343). When Day (1975) had adults interact with two year olds who were sometimes "boys" and sometimes "girls," similar results were found. In teaching situations, men "provided more goal-directed reinforcements to presumed boys and expected them to do better on the tasks than presumed girls" (Block, 1983, p. 1343). Fathers appear to be teaching girls that affectionate relationships are more important than task success, whereas the opposite message is given to boys. Mothers support these differential messages.

Another interesting finding reported by Block comes from a study by Grief (1979). Communication patterns within families were studied. Parents were more likely to interrupt their daughters than their sons. This could convey the message to daughters that what they have to say is less important. Also, mothers are interrupted more frequently than fathers. The message is the same.

TEACHER-CHILD INTERACTIONS

The evidence suggests that the sex-typed patterns are also reinforced in classrooms. In nursery school studies, boys are found to get more attention (both positive and negative). Boys also get more specific help when they ask for it.

In an experimental-teaching study of fifth graders, where groups of boys and girls were classified as *high ability* and *moderate ability,* Frey (1979) found the least amount of reinforcing feedback and support was given to the high-ability girls. They also received the most critical feedback. Others have found a similar pattern. Teachers tend to "interact more with boys, to give boys more positive feedback, and to direct more criticism toward girls" (Block, 1983, p. 1344). A similar neglect of intellectual skills of women are found at the university level (Hochschild, 1975). The potential effects of such interactions are described by Block as follows:

"The greater attrition of women in higher education may reflect, among other factors, the pernicious effects of this pattern of discouragement and negative reinforcement on female intellectual activities" at all educational levels (Block, 1983, p. 1344). These results from the home, laboratory, and classroom settings consistently suggest that girls, even high-achieving girls, are given less encouragement for their efforts than are their male peers. "Gender differences in confidence, self-concept, and problem-solving behaviors noted by L. W. Hoffman (1977), Tyler (1965), and others may well derive from these home and classroom experiences which often discourage and denigrate the efforts of females" (Block, 1983, p. 1344).

The larger school community also supports gender differences of the type just described. Men hold most of the better paying and responsible jobs. Women's roles tend to be devalued. The sociologist Jean Stockard (1984) believes that men's tendency to devaluate women's work is learned in the early years at home and school. She also believes that one thing schools can do about it is to focus on the devaluation of women that goes on in *male peer groups.* Boys are taught "Don't run like a girl!" or "Don't be a sissy!", and when they get older, talk of women as sex objects directly or in jokes. Male peer groups reinforce many attitudes that depreciate women. Stockard believes that schools should attack such practices through group discussions and confrontation, just as racially prejudicial behavior is currently not tolerated in schools.

Block concludes her review of the literature on sex differences in personality development with a hypothesis about *cognitive* differences between the sexes. The greater freedom to explore, experiment, and learn on their own about the physical world makes it more likely that boys will learn better problem-solving strategies and related feelings of competence. In Piagetian terms, boys learn to accommodate better when confronted with discrepant information requiring problem solving. On the other hand, the more restrictive rearing of girls, with an emphasis on proximity to adults, supervision, being nice, less inventive toys, and less freedom to solve problems on their own, can lead to weak problem-solving skills and, in Piagetian terms, behavior that is more assimilating than accommodating. Girls are pre-empted from learning certain cognitive skills by the way in which they are reared.

Given this background, you are ready to examine sex differences in cognitive skills.

SEX DIFFERENCES IN COGNITIVE SKILLS

Sex differences in general intelligence are not found, but the tests were designed that way. Items showing sex differences were either eliminated or balanced by items showing a difference favoring the other sex. Some differences are found on the subtests of the WAIS (Matarazzo, 1972). Men score higher on *Arithmetic,* and women higher on the *Coding* subtest where symbols must be rapidly and accurately copied under the right number. In looking at more specific abilities, Maccoby and Jacklin (1974) summarize the sex differences for school-aged children as follows: (1) boys do better on visual-spatial tasks, (2) girls do better on verbal skills, and (3) boys do better on mathematical tasks.

The basis of these differences is quite unclear. Mothers talk more to their girls than boys, even at very early ages (Fagot & Kronsberg, 1982), and it is consistent with sex stereotypes for girls to do well in English and boys in mathematics. In the 1960s, there was a large gap in high school in the number of math classes taken by girls and boys. This gap had started to close by 1972, and is narrower today, but still significant. A major factor affecting math enrollments in high school appears to be attitudinal. Girls see math, and math-based careers, as more masculine and orient away from them in later adolescence. In the lives of many young women, math is not seen as important to their futures.

Performance of the sexes on math tests produces some conflicting data when number of math courses taken is controlled. Some find no differences (Fenema & Sherman, 1977) and others still find differences (Benbow & Stanley, 1980; Kolata, 1980). But as Shelia Tobias (1982) points out, "Until and unless girls are encouraged to experience the world as boys do, it is unreasonable to assume, as Benbow and Stanley have done, that the boys and girls they tested had identical exposure to mathematics." Patricia Casserly studied twenty high schools where sex differences were not found in math on the Scholastic Aptitude Test (SAT). Common to these schools were teachers who were specialists in mathematics, engineering, or science, and not generalists. Bright students (male and female) were grouped together in special classes with enthusiastic teachers who put an emphasis on logical reasoning (Kolata, 1980).

The evidence just discussed on early exploratory opportunities for boys versus girls could account for differences in visual-spatial skills. The ability to manipulate two- and three-dimensional figures in your head (as an architect or mechanical engineer might have to do), could be strengthened by the kinds of toys and play activities boys get into. Since there is evidence that (for most people) visual-spatial skills have more to do with right-brain functioning, and verbal skills have more to do with left-brain functioning, a potential basis for a biological interpretation of these differences exists. However, there is no evidence to support a biological interpretation at this time.

Steinkamp and Maehr (1984) have reviewed studies of gender differences in school science attitudes and achievement. They summarized the data by using a method called meta-analysis (Glass, 1978). Different studies are added together by converting the differences found to standard scores—that is, the magnitude of the difference between sex groups (called *effect size*) is expressed in terms of the standard deviation of the measure being used. Considering just the large-scale studies in the United States, they found an average difference favoring males in ***science motivation*** ("How much do you like science?") of .29 standard score units. For ***science achievement,*** the effect size was .48 standard score units. Figure 24.1 shows the difference in distributions for science motivation. As you can see, the overlap of the two groups is considerable. A point not made clear in our earlier discussion of gender differences, is that the magnitude of the differences we are talking about are not all that great. When they can be quantified, they tend to range between .25 and .50 standard deviation units.

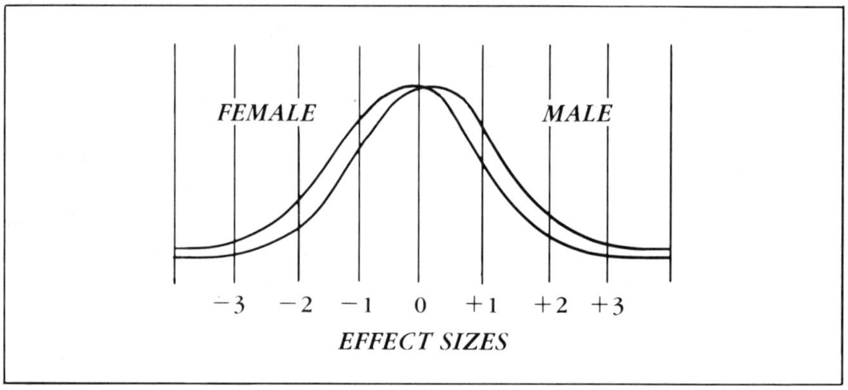

Figure 24-1 *Two normal distributions representing an effect size of .29. This is approximately the magnitude of sex differences in motivational orientation reported in the U.S. large-scale studies sample.*

Women are grossly underrepresented in science and technological fields. In 1972, 18.4 percent of the doctorates in biological sciences were awarded to women, and in physics 4.4 percent (Cole, 1979). Steinkamp and Maehr (1984) found in their analysis of science motivation, girls generally do not favor science careers, but the analysis by disciplines shows them to favor the life sciences (botany, biology) over the physical sciences. Somewhat puzzling was the finding that girls had higher interest in chemistry than boys. Their data show that for lower socioeconomic groups girls' orientation toward science is higher than boys, while boys' orientation is higher in upper middle-class groups.

SUMMARY AND REVIEW OF OTHER DIFFERENCES

Before looking at what can be done to promote equality of opportunity for the sexes, let us summarize the established sex differences and evidence of bias found during the school years and later life. This summary is adapted from Myra and David Sadker's (1982) excellent book entitled *Sex Equity Handbook for Schools*. The reader interested in pursuing this literature is referred to this handbook for detailed reference sources.

Academic Differences

- On standardized achievement tests, the performance of girls declines as they progress through school. The performance of boys improves, especially in math and science.

- Even with the decline on achievement tests, girls get better grades than boys (the reward for docility?).

- Studies of teacher-student interactions show that teachers call on girls less, give them less praise, ask girls fewer complex questions, and give them less guidance in doing things on their own.

- Girls with high math ability are less likely to be identified. Of those identified, fewer are placed in accelerated classes.

- Girls with learning problems are less likely to be detected and given special help.

- Boys are more likely to be disciplined in school, even though their behavior does not differ from that of girls.

- More boys are labeled as having "learning disabilities," "reading problems," and "mental retardation." They are also more likely to be retained in a grade and to "drop out" of high school.

- Between 70 percent and 90 percent of bright high school graduates who do not go on to college are women. Through the high school years, girls' career commitments decline. This decline is presumed to be related to a perception that boys do not like women who use their brains.

Personal-Social Behavior

- Boys show more aggression (including conduct problems), more activity (including hyperactivity), more impulsivity (including emotional problems and suicide). These characteristics make it more difficult for boys to adapt to school expectations, especially at the elementary level. It is possible that the strain of conforming to the male sex-role stereotype is related to males having more serious diseases, being victims of more accidents and violence, and having an average life expectancy that is eight years less than that for women.

- Girls show more dependence, anxiety, fear, and compliance. They are more relationship oriented and less achievement oriented than boys. Women are more likely than men to end up in outpatient therapy for a variety of problems like phobias, depression, anorexia nervosa, and agoraphobia.

Athletic Programs

- Athletic programs for women were minimal until the law changed in 1972. Even with the law change, in 1978–79 athletic budgets for women in U.S. colleges were only 18 percent of those for men.

Careers

- Elementary school girls report sex-stereotyped career goals. In the majority of the cases, they identify teaching and nursing as career goals.

- The advice given to boys on careers is usually sex-role stereotyped, limiting their choices.

- Women are shut out of many choices in science, math, and technical fields because they do not get a solid grounding in math in high school.

- Over 90 percent of women will work on a paid job at some time. The bias they will encounter is shown in the following statistics:
  a. *A third of families with a woman as the head live below poverty level.*
  b. *Women college graduates typically make less than men who drop out of high school.*
  c. *Women earn 59 cents for each dollar a man earns. For minority women the figure is 50 cents when compared to white males.*
  d. *Women are only 5 percent of the craft workers, but 79 percent of the clerical workers.*
  e. *The wage gap has actually been getting larger since 1954.*
  f. *Most women work out of necessity, not just to have "extra cash."*
  g. *Two-thirds of working women are either single, divorced, separated, widowed, or have a spouse earning under $10,000.*

Family Relations

- The male role pressures to suppress feelings may cause difficulties with family and friends.

- There are few programs for teaching parenting skills to boys and men. This may be one reason the typical father interacts with his children only twelve minutes a day on the average.

- Because men and women develop different views of the role of father, family stress is likely. Women want fathers to help in child care and to respond to family emotional needs ("Talk to us."). Fathers see their role as providing income and solving family problems.

These facts point to serious problems for both males and females in achieving the American ideal of equality of opportunity. The biasing effects are particularly great for those whose parents are poor or members of minority groups, and for women. Teachers need to understand that their stereotyped views of racial groups, socioeconomic groups, and sex roles can lead to self-fulfilling prophecies. Beliefs lead to differential treatment, which leads to loss of potential options for further development, and to actual differences in opportunities as adults.

How many women reading this would have had a different attitude about high school core subjects in math and science if they knew the work force statistics just presented?

How many men would have persisted in peer interactions that depreciate women if they understood the potential harm this behavior posed for women and their relations with women?

WORKING TOWARD EQUITY

Change is possible and for many is already happening. Studies at one time showed that boys roles were considered progressively more desirable as one progressed through school and that girls roles were considered less desirable (Smith, 1939). Recent studies (Olsen and Willemsen, 1978; Kuhn, Nash, and Bricken, 1978) suggest that some girls have a more positive self image. However, as recent as 1975, Slaby and Frey asked children the question "If I had a magic wand and I could make you a boy or girl right now, would you like to be a boy or girl?" The children (150 of them) were tested at 18 months and many of them retested over the next two years. Over half of the girls said at some time in that period that they would rather be a boy. *None* of the boys over the age of two ever wanted to be a girl. The problem is not likely to go away quickly.

Earlier we indicated that athletic budgets for college women averaged only 18 percent of that for men in 1978–79. In perspective, this was quite a leap forward. The women's budget was only 2 percent of that for men in 1974 and the number of women in college athletics has increased by 570 percent from 1970 to 1980 (U.S. Commission on Civil Rights, 1980).

Since 1958, the percentage of women in the labor force has increased from 38 percent to 50 percent. While women mostly are in lower-paying jobs, more and more women are entering professional and management positions (U.S. Commission on Civil Rights, 1980).

Change is occurring, but there is much more to be done.

Recognizing Sexism in Education

The first task in working toward equity in education for the sexes is to be able to identify attitudes, materials, behaviors, and policies that are sexist. Rita Bornstein (1982) specifies three assumptions about women that underlie sexism. These are:

1. Women's place is in the home.
2. Women are physically, emotionally, and intellectually inferior to men.
3. Women should cultivate traditionally feminine characteristics. (Bornstein, 1982, pp. 13–14).

Assumption 1 implies that girls should be trained in home economics, parenting, and "nurturance" jobs such as teachers and nurses. They do not need to be trained in physics or calculus. Their main goal should be the skills needed to catch a husband, and be a wife and mother.

Assumption 2 should be apparently true if history is your criterion. Women have not been the great scholars, explorers, or leaders of the past. (But, we know how self-fulfilling prophecies work, don't we?) Following this assumption, women do not need physical strength or to get into competitive games. Being emotional, they can't be good leaders. And, being "not so bright," we should not expect too much from them when faced with complex problems.

Assumption 3 implies that men are primarily attracted to and marry the more feminine women. So training for this role reinforces the compliant, docile, neat, sweet, thoughtful behaviors. Again, self-assertion, intellectuality, ambition, and independence are to be punished.

If women are to truly have equality as our society moves forward, the subtile effects of these assumptions on school programs need to be recognized and removed. According to Bornstein (1982), these assumptions have been hidden in textbooks, curriculum options, teacher behavior, counseling procedures, athletic activity, and special activities. They need to be recognized if they are to be countered.

Textbooks. Studies of stories in readers at the elementary level show male characters to be present more often than female characters by a 2:1 to 6:1 ratio, depending on the categories of central figures used. Males are portrayed with characters fitting the traditional-role ideal—successful, clever, powerful, etc. Girls are portrayed in the traditional feminine, docile, incompetent role (Women on Words and Images, 1974). In a study of high school texts on U.S. history, Weitzmann and Rizzo (1974) found that men dominated in the topics covered. When women were mentioned, they were presented in passive roles. Biased representations of women are so pervasive in textbooks and other instructional materials that we become accustomed to them.

The wide spread use of sexist language in textbooks is another problem. Pronouns like *he, him, mailman, policeman*—even *God* is made male—reveal the male-oriented world in which children are raised.

Publishers have attempted to respond to the criticisms by providing authors with nonsexist and nonracial discrimination guidelines to follow. Some change has occurred, but bias is still there (Tibbetts, 1979).

An analysis of twenty-four widely used texts in teacher education showed that most give little space to the sexist issue, one-third do not mention it at all, and *none* provide guidelines to help teacher counter-act sexism in the classroom (Sadker and Sadker, 1980).

Curriculum options. For a long time there have been special courses for boys and girls, especially at the high school level, such as, physical education, home economics, and vocational education. Sexist language permeates course descriptions, so it is quite clear that a sewing class expects only girls to sign up. Women need to learn about cars and other machines, and most men have to learn to cook and sew sometime in their life. But the sex-related roles tied to such courses serve as barriers.

We have mentioned the math barrier before, but it is worth evaluating further. Boys and girls increasingly rate math as more anxiety-provoking (as opposed to enjoyable) as they go from sixth to twelfth grade, but at every grade level girls find it less enjoyable than boys (Brush, 1985). Enrollment data also show a decline for both boys and girls. Even those who do well in science and math, tend not to take the advanced courses. Chipman and Wilson (1985) interpret these and related data as indicating that the relevance of math in the lives of both boys and girls is not made clear by high school math teachers, and that there are problems in the quality of the teaching going on. While boys tend to take more math because it is required by career choices, neither boys or girls see its relevance to everyday living. One consequence of dropping math early for women is that they are locked out of many fields of college study such as astrophysics, chemistry, computer science, economics, engineering, medicine, and physics. This leads women to important, but lesser-paying jobs in education, social work, and the humanities. It would seem important to encourage women to obtain stronger math science backgrounds, if for no other reason than to ***keep their options open***.

In one study of vocational training, girls were found to be offered opportunities for training in only thirty-three different occupations, whereas boys were offered opportunities in ninety-five occupations (Verheyden-Hilliard, 1977). Bornstein (1982) notes that "Since 1972, there has been an increase of ten percent more boys studying home economics, but less than one percent more girls in trade and industrial programs." (p. 19)

Teacher behavior. The effects of teacher expectations on how hard they will try with some students has been cited. Just as expectations about racial differences and IQ differences influence teacher behavior (and student learning), so do expectations about the sexes. We have already reviewed the data. Boys are expected to be trouble makers (and are disciplined more). Girls are not expected to be good problem solvers and thinkers (but boys are), so girls are treated in ways that challenge them less. Boys are expected to be poor readers and more become so. However, Brophy and Good (1973) find that reading problems are not sex-linked in other countries where teachers expect boys to be good readers.

Counseling and guidance. The tests, the training, and the attitudes of counselors and other advisors often reflect traditional values. The following studies are cited from Rita Bornstein's review (1982):

Thomas and Stewart (1971) had men and women high school counselors listen to taped self-descriptions made by high school girls. Some girls followed the traditional feminine goals and others described traditional masculine goals. Both men and women counselors thought that feminine goals were more appropriate for girls and that those with masculine goals were more in need of counseling.

Friedersdorf (1969) had counselors invent "backgrounds and interests" for college-bound and noncollege bound women (sort of a projective test of attitudes). Male counselors did not offer any traditionally male careers for women. The college bound women were portrayed by men as interested in semiskilled traditionally female careers. The college bound women were portrayed by women as interested in careers that did require a college education.

Bornstein makes these comments about what is needed:

> Girls and boys today need counseling that is free from stereotyped expectations. For example, although 97 percent of high school girls report that they expect to have careers, they are generally more interested in the arrival of Prince Charming and tend to underplan for their educational and occupational goals (National Assessment of Educational Progress, 1977).
>
> This vague, dreamy approach to their adult lives goes unchallenged by many counselors who fail to guide girls toward serious academic and career planning. Counselors, like other adults in education, are operating from the basic assumption that a girl's career will be her husband and not her work. These assumptions do not recognize that nine out of ten young women in today's high schools will work outside the home for a major part of their adult lives. (Bornstein, 1982, p. 21)

Athletic activity. Physical activity is important to mental well-being and general health. Throughout the school years, girls and young women have been short changed when it comes to opportunity for training and competition in athletics. The traditional feminine role model has led to segregated classes, with the avoidance of competition and vigorous action, and in general second-rate training. The evidence indicates that vigorous activity is every bit as good for girls as for boys. During the 1970s, the percentage of athletes who were female at the high school level rose from 7 percent to 30 percent. The athletic skills demonstrated by American women in the 1984 Olympics testify both to the capabilities of women and to the changes in opportunities for good training and coaching that have been going on. There has been improvement, but there still is a way to go to reach equity. Men often credit their training in team athletics for the development of leadership skills and teamwork skills important for management jobs in the competitive business world. Perhaps women will develop more of these skills also if given greater opportunities in sports.

Special activities. Most extracurricular activities have been sex segregated. For girls there was cheerleading, service clubs, future teachers, and so on. For boys there was science clubs, marching bands, chess clubs, and so forth. In student governments, women usually got the offices of secretary and maybe treasurer, with boys getting the presidency and vice-presidency. Again, these traditional patterns are beginning to break down and students are working more in mixed groups. Further progress requires as a first step the recognition of the remaining discriminations that exist.

Title IX

Title IX of the Educational Amendments of 1972 required schools and colleges to implement five procedures by July 1976. These involved self-evaluation of current discrimination practices and steps to be taken to eliminate them, appointment of a Title IX coordinator, development of greivance procedures, dissemination of policy to all involved, and filing an assurance of compliance form. These requirements continue to be in effect. The regulations apply to the admission of students, the treatment of students, and employment of staff.

Does this mean schools must have women on football teams and coeducational classes on human sexuality? Obviously not, because these things are not happening in many schools. The law provides for these exceptions:

- Parts of classes dealing with human sexuality *may be* held separately.
- Choruses may be established on the basis of vocal range (but not be exclusively for males or females).
- Students in physical education classes and sports *may be* grouped by ability for each sport and *may be* segregated for contact sports.

Two other points in the law to note: (1) pregnant students may not be excluded from any programs or activities, and (2) the law requires funds adequate to ensure equal opportunity, but does not require an equal expenditure of funds for male and female programs.

Some Specific Steps You Can Take

Rita Bornstein (1982) concludes her chapter on *Sexism in Education* with these recommendations for educators:

- Examine your own attitudes and behavior continuously for sex bias and stereotyping.
- Help sensitize others to these issues by sharing information and exchanging ideas.
- Don't let biased or discriminatory behaviors go unchallenged.
- Inform others of their rights.
- Continue to inform yourself about the issues of sexism in education by reading the latest news, reports, and research findings in this field.
- Challenge the years of habit and tradition that keep female and male students confined to prescribed roles.
- Keep in mind that you can be a leader in the process of change (Bornstein, 1982, p. 55).

Those interested in developing their skills in non-sexist teaching are referred to Chapters 3 to 5 in *Sex Equity Handbook for Schools* by Myra and David Sadker. Chapter 3 focuses on overcoming sex bias in instructional materials. Chapter 4 focuses on overcoming sex bias in classroom interactions. And, Chapter 5 focuses on many ways in which nonsexist values can be brought into the daily curriculum plan.

SUMMARY

This chapter reviewed the literature on differences in behavior and in opportunities for the sexes and how these differences are related to the traditional sex-role stereotypes that are maintained by parents, teachers, and peers. The traditional stereotypes tend to limit available choices for boys as well as girls.

The evidence on differences in personal-social behavior shows boys and men to be more aggressive, more active, more impulsive, more achievement-oriented, and having concepts of themselves that imply more power and effectiveness in dealing with the environment. Girls and women are more anxious, more compliant, more helpless in the face of problems, and more relationship-oriented. Older boys and men do better in math and tasks involving visual-spatial problems. Girls show higher verbal skills and do better on some clerical-type tasks (such as the WAIS Coding test).

These differences can be directly related to the greater restrictions placed on girls, and to the types of toys and role models boys and girls are provided with in the preschool years. Teachers also contribute to these differences by supporting traditional sex-role stereotypes, attending more to boys both positively and negatively, and by providing greater intellectual stimulation for boys. Jeanne Block hypothesizes that these differences in treatment lead to cognitive differences. With a greater freedom to explore and experiment with their world, boys develop better problem-solving strategies and greater feelings of competence. Girls are more closely supervised, are reinforced for being nice and developing strong social skills, but at the cost of adaptive skills in problem situations. Women are grossly underrepresented in the sciences and many professions. This appears to be a product of traditional sex-typed goals (which are expressed in many girls' attitudes) which lead girls to not take the advanced science and math courses in high school that are needed to gain entry into courses of study in the sciences and professions. Keep in mind that when measurable, the differences being discussed are relatively small, on the order of .25 to .50 standard score units, but still of great social importance. If there was such a difference on a general intelligence test (and there is not because the test was built to eliminate sex differences) there would be a difference of only 4 to 7 points.

Other differences attributable to the traditional sex-role stereotype are:

- Fewer women go to college.
- Fewer women participate in athletics.
- Men tend to hold in feelings, even with family and friends.
- Men are not taught parenting skills and spend little time with their children.
- Family stress is likely because men and women have different views of what a father should be.

In the market place:

- One-third of families with a woman at the head live below poverty level.
- Women college graduates make less than men who drop out of high school.
- Women earn 59 cents for each dollar earned by men.
- Women are only 5 percent of the craft workers, but 79 percent of the clerical workers.
- Two-thirds of the working women are either single, divorced, separated, widowed, or have spouses making less than $10,000.

Title IX of the Educational Amendments of 1972 made it illegal for schools and colleges not to provide equal treatment (with a few exceptions) for males and females. This act has stimulated some changes (most apparently in athletics), but there is much more to be done. The traditional sex-role stereotype assumes that women's place is in the home; that women are physically, emotionally, and intellectually inferior; and that women should be "feminine." In moving to relationships based on equality, these assumptions become untenable.

Sex biases can still be found in textbooks in the ways males and females are depicted and in sexist language usage. They can also be found in curriculum options, in teacher behavior, in counseling procedures, in athletics, and in other special school activities.

Publishers and authors are trying to do their part to eliminate the pervasive biases in instructional materials. Title IX is helping in other areas. Title IX requires elimination of sex-biased practices in the admission of students, the treatment of students, and employment of staff. However, schools, at their choice, may teach about human sexuality in sex-segregated groups, may group chorus members on the basis of voice range, may group for physical education on the basis of skill by sport, and may have segregated contact sports.

Important gains in equal opportunity for women have been made in recent years, but there is still a long way to go. We need to become sensitized to sexist practices, help to sensitize others, keep informed on the subject, and challenge sexist practices when they are found.

CHAPTER

25

SPECIAL NEEDS, APTITUDES, AND THE MAINSTREAMING PROCESS

This chapter examines several issues relating individual differences in capabilities that influence the ability to profit from instruction. It also examines some of the issues relating to the mainstreaming of exceptional students and Public Law 94–142, a law that provides for "free appropriate public education" and that requires the placement of exceptional students in the "least restrictive environment possible."

DIFFERENCES IN APTITUDES

The goal of some day individualizing instruction so that each individual can develop through learning experiences to her or his maximum potential has led educational psychologists to study what are called *aptitude-treatment interactions (ATI)*. In such studies, learners are assessed along some dimension, such as verbal ability. Then the effect on learning outcomes of different teaching methods or atmospheres are studied in relation to the initial differences among the learners. Figure 25.1 shows a hypothetical interaction between vocabulary knowledge and student ability to benefit from text instruction versus a video-tape presentation of the same material. The figure shows that those lower in vocabulary knowledge (taking the same comprehension test) do better with video-tape instruction, while those higher in vocabulary skills do better reading a text. Findings of this sort suggest the need to provide different instruction to students with varied learning backgrounds—a very logical conclusion.

Some of the learner characteristics studied in this context include general ability, specific abilities, specific prerequisite skills, personality traits (such as anxiety), and cognitive styles (such as field-dependence versus field-independence). A wide range of "treatments" have also been studied, including programed instruction, lecture method, group discussion, and variations in teacher personality and presentation. A comprehensive evaluation of this research has been complied by Cronbach and Snow (1981).

Within the mastery learning model presented in Chapter 12, *aptitude for learning* would be concerned with whether or not the student possessed the prerequisite skills required to learn a particular skill by a particular method. Students without the prerequisite skills would not be expected to benefit as well as those with the necessary preskills. These preskills could include motivational variables that might determine the reinforcing conditions under which the student works effectively. For example, a student reinforced by task-completion

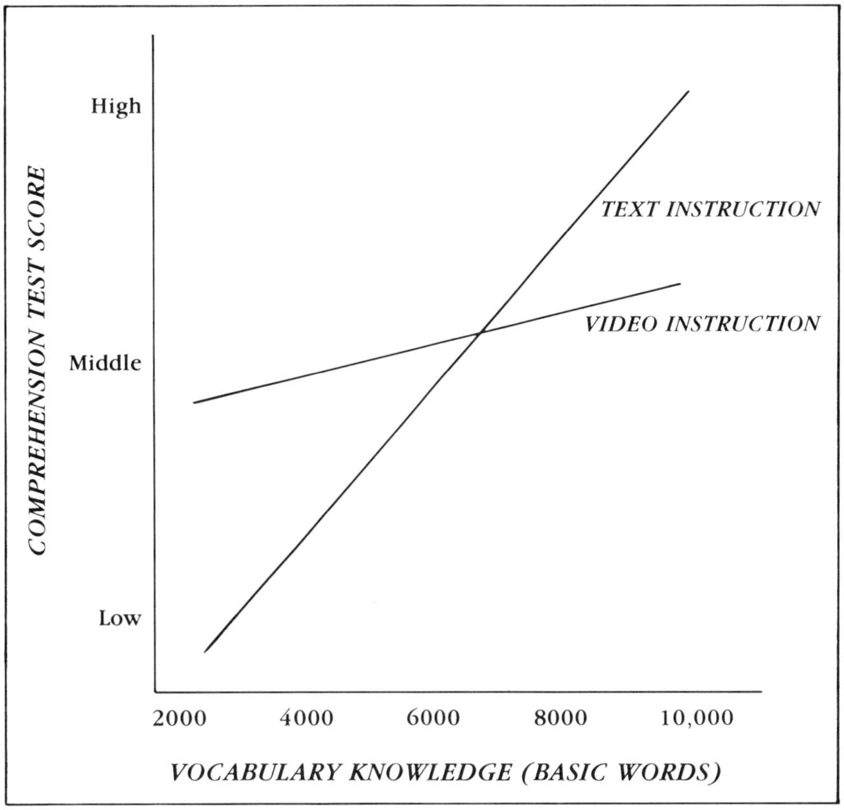

Figure 25-1 *A Hypothetical aptitude-treatment interaction*

might work well independently, while someone more dependent on social reinforcers might work better in group discussion or in teacher-directed instruction. For the most part, however, such motivational variations can be controlled by a good teacher using the variety of strategies covered in this text. Therefore it does not make too much sense to study the "natural variations" of such variables.

The most consistent findings in ATI research relate general verbal intelligence to different teaching approaches. General verbal intelligence reflects the student's knowledge of vocabulary, logical operations, and problem-solving strategies. The research findings suggest that those high in verbal IQ are better able to profit from an opportunity to take in information in their own way. While those low in verbal IQ benefit more from carefully-structured instruction. Preorganizers (lists of key point, study questions, and so on) have been found to help "Lows" learn from text or lecture, but have no effect on, or hinder, "Highs" (Ausubel & Fitzgerald, 1961, 1962; Proger, Taylor, Mann, Coulson, & Bayuk, 1970). However, results on preorganizers, both within and across studies, are quite inconsistent. And, when dealing with difficult materials, even "Highs" may be helped by preorganizers (Cronbach & Snow, 1981). Other kinds of "clarifying devices" (demonstrations, diagrams) seem to help "Lows" more than "Highs." Elaborations involving systematic "explanation" tend to hinder the "Lows" and help the "Highs." In general, "Highs" do better than "Lows" when left to their own devices. This can be attributed to their greater skills in comprehension, reasoning, problem-solving strategies, and so forth.

When other intellectual measures are studied (such as Guilford's specific factors, or Thurstone's spatial ability) consistent aptitude-treatment interactions are usually not found in studies reported to date. Many thought that graphic presentations would be more beneficial to those higher in spatial reasoning. But this is not the case. As Cronbach and Snow (1981) point out, it was also a bad idea. What is measured on a test of spatial reasoning are skills like visualizing in your head what happens if a figure is rotated, or how pieces of a puzzle go together, or how to count hidden blocks. These skills are not necessarily involved in learning from visual displays. The main functions of a visual display are to reduce memory requirements and show relationships.

In the case of mathematical abilities, Wasik (1971) found that students high on SAT Mathematics did better in physics than those who scored low, while a similar relation was not found for SAT Verbal Ability. This outcome should surprise no one, since math skills are critical to physics. Other studies of more specific preskills produce similar outcomes. Students who have the skills necessary to profit from a particular treatment do better. For example, students with high short-term memories did better than "Lows" when instructed to take lecture notes. Students with low short-term memory did better than "Highs" when embedded questions directed the student to important points (Berliner, 1971, 1972). While there was one replication of this finding within a series of studies, there were also many inconsistent findings and failures in replication.

Cronbach and Snow (1981) conclude that the ATI research is generally characterized by "inconsistent results." This outcome is interpreted to result from the interaction of many learner and situation-specific effects on outcomes. As a result, this literature does not lead to many specific recommendations for educators except to be sure the students have the preskills assumed by what you are teaching. Also, much of the ATI research is based on short-periods of experimental instruction that make the results difficult to generalize to classrooms where students have a chance to adapt to different methods over time.

If this research is so inconclusive, why even talk about ATI in a book for beginning teachers? I do so because there is a dogma "out there" about fitting teaching methods to the individual's "learning style," "cognitive style," or "special modalities." Even paper and pencil "learning style inventories" are being marketed which basically ***ask the student*** how she or he likes to learn—alone or with others, with or without teacher, through touch, sight, or hearing (Davidman, 1981). Schools are being sold workshops that do not have a sound scientific basis to them. To put it another way, the "learning styles" approach conflicts with the research findings on effective teaching methods. Once you have your students motivated and are sure they have the preskills for what you are going to teach, go at it as best you can. If you are dealing with physically intact relatively normal students, the major variables that control what you do in teaching lie in the nature of the knowledge to be taught. Most often, the student variable influencing how and what you can teach is likely to be ***vocabulary knowledge.*** This variable is often the critical one in adjusting for differences in students from different social classes, in teaching students grouped on the bases of intelligence test scores, and in teaching groups differing on reading comprehension scores. For some students, it is necessary to preteach critical vocabulary concepts before making a reading assignment, either that or adjust the words you use in lecturing.

HANDICAPPED STUDENTS

Over the past 20 years educators have found ways to keep more and more children and adults with physical and mental handicaps out of institutions and special classes and in the mainstream of society. Those with handicaps are people too. They have desires and feelings similar to our own. They like to be good at things, to show off what they can do, and to learn. And, they can learn—moderately retarded children have been taught to read at third grade level (Booth, Hewitt, Jenkins, & Maggs, 1979) and taught the rule-governed behaviors necessary for beginning programing in BASIC (Berryman & Maggs, 1983). We are all learning to be wary of labels, but there are still many who believe that some children cannot learn because they are brain-injured, retarded, disadvantaged, or disabled. The evidence from the research of the past two decades clearly shows that all of these groups can be taught, and that for the most part, students said to have learning disabilities, usually *just have not been taught* using the most effective methods that are available. While we will be using labels to communicate and help break down our topics for discussion, keep in mind that the label does not tell you who can learn what, or who needs to learn what. These questions are best answered by analysis of the behavior of individual students and by trying to teach with the best technology available.

Intellectual Retardation

In examining the concept of *intelligence* in Chapter 20, you were introduced to three classes of retardation: the mildly retarded, the moderately retarded, and the severely and profoundly retarded. Since you are dealing with a continuum, there will be cases that are difficult to clearly label, but as long as the labels are not taken too seriously there is no harm.

The American Association on Mental Deficiency (AAMD) and the Education for All Handicapped Children Act of 1975 (P.L. 94–142) define mental retardation as "significant subaverage general intellectual functioning existing concurrently with defects in adaptive behavior and manifested during the developmental period which adversely affects a child's educational performance" (Grossman, 1977).

Causes of Intellectual Retardation

Intellectual retardation can be caused by a variety of events. When causes are known, intellectual retardation can often be prevented or remediated.

Physiological Defects. Genetic defects, defective development during pregnancy, and a variety of destructive processes taking place during pregnancy or shortly after birth have been implicated as causes of retardation. For example, Down's syndrome is caused by a defective structure of the chromosomes. A 1984 study by Colleen Jackson-Cook has identified a genetic abnormality in parents (mother or father) that can increase the probability to have a Down's syndrome child by twenty-fold. Jackson-Cook believes at least 30 percent of Down's syndrome births could be prevented with this knowledge. Phenylketonuria (PKU) is due to a genetic defect in the child's metabolism that causes products that are harmful to the brain to enter into the blood stream. Phenylketonuria can now be easily detected in infants and retardation eliminated by diet control.

Many kinds of retardation have their basis in events related to pregnancy. If a child is born prematurely, his chances of being retarded for a variety of reasons are increased. A good diet and good medical care reduce the occurrence of premature births. Diseases such as German measles can produce a retarded child if the mother is infected during pregnancy. This is especially true during the first three months of pregnancy. If steps are taken to insure that women get German measles before having children, this cause of retardation will be eliminated. In the past, syphilis infection in the mother was an important cause of mental retardation. Compulsory blood tests and effective therapy have largely eliminated this condition. Rh blood incompatibility is another former cause of retardation that can now be detected and prevented. In the 1960s and early 1970s, drugs such as LSD and thalidomide used by the mother during pregnancy have been implicated in birth defects. Many other events can happen to injure the brain. The birth process itself can involve mechanical injury or oxygen deficiency.

For a long time, a major form of mental retardation was cretinism, or dwarfism. The lack of iodine, which is important in building the thyroid hormone, leads to defective growth. With the addition of iodine to salt, a major cause of retardation was largely eliminated. Some retardation is related to defective growth of the skull. In microcephaly, the skull is abnormally small. In hydrocephaly, a deformation leads to the excessive accumulation of fluids inside the skull. The skull enlarges and the brain may be damaged if the pressure is not relieved. Surgical treatment of this condition has been fairly successful.

It is not necessary for our purposes to list the many other physiological bases for retarded development that have been identified, such as infections, tumors, and poisons. The main point is that many causes have been found and prevention and treatment programs established. More work in this direction is needed. It is most interesting, however, to recognize that for 75 percent of the retarded, no specific physiological causes can be identified. For some of these, new physiological causes may be found that can be treated or prevented at some time in the future.

Causes Unknown. For the majority of cases, when there is no known basis for the retardation, it is often found that other members of their family are also labeled retarded and their IQ's are usually above 50 (Zigler, 1967). As noted in Chapter 20, there is most likely a combination of hereditary and social learning factors contributing to what has been called "familial retardation." If the parents have been relatively uneducated, this can contribute to their not being able to teach their children as much basic vocabulary skills as more educated parents can. The studies on raising IQ's reviewed in Chapter 20 state that no matter what the cause, there is much that can be done through education to improve social functioning for such children.

Public Law 94–142

The 1975 Education for All Handicapped Children Act provided for a "free appropriate public education" for all handicapped persons in "the least restrictive environment." This law was a major civil rights action on behalf of the handicapped and their parents. Zigler and Muenchow (1979) note that the care of the handicapped has gyrated in cycles. During the last century, for example, state institutions were set up to provide training that would help the retarded become normal. When this did not happen, the attempts to train them were abandoned and state training schools became "human warehouses." Years later, the value of training was "rediscovered," and there was a big push to establish special classes for the handicapped. In the 1960s, special classes were viewed as a means of preventing the retarded from feeling frustrated and inferior because of the inherent comparisons in regular classes they experienced with non-handicapped students (Quay, 1963). Next, special classes were viewed as "inherently stigmatizing" and the political banner was waved for deinstitutionalization and mainstreaming. This move was politically compatible with the other human rights movements of the time and it eventually became law.

Least Restrictive Environment. The requirement that handicapped persons be placed in an environment that provides them with the greatest possible freedom, given their handicaps, provided the thrust for the "mainstreaming" efforts in education today. This requirement does not mean that all handicapped children should be placed in regular classes, but those who can learn and function there (even if requiring special assistance) should be allowed to. A full range of placement possibilities, going from least restrictive to most restrictive would go something like the following:

Least restrictive: Regular classroom
Regular classroom with teacher consultant
Regular classroom with special teacher or aide
Regular classroom with resource room part-time.
Special class part-time, regular class part-time
Special class full-time
Special school, return home at night
Residential school
Homebound instruction
Residential hospital school
Most restrictive: Residential hospital—custodial care

While it is unclear quite where homebound instruction fits into this hierarchy, the goal of special educational programs would be to improve skills to the point of being able to move students to less restrictive settings over time. To implement such goals, while simultaneously protecting parent and student rights, the law requires that IEPs be written for each student.

The IEP. The IEP is an Individualized Educational Program plan for a handicapped student. It is written by a team that includes parents, the student's teacher(s), a qualified school professional, and the student (if appropriate). The IEP is a written document that specifies: (1) current skill levels of the student, (2) year-end goals and the steps (subskills) to be taken to get there, (3) a list of special services the student will receive (counseling, physical therapy), (4) a list of the ways the student will be mainstreamed, and (5) a specification of how progress toward objectives will be evaluated and revised, if necessary, and an estimate of length of time required to complete the plan.

Parent and Student Rights. Parents have many legal rights under the law. Parents may challenge the program developed for their child through legal procedures. Schools must maintain confidentiality and use nondiscriminatory testing practices. Parents have the right of access to school records on their child, the right to obtain an independent evaluation, and the right to representation by an advocate or consultant at the IEP meeting. Where the parent cannot attend a planning meeting, a substitute must be appointed to represent the parent's interest. When evaluations or changes in placement are planned, parents must be notified ahead of time in writing (using a language they can understand).

While it is possible that P.L. 94–142 could be modified or eliminated, regular teachers are likely to be expected to handle more handicapped students in their classes. To facilitate this, more and more colleges of education are offering blocks of special education courses as a part of regular teacher training.

Placement Issues

As we have mentioned in earlier chapters, civil rights issues and special education issues have become entwined. In *Larry P.* v. *Riles* (1979), a federal court judge in California ruled that educational authorities discriminated against black children by using IQ tests that were culturally and racially biased. The basic evidence was that blacks represented only 10 percent of the state's population, but 25 percent of the Educable Mentally Retarded (EMR) (that is, the mildly handicapped) population. Nationwide in 1978, blacks represented 16 percent of the population and 38 percent of the students in classes for EMRs (Messick, 1984). Table 25.1 show the percentages by racial groups and by problem groups. There is also an over-representation of males in special education classes, as you might infer from Chapter 23. The Office of Civil Rights, which is charged with ensuring that the schools comply with equal protection rights of minorities, asked the National Research Council for guidance. The National Research Council appointed a distinguished 15-member panel to examine the issues.

Table 25-1 Nationwide special education placement for specific racial/ethnic groups

	American Indian or Alaskan Native	*Asian or Pacific Island*	*Hispanic*	*Black*	*White*	*All Students*
Percentage of student population	0.79	1.42	6.75	15.72	75.32	100.00
Percentage in special education programs:						
Educable mentally retarded (EMR)	1.73	0.37	0.98	3.46	1.07	1.43
Trainable mentally retarded (TMR)	0.23	0.15	0.24	0.39	0.19	0.23
Seriously emotionally disturbed (SED)	0.33	0.10	0.29	0.50	0.29	0.32
Specific learning disabilities (SLD)	3.49	1.27	2.58	2.23	2.32	2.31
Speech-Impaired (SI)	1.87	1.85	1.78	1.87	2.04	1.99

Report of the NRC Task Force. The approach taken by this task force was not to focus on the simple reduction of numbers of minorities and males placed in EMR classes or to attack the IQ tests used in placement decisions, but to focus on what the students needed in terms of skills and quality services. This approach led to an examination of the validity of the assessment procedures *and* to an examination of the *quality* of the instruction provided in regular and special classes. Messick (1984) and Finn and Resnick (1984) have summarized key chapters from the final report prepared by this group (see Heller, Holtzman, & Messick, 1982).

If you were to take the simplistic solution and just move students out of special education, then the equal protection right might come into conflict with the handicapped person's right to an education as provided by section 504 of the Rehabilitation Act of 1973 and P.L. 94–142. The problem was reformulated into three sources of inequity.

- Are some students more likely to be placed in classes because their regular instruction is of poor quality?
- Are some students placed in classes for the mentally retarded because of invalid testing?
- Does the quality of the special program decrease the probability of some students returning to regular classrooms?

If in fact valid placements showed that effective services were being provided, then inequality in representation of minorities would not be inequitable. Given this analysis of the issue, the panel formulated a two stage assessment procedure for special placements.

Stage 1. Assess the current learning environment. If in fact a large number of minorities are placed in special classes because the regular class instruction is defective, this could be corrected. Thus, before a student is even considered for referral for individual assessment, an evaluation of the quality of current instruction should be undertaken. This evaluation should gather at least four kinds of data according to Messick (1984):

- What is the evidence that the programs being used have been demonstrated to be effective for regular students and special groups? Standardized achievement tests would be helpful here.
- What is the evidence that the student in question has been adequately exposed to the programs (days attended, lessons covered) and the teacher has adequately *implemented* the programs (checks for assumed preskills, has clear presentations, gives appropriate directions, solicits student responses, provides appropriate feedback and reinforcement)? Are other students in the class progressing appropriately?
- Is there evidence the child has failed to learn when the instruction was adequate? Criterion-referenced tests geared to the curriculum would be useful.
- Have efforts been made to identify the learning problem and try other approaches?

Messick and the task force recognized that this is a novel approach, lacking a firm research base and therefore it still needs to be validated. However, it is possible to use the logic and evidence discussed in Chapters 12 to 18 to predict when and where instruction should fail. If that can be done, Messick's proposal should work.

Stage 2. Assessing the student's functioning. If in fact the student's problems cannot be traced to and corrected in the current learning environment, then referral for a special education assessment should be made. The assessment battery should include the following components:

- *Cognitive assessment.* An IQ test may be included as a general measure of past learning, but its limitation for making instructional decisions must be emphasized. Measures of more specific skills related to comprehension, reasoning, memory, reading, math, and so on are also required. Messick also suggests that the assessment include a work sample consisting of intensive "structured teaching for various types of conceptual tasks" (1984). This work sample would provide direct evidence of how well the student can learn.
- *Biomedical measures.* Screening examinations are needed for hearing, vision, motor incoordinations, and so on; for neurological or endocrine problems; and for other potential contributing factors in

the student's history (using an interview with parents and/or medical records).

- *Adaptive behavior measures.* Adaptive behavior scales attempt to identify strengths and weaknesses in taking care of oneself and in social interactions. Some scales are filled out by teachers (Lambert, Windmiller, Cole, and Figueroa, 1975) and some by parents (Mercer and Lewis, 1978). Such scales are normed against an age scale based on the average child. They have proved very useful in assessing degree of retardation as well as in pointing to needed social skills.

Messick concludes his summary of the proposal for equity-based placement procedures by pointing out the importance of continually justifying a special education placement in terms of its current validity and value.

Teaching the Mildly Retarded Student

Finn and Resnick (1984) summarize the research and recommendations on procedures for instructing mildly retarded students. In the past twenty-five years, there was a rash of research trying to demonstrate that special classes were better, and then the reverse, trying to show that mainstreaming was better. The single conclusion from this research is that *setting is not the critical variable* for most outcomes. What is critical is method of instruction. Not surprisingly, the features of effective instruction for the mildly retarded are not different than the features of effective instruction of other high risk groups, and students in general.

> The most consistent finding in these recent studies is that methods of 'direct instruction' tend to be associated with academic gains for [mildly retarded] children. [See Heller, Holtzman, and Messick, 1982, p. 80 for citations of specific studies.] The instructional programs found most effective are those in which (a) the teacher provides daily work assignments and thus determines the pace of work; (b) there is regular recording and reviewing of each child's program, based on tests directly related to the curriculum content; (c) systematic reward for good behavior and learning is offered; and (d) a significant amount of one-to-one instruction, sometimes by peer tutors, is given (Finn and Resnick, 1984, p.10).

These practices have been found effective in regular classrooms, in resource rooms, and in classrooms for the mildly retarded. Direct instruction has also been found effective in social skills training (a topic I will return to later). Finn and Resnick go on to emphasize that the same procedures have been found to be effective with learning disabled and culturally disadvantaged children, leading to the recommendation that students be grouped by *instructional need*, not label. The following conclusion was drawn in the NRC report (Heller et al., 1982, p. 87):

> We can find little empirical justification for categorical labeling that discriminates mildly retarded children from other children with academic difficulties, such as LD children or children receiving compensatory education. . . . The weight of the evidence clearly points to a group of instructional practices that seem to benefit all of these types of children. Intense direct instructional methods . . . seem to be applicable

in a variety of settings . . . and are not different in spirit from the methods that appear to have been generally effective in schools that serve children with poor prognoses for academic success. (Taken from Finn and Resnick, 1984, p. 11.)

Teaching the Moderately and Severely Retarded

While most regular teachers will not be expected to teach the moderately and severely retarded, you should note that the same mastery-learning direct-instruction strategies proven effective with normal students and mildly retarded students have been demonstrated to work with more severely handicapped groups. This point will be illustrated with a few of the many studies currently available.

Chapter 12 described the study by Maggs and Morath (1976), who successfully taught moderately and severely retarded children in a residential school using DISTAR I Language and various reinforcement procedures (see page 167). Booth et al. (1979) followed 12 moderately retarded children (IQs in the low 40s) for 5 years. DISTAR Language I was started in first year and the Reading I was added after Language I was completed (18 months later). The children were reading at the early third grade level at the end of five years and were in DISTAR Reading III. Their mean IQ's had risen from 41.9 to 50.6 (Gersten and Maggs, 1982).

In a series of studies with Down's syndrome children, Graham and Rosemary Clunies-Ross (as reported by Becker, 1982), first demonstrated that by starting training early in the first year, greater developmental progress could be made than if systematic training were started when the children were older. Direct instruction strategies and programs were used when they were appropriate. Eventually the Down's syndrome children were mainstreamed into public schools, but the Clunies-Rosses found that the schools could not handle the children until they helped them set up Direct Instruction groups in reading and math. Groups were formed that included the Down's syndrome children and others with similar reading or math skills.

For many severely retarded persons, especially as they get older, the focus of training is less on reading and arithmetic and more on functional survival skills. For example, Robert Horner and colleagues at the University of Oregon have been using Direct Instruction strategies to teach severely handicapped high school students such skills as street crossing, shopping, receiving and making telephone calls, and skills for use in a sheltered workshop. Various instructional program have been constructed and tested and are available for other teachers to use (Horner, Sprague, and Wilcox, 1982).

Some Issues in Mainstreaming

For handicapped students to be successful in regular classes, they need: "(a) social skills acceptable to teacher and peers, (b) content-based academic skills sufficient to cope with and benefit from the class curriculum, and (c) non-content-based academic skills such as working efficiently, seeking assistance, and writing neat assignments" (Anderson-Inman, 1982).

The potential problems for teachers, handicapped students, and other students that can occur in the area of social skills alone led Hill Walker (1984) to develop the AIMS assessment system. The system evaluates the social behavior *standards* held by the teacher and the social skills of the student. Walker found that teachers vary widely in their tolerance for "deviant" behavior and in the demands they place on students. By assessing student social skills and behavior problems (through ratings and observations), it becomes possible to seek a fit between teacher standards and student behavior, or to train the student in the behaviors needed to function in a particular setting.

Walker, McConnell, Holmes, Todis, Walker, and Golden (1983) developed the *ACCEPTS* curriculum to teach the social and academic survival skills handicapped children would need to function in mainstreamed settings. The skills taught in the ACCEPTS are listed in Table 25.2. (Walker, 1983) Four have to do with teacher interactions. Twenty-four of the skills have to do with peer interactions. A nine-step teaching format is followed using video taped examples (models) of how to do it and how not to do it, prompted practice, and role playing.

Table 25-2 ACCEPTS Skills

Classroom Skills
1. Listening to the Teacher
2. When the Teacher Asks You to Do Something
3. Doing Your Best Work
4. Following the Classroom Rules

Basic Interaction Skills
1. Eye Contact
2. Using the Right Voice
3. Starting
4. Listening
5. Answering
6. Making Sense
7. Taking Turns Talking
8. A Question
9. Continuing

Getting Along Skills
1. Using Polite Words
2. Sharing
3. Following Rules
4. Assisting Others
5. Touching the Right Way

Making Friends Skills
1. Good Grooming
2. Smiling
3. Complimenting
4. Friendship Making

Coping Skills
1. When Someone Says "No"
2. When You Express Anger
3. When Someone Teases You
4. When Someone Tries to Hurt You
5. When Someone Asks You to Do Something You Can't Do
6. When Things Don't Go Right

Anderson-Inman (1982) has identified five approaches to mainstreaming.

1. *A special class is used to catch the students up* in critical reading and math skills so they can be integrated into a regular class. With the success of Direct Instruction programs, this goal appears potentially achievable in some cases. For example, L'E. Stein and Goldman (1980) found that learning disabled students in *Distar Reading* gained fifteen months in reading age over eleven

calendar months. Students in a comparison program (Palo Alto Reading Program) gained only seven months.

2. *Students are accommodated to the regular class.* The Direct Instruction Follow Through model kept students with IQ's as low as 55 in regular classes. If a student was too low to fit into a group, short, individual tutoring was given periodically by the teacher or an aide. Several of the low performers covered only sixty lessons the first year. These children were retained for a second year of kindergarten or first grade so that they would finish Language I and Reading I before going on. By the second year, they would fit into teaching groups and not require special tutoring. Another effective procedure for groups of low performers was to have the teacher or aid *preteach* a math lesson to this group the afternoon before the lesson was taught to the whole class. This approach had two advantages, it provided the additional instruction and practice needed by the low performers and it allowed the low performers to participate more fully with the rest of the class. (Before the researchers got to this strategy they were *reteaching* the low groups rather than *preteaching*. The latter procedures builds self-esteem in the low performers more readily.)

3. Another approach is to teach "*academic support skills*." These are skills such as how to ask for help, how to work efficiently, or how to prepare a neat written paper to turn in to the teacher. For example, some of the component skills involved in neat writing are: "(1) use of margins, (2) starting on the front side, (3) proper placement of the student's name, (4) identification of the assignment's content, (5) leaving the sheet of paper whole, (6) no unnecessary marks or scribbling, (7) writing which stays on the line, (8) use of consistent spacing within and between sections, (9) neat and appropriate use of an eraser" (Anderson-Inman, 1982, p. 9). Skills of this sort can be taught in special classes or regular classes.

4. *The use of a resource-room teacher* to provide skill training part of the day to facilitate functioning in the regular class is a common pattern. Perkins and Anderson-Inman (1981) studied the transfer of skills taught in a resource room to the regular class. Five low performing junior high students were taught a strategy for answering comprehension skills which required making deductions from what was read. Three of the five students had no success in transfering this strategy to text reading in regular classes. Only after further training was given from thirteen different texts used in the classroom, did transfer occur. This is not at all an uncommon finding. One often has to explicitly show the remedial reader that his or her new-found skills in the resource room can be used back in the classroom (where failure was common in the past).

5. It is often useful for the *resource teacher and the classroom teacher to double teach some content areas* for low performer. This is similar to the preteaching discussed under item 2. A major problem is coordinating the work carefully so that the students do not get confused by conflicting approaches.

OTHER SPECIAL GROUPS

This last section briefly looks at six other special groups of students, those with problems of vision, hearing, and speech; learning disabled students; bilingual students, and gifted students.

Problems of Vision

About 1 in 1,000 students have vision impairments requiring special education. Most of these have enough vision to allow them to stay in the classroom if they have large print readers. About 1 in 2,500 are functionally blind and require material in Braille and/or audio recordings. More and more the visually impaired are remaining in regular classrooms but receive specialized training from resource teachers in reading. A variety of special instructional materials are available. Catalogs can be obtained from the Instructional Materials Reference Center of the American Printing House for the Blind, 1839 Frankfort Avenue, Louisville, Kentucky, 40206.

The functionally blind do not, on the average, score lower on IQ tests (as is the case for the deaf). They tend to show the same range of variation as the rest of us. Good hearing is very important to the development of the language comprehension so critical to verbal intelligence. The major problems for the blind are the increased possibility of developing over-dependence on others and the restrictions they face in mobility. Special training is often provided for the blind in learning to get around.

Teachers need to remain alert for mild visual and hearing problems that can interfere with effective school functioning.

Problems of Hearing

Hearing problems may be caused by genetic factors, accidents and infections, birth complications, and other reasons. The control of childhood diseases such as mumps and measles has helped to reduce the frequency of hearing losses. There is still disagreement over the best approaches to the hearing impaired. Oral approaches focus on learning to read lips and manual approaches use sign language and finger spelling. Some approaches combine oral and manual approaches. Most recently direct neural electrical implants are showing promise. The latter offer great hope for achieving closer to normal development for the profoundly deaf. Not being able to hear greatly limits the development of comprehension skills.

Speech Impairments

Speech impairments are quite common in young children and most frequently involve articulation problems and stuttering. In the years of work in Follow Through, my research group found that training in phonics did much to help reduce articulation problems and obviated, in most cases, the need for special remediation. Stuttering problems tend to appear around the age of three or four and tend to disappear in adolescence (Wiig, 1982). Use of delayed auditory feedback, that is gradually changed to normal feedback, has been found effective as a treatment for severe stuttering problems. The delayed feedback leads to talking more slowly during training and facilitates the learning of new speech habits. However, generalization of fluency beyond the training situation is difficult to achieve.

Learning Disabilities

If a student is of normal intelligence, but fails to learn in some basic skills area, she or he is said to have a learning disability. Haring and Bateman (1977) point out that most students said to have learning disabilities have not learned to read, and that there are foolproof methods for teaching them. Haring and Bateman go on to say that a better name for learning disabilities would be "teaching disabilities."

The most commonly *assumed* cause of learning disabilities has been "minimal brain damage"—that is, brain damage for which there is no evidence. However, many other causes have been postulated from chemical imbalances to lack of dominance of one side of the brain. So far, the question of causes has not been answered. However, in the late 1970s, five universities were funded by the government as Institutes for Research on Learning Disabilities. Three of the five institutes (Columbia, Kansas, and Virginia) tested teaching models and variables to find out what worked with LD students. Their findings showed that the most effective procedures were what this text calls mastery-learning, direct-instruction procedures (Stepnoski, 1984).

Bilingual Students

Many languages are spoken in the U.S. other than English. There are a number of Native American languages, Oriental languages, and European languages. The largest group speak Spanish and tend to come from Mexico and other areas of Latin America. Bilingual educational programs were set up in the late 1960s to give children a better chance to learn English without eliminating their own cultural uniqueness. A recent review of studies of programs of limited-English-speaking students, Baker and DeKanter (1982) report that there is a shortage of good empirical findings on effective approaches. There is evidence that structured-immersion approaches (careful teaching in a setting where only the language to be learned is used) were found to be superior to traditional bilingual approaches which sometimes mixed languages during instruction (Lambert and Tucker, 1972; Barik, Swain, and Nwanunobi, 1977).

Four of our Follow Through sites (E. Las Vegas, NM, Dimmitt, TX, Uvalde, TX, and San Diego, CA) had high percentages of Spanish speaking students. Our approach in these setting was first to get English speech and reading strong, and then add oral Spanish, followed by reading in Spanish. This approach was quite successful in reducing the typical "Texmex" confusions of many bilingual settings. The programs in Uvalde and San Diego were validated as effective in teaching math and reading to limited and non-English-speaking students by a panel of the U.S. Government (The Joint Dissemination Review Panel).

A recent norm-referenced study from the Marina Del Mar school in Monterey, CA, (Gersten, Brockway and Henares, 1983), gives further support to the use of Direct Instruction in bilingual settings. The study looked at program effects in grades one and two and three through six. The students were limited-English speaking and non-English speaking, and came from Korea, Vietnam, Japan, the Phillipines, Samoa, Laos, Germany, and Mexico. Comparison students were taken from the traditional bilingual program and matched with DI students on the basis of the Language Assessment Scale score at entry, and ethnic origin.

Scores on the Comprehensive Test of Basic Skills (CTBS) were examined at the end of second grade. On Total Reading, 21 of 28 (75 percent) of the DI students were at or above the median. Only 3 out of 16 (19 percent) of the traditional bilingual students were that high. On Total Math, the percentages above the median were 96 percent (DI) and 62 percent (Bilingual). On Total Language, the percentages were 71 percent (DI) and 44 percent (Bilingual). Only the difference on Language did not reach statistical significance. Follow-up testing of the DI students at the end of third, and for some fourth graders, showed good maintenance of performance on the CTBS.

Table 25.3 (from Gersten et al., 1983) shows norm-referenced comparisons for the older students in grades three through six who were taught in an ungraded setting. Significant gains against the norm group are demonstrated.

Chris van Rensburg (1982) did an experimental comparison of DISTAR with two other programs in South Africa using random assignment to groups of all children in first grade in five schools. The children were from India and bilingual, and the schools had a history of high failure rates. The DISTAR students achieved significantly higher scores on all tests (decoding, comprehension, spelling and writing).

In the past decade, bilingual education has been somewhat of a political football. The government has poured a lot of money into it, but it was often not

Table 25-3 Norm-referenced comparison pre- and post-test scores on the CTBS (percentile equivalents)

	1980-81 School Year: Grades 3 to 6 (N = 15)	
	Pretest (May, 1980) Percentile	*Posttest (May, 1981) Percentile*
Total Reading	4th	19th
Total Language	5th	23rd
Total Math	13th	45th
	1981-82 School Year	
	Pretest (May, 1981) Percentile	*Posttest (May, 1982) Percentile*
Grade 3 (N = 10)		
Total Reading	17th	47th
Total Language	16th	41st
Total Math	39th	50th
Grades 4, 5, 6 (N = 10)		
Total Reading	4th	23rd
Total Language	4th	30th
Total Math	24th	43rd

used effectively. The biggest conflict was between social-cultural goals of multicultural education and English instruction. Our choice has been to give first priority to the English these students must have to further their education, but this does not have to negate multicultural goals. Beginning English language and reading skills can be made quite strong in about six months time. Then the primary language can be brought in (first orally, and about a year later in reading and writing). Features of the bilingual children's parent culture(s) can be a part of the classroom from day one. The bilingual students and their parents offer the teacher a rich resource for teaching about other cultures.

The Gifted and Talented

Attention to the gifted and talented has suffered in the past 20 years as resources were focused on egalitarian goals and away from "ability grouping" which often was discriminatory. But it is also discriminatory to bore brighter students and teach them not to use their capabilities to the fullest. The issues involved here are: How do we identify the gifted? What are they like? And, how can schools facilitate their development?

How Do We Identify the Gifted? Multiple criteria are often used in attempting to identify the gifted in schools. The single instrument that most people will agree should be included in a set of selection criteria is an individual intelligence test. For white, native-born Americans, an IQ of about 130 will select about 3 percent of the students. An IQ of 140 would select the top 1 percent. Most schools with gifted programs take the top 3 percent from each cultural or ethnic group. Because individual IQ tests are costly to give to every student, very often the selection of students for a gifted program will start with a group IQ test and use a low cutoff. According to Fox (1981), a cutoff of 115 will include about 90 percent of the gifted picked up by an individual test, but a cutoff of 130 would miss over half. Teacher recommendations are used, but these can be biased toward the better conforming student. However, teachers can make judgments of quickness in learning, memory, vocabulary, general comprehension, and special talents that may be helpful. There are varieties of giftedness which the verbal IQ test might not pick up. Specialists in artistic and scientific fields might be used to provide nominations. Identifying especially creative skills is not all that easy, but the judgments of experts can help.

What Are They Like? Lewis Terman, the father of the Stanford-Binet, began a study in 1925 of a large group of children with IQ's of 140 or higher. The study is still continuing. The children were identified by teacher recommendations and the Stanford-Binet IQ test. Terman found that those selected had been precocious in physical development also. They walked earlier, were more athletic, and were larger, stronger, and healthier. However, remember we are talking about "on the average." Not all gifted are physically more capable. Terman's gifted were also better adjusted and had fewer social problems. The teacher nominations may have biased the group in this direction. As adults, Terman's gifted (especially the men, as noted in the last chapter) were very productive as scientists, authors, inventors, playwrights, and artists. They were definite assets to our society, a resource worth cultivating.

How Can Schools Facilitate Their Development? The main choices available include special grouping, with enrichment or acceleration, and special teaching methods. A large number of school districts have decided to use special grouping. Gifted students are less bored when they can be challenged and interact with bright peers at least part of the day. There has been considerable resistance to the acceleration of the gifted, although the current evidence suggests that even greatly accelerated programs, leading to entry into college two to four years earlier, does not necessarily lead to poor social development (although it might in individual cases).

In one program (Stanley, Keating, & Fox, 1974; Keating, 1976), mathematically talented youth were identified in junior high using the Scholastic Aptitude Test (SAT). They were placed in accelerated classes in high school and college math. One ninth grader had already completed three courses in calculus. He entered Johns Hopkins at fifteen and a half. Another student skipped 7th, 9th, 10th, 12th and 13th grades, completing his bachelor's degree at 17 and started on his Ph.D. Challenging work that can come through acceleration seems to have benefits that simple enrichment programs have difficulty providing. With flexible planning it is possible to prevent gross social dislocations for such students by spending part of the day with peers—for example, in sports, perhaps social studies, and social events.

Other options for the gifted include courses at local colleges, summer institutes, after-school special programs, independent self-directed projects, etc. It may also be useful to have the students help in planning their own learning goals.

Pushy Parents. A common problem faced by teachers is pressure from parents of "semigifted" students who want their child in the top group of gifted students. It takes considerable tact on the teacher's part to keep from insulting the parents and creating open conflict. Here are some suggestions. Ask about the reasons their child should be in a special group. Listen and be as supportive as you can with honesty. Discuss the criteria your school has for special groups and how their child stands on the criteria. Consider having a re-evaluation if there is justification. Explain that there are always going to be borderline cases and the gifted program has a limit as to the number of students they can take. Your goal should be to be fair and to keep the parents working with you.

SUMMARY

Studies of the interaction of student aptitudes with teacher characteristics and teaching methods have yielded few stable findings. The most consistent findings relate to general verbal ability, where those who score high benefit from being allowed to do more on their own, and those who score low need more carefully structured instruction. The fads based on "learning styles" or "cognitive styles" have very little substance to them and should be treated with caution. The single student variable most likely to prompt differential teacher actions is level of vocabulary (which is, of course, closely related to general verbal ability). Preteaching of vocabulary is often important for the lower performers.

In looking at issues related to mental retardation, the chapter examined some of the causes and the gains in prevention that have occurred over the past half century. You also saw that the majority of mildly retarded students show no known basis for retardation. This group has been called the familial retarded and the basis probably lies in a mixture of adverse hereditary and environmental events.

The requirements of Public Law 94–142 were examined. This law provides for the "free appropriate public education" of every child in "the least restrictive environment possible." It does not mean all retarded children have to be mainstreamed, only that placement should be as normal as possible, given the student's capabilities. The key to implementing P.L. 94–142 is the IEP and the legal rights of students and their parents. The IEP is an Individualized Educational Program plan. It sets goals, time lines, and evaluation procedures. Parents have the right to contest school plans for their handicapped student under the law.

Discrimination issues have been raised in the placement of students in special education. Nationwide, blacks represent 16 percent of the populations and 38 percent of those in special classes. To ensure fairness, a task force of the National Research Council (NRC) recommends a two-stage assessment process. Stage 1 is concerned with the adequacy of the current learning environment. Only if this proves to be adequate and not in need of improved methods does the assessment process move to Stage 2. In this second stage, the recommended assessment is based on cognitive skills (including general intelligence and a learning work sample), biomedical measures and history, and adaptive behavior measures (self care and social skills).

The research studies involving the teaching of mildly retarded student show that the setting is not a critical variable. What is found effective regardless of setting are methods that have been called "direct instruction." These methods have also been show to be effective in teaching social skills. The NRC report concludes that there is no justification for placing mildly retarded students in groups separated from LD students or students receiving compensatory education. Placement should be based on educational need, not categorization.

A few studies with the moderately and severely retarded were discussed to illustrate that effectiveness of direct instruction methods also extends to these groups.

To achieve the mainstreaming ideals of P.L. 94–142, it is necessary to see that handicapped students have social skills that make them acceptable to teachers and peers, that they have basic academic skills, and that they have "academic support skills" (or academic survival skills) necessary to listen to instructions, do assignments, etc.

Walker developed the AIMS assessment system to help fit students and settings together. The system assesses the teacher's judgments on what is acceptable social behavior in the classroom and the student's behavior also. The goal is to tailor the placement to settings where it is most likely to be successful. Walker et al. also developed the ACCEPTS training program to teach academic survival skills and social skills handicapped students might need in less restrictive settings.

A variety of strategies and procedures for approaching mainstreaming were illustrated.

In looking at other special problems, the chapter briefly described some of the problems involved with students with impaired sight and hearing, and with speech problems. It was noted that most learning disabled students are quite teachable if appropriate methods are used. There may be a few "hard core" LD students, but until better methods are used (especially in beginning reading) it will be hard to tell them from the "teaching disabilities." Effective methods for teaching bilingual students are available without sacrificing the goals of multicultural instruction. The key is not to confuse symbols and sounds from two languages during beginning instruction. In my view, since English is likely to be the major language by which non-English and limited English students will be instructed in this country, it should be given initial priority in a structured-immersion program.

This chapter closed by reviewing some of the problems of getting the best out of the gifted and talented. A variety of procedures for identifying these students were discussed. Terman's work on the gifted shows that on the average they are advanced in many areas, physically, socially, emotionally, as well as intellectually. Current research support school practices that focus on acceleration in special classes, especially in math and the sciences.

PART IV

MONITORING AND EVALUATING INSTRUCTION

Part IV consists essentially of two chapters covering tests and monitoring systems that help one to evaluate the progress of instruction. A third and final chapter on "Futures" is also included.

As we have noted many times earlier, systems to monitor student progress through a curriculum are important for the student and teacher. Chapter 26 describes general strategies for building monitoring systems, and for constructing tests geared to a specific curriculum. Chapter 27 deals with norm-referenced tests that might be used for longer-term evaluation of student progress. The chapter focuses on the nature of the tests and how to interpret the various kinds of scores used to report the results of norm-referenced tests. It also considers issues related to the reliability and validity of test scores.

The final chapter examines some technologies that are likely to increasingly play a role in education. Microcomputers, network systems, and videodiscs offer the promise to provide the teacher with better ways to set up mastery-learning classrooms.

CHAPTER

26

MONITORING STUDENT PROGRESS WITH CRITERION-REFERENCED TESTS

Tests are used by educators to help make decisions about individual students, to evaluate innovations, to hold teachers and administrators accountable, and to provide information to teachers on student progress. There are two major types of tests used in education today—*norm-referenced* and *criterion-referenced.* These types of tests differ with respect to the way test scores are interpreted. When the interpretation is based on some specified standard of performance, the test is called *criterion-referenced* (Glaser, 1963). When the interpretation is based on a comparison to the distribution of scores obtained by others taking the test (that is, a norm group), the test is called *norm-referenced.* One type of norm-referenced test, the IQ test, was discussed in Chapter 20. Norm-referenced achievement tests will be discussed in the next chapter. The present chapter will focus on the design and use of criterion-referenced tests by teachers in evaluating and monitoring student performance.

A COMPARISON OF NORM-REFERENCED AND CRITERION-REFERENCED TESTS

Besides differing in the ways scores are interpreted, norm-referenced and criterion-referenced tests differ in their usefulness for various purposes. Norm-referenced tests are especially useful in selecting relatively high- or relatively low-scoring groups. For example, an IQ test might be used as one criterion for selecting students for a "gifted program." The Scholastic Aptitude Test might be used to select promising students for college admission or scholarships. Low scores on IQ tests are usually used as one criterion for placing students in special educational programs. Norm-referenced tests are also often used in the comparative evaluation of longer-term educational outcomes. While there are certain risks in using norm-referenced tests to compare programs (these are discussed in the next chapter), they have often provided a useful framework for making comparisons. Criterion-referenced tests have been found most useful in evaluating whether students meet a standard (as in minimum competency tests) and in monitoring student progress within mastery-learning type programs.

The reason for differences in uses of norm-referenced and criterion-referenced tests lies in the way tests are constructed. The items that make up norm-referenced tests are selected for their ability to discriminate between people. Items that everyone passes or fails *are discarded* because they do not help to spread people out on a score distribution. On the other hand, the items that make up a criterion-referenced test are selected because they represent an important skill the learner is expected to acquire. It would be all right if everyone passed an item after instruction. In fact, that would be a most pleasing outcome. (Return to Figure 12.4 and the discussion of mastery learning to see an example of how the distributions of performances can differ.) If the standards for norm-referenced tests were used to make tests to monitor the learning process, you might be throwing out items that measured what you were most concerned about.

TYPES OF CRITERION-REFERENCED TESTS

Criterion-referenced tests have developed their current applications in education through the growth in the 1960s of the behavioral objectives movement (Mager, 1962) and the reappearance of mastery learning models. An approach to teaching based on testing objectives was advocated by Popham (1973) and called *criterion-referenced instruction.* Popham recommended that teachers follow a strategy of: (1) stating objectives in terms of observable performances, (2) building and giving students a pretest on the objectives, (3) providing instruction, (4) posttesting on the objectives. The potential advantages of this approach in providing feedback to teachers and students alike should be obvious. Over the years, however, it has become increasingly apparent that to be maximally useful, *criterion-referenced tests need to be tied to specific curricula,* not just to objectives (Baker, 1974). When tests are designed for specific instructional programs, it is easier to write items that are logically valid measures of what is being taught. Also, for some kinds of objectives, one cannot construct a fair test without knowing how the objective was taught.

Chapter 14 distinguished between teaching objectives that are general-cases and those that are not. If a general-case has been taught, a test of it can be composed of *any sample of instances* of the general-case that was taught.[1] If a set made up of independent members has been taught, *every member needs to be tested* if you want to be sure it was learned. If your objective is teaching letter sounds, you have an independent-member (IM) set, where every member must be taught. Knowing that Susie can read the sound for *a* does not help you in inferring that she knows the sound for *t.* On the other hand, each sound by itself constitutes a general case, so I can sample the kinds of *a*'s and *t*'s she is to read. Similarly, a set of prepositional concepts—*on, over, under, beside*—is an IM set, but each member concept is a general case.

In dealing with problem-solving routines, you have an additional problem. Consider the objective, "Give the correct answer for any problem of this form (4 + 6 = _) with sums up to 20." If I teach this skill as a problem-solving routine, I can test with a randomly selected sample of problems, including those not used in the instruction. If I teach the same objective as a set of independent rote facts, then *I would have to test for each one* to know if it were learned or not.

The distinction between general-case and independent-member objectives is important in building tests to assess instruction. Given a general case, you can always *randomly sample* to see if it has been learned. Given an IM set, we have two choices: (1) you can *test every member* to insure it has been learned, (2) or you can use a *representative sample* to gain an estimate of *how much* has been learned. Hively et al. (1973) calls this latter procedure "domain-referenced testing." For example, a spelling test might be constructed from every 6th word on the list the students were given to learn. A final exam in algebra might divide the content covered into principles, concepts, and several

[1]However, note that how general a given concept (principle, etc.) is depends on the range of application demonstrated by the range of teaching examples (that is, the range of variation shown for S^+, S^-, and Si).

application categories, and then sample from these according to how much weight the teacher wished to give different categories. Working within a program like Individually Prescribed Instruction, test items might be sampled to cover each subskill in the levels the students have covered (see Figure 12.2). The important point in test construction is to know when and what kind of a *sampling process* is needed, or when *every skill* should be tested.

MONITORING SYSTEMS

A central feature of mastery-learning approaches is a system of criterion-referenced tests for monitoring student progress. In this section we will look at the overall requirements of a good monitoring system and illustrate both informal and formal systems. Ideally, where the option is there, one would select proven instructional materials with *built-in* placement and monitoring procedures. Later, you will look at some issues in constructing your own tests when they are needed.

There are six general steps for building a good monitoring system:

1. Specify a placement procedure.
2. Define progress units.
3. Specify checkout and review procedures.
4. Develop a guide for recording progress through the units.
5. Establish goals.
6. Establish remedial procedures and retesting.

Criterion-referenced testing is involved in steps 1, 3, and 6. Steps 2, 4, and 5 help to motivate the students and help keep track of student progress.

Note: If you happen to be placed in a school that is not using programs with a built-in systematic monitoring system, you can still use mastery-learning monitoring strategies by making use of the suggestions which follow.

Test For Placement

Placement testing is used to see if students have assumed preskills. Where a general placement system is not provided with the program being used, it is necessary to analyze some of the early tasks in the program for their assumed preskills. For example, if the students are required to do problems in addition with sums up to twenty, they would need to be able to count to twenty, read numbers up to twenty, write numbers to twenty, and have a procedure for solving the problems. The program would need to be examined to see whether these skills are taught or not. Where they are not, it would be necessary for the teacher to test for them and teach them as needed. Where individualized instruction is not possible, it is usually economical to spend a few days or more on firming preskills before pushing on. Where there is grouping by skill levels or individualization, the placement procedure should be able to tell you where to start a given student.

When students come from different programs, you need to be careful that test failures are not just due to a change of instructions or test format. Some students may have learned the concepts and skills, but do them a different way. A brief instruction on "the new way" may be all that is needed. In any case, placement decisions should always be made tentatively, using the student's performance in the next few weeks as the test of whether a different placement might be more appropriate.

Define Progress Units

For beginning levels, a *unit* may be defined as completion of certain workbook exercises, by a specified number of pages covered in a text, by specified performance on a test of key concepts, or by the amount of work to be covered in a day or a week. At more advanced levels, the unit may be a chapter in a text.

The units provide the teacher with a metric for measuring progress through the curriculum. By charting this progress (as illustrated later), the teacher is able to keep track of progress of individual students and to take steps to improve this progress when necessary.

Specify Checkout and Review Procedures

For each unit, specify checkout procedures and periodic review procedures. The checkout procedures can consist of a written exercise(s) checked by the teacher, an aide, or by the student. Oral reading progress can be checked by reading a passage to the teacher or aide who charts rate and errors. When writing skills are adequate, comprehension and grammar tasks can be checked by the student. A desk can be placed at the back of the room as a checkout station. An answer key can be provided by the teacher so that the students can correct their answers (using a special colored pencil). The answers can then be turned in for spot checking by the teacher. For some activities the checkout can be given by another student who has completed the unit. Checkouts can also consist of unit tests which are corrected by the teacher or students. The point to note is that monitoring procedures can be individualized and need not involve a lot of extra teacher or aide time except at beginning levels where oral responding is very critical to the objectives.

Develop a Guide for Recording Progress Through the Units

The next step is to develop a guide specifying the steps to be followed in working through the units and taking checkouts. The guide should also serve as a record of progress. One teacher we have worked with had a large group (thirty-three) of fourth graders with reading skills ranging from beginning second to sixth grade. She devised a system that provided small-group instruction and workbook exercises to the lowest group and a more individualized self-directed approach for the more advanced students. The list of tasks to be completed in reading were placed on dittos in order. The tasks covered the basal series from second grade to sixth grade. Each student was provided with materials appropriate to his or her level, and an appropriate dittoed page was stapled to each student's workbook to provide a checklist to be followed and a record of progress. The following is an example of the kind of instructions provided.

Unit 7	Completion Check	Completion Date
1. Read story on pages 36 to 45 in your reader. 2. Answer the questions on page 46 in your reader. 3. Check your answers at checkout station A, and place in box A. 4. Do workbook exercise 7 on pages 14 and 15. 5. Check your answers at checkout station B, and place workbook in box B. 6. Do SRA *Reading Laboratory* level 1b, number 7. 7. Check your answers at checkout station C, and place in box C.		

Establish Goals

With a sequenced list of tasks to be followed for each instructional program, an individualized approach must let the students know what is expected of them. Setting weekly goals for progress is a very effective procedure for increasing motivation. Figure 26.3 on page 406 illustrates a goal chart used within the University of Kansas Follow Through Model.

Establish Remedial Procedures

A monitoring system makes it very evident when students are progressing too slowly through the course or are not learning the material. If the children are progressing too slowly, the solution may involve increasing the amount of instruction provided through the use of an aide or tutor or changing the incentive conditions through any one of a variety of procedures covered in earlier chapters. If some students are having trouble with specific skills, special lessons can be provided, or other solutions. The key is to establish a plan for dealing with errors that provides new instruction and a *new checkout* on the skills.

SOME ILLUSTRATIVE MONITORING SYSTEMS

In illustrating mastery learning models in Chapter 12, you have already seen the monitoring systems used in Individually Prescribed Instruction (Figures 12.1, 12.2, and 12.3), in computer-assisted instruction, Keller's Personalized System of Instruction, and Precision Teaching. Two additional systems used in the Follow Through project by the Behavior Analysis model and the Direct Instruction Model will be described here.

Behavior Analysis Monitoring System

Under the direction of Don Bushell, Jr. and Gene Ramp at the University of Kansas, the Behavior Analysis Follow Through Model has demonstrated the effectiveness of a variety of procedures for building a monitoring system around existing curriculum materials. At one time the program was operating in 300 classrooms in 12 communities where there is a high percentage of disadvantaged children. The goal of the program was to substantially improve the children's mastery of basic skills. Most classrooms had a teacher and two or three aides. Each adult typically worked with six or seven children.

Curriculum materials were selected that could be individualized in their use, that required frequent student response, and that contained periodic criterion-referenced tests. The main programs selected for use were *Programed Reading* (McGraw-Hill), *Sets and Numbers* (Singer), and the *Behavior Analysis Handwriting Primer. Programed Reading* was augmented by a phonics preprogram using DISTAR-type small-group instruction, by SRA Reading Laboratories, and by a recommended list of supplementary texts.

Both the reading and math programs have frequent in-book tests. *Programed Reading* has a test for each one-fourth book and the end of each book. Seven to eight books constitute a school year program. *Sets and Numbers* has in-book quizzes for each unit. These range in number from 13 in Book 1 to 24 in Book 6. Each curriculum series was broken into progress steps, defined by the number of pages to be completed. The steps were constructed to take about the same amount of time to complete on the average, and, where feasible, break at a testing point. Whenever the student reached a check point, the test was taken and checked by the teacher or aide. If it was passed at an 80 percent correct rate or higher, the student went on to the next unit. If the test was failed, an analysis of the problem was made and supplemental materials and tutoring used to teach

the deficient skills. The test was then retaken and if passed, the student progressed to the next unit.

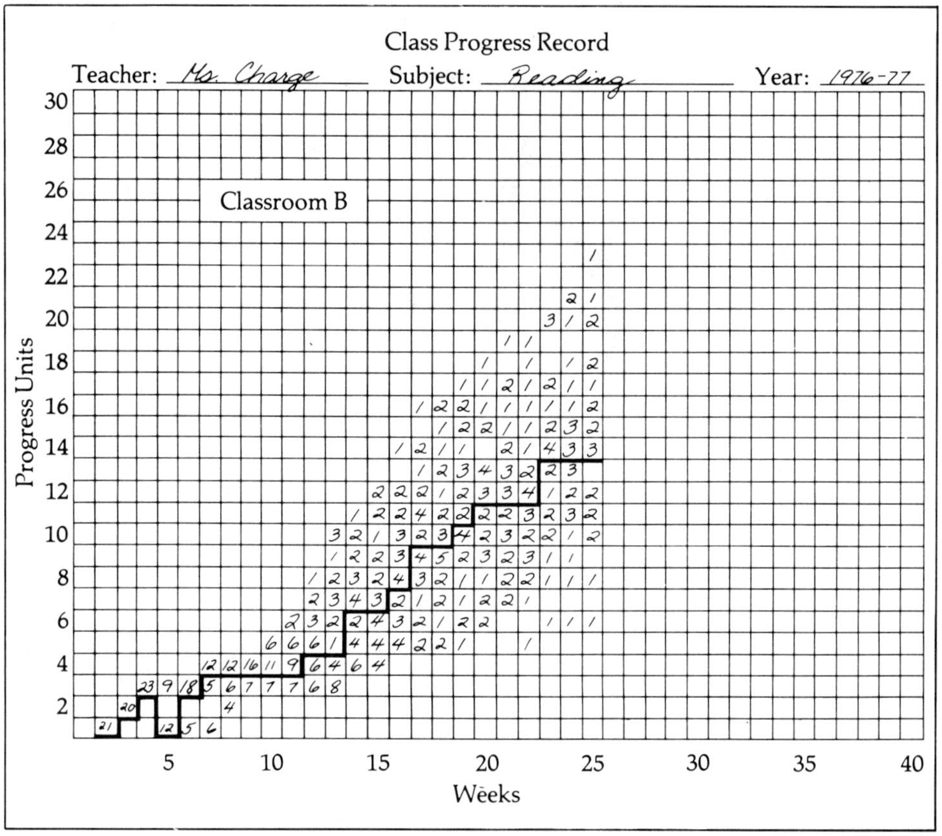

Figure 26-1 *Completed class progress record*

With an individualized program beyond the initial level, and with tests built into the curriculum, it was not difficult to keep track of student progress. Figure 26.1 shows a Class Progress Record for reading (Bushell, 1973). The

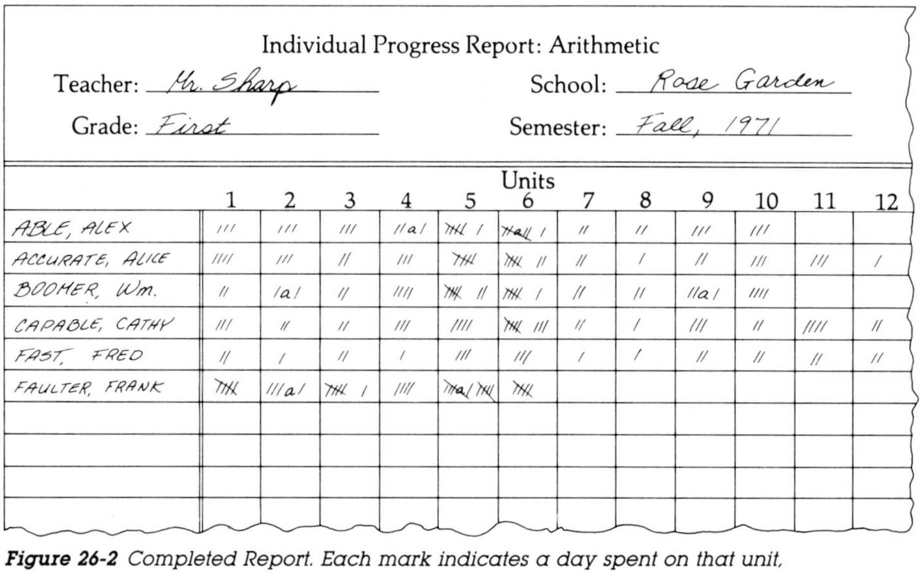

Individual Progress Report: Arithmetic

Teacher: Mr. Sharp School: Rose Garden

Grade: First Semester: Fall, 1971

	Units 1	2	3	4	5	6	7	8	9	10	11	12
ABLE, ALEX	///	///	///	//a/	𝍸 /	𝍸(a) /	//	//	///	///		
ACCURATE, ALICE	////	///	//	///	𝍸	𝍸 //	//	/	//	///	///	/
BOOMER, Wm.	//	/a/	//	////	𝍸 //	𝍸 /	//	//	//a/	////		
CAPABLE, CATHY	///	//	//	///	////	𝍸 ///	//	/	///	//	////	//
FAST, FRED	//	/	//	/	///	///	/	/	//	//	//	//
FAULTER, FRANK	𝍸	///a/	𝍸 /	////	𝍸(a) 𝍸	𝍸						

Figure 26-2 *Completed Report. Each mark indicates a day spent on that unit, a indicates absent*

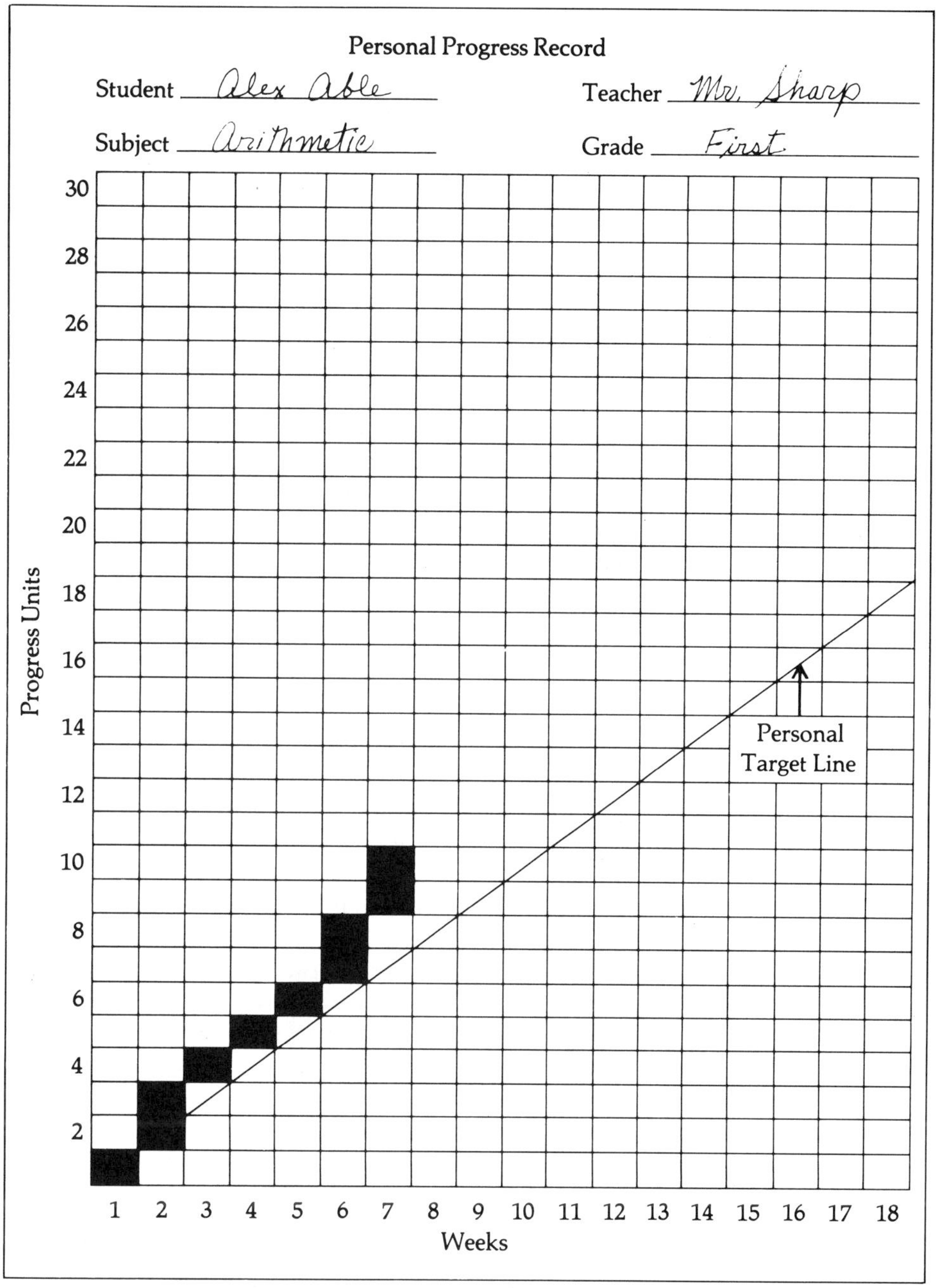

Figure 26-3 *Completed Personal Progress Record. This chart is filled in for Alex by seeing how many units are completed at each five-day point for the data in Figure 26-2*

teacher for this class took the whole class through the first three units and used that as the pretest. By week five the teacher was ready to take twelve of the students back for review of basic sounds. From week 11 on the degree of individualization increased steadily. The dark line on Figure 26.1 shows the progress of the median (middle) child in the class. Progressing at this rate, the median child will complete unit 28 by the end of school. This corresponds to seven books in the *Programed Reading* series and is considered average progress for middle-class children.

Individual progress records are also kept. Figure 26.2 shows an example of a very simple record for six children. The units in arithmetic are listed across the top. A slash is placed in the appropriate box each day to show the unit each student was working on. An *a* indicates an absence. The daily information is readily converted into a weekly or monthly Personal Progress Record as indicated in Figure 26.3 (Bushell, 1973).

The University of Kansas monitoring system contains all of the essential features that we have indicated are required by an adequate monitoring system. There is a specified curriculum, adaptable to individualization, as well as placement procedures, progress measures toward goals, evaluation of student performance and remedial procedures. It should not be too surprising to learn that test data on progress of children in this program are very positive in comparison to control groups (Stebbins et al., 1977). The beauty of the program lies not in the logical niceties of the programing procedures or the completeness of analysis of progress, but in the *simplicity* of the procedures.

Direct Instruction Monitoring System

The system for monitoring student progress in the Direct Instruction Follow Through Model was based on placement tests, criterion-referenced tests (called Continuous Progress Tests), and biweekly reports summarizing testing data and lessons covered in DISTAR Reading, Arithmetic, and Language programs. There was also a system for monitoring teachers and aides to see where they needed help, but that will not be covered here.

Placement Tests. The DISTAR programs were designed so that they covered (in early lessons) the so called "readiness skills" not taught by basal programs. This makes it possible to test entry level students and place nearly all of them in a lesson sequence where they need to be. Those who test below Lesson 1, are given tutoring until they are ready for the programs. Most students at that level would be in special classes.

At advanced levels, the teacher can use several methods to decide on placement. One approach is to take the records of how far the students advanced in the program the year before and start the children back ten to fifteen lessons, using these lessons as "warm up" and review during the first week of school. From then on, decisions on group assignments are made on the basis of individual performances. Another approach is to use the continuous progress tests to determine placement. This may be especially helpful with new children entering the program. A third approach is to use the review lessons, that precede advance level programs, as a testing device to make placement decisions.

Reports of Lessons Taught. Every two weeks a report is filled out showing which lesson each group is on, the number of lessons gained during that two weeks, and lessons gained from the start of the school year. By taking a school calendar and numbering it consecutively from the first day of school to the last day of school, the ***day in the school year*** can be determined for any given report date. By comparing day-in-school year with number of lessons taught, important monitoring information is obtained. From this information, a teacher, supervisor, or principal can easily determine the likelihood of any given group completing one of the programs. Table 26.1 gives an example of a Biweekly Report of Lessons Taught. In that report, by December 10, 70 school days had passed. The children in group 1 started on lesson day 10 in reading (as determined by the placement test). They are now at lesson day (LDIP) 90. During the past two weeks they gained twelve lessons. From the start of the school year they have gained eighty lessons or an averge of 1.14 lessons a day (80/70). If they continue at this rate they will be on lesson 205 (1.14 × 180) by the end of the year. This means they will be 45 days into the level 2 program. Group 1 is making good progress.

Table 26.1 Biweekly Report of Lessons Taught

Teacher Thomas　Grade K　School Marshall
Date Dec. 10　Day in School 70

Group	Reading					Arithmetic					Language				
	L	*SDIP*	*LDIP*	*2 wk Gain*	*Year Gain*	*L*	*SDIP*	*LDIP*	*2 wk Gain*	*Year Gain*	*L*	*SDIP*	*LDIP*	*2 wk Gain*	*Year Gain*
1	1	10	90	12	80	1	40	125	13	85	1	60	150	14	90
2	1	0	70	10	70	1	0	65	9	65	1	0	75	11	75
3	1	0	60	9	60	1	0	50	7	50	1	0	65	10	65
4	1	0	40	5	40	1	0	45	4	45	1	0	55	8	55

L = Program Level
SDIP = Starting Day In Program
LDIP = Lesson Day In Program

Group 4 started the reading program at the beginning. They are now on lesson day 40. They progressed only five lessons in the past two weeks. They are progressing at an average rate of .57 lessons per day (40/70). By the end of the year they will be expected to complete only 103 lessons (.57 × 180). Whether this is an acceptable performance will depend on a more careful analysis of how they are being taught. If analysis shows that the problem is one of scheduling teaching time, or if the teacher's skills with low-performing children are weak, then the supervisor would try to adjust the schedule or provide additional training for the teacher. If the group is in fact being taught each day and the teaching method is adequate, this rate of progress would be acceptable. Many groups of children with low skills at entry progress slowly the first year. After mastering skills in the language of instruction, this rate can be expected to improve to .80 or .90 lessons per day.

It is possible to plot the information from the Biweekly Report of Lessons Taught on a graph each two weeks to show more readily the rate of progress toward a goal.

Reports of Continuous Progress Testing. In the schools that implemented the Direct Instruction Model, the students were tested each two weeks in one subject area. Testing aides would test reading for two weeks, then arithmetic, and then language. This cycle was repeated each six weeks, giving five or six cycles during the school year. The test results go to teachers, supervisors, and sponsor each two weeks as part of the Biweekly Report of Lessons Taught. These test data have been very helpful in pinpointing problems and remedial procedures.

The Arithmetic I Continuous Progress Test will be used to illustrate the monitoring procedure and its uses in decision making. The arithmetic test is made up of tracks which cover the major skills in the program. Figure 26.4 illustrates an Individual Record Form. The abbreviations across the top stand for the track names, such as Object Counting (OC) or Algebra Addition (AA). The testing begins according to the student's current lesson placement in the program. For example, if a student is on Lesson 100, testing would begin with those items in the row identifying the 94–103 lesson range (items 7, 15, 25, 29, 33). The tester goes ahead to the next item in a track if the first is passed, and moves back if it is failed. Since each item (which is actually a set of tasks) is selected to reflect ten days progress in the lessons tested in the track, the scores can be directly interpreted in relation to lesson placement in the program. If a student is two items ahead of where the teacher has him, he is 20 lessons ahead. If a student is two items behind, he is 20 lessons behind. To make the tests useful diagnostically, a key is provided so that for any item missed, the teacher has a direct reference to the tasks which need to be taught. For each new testing cycle, the same form is used, providing a summary of progress over the year.

ARITH 1: 1-220

Arithmetic Record Form

Teacher________________

Child________________

Site ________________

Testing	*Group*	*Lesson*
1st		
2nd		
3rd		
4th		

Lesson Range	*OC*	*CTN*	*CET*	*CFN TN*	*E*	*A*	*AA*	*FA*	*POS*	*SP*	*CB*	*AAF*	*S*	*SF*	*AS*	*C*	*ASF*	
1 43	1 2− 2+	8 9− 9+	17															
44 53	3− 3+	10− 10+	18− 18+															
54 63		11− 11+	19− 19+															
64 73	4− 4+	12− 12+	20− 20+	22														
74 83	5− 5+	13− 13+	21− 21+	23− 23+														
84 93	6− 6+	14− 14+		24− 24+	28	32												
94 103	7− 7+	15− 15+		25− 25+	29− 29+	33− 33+	46											
104 113		16− 16+		26− 26+	30− 30+	34− 34+	47− 47+											
114 123				27− 27+	31− 31+	35− 35+	48− 48+	56										
124 133						36− 36+	49− 49+	57− 57+	67	77								
134 143						37− 37+	50− 50+	58− 58+	68− 68+	78− 78+	87							
144 153						38− 38+	51− 51+	59− 59+	69− 69+	79− 79+	88− 88+	94						
154 163						39− 39+	52− 52+	60− 60+	70− 70+	80− 80+	89− 89+	95− 95+	99					*Lesson Range*
164 173						40− 40+	53− 53+	61− 61+	71− 71+	81− 81+	90− 90+	96− 96+	100− 100+	106	112			164 173
174 183						41− 41+	54− 54+	62− 62+	72− 72+	82− 82+	91− 91+	97− 97+	101− 101+	107− 107+	113− 113+			174 183
184 193						42− 42+	55− 55+	63− 63+	73− 73+	83− 83+	92− 92+	98− 98+	102− 102+	108− 108+	114− 114+	118		184 193
194 203						43− 43+		64− 64+	74− 74+	84− 84+	93− 93+		103− 103+	109− 109+	115− 115+	119− 119+	122	194 203
204 213						44− 44+		65− 65+	75− 75+	85− 85+			104− 104+	110− 110+	116− 116+	120− 120+	123− 123+	204 223
214 220						45− 45+		66− 66+	76− 76+	86− 86+			105− 105+	111− 111+	117− 117+	121− 121+	124− 124+	224 243

Figure 26-4 *Individual Record Form*

Data from individual testing are then summarized on a Biweekly Test Report form covering the whole class. (The Biweekly Report of Lessons Taught, illustrated earlier, goes on the bottom of the test report, so that only one form is needed.) Figure 26.5 gives an example of part of a Biweekly Test Report. For each group, numbers in the shaded area give the items the student should pass. For group 1, all students passed item 11 on track 1 as they should have. For tracks 2, 3, 4, and 5, most students were right on target, and only a few were 10 days (one item) ahead or behind. This is acceptable. For group 2, however, there are problems with tracks 2 and 4. Several students in the group are 20 days behind (circled scores). This performance calls for remediation in sounding out words (track 2) and rhyming (track 4).

In group 3 there are problems with tracks 2, 3, and 4. Tract 3 involves reading new words using sounds which have been taught. Groups 2 and 3 could be combined for review on tracks 2, 3, and 4.

In group 4, Edward needs special tutoring in tracks 1 and 2 or he won't

BIWEEKLY REPORT

SITE: Smithville SUBJECT: Reading REPORT NO: 13 DATE: 3-17-75
TEACHER: Selma Salt GRADE: Kindergarten SCHOOL DAY AT TEST: 132

	Group No.	Days Absn.	LDIP*	TRACKS				
				1	2	3	4	5
Level: Ⓘ II III			100	11**	23	34	44	53
Shauna	1	0	100	11	23	34	44	53
Susan	1	0	100	11	24	35	45	54
Steven	1	0	100	11	23	35	43	53
Sally	1	1	100	11	24	35	45	54
Laura	1	0	100	11	24	35	45	53
Ken	1	2	100	11	23	35	43	53
Mike	1	0	100	11	23	35	45	53
Level: Ⓘ II III			88	10	22	33	43	52
Michelle	2	0	88	10	⑳	33	㊶	52
Shawn	2	0	88	10	⑲	33	㊶	53
Laura	2	1	88	10	⑳	33	43	52
Sandy	2	0	88	10	⑳	33	㊶	52
John	2	½	88	10	22	33	43	52
Level: Ⓘ II III			87	10	22	33	43	52
Penny	3	1	87	9	⑲	㉛	㊶	52
David	3	0	87	9	⑳	㉜	42	52
Tony	3	0	87	9	⑲	㉜	㊶	52
Pam	3	2	87	9	㉑	㉛	㊶	52
Brian	3	0	87	9	22	33	43	52
Joe	3	0	87	9	⑲	㉛	㊶	52
Stan	3	1	87	9	⑳	33	㊶	52
Level: Ⓘ II III			84	9	21	32	42	
Tam	4	1	84	10	21	33	41	
Jim	4	0	84	10	21	32	43	
Charles	4	3	84	10	21	31	42	
Violet	4	0	84	10	21	33	43	
Edward	4	1	84	⑥	⑱	32	42	
David	4	2	84	10	20	32	41	

*Lesson Day in Program

**Numbers in shaded area indicate expected performance for the given LDIP

Figure 26-5 *Sample Biweekly Report*

be able to keep up with the group. He does not know the sounds taught in the past 30 days and cannot sound out words with the sounds he does know. Tam and David need help in track 4.

As noted earlier, from the Report of Lessons Taught, we are able to make projections about where the children will be at the end of the year and to take steps to change those projections if that is needed. However, when we compare the student's *test performance* with *lessons taught,* we are able to get a more complete picture of what is happening. Consider some of the logical possibilities.

Suppose 125 lessons in arithmetic have been taught to the students in the top group and their performance on the addition track indicates that they failed item 29 for lesson days 94–103. The students are performing substantially below (about 25 days) where the teacher has them. This suggests that the teacher may just be taking them through the lessons and not making sure the children have mastered each lesson before going on. It may be necessary to take the students back and reteach some lessons after carefully examining and correcting the teacher's procedures.

Consider a reverse example. The teacher has the students at day 90, but the test shows they can do test items at day 130. The students already have the skills coming up in the program so that it is possible to move them ahead.

Another possibility is that the whole group is behind, but only in one track. In the other tracks, they are at lesson day-in-program on the test. It is likely that the teacher may need specific help in teaching the skills in *that track*.

The test results might also show that one or two students in a group are lagging behind the rest. This could happen because the teacher was not teaching every child in the group or because the children are placed in a group too fast for them. The supervisor would give special attention to such a situation and either give the teacher more training or reassign the children to a lower group.

Again, the reverse could be happening. Two students in a group may be far ahead of where the teacher has them. A placement in a higher group would be in order.

The Continuous Progress Test results in combination with the Report of Lesson Taught provide very critical information for monitoring classroom progress and correcting difficulties.

CONSTRUCTING TESTS

This final section examines a few of the issues involved in constructing criterion-referenced tests. However, learning to build tests should occur within content area courses rather than an educational psychology class, since good tests should be built around specific programs and require detailed analytic knowledge of the content area being tested. For these reasons, this text will only touch on the most general issues in constructing tests for classroom monitoring systems.

The two most fundamental questions to ask about any test are, "Is it reliable?" and "Is it valid?" Reliability is estimated by seeing if different measures of the same thing produce the same result. Validity is concerned with whether the test is measuring what you think it is measuring.

Evaluating Reliability

To examine the reliability of a criterion-referenced test, you would look at the percentage of agreement between two measures of the same thing. To get a percentage of agreement measure, give two measures of the same skill to a group of students. Then, you count the number who *passed both test items or failed both* (the number of agreements) and divide by the number of students tested to get the percentage of agreement. Agreement scores above 80 percent are usually acceptable. In testing relatively discrete or unitary skills (concepts, rules, facts, etc.) with instructional program-based tests, you typically find the agreement so high (95 percent or higher) that you need no longer use multiple measures of the same skill unless you are trying out some new (and complex) type of item. However, there often are problems in evaluating longer open-ended responses, as in essays. We will return to that issue shortly.

Evaluating Validity

Content Validity. The primary validity question to be asked about a criterion-referenced test is: "Does the test item fall in the class of behaviors defined by the objective being tested." A spelling test that contained words not taught would not be valid *unless* the instruction taught a general case. This would be possible for a method that taught spelling-by-sounds for regular sound words. It would also be possible for spelling that was taught using morphographs (re-, un-, -ed, -ing, port, arm, fine). New words made up of morphographs that had been taught would be legitimate. The process of determining content validity is a logical one. It is often helpful to have several people go through the same decision processes to see if they agree. Disagreements are most likely when the objectives are poorly defined (as is often the case in dealing with reading comprehension skills). Besides falling into the skill class being tested, a valid test item must also be consistent with the *direction words* and *response requirements* as taught by the teacher.

Sensitivity to Instruction. Another criterion for test validity is to see if test items failed before instruction are passed after (Burket, 1974; Wilson, 1974; Harris, 1974). This criterion assumes: (1) that you have independent evidence that the instruction is effective, (2) that the simple passage of time does not lead to passing the items, and (3) that the skill was not taught elsewhere.

Deciding What to Test

The progress units in a monitoring system define when tests or checkouts are given, but a major task is to decide which skills to test. It helps to start with the main skills you expect the students to master by the end of the term (or year) in a given area and then work backward to pick up the subskills they are dependent on. This will provide a structure of the more important concepts and skills. A teacher's guide for many texts will sometimes provide an outline of major skills and subskills. Keeping the over all goals in mind will make it easier to decide which skills to focus on during checkout and reviews.

To insure content validity, once a decision has been made on the skills to be covered on a given test, examine more precisely *how they were taught* so that test examples will be compatible with what was taught. Our earlier discussion of general cases and independent member sets should also be kept in mind in deciding when examples not used in the teaching are legitimate and when they are not.

Reviews should be designed to help foster retention of the important terminal skills. When subskills have already been consolidated into a more complex task, just test the consolidated tasks. You should give preference to newer material and *highly similar* content taught earlier. For example, after teaching substraction, test with subtraction and addition items intermixed so the similar kinds of problems become clearly discriminated.

Suppose in a corrective reading program, you are teaching decoding skills focusing on long-short vowel confusion. Long-o and short-o sounds were emphasized first (mod-mode, bon-bone, con-cone). Then long-a and short-a sounds were introduced (mad-made, ban-bane, can-cane). It would be important in testing long-a and short-a words to also test long-o and short-o words that differ only in the vowel. For example, one test item might be:

Say: *Read these words.* Point to each word in order by row.

can	con	cane	cone
bane	bone	ban	bon
mad	mode	made	mod

The only way the student can discriminate words in a given row is to show mastery of the long-o and short-o sounds *and* the long-a and short-a sounds. If the test focused only on long-a and short-a words, it is possible that confusions with long-o and short-o words would still exist and be missed.

Consider another example. In the DISTAR *Reading I* Continuous Progress Test for days 51–61, only five sounds are tested, although twelve sounds have been taught by day 48. The three sounds taught in the past ten days (days 39–48) are tested (*t, n,* and *c*) along with two taught earlier (*m, th*). The *m* sound was included because of its possible confusion with *n*. The *th* sound was included because of its possible confusion with *t*. For days 111–120, four sounds are tested. At this point twenty-five sounds have been taught, two of them in the past ten days (*v* and *g*). The two recent sounds are tested along with *p* and *d*. These were added because of their possible confusion with *g*. Inspection of the DISTAR Reading orthography, shows that *d* and *g* have the same kind of oval shape, and that a rotation of *p* makes a *d*. Thus, the testing attempts to make sure that the most critical discriminations in the set being taught have been mastered. If these are mastered, it is very likely (but not sure) that easier discriminations have also been mastered.

Try to avoid teaching and testing trivial skills. A trivial skill is one that is never used later. For example, in one beginning reading program, the students have exercises where they indicate whether a particular sound occurs at the beginning, middle, or end of a word. This skill is not a reading skill and is never used again. A reading skill would involve being able to say the word no matter where a given sound occurs, not describing the position of a given sound.

Ambiguous instructions are often a problem. To avoid ambiguities, it is helpful to have a student work through a test talking out loud to you about her/his thoughts. Another teacher could go over the test with you and point out ambiguities. You might also just put the test away for awhile and then re-examine it.

Considering Alternative Test Formats

The choice of test formats is often constrained by what is to be tested. However, in general the alternatives are these:

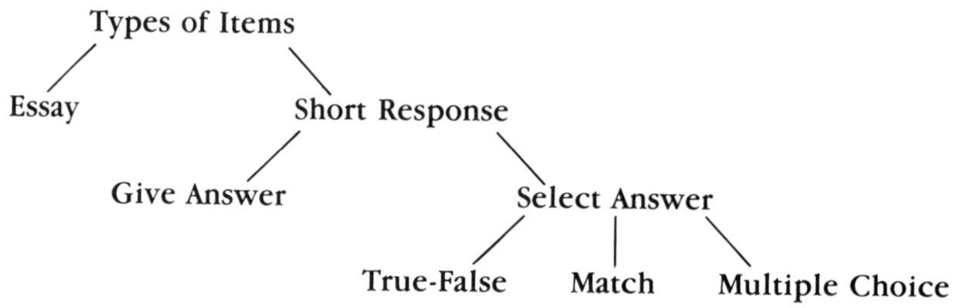

Essay exams have the advantage of being able to sample productive writing skills and higher level thinking such as analysis, synthesis, and evaluation. Also they can be created relatively easily. However, they are rarely consistent with testing for the mastery of specific objectives. Essay tests have a notorious history of being unreliable, in the sense that teachers do not agree on how to score the same questions. They also require a lot of time to score and allow you to cover less material in a given period of time.

Reliability in evaluating essays can be improved by keeping the questions directed, so that the student has clear cues to what you are looking for. It also helps to develop model answers that show how points are given to serve as a guideline in scoring. It would probably help for several people to work together to see if they can get agreement on objectives for essays and evaluation criteria.

The use of shorter-answer forms allows a broader coverage of topic, more reliable scoring, easier scoring, and are suitable to testing key concepts and principles. However, they do take more time to construct. In general, it is better to use a variety question forms. When the student is required to produce the answer, rather than select it, this reduces the possibilities of guessing and usually is a stronger test of mastery. However, tests requiring written responses are more work to score.

SUMMARY

Criterion-referenced tests are most often the test of choice for monitoring student progress. Criterion-referenced tests compare a student's performance with some criterion of mastery (pass-fail). In contrast, norm-referenced tests, such as IQ tests, are useful and selecting students who are relatively high or low on some measure, but are not very useful in making decisions about student placement or skill mastery.

To be maximally useful, criterion-referenced tests should be built around a particular curriculum. In this way, you can achieve a better match between what is taught and what is tested. In selecting legitimate test items for a given objective it is important to discriminate whether the objective is a general case or an independent member set. When you are dealing with a general case, items not used in the instruction can be used in the testing. This is not so for IM sets.

Criterion-referenced tests are a central part of mastery learning systems to monitor student progress. There are six general steps for building a good monitoring system:

1. Specify a placement procedure.
2. Define progress units.
3. Specify checkout and review procedures.
4. Develop a guide for recording progress through the units.
5. Establish goals.
6. Establish remedial procedures and retesting.

The monitoring systems used in the Behavior Analysis and the Direct Instruction Follow Through Models were described in some detail to illustrate some of the potential values and features of such systems. A major advantatge of a good testing system is that it can show where students and/or teachers are having problems *in time to do something about them* before it is too late. A good system not only diagnoses problems, but it specifies remedies.

Some of the more general issues in the construction of criterion-referenced tests were examined. The reliability of criterion-referenced tests can be examined by looking at the percentage of agreement obtained by two measures of the same learning outcome for a group of students. For relatively unitary skills (including problem-solving routines), agreements between different measures are usually so high as to make multiple testing unnecessary. However, there are areas where some objectives (as in reading comprehension, or literary style) are less clearly defined. It may be important in developing mastery testing in these areas to have several people working together to see if they can get agreement in specifying testing goals and in evaluating student performance.

Validity is concerned with whether a test is measuring what one thinks it is measuring. For criterion-referenced tests, this question can be answered by determining if the test items fall *logically* into the sets of objectives being tested.

Deciding what to test requires an analysis of overall goals and critical subgoals in a given content area. Where a lot of subskills are already consolidated in some terminal skills, it is only necessary to test the terminal skills. Periodic reviews help to foster retention and to differentiate newer content from previously learned material with which it might get confused.

Mastery testing programs will typically use relatively specific short-response test items. Essay formats tend to be unreliable. However, there are some objectives relating to analysis, synthesis, evaluation, and productive writing where well-specified essay questions would be desirable. Give the students clear guidelines for what you are looking for. Usually, a sampling of a variety of shorter-answer question will permit a better coverage of objectives than long essays.

CHAPTER

27

NORM-REFERENCED ACHIEVEMENT TESTS

Norm-referenced tests are big business in this country. Millions of tests (often with a computerized scoring service) are sold each year. They are used to help evaluate the educational progress of students, to help evaluate curricula, to evaluate teaching procedures, and to select students for special groups. This chapter examines some of the procedures used to build such tests, the tests themselves, their uses, their administration, and the interpretation of scores derived from such tests.

CONSTRUCTING NORM-REFERENCED ACHIEVEMENT TESTS

Steps followed in building a norm-referenced achievement test are in some ways quite similar to those followed in developing a criterion-referenced test. First there is a concern with the instructional objectives in a particular curriculum area. The test publishers usually convene a group of curriculum specialists in a particular subject matter and use their skills to analyze textbooks and programs most commonly used throughout the country. A list of instructional objectives is developed. Objectives provide the skeleton framework for the development of test items. Classroom teachers and curriculum specialists then write items to flesh out the framework provided by the statement of objectives. Those items are reviewed and edited for logical consistency, difficulty level, and ambiguity. Next, instructions are prepared and the items are given a tryout on an appropriate group. The data are then subjected to an item analysis to weed out poor items and to provide a basis for further editing. Finally, the test is given to a representative sample of students (called a norm population) to provide a basis for constructing test norms.

The key differences in procedures used to construct norm-referenced achievement tests and criterion-referenced tests are these:

1. Objectives for norm-referenced tests *cover more material* that is usually taught over longer time units. Objectives for criterion-referenced tests are usually geared to the goals of shorter units of instruction.

2. Objectives for norm-referenced tests attempt to reflect what is *common to most instructional programs* in a content area. Objectives for criterion-referenced tests are either the basis of an instruc-

tional program in themselves (as in Popham's use), or directly derived from an instructional program (as in DISTAR).

3. Methods of item analysis differ greatly. For example, in selecting items for norm-referenced tests, items are eliminated that most students pass or fail. In selecting items for criterion-referenced tests, you would seek items that are failed by many prior to instruction, but passed by many after instruction.

4. Scores for norm-referenced achievement tests are interpreted in relation to the frequency distribution of scores obtained by the norm group. Scores for a criterion-referenced test are usually interpreted directly in terms of the degreee (percentage) of mastery of an objective.

SOME COMMON ACHIEVEMENT TEST BATTERIES

A *test battery* is a test designed to assess several areas such as reading, arithmetic, and language. The five most frequently used achievement tests batteries are typically known by their abbreviations: the CAT, the CTBS, the MAT, the SAT, and the SRA. The abbreviations stand for:

CAT—California Achievement Tests (1977/78)
CTBS—Comprehensive Test of Basic Skills (1981)
MAT—Metropolitan Achievement Tests (1978)
SAT—Stanford Achievement Tests (1982)
SRA—Science Research Associates Achievement Series (1978)

The Stanford Achievement Tests (SAT) are the granddaddy of them all, first appearing in 1923. The tests are typically revised every seven to ten years to keep up with school changes and population changes. These tests have similar structures and assess similar skills, although they cannot be said to have equal *content validity* for a given instructional program. Generally, they cover reading and mathematics with two or three subtests (for reading—vocabulary and comprehension; for mathematics—computation, concepts, and problem solving). They also cover spelling, grammatical usage (language), science, and social science. Some variations on these themes are found; for example, the SAT has a test called *Environment,* and others include *Study Skills* and *Reference Skills.* For the kindergarten levels and first grade, there are a number of tests of more specific reading or prereading skills such as letter sounds, listening, phonic analysis, etc. Table 27.1 contains an outline of the skills and subskills tested on the CAT. The asterisks show the levels at which different skills are tested. The 10 stands for kindergarten, 11 through 17 for 1st through 7th grades, the 18 stands for grades 8 & 9, and the 19 for grades 10, 11, & 12.

There is a trend in designing norm-referenced tests to provide a basis for grouping items into subclusters within reading or math that can give the teacher better diagnostic information—more like that given by criterion-referenced tests. In evaluating progress or problems for a given classroom, these cluster scores could be quite useful—depending on how well the test matches the curriculum in use. For individual students, however, many clusters have too few items to permit reliable statements about individual students.

Information for evaluating achievement tests can be found in the test manuals themselves and in the *Mental Measurement Yearbook* (Buros, 1978, 1985). The MMYB provides critical reviews of all major tests in print.

Table 27-1 Content of the CAT (form C and D)

Content Area	Test	Level 10	11	12	13	14	15	16	17	18	19
Prereading	Listening for Information	•									
	Letter Forms	•									
	Letter Names	•									
	Letter Sounds	•									
	Visual Discrimination	•									
	Sound Matching	•									
Reading	Phonic Analysis		•	•	•						
	Structural Analysis			•	•						
	Reading Vocabulary		•	•	•	•	•	•	•	•	•
	Reading Comprehension		•	•	•	•	•	•	•	•	•
Spelling	Spelling			•	•	•	•	•	•	•	•
Language	Language Mechanics			•	•	•	•	•	•	•	•
	Language Expression		•	•	•	•	•	•	•	•	•
Mathematics	Mathematics Computation		•	•	•	•	•	•	•	•	•
	Mathematics Concepts and Applications	•	•	•	•	•	•	•	•	•	•
Reference Skills	Reference Skills					•	•	•	•	•	•

GIVING STANDARDIZED NORM—REFERENCED TESTS

Norm-referenced tests are also called *standardized* tests because they have been designed to be given by following a specified procedure (or *standard* of administration). Usually a test coordinator's manual is provided with detailed procedures to follow. A teacher's manual also contains specific procedures for giving a particular test. A training period for those who are to give and monitor the tests is a good idea.

The first step is to prepare the students ahead of time in a way that is reassuring and in a way that reduces possible anxiety about the test. Practice tests are provided with the tests and should be used as part of this preparation. The best anxiety reducer is to know what is going to happen. *It is all right to teach students how to follow the directions required by the test by holding practice sessions.* Just do not use the items actually on the test or give students the answers during the test. It is also important to have a monitor for every ten to fifteen students (high school students, aides, or parents will do). This is especially important with younger students and disadvantaged students. The test scores are useless if the students do not follow the instructions and do not actually spend their time trying to answer the questions. Many a test has returned from the machine-scoring process with chance-level scores because the students answered only the first row of questions on a page and then turned to the next page, or because they circled the right answer, but did not fill in the machine-scored answer sheet. By monitoring whether or not students are following instructions, it is possible to correct some of these problems during a test, or at least to qualify the interpretation of the test results. It is also probably wise to hand score some of the tests before they are sent off for machine scoring to provide a basis for checking the accuracy of the scoring. The people operating scoring machines can make mistakes.

INTERPRETING TEST SCORES

Review

Chapter 19 introduced five statistical concepts: frequency distribution, mean, standard deviation, standard scores, and correlation. A frequency distribution is a graphic representation of how many students achieve scores of particular values. The mean is the average of all the scores, and the standard deviation is a measure of how far ("on the average") the scores spread out from the mean. In norm-referenced tests, the distribution of scores in the normalization sample is used to evaluate the scores for a given individual taking the test. Norm tables are built to allow you to easily convert *raw scores* into various *standard scores.* You can also use mean data to determine *grade equivalent scores* and the frequency distribution to determine *percentiles* and *normal-curve equivalents* of percentiles.

In Chapter 20 you studied the *normal distribution* and learned about its usefulness in interpreting standard scores. If you know someone has an IQ that is two standard deviations above the mean (an IQ of 130), you know that she or he is at the 98th percentile. Remember the numbers 34, 14, and 2 and the rough shape of the normal curve so you can interpret standard scores in terms of percentiles (without a special table). *Return to Table 20.1 (page 300) and Figure 20.3 (page 300) and study them once more.*

Norm Populations

Norm-referenced test scores of all types are determined by first giving the test to a *sample* from a specified population (such as "all second graders in the USA"), and then comparing the performance of a given individual to the distribution of scores for the norm-group sample. Most samples are quite large and well-selected so they are representative. The mean and standard deviation for the norm group (or in the case of percentiles, the distribution) are used to convert a given *raw score* into *norm-referenced scores.* For example, a particular raw score on a reading test is obtained by only 10 percent of *second graders in the United States.* Or, this science score is two standard deviations above the mean of scores obtained by *high school seniors in California.* Local norms can also be used. Local norms are valuable because you can compare a student's performance against that of others in the same curriculum. You cannot do this with national norms. Local norms may be especially important if you are working with a group of students that is quite different from the national average. For example, Southern rural students tend to score lower against national norms, while those from a New England suburb tend to score higher than average. If norms are used to compare teachers or schools, they should be derived from like students in similar programs. Even promotion policy can make a difference. For example, if 90 percent of Spanish-speaking students are retained each year in first grade, the levels of performance at each *grade level* would likely be different than if most of them were promoted. Those with two years of first grade are likely to score higher later because they are a year older and have had an extra year of schooling.

In choosing a norm group, a *representative sample* is sought. Variables such as ethnic group, socioeconomic status, urban-rural residence, section of the country, and so on are used in building a national sample to norm a test. Similar criteria should be considered in establishing local norms.

Finally, keep in mind that grade norms are based on the average performance of the group. This means that if your class average is at grade level, 50 percent of the students will be *below* this grade level and 50 percent above.

Types of Norm-Referenced Scores

Rank-Order Scores. First consider the concept of ranks (rank-order scores) to set the stage for the concept of percentile ranks. In ranking a set of scores, you assign 1 to the highest score, 2 to the next highest, 3 to the next highest, and so on until all scores are ordered. If two scores are tied, we give each of them the average of the next two ranks. If three scores are tied, say taking up ranks 3, 4, and 5, they would all be given rank 4. Note carefully that in dealing with ranks, the *lowest* score (1) is the top rank. In dealing with percentile ranks, the *highest* percentile (99) goes with the highest scores.

Percentile Ranks. Percentile ranks (also called *percentiles* or *centiles*) are often used to interpret test scores to parents and others because they are easy to interpret directly. A percentile specifies the percentage of scores that are *lower* than that percentile. If a student ranks 15 in a group of 20, that means that 5 students (or 5/20 × 100 = 25 percent) have lower scores. Thus, that student would be at the 25th percentile. If a girl outranks 90 percent of her classmates in arithmetic, she would be at the 90th percentile. If in a class of 30, Roger scores above 20 of his classmates, his percentile rank would be 20/30 × 100 = 67. Percentile ranks are expressed on a scale from 1 (low) to 99 (high).

Normal–Curve Equivalents. *Normal-curve equivalents (NCEs)* convert percentiles to standard scores with a mean of 50 and a standard deviation of approximately 21. As with percentiles, the top score given is 99 and the lowest score is 1. Normal-curve equivalents can be used to compare a student's standing in different subject areas (such as reading and math) more readily than percentiles (or expanded-standard scores, which are covered next). Standard scores more closely approximate a scale with roughly equal intervals than is the case with percentiles. An NCE change from 50 to 60 represents a percentile change from 50 to 69. An NCE change from 80 to 90 represents a percentile change from 92.3 to 97.1. Percentiles change rapidly in the middle of a distribution and slowly at the extremes. The relationship between percentiles and NCEs is shown in Table 27.2. Figure 27.1 shows the relationship graphically.

Table 27-2 Normal-Curve Equivalents corresponding to percentile ranks. *(From the Standford Achievement Tests, Primary 2, Form E/F Norms Booklet, National. New York: Harcourt Brace Jovanovich, 1983, 13. Reproduced with permission.)*

Percentile Rank	*NCE*	*Percentile Rank*	*NCE*	*Percentile Rank*	*NCE*	*Percentile Rank*	*NCE*
1	1.0	26	36.5	51	50.5	76	64.9
2	6.7	27	37.1	52	51.1	77	65.6
3	10.4	28	37.7	53	51.6	78	66.3
4	13.1	29	38.3	54	52.1	79	67.0
5	15.4	30	39.0	55	52.6	80	67.7
6	17.3	31	39.6	56	53.2	81	68.5
7	18.9	32	40.1	57	53.7	82	69.3
8	20.4	33	40.7	58	54.2	83	70.1
9	21.8	34	41.3	59	54.8	84	70.9
10	23.0	35	41.9	60	55.3	85	71.8
11	24.2	36	42.5	61	55.9	86	72.8
12	25.3	37	43.0	62	56.4	87	73.7
13	26.3	38	43.6	63	57.0	88	74.7
14	27.2	39	44.1	64	57.5	89	75.8
15	28.2	40	44.7	65	58.1	90	77.0
16	29.1	41	45.2	66	58.7	91	78.2
17	29.9	42	45.8	67	59.3	92	79.6
18	30.7	43	46.3	68	59.9	93	81.1
19	31.5	44	46.8	69	60.4	94	82.7
20	32.3	45	47.4	70	61.0	95	84.6
21	33.0	46	47.9	71	61.7	96	86.9
22	33.7	47	48.4	72	62.3	97	89.6
23	34.4	48	48.9	73	62.9	98	93.3
24	35.1	49	49.5	74	63.5	99	99.0
25	35.8	50	50.0	75	64.2		

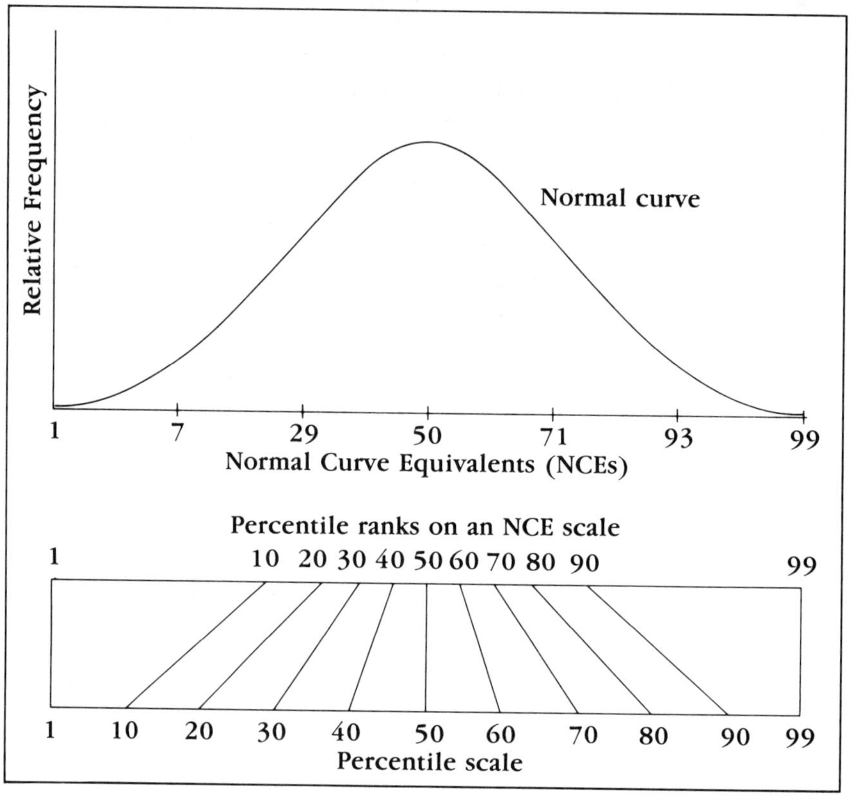

Figure 27-1 *A Comparison of frequency distributions for percentiles and Normal-Curve Equivalents*

Other Standard Scores. Return once again to Chapter 20, page 300, you will find some other standard scores defined and illustrated (such as z-scores, GREs, and stanines). Stanines are especially useful (see Figure 20.3) as a simple way of defining *below average* (stanines of 1, 2, and 3), *average* (stanines of 4, 5, 6), and *above average* (stanines of 7, 8, 9) performance.

Expanded-Standard Scores. NCEs are standard scores that have the same mean and standard deviation for each grade level and each test area. In order to provide scores that increase over grade levels and serve to tie to *one scale* the different test levels in a battery, test designers developed expanded-standard scores. For the SRA test, they are called *growth scale values (GSV),* for most other tests, they are simply called *scaled scores.* Scale scores and growth scale values are expressed as three digit numbers. Expanded-standard scores are derived by giving adjacent levels of a test to the same students. This allows the test developer to statistically link one level of the test to the next. What is sought is a standard score scale that represents the best fit of the data from the overlapping testings. Table 27.3 shows how the mean score grows from grade level to grade level in reading and math for the MAT and the SRA. These expanded-standard scores are very useful in evaluating change over time (a year or more) in student performance even when the level of the test changes.

Next to the scaled scores and growth scale values, you have seen the average *change* from grade to grade. The changes from grade to grade illustrate an important point. As students approach mastery of basic reading and math skills, the amount of change per year decreases. This kind of table serves to illustrate why changes in grade levels (grade equivalent scores) are not a useful way to compare student gains. A change from 1.0 to 2.0 grade equivalents on MAT reading (127

Table 27-3 Scale score values by grade level for the MAT and the SRA Achievement Tests, Total Reading, Total Mathematics

MAT					*SRA*				
	Reading		*Math*			*Reading*		*Math*	
GE	*SS*	*Change*	*SS*	*Change*	*GE*	*GSV*	*Change*	*GSV*	*Change*
K.0	264		264						
		127		81					
1.0	391		345		1.0	109	(GE 1.2)	129	
		167		85			83		(27)
2.0	558		430		2.0	192		156	
		83		91			43		49
3.0	641		521		3.0	235		205	
		38		58			27		53
4.0	679		579		4.0*	262		258	
		22		50			27		29
5.0	701		629		5.0	289		287	
		20		43			24		31
6.0	721		672		6.0*	313		318	
		19		38			32		32
7.0	740		710		7.0	345		350	
		16		28			18		24
8.0	756		738		8.0*	363		374	
		20		24					
9.0	776		762		(9.5	382)			
		19		16					
10.0	795		778		(10.7	398)			
		18		14					
11.0	813		792						
		15		11					
12.0	828		803						

*Values interpolated.

Notes: Figures in parentheses are not based on full years. GE stands for grade equivalent. SS stands for scaled score. GSV stands for growth scale values.

scale score points) is not the same as a change from 7.0 to 8.0 grade equivalents (16 scale score points). Table 27.3 also illustrates the fact that expanded-standard scores in reading cannot be compared with those in math. Only the scores from the different forms of the same subject area test can be compared legitimately.

Grade-Equivalent Scores. Standard scores and ranks allow you to locate a person's position within some reference group. "He is in the top 10 percent of 10 year olds." "She is right in the middle of the group of second graders." Grade equivalent scores assign scaled scores on the basis of the average raw score earned by a group in a given grade. A student with a grade equivalent of 2.0 has a score obtained by the *average* beginning second grader.

Suppose you design a vocabulary test to cover grades 1 to 12. The test is built so that words are ordered from easy to difficult and it contains 100 words. Now, suppose Jimmy, a third grader gets 25 words right. Is that good or bad? To answer that, you need some basis for comparison. You could find out how Jimmy stands in his class by comparing his score to the rest of the class. This could lead to a conversion of his score to a z-score or a percentile. An alternative comparison procedure is to test a number of children at each grade level the test is designed to cover and plot the mean scores obtained by each grade group. Some hypothetical data for such an analysis are presented in Figure 27.2. Grade-equivalent scores are determined by "smoothing out" the plotted mean data (with the best fit line or curve), and then finding a possible grade equivalent for each possible raw score. For example, a raw score of 47 has a grade-equivalent score of 5.0. These equivalences can be placed in a table for easy use.

How are grade-equivalent scores to be interpreted? Can a second grader who scores 6.5 grade-equivalents be expected to do sixth grade work? The answer is no. The second grader was not even tested on sixth grade material. What the score means is that *the second grader can do second grade work about as well as a sixth grader is estimated to do second grade work.* Even here, you are dealing with an extrapolation of trend lines. No six graders actually took the second grade test.

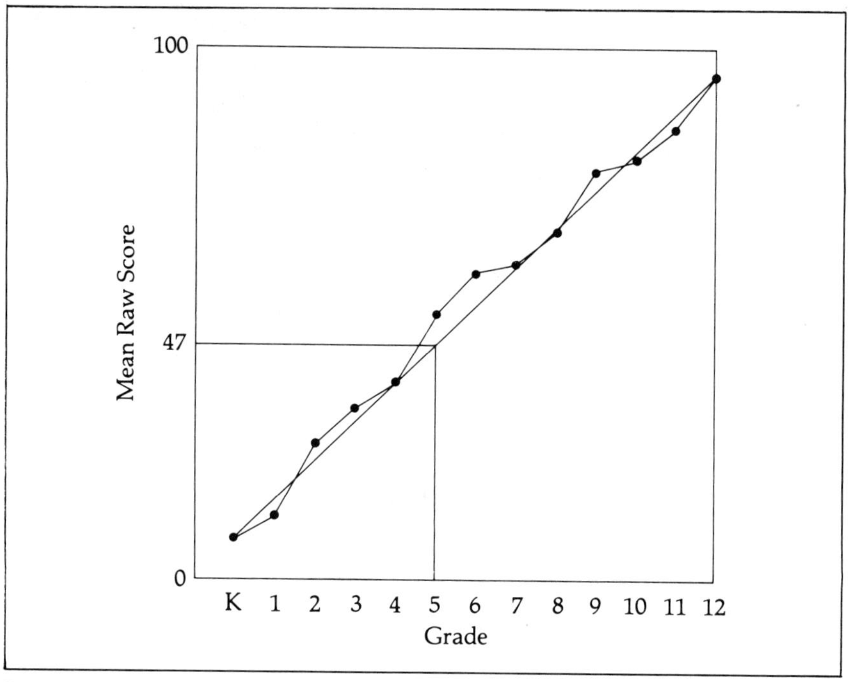

Figure 27-2 *Mean concept mastery score by grade*

Using Norm Tables

After a test is scored, *raw scores* can be converted to a variety of norm-referenced scores by using tables provided in the test manuals. Tables 27.4 through 27.7 are included to show some of the variety of conversions possible.

Raw Scores to Grade Equivalents. Table 27.4 from the CAT is used to convert raw scores to grade equivalents. Suppose Billy, a second grader, scores 65 on Total Reading. Come down the column labeled Total Read until you find 65 and then go to the grade equivalents (GE) given on either side. In this case the GE is 3.7

Note that grade equivalents are constructed so that each tenth is equal to a month of school. The school year is divided into nine months and one month is counted for the summer. Thus a grade equivalent score of 4.2 would be the average score expected from a fourth grader in November. The following table shows the relationship of months to grade placement in tenths:

Date of Testing	Sept.	Oct.	Nov.	Dec.	Jan.	Feb.	March	April	May	June
Grade Placement	.0	.1	.2	.3	.4	.5	.6	.7	.8	.9

Raw Scores to Scaled Scores, Percentiles, and Stanines. Table 27.5 simulates a MAT table that is used to convert raw scores to scaled scores. The number right is found in the left column and the appropriate scaled score is found by moving across until the right test is found. The scaled score can then be used in Table 27.6 to find the equivalent stanine or percentile (%ile rank). What is the percentile if the raw score in Reading is 30? Answer: 54. Find 550 in Table 27.5. Go to Table 27.6 and find the scaled score (or next higher scaled score) under Reading (550), and move left to 54, the percentile.

Another Layout. Just to keep you on your toes, another system has been provided from the SRA Achievement Series (1978), which more simply takes you from raw scores, to growth scale values, to grade equivalents, and to percentiles (by semester) all in one table (see Table 27.7). This table covers *vocabulary* only. In this table, a raw score of 20 is equal to a GSV of 277, a GE of 4.0, and a fall-semester, third-grade percentile of 79.

Reliability

The reliability of a norm-referenced test is concerned with the contribution of errors of measurement to test scores. If there is no error in measurement, reliability is 1. As the proportion of error variance to total variance increases, reliability decreases. The contribution of error to test scores is determined by correlating measures of the same thing. Some of the ways this can be done are:

1. By using equivalent forms of the same tests.

2. By dividing a test into odd- and even-item halves and correlating the halves and then using the Spearman-Brown formula to estimate the reliability of the total test:

$$r_{xx} = \frac{2\,r}{1 + r}$$

   where r is the correlation between the two halves.

3. By computing an alpha coefficient (Cronbach 1970), which gives the average of all possible split halves. Test manuals usually refer to alpha as K-R 20 (Kuder-Richardson formula 20). K-R 20 is a special case of alpha.

4. Reliabilities are sometimes based on using the same test and giving it twice within a relatively short period of time. Be careful of these. Memory effects will tend to increase the obtained correlations and give an inflated estimate of the reliability.

A reliability coefficient, when multiplied by 100, gives the percent of the variance in test scores that can be attributed to true-score variance.

Standard Error of Measurement

When the reliability of a test is known, the standard error of measurement can be computed and used to determine a a confidence interval for a given score. The

Table 27-4 Raw score to Grade Equivalents. *(From the California Achievement Tests, Norm Tables, Level 12, Form C, Page 16. Monterey, CA: STM/McGraw Hill, 1977-78. Reproduced with permission.)*

	Raw Scores											
	Reading				Language			Mathematics				
GE	Read Vocab	Read Comp	Total Read	Spell	Lang Mech	Lang Expr	Total Lang	Comput	Concepts & Applc	Total Math	Total Battery	GE
0.1	0	0	0-11	0-6	0-2	0-5	0-11	0-2	0-7	0-10	0-45	0.1
0.2		1	12			6				11	46-47	0.2
0.3	1		13				12		8	12	48-49	0.3
0.4			14	7							50-51	0.4
0.5					3		13		9	13	52-54	0.5
0.6		2	15							14	55	0.6
0.7	2		16	8			14		10		56-58	0.7
0.8						7		3				0.8
0.9			17		4					15	59-61	0.9
1.0			18			8			11	16	62-63	1.0
1.1			19	9			15		12	17	64-65	1.1
1.2	3	3	20		5		16	4	13	18-19	66-69	1.2
1.3			21-22	10		9		5	14	20	70-73	1.3
1.4	4	4	23		6		17		15-16	21-22	74-78	1.4
1.5			24-25	11		10	18	6	17	23-24	79-82	1.5
1.6	5	5	26-27		7		19	7	18	25-26	83-88	1.6
1.7	6	6	28-30	12	8	11		8	19	27-28	89-94	1.7
1.8		7	31-33		9	12	20	9	20-21	29-31	95-101	1.8
1.9	7	8	34-35	13		13	21		22	32	102-108	1.9
2.0	8		36-37	14	10		22-24	10	23	33	109-113	2.0
2.1		9	38-39		11	14	25	11	24	34-36	114-118	2.1
2.2	9	10	40-41				26	12	25	37-38	119-123	2.2
2.3	10	11	42-44	15	12	15	27	13-14		39-40	124-129	2.3
2.4	11	12	45-47			16	28	15	26	41-42	130-136	2.4
2.5	12	13	48-49		13		29-30	16	27	43-44	137-142	2.5
2.6			50-52	16		17	31	17	28	45-46	143-147	2.6
2.7	13	14	53-55		14				29		148-153	2.7
2.8		15	56				32	18	30	47	154	2.8
2.9			57		15	18	33	19-20		48-50	155-158	2.9
3.0		16	58	17				21	31	51-52	159-162	3.0

Table 27-4 (continued) Raw score to Grade Equivalents. *(From the California Achievement Tests, Norm Tables, Level 12, Form C, Page 16. Monterey, CA: STM/McGraw Hill, 1977-78. Reproduced with permission.)*

	Raw Scores											
	Reading				Language			Mathematics				
GE	*Read Vocab*	*Read Comp*	*Total Read*	*Spell*	*Lang Mech*	*Lang Expr*	*Total Lang*	*Comput*	*Concepts & Applc*	*Total Math*	*Total Battery*	*GE*
3.1			59					22	32		163-165	3.1
3.2			60				34		33	53-54	166-168	3.2
3.3	14	17	61-62		16			23		55-56	169-171	3.3
3.4							35	24	34	57-58	172-174	3.4
3.5			63			*19*		25		59-60	175-177	3.5
3.6		18	64	*18*	17		36		35	61	178-179	3.6
3.7			65					26		62	180-181	3.7
3.8									36		182-183	3.8
3.9			66				37			63	184	3.9
4.0	15				18						185	4.0
4.1		19	67						37		186	4.1
4.2										64	187	4.2
4.3											188	4.3
4.4			68			*20*	38			65	189	4.4
4.5				*19*	19				38		190	4.5
4.6												4.6
4.7			69							66	191	4.7
4.8											192	4.8
4.9		20							39			4.9
5.0											193	5.0
5.1							39					5.1
5.2			70								194	5.2
5.3											195	5.3
5.4												5.4
5.5					20				40		196	5.5
5.6												5.6
5.7											197	5.7
5.8			71									5.8
5.9				*20*								5.9
6.0												6.0
6.1												6.1
6.2												6.2
6.3							40					6.3

Table 27-5 Number right (raw score) to scaled score conversion table (hypothetical example)

	Scaled Scores						
No. Right	Reading	Mathematics	Language	No. Right	Reading	Mathematics	Language
50	650	700	675	25	535	490	410
49	645	690	661	24	532	482	399
48	641	681	649	23	530	475	382
47	637	669	634	22	527	469	367
46	631	660	617	21	523	458	352
45	625	650	600	20	520	450	340
44	617	641	592	19	517	441	331
43	611	631	581	18	513	430	318
42	604	618	571	17	509	422	304
41	597	609	560	16	504	411	292
40	590	600	550	15	500	400	280
39	584	589	541	14	494	394	269
38	580	580	532	13	487	388	258
37	574	572	521	12	482	381	244
36	569	561	509	11	476	376	233
35	565	550	500	10	470	370	225
34	562	542	492	9	466	358	216
33	560	533	481	8	462	349	204
32	556	524	470	7	458	334	195
31	553	516	462	6	451	317	184
30	550	510	450	5	440	300	170
29	547	505	441	4	429	280	157
28	544	501	430	3	410	265	142
27	540	497	419	2	374	248	125
26	538	493	407	1	331	230	110
				0	300	200	90

standard error of measurement (SD_E) is defined as follows:

$$SD_E = SD_x \sqrt{1 - r_{xx}}$$

This is the standard deviation of a person's scores that would be expected if he were tested a large number of times on parallel forms of the same test. The mean of this distribution would be the person's true score. Suppose the internal consistency reliability (r_{xx}) for a MAT Mathematics test is .90, and the standard deviation (SD_x) is 100 using scaled scores. The standard error of measurement (SD_E) would be:

$$SD_E = 100 \sqrt{1 - .90} = 100 \sqrt{.10} = 100 \times .316 = 31.6$$

If a student obtains a scaled score of 550, assuming a normal distribution, you would expect that his or her true score would be within plus or minus 2 standard errors 95 percent of the time. Knowing the reliability of a test score permits you to estimate a score interval in which a student's true score would fall with a certain level of confidence. In this case, it would be 550 + 2 × 31.6. Thus, 95 percent of the time the score would fall between 487 and 613. In grade equivalents this is a range from approximately grade 2.6 to grade 4.3.

Table 27.8 presents reliability and standard error of measurement data

Table 27-6 Scaled Score to Percentile Rank and Stanine conversion table (hypothetical example)

Spring of Grade 4
Scaled Scores

Stanine	%ile Rank	Reading	Mathematics	Language
9	99	716	680	687
	98	702	597	643
	96	679	572	620
8	94	664	552	601
	92	652	538	585
	90	642	527	571
	89	634	522	565
7	88	627	518	559
	86	621	511	549
	84	615	505	540
	82	610	500	532
	80	605	495	525
	78	600	490	518
	77	597	487	515
6	76	595	485	512
	74	590	480	506
	72	585	475	500
	70	581	470	494
	68	577	465	488
	66	573	461	482
	64	569	457	476
	62	565	453	470
	60	561	450	464
5	58	557	446	458
	56	553	443	452
	54	550	439	446
	52	547	436	441
	50	544	432	436
	48	541	428	431
	46	538	424	426
	44	535	420	421
	42	532	416	416
	40	528	412	411
4	38	524	408	406
	36	520	404	401
	34	516	400	395
	32	512	396	389
	30	507	392	383
	28	502	388	377
	26	496	384	371
	24	490	380	364
	23	487	378	361
3	22	484	375	357
	20	478	369	349
	18	471	363	341
	16	464	357	333
	14	457	350	325
	12	450	342	317
	11	446	338	313
2	10	442	333	309
	8	434	323	300
	6	425	313	290
	4	415	298	277
1	2	403	277	261
	1	388	249	241

from the MAT Survey Battery for the fall of grade 4. Just looking at the grade equivalents, plus or minus 2 standard errors cover 2 grade levels in the best case (Reading) and 3.6 in the worse case (Language). With other tests, the 95 percent confidence range is about one-half as large as those shown in Table 27.8. Nevertheless, the message should be very clear, ***making precise predictions about individual students is a bit risky,*** especially if reliabilities get below .90. This is one reason norm-referenced tests are not very useful for placing students in a program. On the other hand, making statements about the progress of the whole class can be fairly precise, since the error term gets smaller as the number of cases get larger. Also, longer tests are likely to be more reliable than shorter tests of the same type. Teacher's manuals which go with norm-referenced achievement tests, and the *Mental Measurement Yearbook* can provide information on test reliabilities.

Table 27-7 Conversion table for Vocabulary. Raw Scores (RS) Growth Scale Values (GSV), and Grade Equivalents (GE) to Percentiles by Grade and Semester. *(From SRA Achievement Series and Conversion Tables © 1979, 1978, Science Research Associates, Inc. Reprinted by permission of the publisher.)*

SRA Achievement Series—National Norms—Level D												
Raw Scores				*Percentiles by Grade and Month*								
Form 1	*Form 2*	*GSV*	*GE*	*2-1*	*2-8*	*3-1*	*3-8*	*4-1*	*4-8*	*5-1*	*5-8*	*6-1*
30	30	393	9.6	99	99	99	99	99	97	95	90	85
	29	379	8.6	99	99	99	99	99	95	92	86	79
29		367	8.0	99	99	99	99	98	92	88	81	73
	28	366	8.0	99	99	99	99	97	92	88	80	72
28		349	7.1	99	99	99	97	95	86	81	71	63
	27	348	7.0	99	99	99	97	95	85	80	71	63
27	26	334	6.5	99	99	99	96	92	78	72	62	54
26		323	6.0	99	99	99	92	87	70	65	54	48
	25	322	6.0	99	99	99	92	87	69	64	54	47
25		314	5.7	99	99	99	87	81	63	58	48	43
	24	311	5.5	99	99	99	85	79	61	56	46	41
24		305	5.2	99	95	93	80	74	56	51	42	38
	23	302	5.1	99	95	92	78	71	54	49	40	36
23		298	4.9	99	94	92	74	67	51	46	38	34
	22	292	4.6	99	94	92	69	62	46	42	34	31
22		291	4.6	99	94	92	68	61	46	41	34	30
21	21	284	4.3	99	93	91	61	54	40	37	30	27
20		277	4.0	99	90	87	54	47	35	32	26	24
	20	276	3.9	99	89	86	53	46	35	32	26	23
19		271	3.7	99	85	81	48	42	32	29	23	21
	19	270	3.7	99	84	80	48	41	31	28	23	21
18		265	3.6	99	79	74	43	37	28	26	21	19
	18	264	3.5	99	78	73	42	36	27	25	20	19
17		259	3.4	84	72	66	38	32	24	23	19	17
	17	257	3.4	82	70	63	36	30	23	22	18	16
16		253	3.2	80	65	57	33	28	21	20	17	15
	16	252	3.2	79	64	56	32	27	21	19	16	15
15		248	3.1	77	59	50	29	24	19	18	15	14
	15	246	3.0	75	56	47	28	23	18	17	15	13
14		243	2.9	73	53	43	25	21	17	16	14	12
	14	241	2.8	72	50	41	24	20	16	15	13	12
13		238	2.7	69	47	37	22	19	15	14	13	11
	13	235	2.6	67	43	34	20	17	14	13	12	10
12		232	2.5	64	40	31	19	16	13	12	11	10
	12	228	2.4	59	36	27	17	14	12	11	11	9
11		226	2.3	57	34	25	16	13	11	11	10	9
10	11	220	2.1	50	29	20	13	11	10	9	9	8
9		212	2.0	42	23	15	10	8	8	8	8	6
	10	211	1.9	41	22	15	10	8	8	8	8	6
8		203	1.8	34	17	11	7	6	6	6	6	5

Validity

Validity is the degree to which a test measures what it is supposed to measure. Tests can have different validities for different uses. When norm-referenced achievement tests are used in the evaluation of instructional outcomes, the question of validity rests largely on the appropriateness of the test *content* and secondarily on the *sensitivity* of test items to instruction. The following quote

Table 27-8 Reliability estimates (Kuder-Richardson formula 20) and standard errors of measurement—fall of grade 4. *(From the* Metropolitan Achievement Tests: *Teacher's Manual for Administering and Interpreting, Elementary Level, Forms JS/KS, page 70. New York: Harcourt Brace Jovanovich, 1978.)*

Test	$r_{K\text{-}R}$	*Standard Error of Measurement* *Raw Score*	*Scaled Score*	*Grade Equivalent*
Reading	.96	2.8	14.8	.5
Mathematics	.90	3.1	28.5	.6
Language	.88	3.4	41.5	.9
Science	.90	2.8	35.9	.7
Social Studies	.90	2.9	34.9	.7
Basic Battery	.97	5.3	14.9	.3
Complete Battery	.98	6.6	12.0	.2

is from the MAT (*Teacher's Manual for Administering and Interpreting,* Elementary Level, Forms JS/KS, page 70, 1978):

> The validity of an achievement test is defined primarily in terms of content validity. A test has content validity if the objectives and items adequately cover the curriculum areas the test is intended to measure. Since each school's curriculum differs from that of other schools, the content validity of the *Metropolitan Achievement Tests* must be estimated by each school. It cannot be claimed that the tests are universally valid.

The manual goes on to point out that in Appendix C (and Special Report 2) there is a full list of all objectives covered by the test. Other test publishers are also furnishing such information. This makes the task of matching school objectives and test objectives considerably easier than had been the case in the past.

In considering norm-referenced tests, another kind of validity (in addition to content validity) is called *criterion validity.* The criterion of *sensitivity to instruction* is considered in evaluating the "goodness" of an item. Items that are passed by more students in higher grades than lower grades are considered more valid than items that do not show an increase in percent passing with grade level.

Other criteria that enter into the question of validity of achievement tests vary with their use. For example, if a test is used to select students for college, you might want to know how well test scores correlate with (predict) college grade-point average (GPA). GPA can be used as a *criterion* for the validity of the achievement test. If an achievement test is being used to diagnose and prescribe remediation, some measure of the remedial successes and failures could provide a criterion for the validity of this use.

USES OF NORM-REFERENCED ACHIEVEMENT TESTS

Many of the studies of effective teaching practices (see Chapter 12 on mastery learning) have used more norm-referenced achievement tests to show which practices produced better outcomes in reading and math. This is a valid use of such tests if the content of the instructional program and the content of the test are covering the same (or nearly the same) skills.

Norm-referenced tests may also be useful in assessing progress in a single class. The students are tested before and after instruction (say spring or fall of one year and spring of the next year) and the gain in scaled score units is examined. An effective program might show more than a year's gain in a year. This approach is called a ***norm-referenced evaluation.*** The norm group is used to make a judgment about the effectiveness of the instruction. In using tests in this way, it is important that testing dates be within a week or two of the norm-group testing dates.

Norm-referenced tests can also be used to compare different programs, again if there is an adequate match up between tests and programs. Norm-referenced tests are also useful for selecting students who score especially high or especially low in a given skill area. And, they are useful in guidance, where knowing more about one's strengths and weaknesses can lead to better career decisions.

Although the aim of the more current approaches to item cluster analysis is to provide teachers with more specific guidance for instruction, most norm-referenced tests are only crude guides for making placement decisions or evaluating the process of teaching. Tests more specifically built around a given curriculum are more likely to be valuable for such decisions.

Finally, norm-referenced tests are inappropriate instruments for the evaluation of teachers. Differences in student outcomes can be produced by many other factors than classroom instruction. The most important of these outside influences (such as the education of the student's mother) was covered earlier under the vocabulary problem (see Chapter 17).

SUMMARY

Norm-referenced achievement tests attempt to test the "common core" of what is happening in elementary and secondary mainline education. The tests are typically constructed by starting with a group of general objectives defined by a group of curriculum experts on the basis of texts and programs in use in schools. Test items are then written, tried out, and edited for ambiguities, logical consistency, difficulty level, and evaluated on item information relating to reliability and validity. Finally, a representative sample of students is tested to provide a basis for constructing test norms. In contrast to criterion-referenced tests, the objectives of norm-referenced tests are usually broader and not specific to particular instructional programs. Items are preferred that discriminate among persons taking the test (some pass and some fail), and scores are interpreted according to a given student's placement in the distribution of scores obtained by the norm group.

The structure of five of the most commonly used achievement test batteries was examined in terms of what was tested at what levels. Each of these tests is technically quite sophisticated. They enjoy a widespread use in the evaluation of educational programs today.

Teachers need to take time to learn the standardized administration procedures before attempting to give norm-referenced tests. The teachers' manuals that come with the tests give the details. It is important in preparing students that teachers use the practice tests provided by the publishers, so that students will learn to follow the instructions. Trained monitors to assist with the testing are also useful.

The normal curve or normal distribution is used in interpreting many norm-referenced scores. This distribution provides a practical basis for converting standard scores into percentiles. By remembering the numbers 34, 14, 2, which correspond approximately to the percentage of cases falling between z-score units starting at the mean (zero), and keeping in mind the bell shape of the normal curve, it is possible to convert a standard score to a percentile estimate in your head.

A representative national sample (the norm group) is used to provide the data to convert raw scores on a test into standard scores and percentiles. The most commonly used norm-referenced scores are:

- Percentile ranks—specify the percentage of scores which are lower than a given percentile. Scores go from 1 to 99.
- Normal-curve equivalents—convert percentiles into standard scores with a mean of 50 and a standard deviation of about 21. Scores go from 1 to 99.
- Expanded-standard scores—by overlapping testing, the various levels of a test series are tied together on one scale that has higher average standard scores each year. These scores are called *scaled scores* and *growth scale values*.
- Grade-equivalent scores—the mean grade level of student obtaining various raw scores is used to produce a smoothed curve relating raw scores to grade levels.

Percentiles are relatively easy to interpret, but they give a distorted picture of differences in scores compared to standard scores. Percentiles make little differences look big near the middle of a distribution and big differences look small near the extremes of a distribution.

Normal-curve equivalents (NCEs) are useful in comparing performance in different subject areas and in showing gains within a grade level. Expanded-standard scores are most useful in determining longer-term gains in a particular subject area. In reading and math, these growth curve values typically show smaller and smaller gains as grade levels increase (as more students approach mastery). A different pattern would likely occur in science and social science.

Grade-equivalent scores are not useful in studying change processes (gains) and are likely to be misunderstood. A score of 5.5 grade equivalents for a beginning second grader means that she can do beginning second grade work as well as a mid-fifth grader is estimated to be able to do beginning second grade work. It does not mean she should be moved to fifth grade work.

Samples of various kinds of tables used to convert raw scores to standard scores, grade equivalents, and percentiles were illustrated. Teachers need to take time to understand these tables before using them.

Test reliability is concerned with the proportion of error in a test score. More reliable tests have a smaller proportion of error in the measurement. Reliability is estimated by making two or more measures of the same thing and then seeing how well they correlate. This can be done by using equivalent forms of the same test, by correlating odd and even halves, by getting an average of the item intercorrelations (coefficient alpha), or retesting with the same test.

The reliability coefficient can be used to calculate the *standard error of measurement*. This standard error can then be used to estimate the range of values a given score might fall within. For making statements about individuals, reliabilities of .90 or above are very desirable.

Tests have different validities for different uses. Most important for achievement tests is content validity. Does the test measure what was taught? Sensitivity to instruction provides another approach to validity of achievement tests. Good test items would be those failed prior to instruction and passed after instruction. A variety of criterion validities are possible when tests are used to predict who will do well at something (like being successful in college).

Norm-referenced tests are sometimes useful in making gross decisions about student placement, but are not designed for use in making precise placement in a particular curriculum. Similarly, they are not sensitive enough nor program-specific enough for use in evaluating short-term instructional progress. The tests have been useful in helping to identify effective teaching practices, and they may be useful in making a "norm-referenced evaluation" within a particular program or in comparing programs, if there is sufficient content validity. Norm-referenced tests are not useful in evaluating teachers (except under very special conditions not dealt with here), but may be useful in selection for special programs and in guidance. There are some ethical issues (discussed in an earlier chapter) that must be kept in mind when tests are proposed for selecting students for special programs.

CHAPTER

28

FUTURES

Most of this chapter's content could just as well have been put in Part II, "The Design of Quality Instruction." It is perhaps fitting that after spending the past twenty years helping to develop and evaluate instructional systems based on mastery-learning and direct-instruction principles, that when I look to the future I see the possibility for even better mastery-learning systems with direct-instruction design technology underlying them. The improvement in interactive communications and computer technologies show great promise as a basis for better mastery-learning systems.

MICROCOMPUTERS

Computer-assisted instruction (CAI) is little more than twenty years old and the age of microcomputers little more than ten years old. Most of the nation's schools have at least one microcomputer available to students, and many have computer laboratories with more than twenty microcomputers. Microcomputers are constantly increasing in speed and memory capabilities, and they are likely to have a significant impact on how teachers, at all levels, use their time. Teachers are more and more going to need computer survival skills. They are going to need to know how, when, and why to use computers; how to select software and hardware; and the basic terminology.

What is happening in this important area now, and what can you expect for the future? While there are issues of cost, access, relative effectiveness, and adequacy of software that remain as problems, computers are gaining wide-ranging applications in schools (for keeping financial records, student records, schedules, career guidance and other information-retrieval systems, computer programing courses, computer literacy courses, and typing courses to name just some). But the main concern here is in the use of computers and related technologies for instruction and the management of instruction. First, examine some of the problems.

Cost

The schools have nowhere near the resources necessary to provide a computer for every student, which some researchers see as the ideal. In Minnesota, which has sophisticated statewide applications of computers, the availability would have to increase by a factor of ten just to give each student one hour per day of computer access. Levin and Meister (1984) estimate that the hardware costs alone represent only *one-fourth* of the cost of operation, which includes trained personnel, maintenance, consumable supplies, security, and software. So, even with a rapidly declining hardware cost, progress is likely to be a bit slower than the often-promised "revolution."

Equity

It appears that equity issues are arising, such that in richer school districts (with higher socio-economic status parents) more is being spent on computers than in districts with more disadvantaged students. In 1983, "80 percent of the 2,000 largest and richest high schools owned instructional computers, while only 40 percent of the smallest, poorest high schools had them" (Robinson, 1984, based on an unpublished report by M. Beatriz Arias). Within schools there is also evidence that the middle-class students are more apt to get access to them because of their greater use in higher-level science and math courses (Robinson, 1984). Later in the chapter you will look at some possible ways around the cost and equity issues in the discussion of Teacher Net, a low-cost system based on one or two microcomputers per classroom.

Relative Effectiveness

A comparison of four interventions by Levin, Glass, and Meister, (as reported in Levin & Meister, 1984) suggested that cross-age tutoring may be still more cost effective than *drill and practice CAI* in raising mathematics and reading scores. However, this comparison of approaches found the CAI more cost effective than using adult tutors or reducing class size. Unfortunately, each "intervention" considered by these authors was based on data drawn from quite different kinds of school districts, making valid comparisons most difficult. Also, it is unlikely that cross-age tutors could compete for effectiveness against courseware that was carefully designed to teach concepts, principles, and/or strategies. The point, however, is that teachers need to stay open to other alternatives. CAI should not be taken as a panacea, however promising.

Adequacy of Software

The issue of adequacy of software is one to look at more closely, because it relates to the analyses of the design of effective instruction examined in Part II of this text.

At the time of this writing, software sales to schools were expected to reach $500 million. In 1981, the Educational Products Information Exchange (EPIE) drew these conclusions, and they remain largely true today:

1. Most programs are drill and practice for supplementary use in the classroom.

2. Most programs specify a target population that represents too wide of an audience.

3. Most objectives have to do with recall of previously learned facts rather than higher-order skills such as comprehension, application, analysis, synthesis, and evaluation.

4. Few preinstructional strategies are used to orient the student to the context.

5. About 50 percent of the programs format the instructional text inadequately, with sentence structure as a major problem.

6. The only program that attempts to teach concepts does not use any systematic method of presentation based on concept-teaching research.

7. Graphics are rarely embedded in the instructional content.

8. Although all programs include a teacher's guide, these do not provide specific lesson plans or activities designed to integrate the programs into the curriculum.

9. Most programs grant user control in only two areas: rate of display and exiting.

10. Although all programs use feedback for both correct and incorrect responses, most of the feedback does not remediate (only one program informs the user why the response is wrong). (From Vachon & Carnine, 1983–84, p.11.)

While some improvements have been made or are in process, there is little disagreement today that most software is drill and practice and not explicitly connected to specific curricula. This does not mean that it cannot be useful, just that its uses are limited. Some of the problems of software can be attributed to the fact that software has been largely developed by computer programers who have not been trained in principles of instructional design. Also, they tend not to field test what they develop to eliminate user problems and to better adapt the programs to teacher needs.

Vachon and Carnine (1983–84) have recommended guidelines for evaluating computer software for use in schools based on the instructional design and mastery-learning principles discussed earlier. Their review process begins with eight screening questions. Since a single evaluation of a piece of courseware can take up to 40 hours, the initial screening can help identify programs meriting a closer evaluation. Each of these eight questions is answered as *Acceptable, Marginal,* or *Unacceptable*:

1. Is the content accurate?

2. Is the content of educational value?

3. Are entry skills specified?

4. Is the presentation of material clear and logical?

5. Is the learning that is to occur generalizable?

6. Is there feedback on all errors?

7. Is review provided?

8. Is the program motivational?
(Vachon and Carnine, 1983–84, p. 11.)

Table 28.1 presents their Courseware Evaluation Form (from Vachon and Carnine, 1983–84, p. 12). It is in the area of Instructional Design that

Table 28-1 Courseware evaluation form

Each item is rated using the following code:
E = Excellent
A = Acceptable
M = Marginal
U = Unacceptable
N.A. = Not Applicable

	Rating
CONTENT	
1. Is the content accurate?	____
2. Is the content of educational value?	____
3. Is the content free of stereotypic bias?	____
INSTRUCTIONAL DESIGN	
1. Objectives	____
a. Are objectives clearly stated?	____
b. Are objectives defined to the learner?	____
c. Is the program content consistent with objectives?	____
2. Individualization	
a. Is the target audience specified?	____
b. Are entry skills specified?	____
c. Is a pretest or placement test provided?	____
d. Are a variety of entry points available?	____
e. Are options for exiting or returning to menu available?	____
f. Can the program be altered?	____
g. Is there a method of record-keeping?	____
3. Presentation	
a. Do the activities optimally match the content?	____
b. All Programs (Tutorials, Drill & Practice/Gaming, Simulation)	____
____ provides opportunity for frequent interaction	____
____ avoids restrictive response formats	____
c. Tutorials	
____ uses consistent wording	____
____ tests learner's ability to generalize	
____ provides review	
(1) Concepts (Discriminations & Relationships)	
____ uses examples & non-examples	
____ demonstrates range variations through examples	
(a) Discriminations (labelling tasks)	
____ sequenced to demonstrate differences (minimally different non-examples)	
____ uses continuous conversion when appropriate	
(b) Relationships (fact systems, science rules)	
____ lists preskills as entry competencies	
____ presents relationships explicitly (e.g., visual displays)	
____ introduces new vocabulary systematically	
(2) Strategies	
____ lists component skills as entry competencies	
____ presents strategy as a series of steps	
____ guides learner in responding to each step	
____ integrates steps into sequence	

____ provides *less* specific direction (hints, clues) as learner progresses
____ provides sufficient independent practice with range of appropriate tasks

d. Drill and Practice/Gaming ____
____ provides varying levels of difficulty
____ problem type ____ rate
____ number of tasks
____ provides cumulative introduction
____ re-introduces missed tasks or equivalent tasks
____ provides tutorial instruction when appropriate
____ sequences tasks unpredictably

e. Simulations ____
____ utilizes valid model
____ informs learner of inherent assumptions
____ informs learner of program variables
____ provides access to explanations
____ includes pre/post activities

4. Feedback
   a. Are all errors corrected? ____
   b. Does the correction fit the context in which the error occurred? ____
   c. Is feedback informative? ____

5. Review
   a. Is review provided for newly acquired skills? ____
   b. Does review incorporate previously-learned skills into more complex applications? ____

6. Motivation
   a. Is the level of difficulty challenging to the learner? ____
   b. Is the material presented at a good pace? ____
   c. Are readability levels appropriate to the target audience? ____
   d. Is user control granted to the learner where appropriate? ____
   e. Does the use of graphics/sound/color increase interest in program content? ____

7. Reinforcement
   a. Is reinforcement age-appropriate? ____
   b. Is reinforcement used appropriately? ____
   c. Is a variety of reinforcement used? ____

PROGRAM UTILITY

1. Are user-support materials included? ____
2. Is there a Teacher's Manual? ____
3. Is the program easy to operate? ____
4. Is the program reliable under normal use? ____
5. Can the program analyze a variety of responses? ____
6. Are information displays attractive? ____

Vachon and Carnine make a distinctive contribution. Note that programs are divided into three major types: Tutorials, Drill and Practice/Gaming, and Simulations. Tutorials are further divided into Concepts and Strategies. In their usage, Concepts include what this text has previously called concepts, rules, and fact systems. Strategies are what have been called problem-solving routines. Simulations involve a model of a set of processes and relationships within which problems can be posed and alternative actions taken. Simulations can be used to teach about "systems" such as ecology, weather, health maintenance, and governments.

A potentially useful software guide is distributed by the International Council for Computers in Education (ICCE) (College of Education, University of Oregon, Eugene, Oregon 97403). The guide called *The 1984 Educational Software Preview Guide* was developed by the Educational Software Evaluation Consortium. It covers some 400 programs that have been "favorably reviewed" by consortium members and others (the criteria specified in Table 28.1 were very likely not used in the evaluations).

LOGO

High on the popularity list of software for children is LOGO, a programing language developed by Seymour Papert. All sorts of claims have been made for the value of LOGO in "disciplining the mind," teaching new and powerful ways of thinking. However, there is little evidence to support this. "The few studies done so far have not verified any of these indirect cognitive outcome." While the data are not in, there is certainly much to support the use of LOGO as an introduction to computer programing. LOGO focuses on graphics. A triangle on the screen (the turtle) is moved about by typing various commands. As the turtle is moved, a line is made. The student starts with a screen like this:

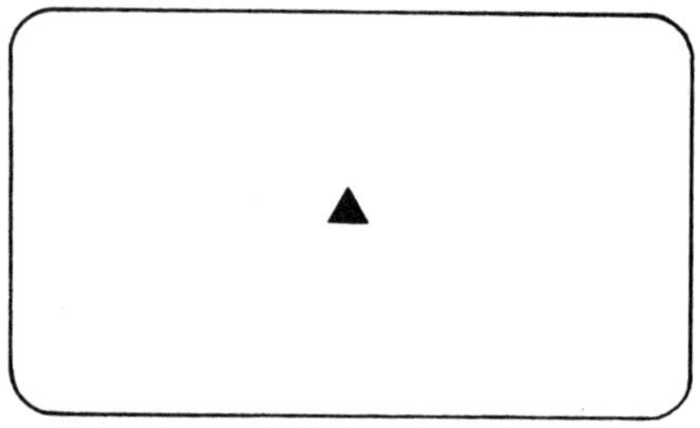

If the student then types FORWARD 60, the turtle moves up the screen. Then, the following commands (a program) will produce a square:

```
RIGHT 90

FORWARD 60

RIGHT 90

FORWARD 60

RIGHT 90

FORWARD 60
```

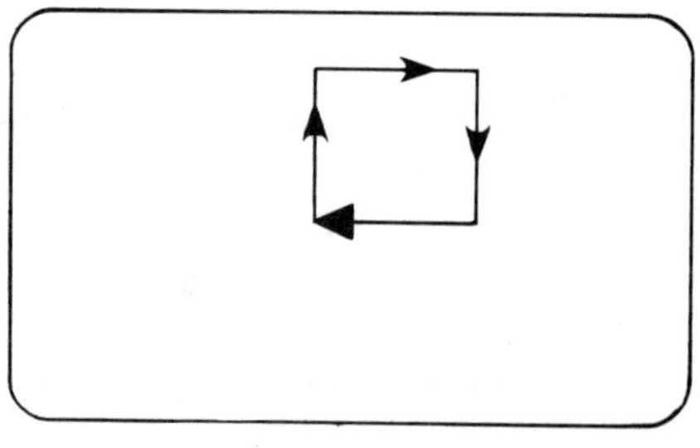

(Note: The arrows have been added to show which way the turtle moved. They would not be on the screen; only the lines and the triangle showing where the turtle is currently are displayed.)

A book published in 1984 by the International Council for Computers in Education, *Logo in the Classroom* (Torgerson, Kriley and Stone, 1984), provides guidelines for teachers in grades 3, 4, and 5 for teaching LOGO in a classroom where there are a few computers. Twenty lesson guidelines are provided. While claims may be overexaggerated, it is certainly clear that the use of a simplified turtle graphics program (LOGO) is a fun way to teach beginning computer programing to young children.

Writing

The use of computers as word processors is coming to dominate the adult world and replace typewriters. Computers are obviously going to be the vehicle for writing in schools also. Programs are available that readily teach keyboarding, monitor the student's rate and errors, and reinforce practice. These programs can operate in a mode that prevents keyboarding of an error (for early instruction with prompting), or they can be set to operate normally showing what is actually typed. Simplified word processing programs are available, as is a variety of software to assist in writing instruction.

Prompted Idea Generation. A number of programs are available that assist the student in writing stories by the use of various questioning strategies. Good software can help define the goal of an essay. It can help to structure the steps to take. It can ask about alternatives to be considered, and so on. And, it can provide a printed copy for editing and revisions. For example, STORYTREE (Scholastic Inc., 1984) allows the student to create stories with multiple endings. Prompts help the student develop a mystery or adventure story with some chance elements in it and then branch to several endings. The research in this area is just developing. To date, the research suggests that prompting programs do not necessarily promote better writing, but may be useful in developing some of the component skills important to writing. Such programs may also help take some of the pain out of early creative attempts and increase motivation to write.

Subskill Development. There are hundreds of drill and practice programs and a few tutorials oriented around the development of spelling skills, vocabulary, and grammar. To date there is little evidence supporting their effectiveness, and the earlier comments about the general inadequacies of current educational software should be kept in mind. Nevertheless, there remains a promise and a hope that systematic approaches to skill development in this complex area will eventually be constructed.

Word processing. Many teachers are interested in using word processors to improve writing skills with upper elementary and secondary students. A number of word processing programs for youth have been developed, such as BANK STREET WRITER (1982) and QUILL (1984) . These are easy-to-use programs. Reports on the use of these programs with students of all ages are generally positive. For example, Bradley (1982) found that sixth grade students readily completed sentence combining tasks, were not limited by lack of typing skills, and were motivated. Kleiman and Humphrey (1982) found that learning-disabled 7 to 12 year olds began writing with enthusiasm when allowed to use word processors. College students have been found to edit and revise more when using a word processor (Schwartz, 1982).

A recent reference in this area that teachers should find helpful is *Computer in Composition Instruction* (Shostak, 1984).

Monitoring Systems

Computer monitoring of student errors and mastery has been an important part of CAI from the beginning. Provision for adequate monitoring and feedback to the student and teacher should be an important component of any courseware. When whole classes are working on computer lessons, efficient monitoring reports become even more important. In the future, the teacher can expect more and more of the tedious recordkeeping and charting of progress to be handled by microcomputers.

Authoring Languages

Authoring languages allows you to use programing instructions closer to natural languages. A number of authoring languages such as PILOT and SUPERPILOT have come on the market to aid in the creation of programs by those teachers and students who are really into computer programing. These languages are easier to learn and use than languages such as BASIC or PASCAL.

Woodward and Carnine (1983) evaluated a teacher's experiences with a number of authoring languages. They found that important features of a good program design (such as reviewing later items with incorrect responses) were often missing. Also, it was very difficult to repair these deficiencies using the languages provided. The prompts, questions, and reinforcers used with some languages became very tiresome. To be useful to teachers, Woodward and Carnine concluded that different systems are needed for different instructional goals (one for tutorials, one for drill and practice, and one for simulations). The different systems need to include the instructional design features critical for teaching the different kinds of knowledge structures.

Carnine and Engelmann are currently working on the development of a Direct Instruction Authoring Language, and Carnine is developing a drill and practice authoring language. These languages systems should be especially useful to teachers. They are called DIAL (Direct Instruction Authoring System) and DRILL AND PRACTICE. DIAL can be used by teachers to construct CAI tutorials following principles discussed earlier in this book. For example, after a student error, the programer can: (a) give an additional explanation, (b) review a sequence or a set of questions, or (c) answer new questions. Also, the amount of review given depends on student errors. Various kinds of reviews can be used depending on what is being taught. A variety of recordkeeping files are built into DIAL.

DRILL AND PRACTICE is very easy to set up and use. The teacher only needs to enter the questions and the answers in a lesson, and the program takes care of the rest—presentation formats, corrections, review of missed items, recordkeeping to determine when the student has reached criterion on one set of questions so a new one can be started, cumulative review, and more.

TEACHER NET

Teacher Net is a computer peripheral for networking that permits many keyboards to function with one microcomputer. For a class of 30, the cost of Teacher Net (the peripheral and 30 numerical keyboards) is about $100 a student (plus the cost of the single microcomputer). Alphanumeric keyboards (which are currently being tested) would raise the cost of the hardware another $30 per student. Teacher Net has the promise of overcoming the cost and access problems discussed earlier.

Teacher Net receives and holds signals from each student keyboard. Each student can send up to sixty characters each second. The computer can store and operate on this information; it can display it on the screen or not, it can print summary reports, and perform other functions. Consider some possible uses.

Application Software

The basic application program (TNBAP) permits the teacher to monitor independent study, testing, and to receive lecture feedback.

TNBAP performs several functions: (1) It collects (and stores) the input data from all of the keyboards in use. (2) It can provide item-by-item feedback to students (during independent work or testing) and to the teacher (during lectures). (3) It can score, analyze, and summarize student input data. Answers may be precoded by skill, allowing a skill-by-skill analysis to be made.

The monitor display is different for each function. During independent study and testing, the monitor screen is divided into sections and each student is assigned his or her own section of the monitor. Within a student's section the number of the question currently answered is displayed. At the teacher's option, the students are assigned a question number, or they are allowed to answer questions in order of their choice. In the latter mode, they can change any answer, at any time, by reanswering the question.

Once the teacher has loaded a list of correct reponses into the computer, TNBAP can score student entries. At the teacher's option, the student may be informed about the correctness of an answer. A symbol indicating "right" or "wrong" can be made to appear as soon as an answer is entered.

In the lecture format, the lecturer can quickly and easily pause in the midst of a lecture to assess student apprehension. The monitor is positioned so that only the instructor can view it. The teacher has options for the display on the monitor. It can provide a list of individual responses, a summary of student input, and an analysis of the data (Carnine, 1985).

The standard TNBAP divides the screen into 16 sections. The individual sections would be hard to read if they were any smaller. Thus, for testing-seatwork uses, a monitor is needed for each 16 students.

The data storage and management program that accompanies TNBAP can automatically collect data keyboarded by students or *data entered by others*. Thus, other file information, attendance, IEP goals, grades, and other records can be managed by the program. Data can be shown in graphic form and reports can be printed when desired. It can communicate with other computers in the school.

Other Software

Other software available for use on the Teacher Net system include a diagnostic math lab, a program for computer-assisted video instruction (CAVI), a keyboarding (typing) program, and group-response-controlled CAI in tutorial or drill and practice models. The computer-assisted video instruction makes it possible to train critical visual discriminations or audio discrimination by presenting instances and not-instances (as single frames or moving sequences) and getting student responses to each example.

The real advantages of the system are that it maintains the group orientation that teachers are accustomed to; it increases the information available to students and teachers; it reduces the amount of information the teacher has to evaluate and record; and it does all of this at a modest cost. At the time of this writing, the system is being field tested in Kent, Washington and Mountain View, California.

VIDEODISCS

A videodisc is shaped like a record and stores images and sounds like a videotape recorder. A popular model uses a low-power laser beam to read the images. Thus, the discs have potentially long lives, since nothing but a light "touches" the disc. A single disc can store 54,000 high-quality individual frames on one side (each frame is a high resolution video screen). Each of the individual frames on the disc can be accessed in a second or two. The frames can be read as moving pictures (moving at 30 frames a second) or as stills. As moving pictures, there are 30 minutes of video on one side of a disc. (Two-sided discs are expected before long.)

Types of Videodisc Systems

Videodisc systems have been classified according to the "intelligence" of the system (Daynes, 1984). The lowest system (level 0) functions like a linear tape player. The highest system (level 4) is integrated with a microcomputer using artificial intelligence software. Two in-between levels (levels 1 and 3) are most likely to dominate the school market. The level 1 system has these functions:

- *Quick frame access.* Each frame can be accessed using a remote control device.
- *Chapter stop.* Instead of going to a specific frame with a 5-digit number), a 2-digit number can take you to the beginning of up to 70 chapters.
- *Picture stop.* This is a place where the player stops automatically. It is a preprogramed stop for a picture to be studied, a problem to be worked in workbooks, or a question to be answered by the group orally. The teacher signals the player to go on when appropriate.
- *Selectable audio channels.* The two audio channels can be selected together or one at a time. One could present a problem on one track while the pictures provide a demonstration, and then the sequence could be replayed to give the solution through audio on other track. (After Hofmeister, Engelmann, and Carnine, 1985.)

The level 3 system links the level 1 videodisc to a microcomputer. It permits both computer and videodisc material to be shown. It permits interactive computer-assisted videodisc instruction. The cost of the system is considerably more than the level 1 system. The level 1 system can be an economical basis for teacher-directed, group instruction.

Videodisc program development is likely to proceed in two stages. First, programs will be built that can be used by the level 1 system. Second, these programs will be adapted to the computer-assisted, level 3 format (Hofmeister et al., 1985).

Core Concepts

The rest of this chapter highlights one ambitious approach to the development of videodisc courseware for high school and junior college science and math courses. These are areas where there are currently critical shortages of qualified teachers, where there is public need for better instruction, and where programed instruction by "master teachers" could be of great benefit. Alan Hofmeister of Utah State University originally proposed to Engelmann and Carnine that they undertake the analysis, design, and initial field testing (using video tape) for a videodisc project. A second group was identified to produce the final tapes to be used to make the discs, and a third group would oversee the project, secure financing, and handle the sales side of the project. The initial set of courses was estimated to require 48 discs, although over 100 might be required to complete the project. The program development is being financed by Systems Impact Inc. The series is entitled *Core Concepts in Math and Science.* The first program (Fractions), was marketed in November, 1985. Each course is made up of several mini-courses. They cover prealgebra, algebra, biology, and physical science.

According to Hofmeister et al. (1985) the development steps include:

- Analyses of curricula and textbooks.
- Initial list of potential core concepts (those with the greatest generalization potential).
- Consultant review of initial selections and revisions.
- Preparing and reviewing trial scripts.
- Constructing lesson prototypes.
- Field testing of lessons with two groups ten lessons apart. (Problems found with the first group are adjusted and tested again with the second group. The lessons are also tested against daily in class exercises, homework, and criterion-referenced tests given as a part of every fifth lesson.)
- Prepare videodiscs and supporting workbooks and manuals.

The discs are designed to use a tutorial approach. Demonstrations are followed by questions and problems for students to do. A high level of student activity is achieved, quite unlike the passive interaction that goes on with movies and TV presentations.

The videodisc permits the careful control of the details of instruction. It permits dynamic presentations that can quickly show a range of samenesses or minimum differences. They permit travel from inside an atom to the far reaches of outer space in seconds.

Problems with Current Math-Science Texts

Engelmann approaches the critical problems of teaching at this level with his typically astute analysis.

> The traditional approaches to high school science instruction are a hodge-podge. One reason is that science instruction mirrors the history of scientific discovery. Geometry springs from Euclid, with its proofs and theorems. Algebra follows the tired route from polynomials to roots of irrational numbers. Overlaying the older traditions are newer orientations—graphing procedures and discrete math. But the new is not embedded in the old. It stands as a separate entity—an add-on occupying its own cubbyhole with its unique notations and conventions.
>
> The conventions may discourage a math student from free substitutions of variables by suggesting that the student must go through

> the ritual of saying, "There is an X such that X. . . . " when all the student needs to say is, "Let X equal V/T." The student, after all, is not "proving" anything or operating on the level of theory, but is just trying to solve a problem (Engelmann, 1983, p. 1).

Engelmann points to the unnecessary teaching of vocabulary and "laws" in math that are nonfunctional in problem solving and to the failure to teach generalizations that cut across topics. Students are continually punished because they can't do something that is expected, but was not explicitly taught. The presentations do not teach generalizations in a simple context before proceeding to more complicated examples; they fail to teach every skill needed; and they teach too much historical information that is not relevant.

> These problems result from a basic confusion that pervades nearly all textbooks in any field. The confusion is between *accuracy* and *completeness* . . . [many believe that] to be accurate is to be complete—to say all, to qualify general statements elaborately, and basically to write for other experts, not for students. For example, it would be considered "inaccurate" by the typical expert to introduce the atom without referring to all its parts and all its basic properties—right now. Even though protons may be perfectly irrelevant to any of the discriminations the student must make in the earlier exercises, the information about protons is presented. However, to introduce atoms without referring to protons is not inaccurate, merely incomplete (Engelmann, 1983, p. 4).

The assumptions made about what a student can learn in a given period is "almost magical." Why does Algebra 2 overlap 70 percent with Algebra 1? The material was not taught the first time around.

> Would the learner have been much farther ahead if, instead of receiving mere exposure to a lot of topics, the learner actually mastered those skills that would make Algebra 2 a series of relatively obvious extensions from known information? . . . The lack of good teaching models is partly a result of the text structure . . . [and] instruction [that] . . . is not consistent with what we know about learning, and certainly not consistent with the principles of instructional design (Engelmann, 1983, p. 5).

A Proposed Solution

Engelmann and Carnine propose to get around these problems by doing appropriate analyses of what is to be taught, by using the graphic capabilities of videodiscs, and packaged programs that will teach. The programs in math and science will not cover all concepts in a field, but will target *core concepts*.

> We have the opportunity to reorganize curricula so they deal more with generalizations and less with associated "facts." And we have the opportunity to be irreverent, to the extent that the irreverence doesn't do violence to the integrity of the topic being presented. We can eschew history. We can speak in plain language. We can present narrators that do not preach from Mount Nowhere . . . We can *show* things that are virtually impossible to present in textbooks, and at the same time, we can orchestrate the presentations so that, in addition to being well-paced and interesting, they are consistent with learning phenomena and

instructional-design principles (Engelmann, 1983, pp. 6–7).

Engelmann illustrates his analysis and design goals by starting with a balance beam. "We can demonstrate all basic principles of simple machines. We show that the product of one side of the fulcrum may be balanced by a number of weight arrangements that create the same product" (Engelmann, 1983, p. 7).

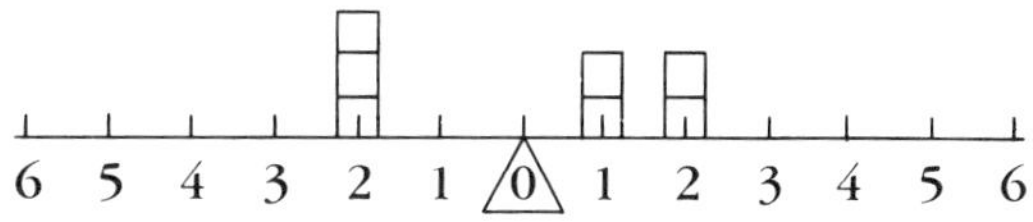

$$3 \times 2 = 6 = (2 \times 1) + (2 \times 2)$$

OR:

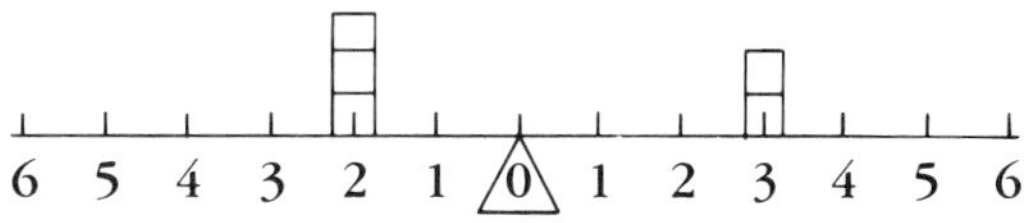

$$3 \times 2 = 6 = 2 \times 3$$

Dynamic presentations can show actual changes and outcomes. Arithmetic operations are reinforced in the process and the stage is set for the relation of distance to force. "The farther the distance from the fulcrum, the greater the force a counter has." Conservation of force can be shown by rotating the beam. The farther a point is from the fulcrum, the greater distance it has to move. Discounting possible friction and bending of the beam, if a force of 4 pounds is exerted at A and moves the beam three yards ($4 \times 3 = 12$), the upward force at B times the distance moved will yield the same product. If B moves one yard, the force at B is 12 pounds ($1 \times 12 = 12$). Obviously, these presentations would be much clearer with video graphics (and dynamic changes).

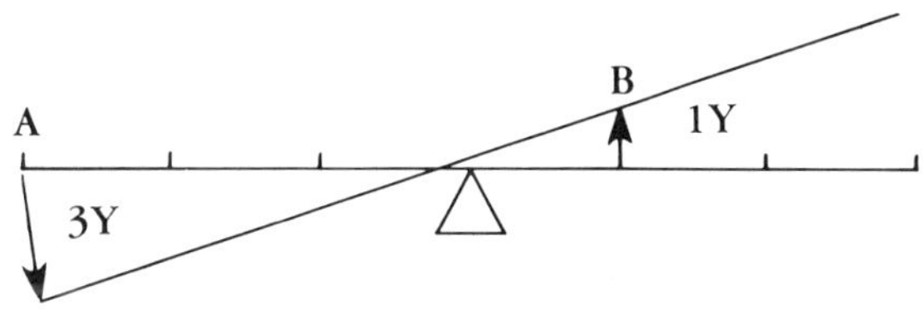

Now consider the next step, once the learner understands that distance times force equals distance times force. We rotate the balance beam and we have a wheel. Put two wheels of different sizes together on a conveyor belt and we have a new kind of magic. The outsides of both wheels are moving at exactly the same speed, but the rate at which the wheels revolve is not the same. . . . We can move the wheels together and eliminate the belt. We now have gears that function the same way the wheels did, except they rotate in opposite directions. But they are still governed by the same rule: Force times distance equals force times distance.

Switch scenes now to a ramp, an inclined plane. Two men are

> lifting 100-pound sacks—one hoisting it straight up, the other wheeling it up the ramp. Using the force-times-distance equation, we see the same relationship. The person going up the ramp covers a much greater distance, but exerts far less force (Engelmann, 1983, p. 9).
>
> Wrap the inclined plane around a pole and you have a screw, and so on. The key in analysis is to find the generalizable relationships that cut across and integrate traditional topics (Engelmann, 1983).

Only time can tell how successful Engelmann and Carnine will be in this new adventure. But it is clear that a technological approach to the problems of good education is going to expand in the future.

A Concluding Note

There are those who are concerned that if students interact more with machines or technological approaches to learning they will become less human. In Follow Through, it was found that the students given the strongest academic skills through Direct Instruction, felt best about themselves in school and felt they were more in command of their own lives (internal locus of control). A recent two-year study by Griswold (1984) found that fourth and fifth graders who participated in a CAI program in math (drill and practice, 10–20 minutes a day) felt more responsible for their success and were more confident about academic success. Americans have been interacting with various machines and technologies now for more than a century. I doubt that this has made us less human. In fact it has probably given us more time to be human. In the case of the computer-videodisc "revolution," students probably will become more competent earlier in life and remain the human beings they are.

SUMMARY

Most of this chapter on "Futures" has actually described events going on right now, some of which have already impacted schools, and others that are in the field test stage. The ideas could have pushed further and considered the potential impact of two-way communication networks using cable video, satellites, and other networking systems. However, I preferred to stay closer to the developments I have had direct experience with, that already have considerable development effort behind them and are aimed at schools.

The key underlying these "futures" is the potential for better mastery-learning systems and for more quality designed instruction at all levels. The microcomputer revolution is in progress. There are problems of costs, equity, effectiveness, and especially the quality of software. The costs are a lot higher than most people think they are, and the resources are not always there. This will slow down the "revolution," and until software gets better, that might not be a bad idea. Equity issues can be handled through better school policy and continued state (if not federal) equalization of school assets. They can also be aided by lower-cost systems like Teacher Net.

The chapter devoted considerable discussion to an approach to software evaluation that grew out of Engelmann and Carnine's *Theory of Instruction.* Instructional software should be built using the best instructional design principles for the kind of learning involved. You should return to Table 28.1 the next time you are involved in a software evaluation decision.

The chapter introduced briefly some software programs involved in problem solving (LOGO), the development of writing skills (where there is a great potential for computer applications), and authoring languages. With the appropriate systems, teachers can readily prepare lessons needed by their students when appropriate software is not available.

Teacher Net is an exciting possibility. While still in need of much testing and development (and some easy way to get rid of all those wires running everywhere!), the potential for low-cost feedback from every student, testing, group CAI, and automated recordkeeping present a real promise of a system that can be most helpful to the teacher.

While they are likely to be costly initially, random access videodisc systems (with or without microcomputer interface) present another promising approach to improving instruction. This is especially exciting to me personally, because I have had a chance to experience the process being followed to ensure that quality programs are produced, and not just more drill and practice under the guise of the queen of technologies. However, teachers can only await the test and verdict of time.

The chapter closed with a thought on the humanity of it all.

FINAL COMMENTS

Through these 28 chapters I have attempted to provide prospective teachers with an understanding of the principles that can generate good student motivation and effective instructional processes. I have also looked at issues in human development and assessment processes. There is no doubt in my mind that the major improvements in quality instruction are going to come from two sources: better designed-pretested curriculum materials and better application of what researchers know about effective teaching practices by teachers. Education is a major and vital industry in this country. Over $200 billion is invested annually on schools and colleges. As recent history has shown, however, school improvement is not going to occur just because the citizens spend more money. Improvement will come when the extensive knowledge researchers have about learning processes is applied by better trained teachers.

Teaching is often a thankless, underpaid job. But for those who get involved and do it well, it can also be one of the most interesting, self-fulfilling, and satisfying careers one could undertake. Be a winner!

Acknowledgements for Illustrative Material

P.14 From Wesley C. Becker, et al., "The Contingent Use of Teacher Attention and Praise in Reducing Classroom Behavior Problems," in *Journal of Special Education,* vol. 1, 3, 1982, 1967. Used by permission of Buttonwood Farms, Inc.

P. 38 From *Hand Writing with Write and See,* by B. F. Skinner and S. Krakower. © 1968, Lyons and Carnahan. Used by permission of B. F. Skinner.

P. 48 From Ronald K. Parker (ed.), *Reading in Educational Psychology.* Copyright © 1968 by Allyn and Bacon, Inc. Reprinted with permission.

P. 59 From *Token Reinforcement Techniques,* By H. M. Walker and N. K. Buckley. © 1974, E-B Press. Used by permission of the publisher.

P. 70 From K. D. O'Leary and W. C. Becker, "Behavior Modification of an Adjustment Class: A Token Reinforcement Program," in *Exceptional Children,* vol. 33, pp. 637-642, 1967. Used by permission of the Council for Exceptional Children.

P. 78 From *Corrective Reading/Decoding B: Decoding Strategies,* Student's Book by Siegfried Engelmann, et al. © 1978, Science Research Associates, Inc. Reprinted by permission of the publisher.

P. 106 From B. S. Rushall, "A Motivational Device for Swimmers," in *Swimming Techniques,* vol. 11, pp. 103-106, 1975. Used by permission of the publisher.

Pp. 108, 109 From J. Komaki and F. Barnett, "A Behavioral Approach to Coaching Football: Improving the Play Execution of the Offensive Backfield," in *Journal of Applied Behavioral Analysis,* vol. 10, pp. 657-664, 1977. Copyright © 1977 by the Society for the Experimental Analysis of Behavior, Inc. Used by permission of the publisher and the author.

Pp. 115, 116, 117, 118, 119 Reprinted by permission of the publisher from R. Douglas Greer, *Design for Music Learning* (New York: Teacher's College Press, © 1980 by Teacher's College, Columbia University. All rights reserved.) Appendix B.

P. 144 From Richard A. Schmuck and Patricia S. Schmuck, *Group Processes in the Classroom,* 4th Edition. © 1971, 1975, 1979, 1983 Wm. C. Brown Publishers, Dubuque, Iowa. All rights reserved. Reprinted by permission.

P. 158 From *Follow Through Grant Proposal to USOE 1975-1976,* by R. T. Eichelberger, 1975. Used by permission of the author.

Pp. 158, 159, 160 From R. G. Scanlon, "Individually Prescribed Instruction." Used by permission of the author.

P. 168 From *Reading Mastery/Distar®* Reading I, Presentation Book "B" by Siegfried Engelmann and Elaine C. Bruner. Copyright © Science Research Associates, Inc. 1983, 1974, 1969. Reprinted by permission of the publisher.

P. 177 Adapted from *Principles of Instructional Design* 2/e, by Robert M. Gagne, and Leslie J. Briggs. Copyright © 1979 by Holt, Rinehart, and Winston. Reprinted by permission of CBS College Publishing.

P. 178 From *The Conditions of Learning* by Robert M. Gagne. Copyright © 1965 by Holt, Rinehart, and Winston. Reprinted by permission of CBS College Publishing.

P. 179 From *Analyzing Instructional Content: A Guide to Instruction and Evaluation* by P. W. Tiemann and S. M. Markle. © 1983, Stipes Publishing Co. Reprinted by permission of the publisher.

Pp. 180, 181, 192, 203, 207, 208, 209 From *Theory of Instruction* by S. Engelmann and D. W. Carnine, 1982. Used by permission of S. Engelmann.

P. 197 From W. C. Becker and S. Engelmann, "Systems for Basic Instruction: Theory and Application," in *Handbook of Applied Behavior Analysis* by Cantania and Brigham. 1978. Used by permission of W. C. Becker.

P. 211 From *Your World of Facts II,* Student Workbook, by S. Engelmann, K. Davis and G. Davis. Copyright © 1983, C. C. Publications, Inc. Used by permission.

P. 212 From *Your World of Facts—Student Workbook,* by S. Engelmann, K. Davis and G. Davis. Copyright © 1982, C. C. Publications, Inc. Used by permission.

P. 243 From *Distar®* Reading I, Teacher's Guide. © 1974, 1969, Science Research Associates, Inc. Reprinted by permission of the publisher

Pp. 244, 245 From *Reading Mastery/Distar®* Reading II, Storybook 1, Siegfried Engelmann and Elaine C. Bruner. Copyright © Science Research Associates, Inc. 1983, 1975, 1969. Reprinted by permission of the publisher.

P. 249 From W. E. Nagy and R. C. Anderson The Number of Words in Printed English: *Reading Research Quarterly 1984, 19,* 304-330. Used by permission of the International Reading Association and the author.

P. 271 From L. B. Resnick and R. C. Glaser, "Problem Solving and Intelligence," in *The Nature of Intelligence,* p. 226. © 1978, Lawrence Erlbuam Associates, Inc. Used by permission of the publisher.

P. 305 From A. Maggs and P. Morath, "Effects of Direct Verbal Instruction on Intellectual Development of Institutionalized Moderately Retarded Children," in *The Journal of Special Education,* vol. 10, pp. 357-364, 1976. Used by permission of Buttonwood Farms, Inc.

P. 304 From S. Engelmann, "The Effectiveness of Direct Instruction on IQ Performance and Achievement in Reading and Arithmetic," in *Disadvantaged Child,* vol. 3, 1971, Bruner/Mazel, Inc. Used by permission of Bruner/Mazel, Inc. and the author.

Pp. 309, 310, 311 From R. M. Gersten, W. C. Becker, et al., "Entry IQ and Yearly Academic Growth of Children in Direct Instructional Programs: A Longitudinal Study," in *Educational Evaluation and Policy Analysis,* vol. 6, 2, pp. 109-121, 1984. Used by permission of the American Educational Research Association.

P. 316 From *Child Development and Relationships,* by Carol Flake-Hobson, Bryan Robinson and Patsy Skeen. Copyright © 1983, Random House, Inc. Used by permission of the publisher.

P. 322 From *Piaget's Theory of Cognitive Development,* Third Edition, by Barry J. Wadsworth. Copyright © 1984 by Longman Inc. Used by permission of the publisher.

P. 328 From Robbie Case, "Piaget and Beyond' Toward a Developmentally Based Theory of Technology of Instruction," in *Advances in Instructional Psychology.* © 1978, Lawrence Erlbuam Associates, Inc. Used by permission of the publisher.

Pp. 340, 334, 345 From unpublished data and charts by James Enochs, 1981. Also the "Phases of the moon" analysis of implementation problems from a paper, "Restoration of Standards," by James Enochs, *Education Week,* Dec. 21, 1981, pp. 17-18. Used by permission of the author.

P. 359 From B. Hart, "Effects of Contingent and Noncontingent Social Reinforcement on the Cooperative Play of a Preschool Child," in *Journal of Applied Behavior Analysis,* vol. 1, p. 1. Copyright © 1968, Society for the Experimental Analysis of Behavior. Used by permission of the publisher and the author.

P. 368 From M. W. Steinkamp and M. L. Maehr, "Gender Differences in Motivational Orientations Toward Achievement in Social Science," in *American Educational Research Journal,* vol. 21, pp. 39-59, 1984. Used by permission of the American Educational Research Association.

Pp. 404, 405, 406 From *Classroom Behavior,* by Donald Bushell, Jr. (Prentice-Hall, 1973) Used by permission of the author.

P. 417 From the *California Achievement Test, Test Coordinator's Handbook, Forms C and D,* 1977/78, p. 22. CTB/Mcgraw-Hill. Reproduced with permission.

P. 419 Reproduced with permission from the *Stanford Achievement Tests,* 7th Edition. Copyright © 1982, 1983, 1984 by Harcourt Brace Jovanovich, Inc. All rights reserved.

Pp. 424, 425 From the *California Achievement Tests, Norm Tables, Level 12, Form C,* 1977/78. CTB/Mcgraw-Hill. Reproduced with permission.

P. 428 From the *SRA Achievement Series, Answer Keys, Norms and Conversion Tables.* © 1979, 1978, Science Research

Associates, Inc. Reprinted by permission of the publisher.

P. 429 Reproduced by permission from the *Metropolitan Achievement Tests,* 5th Edition. Copyright © 1978, 1979 by Harcourt Brace Jovanovich, Inc. All rights reserved.

P. 436 From *Evaluating Software,* by V. Vachon and D. W. Carnine. ADI News, Winter 1983/1984. Used by permission of Douglas Carnine.

Acknowledgements for Quoted Material

Pp. 139, 140, 141 From C. L. Salzberg, "Freedom and Responsibility in an Elementary School," in *Behavior Analysis and Education,* 1972. Reprinted by permission of the author.

Pp. 165, 166 From *Making Schools Work,* by Robert Benjamin, 1981, The Continuum Publishing Co. Reprinted by permission of the publisher.

Pp. 181, 182, 204, 215 From *Theory of Instruction* by S. Engelmann and D. W. Carnine. 1982. Used by permission of S. Engelmann.

Pp. 176, 177 From *The Conditions of Learning,* 2/e, by Robert M. Gagne. Copyright © 1970 by Holt, Rinehart, and Winston. Reprinted by permission of CBS College Publishing.

P. 317 From *Origins of Intelligence in Children,* by J. Piaget, 1952. Reprinted by permission of International Universities Press, Inc.

P. 318 From *Judgment and Reasoning in the Child,* J. Piaget, 1959. Reprinted by permission of Humanities Press International, Inc. and Routledge & Kegan Paul, Ltd.

Pp. 338, 339 From *Restoration of Standards, Fastback 129,* by James Enochs. © 1979, Phi Delta Kappa Educational Foundation. Reprinted by permission of the publisher.

P. 343, The "Phases of the moon" analysis of implementation problems from a paper, "Restoration of Standards," by James Enochs, *Education Week,* Dec. 21, 1981, pp. 17-18. Used by permission of the author.

Pp. 364, 365, 367 From Jeanne H. Block, "Differential Premises Arising from Differential Socialization of the Sexes: Some Conjectures," in *Child Development,* vol. 54, pp. 1335-1354. © 1983, Society for Research in Child Development. Reprinted by permission of the publisher.

P. 429 Reproduced by permission from the *Metropolitan Achievement Tests,* 5th Edition. Copyright © 1978, 1979 by Harcourt Brace Jovanovich, Inc. All rights reserved.

Pp. 443, 444, 445, 446, From *Science, Video Discs, and the Learner,* an unpublished manuscript by S. Engelmann, Nov. 1983. Reprinted with permission.

APPENDIX

Latest Versions of Engelmann Designed Direct Instruction Programs

DISTAR

Engelmann, S. & Bruner, E. *DISTAR Reading I* (2nd Ed.). Chicago: Science Research Associates, 1974.

Engelmann, S. & Bruner, E. *DISTAR Reading II* (2nd Ed.). Chicago: Science Research Associates, 1975.

Engelmann, S. & Carnine, D. *DISTAR Arithmetic I* (2nd Ed.). Chicago: Science Research Associates, 1975.

Engelmann, S. & Carnine, D. *DISTAR Arithmetic II* (2nd Ed.). Chicago: Science Research Associates, 1976.

Engelmann, S. & Osborn, J. *DISTAR Language I* (2nd Ed.). Chicago: Science Research Associates, 1976.

Engelmann, S. & Osborn, J. *DISTAR Language II* (2nd Ed.). Chicago: Science Research Associates, 1977.

Engelmann, S. & Stearns, S. *DISTAR Reading III.* Chicago: Science Research Associates, 1972.

Engelmann, S. & Carnine, D. *DISTAR Arithmetic III.* Chicago: Science Research Associates, 1972.

Engelmann, S. & Osborne, J. *DISTAR Language III.* Chicago: Science Research Associates, 1972.

Reading Mastery

Engelmann, S. & Bruner, E. *Reading Mastery I, DISTAR Reading.* Chicago: Science Research Associates, 1983.

Engelmann, S. & Bruner, E. *Reading Mastery II, DISTAR Reading.* Chicago: Science Research Associates, 1983.

Engelmann, S. & Hanner, S. *Reading Mastery III.* Chicago: Science Research Associates, 1982.

Engelmann, S. & Hanner, S. *Reading Mastery IV.* Chicago: Science Research Associates, 1983.

Engelmann, S., Osborn, J., Osborn, S., & Zoref, L. *Reading Mastery V.* Chicago: Science Research Associates, 1983.

Engelmann, S., Osborn, J., Osborn, S., & Zoref, L. *Reading Mastery VI.* Chicago: Science Research Associates, 1984.

Corrective Reading

Engelmann, S., Becker, W. C., Carnine, L., Meyers, L., Becker, J. & Johnson, G. *Corrective Reading Program.* Chicago: Science Research Associates, 1975.

Engelmann, S., Osborn, J., Haddox, P., & Hanner, S. *Corrective Reading Series: Comprehension A.* Chicago: Science Research Associates, 1978.

Engelmann, S., Osborn, S., & Hanner, S. *Corrective Reading Series: Comprehension B.* Chicago: Science Research Associates, 1978.

Engelmann, S., Hanner, S., & Haddox, P. *Corrective Reading Series: Comprehension C.* Chicago: Science Research Associates, 1980.

Engelmann, S., Carnine, L., & Johnson, G. *Corrective Reading Series: Decoding A.* Chicago: Science Research Associates, 1978.

Engelmann, S., Becker, W. C., Carnine, L., Meyers, L., Becker, J., & Johnson, G. *Corrective Reading Series: Decoding B.* Chicago: Science Research Associates, 1978.

Engelmann, S., Carnine, L., Meyers, L., & Johnson, G. *Corrective Reading Series: Decoding C.* Chicago: Science Research Associates, 1978.

Math Modules

Engelmann, S. & Steely, D. G. *Fractions I.* Chicago: Science Research Associates, 1978.

Engelmann, S. & Steely, D. G. *Fractions II.* Chicago: Science Research Associates, 1978.

Engelmann, S. & Steely, D. G. *Basic Fractions.* Chicago: Science Research Associates, 1978.

Engelmann, S. & Steely, D. G. *Fractions, Decimals, Percents.* Chicago: Science Research Associates, 1978.

Engelmann, S. & Steely, D. G. *Ratios and Equations.* Chicago: Science Research Associates, 1980.

Engelmann, S. & Carnine, D. *Corrective Mathematics: Addition.* Chicago: Science Research Associates, 1981.

Engelmann, S. & Carnine, D. *Corrective Mathematics: Subtraction.* Chicago: Science Research Associates, 1981.

Engelmann, S. & Carnine, D. *Corrective Mathematics: Multiplication.* Chicago: Science Research Associates, 1981.

Engelmann, S. & Carnine, D. *Corrective Mathematics: Division.* Chicago: Science Research Associates, 1981.

Spelling

Dixon, B. & Engelmann, S. *Corrective Spelling Through Morphographs.* Chicago: Science Research Associates, 1979.

Engelmann, S., Dixon, R., & Meier, M. *Spelling Mastery Level A.* Chicago: Science Research Associates, 1980.

Engelmann, S., Dixon, R., & Meier, M. *Spelling Mastery Level B.* Chicago: Science Research Associates, 1980.

Engelmann, S. & Dixon, R. *Spelling Mastery Level C.* Chicago: Science Research Associates, 1981.

Engelmann, S. & Dixon, R. *Spelling Mastery Level D.* Chicago: Science Research Associates, 1981.

Engelmann, S., Dixon, R., Steely, D., & Wells, T. *Spelling Mastery Level E.* Chicago: Science Research Associates, 1981.

Other

Miller, S. & Engelmann, S. *Cursive Writing Program.* Tigard OR: C. C. Publications, Inc., 1980.

Engelmann, S., Davis, K. & Davis, G. *Your World of Facts, Level 1.* Tigard OR: C. C. Publications, Inc., 1982.

Engelmann, S., Davis, K. & Davis, G. *Your World of Facts, Level 2.* Tigard OR: C. C. Publications, Inc., 1983.

Engelmann, S. & Jensen, J. *I Love Library Books.* Tigard OR: C. C. Publications, Inc., 1982.

Engelmann, S., Haddox, P. & Bruner, E. *Teach Your Child to Read in 100 Easy Lessons.* New York: Simon & Schuster, 1983.

Engelmann, S., & Silbert, J. *Expressive Writing, Level 1.* Tigard OR: C. C. Publications, Inc., 1983.

REFERENCES

Abraham, S. & Nordsieck, M. Relationship of excess weight in children and adults. *Public Health Reports,* 1960, *75,* 263-273.

Ainsworth, M. D. Infant-mother attachment. *American Psychologist,* 1979, *34,* 932-937.

Aldrich, C. A., & Aldrich, M. M. *Babies Are Human Beings.* New York: Macmillan, 1941.

Allen, K. E., Hart, J. S., Buell, F. R. & Wolf, M. M. The effects of social reinforcement on isolate behavior of a nursery-school child. *Child Development,* 1964, *35.* 511-18.

Allison, M. G. & Ayllon, T. Behavioral coaching in the development of skills in football, gymnastics, and tennis. *Journal of Applied Behavior Analysis,* 1980, *13,* 297-314.

Anania, J. *The Effects of Quality of Instruction on the Cognitive and Affective Learning of Students.* Unpublished doctoral dissertation, University of Chicago, 1981.

Anderson, B. E. *An Evaluative Study: Teaching Three- and Four-Year Olds in a Structured Education Program.* Unpublished master's thesis, University of Utah, 1971.

Anderson, G. Effects of classroom social climate on individual learning. *American Educational Research Journal,* 1970, *7*(2), 135-152.

Anderson, J. E. The limitations of infant and preschool tests in the measurement of intelligence. *Journal of Psychology,* 1939, *8,* 351-79.

Anderson, L. M., Evertson, C. M. & Brophy, J. E. An experimental study of effective teaching in first-grade reading groups. *Elementary School Journal,* 1979, *79,* 193-222.

Anderson, R. C., Hiebert, E. H., Scott, J. A. & Wilkinson, I. A. G. *Becoming a Nation of Readers: The Report of the Commission on Reading.* Champaign IL: Center for the Study of Reading, 1985.

Anderson-Inman, L. DI and mainstreaming handicapped students. *Association for Direct Instruction News,* 1982, *1*(4), 8-11.

Aragona, J., Cassady, J. & Drabman, R. S. Treating overweight children through parental training and contingency contracting. *Journal of Applied Behavior Analysis,* 1975, *8,* 269-78.

Atkinson, J. W. The achievement motive and recall of interrupted and completed tasks. In D. C. McClelland (Ed.), *Studies in Motivation.* New York: Appleton-Century-Crofts, 1955.

Atkinson, J. W. & McClelland, D. C. The projective expression of needs: II. The effect of different intensities of the hunger drive on thematic apperception. *Journal of Experimental Psychology,* 1948, *38,* 643-58.

Atkinson, R. C. Computerized instruction and the learning process. *American Psychologist,* 1968, *23,* 225-39.

Atkinson, R. C. Teaching children to read using a computer. *American Psychologist,* 1974, *29,* 169-78.

Ausubel, D. P. & Fitzgerald, D. The role of discriminability in meaningful verbal learning and retention. *Journal of Educational Psychology,* 1961, *52,* 266-274.

Ausubel, D. P. & Fitzgerald, D. Organizer, general background and antecedent learning variables in sequential verbal learning. *Journal of Educational Psychology,* 1962, *53,* 243-9.

Ayllon, T. Intensive treatment of psychotic behavior by stimulus satiation and food reinforcement. *Behavior Research and Therapy,* 1963, *1,* 53-61.

Azrin, N. H. & Holz, W. C. Punishment. In W. K. Honig (Ed.), *Operant Behavior.* New York: Appleton-Century-Crofts, 1966.

Back, K. W. Influence through social communication. *Journal of Abnormal and Social Psychology,* 1951, *46,* 9-23.

Baer, D. M. & Wolf, M. M. The entry into natural communities of reinforcement. In R. Ulrich, T. Stachnik, and J. Mabry (Eds.), *Control of Human Behavior* (Vol. 2). Glenview IL: Scott, Foresman, 1970.

Bailey, J. S., Wolf, M. M. & Phillips, E. L. Home-based reinforcement and the modification of pre-delinquents' classroom behavior. *Journal of Applied Behavior Analysis,* 1970, *3,* 223-33.

Baker, R. L. *Measurement Considerations in Instructional Product Development.* Los Angeles: Center for the Study of Education, U.C.L.A., 1974, Monograph No. 3, p. 38.

Baker, K. & DeKanter, A. *Federal Policy and the Effectiveness of Bilingual Education.* Washington DC: National Institute of Education, 1982.

Ballard, K. D. & Glynn, T. Behavioral self-management in story writing with elementary school children. *Journal of Applied Behavior Analysis,* 1975, *8,* 387-98.

Bandura, A. *Principles of Behavior Modification.* New York: Holt, Rinehart and Winston, 1969.

Bandura, A. *Social Learning Theory.* New York: General Learning, 1971.

Bandura, A. Self-reinforcement: Theoretical and methodological considerations. *Behaviorism,* 1976, *4,* 135-55.

Bandura, A. Self-efficacy: Toward a unifying theory of behavioral change. *Psychological Review,* 1977, *84,* 191-215.

Bank Street Writer. New York: Scholastic, 1982.

Barik, H. C., Swain, M., & Nwanunobi, E. A. English-French bilingual education: The Elgin study through grade five. *Canadian Modern Language Review,* 1977, *33,* 459-75.

Baumrind, D. Current patterns of parental authority. *Developmental Psychology Monograph,* 1971, *4* (No. 1, Part 2).

Becker, W. C. Consequence of different kinds of parental discipline. In M. L. Hoffman & L. W. Hoffman (Eds.), *Review of Child Development Research* (Vol. I). New York: Russell Sage Foundation, 1964.

Becker, W. C. Teaching reading and language to the disadvantaged—what we have learned from field research. *Harvard Educational Review,* 1977, *47,* 518-543.

Becker, W. C. (Reporter). Mainstreaming Down's syndrome kids. *Association for Direct Instruction News,* 1982, *2*(1), 3.

Becker, W. C. *Direct Instruction: A Twenty Year Review.* Paper presented at the XVI Annual Banff International Conference on Behavioral Science, Banff, Alberta, March 18-23, 1984.

Becker, W. C. & Carnine, D. W. Direct instruction: An effective approach to educational intervention with the disadvantaged and low performers. In B. B. Lahey & A. K. Kazdin (Eds.), *Advances in Clinical and Child Psychology* (Vol. 3). New York: Plenum, 1980.

Becker, W. C., Dixon, R., & Anderson-Inman, L. *Morphographic and Root Word Analysis of 26,000 High Frequency Words.* Technical Report 1980-1. Eugene OR: University of Oregon Follow Through Project, 1980.

Becker, W. C. & Engelmann, S. *Teaching 3: Evaluation of Instruction.* Chicago: Science Research Associates, 1976.

Becker, W. C., Engelmann, S., Carnine, D. W., & Maggs, A. Direct Instruction technology: Making learning happen. In P. Karoly & J. J. Steffen (Eds.), *Improving Children's Competence: Advances in Child Behavioral Analysis and Therapy* (Vol. 1). Lexington MA: D. C. Heath, 1982.

Becker, W. C., Engelmann, S., & Thomas, D. R. *Teaching 2: Cognitive Learning and Instruction.* Chicago: Science Research Associates, 1975.

Becker, W. C. & Gersten, R. A follow-up of Follow Through: The later effects of the Direct Instruction Model on children in fifth and sixth grades. *American Educational Research Journal,* 1982, *19,* 75-92.

Becker, W. C., Madsen, C. H., Arnold, C. R., & Thomas, D. R., The contingent use of teacher attention and praise in reducing classroom behavior problems. *Journal of Special Education,* 1967, 1(3), 287-307.

Benbow, C. P & Stanley, J. C. Sex differences in mathematical ability: Fact or artifact? *Science,* 1980, *210,* 1262-4.

Benjamin, R. *Making Schools Work.* New York: Continuum, 1981.

Berliner, D. C. *Aptitude-Treatment Interaction in Two Studies of Learning from Lecture Instruction.* Paper presented to the American Educational Research Association, New York, 1971.

Berliner, D. C. *The Generalizability of Aptitude-Treatment Interaction Across Subject Matter.* Paper presented to the American Educational Research Association, 1972.

Berlyne, D. E. *Conflict, Arousal, and Curiosity.* New York: McGraw-Hill, 1960.

Bernstein, D. A. & Borkovec, T. D. *Progressive Relaxation Training: A Manual for Therapists.* Champaign IL: Research Press, 1973.

Berryman, D. & Maggs, A. Using DI to teach computer programming to retarded institutionalized adolescents. *Association for Direct Instruction News,* 1983, *2,* (4), 1 & 12-13.

Birch, H. G. The relation of previous experience to insightful problem solving. *Journal of Comparative Psychology,* 1945, *38,* 367-83.

Block, Jeanne H. Another look at sex differentiation in the socialization behavior of mothers and fathers. In J. Sherman & F. L. Denmark (Eds.), *Psychology of Women: Future Directions of Research.* New York: Psychological Dimensions, 1979.

Block, Jeanne H. *Socialization Influences on Personality Development in Males and Females.* Paper presented at the University of Oregon Pathfinders Conference, Eugene OR, 1981.

Block, Jeanne H. Differential premises arising from differential socialization of the sexes: Some conjectures. *Child Development,* 1983, *54,* 1335-45.

Block, Jeanne H., Block, J., & Harrington, D. *Sex Role Typing and Instrumental Behavior: A Developmental Study.* Paper presented at the meeting of the Society for Research in Child Development, Denver, 1975.

Block, James H. (Ed.), *Mastery Learning.* New York: Holt, Rinehart and Winston, 1971.

Block, James H. & Burns, R. B. Mastery learning. In L. S. Shulman (Ed.), *Review of Research in Education* (Vol. 4). Itasca IL: F. E. Peacock, 1976.

Block, N. J. & Dworkin, G. *The IQ Controversy.* New York: Random House, 1976.

Bloom, B. S. *Human Characteristics and School Learning.* New York: McGraw-Hill, 1976.

Bloom, B. S. Affective outcomes of school learning. *Phi Delta Kappan,* 1977, *59,* 193-98.

Bloom, B. S. The 2 sigma problem: The search for methods of group instruction as effective as one-to-one tutoring. *Educational Researcher,* 1984, *13,* 4-16.

Bloom, B. S., Engelhart, M. D., Furst, E. J., Hill, W. H., & Krathwohl, D. R. *Taxonomy of Educational Objectives: Handbook I, Cognitive Domain.* New York: Longman, 1956.

Bolstad, O. D. & Johnson, S. M. Self-regulation in the modification of disruptive behavior. *Journal of Applied Behavior Analysis,* 1972, *5,* 443-54.

Booth, A., Hewitt, D., Jenkins, W., & Maggs, A. Making retarded children literate: A five year study. *Australian Journal of Mental Retardation,* 1979, *5,* 257-260.

Bornstein, R. Sexism in education. In M. P. Sadker & D. M. Sadker, *Sex Equity Handbook for Schools.* New York: Longman, 1982. (This chapter is adapted from R. Bornstein, *Sexism in Education* sponsored by the U. S. Dept. of Education, Women's Educational Equity Act Program, 1980.)

Bostow, D. E. & O'Connor, R. J. A comparison of two college classroom testing procedures: Required remediation versus no remediation. *Journal of Applied Behavior Analysis,* 1973, *6,* 599-607.

Bradley, V. N. Improving students' writing with microcomputers. *Language Arts,* 1982, *59*(7), 732-43.

Braun, C. Teacher expectation: Socio-psychological dynamics. *Review of Educational Research,* 1976, *46,* 185-213.

Brigham, T. A. & Bushell, D. Notes on autonomous environments: Effects of student-selected and teacher-selected rewards on academic performance. *Educational Technology,* 1973, *13,* 19-22.

Brigham, T. A. & Sherman, J. Effects of choice and immediacy of reinforcement on single response and switching behavior of children. *Journal of the Experimental Analysis of Behavior,* 1973, *19,* 425-35.

Brigham, T. A. & Stoerzinger, A. An experimental analysis of children's preference for self-selected rewards. In T. A. Brigham, R. Hawkins, J. Scott, & T. F. McLaughin (Eds.), *Behavioral Analysis in Education: Self-Control and Reading.* Dubuque IA: Kendall/Hunt, 1976.

Broden, M., Hall, R. V., & Mitts, B. The effect of self-recording on the classroom behavior of two eight-grade students. *Journal of Applied Behavior Analysis,* 1971, *4,* 191-99.

Bronfenbrenner, U. Some familial antecedents of responsibility and leadership in adolescents. In L. Petrullo & B. M. Bass (Eds.), *Leadership and Interpersonal Behavior.* New York: Holt, Rinehart and Winston, 1961.

Brookover, W. B., Erickson, E. L., & Joiner, L. M. *Self-Concept of School Ability and School Achievement.* Educational Research Series, No. 36, Cooperative Research Project No. 2831, Michigan State University, 1967.

Brookover, W. B., Paterson, A., & Thomas, S. *Self-Concept of Ability and School Achievement.* Final report of Cooperative Research Project No. 845, U.S. Department of Health, Education and Welfare, Office of Education. Michigan State University, 1962.

Brophy, J. E. & Evertson, C. M. *Process-Product Correlations in the Texas Teacher Effectiveness Study: Final Report.* R. & D Center for Teacher Education, University of Texas, 1974.

Brophy, J. E. & Evertson, C. M. *Learning from Teaching: A Developmental Perspective.* Boston: Allyn and Bacon, 1976.

Brophy, J. & Good, T. Feminization of American elementary schools. *Phi Delta Kappan,* 1973, *54,* 564-6.

Brophy, J. & Good, T. *Teacher-Student Relationships: Causes and Consequences.* New York: Holt, Rinehart and Winston, 1974.

Brown, A. L. Knowing when, where, and how to remember: A problem of metacognition. In R. Glaser (Ed.), *Advances in Instructional Psychology* (Vol. 1). Hillsdale NJ: Lawrence Erlbaum Associates, 1978.

Brown, M. & Precious, N. *The Integrated Day in the Primary School.* New York: Agathon Press, 1968.

Brown, P. & Elliot, R. Control of aggression in a nursery school class. *Journal of Experimental Child Psychology,* 1965, *2,* 103-7.

Brownell, K. D., Colletti, G., Ersner-Hershfield, R., Hershfield, S. M., & Wilson, G. T. Self-control in school children: Stringency and leniency in self-determined and externally imposed performance standards. *Behavior Therapy,* 1977, *8,* 442-55.

Bruner, J. S. *Toward a Theory of Instruction.* Cambridge MA: Belknap Press, 1966.

Bruner, J. S., Goodnow, J. J., & Austin, G. A. *A Study of Thinking.* New York: Wiley, 1956.

Brush, L. R. Cognitive and affective determinants of course preference and plans. In S. F. Chipman, L. R. Brush, & D. M. Wilson (Eds.), *Women and Mathematics: Balancing the Equation.* Hillsdale NJ: Lawrence Erlbaum Associates, 1985.

Bucher, B. & Schneider, R. E. Acquisition and generalization of conservation by preschoolers, using operant training. *Journal of Experimental Child Psychology,* 1973, *16,* 187-204.

Burke, A. J. *Students' Potential for Learning Contrasted under Tutorial and Group Approaches to Instruction.* Unpublished doctoral dissertation, University of Chicago, 1983.

Burket, G. R. Empirical criteria for distinguishing and validating aptitude and achievement measures. In D. R. Green (Ed.), *The Aptitude-Achievement Distinction.* Monterey CA: CTB/McGraw-Hill, 1974.

Buros, O. K. (Ed.), *Eighth Mental Measurements Yearbook.* Highland Park NJ: Gryphon Press, 1978.

Buros, O. K. (Ed.), *Ninth Mental Measurements Yearbook.* Lincoln NE: University of Nebraska Press, 1985. (This edition was published after Oscar Buros' death by the Buros Institute of Mental Measurements.)

Burtis, P. J. *Two Applications of Measurement Theory in Developmental Psychology.* Unpublished manuscript, York University, 1974.

Bushell, D., Jr. *Classroom Behavior.* Englewood NJ: Prentice-Hall, 1973.

Calsyn, R. J. & Kenny, D. A. Self-concept of ability and perceived evaluation of others: Cause or effect of academic achievement? *Journal of Educational Psychology,* 1977, *69,* 136-45.

Caplan, P. Beyond the box score: A boundary condition for sex differences in aggression and achievement striving. In B. Maher (Ed.), *Progress in Experimental Personality Research* (Vol. 9). New York: Academic Press, 1979.

Carnine, D. *Technology in Education.* Unpublished manuscript, University of Oregon, 1985.

Carnine, D. & Silbert, J. *Direct Instruction Reading.* Columbus OH: Charles E. Merrill, 1979.

Carroll, J. B. A model of school learning. *Teachers College Record,* 1963, *64,* 723-33.

Carroll, J. B. *Learning from Verbal Discourse in Educational Media: A Review of the Literature.* Princeton NJ: Educational Testing Service, 1971.

Carroll, J. B. Psychometric tests as cognitive tasks: A new "structure of the intellect." In L. B. Resnick (Ed.), *The Nature of Intelligence.* Hillsdale NJ: Lawrence Erlbaum Associates, 1976.

Carroll, J. B., Davies, P., & Richman, B. *American Heritage Word Frequency Book.* Boston: Houghton Mifflin, 1971.

Case, R. Validation of a neo-Piagetian capacity construct. *Journal of Experimental Child Psychology,* 1972, *14,* 287-302.

Case, R. *The Process of Stage Transition in Cognitive Development.* Final report, Project HROIHD09148-01, NIMHCD, University of California, Berkeley, 1977.

Case, R. Piaget and beyond: Toward a developmentally based theory and technology of instruction. In R. Glaser (Ed.), *Advances in Instructional Psychology* (Vol. 1). Hillsdale NJ: Lawrence Erlbaum Associates, 1978.

Catania, A. C. & Brigham, T. A. *Handbook of Applied Behavior Analysis: Social and Instructional Processes.* New York: Irvington, 1978.

Cavalli-Sforza, L. L. Problems and prospects of genetic analysis of intelligence at the intra- and interracial level. In J. Hellmuth (Ed.), *Disadvantaged Child* (Vol. 3). New York: Brunner-/Mazel, 1970.

Chall, J. S. *Learning to Read: The Great Debate.* New York: McGraw-Hill, 1967, 1983.

Chipman, S. F. & Wilson, D. M. Understanding mathematics course enrollment and mathematics achievement: A synthesis of the research. In S. F. Chipman, L. R. Brush, & D. M. Wilson (Eds.), *Women and Mathematics: Balancing the Equation.* Hillsdale NJ: Lawrence Erlbaum Associates, 1985.

Coats, D. M. *The Development of Social Responsiveness to Other Children in a Nursery-School Child through Experimental Use of Social Reinforcement.* Unpublished master's thesis, Department of Human Development, University of Kansas, 1969.

Cole, J. R. *Fair Science: Women in the Scientific Community.* New York: Free Press, 1979.

Coleman, J. S., et al. *Equality of Educational Opportunity.* Washington DC: U.S. Government Printing Office, 1966.

Committee on the Judiciary, United States Senate. *Our Nation's Schools—A Report Card: "A" in School Violence and Vandalism.* Washington DC: April, 1975.

Cooke, N. L. Misrepresentations of the behavioral model in preservice teacher education textbooks. In W. L. Heward, T. E. Heron, D. S. Hill, J. Trap-Porter (Eds.), *Focus on Behavior Analysis in Education.* Columbus OH: Charles E. Merrill 1984.

Cooper, K. H. *The New Aerobics.* New York: Bantam Books, 1970.

Coopersmith, S. *The Antecedents of Self-esteem.* San Francisco: W. H. Freeman, 1967.

Cotter, V. & Spradlin, J. E. A nonverbal technique for studying music preference. *Journal of Experimental Child Psychology,* 1971, *11,* 357-65.

Cracklen, C. & Martin, G. L. *To Improve the Performance of Young Swimmers at Practice, "Fun" Should be Earned.* Paper presented at the Annual Conference of the Manitoba Behavior Modification Association, Winnipeg, Manitoba, 1983.

Crandall, V. C., Katkowsky, W., & Crandall, V. J. Children's beliefs in their own control of reinforcements in intellectual-academic achievement situations. *Child Development,* 1965, *36,* 91-109.

Crisp, A. H., Douglas, J. W. B., Ross, J. M., & Stonehills, E. Some developmental aspects of disorders of weight. *Journal of Psychosomatic Research,* 1970, *14,* 313-320.

Cronbach, L. J. *Essentials of Psychological Testing.* New York: Harper and Brothers, 1949.

Cronbach, L. J. *Essentials of Psychological Testing (3rd ed.). New York: Harper & Row, 1970.*

Cronbach, L. J. & Snow, R. E. *Aptitudes and Instructional Methods: A Handbook for Research on Interactions.* New York: Irvington, 1981.

Darsh, C. & Carnine, D. W. *Effects of Explicit Instruction, Visual Displays, and Team Games on Aquisition of Information from Expository Material.* Unpublished manuscript, University of Oregon Follow Through Project, 1981.

Davidman, L. Learning style: The myth, the panacea, the wisdom. *Phi Delta Kappan,* 1981, *62,* 641-645.

Day, K. *Differences in Teaching Behavior in Adults as a Function of Sex Related Variables.* Unpublished doctoral dissertation, University of Washington, 1975.

Daynes, R. Who, what, where, why, and how much of videodisc technology. In R. Daynes and B. Butler (Eds.), *The Videodisc Book.* New York: Wiley, 1984.

Deci, E. L. Effects of externally mediated rewards on intrinsic motivation. *Journal of Personality and Social Psychology,* 1971, *18,* 105-15.

Deci, E. L. Intrinsic motivation, extrinsic reinforcement, and inequity. *Journal of Personality and Social Psychology,* 1972a, *22,* 113-20.

Deci, E. L. The effects of contingent and noncontingent rewards on intrinsic motivation. *Organizational Behavior and Human Performance,* 1972b, *8,* 217-29.

Deci, E. L. *Intrinsic Motivation.* New York: Plenum, 1975.

Dennis, W. & Najarian, P. Infant development under environmental handicap. *Psychological Monographs,* 1957, *71,* No. 7, 60-1.

Desiderato, O. & Miller, I. B. Improving tennis performance by cognitive behavior modification techniques. *The Behavior Therapist,* 1978, *2,* 19.

Deutsch, M. *The Resolution of Conflict.* New Haven CT: Yale University Press, 1973.

Dewey, J. *Human Nature and Conduct: An Introduction to Social Psychology.* New York: Modern Library, 1930.

Dias, S. *Cucui Scale: Technical Manual. Multilingual Assessment Program.* Stockton CA: Stockton Unified School District, 1974.

Dittes, J. E. & Kelley, H. H. Effects of different conditions of acceptance upon conformity to group norms. *Journal of Abnormal and Social Psychology,* 1956, *53,* 100-7.

Dixon, B. & Engelmann, S. *Corrective Spelling Through Morphographs.* Chicago: Science Research Associates, 1979.

Dodds, P. Love and joy in the gymnasium. *Quest,* 1976, *26,* 109-116.

Dollard, J., Doob, L. W., Miller, N. E., Mowrer, O. H., & Sears, R. R. *Frustration and Aggression.* New Haven CT: Yale University Press, 1939.

Donahue, J. A., Gillis, J. H., & King, K. Behavior modification in sport and physical education: A review. *Journal of Sport Psychology,* 1980, *2,* 311-28.

Dougall, J. M. Organizing your classroom for the beginning of the school year. *Association for Direct Instruction News,* 1983, *3*(1), 8-9.

Duncker, K. On problem solving. *Psychological Monographs,* 1945, *58* (5, Whole No. 270), 1-112.

Dupuy, H. J. *The Rational, Development, and Standardization of a Basic Word Vocabulary Test.* Health Resources Administrtation, National Center for Health Statistics, DHEW, Series 2, No. 60. Washington DC: U. S. Government Printing Office, 1974.

Durkin, D. What classroom observation reveals about reading

comprehension instruction. *Reading Research Quarterly,* 1978-79, *14,* 481-533.

Dusek, J. Do teachers bias children's learning? *Review of Educational Research,* 1975, *45,* 661-84.

Eichelberger, R. T. *Follow Through Grant Proposal to USOE, 1975-76.* Pittsburgh: University of Pittsburgh, Learning Research and Development Center, 1975.

Elashoff, J. D. & Snow, R. E. *Pygmalion Reconsidered.* Worthington OH: Charles A. Jones, 1971.

Ellson, D. G. Tutoring. In N. L. Gage (Ed.), *The Psychology of Teaching Methods.* The seventy-fifth yearbook of the National Society for the Study of Education. Chicago: University of Chicago Press, 1976.

Emerson, R. M. Deviation and rejection: An experimental replication. *American Sociological Review,* 1954, *19,* 688-93.

Engelmann, S. Cognitive structures related to the principle of conservation. In D. W. Brison & E. V. Sullivan (Eds.), *Recent Research on the Acquistion of Conservation of Substance.* Educational Research Series No. 2, Ontario Institute for Studies in Education, Toronto, Ontario, 1965.

Engelmann, S. Teaching formal operations to preschool advantaged and disadvantaged children. *Ontario Journal of Educational Research,* 1967, *9*(3), 193-208.

Engelmann, S. *Conceptual Learning.* San Rafael CA: Dimensions Publishing Co., 1969.

Engelmann, S. The effectiveness of direct instruction on IQ performance and achievement in reading and arithmetic. In J. Hellmuth (Ed.), *Disadvantaged Child.* (Vol. 3). New York: Brunner/Mazel, 1970.

Engelmann, S. A study of 4th-6th grade basal reading series. *Direct Instruction News.* 1982, *1*(3), 1, 4-5, 19.

Engelmann, S. *Science, Videodiscs, and the Learner.* Unpublished manuscript, University of Oregon, November, 1983.

Engelmann, S., Becker, W. C., Carnine, L., Meyers, L., Becker, J., & Johnson, G. *Corrective Reading Program.* Chicago: Science Research Associates, 1975.

Engelmann, S. & Bruner, E. *Teacher's Guide for Distar Reading I* (Rev.). Chicago: Science Research Associates, 1974.

Engelmann, S. & Carnine, D. W. *Theory of Instruction: Principles and Applications.* New York: Irvington, 1982.

Engelmann, S., Davis, K., & Davis, G. *Your World of Facts, Level 1.* Tigard OR: C. C. Publications, 1982.

Engelmann, S., Davis, K., & Davis, G. *Your World of Facts, Level 2.* Tigard OR: C. C. Publications, 1983.

Enochs, J. C. *The Restoration of Standards: The Modesto Plan.* Bloomington IN: Phi Delta Kappa Educational Foundation, 1979.

Enochs, J. C. The restoration of standards. *Education Week,* December 21, 1981, 17-8.

Erikson, E. *Childhood and Society* (2nd ed.). New York: W. W. Norton, 1963.

Ernst, G. & Newell, A. *GPS: A Case Study in Generality and Problem Solving.* New York: Academic Press, 1969.

Fagot, B. I. The influence of sex of child on parental reactions to toddler children. *Child Development,* 1978, *49,* 459-65.

Fagot, B. I. & Kronsberg, S. J. Sex differences: Biological and social factors influencing the behavior of young boys and girls. In S. G. Moore & C. R. Cooper (Eds.), *The Young Child: Reviews of Research* (Vol. 3). Washington DC: National Association for the Education of Young Children, 1982.

Fanelli, G. C. Locus of control. In S. Ball (Ed.), *Motivation in Education.* New York: Academic Press, 1977.

Farmer, J., Lachter, G. D., Blaustein, J. J., & Cole, B. K. The role of proctoring in personalized instruction. *Journal of Applied Behavior Analysis,* 1972, *5,* 401-4.

Farnum, M., Brigham, T. A., & Johnson, G. *A Comparison of the Effects of Teacher Determined and Student Determined Contingencies on Arithmetic Performance.* Unpublished manuscript, 1977, (Available from T. A. Brigham, Department of Psychology, Washington State University, Pullman WA 99164).

Feingold, B. F. *Why Your Child Is Hyperactive.* New York: Random House, 1975.

Felixbrod, J. J. & O'Leary, K. D. Effects of reinforcement on children's academic behavior as a function of self-determined and externally imposed contingencies. *Journal of Applied Behavior Analysis,* 1973, *6,* 241-50.

Felixbrod, J. J. & O'Leary, K. D. Self-determination of academic standards by children: Toward freedom from external control. *Journal of Educational Psychology,* 1974, *66,* 845-50.

Fenema, E. & Sherman, J. Sex-related differences in mathematics achievement, spatial visualization and affective factors. *American Educational Research Journal,* 1977, *14*(1), 51-71.

Ferster, C. B. & Hammer, C. E., Jr. Synthesizing the components of arithmetic behavior. In W. K. Honig (Ed.) *Operant Behavior: Areas of Research and Application.* New York: Appleton-Century-Crofts, 1966.

Ferster, C. B. & Skinner, B. F. *Schedules of Reinforcement.* New York: Appleton-Century-Crofts, 1957.

Festinger, L. *A Theory of Cognitive Dissonance.* New York: Harper & Row, 1957.

Fine, M. J. (Ed.). *Principles and Techniques of Intervention with Hyperactive Children.* Springfield IL: Charles C. Thomas, 1977.

Finn, J. D. & Resnick, L. B. Issues in the instruction of mildly mentally retarded children. *Educational Researcher,* 1984, *13,* 9-11.

Fisher, C. W., Filby, N. A., Marliave, R., Cahen, L. S., Dishaw, M. M., Moore, J. E., & Berliner, D. C. *Teaching Behaviors, Academic Learning Time, and Student Achievement: Final Report of Phase III-B, Beginning Teacher Evaluation Study (Technical Report V-1).* San Francisco: Far West Laboratory for Educational Research and Development, 1978.

Fixsen, D., Phillips, E. L., & Wolf, M. M. Achievement Place: The reliability of self-reporting and peer-reporting and their effects on behavior. *Journal of Applied Behavior Analysis,* 1973, *6,* 31-47.

Fixsen, D., Phillips, E. L., & Wolf, M. M. Achievement Place: Experiments in self-government with pre-delinquents. *Journal of Applied Behavior Analysis,* 1972, *5,* 19-30.

Flake-Hobson, C., Robinson, B. R., & Skeen, P. *Child Development and Relationships.* Reading MA: Addison-Wesley, 1983.

Flavell, J. H. *The Developmental Psychology of Jean Piaget.* Princeton NJ: D. Van Nostrand, 1963.

Flavell, J. H. Metacognitive aspects of problem solving. In L. B. Resnick (Ed.), *The Nature of Intelligence.* Hillsdale NJ: Lawrence Erlbaum Associates, 1976.

Flesch, R. *Why Johnny Can't Read.* New York: Harper, 1955.

Flesch, R. *Why Johnny Still Can't Read.* New York: Harper & Row, 1981.

Fletcher, J. D. & Atkinson, R. C. Evaluation of the Stanford CAI program in initial reading. *Journal of Educational Psychology,* 1972, *63,* 597-602.

Fox, L. H. Identification of the academically gifted. *American Psychologist,* 1981, *36,* 1103-11.

Fox, R. G., Copeland, R. E., Harris, J. W., Rieth, H. J., & Hall, R. V. A computerized system for selecting responsive teaching studies, catalogued along twenty-eight important dimensions. In E. Ramp & G. Semb (Eds.), *Behavior Analysis: Areas of Research & Application.* Englewood Cliffs NJ: Prentice-Hall, 1973.

Frey, K. S. *Differential Teaching Methods with Girls and Boys of Moderate and High Achievement Levels.* Paper presented at the meeting of the Society for Research in Child Development, San Francisco, March 1979.

Friedersdorf, N. W. *A Comparative Study of Counselor Attitudes Toward the Further Educational and Vocational Plans of High School Girls.* Unpublished study, Purdue University, 1969. Cited in *Implementing Title IX and Attaining Sex Equity—The Counselor's Role.* Washington DC: Resource Center on Sex Roles in Education, 1977.

Gage, N. L. & Berliner, D. C. *Educational Psychology* (2nd ed.). Chicago: Rand McNally, 1979.

Gall, M. D. & Gall, J. P. The discussion method. In N. L. Gage (Ed.), *The Psychology of Teaching Methods.* The seventy-fifth yearbook of the National Society for the Study of Education. Chicago: University of Chicago Press, 1976.

Gagné, R. M. *The Conditions of Learning.* New York: Holt, Rinehart and Winston, 1965, 1970, 1977.

Gagné, R. M. & Briggs, L. J. *Principles of Instructional Design.* New York: Holt, Rinehart and Winston, 1974, 1979.

Gelman, R. Conservation acquisition: A problem of learning to attend to relevant attributes. *Journal of Experimental Child Psychology,* 1969, *7,* 167-87.

Gerard, H. B. The anchorage of opinions in face-to-face groups. *Human Relations,* 1954, *7,* 313-25.

Gersten, R. M. High School follow-up of DI Follow Through. *Association for Direct Instruction News,* 1982, *2*(1), 3.

Gersten, R. M., Becker, W. C., Heiry, T. J., & White, W. A. T. Entry IQ and yearly academic growth of children in Direct Instruction programs: A longitudinal study of low SES children. *Educational Evaluation and Policy Analysis,* 1984, *6,* 109-21.

Gersten, R. M., Brockway, M. A., & Henares, N. The Monterey DI program for students with limited English (ESL). *Association for Direct Instruction News,* 1983, *2*(4), 8-9.

Gersten, R. M. & Carnine, D. *The Latter Effects of Direct Instruction Follow Through.* Paper presented at the American Education Research Association meeting, Montreal, 1983.

Gersten, R. M. & Carnine, D. *The Lasting Impact of Direct Instruction on 1500 Low Income Students.* Paper presented at the American Education Research Association meeting. New Orleans, 1984.

Gersten, R. M. & Keating, T. DI Follow Through students show fewer dropouts, fewer retentions, and more high school graduates. *Association for Direct Instruction News,* 1983, *2*(3), 1 & 14-15.

Gersten, R. M. & Maggs, A. Five year longitudinal study of cognitive development of moderately retarded children in a direct instruction program. *Analysis and Intervention in Developmental Disabilities,* 1982, *2,* 329-43.

Gibson, E. J., Gibson, J. J., Pick, A. D., & Osser, H. A. A developmental study of the discrimination of letter-like forms. *Journal of Comparative and Physiological Psychology,* 1962, *55.* 897-906.

Gilbert, T. E. Mathetics: The technology of education. *Journal of Mathetics,* 1962, *1,* 7-73.

Gilliam, T. B., Katch, V. L., Thorland, W., & Weltman, A. Prevalence of coronary heart disease risk factors in active children 7 to 12 years of age. *Medicine and Science in Sports,* 1977, *9*(1), 21-5.

Glaser, R. Instructional technology and the measurement of learning outcomes. *American Psychologist,* 1963, *18,* 510-22.

Glaser, R. Adapting the elementary school curriculum to individual performance. In *Proceedings of the 1967 Invitational Conference on Testing Problems.* Princeton NJ: Educational Testing Service, 1967.

Glass, G. V.. Integrating findings: The meta-analysis of research. In L. S. Shulman (Ed.), *Review of Research in Education* (Vol. 5). Itasca IL: F. E. Peacock, 1978.

Glynn, E. L. Classroom applications of self-determined reinforcement. *Journal of Applied Behavior Analysis,* 1970, *3,* 123-32.

Glynn, E. L., Thomas, J. D., & Shee, S. M. Behavioral self-control of on-task behavior in an elementary classroom. *Journal of Applied Behavior Analysis,* 1973, *6,* 105-13.

Goetz, E. M. & Baer, D. M. Social control of form diversity and the emergence of new forms in children's block-building. *Journal of Applied Behavior Analysis,* 1973, *6,* 209-17.

Good, T. Teacher effectiveness in the elementary school: What we know about it now. *Journal of Teacher Education,* 1979, *30,* 52-64.

Gottman, J. M. & McFall, R. M. Self-monitoring effects in a program for potential high school dropouts: A time-series analysis. *Journal of Consulting and Clinical Psychology,* 1972, *39,* 273-281.

Gravel, R., Lemieux, G., & Ladouceur, R. Effectiveness of a cognitive behavioral treatment package for cross-country ski racers. *Cognitive Therapy and Research,* 1980, *4,* 83-9.

Greenwood, C. R., Delquadri, J. C., & Hall, R. V. The opportunity to respond and student academic performance in school. In W. L. Heward, T. E. Heron, D. S. Hill, & J. Trap-Porter (Eds.), *Focus on Behavior Analysis in Education.* Columbus OH: Charles E. Merrill, 1983.

Greer, R. D. *Design for Music Learning.* New York: Teachers College Press, 1980.

Greer, R. D., Randall, A., & Timberlake, C. The discriminate use of music listening as a contingency for improvement in vocal pitch acuity and attending behavior. *Bulletin of the Council for Research in Music Education,* 1971, *26,* 10-18.

Grief, E. *Sex Differences in Parent-Child Conversations: Who Interrupts Whom?* Paper presented at the meeting of the Society for Research in Child Development, San Francisco, March 1979.

Griswold, P. A. Elementary students' attitudes during 2 years of computer-assisted instruction. *American Educational Research Journal,* 1984, *21,* 737-54.

Grossman, H. J. (Ed.), *Manual on Terminology and Classification in Mental Retardation* (American Association on Mental Deficiency). Baltimore MD: Garamond/Pridemark, 1977.

Guilford, J. P. *The Nature of Human Intelligence.* New York: McGraw-Hill, 1967.

Hansford, B. C. & Hatti, J. A. The relationship between self and achievement/performance measures. *Review of Educational Research,* 1982, *52,* 123-42.

Hare, A. P. *Handbook of Small Group Research.* New York: Free Press, 1962, 1977.

Haring, N. G. & Bateman, B. *Teaching the Learning Disabled Child.* Englewood Cliffs NJ: Prentice-Hall, 1977.

Harris, A. J. & Jacobson, M. D. *Basic Elementary Reading Vocabularies.* New York: Macmillan, 1972.

Harris, C. W. Problems of objectives-based measurement. In C. W. Harris, M. C. Alkin, and W. J. Popham (Eds.), *Problems in Criterion-Referenced Measurement.* Center for the Study of Evaluation, UCLA, 1974, Monograph No. 3, 83-91.

Harris, F. R., Johnston, M. K., Kelley, C. S., & Wolf, M. M. Effects of positive social reinforcement on regressed crawling of a nursery-school child. *Journal of Educational Psychology,* 1964, *55,* 35-41.

Harris, M. B. & Bruner, C. G. A comparison of a self-control and a contract procedure for weight control. *Behaviour Research and Therapy,* 1971, *9,* 347-354.

Hart, B. M., Reynolds, N. J., Baer, D. M., Brawley, E. R., & Harris, F. R. Effects of contingent and noncontingent social reinforcement on the cooperative play of a preschool child. *Journal of Applied Behavior Analysis,* 1968, *1,* 73-6.

Hartup, W. W. Peer interaction and social development. In P. Mussen (Ed.), *Carmichael's Manual of Child Psychology* (Vol. 2, 3rd ed.). New York: Wiley, 1970.

Hasazi, J. E. & Hasazi, S. E. Effects of teacher attention on digit-reversal behavior in an elementary school child. *Journal of Applied Behavior Analysis,* 1972, *5,* 157-62.

Hawkins, R. P., Peterson, R. F., Schweid, E., & Bijou, S. W. Behavior therapy in the home: Amelioration of problem parent-child relations with the parent in a therapeutic role. *Journal of Experimental Child Psychology,* 1966, *4,* 99-107.

Heber, R. Sociocultural mental retardation: A longitudinal study. In D. Forgays (Ed.), *Primary Prevention of Psychopathology: Vol. 2. Environmental Influences.* Hanover NH: University Press of New England, 1978.

Heber, R., Garber, S., Harrington, S., Hoffman, C., & Falender, D. *Rehabilitation of Families at Risk for Mental Retardation.* Progress Report, Rehabilitation Research and Training Center, University of Wisconsin (Madison), 1972.

Heckhausen, H. *The Anatomy of Achievement Motivation.* New York: Academic Press, 1967.

Heller, K. A., Holtzman, W. H., & Messick, S. (Eds), *Placing Children in Special Education: A Strategy for Equity.* Washington DC: National Academy Press, 1982.

Helson, H. *Adaptation Level Theory*. New York: Harper & Row, 1964.

Hess, R. D. & Shipman, V. C. Early experience and the socialization of cognitive modes in children. *Child Development*, 1965, *36*, 869-86.

Hess, R. D. & Shipman, V. C. Maternal influences upon early learning: The cognitive environments of urban preschool children. In R. D. Hess & R. M. Bear (Eds.), *Early Education: Current Theory, Research, and Action*. Chicago: Aldine, 1968, 91-103.

Herrnstein, R. J. *IQ in the Meritocracy*. Boston: Little, Brown, 1973.

Heward, W. L. Operant conditioning of a .300 hitter? The effects of reinforcement on the offensive efficiency of a barnstorming baseball team. *Behavior Modification*, 1978, *2*(1), 25-40.

Heward, W. L., Heron, T. E., Hill, D. S., & Trap-Porter, J. *Focus on Behavior Analysis in Education*. Columbus OH: Charles E. Merrill, 1984.

Hilgard, E. R. Methods and procedures in the study of learning. In S. S. Stevens (Ed.) *Handbook of Experimental Psychology*. New York: Wiley, 1951.

Hilgard, E. R. & Bower, G. H. *Theories of Learning* (4th ed.). Englewood Cliffs NJ: Prentice-Hall, 1975.

Hochschild, A. Inside the clockwork of male careers. In F. Howe (Ed.), *Women and the Power of Change*. New York: McGraw-Hill, 1975.

Hoffman, L. W. Early childhood experiences and women's achievement motive. *Journal of Social Issues*, 1972, *28*, 129-55.

Hoffman, L. W. Changes in family roles, socialization, and sex differences. *American Psychologist*, 1977, *32*, 644-657.

Hoffman, M. L. Sex differences in empathy and related behaviors. *Psychological Bulletin*, 1977, *84*, 712-22.

Hoffman, M. L. Development of moral thought, feeling, and behavior. *American Psychologist*, 1979, *34*, 958-66.

Hofmeister, A. M., Engelmann, S., & Carnine, D. *Designing Videodisc-based Courseware for the High School*. Paper presented at the Annual Meeting of the American Educational Research Association, Chicago, March-April 1985.

Honig, W. K. & Staddon, J. E. R. *Handbook of Operant Behavior*. Englewood Cliffs NJ: Prentice-Hall, 1977.

Horner, R., Sprague, J., & Wilcox, B. General case programming for community activities. In B. Wilcox and G. T. Bellamy (Eds.), *Design of High School Programs for Severely Handicapped Students*. Baltimore MD: Paul Brooks, 1982.

Horton, G. O. Generalization of teacher behavior as a function of subject matter specific discrimination training. *Journal of Applied Behavior Analysis*, 1975, *8*, 311-319.

Humphreys, L. G. The misleading distinction between aptitude and achievement tests. In D. R. Green (Ed.), *The Aptitude-Achievement Distinction*. Monterey CA: CTB/McGraw-Hill, 1974.

Hunt, J. McV. *Intelligence and Experience*. New York: Ronald, 1961.

Hursh, L. L. *A School Intervention Program for South-Eastern Rural Primary School Children Referred for Special Education*. Unpublished doctoral dissertation, University of South Carolina, 1979.

Inhelder, B. & Piaget, J. *The Growth of Logical Thinking from Childhood to Adolescence*. New York: Basic Books, 1958.

Inhelder, B. & Piaget, J. *The Early Growth of Logic in the Child*. New York: Norton, 1964.

Jensen, A. R. How much can we boost the IQ and scholastic achievement? *Harvard Educational Review*, 1969, *39*, 1-123.

Jensen, A. R. Another look at culture-fair testing. In J. Hellmuth (Ed.), *Disadvantaged Child* (Vol. 3). New York: Brunner-/Mazel, 1970.

Jensen, A. R. *Genetics and Education*. New York: Harper & Row, 1973.

Johnson, J. M. & O'Neill, G. The analysis of performance criteria defining course grades as a determinant of college student academic performance. *Journal of Applied Behavior Analysis*, 1973, *6*, 261-68.

Johnson, K. R. & Ruskin, R. S. *Behavioral Instruction: An Evaluative Review*. Washington DC: American Psychological Association, 1977.

Johnston, M. K., Kelley, C. S., Harris, F. R., & Wolf, M. M. An application of reinforcement principles to development of motor skills in a young child. *Child Development*, 1966, *37*, 379-87.

Jones, M. C. A laboratory study of fear: The case of Peter. *Pediatrics Seminar*, 1924, *31*, 308-15.

Kagan, J. & Moss, H. A. *Birth to Maturity: The Fels Study of Psychological Development*. New York: Wiley, 1962.

Kazdin, A. E. & Wilson, G. T. *Evaluation of Behavior Therapy: Issues, Evidence, and Research Strategies*. Cambridge MA: Ballinger, 1978.

Keating, D. P. (Ed.), *Intellectual Talent: Research and Development*. Baltimore MD: Johns Hopkins University Press, 1976.

Keller, F. S. "Good-bye teacher . . ." *Journal of Applied Behavior Analysis*, 1968, *1*, 79-89.

Kelley, T. L. *The Interpretation of Educational Measurements*. Yonkers-on-Hudson NY: World Book, 1927.

Kendler, H. H. The concept of the concept. In A. W. Melton (Ed.), *Categories of Human Learning*. New York: Academic Press, 1964.

Kifer, E. Relationships between academic achievement and personality characteristics: A quasi-longitudinal study. *American Educational Research Journal*, 1975, *12*, 191-210.

Kim, Y., Berger, B. J., & Kratochvil, D. W. *Distar Instructional System*. Palo Alto CA: American Institute for Research, Product Development Report No. 14, January 1972.

Kimble, G. A. *Hilgard and Marquis' Conditioning and Learning* (2nd ed.). New York: Appleton-Century-Crofts, 1961.

Kirchenbaum, D. S. & Bale, R. M. *Cognitive Behavioral Skills in Golf*. Paper presented at the First International Symposium on Sports Psychology, Monterey, Mexico, July 1978.

Kleinman, G. & Humphrey, M. Word processing in the classroom. *Computer*, 1982, *22*(3), 96-99.

Kohlberg, L. The development of children's orientations toward moral order: I. Sequence in the development of moral thought. *Vita Humana*, 1963, *6*, 11-33.

Kohlberg, L. Development of moral character and moral ideology. In M. L. Hoffman & L. W. Hoffman (Eds.), *Review of Child Development Research* (Vol. 1). New York: Russell Sage Foundation, 1964.

Kohlberg, L. The contribution of developmental psychology to education: Examples from moral education. *Educational Psychologist*, 1973, *10*, 12-14.

Kohlberg, L. The cognitive-developmental approach to moral education. *Phi Delta Kappan*, 1975, *56*, 670-7.

Kohler, W. *The Mentality of Apes*. New York: Harcourt Brace, 1925.

Kolata, G. B. Math and sex: Are girls born with less ability? *Science*, 1980, *210*, 1234-5.

Komaki, J. & Barnett, F. T. A behavioral approach to coaching footfall: Improving the play execution of the offensive backfield on a youth football team. *Journal of Applied Behavior Analysis*, 1977, *10*, 657-64.

Koop, S. & Martin, G. L. A coaching strategy to reduce swimming stroke errors with beginning age-group swimmers. *Journal of Applied Behavior Analysis*, 1983, *16*, 447-460.

Kounin, J. S. & Gump, P. V. The ripple effect in discipline. *Elementary School Journal*, 1958, *59*, 158-162.

Kreutzer, M. A., Leonard, C., & Flavell, J. H. An interview study of children's knowledge about memory. *Monographs of the Society for Research in Child Development*, 1975, *40* (1, Serial No. 159).

Kuhn, D., Nash, S., & Bricken, L. Sex role concepts of two- and three-year-olds. *Child Development*, 1978, *49*, 445-51.

Kunzelmann, H. P. (Ed.) *Precision Teaching*. Seattle: Special Child Publications, 1970.

Lambert, N. M., Windmiller, N., Cole, L. J. & Figueroa, R. A. *AAMD Adaptive Behavior Scale Manual* (Rev. ed.). Washington DC: American Association of Mental Deficiency, 1975.

Lambert, W. E. & Tucker, G. R. *Bilingual Education of Children: The St. Lambert Experience.* Rowley MA: Newbury House, 1972.

Lauer, R. M., Conner, W. E., Leaverton, P. E., Reiter, M. A., & Clarke, W. R. Coronary heart disease risk factors in school children: The Muscatine study. *The Journal of Pediatrics,* 1975, *86*(5), 697-706.

Leavitt, H. J. Some effects of certain communication patterns on group performance. *Journal of Abnormal and Social Psychology,* 1951, *46,* 38-50.

Lefebvre, M. & Pinard, A. Apprentisage de la conservation des quantites par une methode de conflit cognitif. *Canadian Journal of the Behavioral Sciences,* 1972, *4,* 1-12.

L'E. Stein, C. & Goldman, J. Beginning reading instruction for children with minimal brain dysfunction. *Journal of Learning Disabilities,* 1980, *13,* 219-222.

Levin, H. M. & Meister, G. R. Computers in the balance: Weighing the costs and effectiveness. *IFG Policy Perspectives,* Summer, 1984, 1.

Lewin, K., Lippitt, R., & White, R. Patterns of aggressive behavior in experimentally created "social climates." *Journal of Social Psychology,* 1939, *10,* 271-99.

Lewis, M. & Freedle, R. Mother-infant dyad: The cradle of meaning. *Communications and Affect: Language and Thought.* New York: Academic Press, 1973.

Lewis, M. & Weinraub, M. Sex of parent x sex of child: Socioemotional development. In R. C. Friedman, R. M. Richart, & R. L. Van de Wiele (Eds.), *Sex Differences in Behavior.* New York: Wiley, 1974.

Lewis, R. & St. John, N. Contribution of cross-racial friendship to minority group achievement in desegregated classrooms. *Sociometry,* 1974, *37,* 79-91.

Leyton, F. S. *The Extent to Which Group Instructions Supplemented by Mastery of the Initial Cognitive Prerequisites Approximate the Learning Effectiveness of 1-to-1 Tutorial Methods.* Unpublished doctoral dissertation, University of Chicago, 1983.

Liberman, R. P. & Ferris, C. *Antisocial Behavior and School Performance: Comparison Between Welcome Home and Rancho San Antonio.* Unpublished report to the California Council on Criminal Justice, 1974.

Lindsley, O. R. Precision teaching in perspective: An interview with Ogden R. Lindsley. *Teaching Exceptional Children,* 1971, *3,* 114-9.

Lindsley, O. R. *The History of Precision Teaching.* Paper presented at the XVI Annual Banff International Conference on Behavioral Science, Banff, Alberta, March 18-23, 1984.

Lockery, M. & Maggs, A. Direct Instruction research in Australia: A ten-year analysis, *Educational Psychology,* 1982, *2,* 263-288.

Lockheed, M. E. *The Modification of Female Leadership Behavior in the Presence of Males* (Final Report). Princeton NJ: Educational Testing Service, 1976.

Lohren, C. *One Move to Better Golf.* New York: Signet, 1975.

Lott, T. S., Jr. 60 Houston schools implement Direct Instruction programs. *SRA Reports,* 1979, *1,* (5), 1 & 3.

Lovitt, T. C. Self-management projects with children with behavioral disorders. *Journal of Learning Disabilities,* 1973, *6,* 138-50.

Luchins, A. S. & Luchins, E. H. *Wertheimer's Seminars Revisited: Problem Solving and Thinking.* Albany NY: Faculty-Student Association, State University of New York, 1970.

Maccoby, E. E. & Jacklin, C. N. *The Psychology of Sex Differences.* Stanford CA: Stanford University Press, 1974.

Maccoby, E. E. & Zellner, M. *Experiments in Primary Education: Aspects of Project Follow-Through.* New York: Harcourt Brace Jovanovich, 1970.

MacDonald, W. C., Gallimore, R., & MacDonald, G. Contingency counseling by school personnel: An economical model of intervention. *Journal of Applied Behavior Analysis,* 1970, *3,* 175-82.

Mace, D. *Close Companions: The Marriage Enrichment Handbook.* New York: Continuum, 1982.

Madsen, C. H., Jr., Becker, W. C., Thomas, D. R., Koser, L., & Plager, E. An analysis of the reinforcing function of "Sit Down" commands. In R. K. Parker (Ed.), *Readings in Educational Psychology.* Boston: Allyn & Bacon, 1968.

Madsen, C. K. How reinforcement techniques work. *Music Educators Journal,* 1971, *57*(8), 38-41.

Madsen, C. K., Greer, R. D., & Madsen, C. H., Jr. (Eds.). *Research in Music Behavior: Modifying Music Behaviors in the Classroom.* New York: Teachers College Press, 1975.

Mager, R. F. *Preparing Instructional Objectives.* Belmont CA: Fearon, 1962.

Maggs, A., McMillan, K., & Patching, W. Increasing academic achievement in neurologically impaired children. *A.S.E.T. Journal,* 1980, *12,* 47-53.

Maggs, A. & Morath, P. Effects of direct verbal instruction on intellectual development of institutionalized moderately retarded children: A two year study. *The Journal of Special Education,* 1976, *10,* 357-364.

Mahone, C. H. Fear of failure and unrealistic vocational aspiration. *Journal of Abnormal and Social Psychology,* 1960, *60,* 253-61.

Mahoney, M. J. *Cognition and Behavior Modification.* Cambridge MA: Ballinger, 1974.

Maier, N. R. F. *Problem Solving and Creativity in Individuals and Groups.* Belmont CA: Brooks/Cole, 1970.

Maloney, K. B. & Hopkins, B. L. The modification of sentence structure and its relationship to subjective judgments of creativity in writing. *Journal of Applied Behavior Analysis,* 1973, *6,* 425-33.

Mann, R. A. The behavior-therapeutic use of contingency contracting to control an adult behavior problem: Weight control. *Journal of Applied Behavior Analysis,* 1972, *5,* 99-111.

Margolin, G. & Patterson, G. R. Differential consequences provided by mothers and fathers for their sons and daughters. *Developmental Psychology,* 1975, *11,* 537-8.

Markle, S. M. *Designs for Instructional Designers.* Champaign IL: Stipes, 1983.

Martin, B. Parent-child relations. In F. D. Horowitz (Ed.), *Review of Child Development Research,* (Vol. 4). Chicago: University of Chicago Press, 1975.

Martin, G. L. & Hrycaiko, D. *Behavior Modification and Coaching.* Springfield IL: Charles C. Thomas, 1983.

Maslow, A. H. *Motivation and Personality.* New York: Harper & Row, 1954.

Maslow, A. H. *Toward a Psychology of Being.* New York: Van Nostrand Reinhold, 1968.

Masur, E. F., McIntrye, C. W., & Flavell, J. H. Developmental changes in apportionment of study time among items in a multitrial free recall task. *Journal of Experimental Child Psychology,* 1973, *15,* 237-46.

Matarazzo, J. D. *Wechster's Measurement and Appraisal of Adult Intelligence* (5th ed.) Fair Lawn NJ: Oxford University Press, 1972.

Mawhinney, V. T., Bostow, D. E., Laws, D. R., Blumenfeld, G. J., & Hopkins, B. L. A comparison of students' studying-behavior produced by daily, weekly, and three-week testing schedules. *Journal of Applied Behavior Analysis,* 1971, *4,* 257-64.

McClelland, D. C. Measuring motivation in fantasy: The achievement motive. In H. Guetzkow (Ed.), *Groups, Leadership, and Men.* Pittsburgh PA: Carnegie Press, 1951, 191-205.

McDermott, J. R1: a rule-based configurer of computer systems. *Artificial Intelligence,* 1982, *19* (1).

McGraw, M. B. *Growth: A Study of Johnny and Jimmy.* New York: Appleton, 1935.

McKeachie, W. J. Research on teaching at the college and university level. In N. L. Gage (Ed.), *Handbook of Research on Teaching.* Chicago: Rand McNally, 1963.

McKenzie, T. L. & Rushall, B. S. Effects of self-recording on attendance and performance in a competitive swimming training environment. *Journal of Applied Behavior Analysis,* 1974, *7,* 199-206.

Meichenbaum, D. *Cognitive-Behavior Modification.* New York: Plenum, 1977.

Meichenbaum, D. & Goodman, J. Training impulsive children to talk to themselves: A means of developing self-control. *Journal of Abnormal Psychology,* 1971, *77,* 115-26.

Mercer, J. R. & Lewis, J. F. *System of Multicultural Pluralistic Assessment.* New York: Psychological Corporation, 1978.

Messer, S. The relation of internal-external control to academic performance. *Child Development,* 1972, *43,* 1456-62.

Messick, S. Assessment in context: Appraising student performance in relation to instructional quality. *Educational Researcher,* 1984, *13,* 3-8.

Meyers, L. *Comparison of Learning Rate and Retention Between a Mongoloid and Normal Population.* Unpublished master's thesis, University of Illinois, 1968.

Miller, G. A., Galanter, E., & Pribram, K. H. *Plans and the Structure of Behavior.* New York: Holt, Rinehart and Winston, 1960.

Mitnick, L. L. & McGinnies, E. Influencing ethnocentrism in small discussion groups through a film communication. *Journal of Abnormal and Social Psychology,* 1958, *56,* 82-90.

Morgan, M. Reward-induced decrements and increments in intrinsic motivation. *Review of Educational Research,* 1984, *54,* 5-30.

Morris, L. & Resnick, L. B. *Assembling Component Processes In Problem Solving.* Paper presented at the meeting of the Midwestern Psychological Association, Chicago, May 1974.

Morrison, H. C. *The Practice of Teaching in the Secondary School.* Chicago: University of Chicago Press, 1926.

Mulholland, T. M. *Availability Versus Accessibility of a Subroutine in Problem Solving.* Unpublished masters thesis, University of Pittsburgh, 1974.

Nagy, W. E. & Anderson, R. C. How many words are there in printed school English? *Reading Research Quarterly,* 1984, *19,* 304-30.

National Assessment of Educational Progress. Essay task: A woman's place is (Where?). *NAEP Newsletter,* June 1977.

Nawas, M. M. Change in efficiency of ego functioning and complexity from adolescence to young adulthood. *Developmental Psychology,* 1971, *4,* 412-5.

Neef, N. A., Iwata, B. A., & Page T. J. The effects of interspersal training versus high-density reinforcement on spelling acquisition and retention. *Journal of Applied Behavior Analysis,* 1980, *13,* 153-8.

Newell, A., Shaw, J. C., & Simon, H. A. *Preliminary Description of a General Problem Solving Program-I (GPS-I).* Report CIP Working Paper 7, Carnegie Institute of Technology, Pittsburgh PA, 1957.

Newell, A. & Simon, H. A. *Human Problem Solving.* Englewood Cliffs NJ: Prentice-Hall, 1972.

Nicklaus, J. *Golf My Way.* New York: Simon & Schuster, 1974.

Notz, W. W. Work motivation and the negative effects of extrinsic rewards. *American Psychologist,* 1975, *30,* 884-91.

O'Brien, R. M. & Simek, T. C. *A Comparison of Behavioral and Traditional Methods of Teaching Golf.* Paper presented at the meeting of the American Psychological Association, Toronto, Ontario, August-September, 1978.

Odgen, C. K. *The Basic Words: A Detailed Account of Uses.* London: Kegan Paul, 1932.

O'Leary, K. D. Pills or skills for hyperactive children. *Journal of Applied Behavior Analysis,* 1980, *13,* 191-204.

O'Leary, K. D. & Becker, W. C. Behavior modification of an adjustment class: A token reinforcement program. *Exceptional Children,* 1967, *33,* 637-642.

O'Leary, K. D. & Becker, W. C. The effects of intensity of a teacher's reprimands on children's behavior. *Journal of School Psychology,* 1968, *7,* 8-11.

O'Leary, K. D., Kaufman, K. F., Kass, R. E., & Drabman, R. S. The effects of loud and soft reprimands on the behavior of disruptive students. *Exceptional Children,* 1970, *37,* 145-55.

O'Leary, S. G. & Dubey, D. R. Applications of self-control procedures by children: A review. *Journal of Applied Behavior Analysis,* 1979, *12,* 449-465.

Olsen, N. & Willemsen, E. Studying sex prejudice in children. *Journal of Genetic Psychology,* 1978, *133,* 203-16.

Osgood, C. E. *Method and Theory in Experimental Psychology.* New York: Oxford University Press, 1953.

Paine, S. C., Radicchi, J., Rosellini, L. C., Deutchman, L., & Darch, C. B. *Structuring Your Classroom for Academic Success.* Champaign IL: Research Press, 1983.

Parke, R. D. & Sawin, D. B. The father's role in infancy. *Family Coordinator,* 1976, *25,* 265-371.

Parkinson, G. M. *The Limits of Learning.* Unpublished doctoral dissertation, York University, 1976.

Pascual-Leone, J. *Cognitive Development and Cognitive Style.* Unpublished doctoral dissertation, University of Geneva, 1969.

Pascual-Leone, J. A mathematical model for the transition rule in Piaget's developmental stages. *Acta Psychologica,* 1970, *63,* 301-45.

Pascual-Leone, J. *A Theory of Constructive Operators, A New-Piagetian Model of Conservation, and the Problem of Horizontal Dècalages.* Unpublished manuscript, York University, 1972.

Pascual-Leone, J. A view of cognition from a formalist's perspective. In K. F. Riegel & J. Meacham (Eds.), *The Developing Individual in a Changing World.* Hague: Mouton, 1976.

Patterson, G. R. A learning theory approach to the treatment of the school phobic child. In L. P. Ullmann & L. Krasner (Eds.), *Case Studies in Behavior Modification.* New York: Holt, Rinehart and Winston, 1965a.

Patterson, G. R. An application of conditioning techniques to the control of a hyperactive child. In L. P. Ullmann & L. Krasner (Eds.), *Case Studies in Behavior Modification.* New York: Holt, Rinehart and Winston, 1965b.

Pavlov, I. P. *Conditioned Reflexes.* (G. W. Anrep, trans.) Oxford, England: Oxford University Press, 1927.

Pellegrino, J. W. & Schadler, M. *Maximizing Performance in a Problem Solving Task.* Unpublished manuscript, University of Pittsburgh, Learning Research and Development Center, 1974.

Perkins, M. L. & Anderson-Inman, L. *Transfer of Training as a Technique to Promote the Application of Learned Skills to New Material.* Paper presented at the annual conference of the Council for Exceptional Children, New York, April 1981.

Persig, R. M. *Zen and the Art of Motorcycle Maintenance.* New York: Bantam Books, 1974.

Phillips, E. L. Achievement Place: Token reinforcement procedures in a home-style rehabilitation setting for predelinquent boys. *Journal of Applied Behavior Analysis,* 1968, *1,* 213-23.

Phillips, E. L., Phillips, E. A., Wolf, M. M., & Fixsen, D. L. Achievement Place: Development of the elected manager system. *Journal of Applied Behavior Analysis,* 1973, *6,* 541-61.

Piaget, J. *The Origins of Intelligence in Children.* Translated by Margaret Cook. New York: International Universities Press, 1952.

Piaget, J. Structures opèrationelles et cybernètique. *Annèe Psychology,* 1953, *53,* 379-88.

Piaget, J. *The Construction of Reality in the Child.* New York: Basic Books, 1954.

Piaget, J. *Judgment and Reasoning in the Child.* Paterson NJ: Littlefield, Adams and Company, 1959.

Piaget, J. *The Child's Conception of the World.* Paterson NJ: Littlefield, Adams, 1960.

Piaget, J. *The Moral Judgment of the Child.* New York: Collier, 1962a.

Piaget, J. *Play, Dreams, and Imitation in Childhood.* New York: Norton, 1962b.

Piaget, J. *The Origins of Intelligence in Children.* New York: Norton, 1963.

Piaget, J. *The Child's Conception of Number.* New York: Norton, 1965a.

Piaget, J. *The Child's Conception of Physical Causality.* Paterson NJ: Littlefield, Adams, 1965b.

Piaget, J. *The Child's Conception of Space.* New York: Norton, 1967.

Piaget, J. *The Child's Conception of Movement and Speed.* New York: Basic Books, 1970.

Piaget, J. *The Child's Conception of Time.* New York: Ballantine, 1971.

Popham, W. J. *Criterion-Referenced Instruction.* Belmont CA: Fearon, 1973.

Pople, H. E., Jr. On the mechanization of abductive logic. *Third International Conference on Artificial Intelligence.* Stanford CA, 1973.

Postman, L. The present status of interference theory. In C. N. Cofer (Ed.), *Verbal Learning and Verbal Behavior.* New York: McGraw-Hill, 1961.

Premack, D. Reinforcement theory. In D. Levine (Ed.), *Nebraska Symposium on Motivation.* Lincoln NB: University of Nebraska Press, 1965.

Pressey, S. L. A simple apparatus which gives tests and scores—and teaches. *School and Society,* 1926, *23,* 373-376.

Proger, B. B., Taylor, R. G., Jr., Mann, L., Coulson, J. M., & Bayuk, R. J. Conceptual pre-structuring for detailed verbal passages. *Journal of Educational Research,* 1970, *64,* 28-34.

Purkey, W. *Self-Concept and School Achievement.* Englewood Cliffs NJ: Prentice-Hall, 1970.

Quay, L. C. Academic skills. In N. R. Ellis (Ed.), *Handbook of Mental Deficiency.* New York: McGraw-Hill, 1963.

Quill, Cambridge MA: D. C. Heath, 1984.

Reith, H. J. A behavioral approach to the management of hyperactive behavior. In M. J. Fine (Ed.), *Principles and Techniques of Intervention with Hyperactive Children.* Springfield IL: Charles C. Thomas, 1977.

Resnick, L. B. & Glaser, R. Problem solving and intelligence. In L. B. Resnick (Ed.), *The Nature of Intelligence.* Hillsdale NJ: Lawrence Erlbaum Associates, 1976.

Robin, A. L. Behavioral instruction in the college classroom: A review. *Review of Educational Research,* 1976, *46,* 313-54.

Robinson, H. M. Access: The time has come to talk of policies governing who acquires computers and who uses them. *IFG Policy Notes,* 1984, *5*(3), 4-5.

Robinson, F. P. *Effective Study.* New York: Harper & Row, 1946.

Rogers, C. *Freedom to Learn,* Columbus OH: Charles E. Merrill, 1969.

Rohwer, W. D., Ammon, P. R., & Cramer, P. *Understanding Intellectual Development.* Hinsdale IL: Dryden Press, 1974.

Rolider, A. *Effects of Modeling, Instruction, and Grade Incentive on Supportive Verbalization Among Peers in a College Physical Education Class.* Paper presented at the meeting of the Midwestern Association of Behavior Analysis, Chicago, May 1978.

Rosen, R. & Hall, E. *Sexuality and Modern Life.* New York: Random House, 1983.

Rosenbaum, M. S. & Drabman, R. S. Self-control in the classroom: A review and critique. *Journal of Applied Behavior Analysis,* 1979, *12,* 467-485.

Rosenshine, B. V. Classroom instruction. In N. L. Gage (Ed.), *The Psychology of Teaching Methods.* Seventy-fifth yearbook of the National Society for the Study of Education. Chicago: University of Chicago Press, 1976.

Rosenshine, B. V. *Direct Instruction for Skill Mastery.* Paper presented to the School of Education, University of Wisconsin at Milwaukee, April 1979 (revised January 1980).

Rosenshine, B. V. Teaching functions in instructional programs. *The Elementary School Journal,* 1983, *83,* 335-51.

Rosenthal, R. & Jacobson, J. *Pygmalion in the Classroom.* New York: Holt, Rinehart and Winston, 1968.

Rosenthal, T. L. & Zimmerman, B. J. Instructional specificity and outcome expectation in observationally induced question formation. *Journal of Educational Psychology,* 1972, *63,* 500-504.

Ross, D. M. & Ross, S. A. *Hyperactivity: Research, Theory, and Action.* New York: Wiley-Interscience, 1976.

Rotter, J. *Social Learning and Clinical Psychology.* Englewood Cliffs NJ: Prentice-Hall, 1954.

Rubin, R. A., Dorle, J., & Sandidge, S. Self-esteem and school performance. *Psychology in the Schools,* 1977, *14,* 503-6.

Rushall, B. S. A motivational device for competitive swimming training. *Swimming Technique,* 1975a, *11,* 103-6.

Rushall, B. S. Applied behavior analysis of sports and physical education. *International Journal of Sports Psychology,* 1975b, *6,* 75-88.

Rushall, B. S. Coaching styles: A preliminary investigation. *Behavior Analysis of Motor Activity,* 1981, *1,* 3-19.

Rushall, B. S. Using applied behavior analysis for altering motivation. In G. L. Martin and D. Hrycaika (Eds.), *Behavior Modification and Coaching: Principles, Procedures, and Research.* Springfield IL: Charles C. Thomas, 1983.

Rushall, B. S. & Pettinger, J. An evaluation of the effects of various reinforcers used as motivators in swimming. *The Research Quarterly,* 1969, *40,* 540-45.

Sadker, M. P. & Sadker, D. M. *Beyond Pictures and Pronouns: Sexism in Teacher Education Textbooks.* Washington DC: Dept. of Education, Women's Educational Equity Act Program, 1980.

Sadker, M. P. & Sadker, D. M. *Sex Equity Handbook for Schools.* New York: Longman, 1982.

Salzberg, C. L. Freedom and responsibility in an elementary school. In G. Semb (Ed.), *Behavior Analysis & Education.* Lawrence KA: University of Kansas Support and Development Center for Follow Through, 1972.

Satterfield, J. H. & Cantwell, D. P. Pathophysiology of the hyperactive child syndrome. *Archives of General Psychiatry,* 1976, *31,* 839-44.

Sayegh, Y. & Dennis, W. The effect of supplementary experience upon the behavioral development of infants in institutions. *Child Development,* 1965, *36,* 81-90.

Schachter, S. Deviation, rejection, and communication. *Journal of Abnormal and Social Psychology,* 1951, *46,* 190-207.

Scheirer, M. A. & Kraut, R. E. Increasing educational achievement via self concept change. *Review of Educational Research,* 1979, *49,* 131-50.

Schmuck, R. A. & Schmuck, P. A. *Group Processes in the Classroom* (4th ed.). Dubuque IA: Wm. C. Brown, 1983.

Scholastic, Inc. *Storytree.* New York: Scholastic, 1984.

Schwartz, M. Computers and the teaching of writing. *Educational Technology,* 1982, *22*(11), 27-29.

Semb, G., Hopkins, B. L., & Hursh, D. E. The effects of study questions and grades on student test performance in a college course. *Journal of Applied Behavior Analysis,* 1973, *6,* 631-42.

Shavelson, R. J. & Bolus, R. Self-concept: The interplay of theory and methods. *Journal of Educational Psychology,* 1982, *74,* 3-17.

Shavelson, R. J., Hubner, J. J., & Stanton, G. C. Self-concept: Validation of construct interpretations. *Review of Educational Research,* 1976, *46,* 407-41.

Sheinker, J., Sheinker, A., & Stevens, L. J. *Study Strategies: A Metacognitive Approach.* Rock Springs WY: White Mountain Pub. Co., 1983.

Shostak, R. (Ed.). *Computers in Composition Instruction.* Eugene OR: International Council for Computers in Education, 1984.

Shulman, L. S. Psychological controversies in the teaching of science and mathematics. *Science Teacher,* 1968, *35,* 34-8 & 89-90.

Siedentip, D. & Taggart, A. Behavior analysis in physical education and sport. In W. L. Heward, T. E. Heron, D. S. Hill, & J. Trap-Porter (Eds.), *Focus on Behavior Analysis in Education.* Columbus OH: Charles E. Merrill, 1984.

Silbert, J., Carnine, D., & Stein, M. *Direct Instruction Mathematics.* Columbus OH: Charles E. Merrill, 1981.

Simon, H. A. *The Sciences of the Artificial.* Cambridge MA: MIT Press, 1969.

Simon, H. A. Identifying basic abilities underlying intelligent performance of complex tasks. In L. B. Resnick (Ed.), *The Nature of Intelligence.* Hillsdale NJ: Lawrence Erlbaum Associates, 1976.

Skeels, H. M. Adult status of children with contrasting early experiences. *Monograph of the Society for Research in Child Development,* 1966, *51,* No. 3.

Skinner, B. F. *The Behavior of Organisms: An Experimental Analysis.* New York: Appleton-Century-Crofts, 1938.

Skinner, B. F. *Walden Two.* New York: Macmillan, 1948.

Skinner, B. F. *Science and Human Behavior.* New York: Macmillan, 1953.

Skinner, B. F. The Science of Learning and the Art of Teaching. *Harvard Educational Review,* 1951, *24,* 86-97.

Skinner, B. F. *Verbal Behavior.* New York: Appleton-Century-Crofts, 1957.

Skinner, B. F. Teaching machines, *Science,* 1958, *128,* 969-977.

Skinner, B. F. *The Technology of Teaching.* New York: Appleton-Century-Crofts, 1968.

Skinner, B. F. *Contingencies of Reinforcement: A Theoretical Analysis.* New York: Appleton-Century-Crofts, 1969.

Skinner, B. F. & Krakower, S. *Handwriting with Write and See.* Chicago: Lyons and Carnahan, 1968.

Slaby, R. G. & Frey, K. S. Development of gender constancy and selective attention to same-sex models. *Child Development,* 1975, *46,* 849-56.

Smith, S. Age and sex differences in children's opinion concerning sex differences. *Journal of Genetic Psychology,* 1939, *54,* 17-25.

Sommer, R. Classroom ecology. *Journal of Applied Behavioral Science,* 1967, *3,* 328-42.

Spearman, C. *The Abilities of Man.* New York: MacMillan, 1927.

Sprick, R. S. *A Comparison of Recall Scores for Visual-Spatial, Visual-Serial, and Auditory Presentation of Intermediate Grade Content.* Unpublished doctoral dissertation, University of Oregon, 1979.

Sprick, R. S. *The Solution Book.* Chicago: Science Research Associates, 1981.

Sprick, R. S. Classroom management: Strategies for the beginning of the year. *Association for Direct Instruction News,* 1983, *3*(1), 7.

Sprick, R. S. *Discipline in the Secondary Classroom: A Problem-by-Problem Survival Guide.* By the Center for Applied Research in Education, Inc. Englewood Cliffs NJ: Prentice-Hall, 1985.

Stake, J. E. & Stake, M. N. Performance, self-esteem and dominance behavior in mixed-sex dyads. *Journal of Personality,* 1979, *47,* 71-84.

Stallings, J. A. & Kaskowitz, D. *Follow Through Classroom Observation Evaluation, 1972-73.* Menlo Park CA: Stanford Research Institute, 1974.

Stallings, J. A., Needles, M., & Stayrook, N. *How to Change the Process of Teaching Basic Reading Skills in Secondary Schools.* Menlo Park CA: SRI International, 1979.

Stanley, J. C., Keating, D. P., & Fox, L. H. (Eds.), *Mathematical Talent: Discovery, Description and Development.* Baltimore MD: Johns Hopkins University Press, 1974.

Stanton, T. F. *How to Study.* Montgomery AL: Stanton, 1968.

Staw, B. M., Calder, B. J., Hess, R. K., & Sandelands, L. E. Intrinsic motivation and norms about payment. *Journal of Personality,* 1980, *48,* 1-14.

Stebbins, L., St. Pierre, R. G., Proper, E. C., Anderson, R. B., & Cerva, T. R. *Education as Experimentation: A Planned Variation Model* (Vol. IV). Cambridge MA: Abt Associates, 1977.

Steinkamp, M. W. & Maehr, M. L. Gender differences in motivational orientations toward achievement in school science: A quantitative synthesis. *American Educational Research Journal,* 1984, *21*(1), 39-59.

Stepnoski, M. Instructional interventions for LD students: A review of recent research. *Association for Direct Instruction News,* 1984, *3*(3), 18-20.

Stern, G. G. Environments for learning. In N. Stanley (Ed.), *The American College.* New York: Wiley, 1962.

Stockard, J. Toward equality of the sexes: Should schools take a new approach? *Outlook,* DEPM, College of Education, University of Oregon, Fall 1984.

Strodtbeck, F. L. The hidden curriculum in the middle-class home. In J. D. Krumboltz (Ed.), *Learning and the Educational Process.* Chicago: Rand-McNally, 1965, 91-111.

Stuart, R. B. A three-dimensional program for treatment of obesity. *Behaviour Research and Therapy,* 1971, *9,* 177-186.

Stuart, R. B. & Davis, B. *Slim Chance in a Fat World: Behavioral Control of Obesity.* Champaign IL: Research Press, 1972.

Suppes, P. The uses of computers in education. *Scientific American,* 1966, *215,* 206-20.

Taggart, A. C. *The Effects of a Home Based Activity Program on Low Fitness Elementary School Children.* Unpublished doctoral disseration, Ohio State University, 1980.

Teitelbaum, P. T. Levels of integration of the operant. In W. K. Honig & J. E. R. Staddon (Eds.), *Handbook of Operant Behavior.* Englewood Cliffs NJ: Prentice-Hall, Inc., 1977.

Tennyson, R. D., Wooley, R. R., & Merrill, M. D. Exemplar and nonexemplar variables which produce correct classification behavior and specified classification errors. *Journal of Educational Psychology,* 1972, *63,* 144-52.

Terman, L. M. *The Measurement of Intelligence.* Boston: Houghton Mifflin, 1916.

Terrace, H. S. Stimulus control. In W. K. Honig (Ed.) *Operant Behavior: Areas of Research and Application.* New York: Appleton-Century-Crofts, 1966.

Thomas, A. & Stewart, N. Counselor response to female clients and deviate and conforming career goals. *Journal of Counseling Psychology,* 1971, *18,* 352-7.

Thomas, D. R., Becker, W. C., & Armstrong, M. Production and elimination of disruptive classroom behavior by systematically varying teacher's behavior. *Journal of Applied Behavior Analysis,* 1968, *1,* 35-45.

Thompson, S. B. Do individualized mastery and traditional instructional systems yield different course effects in college calculus? *American Educational Research Journal,* 1980, *17,* 361-75.

Thorndike, E. L. Animal intelligence: An experimental study of the associative processes in animals. *Psychological Review, Monograph Supplement,* 1898, *2.* No. 8.

Thorndike, E. L. & Lorge, I. *The Teacher's Word Book of 30,000 Words.* New York: Teacher College Press, Columbia University, 1944.

Thorndike, R. L. & Hagen, E. *Cognitive Abilities Test.* Boston: Houghton Mifflin, 1971.

Thorne, G. L., Tharp, R. G., & Wetzel, R. J. Behavior modification techniques: New tools for probation officers. *Federal Probation,* 1967, *31,* 21-7.

Thurstone, L. L. Primary mental abilities. *Psychometric Monographs,* 1938, No. 1.

Tibbetts, S. Sex-role stereotyping in children's reading material: Update. *Journal of the National Association for Women Deans, Administrators, and Counselors,* 1979, *42.*

Tiemann, P. W. & Markle, S. M. *Analyzing Instructional Content: A Guide to Instruction and Evaluation.* Champaign IL: Stipes, 1983.

Titley, R. W. The loneliness of a long distance kicker. *The Athletic Journal,* 1976, *57,* 74-80.

Tobias, S. When do instructional methods make a difference? *Educational Researcher,* 1982, *11,* 4-10.

Torgerson, S., Kriley, M. K., & Stone, J. *Logo in the Classroom.* Eugene OR: International Council for Computers in Education, 1984.

Touissaint, N. A. Analysis of synchrony between concrete-operational tasks in terms of structural and performance demands. *Child Development,* 1974, *45,* 992-1001.

Tuddenham, R. D. Soldier intelligence in World War I and II. *American Psychologist,* 1948, *3,* 54-6.

Tyler, L. E. *The Psychology of Human Differences.* New York: Appleton-Century-Crofts, 1965.

Tyler, L. E. The intelligence we test: An evolving concept. In L. B. Resnick (Ed.), *The Nature of Intelligence.* Hillsdale NJ: Lawrence Erlbaum Associates, 1976.

Underwood, B. J. The representation of rote verbal learning. In A. W. Melton (Ed.), *Categories of Human Learning.* New York: Academic Press, 1964.

U.S. Commission on Civil Rights. *More Hurdles to Clear.* Washington DC: U.S. Government Printing Office, 1980.

U.S. Public Health Service. *Obesity and Health.* U.S. Department of Health, Education and Welfare. Washington DC: U.S. Government Printing Office, 1966.

Vachon, V. & Carnine, D. W. Evaluation of computer software. *Association for Direct Instruction News,* 1983-84, *3*(2), 11-15.

van Rensburg, C. Comparative Distar results from five South Afrikaans schools. *Association for Direct Instruction News,* 1982, *1*(4), 4.

Vargus, J. S. *A History of Programmed Instruction.* Paper presented at the XVI Annual Banff International Conference on Behavioral Science. Banff, Alberta, March 18-23, 1984.

Verheyden-Hilliard, M. E. *Cracking the Glass Slipper: PEER's Guide to Ending Sex Bias in Your Schools.* Washington DC: Project on Equal Educational Rights, 1977.

Vinsonhaler, J. F. & Bass, R. K. A summary of ten major studies on CAI drill and practice. *Educational Technology,* 1972, *12,* 29-32.

Walden, E. L. & Thompson, S. A. A review of some alternative approaches to drug management of hyperactive children. *Journal of Learning Disabilities,* 1981, *14,* 213-7.

Waldrop, M. F. & Halverson, C. F. Intensive and extensive peer behavior: Longitudinal and cross-sectional analyses. *Child Development,* 1975, *46,* 19-26.

Walker, H. M. The aims assessment system. *Association for Direct Instruction News,* 1984, *3* (3), 11-4.

Walker, H. M. The social behavior survival skills program (SBS). *Association for Direct Instruction News,* 1983, *2*(3), 36-7.

Walker, H. M. & Buckley, N. K. *Token Reinforcement Techniques: Classroom Applications for the Hard-to-Teach Child.* Eugene OR: E-B Press, 1974.

Walker, H. M., Fiegenbaum, W. E., & Hops, H. *Components Analysis and Systematic Replication of a Treatment Model for Modifying Deviant Classroom Behavior.* Report No. 5, Center at Oregon for Research in the Behavioral Education of Handicapped, University of Oregon, 1971.

Walker, H. M., Mattson, R. H., & Buckley, N. K. The functional analysis of behavior within an experimental class setting. In W. C. Becker (Ed.), *An Empirical Basis for Change in Education.* Chicago: Science Research Associates, 1971.

Walker, H. M., McConnell, S., Holmes, D., Todis, B., Walker, J., & Golden, N. *The Walker Social Skills Curriculum: The Accepts Program.* Austin TX: Pro-ed, 1983.

Walters, R. H. & Brown, M. A test of the high-magnitude theory of aggression. *Journal of Experimental Child Psychology,* 1964, *1,* 376-87.

Washburn, C. W. Educational measurements as a key to individualizing instruction and promotions. *Journal of Educational Research,* 1922, *5,* 195-206.

Wasik, J. L. A comparison of cognitive performance of PSSC and non-PSSC physics students. *Journal of Research in Science Teaching,* 1971, *8,* 85-90.

Watson, J. B. *Psychology from the Standpoint of a Behaviorist.* Philadelphia: Lippincott, 1919.

Watson, J. B. & Rayner, R. Conditioned emotional reactions. *Journal of Experimental Psychology,* 1920, *3,* 1-14.

Weinberg, R. S., Seabourne, T. G., & Jackson, A. Effects of visuomotor behavior rehearsal, relaxation, and imagery on karate performance. *Journal of Sports Psychology,* 1981, *3,* 228-38.

Weiner, B. *Theories of Motivation: From Mechanism to Cognition.* Chicago: Markham, 1972.

Weiner, B. *Achievement Motivation and Attribution Theory.* Morristown NJ: General Learning, 1974.

Weiner, B. An attributional approach for educational psychology. In L. S. Shulman (Ed.), *Review of Research in Education* (Vol. 4). Itasca IL: F. E. Peacock, 1977.

Weiner, B. A theory of motivation for some classroom experiences. *Journal of Educational Psychology,* 1979, *71,* 3-25.

Weisberg, P. Reading instruction for poverty-level preschoolers. *Association for Direct Instruction News,* 1984, *3*(2), 1 & 16-19.

Weitzman, L. & Rizzo, D. *Biased Textbooks.* Washington DC: Resource Center on Sex Roles in Education, 1974.

Wendt, H. W. Motivation, effort, and performance. In D. C. McClelland (Ed.), *Studies in Motivation.* New York: Appleton-Century-Crofts, 1955, 448-59.

Wertheimer, M. *Productive Thinking* (enlarged ed.). New York: Harper & Row, 1959. (Originally published in 1945.)

West, C. K., Fish, J. A., & Stevens, R. J General self-concept, self-concept of academic ability and school achievement: Implication for causes of self-concept. *Australian Journal of Education,* 1980, *24.*

White, R. W. & Lippitt, R. *Autocracy and Democracy.* New York: Harper & Brothers, 1960.

White, W. A. T. & Gersten, R. M. DI Follow Through students follow-up in high school—The Uvalde study. *Association for Direct Instruction News,* 1983a, *2*(3), 16.

White, W. A. T. & Gersten, R. M. The follow-up of Follow Through students in high school. *Association for Direct Instruction News,* 1983b, *3*(1), 1 & 16.

Wiig, E. H. Communication disorders. In H. Haring (Ed.), *Exceptional Children and Youth.* Columbus OH: Charles E. Merrill, 1982.

Wilson, H. A. A judgmental approach to criterion-referenced testing. In C. W. Harris, M. C. Alkin, and W. J. Popham (Eds.), *Problems in Criterion-Referenced Measurement.* Los Angeles: Center for the Study of Evaluation, UCLA, 1974, Monograph No. 3, 26-36.

Winston, P. H. *Artificial Intelligence* (2nd ed.). Reading MA: Addison-Wesley, 1984.

Withall, J. The development of a climate index. *Journal of Educational Research,* 1951, *45,* 93-99.

Wolf, M. M., Giles, D. K., & Hall, R. V. Experiments with token reinforcement in a remedial classroom. *Behavior Research and Therapy,* 1968, *6,* 51-64.

Women on Words and Images. Look Jane look. See sex stereotypes. In J. Stacey et al. (Eds.), *And Jill Came Tumbling After: Sexism in American Education.* New York: Dell, 1974.

Woodward, J. & Carnine, D. *What Do Today's Authoring Languages and Authoring Systems Mean to Today's Educators?* Unpublished manuscript, University of Oregon, 1983.

Wright, M. E. The influence of frustration upon the social relations of young children. *Character and Personality,* 1943, *12,* 111-22.

Wysocki, T., Hall, G., Iwata, B., & Riordan, M. Behavioral management of exercise: Contracting for aerobic points. *Journal of Applied Behavior Analysis,* 1979, *12,* 55-64.

Yoakum, C. S. & Yerkes, R. M. *Army Mental Tests.* New York: Henry Holt, 1920.

Young, R. *The Effects of Various Reinforcement Contingencies on a Second Grade Physical Education Class.* Unpublished doctoral dissertation, Ohio State University, 1973.

Zigler, E. Familial mental retardation: A continuing dilemma. *Science,* 1967, *155,* 292-98.

Zigler, E. & Muenchow, S. Mainstreaming: The proof is in the implementation. *American Psychologist,* 1979, *34,* 993-6.

Zigler, E. & Valentine, J. *Project Head Start: A Legacy of the War on Poverty.* New York: Free Press, 1979.

Zimmerman, B. J. & Rosenthal, T. L. Observational learning of rule governed behavior by children. *Psychological Bulletin,* 1974, *8,* 29-42.

Zimmerman, E. H. & Zimmerman, J. The alteration of behavior in a special classroom situation. *Journal of the Experimental Analysis of Behavior,* 1962, *5,* 1.

AUTHOR INDEX

SUBJECT INDEX